D1713617

NEW ASTROLOGY FOR THE 21ST CENTURY

A Unique Blend Of Chinese And Western Astrology

BY
SUZANNE WHITE

Dedication

This book is dedicated to my mother, Elva Louise McMullen Hoskins, who is gone from this world, but who would have been happy to share this page with my courageous kids, April Daisy White and Autumn Lee White; my brothers, George, Peter and John Hoskins; my niece Pamela Potenza; and my loyal friends Kitty Weissberger, Val Paul Pierotti, Stan Albro, Nathaniel Webster, Jean Valère Pignal, Roselyne Pignal, Michael Armani, Joseph Stoddart, Couquite Hoffenberg, Jean Louis Besson, Mary Lee Castellani, Paula Alba, Marguerite and Paulette Ratier, Ted and Joan Zimmermann, Scott Weiss, Miekle Blossom, Ina Dellera, Gloria Jones, Marina Vann, Richard and Shiela Lukins, Tony Lees-Johnson, Jane Russell, Jerry and Barbara Littlefield, Michele and Mark Princi, Molly Friedrich, Consuelo and Dick Baehr, Linda Grey, Clarissa and Ed Watson, Francine and John Pascal, Johnny Romero, Lawrence Grant, Irma Kurtz, Gene Dye, Phyllis and Dan Elstein, Richard Klein, Irma Pride Home, Sally Helgesen, Sylvie de la Rochefoucauld, Ann Kennerly, David Barclay, John Laupheimer, Yvon Lebihan, Bernard Aubin, Dédé Laqua, Wolfgang Paul, Maria José Desa, Juliette Boisriveaud, Anne Lavaur, and all the others who so dauntlessly stuck by me when I was at my baldest and most afraid.

Thanks, of course, to my loving doctors: James Gaston, Richard Cooper, Yves Decroix, Jean-Claude Durand, Michel Soussaline and to all those daring women in the white crepe-soled shoes who change tangled sheets and murmur comfort in the dead of night.

2016 - Updated thanks to Dorothy Bray of Mill Valley, California without whose loving friendship, hospitality and support, I would have long since been obliged to stop writing books.

Introduction
Why me?

S ome years ago I ran way from Paris, France, to live in the glistening outer reaches of mythical Long island, New York, U.SA. I was 38. Perhaps I thought I'd languished in Paris long enough—too long, in fact. My daughters spoke accented English. I missed milkshakes and back porches. The Hamptons, they told me, was the "in" place for writers to hang out. Now, after much diligence and uncanny good luck, I'd written a couple of successful books. Noblesse oblige, I moved directly to the Hamptons, where the real writers lived. I sincerely believed I had "arrived." My daughters were cheerful and balanced. Their French accents disappeared overnight. The streets flowed with milkshakes. I had not yet really written a bestseller, but that could wait. I had just fallen plumb in love with a gorgeous tennis pro!

It was June. The endless Long Island beaches with their stilted dune houses and generous expanses of white sand were already beckoning, promising a summer thick with golden bodies and chic folks from the city. My new house, a picturesque replica of a 17th-century pioneer's salt box, amalgamated all my dreams into one cozy cottage: two fireplaces, a brand new kitchen, an office for Mom (me), and a sweet bedroom under the eaves for each of the prettiest new girls in town, Daisy and Autumn White. Naturally there was a back porch.

I really believed I had, after all the difficult years on my own trying to become a published writer, made it. My life was so complete that I had hardly noticed how skinny I had become. Over the past couple of months I'd been jogging regularly and moving a lot of furniture and hanging pictures and curtains. I guess I figured it was normal to have lost some weight. "You can never be too thin or too rich," I would quip to my strapping new boyfriend, so sure of myself, so cocky—until the day I sat splashing in my lovely new beige bathtub, examined my favorite right breast, and found a lump the size of my thumbnail sitting right up there next to the axillary nodes. From that day forward, the beautiful June sunshine wept onto my perfectly grained authentic broad oak parquet floor. The jig was decidedly up.

Obviously it was serious. This time, I could not just flail about looking for solutions in the eyes of some wise old sage who might tell me I ought to consider a career change. You don't go to an astrologer for a breast lump. So I went to a hospital and had my breast removed. Then, I lay slowly dying under the debilitating spell of twelve months of chemotherapy treatments. I lost my lovely house and my tennis pro. And, being too sick to take care of them, I even lost my kids for a few months. They were sent far away to boarding school.

By the end of that siege on body and soul, my objectivity meter not only registered below zero, it read "tilt." Everywhere I looked were side effects of the poisonous drugs. Crippling arthritis had invaded my every joint. All my beautiful, thick dark hair had departed my scalp. Unable to retain anything but starches and sugars for over a year, I had gained fifty pounds. My teeth were all loose. I knew what it felt like to be old.

Nevertheless, as soon as both arms were free of intravenous devices, I grabbed a pretty little girl under each of them, borrowed air fare, and flew us all back to Paris whence I had emerged so naively enthusiastic but four years earlier. On the way in from the airport I leapt from the cab and kissed the lion at *Denfert-Rochereau.* The kids munched soulfully on *pains au chocolat.*

What does this have to do with The New Astrology? Well, when you are ill, you tend to lie around a lot thinking about what it must be like to be dead. Sooner or later you notice you have what is known as "time on your hands." If I only had a few months left, I didn't see why I should waste them mooning over worms and urns or sizes of headstones.

But fret I did, nevertheless. I was scared and worried and not ever certain that I'd be around long enough to see my kids grow up. I'd lost my punch, my strength had ebbed, my dreams had been dashed on the ragged rocks of truth. The doctors assured me that with a little luck and plenty of patience I would be perfectly all right from then on. I'd done what 1 could to stem the dangerous illness. I was mending nicely.

But my heart was broken. I'd lost everything I'd built up. Even if cancer had not killed me, it had ruined my life. What was I to do? Boo hoo. "Well, you certainly can't be a stripper or a centerfold now," said my favorite Leo/Monkey friend, Kathryn. "So you'd better write another book."

"But all I do is cry," I moaned at her.

"So when you stop crying you'll write another book," she snapped back.

So slowly, painfully, I set about trying to stop my marathon weeping spell. As friend Kathryn the Leo/Monkey had always been my arch problem-solver, I figured she was right. If I could stop crying. I could write another book. Luckily, about that time, a strange phenomenon occurred to help me. I hadn't counted on this at all. It's called fan mail. Yes. When I returned to France from the States, I found out that my first book, Chinese Astrology, which had been translated in my absence from the original American text into mellifluous French, was selling like croissants. My publisher dumped piles of readers' letters in my lap. In time, as sales kept increasing, so did my volume of mail.

Of course, a few of my readers only needed to know whether or not they should marry their best friends' wives or husbands. But most of them really wanted more information about themselves, their signs, their husbands and wives and cousins and children and aunts and pets and bosses and friends. "If I am a Taurus born in 1928, why do I have so much trouble getting along with my son-in-law, who is a Gemini born in 1952?"

Often, I would write back, "Well, Madame, for a start you and your son-in-law are both Dragons. Dragons like to have center stage all to themselves. Moreover, as a Taurean you are possessive and not too rapid. Your son-in-law, the Gemini, seems too light-headed to you. You find his shiftiness unbearable. He probably finds your stodginess revolting too. The harmony between Taureans and Geminis—especially Dragons!—is never overwhelming. I'd suggest one of you move out." So, thanks to my readers' queries, I was writing to people all the time about the New Astrology. And little by little, unwittingly, I had stopped crying. It was time to write another book.

What Is the New Astrology?

The New Astrology compares Western signs to Chinese signs and comes up with 144 new signs. If you are a Sagittarius and were born in 1949, then you are a Sagittarius/Ox. Simple. Take your regular, familiar astrological sign and match it with the animal sign of the year you were born. Now you have your New astrological sign.

Everybody has a dual nature. Some people are naturally greedy and grasping about money. But surprise! These same people can be generous to a fault in emotional ways, strewing sentiment and affection on their entourage like Santa Claus on a gift binge. People are complicated. They baffle us with their contradictory behavior. We even confuse ourselves with our own haunting ambivalences. How come you get along with Jack and care so much about him when in fact he gets on your nerves? Jack has an abrasive personality.

You know that. But you can't help liking the guy. He fascinates you. Why? It's a dilemma. With a solution.

In order to understand your attraction for the difficult Jack, so as to comprehend the opacities of your own soul, by yourself, without the aid of a shrink or a psychiatrist, all you have to do is read The New Astrology, apply it to your day-to-day life, and you're off and running, I can hear it from here. Is Suzanne White crazy? Who does she think she is comparing astrology to science or religion? What bill of goods is she trying to sell us now? What is this marginal balderdash that Suzanne White expects us to fall for? Is she some kind of retarded hippie? It's a con. Don't believe that garbage. It's bohemian. It's not accepted by the AMA, the Food and Drug Administration, the Council of Churches or the Vatican. Beware, dear reader. A witch is among you, a temptress who will warp and mold your unsuspecting mind with her sorcery. Astrology is hogwash and that is all there is to it!

All right, killjoy. You're right. Astrology is nonsense. Now may we get on with our fun?

How Does the New Astrology Work?

The New Astrology attempts to help us understand human behavior within the universe through the "marriage" of occidental and oriental astrologies.

The Chinese have divided time differently from us Westerners. Whereas we have 100-year centuries, the Chinese have periods of sixty years. We divide our centuries into ten decades. The Chinese divide their sixty-year spans into "dozencades" or twelve-year periods.

In the West, we divide our year up twelve times by its moons. Each 28- to 30-day month has its own astrological name. Every year our cycle begins anew. In the East, each year within the twelve-year dozencade has its own astrological name. At the end of each twelve-year period the Chinese cycle begins anew.

The twelve occidental months have celestial sign names: Aries, Taurus, Gemini, Cancer, Leo, Virgo, Libra, Scorpio, Sagittarius, Capricorn, Aquarius, Pisces. The twelve oriental years have animal sign names: Rat, Ox, Tiger, Cat, Dragon, Snake, Horse, Sheep, Monkey, Rooster, Dog, Pig. In both cases the astrological sign name refers to the character of people born under its influence.

So, in fact, everybody in the world has not just one but two main astrological signs. A Western "month" sign and an Oriental "year" sign. One sign is complementary to the other. Taken together, they show us more about the individual than either one can on its own.

In the New Astrology, if someone is born in Aries and is also born in a Horse year, that person's New Astrology sign is Aries/Horse. Aries/Horses, as you will see, are not the same as Aries/Cats or Aries/Tigers.

There are 144 New Astrology signs. Each is a combined East/West sign. The point of this exercise is to refine our understanding of human nature. Through the New Astrology we can learn to get along better with our friends, family and loved ones. We can find out why we tend not to harmonize with certain people. We can improve our knowledge of them, and of ourselves.

Ruling Elements

Western astrology uses four ruling elements: **Fire, Air, Earth, Water**. Each Western astrological sign is ruled by one of these elements.

FIRE: *Aries, Leo, Sagittarius.* Fire signs are characterized by Movement, Obsession, Energy.

AIR: *Gemini, Libra, Aquarius.* Air signs are characterized by Receptiveness, Intellect, Aspiration.

EARTH: *Taurus, Virgo, Capricorn.* Earth signs are characterized by Function, Practicality, Solidity.

WATER: *Cancer, Scorpio, Pisces.* Water signs are characterized by Emotion, Compassion, Perception.

Chinese astrology uses five ruling elements: **Metal, Water, Wood, Fire and Earth**.

The Five Elements—Wood, Fire, Earth, Metal, Water

To allow for movement to occur and bring about change, Chinese philosophy calls upon the five elements as agents of change and reaction. Change, the Chinese think, derives from the influence of the five main elements—Wood, Fire, Earth, Metal and Water—on the basic Yin or Yang energies. Like in the old rock, paper, scissors game that we played as kids, each of these five Chinese elements has the ability to control and/or destroy the previous element, and is capable of producing the element that directly follows it. In the regenerative cycle of the elements, Water engenders Wood. Wood begets Fire. Fire burns to Earth. Earth creates Metal and Metal gives way to Water.

Wood is characterized by the color green. Wood heralds the beginning of life, springtime and buds, sensuality and fecundity. Wood's influence affects the liver, the gallbladder and, by extension, the digestion. Wood needs moisture to thrive. Its two opposite yet equally emotional forces are rage and altruism. The Wood person will be expansive, outgoing and socially conscious.

Wood, in its turn, can create and nourish Fire. Fire's signatory color is red. Fire is hot weather, satisfaction of nature, aridity and dust. The tongue and the small intestine are the centers of attention in the Fire person's body. Fire makes heat, which either warms or burns. The Fire person must constantly seek to balance a tendency to explode and possibly destroy, against a desire to create coziness and warmth. Passionate by nature, this impatient, ebullient person must strive to keep his flame under control.

Earth is created from the ashes of the Fire. Now we are in the soothingly satisfying late summer cycle. Earth's favorite color is yellow, which represents the equanimity between beginnings and. endings. The weather of Earth is mild or temperate. In the human body, Earth influences spleen, pancreas and mouth. Earth's two opposite but equal forces which need to be kept in constant balance are enhancing and smothering. On the one hand Earth gives care and allows for growth and improvement. On the other, Earth buries roots and snuffs out breath. Earth people are gifted for fairness and have the ability to commit themselves to protracted projects and complete Herculean tasks with ease. They must struggle against a penchant for worry.

The Earth grows Metal in her veins. Metal says white and autumn. Metal is cool, crisp weather. Metal's effect on the body centers in the lungs and respiratory system. It only secondarily rules the large intestine and the nose. Metal people like to communicate. They need to keep discord and harmony in constant balance. Metal signifies the onset of winter. Its influence can sometimes add sadness or gloom to an astrological chart. Two of Metal's emotional forces are melancholy and romance. I see Metal as Wagnerian. Metal people must guard against a tendency to wallow in nostalgia.

Lastly, Metal begets Water—groundwater trickling its way through layers of the Earth's ore. Water's color is blue. Its season is full-blown winter. Water is always moving, fluid, and mutational. In our bodies, water's influence affects our plumbing systems, the kidneys and the bladder. The ear, too, comes under the spell of Water. Hence people born in Water-ruled years are frequently musical. They pick up on everything. Be it good or bad, they never miss a vibe. Water-ruled creatures are always very sensitive and sometimes even mentally fragile. The downside of Water's influence, then, is a stressful nervousness. To balance that fidgety, squeamish, overly sensitive side, Water endows its subjects with the noblest quality of all, kindness and sympathy. Sometimes too permeable, the Water-ruled must take precautions against drowning in the chagrin of those they see as less fortunate than themselves.

So, the five elements cause the commotion and are responsible for creating and maintaining both balance and imbalance—for moving things around and making life interesting. These purveyors of change can be controlled or not, depending on how one manages them.

Each animal year of the Chinese zodiac has been assigned one of the five elements. That element turns up twice in the cycle going away for another ten years. The five elements are always presented in the above order. Once we know this, we can understand how the elements directly affect us and pertain to individual characters.

Planets

Each sign in Western astrology is ruled by one or more of ten planets or heavenly bodies. These are the "stars" astrologers are always said to be gazing at. The planets influence a sign's character. Their position in the heavens helps to predict the future.

Aries *is ruled by Mars representing: Impulse, Action, Bravery*

Taurus *is ruled by Venus representing: Acceptance, Vanity, Love*

Gemini *is ruled by Mercury representing: the Intellect, Change, Adaptability*

Cancer *is ruled by the Moon representing: Receptivity, Emotion, Viscera*

Leo *is ruled by the Sun representing: Assertiveness, Will, Majesty*

Virgo *is ruled by Mercury representing: Analysis, Absorption, Logic*

Libra *is ruled by Venus representing: Sociability, Persuasion, Luxury*

Scorpio *is ruled by Mars and Pluto representing Courage, Creation, Passion*

Sagittarius *is ruled by Jupiter representing: Expansion, Vision, Justice*

Capricorn *is ruled by Saturn representing: Solitude, Rigidity, Ambition*

Aquarius *is ruled by Saturn and Uranus representing: Individuality, Cosmic Consciousness, Obligation*

Pisces *is ruled by Neptune and Jupiter representing: Enigma, Inspiration, Compassion*

Chinese astrology does not concern itself with celestial bodies. If Chinese astrologers look to nature for influence, they consult the climatic changes on Earth, the seasons or the moon's effects on the Earth.

Qualities
Western astrology uses three different qualities: **Cardinal, Fixed and Mutable**.

CARDINAL: Aries, Cancer, Libra, Capricorn—*Dynamic, Authoritative, Active, Energetic*

FIXED: Taurus, Scorpio, Leo, Aquarius—*Concrete, Limited, Purposeful, Conscientious*

MUTABLE: Gemini, Virgo, Sagittarius, Pisces—*Moving, Adaptable, Harmonizing, Versatile.*

Are the *Yin* and the *Yang* Qualities Too?
Yes. In Chinese astrology, yin and yang are qualities. But yin and yang are far more powerful than our qualities because yin and yang are the two major and *only* forces in the Chinese philosophical universe. For them, everything present in the universe is either yin or else it is yang. Everything. Tables. Chairs. Light bulbs, cousins, aunts, uncles and kitchen sinks!

In a way, yin and yang can be compared, in Western culture, to the application in certain languages of the qualities of "masculine" or "feminine" to inanimate objects or intangible nouns. Though it does not seem to make sense, in French a table is feminine. A log is feminine. A shoe is also feminine. Parks are masculine. Lakes too. Feet are masculine. So are eyes and foreheads. But mouths and even teeth are feminine. Worry is masculine. So are gossip and lipstick and panty hose.

Though we may want to look for sexual significance in the application of gender to nouns, there is none. That's what makes it so difficult to remember from one language to the next whether a noun is considered masculine or feminine. Is the application of gender to nouns then perfectly arbitrary? Well, it must have come from somewhere. But nobody knows exactly how, when or why.

There are no genders in the Chinese language. But, without saying how, when or why, Chinese philosophers can feel whether a thing or a person or an idea is yin or yang. It's just there. A known fact. Yin is rooted in the sun. Its goal is darkness. Yang is rooted In the Earth. Its goal is light.

Like everything else Chinese, each Chinese animal sign is either yin or yang.

Rat - Yang
Ox - Yin
Tiger - Yang
Cat/Rabbit - Yin
Dragon - Yang
Snake - Yin
Horse -Yang
Sheep -Yin
Monkey - Yang
Rooster - Yin
Dog - Yang
Pig - Yin

What Does It Mean? What Is Yin? What Is Yang?

To be perfectly frank, I am not even sure what yin is or what yang means. I have read a lot of books on the subject. Still, the concept is not easy for my logical little occidental brain to grasp. Chinese philosophy is complicated - even for Chinese people! I'll be brief.

What Is Yin?

The Chinese say that yin people are mainly interested in what happens in groups. They are frequently preoccupied with the organization of collective or communal events. They are attracted to politics. They are self-confident. They trust nobody. They need success to survive. They worship efficiency. They are always questing after well-being for themselves and for those they love or like. They have good health and long life but may be prone to accidents. They don't smile a lot. They dress conservatively. They are not spiritual. They love their families. They are material.

The way I see it, yin is open, civilized, interested in the good of others. Yin likes parties, feasts, holidays, sex and anything else that provides it with intense company. Yin is not feminine. But it is sometimes said to be subjective. Yin is active in the world. Other-directed. Public. It is different from and equal to yang.

What Is Yang?

The Chinese say that yang people are loners. They are individualistic. They are meditative. They are spiritual. They smile a lot. They have no sense of groups or family. They have delicate health. They like to dress for show. They eschew chains of command. They love nature. They are nonmaterial. Their only goal in life is personal development. They are objective. They keep their own counsel.

The way I see it, yang is closed, unsociable, private. Yang likes books, music, gardening, long walks or anything that brings him closer to himself and nature. Yang is solitary. Self-directed. Yang's equilibrium comes from within.

And Rising Signs? What About Ascendants?

In occidental astrology everybody has a rising sign. This is a sub-sign found by calculating which planet was rising in the sky at the time of a person's birth. Rising signs or ascendants are said to influence one's inner nature. In other words, a peace-keeping Libra with Leo rising will be more majestic, willful and good-natured than a Libra with, say, a sadistic Scorpio rising.

As the New Astrology already has 144 different signs to talk about, we cannot concern ourselves here with rising signs. Do the arithmetic. You will see that in order to include rising signs in our study our book would have weighed as much as your brother-in-law.

So the New Astrology is simply the "marriage" of Western astrology with Chinese astrology. Read on. I'm sure that you will agree they make a lovely couple.

Reference Charts and Birth Date Listings

As you can probably tell by now, I *love* astrology. Particularly New Astrology. In fact, I'm so childishly enthusiastic about my subject that when I meet a new person, I can rarely let five minutes pass before I get the unsquelchable urge to snoop into his or her private self. I'm always blurting, "What's your astrological sign" to unsuspecting newcomers. They usually tell me right off. No problem. "I'm Aquarius." I smile my knowingest smile. Now the plot thickens, "What year were you born?" I always ask right away. Here, the answers vary.

Some people want to hide their real age. That's all right. I just have to help them along. Assure them I don't care about how old they are. (It always shows anyway, right?) I cajole them with the "all ages are the best ages" speech, swoon over their graying temples, rave about the glories of true wisdom and the benefits of experience over callow youth. It doesn't take more than a few seconds. "Well, I was born in 1913," they finally admit. My job here is to drop my jaw and exclaim, "My goodness, you look young for your age." So much for initial interrogation of that sort of person.

There is a second sort of dodgy reply to the "What year were you born?" query. It's unintentional and really rather sweet. Say I ask a nice person I meet at a party, "What's your astrological sign?" She's not too sure. "I think it's Taurus," she offers apologetically. "And what year were you born then?" "Taurus," she insists, "I'm Taurus." "And the year? What *year* were you born in?" She smiles and says more emphatically than before, "I'm Taurus." Obviously this woman is not intimately acquainted with any kind of astrology. So for her, being Taurus should be enough. Of course, when I talk about New Astrology and all of its uses, she will loosen right up and tell me all I need to know. If you give them half a chance, people are surprisingly interested in themselves.

Thing is, as it stands, whether I meet somebody new on the beach or in an elevator or on a bus, if I want to know more about them or tell them some news about themselves, I have to wait till I get home, where I can consult ten or twelve heavy astrology books and come up with some answers. At best, this is an unwieldy method of quick "astrologizing." I've often thought it would be much more efficient to have one portable astrology book, a distillation of the ten or twelve tomes to keep at home plus a carryall of my own deductions and charts, to go with me wherever. For me, *The New Astrology* is just that book—and more!

Discover your inner workings. Now, read about your character, your love, family and professional life, and check out the New Astrology signs that are compatible with yours. Find out which famous people were born with your same New Astrology configuration and see if you have anything in common. If you are interested in your ancestors' character or those of historical figures, you will find their signs in the appendix under *Western Astrological Reference Chart* and *Chinese Horoscope Historical Reference Chart.*

Now it is time to start on family and friends. Look up their dates, jot them in on your *Personal Birth Date Listing.* Then turn to the chapters concerning each person's sign and read up on them.

The New Astrology is really good, clean, informative fun. And your book belongs exclusively to you. In it are recorded all the names and birthdays of the people you know. Take it with you on vacation, to the office, on business trips and even picnics. *The New Astrology* will help you to understand the character of people you meet. Should you have an affair with the chap you met in Acapulco or would it be wiser to let that one slide? Is that blond girl in the office to be trusted? Look her up in *The New Astrology*, put her on your chart and take a look at which of your acquaintances she resembles. With the aid of *The New Astrology* you can now check people out instantly, know on the spot if they're your type. *The New As-*

trology will be your constant faithful companion and guide through the perilous rest of your modern life. Don't lend it to a friend. And never leave home without it.

Why not make your own Birthday List?

Start now. Keep a record of the "New Astrology" signs of your Friends, Lovers, Family, Colleagues and even your Enemies. Check out your compatibility with them. See why you do or don't get along with them. Find out their secrets to better understand who they are.

The Western Astrological Reference Chart

In a Western astrological year there are twelve signs. Each sign lasts for about one month. They are established in the following order:

1. **Aries:** March 21 to April 20
2. **Taurus:** April 21 to May 21
3. **Gemini:** May 22 to June 21
4. **Cancer:** June 22 to July 23
5. **Leo:** July 24 to August 23
6. **Virgo:** August 24 to September 23
7. **Libra:** September 24 to October 23
8. **Scorpio:** October 24 to November 22
9. **Sagittarius:** November 23 to December 21
10. **Capricorn**: December 22 to January 20
11. **Aquarius:** January 21 to February 19
12. **Pisces:** February 20 to March 20

The Chinese New Year Calendar 1900 through 2050

Your Chinese Animal Sign is based on the year of your birth. It's easy. If you were born in the year of the Horse, you are a Horse. There is, however, an exception to this simple rule. The Chinese New Year doesn't start until mid January or February. Moreover, every year it falls on a different date. So if you are a Capricorn born in January or an Aquarius born in either January or February, you may have been born at the end of the current Chinese year and, of course, wear the animal sign of that year. To find out the exact date of the Chinese New Year in your case, you must consult the following charts to see where your birth date falls in the appropriate Chinese Year.

To find out the New Astrology sign of some older people we know or historical personages we read about, we need to know their birth dates. It's easy to see from "April 15, 1776" that a person born on this date is Aries. There are twelve Western astrological signs and as many months in each year. But to find out the Chinese sign of this person born so long ago, we must calculate backward to find which animal of the twelve Chinese animal signs ruled the year in question. Many readers wrote to me after reading *The New Chinese Astrology* asking me to tell them which signs their grandfather born in 1906 might have been. I get bored calculating backward each time so I drew up charts of each century since the 1500's, with the year and their signs clearly calculated ahead. If you want to know more about a certain person in history, instead of getting out your pencil and paper to count backward from 1900, open to the end of your book and consult the Chinese Historical Reference Chart. Otherwise, for dates in the 20th and 21st centuries, consult the Chinese Astrology Chart on the next page.

Year | Sign | Year begins | Year ends
1900 | Rat | 1/31/1900 | 2/18/1901
1901 | Ox | 2/19/1901 | 2/7/1902
1902 | Tiger | 2/8/1902 | 1/28/1903
1903 | Cat | 1/29/1903 | 2/15/1904
1904 | Dragon | 2/16/1904 | 2/3/1905
1905 | Snake | 2/4/1905 | 1/24/1906
1906 | Horse | 1/25/1906 | 2/12/1907
1907 | Sheep | 2/13/1907 | 2/1/1908
1908 | Monkey | 2/2/1908 | 1/21/1909
1909 | Rooster | 1/22/1909 | 2/9/1910
1910 | Dog | 2/10/1910 | 1/29/1911
1911 | Pig | 1/30/1911 | 2/17/1912
1912 | Rat | 2/18/1912 | 2/5/1913
1913 | Ox | 2/6/1913 | 1/25/1914
1914 | Tiger | 1/26/1914 | 2/13/1915
1915 | Cat | 2/14/1915 | 2/2/1916
1916 | Dragon | 2/3/1916 | 1/22/1917
1917 | Snake | 1/23/1917 | 2/10/1918
1918 | Horse | 2/11/1918 | 1/31/1919
1919 | Sheep | 2/1/1919 | 2/19/1920
1920 | Monkey | 2/20/1920 | 2/7/1921
1921 | Rooster | 2/8/1921 | 1/27/1922
1922 | Dog | 1/28/1922 | 2/15/1923
1923 | Pig | 2/16/1923 | 2/4/1924
1924 | Rat | 2/5/1924 | 1/23/1925
1925 | Ox | 1/24/1925 | 2/12/1926
1926 | Tiger | 2/13/1926 | 2/1/1927
1927 | Cat | 2/2/1927 | 1/22/1928
1928 | Dragon | 1/23/1928 | 2/9/1929
1929 | Snake | 2/10/1929 | 1/29/1930
1930 | Horse | 1/30/1930 | 2/16/1931
1931 | Sheep | 2/17/1931 | 2/5/1932
1932 | Monkey | 2/6/1932 | 1/25/1933
1933 | Rooster | 1/26/1933 | 2/13/1934
1934 | Dog | 2/14/1934 | 2/3/1935
1935 | Pig | 2/4/1935 | 1/23/1936
1936 | Rat | 1/24/1936 | 2/10/1937
1937 | Ox | 2/11/1937 | 1/30/1938
1938 | Tiger | 1/31/1938 | 2/18/1939
1939 | Cat | 2/19/1939 | 2/7/1940
1940 | Dragon | 2/8/1940 | 1/26/1941

1941 | Snake | 1/27/1941 | 2/14/1942
1942 | Horse | 2/15/1942 | 2/4/1943
1943 | Sheep | 2/5/1943 | 1/24/1944
1944 | Monkey | 1/25/1944 | 2/12/1945
1945 | Rooster | 2/13/1945 | 2/1/1946
1946 | Dog | 2/2/1946 | 1/21/1947
1947 | Pig | 1/22/1947 | 2/9/1948
1948 | Rat | 2/10/1948 | 1/28/1949
1949 | Ox | 1/29/1949 | 2/16/1950
1950 | Tiger | 2/17/1950 | 2/5/1951
1951 | Cat | 2/6/1951 | 1/26/1952
1952 | Dragon | 1/27/1952 | 2/13/1953
1953 | Snake | 2/14/1953 | 2/2/1954
1954 | Horse | 2/3/1954 | 1/23/1955
1955 | Sheep | 1/24/1955 | 2/11/1956
1956 | Monkey | 2/12/1956 | 1/30/1957
1957 | Rooster | 1/31/1957 | 2/17/1958
1958 | Dog | 2/18/1958 | 2/7/1959
1959 | Pig | 2/8/1959 | 1/27/1960
1960 | Rat | 1/28/1960 | 2/14/1961
1961 | Ox | 2/15/1961 | 2/4/1962
1962 | Tiger | 2/5/1962 | 1/24/1963
1963 | Cat | 1/25/1963 | 2/12/1964
1964 | Dragon | 2/13/1964 | 2/1/1965
1965 | Snake | 2/2/1965 | 1/20/1966
1966 | Horse | 1/21/1966 | 2/8/1967
1967 | Sheep | 2/9/1967 | 1/29/1968
1968 | Monkey | 1/30/1968 | 2/16/1969
1969 | Rooster | 2/17/1969 | 2/5/1970
1970 | Dog | 2/6/1970 | 1/26/1971
1971 | Pig | 1/27/1971 | 2/14/1972
1972 | Rat | 2/15/1972 | 2/2/1973
1973 | Ox | 2/3/1973 | 1/22/1974
1974 | Tiger | 1/23/1974 | 2/10/1975
1975 | Cat | 2/11/1975 | 1/30/1976
1976 | Dragon | 1/31/1976 | 2/17/1977
1977 | Snake | 2/18/1977 | 2/6/1978
1978 | Horse | 2/7/1978 | 1/27/1979
1979 | Sheep | 1/28/1979 | 2/15/1980
1980 | Monkey | 2/16/1980 | 2/4/1981
1981 | Rooster | 2/5/1981 | 1/24/1982
1982 | Dog | 1/25/1982 | 2/12/1983

1983 | Pig | 2/13/1983 | 2/1/1984
1984 | Rat | 2/2/1984 | 2/19/1985
1985 | Ox | 2/20/1985 | 2/8/1986
1986 | Tiger | 2/9/1986 | 1/28/1987
1987 | Cat | 1/29/1987 | 2/16/1988
1988 | Dragon | 2/17/1988 | 2/5/1989
1989 | Snake | 2/6/1989 | 1/26/1990
1990 | Horse | 1/27/1990 | 2/14/1991
1991 | Sheep | 2/15/1991 | 2/3/1992
1992 | Monkey | 2/4/1992 | 1/22/1993
1993 | Rooster | 1/23/1993 | 2/9/1994
1994 | Dog | 2/10/1994 | 1/30/1995
1995 | Pig | 1/31/1995 | 2/18/1996
1996 | Rat | 2/19/1996 | 2/6/1997
1997 | Ox | 2/7/1997 | 1/27/1998
1998 | Tiger | 1/28/1998 | 2/15/1999
1999 | Cat | 2/16/1999 | 2/4/2000
2000 | Dragon | 2/5/2000 | 1/23/2001
2001 | Snake | 1/24/2001 | 2/11/2002
2002 | Horse | 2/12/2002 | 1/31/2003
2003 | Sheep | 2/1/2003 | 1/21/2004
2004 | Monkey | 1/22/2004 | 2/8/2005
2005 | Rooster | 2/9/2005 | 1/28/2006
2006 | Dog | 1/29/2006 | 2/17/2007
2007 | Pig | 2/18/2007 | 2/6/2008
2008 | Rat | 2/7/2008 | 1/25/2009
2009 | Ox | 1/26/2009 | 2/13/2010
2010 | Tiger | 2/14/2010 | 2/2/2011
2011 | Cat | 2/3/2011 | 1/22/2012
2012 | Dragon | 1/23/2012 | 2/9/2013
2013 | Snake | 2/10/2013 | 1/30/2014
2014 | Horse | 1/31/2014 | 2/18/2015
2015 | Sheep | 2/19/2015 | 2/7/2016
2016 | Monkey | 2/8/2016 | 1/27/2017
2017 | Rooster | 1/28/2017 | 2/15/2018
2018 | Dog | 2/16/2018 | 2/4/2019
2019 | Pig | 2/5/2019 | 1/24//2020
2020 | Rat | 1/25/2020 | 2/11/2021
2021 | Ox | 2/12/2021 | 1/31/2022
2022 | Tiger | 2/1/2022 | 1/21/2023
2023 | Rabbit | 1/22/2023 | 2/9/2024
2024 | Dragon | 2/10/2024 | 1/28/2025

2025 | Snake | 1/29/2025 | 2/16/2026
2026 | Horse | 2/17/2026 | 2/5/2027
2027 | Sheep | 2/6/2027 | 1/25/2028
2028 | Monkey| 1/26/2028 | 2/12/2029
2029 | Rooster | 2/13/2029 | 2/2/2030
2030 | Dog | 2/3/2030 | 1/22/ 2031
2030 | Pig | 1/23/2031 | 2/10/2032
2032 Rat | 2/11/2032 | 1/30/2033
2033 | Ox | 1/31/2033 | 2/18/2034
2034 | Tiger | 2/19/2034 | 2/7/2035
2035 | Rabbit | 2/8/2035 | 1/27/2036
2036 | Dragon | 1/28/2036 | 2/14/2037
2037 | Snake | 2/15/2037 | 2/3/2038
2038 | Horse | 2/4/2038 | 1/23/2039
2039 | Sheep | 1/24/2039 | 2/11/40
2040 | Monkey 2/12/2040 | 1/31/2041
2041 | Rooster | 2/1/2041 | 1/21/42
2042 | Dog | 1/22/2042 | 2/9/2043
2043 | Pig | 2/10/2043 | 1/29/2044
2044 | Rat | 1/30/2044 | 2/16/2045
2045 | Ox | 2/17/2045 | 2/5/2046
2046 | Tiger | 2/6/2046 | 1/25/2047
2047 | Rabbit | 1/26/2047 | 2/13/48
2048 | Dragon | 2/14/2048 | 2/1/ 2049
2049 | Snake | 2/2/2049 | 1/22/50
2050 | Horse | 1/23/2050 | 2/11/2051

THE WESTERN ASTROLOGICAL SIGNS

Aries
March 21 to April 20
Ruler—Mars
Element—Fire
Quality—Cardinal
Aries is the first sign of the occidental zodiac.
Aries have the following characteristics:
COURAGE - AFFABILITY
DRIVE - TALENT
HEARTINESS - ENTERPRISE
Aries sins may include:
NAÏVETÉ - EXCESS
OSTENTATION - SANCTIMONY
WILLFULNESS - DOMINATION

Aries is the first of the twelve Western zodiacal signs. And although it comes first, it is often thought of as the baby of the family. Aries respond to stimuli in an impulsive and headstrong manner. The complexities of cunning, deceit and duplicity don't appeal to Aries. The Aries person likes to operate out of righteousness (self- and the other kind), wherein he feels safe. The danger is that he can also feel a mite too complacent.

It's a sorry day indeed when Aries finds out that her "best friend" at work has wangled the promotion she herself has been drudgingly seeking through the conventional channels: filling in endless forms, waiting for the snooty personnel manager to give her an interview and hanging on every ring of the intercom in the hope that it will be good news. "Janet's been promoted," announces Aries' nearest neighbor. "Isn't that fabulous?"

The bad news really flummoxes Aries. She feels like crying. Why didn't Janet tell her she wanted the job? Why hadn't she noticed Janet's seductive new wardrobe? Of course that was why Janet had been putting in so much zealous overtime lately, Aries chews at a hangnail and worries, "How could I be so stupid?" Don't fret, Aries, you are far from dumb. But you are sometimes blindly naive. Because you have no ulterior motives of your own and like to be "up front" about your personal wants and needs, other people's machinations baffle you.

Take my advice. Put your forthrightness in your back pocket and sit on it once in a while. Sometimes life is just plain not fair. Be on your guard. Check out subtleties while they're happening. Head disappointment off at the pass. Don't wait until the bad movie is over and the plot has thickened to a clot.

Talent is awarded all Aries at birth. If developed at an early age Aries' talents in artistic fields may lead them to solid careers in music, graphic arts or artisanry. The Aries youngster may spend hours practicing alone in a room just to perfect a single musical phrase. Believe me, this kid is not worried about peer pressure or popularity—everybody likes Aries children anyway. They inspire confidence and are pleasant to be around. The child practicing his Mozart is probably president of his class as well as concertmaster of the school orchestra and head of the scenery committee for the senior play. Busy, busy, busy Aries never stops. "Achieve and go on to achieve again" is Aries' unshakeable motto.

As a result of Aries' sound sense of self, he prefers not to be told what to do. Aries is a natural leader and often the most creative thinker in a given group. Originality is his byword. Confront Aries with chaos and he will leap right in and begin putting things to rights. Aries is not afraid to delegate authority and makes a fair and just effort in the exercise of power. Aries are not easily swayed by others. Although they are naive, they are also both stubborn and egocentric.

Aries people are blurters. Again, their childlike earnestness prompts them. Aries is the dinner guest who points out the hair in the soup before it leaves the kitchen. Aries mean no harm. They can usually be trained by about age fifty to turn their tongues around twice before babbling untoward truths.

So Aries has the character of a feisty youngster. He seeks recognition in positive and assertive ways. He does not shrink in the face of conflict. Nor does Aries take a back seat gracefully. If Aries were offered a part in a film about cowboys, he would invariably want to play the U.S. marshal in the white Stetson on the white horse. Aries is an incurable good guy.

Taurus
April 21 to May 21
Ruler—Venus
Element—Earth
Quality—Fixed
Taurus is the second sign of the occidental zodiac.
Taureans have the following characteristics:
ARDOR - PATIENCE
DETERMINATION - LOGIC
INDUSTRY - SENSUALITY
Taurean sins may include:
LANGUOR - GLUTTONY
PREJUDICE - COMPLACENCY
INTRACTABILITY - JEALOUSY

Taureans never slap or sting. Rather, they creep up on you, affect you deeply and leave their indelible impression on your soul. Think of Taurus as a long sensual kiss. A huge tender bear hug. Or an eiderdown on a cold alpine night. Taureans are warm (but sometimes stodgy) customers.

Taurus people make excellent executives. They love money and enjoy earning piles of it. When a Taurus person gets rich, he hangs on to his money, investing it in sound stocks and bonds, building solid houses, and even storing gold sovereigns in a mattress. The key word here is *substantial*. Taureans do not have confidence in lightheadedness. Frivolity doesn't come naturally to them.

Many Taureans work with their hands. Even if a Taurus is a computer expert and seems more cerebral than manual, nine times out of ten there is a hidden craft or hobby lurking behind the scenes. Taureans enjoy forging beautiful things from natural materials. In fact, they are attracted to all sorts of beauty. Music thrills them. Flowers enchant them. The countryside seduces them. And art is their natural habitat.

Taureans are forever building their own workshops and renovating barns and old churches. They are not only home-loving, they like to get their hands into the cement and slather on the plaster, if only for the tangible joy of playing in the mud.

Taureans do not take kindly to sudden change. They like to be wherever they are supposed to be when it is time to be there. Taureans readily adjust to routine and for that reason make fabulous employees. Precipitous and unexpected events requiring flexibility and resilience may cause Taureans to dig in their hooves and refuse to budge. Bulls are obstinate and determined to hold their ground. It is wiser not to try to talk Taurus out of a sulk. Just let him paw the earth and snort and seethe on his own. Take a tranquilizer and a walk. Soon, when the inevitable becomes blatantly inevitable, Taurus will budge of his own accord, come out of his sulk and go with the flow.

Sensuality belongs to Taurus. Wherever there is pleasure you will find a Taurean plunk in the middle of it all. They love to bask in the "good life." Taureans cannot resist the tug of the opposite sex. When an attractive newcomer arrives on the scene, count on Taurus to see to it that the outsiders have a drink, are made comfortable and have slipped Taurus a telephone number or two.

Taureans are amorous and romantic without being flighty or maudlin. They are tender and don't mind public displays of affection. Love and all of its expressions appeal to the Bull. Taureans can be counted on to stray a bit where sex is concerned, but they never flaunt their infidelities and usually avoid sticky extracurricular entanglements. If you love a Taurus, feed him.

Gemini
May 22 to June 21
Ruler—Mercury
Element—Air
Quality—Mutable
Gemini is the third sign of the occidental zodiac.
Gemini have the following characteristics:
QUICK-WITTEDNESS - VERSATILITY
PERSPICACITY - PERFORMANCE
FLEXIBILITY - DEXTERITY
Gemini sins may include:
IMPATIENCE - SELF-DECEPTION
GLIBNESS - SUPERFICIALITY
INCONSTANCY - INDECISIVENESS

Gemini people are brought to you by the famous ruling planet Mercury. In astrology, Mercury represents the intellect, the mind, perception. Nobody thinks more quickly or perceives more rapidly than the Gemini. Endowed with an uncanny ability to relate to others, the Gemini person is always "on".

Geminis are active in the extreme. They love a joke and enjoy silliness. Ordinarily, Geminis want to he smack in the center of all the folly there is to be had. Geminis are always at home performing skits or dancing on the tables or recounting their latest monologue. Born actors and actresses, Geminis may not always invent their own stories, but they sure know how to tell them.

Because theirs is a twin sign, many Geminis suffer from the inability to make life-altering decisions and stick to them. They are so open to change and so adore newness that sometimes they get distracted and won't stick to routine long enough to succeed. What every Gemini needs is a strong-minded parent or mate to literally *force* him to complete projects before going on to other ones.

As the Gemini is usually attractive and exudes a special form of magnetism, he is not infrequently drawn to politics. As a candidate, with his eloquence and that tinge of childlike charm, he can hardly miss—that is, if he can decide which political party he belongs to and whether or not he will care enough to adhere to its tenets tomorrow.

I suppose the word is restless. Geminis have difficulty sitting still. They need change and are impatient with stodgy people who never appear to vacillate. Trouble is, the stodges are very often those who have succeeded through perseverance. The Gemini is not perseverant. He doesn't need to belong to any group where rules and ideals are imposed and clung to. He hankers after the luxury of change and wants the independence to say "Ciao!" to anyone who threatens to tie him down. Gemini is not a loner. He needs people. But not dull people.

Emotionally, too, Gemini is a performer. On certain mornings he is a moody Hamlet and by afternoon he's an optimistic Ulysses forging through the high seas on his way to literary stardom. Whatever he does, he's bound to be the star of the show.

When the evening comes around and the lights go up, he may stun you with his seriousness, his ability to interpret lines, to touch your most sensitive heartstring and raise goose bumps with his eloquence. Next time you see him, Gemini may be worried, lost. Frightened. The magic of emotion—all emotion—lives very close to Gemini's sparkling surface.

Because they are so adaptable, Geminis are extremely versatile. They can excel at almost any career as long as it offers a chance to perform— anything from a top drawer brain surgeon to an operatic garbage man.

Cancer
June 22 to July 23
Ruler—Moon
Element—Water
Quality—Cardinal
Cancer is the fourth sign of the occidental zodiac.
Cancerians have the following characteristics:
IMAGINATION - AFFECTION
INSIGHT - CARING
TENACITY - CAUTION
Cancerian sins may include:
AVARICE - POSSESSIVENESS
IRRITABILITY - MOODINESS
DESPONDENCY - HYPERSENSITIVITY

E motion is the pitfall of Cancer people. As changeable as their ruler, the Moon, these subjects may shift in minutes from stable, normal, "happy" individuals into victims of deep navy blue feelings of gloom and doom. There's a quality of charming despair in Cancerian moodiness which can not only break hearts, but can sometimes actually win them.

Cancers make fabulous partners for home-loving people. The Cancer's nest is where he feels safest and at his most secure. As security is the main preoccupation of most Cancers, a good home with comfy furnishings, a few kids and dogs and a built-in wall safe is about the best thing that can happen to them. In this atmosphere of cushions and curtains Cancer thrives. For the Cancer subject, home is love is home is love, etc.

Cancers are good at making money; they hold executive positions and assume responsibilities with aplomb. You will rarely find a poor-but-happy Cancer. Cancerians very seldom decide to throw it all up and become a hippie or a freelance bohemian. They don't necessarily like the system or the constraints it places on them, but of all the signs of the Occidental zodiac, Cancers are the most capable of placing nose to dull old grindstone and keeping it there. The Cancer wants comfort for himself, but he also enjoys providing for his family in a generous way

Cancers are traditionalists. Where you might have hung a supremely abstract painting over your mantelpiece, the Cancer will have put portraits of his dour-looking grandparents, which he dug out of the attic because nobody else wanted them. They will surely be framed in antique frames and will hold the place or honor in Cancer's heart. Cancer prefers antiques to Formica and longs for his son or daughter to become a doctor, a lawyer or a sure-fire accountant.

If you have a Cancer for a friend, you know what loyalty and devotion mean. Cancer people usually make their friends young and keep them for life. And, as Cancers are fairly intransigent, they are easily hurt if the friends in question do not return their devotion. They will forgive. But Cancers never forget.

If someone asked me to describe the worst aspect of Cancer subjects, I would not say "moods" or "grabbiness." Instead I would have to speak of the Cancer's tendency to hypersensitivity. Cancer is easily offended and susceptible to criticism the way six-year-olds are susceptible to chicken pox. A tiny word of criticism can bring on one of Cancer's legendary moods and the criticizer may go on the black list for quite a long time.

Cancers are jealous too. They own the people they live with and are possessive to a fault about their loved ones. They are not, however, tyrannical about this weakness. The idea is not "I bought you and therefore I own you." No. It's more like "I love you so much and care so profoundly that I cannot believe you dared be attracted to that other (less serious) person." Cancer is also easily hurt by cutting remarks. In love, Cancer gives his all. It's impossible for him to understand someone who doles out their love in tiny eyedropper doses.

Leo
July 24 to August 2
Ruler—Sun
Element—Fire
Quality—Fixed
Leo is the fifth sign of the occidental zodiac.
Leos have the following characteristics:
NOBILITY - PHILANTHROPY
POWER - WARMTH
LOYALTY - PROTECTION
Leo sins may include:
ARROGANCE - TYRANNY
SELF-SATISFACTION - PROMISCUITY
VANITY - IMMODESTY

The Leo subject, like the king of the jungle, is all power and innate substance. No Leo lacks for bravery or courage. Leos are willful and belong to the sign that most characterizes ego and self-esteem. The Leo person is determined and able. He will always find a bevy of loyal subjects who adore and adulate him. In the role of guide and pontiff of their lives, Leo can be both severe and indulgent.

Most Leo people look a little like lions. Often they have huge lovely manes of thick curly hair and their manner of standing or sitting shows self-assurance and dignity. Lions are regal. Sometimes they appear overly confident and even arrogant. Lions are also identifiable by their sunny, superior demeanor.

Leo people are generous with both their fortunes and their affection. Because of their innate superiority, they feel they can afford to be giving. You can practically always count on Leo friends for their aid in times of need. Not only does it come naturally for them to bestow good turns on friends, but with each favor Leo enjoys gaining advantage and is not above taking an "I told you so" attitude.

Leos enjoy being surrounded. They often come visiting with an entourage. The sense of family is very strong in their lives. Leos love to entertain and even to "hold court" with guests who will laugh at their jokes and nod at their outlandish declarations.

You won't find Leos in snap jobs. Find Leo a citadel to conquer, a cause to embrace or a worthy enemy to track and destroy and the Leo subject will be content. Leo is a conqueror. Triumph is his middle name, failure his mortal foe.

Nothing inspires more pity than a downtrodden or beaten Leo. Defeat doesn't sit well with Leo, gives him indigestion and depresses him. I know Leos who are forever telling me how they got wounded in this or that professional or romantic situation because their adversary was wily or cunning and did not operate out of strength alone. Subtlety is not the Leo's strong suit.

Leos are spendthrifts. Money, come by without too much struggle by the prodigious lion, eats away at the bottoms of Leo's pockets. Then, when he's spent it all on what he deemed so "important and essential," Leo complains bitterly. "Where is my money? My lovely money." Thing is, Leo is serious about family matters and also about business responsibilities. He hates to be in debt and hastens to pay off in full whomever he owes, sometimes to the detriment of his cash flow.

Leos are extremely vain people. It isn't surprising, then, that extramarital affairs tend to creep into their lives. Leos have energy and tenderness to burn. If they are not sufficiently adored and worshiped at home, Leos might just go looking elsewhere,

Leo friends are an asset to anyone's life. Their innate sense of pre-eminence is comforting. To please Leos, tell them that they are fantastic and magnificent. And remember that with all his apparent panache and pride, Leo was once just a kitten.

Virgo
August 24 to September 23
Ruler—Mercury
Element—Earth
Quality—Mutable
Virgo is the sixth sign of the occidental zodiac.
Virgos have the following characteristics:
LUCIDITY - PRACTICALITY
DISCRIMINATION - SERVICE
COURTESY - DECORUM
Virgo sins may include:
NIT-PICKING - METICULOUSNESS
NEGATIVISM - CRANKINESS
SNOBBERY - RESERVE

S how me the upstanding citizen whose "rightness" and probity put every other sign to shame and I will show you a Virgo. No other sign of the occidental horoscope system (except at times the Capricorn) has such a well-developed sense of what is proper and meet in any situation. The Virgo is clear-thinking and almost never misses the mark. Virgo is logical, analytical and keeps a cool head.

Virgos are not coldhearted or indifferent. They are loving and even slightly grasping about their love objects. Virgos are both sensual and gentle people. But what is so peculiar to Virgos is their ability to penetrate the fog of subjective thinking that surrounds emotion-laden situations. Run up to a Virgo and cry, "My house is ablaze! My children are inside! Help! Do something!" The Virgo: "Where do you keep your ladder?" Practical and down-to-earth, the Virgo can be looked to by almost any of the rest of us hysterics to keep calm and do the right thing.

Because Virgo people are methodical, they enjoy living in organized and pleasantly decorated surroundings. They are concerned with precision and enjoy keeping order. Meticulous to a fault, Virgo has to struggle to accept untidiness. Virgo eschews mess.

Often people in high positions in industry turn out to be born under the sign of Virgo. In power, however, Virgos sometimes have trouble getting along with their coworkers. They have difficulty communicating their displeasure without being biting and critical. If a Virgo boss thinks John acted badly at the office party, he may call him on the carpet, saying something like "John, you acted like a perfect idiot last Friday night. This behavior of yours is pathological. You had seventeen Scotches." Diplomatic, Virgos are not. But their ability to analyze complex situations is at the least astute.

Virgos are gifted for art appreciation and are very often creative. They have good taste and know how to judge fine quality. Often Virgos have collections of delicate antiques or precision instruments. They know how to take care of things and can be trusted to return borrowed items.

In the shortcoming department, Virgos may like to gamble, try drugs or dabble in the seamier sides of life. Virgos can become addicts and near-residents of casinos. Drugs have a sedative effect on them. A desire to alter Virgo's rigid consciousness? A need to vacate? *La nostalgie de la boue*? Whatever. Virgos must be on guard against self-destructive tendencies.

Virgos can be terrible snobs. For some reason, Virgos often think themselves separate and not-so-equal beings in relation to the rest of the world. They like to have "important" friends and tend to stick up their noses at "trashy" people. Perhaps, as Virgos are so orderly, anybody slightly less exacting seems beneath them. In any case, I always feel that Virgos need a good tickle. They are a bit on the stiff side and could stand to have a turquoise popsicle melted over their heads.

Libra
September 24 to October 23
Ruler—Venus
Element—Air
Quality—Cardinal
Libra is the seventh sign of the occidental zodiac.
Librans have the following characteristics:
JUSTICE - GENTILITY
AESTHETICS - EQUILIBRIUM
CHARM - IDEALISM
Libra sins may include:
QUARRELSOMENESS - SELF-INDULGENCE
MANIPULATION - INDECISION
PROCRASTINATION - TALKATIVENESS

Have you ever met a person who seems to find everything horrid wonderful and everything wonderful horrid? Have you ever known anyone who finds hidden beauty and grace in people you wouldn't want to take the bus with? Do you know a person who always invariably and constantly alters his or her viewpoint to suit the moment? If the answer to these questions is "yes," you probably know a Libran.

Faced with conflict. Libra never exhibits cowardice. Nor does Libra charge ahead willy-nilly with guns blazing. Instead, Libra attempts to establish negotiations. Libra wants to settle things amicably. Consider first one side, then the other. Libra says, "Don't be too quick to judge people on their face value. Give it time." In fact, by the time Libra has finished flitting from one side of the argument to the other and back forty billion times, the war is very often over.

Libra knows that life is loaded with undercurrents of evil and mined with trouble spots. But the Libran attitude is "Why look for the bad things? Why consider the evil and wretched side of life? Let's put up another watercolor or run out and buy ourselves a lovely new negligee. You'll see. We'll all feel much, much better."

Librans themselves always try to remain on an even keel. They soothe the ill-tempered and cause raging rivers of dissension to flatten out and run smoothly. By means of their good humor and fine sense of what is pleasurable, Librans urge us gently along toward human understanding, beauty and righteousness.

Yet, Librans are capable of being annoyingly argumentative It seems out of character, but there it is. Sometimes the gentle, diplomat needles others. He doesn't want to win arguments. Just wants to find out what you're thinking. Head him off at the pass. Caress the picky Libra's forehead with hundred dollar bills soaked in *Givrey Chambertin*.

Librans love *luxe*. They surround themselves with prettiness and seem to require a comfortable, well-designed frame in which to picture themselves happy. Because of this excessive desire for "the finer things," Librans, if they are sufficiently well looked after, might grow lazy. Perhaps it is unjust to say this as Librans are capable of hard work and tend to be serious about it. But in an ambience of charm and gentility, the Libran revels. In rustic or sparse surroundings the Libran feels cold and longs to return to the land of fashion and folderol.

I have always felt that Librans talked too much. This opinion may be misguided. But still, I do find when I meet Librans for the first time that they have this annoying tendency to over-relate, to recount their life stories and all the details complete with sufferings and losses, injustices and wrongdoings, fears and doubts in Technicolor and Cinemascope. What I want to say to them is "Hey, maybe I don't want to know about every hard-boiled egg you ever ate." Hardly the strong silent type, Libra is placid (except when in a steaming rage) but blabby.

Libras are not in a hurry, nor do they think other people ought to be. My Libra mother asked me once, "Why do you wash the dishes so fast?" I answered tersely, "Because I *hate* washing the dishes." "Oh," she said, with a pretty smile out of which I expected to see a flower grow. "I see." She didn't see at all. But to keep the peace . .

Scorpio
October 24 to November 22
Ruler—Mars
Element—Water
Quality—Fixed

Scorpio is the eighth sign of the occidental zodiac.
Scorpios have the following characteristics:

DEDICATION INSPIRATION
SOVEREIGNTY TENDERNESS
MAGNETISM DISCIPLINE

Scorpio sins may include:

MERCILESSNESS SADISM
FANATICISM SUSPICION
REVENGE INTRANSIGENCE

Just yesterday, for the first time in my life, I saw a real live scorpion. It was smallish, about as long as half of your pinkie. The beast was blackish blown and cowering in the corner of a friend's tennis court changing room. The au pair girl stood nearby with a large broomstick and fire in her eyes, How long the scorpion would have gone on cringing I will never know. Hermione, the girl in question, squashed it dead. It did not have time to sting itself

I had always imagined a scorpion as a sort of giant crablike combination lizard/hippopotamus/lobster snorting flames from a poisonous tail ready to strike at all times. The poor insignificant creature so readily squashed with a broom handle made me feel sorry for it, although I'm certain that had I found this same creepy-crawly in my bed or shoe, my heart would not have gone out to it.

The point here is that Scorpio people bear a very close resemblance to the scorpion in this story. At first they seem all shiny and cute and not too significant. They give the impression you could do them in with a toothpick. They are sensitive, retiring, reserved and mysterious. If you see Scorpios at a party or in public, you may hardly notice them at first. They don't appear to pose a threat. But find a Scorpio in your bed, and right away you'll start to notice how dangerous they can be.

It is said Scorpios are self-destructive, I don't know many completely self-destructive Scorpios. In fact, with the exception of my cousin Phyllis, who is addicted to chocolate bars and hates real food (or all kinds of complex psychological reasons I won't bore you with), and my old friend Gladys, who drinks rather more than she should, I only know positive, go-ahead Scorpios, And even my two "self-destructors" are busy bees, always doing things and making things happen around them.

One of my Scorpio friends is a famous food person in the United States. She's made a million dollars a minute since she started a business a few years ago. She's unbeatable. Another one is a lawyer. Every time I hear from him, he's had another promotion. My brother John's a Scorpio and practically owns the world. I know sculptors and photographers and chefs who are Scorpios. They are all in positions of authority and know how to take (and keep) responsibility.

The reason I defend Scorpios so heartily is that I am one. From the moment I knew I was Scorpio (about twenty-five years ago) I've heard people say awful things about my sign. Some say we are cruel. Some claim we are dictators. Others tell us we're vengeful and attack only the weakest spot in others. In fact, it got so had at one point that whenever people asked me my sign and 1 answered, "Scorpio," a look of horror would seep in from behind their eyes. From that moment on, they treated me with great deference, as though I were a hungry boa constrictor. "A Scorpio?" they would whisper reverently. Now, when people ask my sign, I say, "I am an inoffensive Scorpio."

Because Scorpios have the reputation for being ultra sexy, I have also noticed that sexually insecure folks sometimes pipe up with "I have Scorpio rising" when they announce their astrological sign. It sounds so terrific to be a Scorpio. But let me tell you that just because Scorpios are sexy doesn't mean they have more fun. Imagine all the tight spots being sexy gets you into. Think of all the people who end up hating or being hated by you. Try to conjure the responsibility of having to fulfill the sex-bombshell image of Scorpio when you have a headache. Being a Scorpio is not all that it's cracked up to be. It's a lot of hard work.

Scorpions are definitely vengeful. And they are domineering and self-centered and, well, colorful, Scorpions like to see inside other people's heads and then see how they can direct that person's life.

Scorpios are self-confident to a fault. They love the occult and crave mystery and intrigue. They are determined and impulsive. Frankly, I think Scorpios are adorable. But I concede it's a matter of opinion.

Sagittarius
November 23 to December 21
Ruler—Jupiter
Element—Fire
Quality—Mutable
Sagittarius is the ninth sign of the occidental zodiac.
Sagittarians have the following characteristics:
OPTIMISM – VALOR
GENEROSITY- HONOR
SOLICITUDE - REASON

Sagittarian sins may include:
OUTSPOKENNESS - VACILLATION
RECKLESSNESS - CARELESSNESS
BAD MANNERS - CONTRADICTION

The first thing I notice as I glance down my list of Sagittarians is that they all have an amazing ability to care for others. I've been to about a hundred doctors in my frail little life and about fifty of them have been Sagittarians! These people just love being helpful.

Many Sagittarians are bachelors. I know quite a number of Sagittarian subjects who never got married or else got married once and after three days ran off and never tried it again. The Sagittarian is an independent human being who seeks adventure even in the banal. Seeing the same face every day in the same surroundings doing and saying the same things is not the Sagittarian's idea of paradise. Rather, he or she could be content with a roof, a dog, plenty to eat (but nothing too exorbitantly expensive), a good position in the world and lots of dear friends around him to accept all his moral and material handouts.

Sagittarians are often planning or returning from a trip. They are drawn to travel and motion, always seeking to grow their knowledge of unusual cultures and exciting new places. Those group holidays where people tap on rocks in the Sahara or clamber over miles of rugged terrain to locate a lost shrine are loaded with curious Sagittarians.

As a result, Sagittarians prosper in jobs that permit mobility and allow them to meet new people. They function best in relationships which leave them lots of leeway to come and go as they please. They are happiest when learning and growing and are repelled by sameness and routine.

Sagittarian women are particularly success-oriented. They like to run things, *their way*, and are not usually squeamish about how many dead bodies they have lo walk over in the process.

Need some advice on a dicey sublet or a special color of typewriter ribbon made only in the Philippines? Ask a Sagittarian. They will bounce right out and find you exactly what you want. Then, proudly and with almost childlike enthusiasm, old Sag will ring you up to ask, "How many of those ochre typewriter ribbons did you want?" You ask for it. He's got it. Sagittarius notices everything, pays close attention to details and remembers everybody's birthday. If not by heart, then jotted down in a little date book specially kept for this purpose.

My Sagittarius sister-in-law, Nicole, not only remembers everybody's birthday, but she knows how many times you have bought this certain kind of perfume since last June and whether or not you are the kind of person who likes Breton oysters. It's not that Nicole's memory is so fantastic, although she's very clever. It's that she really, really cares. "Oh..." she'll say after I haven't seen her for ten months and she visits me in Paris. "You cut your hair and had it pushed back over the ears. You lost a pound and you moved the couch. I think you look terrific. How did you ever get that makeup to be so smooth?" When Sagittarius women love somebody, they are not afraid to show it.

Sometimes, because they are very direct, Sagittarians tend to blurt out remarks that might have been better left unsaid. "You had your eyes done!" cried a Sagittarian friend when I met him at Orly Airport. I nearly fainted. Worse, I hadn't had my eyes done at all. He was so embarrassed, poor thing. He meant well. He meant to say, "You look terrific," the way my discreet sister-in-law has learned to. But instead, he mentioned my eyes, which 1 always think have giant bags under them and are better not discussed.

Even so, Sagittarian people have an outstanding ability to cheer one up. If I am ever sad or feeling sorry for myself, I call up my Sagittarian friends. They love to chat and will always have a funny story to tell, a nice cup of hot tea prepared for you or a bottle of

your favorite rosé on ice. You can tell your Sagittarian friend anything you are feeling and he won't be shocked. The Sagittarian is
the soul of comprehension and exudes good will. Find yourself one
for a friend. You won't regret it.

Capricorn
December 22 to February 20
Ruler—Saturn
Element—Earth
Quality—Cardinal
Capricorn is the tenth sign of the occidental zodiac.
Capricorns have the following characteristics:
RESOLVE - GENEROSITY
WISDOM - SUPERIORITY
AMBITION - DEPENDABILITY
Among their sins are:
STIFFNESS - LONELINESS
CLUMSINESS - EPICUREANISM
PRETENSION - SELF-DOUBT

The animal symbol applied to Capricorn is the Sheep. Unlike the dependent, creative and countrified Sheep in the Chinese horoscope, the Capricornian mountain Sheep is a striver and a loner, an ambitious, deliberate achiever and an adorable person to know. It's true that Capricorns can be bossy and self-confident in the extreme. But probe a stiff-upper-lipped Capricorn and you'll find there lives under all that tension and apparent angularity a sentimental and warm-hearted darling.

The way to handle Capricorns is to show them from the beginning that you are as strong and self-willed as they are. And should you not feel sufficiently strong and self-willed, you'd better pick on someone your own size. Capricorns prefer competition. The Capricorn subject is always either on top of the heap or moving—slowly but certainly—toward the summit of his field. Like tall evergreens, they withstand the snows and heat, the wind and rain. Capricorns are winter people. They can hold their heads higher longer than all the others and somehow never appear to be pushing.

In general the Capricorn subject is as rigid in his body as in his high-minded principles. He may be good at games that demand corporal discipline, but in areas that call for supple smooth body movement, Capricorns are challenged. Capricorn children fall a lot.

Capricorn adults are clumsy. You want to warn them, "Be careful. Watch where you're going. Take smaller steps. Slow down. Relax." It is of course impossible for Capricorn to relax. He is always on the qui vive, responsive to each new invitation to achieve.

The Capricorn loves to entertain and adores food. He receives guests with a spirit of generosity in both the welcome he offers and the fare he prepares. Often, Capricorns make fantastic chefs and know how to cook the most complicated foods. Partly, this devotion to fine cuisine comes from the Capricorn's desire to please. But mostly the attention to food native to every Capricorn soul arises from pure joy in eating. Capricorn babies rarely have feeding problems. They chow down with gusto just about anything put within their reach.

Success often comes to Capricorn because he was paying attention while everyone else was goofing off. But if, *God forbid*, he misses the boat —was not even goofing off and still fails—then the ordinarily well-arranged marbles inside the pretty Capricorn head begin to shift dangerously, and melancholy sets in. Capricorns hate failure.

Capricorns are very conscious of the impression they make on others. They are allergic to vulgarity and bad manners. Society judges. Others of us may say, "What do I care for society? I am a free agent." Not your social-conscious Capricorn. If only for the sake of the gallery's approbation, Capricorn will conform.

You can always count on Capricorns to come through in times of trouble or need. They are charitable to others and eager to assist those in difficulty or illness. Sometimes they are hard to reach emotionally and seem rather "pent-up" and stiff inside. But if you can break the hermetic barrier, you will be pleasantly surprised. Physical contact can be a bit on the bony side at first but the Capricorn's enthusiasm soon takes the edge off.

Aquarius
January 25 to February 19
Ruler—Saturn/Uranus
Element—Air
Quality—Fixed
Aquarius is the eleventh sign of the occidental zodiac.
Aquarians have the following characteristics:
VISION - TOLERANCE
ORIGINALITY - INDEPENDENCE
CHARITY - INDIVIDUALITY
Aquarian sins may include:
ECCENTRICITY - DISOBEDIENCE
SEPARATENESS - THOUGHTLESSNESS
NEUROSIS - CRUELTY

A tendency to human love and understanding is decidedly Aquarian. Aquarians are people who care about the sorrows and poverty of others. Aquarians are Samaritans who lie awake nights worrying about starvation and drought. Aquarians wish they might do something about the miseries of their fellow men. Aquarians care.

As Aquarians dream of reaching out to help and are thus crusaders for the good of mankind, they don't always have a tremendous amount of time to spend at home. Aquarians are worldly and other-oriented. Sometimes, their families come last. In their zeal to save the world Aquarians often forget to buy the dog food.

Aquarians are cool customers. Before committing any act or making any major decision, Aquarians think things through. They prefer peace to conflict. It's not that they don't have strong opinions or shrink before confrontation. It's just that Aquarians like to remain detached and aloof from banalities. For that reason, they prefer not to get involved in terrestrial "nonsense" such as petty arguments or domestic tumult.

Aquarians need no one. You will often find them living alone or as an aloof partner in marriages where their mate travels a lot. It is easy for Aquarians to have a few parallel lives, as they never let one hand know what the other is doing. They are pleasant people and usually very honest—in their own way. They can, however, be considered selfish, as they like to behave according to their personal style. They don't enjoy being told what to do. Aquarians are not dictatorial. But they like power. Yet they won't use force to achieve their goals. Aquarians are clever and elusive characters to whom stratagem is second nature.

They surround themselves with friends and are usually liked by all. But, in a strange way, Aquarians are not really *connected* to terrestrial matters. They tend to hover about three feet over their own heads all the time and seem to be observing life from a silent helicopter position. It is said that Aquarius is the sign of madness or great power. More United States presidents were born in Aquarius than in any other sign.

You can be the intimate friend of an Aquarian and expect to see him once a year. Aquarius won't require too much of their mates. Aquarians are really very eccentric.

If you love an Aquarian, don't hang on him or her. Don't pry into her private life, and above all, when your Aquarian shows up after a two-month absence from your life, don't ask questions. Just "Hello. How are you?" Aquarians detest rendering accounts.

Pisces
February 21 to March 20
Ruler—Jupiter/Neptune
Element—Water
Quality—Mutable
Pisces is the twelfth sign of the occidental zodiac.
Pisces have the following characteristics:
UNDERSTANDING - COMPATIBILITY
PERCEPTION - AWARENESS
CREATIVITY - SPIRITUALITY
Piscean sins may include:
DIFFIDENCE - SMUGNESS
LACK OF WILL - RAGE
FEARFULNESS - INDECISION

As the twelfth and final sign of the occidental zodiac, Pisceans make comfortable followers. Pisces people don't find their direction easily. They are not self-propelled and they feel a certain distance from the rest of the human race. When things don't go their way, Pisceans may surrender to self-pity.

Pisces is the soul of sensitivity. Nothing escapes his notice. The faint rustle of a falling leaf that kisses the earth sounds, to a Pisces, like a huge truck smashing into a brick wall. Baby's whimpering in his crib is, to a hyper-susceptible Pisces, the wail of a thousand hungry infants. Pisces is born this way. Overly, tenderly, pricklingly, unrestrainedly sensitive. Pisceans tend toward all that is beautiful, gravitate to loveliness and crave the artistic. Pisceans are the sleepy, languorous, irresistible creators of whom we frequently don't hear a syllable. Not power-hungry, Pisceans are mostly humble and modest about achievements. They are not interested in fame. If fortune comes their way, they'll accept it. But Pisceans usually don't go after glory.

Pisceans are very proud people. They are not cocky, nor do they go around boasting of their conquests and masterpieces. Pisceans are easygoing and seem to be made of butter. Ask them to move an inch left because they're blocking your view. Without a word, Pisces shifts to the left. Suggest a new way of eating snails with a shovel. Pisces is right up there in the front of the queue, raring to please and adjust to whatever is required. But dare to challenge Pisces's deepest beliefs, disagree with his sense of taste or the spiritual tenet by which he lives, and the fish may well turn into a shark before your rapidly blinking peepers. Pisceans have profound personal integrity.

It's not uncommon for Pisceans to suffer. First, they are easily hurt. Secondly, they are afflicted with overwhelming self-doubt. Worldly accomplishment is beyond Pisces because it requires a firm connection to hard reality, which Pisces would rather avoid. Tough and ruthless competitors disguised as friendly warmhearted colleagues or companions may hoodwink the earnest Piscean and leave him beside himself in a heap of disappointment and bafflement He doesn't handle tactics or strategies well. He wants to remain aloof so he can dream and imagine and let his mind wander.

You can be sure to find Pisceans wherever the water is. Pisceans love the soothing silence of water and will go to great lengths to plunge themselves into anything from a stream to an ocean, a bathtub or a Jacuzzi.

Pisceans take all emotional involvement seriously. Whether it's a love affair or a friendship, a child-parent relationship or some other family tie, you can be sure Pisces will nurture the link. The Pisces person loves unconditionally will alter viewpoints or swim willingly in the opposite direction just to please a loved one. If you are enamored of a Pisces, grab your snorkel and flippers and paddle after your fish to the ends of the sea.

THE CHINESE ANIMAL SIGNS

Rat
1900, 1912, 1924. 1936, 1948, 1960,
1972, 1984, 1996, 2008, 2020, 2052,
2044, 2056, 2068, 2080, 2092
Rat is Yang. Rat is the first sign of the Chinese horoscope.
Rats have the following characteristics:
APPEAL - SOCIABILITY
INFLUENCE - INTELLECTUAL SKILL
THRIFT - CHARISMA
Rat sins may include:
NERVOUSNESS - THIRST FOR POWER
VERBOSITY - GUILE
ACQUISITIVENESS - MEDDLING

C hinese astrology, like the rest of life, is really just another rat race. According to legend, many many years ago Buddha summoned all the animals in the kingdom to his side. Only twelve showed up and the rat got there first. To compensate the dozen animals who answered Buddha's behest, their leader awarded one year of the Chinese calendar to each. As the rat had won the race, he got to have his name on the first year out of twelve. How Buddha classed the rest of the animals I don't know, except that they trail in this order; Ox, Tiger, Cat, Dragon, Snake, Horse, Goal, Monkey, Rooster, Dog, Pig, following the Rat. Each gives his name to a year.

Whenever I inform people that their Chinese astrological sign is Rat, they squiggle up their little snouts in disgust. "Ugh!" They don't want to be Rats. They'd rather be something less revolting. A hummingbird? A hamster? Let's face it. Rats don't have a very elegant reputation in our occidental, urbanized society.

But think for a moment of the clever farm rat. It is this rat, the collector, the deft and admirable country rat, whom Buddha honored. This rural rat is, to this day, a scrounger for food, finder of places to nest and procreator par excellence. For the purposes of this book, let's put aside our base image of the repellent city rat and concentrate on his country cousin.

The key words I always use for Rat people are "charm" and "aggressiveness." You'll never meet an unattractive Rat. Nor will you find a Rat person who does not seek to achieve and succeed, stand out from the crowd and even assume power over others. Rats are movers and drivers. They are born with leadership qualities and a hefty measure of guile. The Rat's ends frequently justify his means.

Rat people usually appear calm and at ease in company. They're talkative (to a fault sometimes) and make pleasant conversationalists. But take a closer look. That Rat has a rubber band in his hand which he incessantly snaps back and forth between two fingers. The Rat woman keeps jiggling the fastener on her handbag. Rats only *seem* tranquil. Inside, they are like nuclear reactors: churning, bubbling, twisting and steaming.. Rats never—or rarely—explode.

Rats are not only stashers of food, they have a well-developed sense of economy. They know where their money goes and for which frivolities they are willing to spend lavishly. Parties and gatherings of all sorts please the Rat. In fact, any chance to communicate with others is seen as a joyful occasion. Rats love—no, *need*—to talk. If Rats have problems, they talk them through. If they are depressed, they blab it out. If they lose a lover, they can only cure themselves of heartbreak by exposing the whole gory story until the listener's ears are red with compassion and the Rat has emptied his despondent soul. If you have a gabby Rat pal, keep your Walkman handy and turn up the volume.

If you are loved by a Rat, consider yourself lucky. Rats will defend and spoil the people they love without hesitation. Outsiders don't count. The Rat wants to be surrounded with those who like and admire him. He will lavish presents on them and feed them all till they burst from admiration. Companionship is the Rat's idea of contentment.

Rats are not necessarily high-minded. Nor are they artistic dreamers. Rats are simply smart. They make excellent lawyers and executives. Rats dabble more than a little in politics. They crave power. Richard Nixon, Jimmy Carter, George Bush Sr. – all Rats.

Rats are not infrequently found meddling in other peoples' lives. They get overly involved with friends and neighbors. Rats are not quite busybodies, but almost. They love to be engaged in the running of some committee or the administration of a board of directors. Rats will not volunteer to be on the cleanup committee. No. It's power they are after—power and influence and lots of praise and kudos.

Ox

1901, 1913, 1925, 1937, 1949, 1961,
1973, 1985, 1997, 2009, 2021, 2033,
2045, 2057, 2069, 2081, 2093

Ox is Yin. Ox is the second sign of the Chinese horoscope.
Oxen have the following characteristics:

INTEGRITY - INNOVATION
STRENGTH OF PURPOSE - DILIGENCE
STABILITY - ELOQUENCE

Ox sins may include:

STUBBORNNESS - STANDOFFISHNESS
BIGOTRY -BIAS
PLODDING - VINDICTIVENESS

O xen are worker beasts. As the ox is in nature, so it remains in the symbolic horoscope, the creature who works hard, gets results and has little patience with those who don't. Ox people are always most capable. They have fine imaginations for dreaming up new schemes and methods and can usually put them directly into practice.

So far, this Ox fellow sounds pretty nearly perfect, doesn't he? Stable, hardworking, creative and practical. What more could a human being wish for? Well, how about a little flexibility? Some tenderness? A tad of fancy? Unfortunately, frivolities are not among the Ox's strong points. Oxen, as their name implies, tend to be thick, heavy, slow and exasperatingly stubborn.

Mind you, Ox people don't mean to be stodgy. Underneath the solid Spartan exterior lives a tiny giggling gnome who, when no-body is looking, sticks his nose into all kinds of mischief. As a re-lease from their normal rigor, some Oxen have secret torrid affairs. Or else they write maudlin love poetry and take clandestine tango lessons. In any case, there is always a twinkle in the steadfast Ox's eye, a peephole to merriment.

The dense camouflage of austerity that the Ox wears is very diffi-cult to pierce. Rush up and embrace a strong, silent Ox and watch the trap door to jolliness slam shut with a bang. Ask the Ox to frolic through Cartier's or Tiffany's with you, pretending to be rich and asking to see thousands of diamond rings. The serious Ox will feel obligated to say "No." He doesn't understand silliness. What if Tiffany's discovered his true identity? The average Ox would perish from embarrassment.

Oxen are not shy. They seek approval from their peers and do not balk if they receive public acclaim. On the contrary. Oxen work toward success. Through diligence and perseverance, they prove over and over again that they are worthy of their gains.

There have been some very powerful and dangerous Oxen leaders in the world. Take, for example, Hitler and Napoleon. How's that for hard-headed tyranny? Very little foolishness. No jokes, just plod and drudge and boss and palaver.

Eloquence is given to all Oxen. It's funny—Oxen don't talk much. But without speech training or acting lessons, the average Ox can spin you a yarn as long as the Mississippi. He or she will keep you riveted to your chair while recounting every detail of baby's new trick or describing the open-heart surgery performed on grandmother last year. Many famous writers are Oxen.

Overt tenderness is not a favorite pastime for Ox people. Your friend Jane Ox will probably not be a "gusher." No. Jane is reserved. She loves in a quiet, stolid manner. She will invite you for tea and bake you cakes to show her affection. But she'll never shower you with kisses. Although Oxen don't often show their emotions, they love with a kind of deep-burning ardor that natives of many other signs might never match.

Oxen people are not outrageously sexual. They don't feel obliged to rabbit around from bed to bed in order to feel self-confident. This ability to do without sex can prove a handicap in relationships where the other partner is extremely demonstrative and feels, because of the Ox's standoffishness, that he is being rejected. Ox love affairs require a lot of patience. If you love an Ox, you must wait and woo and seduce.

Tiger

1902, 1914, 1926, 198, 1950, 1962,
1974, 1986, 1998, 2010, 2022, 2034,
2046, 2058, 2070, 2082. 2094

Tiger is Yang. Tiger is the third sign of the Chinese horoscope.
Tigers have the following characteristics:

FERVOR - GOOD LUCK
BRAVERY - BENEVOLENCE
MAGNETISM - AUTHORITY

Tiger sins may include:

IMPETUOSITY - SWAGGER
HOTHEADEDNESS - INTEMPERANCE
DISOBEDIENCE - ITINERANCY

Tiger people are hasty and passionate. Their judgment isn't always perfect and they hate rules unless they make them themselves. It's common to meet Tigers who have held many different (and sometimes very responsible) jobs in their lives. Tigers need change and movement. They hate to stand still or feel confined by outside forces.

Tigers are frequently identifiable by their velvet-footed tread. They move in a rather liquid fashion, arms out slightly, shoulders thrown back.

To the Tiger, all fashion is snobbery. He wouldn't be impressed if Saint Laurent were holding a press conference in his bathroom. Yet, Tiger people love to think of themselves as innovators and pacesetters. And the Tiger's pace is indeed frequently more avant-garde than the current mode. The Tiger seeks out the unusual and then tries to call it his own.

Tigers are go-ahead people. They rush headlong into nests of hungry piranhas that even a killer shark would give a wide berth. Attracted to the zany and outrageous in both friends and mates, the Tiger frequently finds himself hitched to a loony. There's something about this tawny beast that says, "Come along, Nutcase. I'll take care of you. Just amuse me with your crazy antics and we will live happily ever after."

Months or even years later, when the Tiger finds himself being held by the throat against the wall of his lair, threatened both mentally and physically, he simply gives a push with his hind legs and leaps to safety—always landing on his feet. Relationships and circumstances that would drive anyone else to the brink of suicide leave the Tiger person unshaken and even smiling. How does he do it? Let's just say that when the going gets rough, the Tiger's well-developed self-preservation instinct comes to the rescue and, in a rush of adrenalin, he lopes off into the hills.

The Tiger subject is not interested in money (I say this in full knowledge of the fact that some Tiger subjects are lusciously rich and prowl around in luxury.) But what I mean is that Tiger people are not *conscious* of money. They like to have enough—even a lot—of money. But they are not unduly preoccupied by the acquisition of it. For the Tiger, no matter what he does, there will always be ample—until one day there is no more. When they have it, Tigers spend it. And when they have no more, they get more. This does not mean that Tigers are always industrious. But it does mean they are very, very lucky.

Tigers like to be honest. But sometimes circumstances push them to commit small crimes. They cannot tolerate either authority or "unfair" laws. They hate injustice and will fight to the death defending their opinions. As Tigers have natural authority, they are often found in positions of influence or power. But because they are so mobile and fond of change, many intemperate Tigers find themselves at age fifty without a position of importance worthy of their talents. Curiously, the secret of Tiger success lies in his ability to cultivate solid, serious and sound- thinking advisers and friends. If he chooses his lieutenants wisely, the Tiger will always be a winner. He must learn to ask for counsel and help, to learn from experience and derive lessons from all his mistakes. Then, and only then, when the Tiger learns moderation, will he succeed.

Cat/Rabbit*
1903. 1915, 1927. 1939, 1951, 1963,
1975, 1987, 1999, 2011, 2023, 2035,
2007, 2059, 2071, 2085, 2095
Cat is Yin. Cat is the fourth sign of the Chinese horoscope.
Cats have the following characteristics:
TACT - PRUDENCE
FINESSE - LONGEVITY
VIRTUE - AMBITION
Cat sins may include:
SECRETIVENESS - DILETTANTISM
SQUEAMISHNESS - HYPOCHONDRIA
PEDANTRY - COMPLEXITY

Since first I began to be identified with Chinese astrology, some Asian people have written, phoned and practically threatened my life because I call the fourth Chinese sign Cat instead of what they know as the traditional Rabbit or Hare. You may call it Hippopotamus if you want, but I learned Asian Astrology from the Vietnamese who, like some other Asians call this sign Cat. So what if it's Cat to me and Rabbit to you? It's the character that counts.

The Cat person is immediately identifiable by his air of refinement. Cats don't favor ostentation. Be he a lumber-jacketed colossus or a peasant woman in Burgundy, the president of a bank or a ballerina, the Cat bespeaks good taste and chic. Cats are drawn to the classical and tend toward clothing and furnishings, cars and even mates of the low-key variety. Cat interiors reek comfort and elegance. Velvets and earth colors and beiges. Deep armchairs and buttery leather couches.

Cats are never boring. They are sincerely interested in history, art, music, the theater, dance, cuisine and so on, and never tire of companionable discussion. Although this curiosity about the finer things in life is very real, the Cat is not likely to appear in a long red sequined gown at the premiere of *Aida* at the Met. Cats prefer to steer clear of crowds. Instead of attending the premiere, a Cat will usually stay at home in a sumptuously understated decor and listen to a perfect recording.

Cats avoid almost all conflict. They prefer peace and quiet to noise and hubbub and they refuse involvement in situations or relationships that threaten to be stormy. You can tease and taunt a Cat person but you will rarely get much of a reaction. The Cat will lift his head, shiver his whiskers, slither out between your ankles and go lie by the fire—alone.

Tradition and custom are important to the Cat. Celebrations in Cat families are usually in honor of real holidays. Picture a home where everyone is dressed to the nines. Papa is carving the turkey. Momma sets the plum pudding alight and the children sit up straight in their chairs with wonder shining forth from their well-behaved stares. *Chez le Chat* it always seems as though there's enough money and plenty to eat and God in His Heaven.

Some people think Cats are snooty. They aren't. They are however a bit on the distant side. Cats do a lot of "slip-sliding away," and for this reason they sometimes seem a bit distant. But really Cats are shy of strangers and do not value novelty. Therefore, if you meet an attractive Cat, don't throw yourself at him or her. If you appear mannerly and refined, the Cat may just crawl into your lap and purr.

Cats are very generous. If there are a few complications in a loan, you can count on a Cat friend for help. Cats make money and very often keep it. They are careful about spending and never waste funds. Moreover, should yon borrow from a Cat, you *must* pay the money back. Cats are meticulously careful about such things as interest and deadlines.

Cats are wise. They give good advice and will follow up their own counsel with action. They may seem a bit prissy and too well-dressed to pitch in and do their part. But watch the Cats' style when they tie an apron over their designer clothes and dig into a pile of dirty dishes. Cats are healthy and all-around good guys. They might go a bit pale at the hint of a clash or the sight of blood. But never mind. When Cats get back on their paws, in their gentle, strong way they prove to be some of the best leaders and organizers in all of humankind.

Dragon

1904, 1916, 1928, 1940, 1952, 1964,
1976, 1988, 2000, 2012, 2024, 2006,
2048, 2060, 2072, 2084, 2096

*Dragon is Yang. Dragon is the fifth sign
of the Chinese horoscope.
Dragons have the following characteristics:*

**STRENGTH - ENTHUSIASM
SUCCESS - PLUCK
GOOD HEALTH - SENTIMENTALITY**

Dragon sins may include:

**RIGIDITY - INFATUATION
MISTRUST - BRAGGADOCIO
DISSATISFACTION - VOLUBILITY**

You can always tell a Dragon. But you can't tell him much. People born under the flashy and brilliant sign of the immortal and tireless Dragon are most of all noticeable. For a start, they are rarely silent. Secondly, they are almost always highly attractive and magnetic. There is something about Dragon people that say, "I am the majestic one. I rule all men. I am invincible."

Dragon people possess natural authority. Even if you cannot stand them, Dragons command your attention. And once they have you under their spell, you cannot take your ears off their fiery discourse. Dragon enthusiasm is contagious. Their big green hearts are set on giving you the same virus they have.

Nothing, in fact, daunts this marvelous beast of mythical renown. Dragons know best. And most. About everything that applies to their own destinies. They usually have a mission or a goal so ambitious as to frighten three lions and a gorilla. Fearlessly, without blinking an eyelid, the Dragon will slink through the fire and up the mountainside inside into any battle—and he usually emerges victorious.

The Dragon is irresistible. He does not possess mere magnetism. Oh no. The Dragon subject has the power to cloud your mind, put you off guard and tumble you squealing with joy to the floor of his cave. Dragon women are so attractive that even when they are not particularly beautiful, all eyes are on them when they enter a room. It's a question of bearing.

This magnificent presence is not only useful to the Dragon in affairs of the heart. Dragons employ their magic in professional ways too. I wouldn't say that Dragons arc power-hungry. They don't set out to pursue influence and conquer others to acquire it. Dragons are born with their power.

Energy and health fairly beam from all Dragon people. Even apparently reluctant Dragons carry their vigor on their sleeves. They are tireless, going from work to meetings and back to work and then to a party and afterward home to bed down the kids and then out to another gathering and finally home to stay up and listen to some music and chat with their spouse. Ask the next vital, busy, noisy person you meet what their Chinese sign is and they will very likely tell you "I'm a Dragon!" in no uncertain terms.

If yon have a Dragon in your life and you consider that Dragon to be insensitive to your needs, take my advice—weep! That's right. Snivel. Sob. Bawl. Then through the cloud of your tears, watch the seemingly impenetrable Dragon begin to warm up, glow with pity and finally melt into a greenish heap of altruism at your feet. Tears will melt even the scaliest Dragon heart. They are all terminally sentimental.

Finally, what the Dragon needs most from those who live with him and share his life is indulgence. If Dragons make too much brouhaha and wake the baby, they don't do it on purpose. They just have to turn up the radio and rumple the newspaper and make loud pronouncements. They really can't help it if they disturb. They like parties, festivals, holidays, picnics, fireworks and roller coasters. Give them a crepe paper streamer and a paper hat and they'll love you forever.

Snake
1905, 1917, 1929, 1941, 1953, 1965,
1977, 1989, 2001, 2013, 2025, 2037,
2049, 2061, 2073, 2085, 2097
Snake is Yin. Snake is the sixth sign of the Chinese horoscope.
Snakes have the following characteristics:
INTUITION - SAGACITY
ATTRACTIVENESS - CLAIRVOYANCE
DISCRETION - COMPASSION
Snake sins may include:
DISSIMULATION - CUPIDITY
EXTRAVAGANCE - PRESUMPTION
LAZINESS - EXCLUSIVENESS

In our Judeo-Christian society, snakes don't have a terrific image. It was, after all, the snake's body in which our charm-crazy devil chose to hide whilst tempting poor Eve with an apple. But in the Chinese culture, snakes are considered both wise and beautiful, beneficial and sensual. Therefore, my Aunt Florence's comment about her handsome neighbor who made off with his wife's hairdresser, "That snake!" doesn't always hold true. Snakes can be ultra-virtuous people. Except of course when they are lying.

Snakes are always beautiful. Even if they are not classically pretty to look at, there is a quality about Snakes that makes them lovely to look at. Snakes dress well and even a bit ostentatiously. They apply cosmetics and drape jewelry and fix up this and tack up that just the way it should be. Snakes have a natural talent for elegance. They adore accessories, scarves gloves, hats, Cartier watches, Louis Vuitton luggage and—well—money.

In China, to tell a woman that she is a "veritable snake" is the summit of all compliments. And why not? Snakes are fabulous people. No only do they look sensational, but they are wise. Ask a Snake for advice and he will sit down, ponder and consider before replying. Because Snakes have inborn intuition about almost everything, they get a lot or hunches. They are frequently clairvoyant. What's more, they can strike with unmitigated cheek at a moment's notice, cut an adversary to the quick and slink away with impunity.

Why do you suppose almost all Snake people are rich? They always seem to have money coming out of their silken sleeves and yet, when you take a good look, they don't seem to have to work too hard to come by their wealth. It must be the charm and the inimitable attractiveness that causes the pennies to rise from the pockets of others and float into those elegant, decorative purses Snakes are so famous for.

In fact, if I tell you the whole truth about Snakes, I have to admit that although some of my best friends are Snakes, they all have a dreadful streak of laziness. Indolence is the Snake's real and only enemy. He or she must fight every day to move up and forward and go and do. Inside, the Snake has enormous ambition. But the will is not always the way. Snake people must do daily battle with the great god gravity, get out of their cozy beds and slither out into the big cold world.

Snakes are possessive. No. Not possessive. Snakes are positively *feudal* about their mates. They are said to roll themselves around the loved one until the person is smothered by their enchanting beauty and charm. Certain unsuspecting people are well-advised to stay away from Snakes.

Snakes are extravagant and are known to purchase enormously expensive items without a qualm. However, much of the time the Snake is close with his wealth and is loath to spend money on day-to-day routine items. Splurging is fun but buying the milk is a chore. The Snake likes to recline and prefers cake to milk anyway.

Horse

1906, 1918, 1930, 1942, 1954, 1966,
1978, 1990. 2002, 2014, 2026, 2058,
2050, 2062, 2074, 2086, 2098

Horse is Yang. Horse is the seventh sign of the Chinese horoscope.
Horses have the following characteristics:

PERSUASIVENESS - STYLE
AUTONOMY - DEXTERITY
POPULARITY - ACCOMPLISHMENT

Horse sins may include:

SELFISHNESS - HASTE
UNSCRUPULOUSNESS - ANXIETY
REBELLION - PRAGMATISM

Horse people make difficult children, tormented adolescents who refuse to grow up and talented middle-agers who turn out to be damned extraordinary folk.

Horses cannot bear to be held in check. They must express themselves, feel free and operate in an atmosphere that reflects them—and only them. At home, the vases should be filled with bouquets of their favorite flowers. The food should consist only of the Horse's favorites. It's tough for the Horse to see other people's points of view. *His* way is so obviously the *best* way. Why, he wonders, should anyone go looking for a better solution?

Very often, immediately following childhood, whenever they can, Horses leave home. It is thought, for their well-being, that Horses ought rather to evolve directly from home into a marriage where solidity and stability, children and responsibility will keep them from self-destruction. But, as Horse people are essentially rebellious, they don't often take the counsel of the sages. They decide to be free and strike out on their own; they rent their own apartment in a city far from home where they can breathe the purest air of independence without some parent or sibling knocking on their privacy and meddling in their affairs.

Freedom from all constraint is, in fact, the young Horse's dream.

Trouble is, sometimes his dreams are bigger than his stomach, and when he gets out there on his own, he can't handle it.

Horses often imagine the impossible to be at the tips of their busy fingers. They might pilot an airplane single-handed without so much as one lesson in flying. Or why not schuss down Mont Blanc one Friday afternoon nest week? Do they know how to ski?

"No. But it can't be that hard. Everyone does it."

In fact, horses *can* learn to do almost any sport or craft. They are talented for everything from building their own houses to whipping up a salmon mousse for a hundred people. They have clever hands and can turn the least attractive piece of yarn left over from the afghan your Aunt Ethel knitted in 1943 into a sweater or a bathing suit fit for royalty. Whatever they may do, Horses are never awkward. They dress well and carry themselves with dignity.

Horses make delightful companions and excellent friends. They are built for hard work. Once they get off the ground and out of the long-suffering adolescent stage, most Horse people are on the way to surefire success.

Above all, the Horse is a rank pragmatist. If marriage is not exactly as prettily idyllic as the Horse had in mind, it's okay. The Horse will make do. He'll find a rationale to help him cope. Horses are troupers, practical in the extreme and only idealistic to a point.

Sheep

1907, 1919, 1931, 1945, 1955, 1967,
1979, 1991, 2003, 2015, 2027, 2039,
2051, 2063. 2075, 2087, 2099

Sheep is Yin. Sheep is the eighth sign of the Chinese horoscope.
Sheep have the following characteristics

INVENTION - WHIMSY
SENSITIVITY - GOOD MANNERS
PERSEVERANCE - TASTE

Sheep sins may include:

PARASITISM - PESSIMISM
LACK OF FORESIGHT - IMPRACTICALITY
TARDINESS - WORRY

Sheep need security. Yet most of the time they don't know how to create it for themselves. They like to feel that whatever it takes to keep them comfortable and warm will always be available for the taking. Sheep are peace-loving and dependent souls who, according to the Chinese, thrive best in fertile fields belonging chiefly to other more go-getting people.

The Sheep lives in the present. He is capable of enormous protracted effort and can work steadily round the clock day after day, night after night, until he drops. Then for three weeks he may not get out of bed. Time, in the way others conceive it, doesn't exist for Sheep. Now is now and there is no future or past. Sheep don't have much sense of consequence. If they paint a wall, they are painting *that* wall. And it will be

beautifully smooth. But Sheep don't necessarily see that their wall relates to surrounding walls and that if they paint theirs blue, it might not match the others. Blue is pretty. Blue is now.

Matching is however something that Sheep people do very well— and often. They are practically never unattached. Either they remain part of a tight, united family unit or else they evolve from that into a strong couple commitment. Sheep don't like to be on the loose.

So far, Sheep sound exasperating, don't they? Well, don't despair yet. Sheep are also wonderful. They are enormously creative. They can invent almost anything from scratch, and whatever they make with their hands is lovely. They *can* build and repair and craft better than anybody else. Goals are gifted for fantasy and bring into the lives of all who surround them a touch of fancy and an atmosphere of charm unparalleled.

As I have had my share of Sheep littering my living room (my father, my ex-husband), I feel I have earned the right to claim that Sheep have always given me the distinct impression, while embellishing my life, that I am a combination of Julius Caesar and Attila the Hun. Warm, accommodating, easygoing, inertia-worshiping Sheep people bring out the worst in intrinsically active, bossy folks like myself. What's worse, Sheep don't really mind if you yell at them and tell them off. It's all right if the kitchen's on fire. Go ahead and scream. The Sheep will bring the bandages and drive the ambulance. But he will not join you in your hysteria,

The quotient of impracticably among Sheep is very elevated. Sheep people don't cotton to rules and regulations. If it is going to take three years for them to finish a task, then it will take three years. They don't want to know about deadlines. Sheep can't stop their lofty creative pursuits for something so banal as work!

Need I add that Sheep need to be pushed in order to succeed? Usually Sheep are so talented at what they do that you cannot imagine why they aren't famous. (And sometimes they are very famous). But most times they can't cut through the difficult red tape and string-pulling necessary for success in the big bad world. Sheep don't like to hurry or plan. They prefer to do their own work at home, show it to a chosen few friends and starve until you show up with the groceries.

The rare times when Sheep really want something, they do know how to go after it. They also make formidable enemies. As they are dreamers and musers, Sheep spend a lot of time thinking up baroque schemes designed to unhinge their adversaries.

Monkey

1908, 1920, 1932, 1944, 1956, 1968,
1980, 1992, 2004, 3016, 2028, 2040,
2052, 2064, 2076, 2088, 2100

Monkey is Yang. Monkey is the ninth sign of the Chinese horo-
scope.

Monkeys have the following characteristics:

IMPROVISATION - LEADERSHIP
CUNNING - WIT
STABILITY - ZEAL

Monkey sins may include:

DECEIT - SELF-INVOLVEMENT
RUSE - SILLINESS
LOQUACITY - OPPORTUNISM

There is absolutely nothing wrong with Monkeys. They are stable, upstanding creatures who blaze trails, love children and animals, take trouble with detail, and, one is tempted to say, "see no evil, hear no evil, speak no evil." When they are not tempted to be "naughty," Monkey people are the nicest people you would want to know. Trouble is, Monkeys are a mite childish and, like kids, are often drawn to mischief. And when Monkeys get into mischief, hold your hats!

The thing about Monkeys that charms the pants off almost anybody who encounters them is that they are adorable. Monkeys, even at their most vain and chattery, are irresistibly lovable. They make you laugh and are often informative; they are pleasant to look at as they care enormously about their appearance, and. most of all, Monkeys are nice. They make super, long-lasting friends, fine neighbors and excellent employees. Monkeys are naturally conscientious and always prefer to see a job well done rather than sign their name to a slapdash piece of work.

Take a look at the person who cracks the most jokes at the next party you attend. Does he or she have simian features? Is there anything wiry and agile about his morphology? Moving from audience to audience, the Monkey seeks out his most appreciative public and then proceeds to dazzle with rib-tickling tales of experiences he's had or eccentric people he's known. And if this tactic, that of the charming raconteur, doesn't work, don't put it past the Monkey to unbutton his shirt, put it on backward and clown around that way. If you don't pay attention to a Monkey, trust him to find a way to see that you do.

Most admirable about Monkey people is their ability to solve problems. It is difficult to imagine a dilemma wherein the Monkey cannot take the upper hand, wade through the gory particulars, think up new and exotic ways to get at the pith of the problem and come triumphantly, if somewhat the worse for wear, out the other side.

Monkeys make excellent business people. They are apt at negotiating deals and finding little ways to beat their adversaries at their own game. Monkeys like sports and are usually very fit. If they gain too much weight or notice a paunch forming atop their waistline, Monkeys are the first to go on diets, work out and find a way to solve the fat problem.

Deep inside of Monkeys runs a current of equilibrium. No matter how crazy they go; or how much they overindulge, Monkeys always land on their feet. They never sink into self-destruction and are gifted with an uncanny ability to stand back from themselves, appraise the results of their follies and pull themselves together. In the pit of their most profound selves lives a little watcher whose job it is to warn the Monkey of danger. If he listens to his watcher and heeds the watcher's advice, the Monkey will never fall apart.

Finally, if you have a Monkey close to you, my advice is, let him swing. He can go out and stay out and carouse and philander. But the essentially good Monkey will always come home to his favorite tree. Monkeys often have lots of children and make exceptional parents, taking original stands where child-rearing is concerned, helping them over hurdles in adolescence and always being able to recall their own childhoods—hence understanding and communicating, endlessly communicating.

Rooster
1909, 1921, 1933, 1945, 1957, 1969,
1981, 1993, 2005, 2017, 2029, 2041,
2053, 2065, 2077, 2089

Rooster is Yin. Rooster is the tenth sign of the Chinese horoscope.
Roosters have the following characteristics:

RESILIENCE - CONSERVATISM
ENTHUSIASM - CHIC
CANDOR - HUMOR
Rooster sins may include:
COCKINESS - PEDANTRY
BOASTFULNESS - BOSSINESS
BLIND FAITH - DISSIPATION

To his exaggerated sense of style, the Rooster may bring a smidgen of boastfulness. Roosters like to discuss what and whom they know, where they buy their fishing gear, telescopes and kitchen equipment. In all cases, only the most "a la mode" shops will do. Roosters stay abreast of fashion and are some of the quickest to be the first on their block to own whatever new gadget is going. In fact, all Roosters are dandies and feel that appearance is everything in life.

Aside from a burning desire for novelty and facade, Roosters are quite independent. Roosters don't need people around them applauding their every move. In their own right, they are strong and resilient. Reversals never finish off Rooster people. Roosters will repeatedly rise from the ashes of bankruptcy. They can bounce back within hours after a broken heart. Roosters are scrappers with life. They know how to resist despair.

All Roosters should have at least one secretary. They hate and despise bureaucratic chores and paperwork. They don't believe in filling in forms waiting in line for a driver's license or putting in an insurance claim.

Roosters don't mind any new activity, adventure, trip, project, purchase or plan. When they get a bee in their bonnet about doing something, whether it's flying helicopters or learning to play the medieval harp, Roosters go right ahead and do it. Nothing daunts the Rooster.

Roosters are generators. Energy radiates from them. They are perpetually on the move, ready for action and aware of everything—and I mean everything—around them.

Roosters don't cotton to authority either. It they are in command, then things will run smoothly—their way. Otherwise, bigwig beware! Roosters hate to obey. Essentially, the Rooster is a candid person. He wants to speak the truth at all costs.

Roosters are helpful. They go out of their way to assist friends and even strangers in all kinds of altruistic ways. They are funny and enjoy amusing others at parties or even at the office. Roosters are generous too. They will give loans or carry packages, drive you to the dentist and pick up your groceries – as long as you don't try to boss them around.

The most extraordinary thing about Roosters is their multitude of talents. Roosters can do anything they set their minds to do and do it well. I am always running into Rooster people who know how to tap dance, have just won a baking contest and have entered the Boston Marathon. In real life, they may be lawyers or doctors or actors or garbage people. But just to keep their hand in they may decide to give a piano concert in Carnegie Hall.

A penchant for things creative is not unusual in Roosters. But despite an often near-genius for art or music or the pen, it's the rare Rooster who chooses an artistic career. Roosters are found in professions where security is assured without excessive risk-taking. Although Roosters seem outlandish and somewhat eccentric in dress or life style, deep down they are extremely conservative.

Dog

1910, 1922, 1934, 1946, 1958, 1970,
1982, 1994, 2006, 2018, 2050, 2042,
2004, 2066, 2078, 2090

Dog is Yang. Dog is the eleventh sign of the Chinese horoscope.
Dogs have the following characteristics:

CONSTANCY - DUTY
HEROISM - INTELLIGENCE
RESPECTABILITY - MORALITY

Dog sins may include:

UNEASINESS - CYNICISM
CRITICISM - UNSOCIABILITY
SELF-RIGHTEOUSNESS - TACTLESSNESS

People born in Dog years spend much of their time in an advanced state of suspicious outrage. Dogs think the evil world is plotting against them, that life is a dreadful place to live in and that it's up to them to put things to rights. Dogs are crusaders. Give a Dog a cause to campaign for and he'll unearth every bone he's buried for the last ten years in order to see that justice is done. Thorough, diligent, faithful, honest, loyal and devoted—all of the above apply to Dog subjects.

Even at his grumpiest, the Dog is a lovable, if somewhat intractable, beast. He cannot be bothered with trifles because he is intensely involved in constructing an airtight case for his lawsuit against the toy manufacturer who made the flimsy space capsule he bought his son for Christmas. The workmanship is shoddy. The 100 percent virgin polyester plastic is toxic and should never be eaten by a two-year-old. Mr. Dog has the toy laboratory-tested. This time the toy company is in big trouble.

Poor Doggie, you drag yourself away from your desk, exhausted after writing twenty angry letters to school boards around the country warning them of the dangers of frozen pizza in their cafeterias, and you need to be loved. You seek comfort and understanding. You sit down at the knee of your favorite companion and lay your furry head in a welcoming lap. Your big liquid eyes stare beseechingly upward. You sigh and wonder, "Why doesn't somebody stop the lumbering industry from despoiling our forests?"

Because of this crusader side to their character, Dogs are often found in jobs where helping others makes up a large part of their responsibility. They are nurses or doctors or lawyers or architects— or poets. But they are usually not politicians or gangsters. Dogs don't take to crime. They are not after easy gain. They just want a quiet life with a nice family where they will be left undisturbed by the roiling world of scandal and scum.

Trouble is, Dogs are so busy rescuing others and caring about causes, they forget to take care of Number One. They don't look out for their own interests and are surprised and hurt when they realize they've been double-crossed or taken to the cleaners by ruthless characters. Dogs even wear a look of hurt on their faces, a perplexed near frown that says, "Don't hit me again, I'm sorry. I'll be quiet. I won't chew up slippers anymore." It's adorably touching.

This air of the beaten Dog, is even endearing. People are attracted to Dogs. Dogs are nice, friendly, loving souls. Only thing is, they have frequent attacks of snappishness. The most placid peace-loving Dog person may suddenly blurt, "Why do you wear you hair like that?"

It's baffling. Where did this disobliging remark come from? You thought Doggie loved your hair. You react, give him a hurt look and he backs right down., "I'm sorry," says Doggie apologetically. "I didn't mean that about your hair. I really like your hair that way." Dogs must play a lot of "catch-up" because they simply can't keep their yaps shut.

Dogs are basically too nice to be really nasty. But they are critical and very cutting. They reason too much, take things to pieces instead of looking at them globally and eschew fancy because they fear it. They are not mean though. Basically, Dogs are afraid of their own shadows. They lack confidence and are terminally disquiet.

Dogs might be said to blame others for their own shortcomings. We all know that our failings are always partially our own fault. Not Dogs. They frequently cry victim and must made to cop to their mistakes. They have tons of charm and masses of ability. They are noble, upstanding, moral and generous. They make a terrific mates for those who have a mission or want to spend all their time creating In fact, I was just wondering what that handsome Dog I saw in the supermarket yesterday is doing for dinner tonight.

Pig
1911, 1923, 1935, 1947, 1959, 1971,
1983, 1995, 2007, 2019. 2031, 2043,
2055, 2067, 2079, 2091
Pig is Yin. Pig is the twelfth sign of the Chinese horoscope.
Pigs have the following characteristics:
SCRUPULOUSNESS VOLUPTUOUSNESS
GALLANTRY CULTURE
SINCERITY HONESTY
Pig sins may include:
CREDULITY MATERIALISM
WRATH GOURMANDISE
HESITATION PIGHEADEDNESS

P ig people can be awesome. They are strong and warm, loving and sensual, honest—and often rich. Of all the favors life has to offer, Pigs love luxury the best. They wallow in their comfort, which always shows off their own impeccable taste. Give a pig a rotten, falling-down hut and he will transform it into a palace.

Since Pigs often have to suffer many vicissitudes in their young lives, as adults they seek out security as a defense against hardships. They strive for safety, are not afraid of hard work and are, moreover, despite their amazing credulity, shrewd. Pigs are pure of heart and lacking in guile. Even a hint that they might be guilty of an act of dishonesty worries them enormously. Pigs deal in a straight-ahead fashion—but deal they do.

Pigs crave culture and knowledge. Pigs are the people you see lurking about museums every day, all day, dragging their kith and kin to every exhibition and concert and ballet in town. Pigs are the type people who endow symphony orchestras and set up trust funds to assist the local amateur theater group. Philanthropic and significant, Pigs are not just anybody.

Most Pigs I know eat too much. And they make noise when they chew. Pigs adore good food. They quest after all manner of goodies and in a pinch—because they are *always* hungry—may just be discovered ingesting forbidden junk food. It isn't necessarily the quality of the food that counts with Pigs. It's the actual *eating* of it.. As soon as they've finished lunch, they start thinking about the snack they'll be chowing down at tea time.

You won't find many Pigs in crime. Malefaction of all sorts makes Pigs extremely nervous. If you tell a Pig a story about someone who cheated on his income tax, you can literally watch him go pale at the very thought. If a Pig is involved in any scandal or improbity, even unwittingly, it can erase him from the world of the sane. Pigs cannot tolerate chicanery. A parking ticket may be enough to make the average Pig person doubt his own virtue for weeks.

Pigs are not eloquent. They tend rather to lean toward taciturnity. They prefer country to city living. Although they are frequently successful in business and know how to defend themselves where material gain is concerned, in private, Pigs have lots of trouble saying no. You can ask a Pig practically any favor and the answer will be, "Of course. Why, sure, I'd be glad to invite a hundred people to my place for dinner because your refrigerator is on the blink." Pigs are too nice. Other people take advantage of their giving nature.

However sweet they might be. Pigs do have one little fault. They fly into the most excessive and impressive rages you will ever see on this planet. For a long time everything goes along smoothly, the Pig is nodding his head "yes" all over the lot and you think he's just the most pleasant and intelligent and warmhearted soul alive. Then, suddenly, the moment arrives when the Pig reaches his limit. What you think is a wounded moose bouncing off your living room walls is just old Piggy having one of his moments. Head for the kitchen. Open the fridge and start throwing food his way. Food is the only cure I know for Pig fury.

THE 144 NEW ASTROLOGY SIGNS

ARIES
QUALITIES
COURAGE, DRIVE, HEARTINESS,
AFFABILITY, TALENT, ENTERPRISE
QUIRKS
NAÏVETÉ, OSTENTATION, WILLFULNESS,
EXCESS , SANCTIMONY, DOMINATION
Motto: *"I am"*
Elements: *Fire, Mars, Cardinal*

--

RAT
QUALITIES
NERVOUSNESS, INFLUENCE,
ACQUISITIVENESS, THIRST FOR POWER,
INTELLECTUAL SKILL, CHARISMA
QUIRKS
APPEAL, VERBOSITY, THRIFT,
SOCIABILITY, GUILE, MEDDLING
Motto: *"I rule"*
Elements: *Positive Water, Yang*

Who is that Aries I saw you with? It's not just any old Aries. That's an Aries/Rat, the cleverest, wiliest and most loquacious of Aries alive.

Rats are sociable. Aries are affable. Put the two together and you come up with personality plus. Blend the Rat's inimitable charisma with the dauntless self-assurance of Aries and, well, see for yourself. This person is vitality incarnate.

Plans and projects boil over in the lives of Aries/Rats. On the desk in the den there are plans for a new wing on the old new wing, which Aries/Rat has drawn up in a fine deft hand. In the workshop there are four-scale model villages Aries/Rat has designed and will present to the city council for possible use as housing projects. Upstairs, next to the bed, sits a thick notebook full of Aries/Rat's first novel. Down in the kitchen you will find the fridge overflowing with carefully wrapped planned meals for the week. It is impossible to keep up with this subject. Don't try.

But don't sit around and look unbusy either. Aries/Rats cannot tolerate idleness in others. They are kindly and will assist their loved ones in enterprises of all variety, but they will not invest time or funds in your plan while you lie on the couch for ten days watching your toenails grow.

Aries/Rats love a challenge. They are not afraid to take off into a strange cold land by themselves. They could open the market for humidifiers in the Amazon basin. Aries/Rats inspire confidence. They are not just good salespeople. But they are brilliant at the trappings that go with selling: expensive business lunches, gifts for the executives' wives, champagne delivered to your hotel room and truffles for breakfast. Who could resist such openhandedness?

As for open-mindedness, well, that's another story. Aries/Rats, despite their amiability and charm, are slightly on the old-fashioned side—especially where the fashion concerns a member of their family. Call it hypocrisy. Aries/Rats may enjoy a wild "social" life, rife with lovers and thick with intrigue, but they prefer that their mates and kinder remain straight arrows all the way down the line. "Do as I say, not as I do."

Aries/Rat is a nervous type. If he appears calm and exudes peacefulness, it's forced and false. Neuroses are always a simmer in the background. Life is never nearly so terrific as Aries/Rat likes to make it appear. Aries/Rats are impatient and sizzling with the spirit of "let's get going." They hate to be late and never waste time.

Aries/Rat wants power. But he is not willing to take the heat that goes with the dominion over others. The Aries/Rat character is that of a slightly naïve monarch. The Aries/Rat character lends itself to ruling. But to be a boss you must also be a meany, play policeman, enforce rules and regulations. On the whole, subjects don't "like" those who lead them. Aries/Rat, although position appeals to him or her, will not be able to be put up with being hated. The loneliness of sovereignty would kill Aries/Rat. It he were king or she were queen who would they talk to?

Aries/Rat is in a hurry. Lending a quick nervous mind to so many different plans and projects causes this person to wax edgy and grow persnickety at times. Aries/Rat is efficient. Why does the rest of the world have to be so indolent, so uninvolved, so free from worry and care? How dare they take the time to smell the roses? There is no time. It's already scheduled for a meeting, an errand, a buying spree, a committee luncheon or a ceremony. Aries/Rats don't give poetry much quarter. They can't. They really are too busy being busy.

Aries benefits from being born in Rat years. The added Rat guile gives the Ram a better chance of success. With a dose of Rat wisdom thrown in, the excessive Aries will be curtailed. Aries/Rat knows how to fight. But unlike other Aries subjects, he will never stoop to street scrappings or conscious vulgarity. The Aries/Rat is after bigger quarry than a mere physical victory. Aries/Rat wants moral triumphs—and lots of money to go with them.

Love

In the beginning, Aries/Rat never has much trouble with love. The young Aries/Rat is energetic, attractive and wily enough to seduce and conquer easily. Moreover, the younger they are, the more flexible and gentle Aries/Rats allow themselves to be. So parties and dancing, dates galore and even some social drinking will play a big part in the Aries/Rat's early adult life.

But middle age, work, responsibility, kids, social status and the necessity to acquire material wealth has a toning-down effect on this subject. Aries/Rats mellow backward. That is, they start off tender and gentle, funny and silly, and by middle age take every love affair as seriously as Hiroshima.

This reversal in the fun-in-love pattern stems from the grown-up Aries/Rat's unhealthy preoccupation with doing the right thing. Where most people loosen up as they grow into their thirties and forties, the Aries/Rat tightens, stiffens and panics. Am I old? Am I ugly? Should I diet? Will I be attractive enough? As an adult, the Aries/Rat is plagued by self-doubt in love. For this reason, when an Aries/Rat of a certain experience falls in love, you can hear the thud for a thousand miles around. Beware of the elder Aries/Rat who adores you, calls you thirty times a day and sends you so many flowers you'll wake up one day and think you're already in a coffin...wreaths of roses, baskets of posies, truckloads of gladiolas. It's love, Aries/Rat style.

Compatibilities

You ought to go looking for a Gemini/Dragon or Ox, a Leo/Dragon or Leo/Ox, or even a rollicking Sagittarius/Monkey whose antics will be sure to keep you on your toes. Aquarians of the Pig or even Dog persuasion will lighten your spirits and never bore you. Stay away from Cancer/Cats and Horses and avoid Capricorns born in Horse or Tiger years. You don't see eye to eye on important subjects—like money! Librans will beguile you. But don't bank on a Libra to keep you on the straight and narrow. Avoid all Horses. They, too, attract you like mad. But, for Rat people, Horses are eventual poison.

Home and Family

Oh, to have an Aries/Rat parent! Talk about involved—this person digs in with both hands and lives vicariously everything the children do, from their first drool to their final wave as they go off to college. Mother Aries/Rat makes clothes for her children and costumes for the school play. She bakes cookies for the Sunday School bazaar and volunteers to direct and produce the kids' senior play. Father Aries/Rats heft their kids over rocks and rills at age two just to get them out into nature, teach them about birds—and to show them all the property they will inherit one day. As a parent, Aries/Rat is wonderful, responsible and lovingly strict.

As sister and brothers Aries/Rats are not so laudable. They tend to be critical of their siblings and feel superior to them. Aries/Rat might be the one to take on the raising of a nephew or niece because the child is difficult at home, or because of illness or divorce. But don't think that Aries/Rat charity is free. The Aries/Rat will never let you forget how "good" he has been.

Aries/Rat children are great fun. They are energetic in the extreme, but they usually are not naughty or unruly. Aries/Rat kids love taking part in sports or other extracurricular activities. They will be popular and work well in class. At home, they must be reminded to take time away from hobbies to do homework. They will be talented for art. This must be encouraged. Never humiliate an Aries/Rat child. You will not be forgiven.

Profession

It's hardly necessary to tell you that Aries/Rats are incurably ambitious. They like to work—on anything and everything. They are always gifted for their profession. They take joy in planning and organizing, finding things out and even in filling out boring administrative forms. Success arrives at Aries/Rat's doorstep without any apparent effort being made to attract it.

Aries/Rat is not interested in living poorly or in feeling inferior to his neighbors and coworkers. Therefore, Aries/Rat, who has energy to expend anyway and never shirks chores, is a natural achiever.

If I had to hire someone and I had to choose among several candidates I'd look for the Aries/Rat in the lot. They are not only vibrant and intelligent, but they are loyal to any cause they take up. You couldn't ask for a more committed employee. You might, however, be surprised at the cost of this commitment to your monthly payroll. Aries/Rats do not work for peanuts. They do wonderful jobs at whatever they do, so it's probably worth it. But if you're looking for a bargain basement sales manager, don't hire an Aries/Rat. They never give up until they have earned "enough" money, which is about one million more than is "enough" for me or you. Aries/Rats like luxury and are not afraid to go after it.

Famous Aries/Rats:
Abigail Breslin, Al Gore, America Ferrera, Andrew Lloyd Webber, Ayrton Senna, Bonnie Bedelia, Brooke Anne Smith, Carmen Electra, Catherine McCormack, Claire Foy, Eli Roth, Gregory Itzin, Helena Mattsson, Hugo Weaving, Jennie Garth, Jennifer Garner, Jennifer Grey, Jennifer Taylor, Jeremy Clarkson, John Cheever, Karl Malden, Katharine McPhee, Kelli Garner, Kelly LeBrock, Kim Il Sung, King Philippe of Belgium, Kirsten Storms, Leslie Mann, Mandy Moore, Marcus Allen, Marlon Brando, Mili Avital, Nelly Kaplan, Nick Frost, Raymond Barre, Sarah Vaughan, Shawn Roberts, Spencer Tracy, Victor Feldbrill, Wernher Von Braun.

ARIES
QUALITIES
COURAGE, DRIVE, HEARTINESS,
AFFABILITY, TALENT, ENTERPRISE
QUIRKS
NAÏVETÉ, OSTENTATION, WILLFULNESS,
EXCESS , SANCTIMONY, DOMINATION
Motto: *"I am"*
Elements: *Fire, Mars, Cardinal*

--

OX
QUALITIES
STUBBORNNESS, STRENGTH OF PURPOSE,
ELOQUENCE, STANDOFFISHNESS, INNOVATION,
VINDICTIVENESS
QUIRKS
INTEGRITY, BIGOTRY, PLODDING,
DILIGENCE, BIAS, STABILITY
Motto: *"I preserve"*
Elements: *Negative Water, Yin*

The powerful Aries/Ox can wither a mountain in a half-hearted shrug. This is a mighty combination, doomed to achievement. The stalwart Aries character sallies forth into the world full of vigor and hope at a tender age. The Ox, solid and diligent, carries young Aries, head high, sword drawn, slowly but surely toward serious, demanding goals. Aries/Oxen are winners.

But Aries/Ox is about as subtle as a ten-ton truck in a mud slide. His accomplishments are many. But his friends may be few.

People don't hate the Aries/Ox, but this tender-hearted behemoth cannot communicate with ease. Shy? Yes. And reserved and even forbidding. The Aries/Ox can be an eloquent raconteur. But he just cannot make small talk with the grocer. Aries/Oxen are clumsy. Expression, for Aries/Oxen, depends instead on a tangible physical re-

78

sult. And I don't mean sports scores. The Aries/Ox must be allowed to put his shoulder to the wheel, apply elbow grease, pitch in and get things done, solve real problems. Through deeds, Aries/Ox can shine.

Of course our urban-worshiping world of today gives little opportunity for exhibitions of brute force. Gone are the days when a homely young woman who could carry babies and bucketfuls of water in the same load up the steepest hill was preferred over her weak beautiful fairy princess sister. Nowadays people are rewarded for their grasp of the artificial. The girl with the prettiest makeup job is luckier in love than the industrious Cinderella who takes in laundry to help her widowed mother. Our modern hero is the chap with the zippy sports car and the plastic smile. The one in the toothpaste commercials.

So it is that Aries/Ox becomes disenchanted with life and its superficialities. Where are the values of yesteryear? wonders the disgruntled Aries/Ox, embittered and finally alienated. I shall move to the country. I'll get an unlisted address. Who needs this phony baloney world?

A couple of celebrated examples of Aries/Oxen will give you an idea what this phenomenon is like. Take Charlie Chaplin (Aries/Ox 1889). Read his biography. Chaplin came from less than nothing—the streets of London. No money. No education. No serious parenting or direction. But the brave young Chaplin supplied his own direction. He got out on the boards and did his act. He was funny. But not everybody thought so at first.

Chaplin finally went to Hollywood, made a few pictures and was hailed a genius. Then came the fifties, the witch hunts, the black lists, disloyal friends, paranoia and eventually a retreat—to Switzerland.

Finally, Chaplin retired from society and the film world. He lived the rest of his days with his younger wife and many children high atop an alp in air so crystalline that the plastic world couldn't seep through. He made a few more sallies into the world of show biz after that. They were clumsy. He died in a kind of voluntary exile.

I know a couple of Aries/Oxen. They are both around fifty. They have both quit the real world. One is stoned day and night and cannot work. Another sails his yacht around the world looking for peace and finding it nowhere.

Love

No ideal love is too ideal, no miraculous fidelity more faithful than that which Aries/Ox offers a mate. Aries/Oxen love with quiet compact passion. This is a forceful lover on whom you can count for security.

You cannot, however, count on Aries/Ox for imaginative loving. He won't go out of his way just to please or seduce you. Remember that sex is of secondary importance to the Aries/Ox. First comes achievement (or disgruntlement, depending on the stage). Syrupy poetry makes Aries/Ox want to puke. Aries/Ox will take his or her love straight up without so much as a lemon twist. Oh yes, thanks, maybe an ice cube or two. What appeals to Aries/Ox partners are qualities like folksiness and hominess and coziness and earnestness. Fill their beds with hot water bottles and dab essence of vanilla behind your ears. Eschew frippery. To turn on an Aries/Ox you needn't gild the lily. Just get out there in the woods and start gathering nuts and berries. A love affair with an Aries/Ox saves on perfume and coiffure costs. Buy her a garbage disposer for her sink, a new sump pump for Christmas, and Aries/Ox will give years of trouble-free service.

Compatibilities

Your best bet for partners live among Leo/Roosters, Rats and Monkeys. Virgo/Pigs like your solidity, and you will be attracted to Sagittarians, both Dragon and Monkey variety. Gemini/Snakes melt your concrete heart. But Virgo/Tigers get on your nerves, as they tend to snobbery. Cancer/Tigers, Dogs and Horses are too impetuous. Hands off finery- oriented Libra/Cats and ethereal Pisces/ Sheep.

Home and Family

Home is where the Aries/Ox feels safest. Home is where his or her heart beats fastest and most regularly. When the family is nestled all snug in its roost, you can be sure that Aries/Ox is sleeping peacefully. Anything short of domestic perfection is impossible for the Aries/Ox to tolerate.

Nor can the Aries/Ox accept not wearing the pants. At home, this person runs the show. Any attempt at competition will net the remaining family members one real grouchy Aries/Ox. If you don't want to relinquish the throne, Aries/Ox will sulk and fester until you either say "uncle" or walk out. If you leave them, Aries/Oxen grow even angrier and are capable of saying rotten things about you. But if you don't care to give up your beautiful home and comforts provided by the Aries/Ox, tickle him by serving feather pie every night for a week. It will help loosen him up.

Aries/Ox children will be talented and stubborn. They will not take kindly to discipline unless it seems to be their own idea. School will be a breeze for this child so long as his teachers understand his taciturn nature and don't mistake it for sulking. Tenderness is the best weapon against a wall of Aries/Ox grump. Lots of jam on that toast too. Aries/Ox loves sweets.

Profession

The Aries/Ox has the wherewithal to earn and keep a lot of money. So long as the energy spent during the youthful years is effort toward gain, no Aries/Ox will ever go hungry. But as laziness doesn't suit this character, should the early years be wasted, it will be difficult for Aries/Ox to reenter the working world. By age thirty, this subject's natural caution and deliberation will have taken on enormous proportions The cheerful Aries credulousness will have rubbed off. And nobody wants to buy anything from a grouch.

Aries/Ox is best off in jobs where there is no superior. Insubordination is Aries/Ox's middle name. How can a ten-ton truck take orders from a tricycle? To succeed well, Aries/Ox should try starting a business, or opening a school or even a restaurant or laundry. Hard work is no stranger to natives of this sign. But getting along with others in harmony and cooperating in a group effort is dicey. Aries/Oxen are loners.

Oddly, despite their retiring personalities, Aries/Oxen usually manage to retain a few very good close friends. It is with their help that this subject can avoid both moral and financial ruin. If you know any Aries/Oxen in need, go and give them a hand. They are too shy and proud to ask. But your gesture will not be forgotten.

A third famous Aries/Ox is the deliciously hardworking and talented Jessica Lange. You can be certain this girl is no sprinter.

Famous Aries/Oxen:

Adam Scott, Adrien Brody, Aimee Boorman, Ali Hewson, Charlie Chaplin, Christie Laing, Christopher Meloni, Claude Allègre, Colin Powell, Don Mattingly, Eddie Murphy, Emma Caulfield, Guy Laroche, Jane Leeves, Jennifer Esposito, Jessica Lange, Jessica Lu, Jim Parsons, Johann Sebastian Bach, Jonathan Groff, Josh Zuckerman, Karl Malden, Keira Knightley, Lionel Hampton, Lizzie Brocheré, Luke Mitchell, Maisie Williams, Matt Grevers, Melvyn Douglas, Merle Haggard, Paloma Picasso, Pamela Reed , Robert Carlyle, Rooney Mara, Roselyn Sanchez, Sonequa Martin-Green, T.R. Knight, Veronica Cartwright, Vincent Van Gogh, Warren Beatty.

ARIES
QUALITIES
COURAGE, DRIVE, HEARTINESS,
AFFABILITY, TALENT, ENTERPRISE
QUIRKS
NAÏVETÉ, OSTENTATION, WILLFULNESS,
EXCESS , SANCTIMONY, DOMINATION
Motto: *"I am"*
Elements: *Fire, Mars, Cardinal*

--

TIGER
QUALITIES
FERVOR, BRAVERY, MAGNETISM,
GOOD LUCK, BENEVOLENCE, AUTHORITY
QUIRKS
IMPETUOSITY, HOTHEADEDNESS,
DISOBEDIENCE, SWAGGER, INTEMPERANCE,
ITINERANCY
Motto: *"I Watch"*
Elements: *Positive Wood, Yang*

The Tiger's taste for risk couples nicely here with the Aries' boyish courage. An Aries/Tiger is always someone nice to know, fun to be with and easy to like. Aries/Tigers are brimming with schemes and ideas. When they apply their multiple talents and energies, Aries/Tigers are unbeatably effective people.

We know that Aries are serious folks. They do not undertake projects lightly. They attack and carry through. Tigers, on the other hand, frequently attack, immediately lose interest, turn their backs and lope away. So the coupling of Aries with Tiger has all the potential for the effectiveness we expect from other Aries. But there is always a pulling away from responsibility and an edge of rebellious excess to watch out for.

Don't get me wrong. Tigers are very serious people too, but to be quite frank, they don't like to be bored. Aries is capable of tolerating dullness. Tigers can't. They flip. They flee. And they split.

So the Aries/Tiger wants excitement. But because he's Aries he thinks excitement may be a bit too much to ask in life. This makes a reluctant Tiger. The ambivalence may just do the poor Aries/Tiger in.

Talented in the extreme, there is nothing an Aries/Tiger cannot do. There is no chore, no craft nor enterprise too complex or difficult for this subject to excel at. Not only are Aries/Tigers skillful,

but they are conscientious. So everything is open to them. Except perhaps politics.

Politics requires a more supple and strategic approach than the Aries/Tiger wants to take. This is a direct, no-nonsense character who believes in man's basic goodness. Aries/Tiger will be sorely disappointed by scrapes with crafty brigands who commit petty crimes against law and order. To an Aries/Tiger, what is right is right. There are no shortcuts.

The subject will be happiest owning a shop or running a factory, sailing a ship or even organizing tour groups. Not a natural subordinate, Aries/Tiger is able to take orders from higher-ups, but it isn't very good for the Ram/Tiger soul. This person is a true independent. Shackles are his nemesis.

And when the Aries/Tiger gets to feeling cramped, watch his dust! The shop gets sold, the boat given away, the dog farmed out with friends in the country and the Aries/Tiger is gone. To the new world? The old? To sea? Forever? I warned you. Aries/Tiger finds boredom intolerable. Here is the real capacity for revolutionary behavior. Aries/Tigers combine the soldierly with the fervent. They are truly warriors in life, believing passionately in freedom and justice for all. Moreover, Aries/Tigers don't mind sharing their ideals with the world.

Take Hugh Hefner as an example of the intrepid Aries/Tiger. Though criticism and calumny followed him throughout the building of Playboy magazine and its enterprises, Hefner never flinched. The conflict kept him interested. Playboy was his ship. He was at the helm. He had surrounded himself with excellent advisors and hired dynamic lieutenants. With his touch of Aries/Tiger magic, Playboy was a surefire success from the start. And you can be certain that Hugh Hefner saw to it that he was never bored.

Love

Lots of affection and tenderness surround those born under the combined signs of Aries and Tiger. How can anyone resist the slightly callow, yet mellow, boyish or girlish, dominant and strong Aries/Tiger? It's a swell combination of the holy and the profane. I'd say the proverbial Sunday-school teacher/prostitute "ideal woman" about whom my father used to dream incarnates Aries/Tiger.

There will be much movement in the Aries/Tiger's love life. Inconstancy is to be expected, not for the sake of infidelity or spite, but simply for change's sake. The Aries/Tiger will not stick to one mate. This person needs novelty. This character is by turns disobedient, intemperate and excessive. It sounds as though it would be difficult to hope for more than a very torrid affair from Aries/Tiger. But don't forget that this Tiger is an Aries. And that Aries is a "good guy." Whatever indiscretions he or she may commit will be handled discreetly and with savoir faire.

If you love an Aries/Tiger and really want to hang on to him or her, then you must learn to let go. It is only when the Aries/Tiger feels completely free that the partner becomes irresistible. Don't call him. He'll be bound to call you.

Compatibilities

Your heartthrob may be found among Gemini/Horses and Dogs. Leo/Dogs or Sagittarius/Dragons or Horses or Dogs. Aquarian/ Dogs or Pigs—even Aquarians born in Dragon—will enthrall you. Resist the wiles of Librans born Ox, Capricorn/Monkeys, and their star-studded Snake counterparts. Cancer/Snakes are too moody and complex for your simple tastes, too.

Home and Family

You cannot ask for a more dedicated family member than Aries/ Tiger. No matter how far they may roam, no matter what heights they reach or to what depths they dip, Aries/Tigers always remember their mothers' birthdays.

As parents, Aries/Tigers are serious, if a bit long-winded. They feel they must explain everything to their kids and that if they do so, the kids will allow them to dominate and will never talk back. It doesn't always work out that way. The Aries/Tiger parent gains his or her children's utter and unmitigated respect. But behind the scenes the kids might wish the Aries/Tiger parent were a little less sure of the rules and regulations.

Aries/Tiger kids are delightful. They're into everything and full of love and warmth. People are drawn to their charms so they hardly ever have trouble with teachers or other kids in school. The Aries/Tiger child is a love bug. And so-o-o-o talented. Music lessons. Tennis camps. Speech classes. Computer classes. Everything interests Aries/Tigers. And they are so capable that providing access to activities will be a pleasure for the parent.

Profession

Tigers exude ambition. They want to get places, accomplish things, build plans out of dreams and always improve their own lives and the lives of those they love. Money? Well, it isn't all that important to the Aries/Tiger. Both Aries and Tiger are non-money signs. I don't mean that they won't have enough money, although frequently Aries really can go without. But the Aries/Tiger will not ruin his health or destroy his home life for the sake of money. Aries/Tiger figures there will always be money to go around as he or she is energetic and active in the extreme and will always be able to earn money. Thing is, Aries/Tiger doesn't like to stalk money, fight for his share or grab at that of his neighbor. It's beneath Aries/ Tiger's dignity to scrap for personal gain. An honest day's work should do the trick. If it doesn't, then he'll wait around till it does. Aries/Tiger prefers to save his integrity. His bank account will take care of itself.

Famous Aries/Tigers:

Adrian Holmes, Agnetha Faltskog, Alec Guinness, Alexandra Billings, Ali McGraw, Alyson Hannigan, Amanda Bynes, Bud Court, Christine Lahti, Clark Gregg, Commodore Perry, David Cassidy, Drew Van Acker, Elle Fanning, Jeff Dunham., Jenna Jameson, Jerry Brown, John Fowles, Kofi Annan, Lady Gaga, Lara Dutta, Leighton Meester, Marcia Cross, Marley Shelton, Martin Short, Matthew Broderick, Natasha Leggero, Paris Jackson, Robbie Coltrane, Romain Grosjean, Rosie O'Donnell, Scott Eastwood, Steven Strait, Teddy Pendergrass, Tricia Helfer, Vicki Gunvalson, Victoria Beckham.

ARIES
QUALITIES
COURAGE, DRIVE, HEARTINESS,
AFFABILITY, TALENT, ENTERPRISE
QUIRKS
NAÏVETÉ, OSTENTATION, WILLFULNESS,
EXCESS , SANCTIMONY, DOMINATION
Motto: *"I am"*
Elements: *Fire, Mars, Cardinal*

--

CAT/RABBIT
QUALITIES
TACT, FINESSE, VIRTUE,
PRUDENCE, LONGEVITY, AMBITION,
QUIRKS
SECRETIVENESS, SQUEAMISHNESS,
PEDANTRY, DILETTANTISM,
HYPOCHONDRIA, COMPLEXITY
Motto: *"I Retreat"*
Elements: *Negative, Wood, Yin*

C aring is the Aries/Cat's specialty. Not only does this native care about everything solid and traditional and valuable, he also enjoys the capacity to care for those elements. This person is a generator of refinement, an accumulator of wisdom, a dispenser of metaphysical energy and a preserver of life's finer things. The Aries/Cat is a Cat's Cat.

Cat virtue lends itself willingly to Aries' vigorous courage. This person sets about each day on an intense search for peace and beauty. Aries gives him punch. The Cat confers prudence, taste and independence.

You won't find Aries/Cats managing your local supermarket or hawking rugs in a souk. If you are looking for one of these characters; you'd be better off hunting in an art museum. You see, the cultural bent in Aries/Cat people is never just a hobby. Refinement, beauty and the pursuit of the civilized are the real goals of an Aries/Cat.

Gain, of course, enters the picture too. But this person demands that his wealth come from solid, classical sources. Aries/Cats are not tricksters who long for the coup that will bring them a windfall so they can rush off to South America and cha-cha with a bevy of dark-eyed senoritas. Instead, the Aries/Cat is a model of perseverance. He doesn't plod the way an Ox or a Taurus can. The Aries/Cat pads gently but diligently along on velvet paws. His back curves upward from time to time when danger approaches. The hairs on his neck stand up. But Aries/Cat doesn't hiss or spit. This is not a rowdy breed. Vigorous, but never rude or aggressive, the Aries/Cat is a study in moderation.

The addition of the Cat qualities to the dauntless Ram's heredity lends a quality of refinement not given to every Aries. Aries, as we know, can be a bit on the lumpy side—gauche or even ostentatious. The Cat brings Aries finesse, gentility and prudence. What more could a swaggering warrior want?

Not that Aries needs any, but the Cat certainly comes equipped with a lion's share of virtue. Cats like to think of themselves as credible and fair in all matters human. For the Aries, who is also a solid citizen type, albeit a most noisy one, the Cat identity comes easy. In the Cat sign there are no major juxtapositions of character trait to which the Aries cannot easily adjust.

Comfort is excessively important to this person. Aries/Cats surround themselves with plants and cushions, divans, pillows and elaborate hot water systems with matching bathrooms. At Aries/Cat's house the stereo system is always top-of-the-line. There may not be other luxuries—I do not claim the Aries/Cat is merely a materialist—but there will always be deep comfy armchairs where one may sit and listen to the finest music chosen by our friend Aries-the-Cat himself.

Food is not crucially important to this Cat. Aries/Cat enjoys fine cuisine, but if there are only bacon and eggs or corn flakes, Aries/Cat will settle for that. Usually, rather than spend hours in the kitchen or marketplace, Aries/Cat prefers visiting other people's dining rooms. Time spent preparing meals is time in which the Aries/Cat might have gone to an exciting new exhibition, chatted with a fascinating scholar, bought an antique Recamier or grand piano. First, Aries/Cat soaks up the situation through ultrasensitive eyes and ears. Only after "casing the joint" is Aries/Cat ready to embark on any given plan.

Aries/Cats are capable. They can do all manner of work. But Aries/Cat is not what I would call a "creative" sign. Rather, these people lift beauty and ideas from life, polish them in the comfort and beauty of their own homes and refine them for their own use. Aries/Cat is a collector of liveliness, a natural dilettante.

Love

Do I dare say it? Aries/Cat is not very faithful in love. Rather, Aries born a Cat is constantly in love. Aries and Cat together form an emotional independent. Neither of these signs is really the clinging-vine type. Having a partner with whom one makes a home, spends holidays and eventually has children seems on the surface to Aries/Cat like a good idea. But in the doing, Aries/Cat cannot "hack" dense thickets of emotional pushings and shovings. Cats hate conflict, remember? And Aries is ill-equipped to deal with the wars he dreams of fighting. So one-on-one, hard-hitting emotional rows, such as life dumps in the laps of those who cohabit for love's sake, send the Aries/Cat packing. Or rather, it's the other way around. Aries/Cat stays. You go. Out!

Now there are ways to deal with Aries/Cat's reluctance to roll in the mud of emotion. If you love an Aries/Cat and long to take her for your bride, keep your distance. Be the first to back off. "I'm sorry, darling. I just can't make it Tuesday. I have to go to San Francisco for the whole week." You may not really have to go to San Francisco. But it doesn't matter. The Aries/Cat will buy your story. He or she won't even ring you to see if it's true. Oh no. Aries/Cat is delighted for a little space in which to plan and do and absorb in his/her own room with books and paintings and music and maybe a few cats lolling decoratively about the comfortable nest he's made for himself.

Compatibilities

Try going out with Leos born either Dog or Pig. You'll be attracted to Sagittarius/Sheep and Gemini/Pigs and Sheep. You'll fall for handsome Aquarius/Snakes and their cultured Pig brothers too. If I were you, I'd leave Cancer/Dragons, Rats and Roosters alone, give Capricorn/Tigers a wide berth, and avoid all (beautiful but feisty) Libra/Dragons and their lusty Tiger counterparts.

Home and Family

The individualism present in every Aries/Cat subject's nature augurs a problematic family life. Aries/Cat is home-loving and careful, sensible and only slightly mad. But this person is so enormously occupied with his world as it has been engineered by him, for his comfort and quietude and well-being, that he cannot always exteriorize emotion well enough to maintain a family unit. I don't mean that Aries/Cats are not conscientious parents or responsible mates. They are. But they are distant.

But there is more than one way to skin an Aries/Cat. They are almost too cool. The other members of the family will need both patience and the ability to distract and amuse Aries/Cat away from his personal pursuits. Amuse an Aries/Cat and you'll get to keep him for his nine lives.

Aries/Cat children have a pleasing quality. These kids are born curious. They are eager to visit and see every monument, museum, theme park, movie, fireworks show, and so on. From the moment they are born, Aries/Cats absorb prettiness. Make them comfortable. Give the Aries/Cat child his or her own beautiful space to evolve in. Take him or her on trips and get him subscriptions to good magazines. You will not regret a minute you spend with this bundle of sensitivity.

Profession
Nothing to worry about with Aries/Cat. There is enough ambition here to share with a few more "laid back" signs.

Mind you, don't go looking for the world-beater, leader-of-the-pack type in Aries/Cat people. Their goals have little or nothing to do with public acclaim. Aries/Cats want to know more, see more and do more than other people. They are forever delving into a new area, picking up a few books on speed skiing or figure skating, or gathering information on famous painters of nudes in order to write the definitive book on the subject. But remember, Aries/Cats make their own success. Where the world is concerned the Cat could not care less. His objectives are security without conflict, comfort without interference, and a reassuring bank balance.

Famous Aries/Cat/Rabbits:
A. Michael Baldwin, Adam Rodriguez, Anne Dudek, Arturo Toscanini, Billie Holiday, Brooklyn Decker, Claudia Cardinale, Cole Hauser, Conan O'Brien, David Frost, David Harbour, Dean Norris, Eric McCormack, Fergie, Francis Ford Coppola, Gary Kasparov, Heather Burns, Isaac Hempstead-Wright, Jacques Borel, Janis Ian, Joel Murray, Joyce Giraud, Larry Fessenden, Mackenzie Davis, Michelle Harrison, Muddy Waters, Olivia Hussey, Pedro Pascal, Pope Benedict XVI, Quentin Tarantino, Raúl Méndez, Rosie Huntington-Whiteley, Sarah Gadon, Shay Mitchell.

ARIES
QUALITIES
COURAGE, DRIVE, HEARTINESS,
AFFABILITY, TALENT, ENTERPRISE
QUIRKS
NAÏVETÉ, OSTENTATION, WILLFULNESS,
EXCESS , SANCTIMONY, DOMINATION
Motto: *"I am"*
Elements: *Fire, Mars, Cardinal*

--

DRAGON
QUALITIES
STRENGTH, SUCCESS, GOOD HEALTH,
ENTHUSIASM, PLUCK, SENTIMENTALITY
QUIRKS
RIGIDITY, MISTRUST, DISSATISFACTION,
INFATUATION, BRAGGADOCIO, VOLUBILITY
Motto: *"I Preside"*
Elements: *Positive Wood, Yang*

Here, in the Aries/Dragon, we find a crackling combination of raw Aries energy and Dragon pluck and guile. It's an unbeatable concoction. Aries/Dragon burns to get ahead in life. Nothing can stop the brand of will and enterprise born into this subject.

Guile, normally so foreign to the Aries' basic nature, will color every stone the Dragon born an Aries overturns. These people are not only devious; they are not just crafty; they are so self-confident that you hardly notice your silverware is missing. Aries/Dragons don't ever appear shifty. They behave as ladies and gentlemen. And to hear them talk you might think they are positively callow!

"Did that Aries/Dragon woman really wait till her husband was away on business to rob the whole household of its furniture, kidnap the children and abscond with the bank balance? Did she really move to Hong Kong with her lover?"

"Oh yes. She really did that. She picked up and she left. With a forwarding address."

"Did she leave her husband a note?"

"No. Just the dog. She knew that he was very fond of the dog. A dachshund named Darling."

"How strange. Why do you suppose she lifted everything but the dog?"

"She's very sentimental. 'Couldn't bear to think of her husband losing his beloved dog."

The impeccable Aries/Dragon melts when confronted with sadness. Aries/Dragons fall for all sob stories. Sentimentality is, in fact, very often their undoing. An Aries/Dragon boss may hate his employee with a green disgust. But if said employee comes crying for a raise, Aries/Dragon sends out for Kleenex and a fountain pen to sign the guy's check.

There's no other way to tell it. Aries/Dragon are irresistible. They possess unmitigated attractiveness. They give off a kind of brute heat that topples even the iciest opposition. Don't leave your wife in the same room with an Aries/Dragon if you want to get her home intact. Even a five-minute exposure to the rays emanating from the boyish Aries/Dragon will invest her eyes with blinding stars. And Aries/Dragon women are so gorgeous! Oh, it's awful. When a certain Aries/Dragon woman I know comes onto the beach, all the other women bury themselves in the sand.

There is, of course, the danger of arrogance here. So much fire and so little temperance coupled with looks and taste and success— well, it's an incendiary combination.

Aries/Dragons may inspire envy. Their inveterate cunning drives strong, direct people to distraction. Why, wonders the plain-spoken hard-driving straight arrow, does the Aries/Dragon always try to get away with trickery? Can't he tell that after years we've been vaccinated from his wiles?

Answer: Yes.

Aries/Dragon can see that the straight-shooting Sheriff John Wayne-type character has got his number. But that will never deter Aries/Dragon from trying to have a little fun at the Sheriff's expense. To the Aries/Dragon it's all a game anyway. He has the magic touch. So why should he deprive himself of flaunting it?

Actually, underneath the slick exterior, the Aries/Dragon is touchingly sincere. He doesn't make friends easily. He cares deeply about everyone he undertakes to love. (And Aries/Dragons are capable of true flaming passionate attachments.) They are essentially good and well-meaning. But they cannot resist their own adorableness. They like to bask in their own sunshine, get the most out of life and tear into everything they do with living.

Love

In love with love, the Aries/Dragon never misses a chance to seduce or to be seduced. Fidelity? Never heard of it. But that doesn't really matter. Intimate moments passed with an Aries/Dragon will be of such intensity that, well . . . who cares what they get up to the rest of the week?

As I said above, the Aries/Dragon is sentimental in the extreme. If you love an Aries/Dragon and feel he or she is erring and straying just a bit too frequently, you can always appeal to him or her through the maudlin. Stand at the dining room table, white knuckles gripping the edge, head down, and sob. Yes. Snivel and heave your shoulders a lot. Your Aries/Dragon may have been on the way out of the house when suddenly there comes this choking sound. "My love is crying!" Dragon swashbuckles back up the steps, cuddles you close and asks, "What can I do?"

Stay home once in a while, Aries/Dragon. Stay home and learn to like it. Play with your toys. Dig in the garden. Enjoy the little pleasures of workaday life. If you care about forming a united couple, then you have to do at least half of the uniting.

Compatibilities

You'll have a lot of fun with Gemini/Rats, Snakes and Monkeys. Aquarius/Monkeys, Sagittarius/Rats, and Leo/Rats and Monkeys will thrill you. But nix on Cancer/Dogs and Oxen. Ditto nix on Capricorn/Ox and Libra/Dog. You're too presumptuous for them. They'll find niggly ways of squelching you – especially in public.

Home and Family

Aries/Dragons are so attracted by the outside world that their need to shine and perform miracles for the gallery may draw them away from their families. I'm not saying Aries/Dragons don't make good parents or siblings. But they are not the type to be content solely with the admiration of family members. That's too easy. Aries/Dragon needs universal acclaim. And knows how to go after it. This has to cut down on the number of times he or she will agree to do drudgery. You won't find many Aries/Dragons pushing a cartful of family necessities at the supermarket. You are not going to find masses of Aries/Dragons at the laundromat either. They love their families. But they are not particularly interested in catering to them.

Aries/Dragons have a tendency to make rigid rules for their children "Don't talk back. Keep your elbows off the table. Wipe that smile off your face!" are Aries/Dragon phrases. As appearance is of the utmost importance to Aries/Dragons, they want their kids to put on a good show as well.

Aries/Dragon kids will be turbulent, noisy and demanding. But they are so loving and tenderly sweet that you cannot stay angry with them Usually Aries/Dragon children are precocious in ways both intellectual and social. They are leader types but not always the most popular kids in the class.

Profession

The Aries/Dragon is synonymous with ambition. Aspiration is the most important part of this character's life plan. First, Aries/Dragon will undertake to get through the most difficult schools, graduating with top honors and using diplomas wisely to find jobs they deem worthy of their brilliance.

As a young adult, the Aries/Dragon often finds a difficult and taxing pursuit, like buying a defunct mine and trying to start it producing again—or borrowing a huge sum of money to invest in a broken-down building, fix it up and sell it. Or maybe he'll set about producing books of enormous difficulty and size, which nobody is sure will find an audience. The Aries/ Dragon lives for such challenges. And if challenges don't present themselves, Aries/Dragons will go out and dig them up.

Success is guaranteed this subject provided pride and debauchery are kept at a safe distance. Aries/Dragons tend to excessive belief in self. If they find themselves in shady deals or are drawn to lubricity they must take care to slither right out again. Go back to the office and apply shoulder to wheel. It's good for the soul. For this brand of Dragon honesty really is the best—and only—real insurance policy.

Famous Aries/Dragons:

Allison Williams, Amy Smart, Anita Bryant, Astrud Gilberto, Bob Bowman, Brenda Song, Candace Cameron Bure, Chris Wood, Crispin Glover, David Cross, Diana Krall, Elle Macpherson, Erick Avari, Finn Jones, Gabriela Isler, Grégory Peck, Haley Joel Osment, Herbie Hancock, Hope Davis, Irving Wallace, Jesse Plemons, Keri Russell, Maria Schneider, Marie Princess of Liechtenstein, Marilu Henner, Maxim Gorky, Michelle Monaghan, Philip Troy Linger, Reese Witherspoon, Russell Crowe, Serge Gainsbourg, Steven Seagal, Tania Raymonde, Tracy Chapman, Verlaine.

ARIES
QUALITIES
COURAGE, DRIVE, HEARTINESS,
AFFABILITY, TALENT, ENTERPRISE
QUIRKS
NAÏVETÉ, OSTENTATION, WILLFULNESS,
EXCESS , SANCTIMONY, DOMINATION
Motto: *"I am"*
Elements: *Fire, Mars, Cardinal*

--

SNAKE
QUALITIES
INTUITION, ATTRACTIVENESS, DISCRETION,
SAGACITY, CLAIRVOYANCE, COMPASSION
QUIRKS
DISSIMULATION, EXTRAVAGANCE,
LAZINESS, CUPIDITY, PRESUMPTION,
EXCLUSIVENESS
Motto: *"I sense"*
Elements: *Negative, Fire, Yin*

The juxtaposition of Aries to Snake is so paradoxical that I scarcely know where to begin. Both signs are ruled by fire. Oh, all right, Snake is little fire and Aries big fire. Obviously, this character is not a cold fish.

A Snake born Aries suffers pangs of inner contradiction. Does she tend the little fire or burn brightly with the big blazing one? Fiery Aries always wants to rush out and do and go and experience. The chilly Snake wants, on the other hand, to sit back and ponder, intuit and judge whilst warming her toes before her tiny fire. Whichever of her influences happens to be feeling stronger on any given day gets the upper hand.

Schizoid? Well, not exactly. No Snake is ever very far removed from reality. Snakes are wise. They don't much rush in where angels fear to tread. They weigh everything forty times and then sleep on it again to be dead sure. So if Aries is born in a Snake year, the benefits in the profundity department are many.

As I see it, the Aries' headstrong ambition will be nipped in the bud by the addition of the languorous Snake to his character. Being a Snake, this Aries will lean toward creative elements, develop talents and seek wealth and wisdom.

Physically, there is something of the Boy or Girl Scout in all Aries. But here, with the help of the elegantly accessorized Snake, Aries will sport an air of coquetry and be drawn away from hardy sensible shoes and backpacking to more sophisticated city life. Aries' proud self-righteousness will be tempered by the Snake's circumspection, too.

The worst that can happen with this combination of Aries and Snake is that the normally energetic and straightforward Aries might develop into a lazy bum who tells a lot of fibs. That's an exaggeration, but sloth is the built-in enemy of the Snake. Although Aries is not traditionally easy to discourage from leaping into action at the slightest stimulus, the old Snake is intuitive and knows how to persuade. He may be able to con Aries out of his natural drive. Aries, in his rank naiveté, is such an innocent target for the slender Snake! How can any Aries be expected to resist this delightfully attractive cohort?

With determination and lots of encouragement the Aries/Snake can enjoy a secure and very pleasant life. This person will surely be gifted for things artistic and would be well advised to launch an early career, buy a very reliable alarm clock and hire a nanny to keep him or her on the move.

In someone like Paul Baudelaire, the French poet of the nineteenth century (Aries/Snake 1821), we see very clearly how the Aries side of his nature struggled valiantly against his darker serpent side. The Snake provided Baudelaire with all the necessary seaminess and secrecy to write his roiling poetry. But when we read his biography, we find out that Baudelaire was a respected art and music critic in his day, not just a decadent poet who wrote reams about evil.

Love

All Snakes desperately need to be loved and Aries/Snakes are no exception to the rule. What sets Aries/Snakes apart from other Aries in matters of the heart is their real touch with the deepest resources of human nature. Snakes don't miss a trick. They are not only observant, but they are so instinctive. Spookily so. Snakes feel things in a way that Aries rarely can. So again, Aries benefits from his Snakeism. Ardor and caring, not always native to Aries, will be omnipresent in the Aries/Snake. What's more, the otherwise ego-centric Aries personality will be tempered by the Snake's real ability to create and maintain love relationships.

Contrarily, the Snake's graspingness will be held in check by Aries' good-scoutism. The Aries/Snake will no be so all-fired possessive of his loved ones as are so many other Snakes. Finally, the candor of Aries causes the Snake to moderate his tendency toward infidelity. Aries turns Snake's promiscuity into a quest for brotherhood. All the better for Snake, I would say.

Compatibilities

A wise choice for you lives among Gemini/Roosters or Oxen. Or... the love of your life may be hiding out in the Sagittarius/ Dragon or Rooster camps. You can search out Leo/Dragons or Pigs, Aquarius/Oxen or Roosters. Cancer/Tigers are a "no-no" (except for a fling). You will be able to swallow Libra/Pigs whole for breakfast and enchanting Librans born in Snake years will compete with you.

Home and Family

Here is where the Aries/Snake really shines. For home life and child-rearing, decoration and embellishment, caring and feeding, the Aries/Snake is one of the most doting and capable signs.

Imagine the industrious "I am" of Aries married within one person to the Snake "I intuit." It's perfect. Aries/Snake could give lessons in the creation and maintenance of family life.

Aries likes to build and invent and start projects. Snakes like to make things (and not just hire people to make things) pretty. The Aries enjoys exteriorizing. The Snake is just the opposite. In order to run a good family unlike people are frequently preferable to two similar souls. The Aries/Snake could probably dispense with the other half of a couple and manage beautifully, provided he or she remembers to get out of bed in the morning.

The Aries/Snake child will be bright and energetic. But the tendency to indolence must be curbed young. Don't allow Aries/Snake children to spend all their time reading with a flashlight under the covers day and night. Push them out into the sunlight. Encourage the Aries side of their natures. The Snake will take care of itself.

Profession

Where there is Snake there is always money, beauty and elegance. This Aries/Snake character is more affable and pleasant than most. It seems unlikely any Snake would go so far as to become a salesperson. But there is a leaning here toward commerce and away from pure intellect.

The Aries/Snake will have to look as if he or she is busy. But don't fall for it for a minute. Those business trips he pretends to be on are mini-vacations. Snakes don't like to be kept captive. They do the capturing. The earnest desire to sit down and relax may get in the way of this Aries' normal activities. But it won't last long. Aries may be childlike and impetuous but they are also brave and strong. The Snake has a hard time pinning the Aries shoulders to the mat for any kind of significant count.

Whatever happens, the Aries/Snake will always have enough money—and that means more riches than you or I ever dreamed of having. So Aries/Snakes will be richer—and more spendthrift—than other Aries. They will also be generous to a fault and eager to please. The Aries/Snake seems to waft to the top of the heap through his own aura of superiority. Not to worry. There'll always be caviar in the fridge.

Famous Aries/Snakes:

Alia Shawkat, Amy Van Nostrand, Angela Featherstone, Artur Szpilka, Barry Sonnenfeld, Béla Bartok, Edgar Ramírez, Jane Adams, Jessica Chastain, Joan Miro, Jon Cryer, Julie Christie, Juliet Landau, Lily James, Louie Anderson, Marshall R. Teague, Martin Lawrence, Max Von Sydow, Michael Fassbender, Milan Kundera, Pete Rose, Philip Austin, Richard Dawkins, Rick Moranis, Robert Downey Jr., Ryan O'Neal, Sara Shepard, Sarah Jessica Parker, Sarah Michelle Gellar, Tyler Oakley.

ARIES
QUALITIES
COURAGE, DRIVE, HEARTINESS,
AFFABILITY, TALENT, ENTERPRISE
QUIRKS
NAÏVETÉ, OSTENTATION, WILLFULNESS,
EXCESS , SANCTIMONY, DOMINATION
Motto: *"I am"*
Elements: *Fire, Mars, Cardinal*

--

HORSE
QUALITIES
PERSUASIVENESS, UNSCRUPULOUSNESS,
POPULARITY, STYLE, DEXTERITY,
ACCOMPLISHMENT
QUIRKS
SELFISHNESS, AUTONOMY, REBELLION,
HASTE, ANXIETY, PRAGMATISM
Motto: *"I demand"*
Elements: *Positive Fire, Yang*

There is something of the victorious athlete in all Aries/ Horses. They play a mean game, are both fast on their feet and quick of wit. But they don't always carry through on their serve. Herein lies the first and most bothersome of Aries/Horse faults. Both Aries and Horse are pushy and active. Both signs are ego-oriented. Both Aries and Horse are guilty of willfulness. Couple them and you come up with a mighty character prone to demanding what he wants when he wants it, putting down his foot—after removing it from his mouth of course.

Some of the positive qualities of Aries/Horse are rank enthusiasm, a certain charming naiveté and pure energy. These people are apparent dauntless, and give the impression of great strength of purpose. They'll always be the first to tell you how fabulous the day has been, how terrific the world could become and how marvelous life would be if only you know how to look on the bright side. Aries/Horses want to believe. They care about goodness and virtue and really can buckle down and work toward noble and lofty goals. They love truth and are wont to blurt more than their share. And Aries/Horses are incorrigibly practical. They can fix almost anything with their hands, build houses and remodel rooms in a trice; rearrange the furniture and set up new household traffic patterns that nobody else could have dreamed up.

If there is a conclusion hanging about anywhere, you can be sure the Aries/Horse will jump to it. Both Aries and Horse tend to use their energies more readily than their thinking processes, so they are always tempted to try and hit the nail on the head fast and without reflection—and often because of hastiness, they fall short of their ideal.

Aries/Horses are sore losers, too. If they don't get the applause or approval they are so eagerly seeking in life, they have been known to kick and pout and truly carry on. Failure, for an Aries/Horse, constitutes a personal affront. He doesn't take kindly to setbacks.

Soldiers to a man, Aries enjoy tilting at large obstacles in hopes, of course, of conquest and eventual annihilation. The Horse character, although far more canny, includes a similar tendency to engage in headlong turns at one's adversaries. As you can readily see, an Aries/Horse person will be full of dauntlessness.

Trouble is, underneath Aries/Horse is just another "nice guy" who would rather live in peace and quiet than have to survive in a war zone. Aries/Horse always has a secret hiding place carved out for himself in the countryside or even in the city, ready at all times to enwomb his frayed nerves.

Never try to reason with an Aries/Horse. It's a waste of your precious time. Aries/Horses understand power and strength and (unfortunately) brutality. They are not expertly subtle about their own needs and demands. So they can't take hints about what it is you might be after. The abstruse won't reach them. Forget beating around the proverbial bush—chop the damn thing down and walk straight up to the Aries/Horse with your axe visible. If you want to convince the Aries/Horse of anything, you will have to engage in some very direct behavior.

Provided bad luck is not too intrusive, the Aries/Horse will get on smoothly with tasks at hand. He will be amusing and easy to be around. Aries/Horses are quick to make friends and don't mind small talk. Take an Aries/Horse on a picnic or include him in your next swimming party. He is the helpful sort who enjoys deriving praise and respect from his fellows through his ready application of hands to menial or manual tasks. He will dig you the barbecue pit and drive the whole gang in from the rail station and make everyone laugh because the hostess forgot to buy hamburger buns. Aries/Horse is delightfully accessible and does not suffer from an excess of profundity.

By the end of the party you will find him sprawled on the couch in the living room, snoozing away the exhaustion of a busy, busy day wherein all the activity has in some way concerned him. He's a pitch-inner, a born hardhat. Even in a topless bikini, the Aries/ Horse is both willing and capable of chopping the wood.

Love

Enthusiasm can, as well we know, be the enemy of lasting love as it is often the soul of infatuation. Aries/Horse's romantic foible is his dauntless enthusiasm. In two seconds the Aries/Horse falls in love. What is it? That skin, those shoulders, the way he slurs his esses, a little je ne sais quoi that is guaranteed to turn our Aries/ Horse friend into a veritable abyss of infatuate sentiment. We know that Aries/Horses are not overly sentimental. And hesitation is not their problem. This quick impulse-buying in the love department rarely works, so over the long run, Aries/Horse can be disappointed. Those shoulders were only part of a chic new couture shirt design, that smooth skin was achieved with makeup, and the cute way he slurred his esses? You guessed it. He was drunk. Aries/ Horse should learn early on to watch out for red flags in relationships – otherwise he may find himself strangled with one.

Aries/Horses are sexy people. If you love an Aries/Horse, take him to bed. In intimate circumstances you'll discover a whole new being. Remember that Aries/Horse is quick on the uptake and a blurter and a sprinter. Any preliminary out-of-sheets foreplay will naturally confound him. But Aries/Horses, remember, are skillful with their hands and tend to be, although not truly athletic, agile and supple-bodied. Are they romantic? Not really.

Compatibilities

You'll certainly enjoy the company of a Leo/Tiger or Dog. You may also fall for Sagittarius/Sheep, Gemini/Tigers or Dogs. Ethereal Aquarian/Sheep may make you feel a bit faint. As for Libra/ Pigs and Monkeys, they are out of the running, as are Cancer and Capricorn/Pigs. Generally speaking, avoid alluring Rats. Long term, you will come to blows over power.

Home and Family

The Aries/Horse abode will be practical. The drapes and carpet may be carefully color-coordinated. The furniture will be high quality and sturdy. The general Aries/Horse decor is frill-free, comfortable and serviceable. Aries/Horse people have a lot of imagination but they like to apply it sensibly.

Aries/Horse people make bossy family members. As their specialty is getting things over and done with, they cannot tolerate slow, deliberate methods in others. Around the house, Aries/Horse feels things ought to go his way. He is also convinced that his is the only way. It's not always restful to live with Aries/Horses. They want everybody to gather at the table at the same time and are always in a rush to get on with the day at hand. God forbid you should be resting in a deep armchair with your feet up, your thumb in your mouth and your eyes glued to a book. Aries/Horse wants you to be more productive. Mind you, if you wish to you may ignore Aries/Horse's entreaties. He'll get bored with nagging you after a few minutes.

As a kid, the Aries/Horse will show early talent for instant excellence. He'll be adaptable and very charming, open and sociable. All artistic bents should be encouraged. The Aries/Horse needs to be occupied and finding a passion early on may save him from much idle boredom in later life.

Profession

The avenues on which Aries/Horses are most successful are not always the ones they choose to plod along. There is an early desire here to get involved in artistic careers. At first, when young and inexperienced, Aries/Horse may think of himself as an actor, singer or even a painter. He may enjoy early competence at these disciplines. But later on, as his understanding of self and of the world accrues, the Aries/Horse is more likely to choose a more secure career where his easy enthusiasms and capacity for rapid decision-making are called to the fore. Given the Aries/Horse's capacity for leaping before looking, she will be more successful, if she has something solid to fall back on.

The Aries/Horse makes a better boss than employee and even more important than that, he makes a terrific independent worker. Working from home might suit him or her down to the ground. Aries/Horse people can gallop along in all fields requiring snap decisions and pleasant working conditions. He can be a computer programmer or a journalist. Aries/Horses make good pilots and translators and policemen. She can do very well in advertising. A job, a campaign and on to the next job, campaign, etc. I don't advise long-suffering professions such as writing historical treatises for Aries/Horses. The clergy too would be a mistake. They like their share of instant satisfaction and long-winded sermonizing is not their forte.

Famous Aries/Horses:

Alex Pettyfer, Aretha Franklin, Arthur Zanetti, Britt Robertson, Carly Chaikin, Charlie McDermott, Clayne Crawford, Cynthia Nixon, David Bradley, David Janssen, Dennis Quaid, Ellen Barkin, Emma Watson, Georges Wolinski, Helmut Kohl, Herbie Mann, Jackie Chan, James Franco, Jean Rochefort, John Astin, Kristen Stewart, Leopold Stokowski, Lindsay Hartley, Matthew Goode, Michael Imperioli, Michael York, Nikita Khrushchev, Pearl Bailey, Princess Eugenie of York, Richard O'Brien., Riley Smith, Robert Carradine, Robin Wright, Samuel Beckett, Sandra Day O'Connor, Stephen Sondheim, Steve McQueen, Yaguel Didier, Zoella.

ARIES
QUALITIES
COURAGE, DRIVE, HEARTINESS,
AFFABILITY, TALENT, ENTERPRISE
QUIRKS
NAÏVETÉ, OSTENTATION, WILLFULNESS,
EXCESS , SANCTIMONY, DOMINATION
Motto: *"I am"*
Elements: *Fire, Mars, Cardinal*

--

SHEEP
QUALITIES
INVENTION, LACK OF FORESIGHT,
PERSEVERANCE, WHIMSY, GOOD MANNERS,
IMPRACTICALITY
QUIRKS
PARASITISM, SENSITIVITY,
TARDINESS, PESSIMISM, TASTE, WORRY
Motto: *"I depend"*
Elements: *Negative, Fire, Yin*

This character needs "social security" in order to survive. The nature of Aries/Sheep is free-thinking, eccentric, and rebellious. But without an atmosphere of total safety and freedom from want in which to evolve without being forced to involve, this person will suffer. The talented Aries/Sheep performs best with a safety net.

The Sheep is a bit of a bohemian. His nature is easygoing and pleasure-seeking. Aries is a soldier. Aries is enterprising and willful in the extreme. Herein lies the paradoxical character of Aries/Sheep. The gentle Sheep side of Aries/Sheep wants to lie in the sun and dreams of greener pastures and happier days, while the vigorous Aries tugs persistently on the Sheep's tether urging, "Get up! Hurry! Make that phone call. Finish the lunch dishes. It's time to bake a cake now. You forgot to write that important business letter." Poor old laid-back Sheep doesn't have a chance in this busy person's life. The Aries is always mixing cold water in the Sheep's suntan oil.

What happens with Aries/Sheep people is interesting. They tend to be creative in the extreme. They dress well and take great care about their appearance. They are poised and affable. They are fun to be with. And they are usually more jaunty and optimistic than other Sheep subjects.

I say "usually" because the worst thing that can happen to Aries/Sheep is to stand by and watch his own well dry up. If poverty strikes the source of the Aries/Sheep's security, he will sink into abject pessimism. Aries/Sheep can become physically ill from want of prettiness and comfort. They care more about their own well-being (and of course that of their benefactor) than any other value in life. They depend on sumptuousness.

The Aries side of this subject's nature lays him open to outside influence. The Aries, remember, is naive and believing. Sheep are a bit more skeptical but they are not very industrious. Therefore, if a foul influence wafts over the life of an Aries/Sheep, he may very well fall victim to it. What I mean is that Aries/Sheep must be protected. He or she does not want to live alone, to go out in the world and fight for crusts of day-old bread or worry about whether those diamond earrings have made a hole in the family budget.

However, with all this relying on others for safety, the Aries/Sheep behaves in what seems to be an extraordinarily independent fashion. Aries/Sheep have snappy tongues. They say what they think and don't mind shocking others whom they consider less clever than they.

If the Aries/Sheep is born into a climate of jollity and casualness, he may never want to leave home. But if he enters a cold unfriendly world where gray winter prevails, he will do everything in his power to seek a new life in a warmer, more sensitive place. Most often, if Aries/Sheep leave home, they do so with their partner and their children and pets. They may hate their surroundings. But Aries/Sheep rarely leave their kith and kin.

The Aries/Sheep gives an outward impression of simple gaiety. Smiles and handshakes, jokes and pleasantness abound. Don't be fooled. The Aries/Sheep is not your average hail-fellow-well-met. This is a complex soul who, in order to keep up appearances and not rub people the wrong way, will affect a sunny disposition. Look harder the next time you run into one of these people. Behind that crinkly smile lies a note of disquiet, a hyper-sensitive area that can be hurt so easily—too easily. It's better to resist harsh criticism with Aries/Sheep. They are a lot more vulnerable than they look.

Aries/Sheep can be gossipy. They need friends. So they may just be tempted to pretend to be the "best friend" of whomever they are talking to at the moment. They chatter a lot and easily divulge "classified" information such as how much their mate earns every month and who is sleeping with whom.

Love

The Sheeply Ram is love-oriented. In fact, emotionally, Aries/Sheep depend almost entirely on love and the security it brings them. Possessive in the extreme, the Aries/Sheep will not like letting his or her partner out of sight. Unless, of course, the partner has had to go somewhere far away in order to make money so as to bring it home and give it to the Sheep.

If you are Aries/Sheep, you should make sure before you marry or set up housekeeping that your choice of partner is adept at earnest monogamy You should also take care to hitch up with a person whose outside interests lie where yours do, in the creative sector. Aries/Sheep don't make excellent life mates for playboys, scientists or Archie Bunker types. You need to be understood and cheered—not constantly fraught and worried.

Aries/Sheep emanates a languorous passion. No quickies for this subject. Aries/Sheep longs to live in a state of constant foreplay whose sensuality lingers in every syllable and fills the very air with its musky aroma. So make sure Aries/Sheep sleeps on the outside of the bed. That way you can just give him a shove and roll him to his feet in the morning.

Compatibilities

It's love at first sight with Aquarius/Pigs and Cats. Sagittarius/Cats and Horses also enchant you. Gemini/Cats will make you laugh and appreciate your love of beauty and need for stability. Leo/Horses and Cats will pep up your social life. But if I were you, I'd give up on Capricorns, especially Dogs and Tigers. Cancer and Scorpio/Oxen will be your nemesis. They demand too much in return for any security they may be willing to provide.

Home and Family

Surrounded by family and friends, living in a comfortable house in a friendly neighborhood in a warm climate and adhering to a routine (preferably imposed by a mate or the kids' schedules), the Aries/Sheep will shine. It is at home that the Aries/Sheep feels sufficiently secure and warm to really dig in and get at some of the wealth of creative talents he or she owns. Aries/Sheep will knit sweaters in crazy difficult patterns for the whole family. They like to dig in flower beds and apply their imaginations to planning new ways to show off their prize magnolias. Aries/Sheep simply love to live for others—especially others who appreciate them for who they are and don't ask them to try to be what they are not.

For the Aries/Sheep's sense of self to thrive, it will be best to reside in a posh neighborhood. Aries/Sheep wants to shop at the best gourmet food stores, provide the family with the finest in every available product and will not be above a little showing off for the sake of chic neighbors.

In such an atmosphere of luxury and plenty, the Aries/Sheep will be able to exercise his or her remarkable talent at parenting. When you think about this person's extreme duality—the Sheep sensitivity vs. the brave drummer boy Aries—you can see why this person deals well with children. Understanding? Yes. But only to a point.

Aries/Sheep children must be made to feel safe. They will suffer enormously from divorce or family separations. This is a sensitive and trusting nature. Don't change his school too often or uproot the Aries/Sheep child if you can help it. Instead, try to keep everything running smoothly so Aries/Sheep will develop his multiple talents and fine intellect.

Profession

Personal gain is not necessarily this native's most urgent need. The average Aries/Sheep doesn't dream of making a million dollars, having a yacht and thirty nubile slave girls running around on that yacht waving fans—or fannies. No. The Aries/Sheep is not a grasping, vaulting Onassis type.

The Aries/Sheep will however be willing to die for the success and achievement of someone he loves. There are two reasons for this willingness to take a back seat to another's spotlight: 1) Aries/Sheep depends on others for security. 2) Aries/Sheep is most talented at loving. To watch somebody he loves rise to the heights he has always wished for is one of the true dreams of the happy Aries/Sheep.

So, ideally, the Aries/Sheep should either be cared for by the loved ones he or she has encouraged and nurtured along or be the beneficiary of a large trust fund. But if for some reason either of those solutions is impossible, if Aries/Sheep finds himself on his own and penniless, I suggest he go instantly to the nearest bank, borrow a lot of money and open a flower shop. Beautiful things and Aries/Sheep make excellent companions. They can be superlative decorators and savvy designers – even trend setters. Obviously, they work best in "glamour" jobs.

Famous Aries/Sheep :
AJ Michalka, Austin Butler, Benicio del Torro, Bill Cullen, Brendan Gleeson, Christina Ricci, Christopher Walken, Claire Danes, Conchata Ferrell, Eddie Bracken, Eileen Farrel, Grace Hightower, Hayley Kiyoko, Hayley McFarland, Heath Ledger, Henry Ian Cusick, Hugh Carey, Jennifer Morrison, John Major, Kate Hudson, Kourtney Kardashian, Lake Bell, Lee Pace, Leonard Nimoy, Leslie Bega, Lindy Booth, Luke Evans, Maria Bello, Marina Sirtis, Matt Lawrence, McGeorge Bundy, Melissa Gorga, Merce Cunningham, Michael Rooker, Natasha Lyonne, Norah Jones, Seychelle Gabriel, Talisa Soto, Thomas Edison, William Shatner, Zhang Ziyi.

ARIES
QUALITIES
COURAGE, DRIVE, HEARTINESS,
AFFABILITY, TALENT, ENTERPRISE
QUIRKS
NAÏVETÉ, OSTENTATION, WILLFULNESS,
EXCESS , SANCTIMONY, DOMINATION
Motto: *"I am"*
Elements: *Fire, Mars, Cardinal*

--

MONKEY
QUALITIES
IMPROVISATION, CUNNING, STABILITY,
SELF-INVOLVEMENT, WIT, OPPORTUNISM
QUIRKS
DECEIT, RUSE, LOQUACITY,
LEADERS, SILLINESS, ZEAL
Motto: *"I plan"*
Elements: *Positive, metal, Yang*

Talkers one and all, Aries/Monkeys are among the finest, most forthright people around. If you ever get to know one and then leave her behind, I believe your most intense souvenir of her personality will be the things she said. Aries/Monkeys are noted for their directness in speech. They can talk your leg off. But they are almost never boring.

Bright and garrulous, Aries/Monkeys are also gifted with the ability to feel for others. They have built-in compassion and truly care for those they love. Coupled with the wit and intelligence of a Monkey nature, this Aries subject's drive is unbeatably attractive. However, you sometimes feel as though you can't turn this person off, that inside your Aries/Monkey friend is a really just a non-stop radio talk show. This garrulousness can be charming—or exhausting. Talkative Aries/Monkeys are not exempt from repetition for the sake of emphasis either. There comes a moment when you might want to flick the "on/off" switch and hear some soothing silence for a change.

There is little an Aries/Monkey can do that won't lead to success. Accomplishment is this person's middle name. They are not exactly your average hard-driving-killer-scrambler-elbow-the-others-out-of-the-way-get-ahead achievers either. No. Aries/Monkeys achieve in areas where they choose to excel. They are not compelled by gain or social approbation. Instead, they measure success by their own built-in standards. What you or I may think really is immaterial.

Aries/Monkeys have second sight. They can see around corners. This sign endows its owners with an uncanny ability to judge the worth and wiles of others. I have seen Aries/Monkeys cut through more bunk than twelve brand new razor blades. Watch them. When they are confronted with a new acquaintance Aries/Monkeys are pleasant and polite and nod their simian little heads, "Yes. Mmmmm. Hmmm. I see," while the other person is blathering away some nonsense.

Afterward, when the blatherer leaves and you are alone with your Aries/Monkey, he or she will eye you, gauge your approachability and then say, "Did you see that guy who just left?" Yes. You saw him. What about him? (And here comes the good part.) Aries/Monkey pulls up his wiry frame and leans over to your ear in a confidential pose. "That man is a charlatan!" says Aries/Monkey. "He told me had gone to Yale. But he'd never heard of Old Eli and he claimed that the name of his dormitory was Holiday Inn."

It's hard to fool the cunning Aries/Monkey. Obviously, the Aries trait of naiveté is overruled by the Monkey's extreme guile. And it's a good thing. A skeptical Aries is a happy Aries.

The Aries/Monkey is also a firm individualist. Although gregarious, this person is capable of solitary forays inside himself, whence he is sure to dredge up many cunning ideas. Aries/Monkeys can study hard and achieve excellent results where application of derrière to seat of chair is a prerequisite. They are patient. Not slowly and deliberately patient. But patient nonetheless.

Aries/Monkeys go out of their way to be seductive and charming. If they are not naturally attractive, they get themselves up in ways that ensure appeal. They are what we used to call "striking" people. Unforgettable.

One of the pitfalls Aries/Monkeys must watch for is their excessive superstition. People born under this sign tend to be drawn to the mystical rather than the logical solution in an emotional dilemma. They must learn to consult those wiser and more down-to-earth than they. Aries/Monkeys are perfectly capable of heeding good counsel. But they must learn to go out and seek it, not be afraid to appear foolish or untrained in any area at all. This person is able to assimilate anything, but sometimes he goes looking for knowledge in the wrong places.

The Aries/Monkey is basically balanced and stable. But little creeping superstitious doubts can creep in, which will temporarily flummox Aries/Monkeys, cause them to waste time in futile equivocation and tire them uselessly.

Love

In matters of the heart Aries/Monkeys are not, by nature, constant. They can, however, learn to play at being monogamous with great conviction and success. They usually have spouses. But that doesn't always mean they spend long evenings by the fireside reading the Bible to their faithful mates. Not Aries/Monkeys. They like to be out in the world, chatting at everybody and getting chatted back at by lots of people. Aries/Monkeys love contact.

The tinge of infidelity of which I speak does not prevent our Aries/Monkey subject from indulging in relationships of long-standing worth where passion is the main driving force. Aries/Monkeys are, on the contrary, very fiery and involved lovers. They can get so interested in the dynamics of their relationships that sometimes they can't even remember to find others more attractive.

If you love an Aries/Monkey, don't be boring. Keep moving and shaking. Hanging around the kitchen baking cakes will not do the trick. To amuse an Aries/Monkey you have to be on your toes all the time, traveling and entertaining, giving parties, and attending bashes and dos. The Aries/Monkey is a tireless consumer of company. Rent a circus tent and put it in the backyard. Fill it up with new acts and audiences every day. A do-it-yourself three-ring circus might keep the Aries/Monkey content for about a week. But don't count on it.

Compatibilities

Go for a Leo/Dragon or Rat. They will find you irresistibly charming. You are drawn to their power. Rats and Dragons in general leave you anything but cold. But you will find particular pounding in your chest cavity over Geminis, Aquarians and Sagittarians of those same animal sign groups. Stay away from Capricorn and Cancer/Tigers and Pigs, and don't become bewitched by the luscious Libra/Snake or you'll be sorry you did.

Home and Family

This heady talker will be the happy center of his or her family group. Monkeys tend to have a lot of children and spend untold hours teaching and showing their kids new things. An Aries/Monkey may even pillow fight and roller skate with offspring. The Aries/Monkey enthusiasm for communication is such that he'll put up with almost any activity as long as he gets to play, too. I've said it before. Aries are boyish. Monkeys tend to silliness and juvenility. Imagine the gags at the dinner table, the tricks played on grandma and the giggles while hiding under the bed so Nancy won't find you. I know an Aries/Monkey who, when he was a kid, filled up his father's glassed-in shower stall with canned aerosol whipped cream. The father was the type who blindly crashed from his bed at six and never opened his eyes till he was under the stinging shower's invigorating splash. You can picture this middle-aged executive type, stark naked and spluttering, with whipped cream everywhere, in his ears and under his fingernails . . . everywhere! The Aries/Monkey was doubly proud of this caper because as he told me, "Dad had to go right out and play tennis. He was already late. So he left with half the cream still sticking to him. The cream soured in the sunshine on the court. And he smelled awful. Rancid! It was a riot!"

Typically, Aries/Monkeys love fun. The more the merrier. It's difficult to upset the natural equilibrium of an Aries/Monkey child. But keep him safe from superstition, watch out for an attraction to sects and excessive attention to mysticism.

Profession

Do-it-yourself projects and manual efforts do not daunt the spirited Aries/Monkey. Yet this person is not likely to choose a thoroughly manual career for life. However, if obliged by circumstances, Aries/Monkeys can do everything well.

The Aries/Monkey's outgoing personality can take him or her far in almost all jobs. It will be Aries/Monkey who organizes the picnics and invites everybody back to his place for coffee. People are drawn to and enjoy gathering at Aries/Monkey's house. His wiliness and ability to swerve precisely at the right moment, although useful to any boss, may cause some office jealousies. Aries/ Monkeys are well advised not to volunteer for every chore, and to resist the temptation to play the willing employee else he might be accused of boot-licking.

A useful character trait in Aries/Monkey people is that of be willing to take a back seat. It doesn't bother the clever, capable Aries

Monkey to be the brains behind a whole complex operation and not have his name appear in gold letters on the office door. For Aries/Monkey the important thing is achievement—not what the achievement means to outsiders.

Many Aries/Monkeys hold important independent positions, opening their own companies or running their own shops. They are attracted to career fields where perspicacity counts—fashion, psychology, teaching, medicine, commerce. Whatever career this subject chooses will eventually work out for him. The Aries/Monkey is a natural.

Famous Aries/Monkeys:

Andy Garcia, Anthony Michael Hall, Ashley Judd, Barry Nelson, Bette Davis, Bijou Phillips, Céline Dion, Chad Le Clos, Charlie Hunnam, Chloe Bennet, Claude Cheysson, Daisy Ridley, David E. Kelley, David M Brown, Edmonde Charles-Roux, Eric Roberts, Gerhard Schroeder, Jack Webb, Jean Cacharel, Jim Piddock, Joan Crawford, John Laughlin, Kate Micucci, Katee Sackhoff, Lionel Hampton, Lucy Lawless, Maria Teresa Grand Duchess of Luxembourg, Matthew Garber, Melody Thomas Scott., Nicolas Hamilton, Omar Sharif, Patricia Arquette, Randy Orton, Ravi Shankar, René Descartes, Sergio Sasaki Jr., Sue Barker, Timothy Dalton, Toshiro Mifune, Vanessa Morgan, Victor Vasarely.

ARIES
QUALITIES
COURAGE, DRIVE, HEARTINESS,
AFFABILITY, TALENT, ENTERPRISE
QUIRKS
NAÏVETÉ, OSTENTATION, WILLFULNESS,
EXCESS , SANCTIMONY, DOMINATION
Motto: *"I am"*
Elements: *Fire, Mars, Cardinal*

--

ROOSTER
QUALITIES
RESILIENCE, ENTHUSIASM, CANDOR,
CONSERVATISM, CHIC, HUMOR
QUIRKS
COCKINESS, BOASTFULNESS, BLIND FAITH,
PEDANTRY, BOSSINESS, DISSIPATION
Motto: *"I overcome"*
Elements: *Negative, Metal, Yin*

Like all Roosters, the Aries/Rooster is a boiling teakettle of enthusiasm. Every single second of life for this character is full to overflowing with activity and eagerness. Aries/Roosters would like to try everything at least once. And if these tests bring them pleasure or intense experience, they would like to try them again, please. This Aries is generous and outgoing, talented, versatile and curious to a fault.

You'll never see an idle Aries/Rooster. Lying down or sitting still for long periods of time tends to create a malaise in the ever-whirling Aries/Rooster soul. Exoticism magnetizes this subject. Would you like to go across Siberia to China on foot, but cannot find anyone to accompany you because they're afraid they won't like the food? Ring up an Aries/Rooster. Or maybe you have this fabulous plan to buy a house on an island in a fjord in Norway, but you're afraid nobody will come and visit you because it seems too cold there. Invite an Aries/Rooster. He'll be on the next plane to Oslo. And don't bother to fetch him at the airport either. He'll trek to your Nordic hut on his own without a hitch, smiling and whistling hiking songs all the way.

Aries/Rooster people are gregarious, too. They love company and are forever inviting friends to their place for meals and festivities. They like decorating and will only live in surroundings that they have improved to please their own flawless personal good taste. An Aries/Rooster may prefer "minimal" or "high tech" or "French Provincial", but whatever his or her preference, you can be certain it's personal and definitive.

Clothes are vitally important to Aries/Roosters. I won't say they live to adorn their bodies—but practically. The Chinese say that Roosters are never satisfied with their bodies. Aries are not terribly body-conscious, but I have found that my own Aries/Roosters follow the Rooster trait in this regard, covering themselves in finest leathers and silks, primping and preening a lot after they have gotten dressed, checking themselves out in mirrors. Yes. Aries/ Roosters are vain. But they don't make you feel it. They aren't "Whoosh! Look at ME" vain the way a Dragon can be. Aries/ Roosters are more subtly conceited. To this subject a well-clad body is what makes or breaks you in life. Watch him strut his stuff.

Aries/Rooster like the luxury of frankness too. They prefer to keep everything on the up and up in their lives. They don't like fakery and eschew improbity. Yet, because they live in this crooked world, they are sometimes forced by circumstance into corners where it would be wiser to tell white lies than to topple beak-first into the hottest of human soups.

Nonetheless, even when the you-know-what is treacherously close to the fan, Aries/Roosters blurt out the truth. As they don't particularly cotton to tight spots, this bad habit of telling the whole truth and nothing but (which under most conditions would be considered a good habit) often finds our Aries/Roosters up to their scarlet cockscombs in trouble.

But never mind. When an Aries/Rooster meets with a snag, suffers a setback or decides that he's seen all he wants of the neighbors, he knows how to drop everything, sell the house and the cars, crush the last Ping-Pong ball, and pick up and move to the South Seas. Aries/Roosters are resilient. They never allow trouble to cripple them permanently. It's pick yourself up, brush yourself off, and start all over again time.

Aries/Roosters do not brood. They live in the moment at hand and do so with aplomb, grace and class. They seem to be afraid of nothing. Poverty inspires them to want to make money. Adversity brings out their knack for survival. Aries/Roosters benefit from the double energy of both their native signs. The rigor and finesse comes from the Rooster side, the daring go-getting from Aries. It is a dauntless and agreeable combination.

Watch out for a tendency to boasting in this subject. Aries/ Roosters like to show off their achievements, their elegant surroundings, and their bodies, remember? Well, they don't mind telling you about their yacht and their four mistresses either. They must guard against pedantry and bossiness. And most of all, they must take care not to allow addiction to drugs or alcohol to take over their lives. Of course, were an Aries/Rooster addicted to a harmful substance, he or she would more than likely be able to kick the habit and move ever forward alone, head high, and once more into the fray.

Love

Aries/Rooster's stability depends a lot on having a ready outlet for affection. Solitude is not the Aries/Rooster's deepest desire. Rather, the identity, the image of inner self, relies on the reactions of others to Aries/Rooster's behavior. Mirrors, for an Aries/Rooster, are sorely deficient as a method of looking at oneself. He or she believes that the look in an honest interlocutor's eye will tell more about whether or not his hair transplant or her silicone implants really show, than all the looking glasses in Wonderland.

The Aries/Rooster's innate candor and credulity get him into frequent amorous scrapes. Lovers and mistresses will take advantage of this believer in right and justice and truth. He can be made to feel sad and guilty and even allow himself to be criticized for things he didn't do. Aries/Rooster in. may even grow so depressed over a failed love affair as to appear suicidal.

But as we already know, the Aries/Rooster cannot be kept down for long. Resilience and brilliance are not traits that sink into ignominy without bobbing back to the surface. Aries/Roosters always pull themselves out of the depths and triumph over broken hearts. They are survivors. Not long sufferers. Their motto is: "If this isn't working and it's causing me too much angst, I'll just leave, thank you." So if you love and Aries/Rooster don't deride her and don't nag her either. If he seems too independent to you, it's probably because you haven't got enough to do yourself. These people need a large, expansive barnyard in which to rooster around...don't ever hem them in.

Compatibilities

The Gemini/Snake and Ox will excite your interest, but your real mates live in Leo/Ox or Leo/Snake or even Aquarius/Snake or Dragon. Watch out for Cancers in the form of Cats or Snakes. You'll be attracted. But they may break your brittle little heart in a trice. Keep your claws off Libra/Snakes, too, and eschew Leo/Dogs. Don't fall in love with Capricorns, especially Dogs. You like Sagittarian/Snakes and Oxen and they like you back. Tigers can be fun too. Especially Geminis.

Home and Family

I'm not about to declare that Aries/Roosters don't like to have families. They do. They enjoy the security of family. Christmas dinners, although they may bore the Aries/Rooster unless he or she is the engine behind the repast, please them. Yes, Aries/Rooster will take his mother to Venice and walk her around, patiently explaining all the sights and sharing his enthusiasm for the excellent cuisine. Aries/Rooster adheres closely to the rules of duty. Basically conservative, this person will always do what is right—publicly.

Thing is, this busy and talented person doesn't have all that much time to spend hovering over fancily decorated baby cradles or pacing the floor all night with colicky infants. In other words, Aries/Rooster is traditionally an easier sign for a man to inhabit than for a woman to live with. An Aries/Rooster woman may choose motherhood as one of her talents to develop. But nurturing children is never a complete lifestyle for this versatile person.

Aries/Rooster children require much tenderness. They should be taught very young about art and encouraged in all their various curiosities. In order to grow up a solid citizen, this kid needs applause, input, cheers and appreciation from parents. Discipline him. But don't pick on him. If you do, you'll be rewarded for your nagging by watching him walk out the door at age eighteen, only to return when he's good and ready.

Profession

A wise career choice may prove difficult to pin down for this multifaceted character. Aries/Roosters know how to do almost anything. I know an Aries/Rooster who is all of the following: eye surgeon, pianist, artist, horticulturist, carpenter, electrician, chef, calligrapher, tailor, tap dancer. I'm not exaggerating. Another of my Roosters born in Aries is a pianist too. He is also a composer, an actor, a script writer, a translator, a dialogue coach for movies. True, unlike my first Aries/Rooster example, this one seems to work in and around cinema. But he's also a semi-professional baseball player. I tell you, Aries/Roosters can't sit still for a minute.

Rivalry in work situations will cause this subject no little grief. Aries/Roosters can incite jealousy in their coworkers. Of course they are so versatile and able that anyone even slightly self-doubting will succumb to sinking spells in their presence. Independent careers such as medicine and law, show business or the upper military echelons will appeal to these people. You won't find many Aries/Roosters in menial jobs. And if you do, you can be sure that that Aries/Rooster washing the floor is concocting some scheme which will rocket him or her out of that dump through the ceiling and into a more prestigious position.

Famous Aries/Roosters:
Alain Poher, Amanda Plummer, Ben Mendelsohn, Christopher Lambert, Chuck Connors, Cobie Smulders, Daniela Bobadilla, David S Taylor, Dirk Bogarde, Eliza Coupe, Eric Clapton, Gayle Storm, General Patton, Graham Phillips. , Hannah Marks, Hannah Spearitt, Hayden Christensen, Jan Minar, Jean-Paul Belmondo, Julia Stiles, Katy Mixon, Kevin Corrigan, Madeleine Martin, Michel Guérard, Nathan Sykes, Paul Rudd, Pauley Perrette, Peter Ustinov, Sergei Rachmaninoff, Seth Rogen, Severiano Ballesteros, Simone Signoret, Skyler Samuels, Stephen Dillane, Suraj Sharma, Taylor Kitsch, Tulsi Gabbard.

ARIES
QUALITIES
COURAGE, DRIVE, HEARTINESS,
AFFABILITY, TALENT, ENTERPRISE
QUIRKS
NAÏVETÉ, OSTENTATION, WILLFULNESS,
EXCESS , SANCTIMONY, DOMINATION
Motto: *"I am"*
Elements: *Fire, Mars, Cardinal*

--

DOG
QUALITIES
CONSTANCY, UNSOCIABILITY,
RESPECTABILITY, SELF-RIGHTEOUSNESS,
INTELLIGENCE, TACTLESSNESS
QUIRKS
UNEASINESS, CRITICISM, DUTY,
CYNICISM, HEROISM, MORALITY
Motto: *"I worry"*
Elements: *Positive, Metal, Yang*

Take one sweet-natured, hardworking, ambitious believer, add a cup of kindness, a pound and a half of disquiet and tons of tactlessness and you've got yourself an Aries/Dog.

Aries and Dog both call up a spirit of naiveté. In the case of Aries there is the ever-present quality of soldierliness. Aries is a scout, a pioneer and as credulous as they come. He is so nice. Why shouldn't everybody else be nice too? The Dog is also quite nice. But he is also a nervous and skeptical soul. Like Aries, the Dog wants to believe in the basic goodness of mankind. But he knows better. And that very knowledge can make him or her a nervous wreck.

Now, what you come up with when you match these two signs is quite plain: dynamic faith. Capability combined with a well-developed sense of realism. The Aries wants to believe in goodness and truth but the skeptical Dog won't let him. The Dog wants to tilt windmills but the down-to-earth Aries holds him back. So what happens? The Aries/Dog goes trotting along down the very middle of road, applying his genius and making do with what is given him in life.

There is a natural uneasiness in all Dog subjects. The Aries probably hides this disquiet better than all other Dogs. Aries is a bubbly sign. Whenever the Dog gets to feeling paranoid and worrying that every single person he sees is after his job or his wife or his skin, along comes effervescent Aries to say, "Come on Doggie! It's lunchtime. Let's go out and get ourselves a nice big sandwich." Action is a savior of this Dog personality. I do not see any Aries/Dog languishing in satiny eiderdowns eating bonbons and reading dime novels. These people need to move.

The Aries/Dog seems to care little for his own comfort but may find it necessary to call attention to how badly he was treated in such and such a situation. Aries/Dog can be one of those people who complains because others get more and he didn't do so well. He doesn't mind being handicapped, but let's at least notice how badly he has fared.

Because of this streak of self-pity, Aries/Dogs often cope well with adversity. They almost seem to seek out obstacles and go looking for complexity. Aries/Dogs are not really peace-loving. They like a battle and thrive in situations where they are obliged to deal with feistiness in others. Often, they come pretty close to being feisty themselves.

Aries/Dog likes to find in others the goodness he carries around inside himself. This person looks for the best side of everyone and every situation. He's almost Pollyannaish—a bit too kind and loving. It may seem naïve. But it's refreshing, damn it. And it is also curious that in digging for the good in others, Aries/Dog often finds it.

There is a moralizing streak in Aries/Dog that we could all do without. These people like to teach others about "right and wrong". This sanctimonious side can be grating and can cause an Aries/Dog to be excluded from social gatherings and even to lose friends who prefer not to be preached to.

Love

In his personal life the Aries/Dog doesn't like to make waves. Although most Aries/Dogs do settle down to live with one person after a while or are eventually happily married, this may take time.

Early in their adult lives, Aries/Dogs tend to exaggerate the necessity for dealing out the whole truth and nothing but the truth. And since love affairs are peppered from start to finish with all matter of petty hypocrisies, this puts the candid Aries/Dog off his feed. He or she may not only censure a dishonest partner, but may up and walk away from relationships where straight-ahead truth is not the order of the day.

As they get older (and wiser?) Aries/Dogs cease demanding of others the same candor of which they alone are capable. They catch on to life's many grays and relinquish their childish notions about purity in love.

Aries/Dog, maybe without realizing it, is a bit of a heartbreaker. His snappy ways and easy dispatch in romance seem superficial to people born in less "efficient" signs. The feminine variety of this creature is frequently criticized for being too openly attractive. There is an undeniable need for attention in Aries/Dog people which, if it is not satisfied, can make her bitter and old before their time.

Compatibilities

Gemini/Cat or Tiger is a good match for you. Or try a magnanimous Leo in Horse or Tiger clothing. Sagittarius/Horses and Tigers please you as well. But they are a bit on the extravagant side for your Spartan tastes. You admire Aquarius/Horses. And Aquarius/ Tigers thrill you; but it can't last. To be eliminated are Cancer/ Rooster, Dragon, and Sheep. Libra/Sheep and their frills annoy you. Capricorn/Dragons give you scruple competition, and their Sheep brothers and sisters test the limits of your genuinely good nature.

Home and Family

The Aries/Dog will know every inch of his environment by heart and take it upon him- or herself to supervise the decoration and up-keep of same. As long as he has plenty of room for the others in his family and a bit of space for his own things, the Aries/Dog does not complain. Aries/Dogs are not creatures of luxury. They like their comfort but they are very lucid people and know that opulence carries a large price tag in the worry department.

The Aries/Dog's worst habit is his unintentionally wounding comments. For some reason or other all Dogs have this nasty habit. But some Dogs, notably Aries, have it worse. They say anything that shoots into their brain at any moment without filtering it through their tact meter. Aries/Dogs, underneath, are truly very sensitive people. But every day, without seeming to ponder at all, they blurt things like, "You sure have a fat derrière" and "Must be pretty windy out there the way your hair looks today." This habit can take its toll on the family. My advice? Mouth clamps.

Aries/Dogs are generous and good providers. They easily feel guilt over not spending enough time with kiddies or hubby.

An Aries/Dog child should be encouraged to cultivate spontaneity, yet discouraged from making disparaging remarks. He'll be loving in the extreme and too quick to care for people who later may abuse his good nature. Despite his natural penchant for panic, the Aries/Dog should be allowed to dare. Sports and adventure tempt this child. He will need much unsolicited affection.

Profession

Aries/Dog is talented for organizing others. He is usually artistic and always interested in causes and the betterment of humankind and nature. No occupation really daunts this subject—just his own occasional pessimism.

The Aries/Dog can be both boss and employee with great success. If the boss doesn't fire him for remarking on her hairdo, he will be a devoted and able worker whose loyalty can be trusted. As a boss, Aries/Dogs will make those nasty digs at their employees, but their hearts are really in the right place; so most employees learn not to listen. Generosity goes a long way in work situations and the Aries/Dog is fair and open-handed. "Let me pay for that coffee" is a typical Aries/Dog reflex.

I see the Aries/Dog as an independent sort of worker. Solo acts are the order of the day. Bookstore owner, film director, commercial artist, musician or magician would do nicely.

Famous Aries/Dogs:

Akira Kirosawa, Alec Baldwin, Barry Pepper, Bridger Zadina, Carmen McRae, Chyler Leigh, Cobie Smulders, Dakota Blue Richards, David S Taylor, Eileen Ford, Elizabeth Mitchell, Gary Oldman, Gina Carano, Gloria Steinem, Harry Houdini, Hayley Atwell, Henry Luce, Lara Flynn Boyle, Mariah Carey, Maurice LaMarche., Miranda Kerr, Paul Robeson, Peter Capaldi, Richard Edwards, Rick Schroder, Saoirse Ronan, Sean Bean, Seth Rogen, Shemar Moore, Skyler Samuels, Sofia Boutella, Ved Mehta, Vince Vaughn, Yannick Caballero.

ARIES
QUALITIES
COURAGE, DRIVE, HEARTINESS,
AFFABILITY, TALENT, ENTERPRISE
QUIRKS
NAÏVETÉ, OSTENTATION, WILLFULNESS,
EXCESS , SANCTIMONY, DOMINATION
Motto: *"I am"*
Elements: *Fire, Mars, Cardinal*

--

PIG
QUALITIES
SCRUPULOUSNESS, GALLANTRY, SINCERITY,
VOLUPTUOUSNESS, CULTURE, HONESTY
QUIRKS
CREDULITY, WRATH, HESITATION,
MATERIALISM, GOURMANDISM, PIGHEADEDNESS
Motto: *"I civilize"*
Elements: *Negative Water, Yin*

Aries coupled with the Pig sign bespeaks an aura of comfort overlaid with rural enterprise. This is a sign whose subjects will not have an easy time, but the person's entourage, family, friends and colleagues will benefit from the most extraordinary friendship they may ever know. Aries/Pigs are kindness incarnate. They take bunches of squealing brats to movies and buy them all ice cream and let them drip it all over their clothes. The help out on every possible committee—including cleanup—and seem tireless about it all.

These people are so popular that they are often elected class president or camp monitor before they are old enough to read the rule books Everybody trusts an Aries/Pig. With reason, too. Their capabilities, their sense of organization and their delight in pleasing and entertaining others make them some of the finest and most truly altruistic souls ever.

My sister. Sally, was an Aries/Pig. She died an untimely death not too many years ago at age forty-one. Sally was a monster of abilities. She painted the most extraordinary paintings, decorated her house with impeccable taste, flattered and catered to her friends with everything from birthday parties to clever gifts of homemade jams and oregano tomato sauces. Sally was a fabulous mother and a patient, loving, long-suffering wife. We all miss her sorrowfully.

I could write an entire book about the progression in Sally's life from simple housewife to famous abstract painter, president of the city art society and curator of collections of paintings and sculpture worthy of kings. Sally was brilliant at both art and management. That is definitely an Aries/Pig talent. And all of this talent is applied with good cheer and optimism.

People love Aries/Pigs. They never get jealous of them. They never want to take their jobs away. They never really want to steal their husbands or wives. People just want Aries/Pigs to like them, to notice them, to say "Hi" to them and to spread a little of the Aries/Pig sunshine.

A brief anecdote may best illustrate this point. It happened at my sister's house after her funeral. There were hundreds of people there and not enough tears in our collective bodies to do justice to our sorrow. My eyes were slits from crying. But I mingled. Roomful after roomful of guests drank and ate neighborly potato salads and baked hams. Everyone talked about Sally.

Nobody knew me very well. I had always lived in Paris. 'How do you do?' I would walk up to strangers, shake hands and introduce myself. "I'm Sally's sister, Suzanne." Warmly and with true love in their eyes, at least thirty different people shook my hand heartily and said, "How do you do? Sally was my best friend." And they all believed it, too. Sally could make you feel as though you were the only person on earth beside herself. Everybody wanted to be Sally's favorite.

Charisma is not the word. Aries/Pigs have more than just charm or appeal. Aries/Pigs have magic! They are born with it and they die with it. People have set up funds in my sister's name for art scholarships. Every year there are more memorial dinners held in her honor. It's amazing! Sally could have run for president . . . and she might just have won.

A serious flaw exists in the best of us. Aries/Pigs have a biggie. If an Aries born Pig suffers a major setback or is done in by someone else's selfish scheme, his reaction will be called anger. But it will transcend anger and fury. It will instead be a kind of blind, dumb, stupid and steaming "state of rage." It can do him in. It will do him in. Aries/Pig, beware! You are a sitting duck for your own undoing. When you feel that wave of pigheaded fury waft over you and set up housekeeping in your body and soul, move off. Take a trip. Take a walk. Take a tranquilizer. You will die from rage if you aren't careful. I've seen it happen.

Love

The romance part of Aries/Pigs' lives is often fraught with frustration. As this subject starts to befriend everybody he meets from nursery school onward, he is a natural for early marriage. In the ease of the slow-growing Pig nature, where developments happen oh-so-gradually over a long period of time, a precipitous wedding will stand for sure disaster.

Trouble is the Aries/Pig is a believer in his own capacity for "dealing" with everything. He can do it. He can find a way to get along with his mate. He can find a way to keep her home and tie her down with a variety of fascinating ropes. But the truth is that Aries/Pigs cannot manage shaky relationships. They lack subtlety for the sort of connivance necessary to judge other peoples' motives—ulterior and other. The Aries/Pig will, moreover, always blame himself if things go wrong in love relationships. And then comes the rage ... the killer rage. But the unfaithful husband or wife doesn't die. Aries/Pig takes the guilt with him to the grave.

If you love an Aries/Pig and you are any kind of meanie, lay off! Aries/Pig makes for such a delightful companion, who gives so much more than he gets, that often mates take advantage of him. Aries/Pig works hard, makes do, remains cheerful through the worst adversities, saves money and time. Don't misuse this character.

The world needs him to lead and preside and most of all to preserve what is beautiful.

Compatibilities

I'd say you can safely take up with Gemini or Leo/Dragons and Cats. They keep you interested. Sagittarius/Cats make long-lasting partners for you too, as do Aquarius/Cats and Dragons. I'd resist all manner of Snake if I were you. Cancers of the Monkey, Dog or Horse school are not beneficial to you. Nor should you toy with Libra/Roosters or Capricorn/Tigers or Roosters. Follow your best instincts and don't be bamboozled by Libra/Tiger's apparent good-heartedness.

Home and Family

Ah, the talented Aries/Pig! Family for this subject is everything—and frequently everything is Aries/Pig's nemesis. The Aries/Pig loves home. He knows how to care about his home and family in such an original way that children and mates, fathers and mothers and cousins become entirely dependent on him. It's natural too. The Aries/Pig is the basic center of every group in which he finds himself. It's undeniable and indelible.

So what's wrong with this picture? Plenty. Aries/Pig does not take kindly to being crossed. The striking out of an independent child may cause the Aries/Pig so much pain as to make him physically ill. As a parent, or even a sibling, the Aries/Pig hates to lose control. When the reins begin to slip from his fingers, the Aries/Pig starts to go slightly crackers. Look at Tennessee Williams's story (Aries/Pig 1911). He died and left nothing to his brother in his will. All of his money would go to a sister in a mental institution until she died. After that, his brother would be able to have some money. The brother fought the will and won a minor victory. He was allowed a settlement of money by the courts. And as it turned out, at least one reason Williams made the will was that he was furious at his brother for institutionalizing him some years before his death in order to try and get Williams to stop drinking and taking drugs.

An angry Aries/Pig is the angriest thing I know. As kids, Aries/Pig will show early promise. They will eventually shine no matter what happens, but it is best to encourage them in everything artistic and cultural. They will be given to frequent embarrassing rages. My mother actually used to get off the bus and leave my sister to ride home alone when we were small.

Sally could turn a quiet city bus into an instant psychodrama with her quirky angers. My mother, a Libra (and also a Pig), didn't want any part of it. She'd grab me up and take my brother by the hand and say, "When you get over your fit, Sally Ann, you may come home." Hours later, little Sally, pouting, would come through the door. "I'm home," she'd say, and go straight to her room.

Profession

Here is where the Aries/Pig gets to really absorb himself. Ah, work! Ah, creation! Ah, enterprise! Ah, management! Ah, business! They love it all. Aries/Pigs, if they can learn to follow through on the myriad projects they undertake in their lives, will make excellent careers for themselves.

Bosses and personnel managers toss jobs into Aries/Pigs laps. These subjects exude such an incredible aura of capability and good humor that everyone wants them to work on their staff. I'd be willing to bet that no matter how sky-high the rate of unemployment is, no matter how many jobs don't exist, the Aries/Pigs of this world will be employed.

Aries/Pigs should always try to be sure that their job in some way allows them contact with what is cultural and opulent. These people are perhaps the most bohemian of the materialistic Pigs. Nonetheless, objets d'art and beautiful surroundings are of the utmost importance to this person. Aries/Pigs make good artists of all kinds, leaders of anything—including wars!—and they also make excellent public relations agents and advertising executives, journalists and, well, just about anything that doesn't require excessive subordination. Not that Aries/Pigs cannot take orders. But they will always rise to the top from whatever subordinate position they start out in, so why not begin at the top?

Famous Aries/Pigs:
Bismarck, Catherine Keener, David Tennant, Dudley Moore, Ed Skrein, Elton John, Emma Thompson, Ewan McGregor, Guillaume Depardieu, Hervé Bazin, Jamie Chung, Kareem Abdul Jabbar, Marcel Marceau, Matt Lanter, Matthew Modine, Megyn Price, Michèle Torr, Miranda Kerr, Modest Mussorgsky, Nathan Fillion, Phil Morris, Reeve Carney, Richard Edwards, Sean Bean, Shannen Doherty, Tennessee Williams, Thomas F. Wilson, Thomas Jefferson, Yannick Caballero.

TAURUS
QUALITIES
ARDOR, DETERMINATION, INDUSTRY,
PATIENCE, LOGIC, SENSUALITY
QUIRKS
LANGUOR, PREJUDICE, INTRACTABILITY,
GLUTTONY, COMPLACENCY, JEALOUSY
Motto: *"I have"*
Elements: *Earth, Venus, Fixed*

--

RAT
QUALITIES
NERVOUSNESS, INFLUENCE,
ACQUISITIVENESS, THIRST FOR POWER,
INTELLECTUAL SKILL, CHARISMA
QUIRKS
APPEAL, VERBOSITY, THRIFT,
SOCIABILITY, GUILE, MEDDLING
Motto: *"I rule"*
Elements: *Positive Water, Yang*

Taureans born in Rat years benefit from a happy accident. Rats are often hyper. The Taurus mitigates the Rat's piano-wire nervousness. But to the lumbering Taurus personality, Ratso adds spice, pizzazz and a hefty pinch of calculation. The Taurus /Rat is a combination of William Shakespeare and Mark Zuckerberg : tough, bright, with nerves of steel and natural superiority. Real genius is frequently found among Rats born in Taurus.

It is the maintenance of well-earned position that essentially interests the Taurus/Rat. He likes power. But he doesn't necessarily want dominion over others. He can be ardent. But he will not step down from his pedestal of dignity to openly weep over a lost love affair. I doubt that you will ever see a "sloppy" Taurus/Rat.

Taurus/Rats have enormous appeal and are capable of ruse the likes of which you are unlikely to encounter in any other sign. They are strong-minded and strong-willed. But rather than mashing on the accelerator in order to win the race, the Taurus/Rat may lean back in the driver's seat, ponder, then slowly, deliberately, deliver just the razor-sharp tactical stroke of genius necessary to come in first without even lifting a toenail.

Taurus/Rats make redoubtable foes. As they hardly ever seem to take anything personally and never exhibit their vengeances publicly, you cannot ever really tell what they're thinking. All you know is that they are thinking fast and effectively.

Taureans born in Rat years are walking file cabinets. They have infallible memories. What may seem like a petty detail to any normal person is, to the Taurus/Rat, a paramount fact. Complicated names return to their lips after ten years, as though they had seen the person yesterday.

The Taurus/Rat is definitely a master and not a slave. Yet, if need be, he can appear to humble, bat his eyelashes and even titter in his corner if he knows it's necessary to reach his goal. I will not go so far as to say he is ruthless—but almost.

Taureans born in Rat years are protective of those they care about. They can show enormous generosity toward people they want to help, although, being industrious by nature, the Taurus/Rat is inclined to help only those who help themselves.

The Taurus/Rat carries himself with dignity, behaves impeccably in company and appreciates good manners in others. It is obvious wherever he is that he is the one around whom everyone in his vicinity gravitates. Taurus/Rats look as if they have "got it together." But if you penetrate a bit deeper you'll note a hidden spark of fun lurking under the sleek façade. Unless you are part of the Taurus/Rat's select entourage, however, you may never get to share any of that playfulness.

Love

The Taurean Rat subject loves with the constancy and steadiness of an old stone wall. He or she is bound to be a highly sensual soul and for this reason may be given to occasional dalliance. But dalliance is not real life. And what interests the Taurus/Rat is bite-the-coin-real-honest-to-God-solid-to-the-core reality of LOVE.

If you love this person, be faithful. Don't try any funny business. Oh, you can be amusing and even a little light-headed from time to time. But you cannot be disloyal.

Taurean Rats are jealous and grasping and so involved in their relationship, so committed to the perpetuation of that unit, that any deviation seems to them perfectly implausible. So... if you have caught yourself a Taurus/Rat, stay close to home.

Compatibilities

I see you with a strong but gentle Pisces/Ox or Tiger. But you could very well couple with Cancer, Virgo or Capricorn/Monkeys and Pigs. The Ox gives you competition but you don't mind that so long as he doesn't thwart your power trip. Horses don't work for Rats, but you should particularly shun Leo, Scorpio and Aquarius/ Horses. Cats are too cool to keep you fascinated forever. They exasperate you with their eternal reserve. Aquarius/Cats unnerve you the most. They're so calmly clairvoyant and laid back. You hate inertia.

Home and Family

The Taurus/Rat's home will be, first of all, traditional. Even if the lamps seem a little on the ultramodern side and the chairs smack of some posh up-to-the-minute designer's deft hand, look at the Louis XV commode over against the wall. And on its marble top? Copies of publications read only by top-drawer people with good taste in everything.

The family life will (even though Taurus/Rat is so frequently away at work) revolve around the Taurean born Rat member of the family. Bottom line, it is always up to the Bull/Rat whether the family summers in Maine or in Brittany. It's not exactly egomaniacal despotism, because Taurus/ Rat gives space to those he loves and allows room for them to measure up to very high standards. Let's just say that Taurus/Rats choose - benevolently but inevitably – to be boss.

A Taurus/Rat's childhood is meaningful in the extreme. You must first allow him to express opinions and draw his own conclusions. Taurus/Rats are frequently not the best students in the class. They are often bored by the triviality of school routines and prefer to approach study in their own steady, steely manner—independent of petty regulations. Frankly, Rat Taurean kids know the rules down to the ground. But they'd rather work out some system of their own, and often do.

Profession

Few professions are not open to this sturdy, bright nature. The Taurean born Rat is gifted for all jobs that require a strong sense of duty combined with exertion of power.

He likes money and is able to keep thousands of facts in his head at once and concentrate on at least five different pursuits at a time. Taurus/Rats are those people you see with four telephone receivers under their chins, signing documents on their desks and discussing a deal with a client in their office—multifaceted and not for a minute superficial.

As an employee, Taurus/Rat will only be biding his time till he can become the boss. This is a pragmatic person whose common sense far outweighs his urge for spontaneity. Taurus/Rats do make very hard-driving bosses, but their employees respect and like them and will rush around handing them things and making them tea. The natural superiority is undeniable in this character. He will always maintain dignity and keep a safe distance from his employees. But he's not afraid to smile and say thank you.

Famous Taurus/Rats:

Ayatollah Khomeini, Bailey Chase, Bono, Charles Aznavour, Charlotte Brontë, Clare Bowen, Craig Sheffer, Dwayne Johnson, Emily Wickersham, Grace Jones, Irving Berlin, Jesper Christensen, Jesse Lee Soffer, Joseph Haydn, Julie Benz, Kurt Sutter, Mark Zuckerberg, Meg Foster, Michelle Ryan, Naturi Naughton, Noah Centineo, Pam Ferris, Roma Downey, Taylor Cole, Tchaikovsky, Teresa Guidice, Tony Goldwyn, Tony Gwynn, Valerie Bertinelli, William Shakespeare, Zubin Mehta.

TAURUS
QUALITIES
ARDOR, DETERMINATION, INDUSTRY,
PATIENCE, LOGIC, SENSUALITY
QUIRKS
LANGUOR, PREJUDICE, INTRACTABILITY,
GLUTTONY, COMPLACENCY, JEALOUSY
Motto: *"I have"*
Elements: *Earth, Venus, Fixed*

--

OX
QUALITIES
STUBBORNNESS, STRENGTH OF PURPOSE,
ELOQUENCE, STANDOFFISHNESS, INNOVATION,
VINDICTIVENESS
QUIRKS
INTEGRITY, BIGOTRY, PLODDING,
DILIGENCE, BIAS, STABILITY
Motto: *"I preserve"*
Elements: *Negative Water, Yin*

It would seem at first glance that the combination of Taurus the Bull and his soul mate, the ominous Ox, might indeed be born so unwieldy and ponderous as to sink into extinction at the age of two months. The opposite, however, is true. Taureans born in Ox years do tend to be big, heavy characters. But they endure.

Taurus is, of course, taciturn and grounded. Oxen, though eloquent and steadfast, are just plain slow. They take their time about life and go at each task as though it were coated in sticky paper. The key words with Oxen are deliberation and foresight. Closing the door can take quite a while. They take hold of the handle and push ever so gently but firmly, shutting the door panel without a sound and listening for the click that means it is soundly latched.

SUZANNE WHITE

By this time, most other people have been through five doors and out of the building.

No. This character is not in a hurry. Nor, therefore, is he impatient, hotheaded or impulsive. Taurean Oxen think first and leap into the fray after they've had dinner, a long sit and forty winks. As a result, they often make wise long-term decisions. Or at least considered decisions. Sometimes however, their wisdom (in the case of Hitler, for example) can be questionable.

There is little time for nonsense in the life of a Taurean Ox. She will appreciate poetry and enjoy watching ballet but she doesn't really feel she ought to take time away from her more serious work for such frivolities. Taurus/Ox is not a stuffy sign. Far from it. The sensuality quotient is high among Taureans of all persuasions. But the Ox/Taurus will he able to postpone his sensual requirements, delay his gourmet indulgences, stave off the raging desire for passion—because his first aim is to succeed and to gain fame and respect from his fellows. He's not striving for power over others. He is after power among his peers, esteem, admiration. Self-indulgence can wait.

I wouldn't like to be in a job competition with Taurus/Ox. If for one moment I let down my guard and did not stay up day and night to complete the project at hand I would definitely be the loser. Taurean Oxen can outlast anybody at almost any job that promises to take them a notch further toward their struggle's end. Of course there is no "end" as such. Taurean Oxen keep pushing ahead till they keel over and stop breathing.

This person will not be adversely affected by criticism. He may dress badly and forget to comb his hair. He may not shave for a few days while busy at some urgent pursuit. She may not bother to pluck her eyebrows or shave her legs. Again, the paramount motive is the goal.

For all his devil-may-carelessness about dress and grooming, the Taurean Ox can be both attractive and seductive People are drawn to his innate seriousness and ability to make others feel good about themselves.

Love

As we already know, cold-heartedness is one of Taurus/Ox's strong suits. If cornered by a lover or mate, this person is guaranteed to fight, and fight both hard and dirty. Taurean Oxen are capable of profound and somber love with regard to their paramours. But watch out for their cruel streak. It's always ready to clamp down hard on your heart and stay there for as long as it takes to demolish your equilibrium. Otherwise, as long as you don't try to outdo this sensuous creature, you may be rewarded with enduring and profound tenderness.

If you love one of these people, allow him or her to shine. Make room for this character to develop its slow but steady superiority and you will never have to weather a cloudy day. Don't, for Heaven's sake, ask your Taurean Ox to empty his or her heart of "feelings", or beseech him tell jokes and off-color stories at parties. If a Taurus/Ox wants to perform, he'll become an actor and rise inexorably to receive an Academy Award in his own sweet time. He does not need either urging or approval from you. He wants acclaim from the whole wide world.

Compatibilities

You'll not be bored with either Pisces or Cancer/Rats or Snakes. Roosters from these two signs please you, too. They are industrious, but still have "soul." I'd advise you to look into Capricorn and Virgos of the Rat, Snake and Rooster categories. They can be dour, but then so can you. You might try a Pisces or Capricorn/Monkey but only for brief flings. Give Leo, Aquarius and Scorpio of either Tiger or Sheep families a wide berth. They are all too heady to be your steady.

Home and Family

Decor is not all-important to the Taurean Ox. As long as the surfaces are not too cluttered and necessities are more or less functional, this person will not rush out and order new furniture or fabrics so he can impress the neighbors. The Taurus/Ox's goal, remember, is achievement. Surroundings are only useful insofar as they assist him in reaching his goal. Oh, he will not live in a sty or accept to inhabit outrageously humble dwelling places. His self-image is in unusually good shape but nonetheless, he adores comfort. So a couple of deep comfy armchairs and a large oak desk with plenty of room for his papers and books might best characterize the Taurus/Ox's choice of backdrop.

With family, the Taurean Ox is not likely to be overly demonstrative. He will, however, tend toward the tyrannical and must be "handled". The kids will probably not be allowed to make noise while Taurus/Ox parent is toiling over some hefty problem. He or she will also be attached to earthy traditions and hope for offspring and/or siblings to share in this enthusiasm for things natural.

As a kid, the Taurean Ox will likely spend quite a lot of time on his own. He won't be completely solitary. But he will always prefer the company of his cronies to that of his parents or brothers and sisters. When his talents lean toward the artistic, he must be encouraged. Whatever he does choose to pursue—a sport, mastery of a musical instrument or the ballet, he has the innate strength of purpose to persevere and excel.

Profession

Jack Nicholson, a famous Taurus/Ox actor, said recently in a newspaper interview that he felt there was no such thing as "the best age" for success and happiness. He claimed that one should feel good about oneself at all ages and that achievement ought never to depend upon something so transient as "youth" or "beauty" or "charm."

This attitude is typical of the Taurean Ox personality. In work situations, no matter what a Taurus/Ox is aiming for, there is no substitute in his mind for hard work, diligence and might. Age shouldn't have anything to do with it. Nor, according to the Taurean Ox's workaholic creed, should any trifles such as ethnic background, social position or, God forbid, sexual attraction! prevent success.

What can a Taurean Ox do for a living? Answer: anything, as long as it's not insignificant. These natives should be guided into careers where tenacity and drive get you furthest. They might choose athlete, reporter, salesperson, actor, musician or researcher.

Famous Taurus/Oxen:

Adolf Hitler, Billy Joel, Bruno Kirby, Danila Kozlovsky, Dennis Rodman, Elisabeth Röhm, Enya, Fares Fares, Gal Gadot, Gary Cooper, George Clooney, Indira Varma, Isiah Thomas, Iwan Rheon, Jack Nicholson, Jemima Kirke, Joan Chen, Joël and Jean-Pierre Beltoise, John Corbett, Jorge Garcia, Joyce DeWitt, Kristian Lundin, Ludwig Wittgenstein, Madeleine Albright, Matthew McGrory, Nicole Graf, Odette Annable, Patti LuPone, Peter Doohan, Rachel Skarsten, Ricardo Hocevar, Saddam Hussein, Sasha Alexander, Tim Roth, Tori Spelling, Véronique Sanson.

TAURUS
QUALITIES
ARDOR, DETERMINATION, INDUSTRY,
PATIENCE, LOGIC, SENSUALITY
QUIRKS
LANGUOR, PREJUDICE, INTRACTABILITY,
GLUTTONY, COMPLACENCY, JEALOUSY
Motto: *"I have"*
Elements: *Earth, Venus, Fixed*

--

TIGER
QUALITIES
FERVOR, BRAVERY, MAGNETISM,
GOOD LUCK, BENEVOLENCE, AUTHORITY
QUIRKS
IMPETUOSITY, HOTHEADEDNESS,
DISOBEDIENCE, SWAGGER, INTEMPERANCE,
ITINERANCY
Motto: *"I Watch"*
Elements: *Positive Wood, Yang*

Here is the down-to-earth Tiger, the only Tiger who manages to keep all four paws on the ground and his head together at the same time. A steadier Tiger. A more vigilant Taurus.

The mind of the Taurean born Tiger is both tight and shipshape. Nothing that enters there gets out the other side without being carefully recorded. Tigers like to experience new things. Taureans want to keep everything. The combination results in a redoubtably savvy character who, although he may seem slightly eccentric and just a smidgen too easygoing, is really keeping score while you're busy watching the grass grow.

All in all, the Taurus/Tiger is a serious person. There may be something lighthearted in his manner, a certain jauntiness in his gait, a twinkle in the eye. But don't be fooled. The Tiger born Taurus never really lets down his guard. He's wily and he's wary. He's capable and truly enjoys leading. Don't attempt to get ahead of this creature or he'll be likely to pounce.

Tiger Taurean people are rarely haughty. She may be the Queen of England (as it just so happens) but she doesn't have much pretense or snobbery about her. These people favor simple pleasures.

Tigers born in Taurus love crowds. They don't have to be the center of attention, yet they get a kick out of watching others perform without feeling ego-threatened. This subject possesses natural nobility. It comes with the territory. Taurus/Tigers are modest people who plod with panache.

The Taurus/Tiger loves to be mobile. Ask him or her to take a trip tomorrow and the bags will be packed before you can buy the tickets, They are gregarious in a pleasant, settled way, and can be taken absolutely anywhere. They have excellent manners and good common sense about the polite pose to strike in any given company.

Tigers born in Taurus are far from perfect. They tend to excessive individuality. It can be unnerving. Taurean Tigers like things their way and see no reason why they cannot have their druthers. They are the kind of people who will prefer some cheap but exotic tea drink from Lisbon where they were once stranded overnight, to the best champagne money can buy. They may show up at your house for lunch with a quart of ice cream, which they will insist on eating instead of your painstakingly-prepared soup and salad. They don't care what anybody thinks.

Taurean Tigers may be able to get along on very little money. Their needs can he pared down to the barest essentials. They don't mind if you want to spend a cool million dollars a year. They mostly prefer to keep expenses down and get by with less. It's part of their eccentricity. Taurean Tigers want to be expansive without being expensive.

You will not regret befriending a Taurus/Tiger. They are easy to get along with because they find it less complicated to let others know their limits from the start than to suffer unpleasant surprises later. If they don't want your screaming kid in their house, they are most likely to tell you in a nice way that little Shelly is simply impossible. No hard feelings.

Another Taurus/Tiger trait is courage. These people have the grit of a foot soldier and the mind of a Roman general. Like good, hearty red wines, they travel well, age impeccably and enhance just about any activity you can dream up.

Love

The brand of burning passion with which Taurus/Tigers are gifted from birth makes love look like a word to describe apathy. Tigers born in Taurus really fall in love. They find someone to whom they give everything, follow everywhere, involve themselves with self-lessly and with an uncommon ardor, defending that person down to the very last bullet in their gun belts. Trouble is, if anything should happen to said person or a cloud settle over the relationship, Taurus/Tiger can slip into a yellow-and-black-striped despair out of which it is mightily tough to dislodge him. When the love is gone, an integral part of the Taurus/Tiger leaves with it.

In order to love one of these singular souls, you need nor really do any more than be. The Taurean Tiger figures it's up to him or her to do the adoring. "You just sit there while I go get us some drinks." Taurean Tigers like to care for others in a metaphysical or mental way. I wouldn't put my daily diet into their hands—you might be condemned to eating only beans or tomato soup. Taurus/Tiger is not fussy about variety or gourmet preparations. One must eat to live and not live to eat, is his motto. So don't fuss. And don't worry about whether your Taurus/Tiger is comfy or happy or worried—he'll let you know of his own accord. These subjects do not shy from expressing themselves.

Compatibilities

Cancer, Virgo and Capricorn appeal to your earthly side. In their ranks you're best off with Dragons, Dogs or Horses. A flight-of-fancy love life might include the watery Pisces born in Dragon or Dog years. Scorpios are not to be excluded either, particularly those of the Dog variety. Don't bother with Scorpio/Monkeys or Snakes, though, and refrain from Leo and Aquarius/Snake, Ox and even the mellow Monkey. But be your own person first. And in choosing a mate, remember to retreat from the headlong lickety split types. Seek wiser souls than you.

Home and Family

The home life of a Taurus/Tiger is not exactly paradise. Why is it so turbulent? So changeable? So fraught?

I think it might have something to do with the combination of Tigerish hotheadedness and Taurean stubbornness. Taurus/Tigers like things their own way, remember? Now, we all know that happy households depend greatly on compromise, give and take, mutability and shifting of sights. None of the above appeals to the feisty Taurus/Tiger. He plans to have his home as he sees fit. My way or the highway time.

As a parent this person will try very hard to be fair and never to mete out punishments unless no other reasonable solution has worked. Taurean Tigers are serious about their duties and want to make certain their kids achieve and behave. But sometimes their own rather unusual lives and destinies carry them far away across many lands and into fierce and exciting places. The children may be left to manage quite on their own. As everyone knows, a kid on its own can be good or can be a disaster. That's about what happens to Taurus/Tiger's kids. All or nothing.

The Taurus/Tiger child will be eccentric and self-propelled. He should be fun and like the family group as long as he is young and still dependent. As he grows older he will pull at the reins and insist on more independence than one normally wants to accord a child. Let him go. He has bigger fish to fry than a mere parent can imagine.

Profession

This person's creativity lies in his individuality. He doesn't like to think according to someone else's plan. He wants to jump in and find out for himself (even if it hurts) if the fire is really hot.

Employing such a freaky person is not very restful. Yet, the Tiger/Taurus's talents may be worth the few problems you will have getting him or her to adapt to rules and settling into routines. Once convinced that his purpose here in said office or home or shop or restaurant and brings good to the order, the Taurean Tiger will see each task through with remarkable sagacity and fervor. Of course Taurean Tigers prefer to be boss. They like to exert their gentle authority and even quite enjoy collecting the shekels that go with being a part of management. Mind you, they don't really intrinsically care about the damned money. But if it comes with the territory, so much the better.

Some jobs suitable to the Taurus/Tiger: missionary, writer, policeman (Interpol), general, political adviser, journalist, ruler.

Famous Taurus/Tigers:

Amber Heard, Barry Watson, Breckin Meyer, Bruce Boxleitner, Craig Ferguson, Danny Huston, Derek Luke, Emilio Estevez, Emily VanCamp, Fernand Raynaud, Gabriel Byrne, Grace Gummer, Ho Chi Minh, Ivana Milicevic, James Le Gros, James Monroe, Jay Leno, Jenna Coleman, John Hannah, Karl Marx, Marcheline Bertrand, Marina Vlady, Martin Gray, Megan Fox, Nicholas Hammond, Penelope Cruz, Peter Frampton, Queen Elizabeth II, Randall 'Tex' Cobb, Robert Pattinson, Robespierre, Romain Gary, Sendhil Ramamurthy, Stevie Wonder.

TAURUS
QUALITIES
ARDOR, DETERMINATION, INDUSTRY,
PATIENCE, LOGIC, SENSUALITY
QUIRKS
LANGUOR, PREJUDICE, INTRACTABILITY,
GLUTTONY, COMPLACENCY, JEALOUSY
Motto: *"I have"*
Elements: *Earth, Venus, Fixed*

--

CAT/RABBIT
QUALITIES
TACT, FINESSE, VIRTUE,
PRUDENCE, LONGEVITY, AMBITION,
QUIRKS
SECRETIVENESS, SQUEAMISHNESS,
PEDANTRY, DILETTANTISM,
HYPOCHONDRIA, COMPLEXITY
Motto: *"I Retreat"*
Elements: *Negative, Wood, Yin*

S ecurity-oriented and vulnerable, this is a risky combination. The Taurean born Cat requires safety and pledges and assurances and guarantees in all aspects of his life. He cannot function properly if the rent isn't paid and the kids don't all have new shoes. Taurus/Cat is not, by any stretch of the imagination, a bohemian.

While we are on the subject of imagination, let's remember that Taurus/Cats receive a lion's share of that commodity at birth. They are first inventors, innovators and breakthrough thinkers on subjects both artistic and creative. They seek their fortunes by means of their vision and inspiration. Frequently, they succeed.

Taurus/Cats are settlers. Once the fire is in the hearth and their feet are on the fender, you'll have a hell of a time wrenching one of these people loose to take in a movie or drive a few hundred miles for a beer. Taurus born Cat likes to stay at home. They are nesters and snugglers and careful collectors.

The risky business about which I spoke earlier usually arises in the life of Taurean Cats after they have arrived at some of their lofty goals. You see, success is like anything else that appears all good on the surface. We hear "success" and we think, "Ah, comfort! Ah, money! Ah, popularity!" And it's true. Yet, as all coins have a reverse side, so too does success.

If you have made it, then you can't call your life your own any longer. If your records are a hit and it looks as if you're making a mint, the taxman may come and stay for three months in your very own home! People write to you asking you to send them a lock of your hair, one of your baby teeth, and on and on.

Taurus/Cats abhor indiscriminate mingling. They enjoy having a few close acquaintances or friends in for dinner. But they don't really love having crowds surrounding their bathtubs while they bathe. So, as they are artistic people and frequently seek success with the public, these folks have quite a problem.

What has been known to occur with the ragingly successful Taurus/Cat is that once he has made it and tasted the fruits of real success, he contentedly sinks into obscurity, goes back to sitting by the fire and stays there forever. He's not a comeback person at all. He's been there. He's seen and he's conquered. That will be quite enough, thank you.

The Taurean Cat is easily hurt. It's hard for this creature to put up with the rotten world in which we all live. He doesn't hanker after rococo schemes or conjure up secret strategies. Business sharks or gangsterish types grate on the Taurus/Cat's tender nervous system and make him feel that the world is a desperate and dangerous place. He may hole up forever in a tiny town next to nowhere if only so he never has to rub elbows with lowlifes again. Taurus/Cat is a peace and love sign.

Love

A gracious and refined Taurus and a stubborn and sensuous Cat, this person will prefer uncomplicated love affairs to baroque and complex affairs of the heart. Taurus/Cats don't enjoy suffering and are not given to self-pity or sniveling. They adhere rather to the charming and comforting in love relationships.

If you love a Taurean Cat, don't provoke him or her or nag about details. The Taurus/Cat generally looks after details in his own fashion and in his own time. If you can adjust to the routines of your Taurean Cat, move ahead at the pace he or she has chosen, you'll be a lot happier for it.

Taurus/Cats are generous and expansive while on the way up. But don't be fooled into thinking this is their true nature. They are given to long spells of silence and they require calm in which to ponder their flowers growing. It is not exactly Disneyland to live with such a person. If you want somebody to tell you funny stories, there's always "Dial-a-Joke" or "Jokes.com".

Compatibilities

For you I would advise seeking partners in Capricorn or Cancer among Sheep, Dogs or Pigs. You may be enticed by the self-simi-larity of a Virgo/Cat, down-to-earth like you yet more analytical. Pisces/Sheep and Pigs make fine mates for Taureans born Cat. But don't be seduced by dashing Leos, Scorpios or Aquarians born in Rooster or Tiger. Scorpio/Rats will overpower you, too, not to men-tion the disastrous combination of yourself and the Scorpio/ Dra-gon. Ugh.

Home and Family

The decor is always splendid, cozy, warm, pleasant and welcom-ing around a Taurus/Cat's home. Luxury will be omnipresent but it will not show itself through the unbecoming appearance of golden angel sconces or showy, meltdown sterling silver firedogs. Subtle grace and inherent good taste will sing forth from all the furniture and objects about the place. Culturally acceptable magazines like National Geographic and Architectural Digest probably figure among the Taurus/Cat's favorite coffee table literature.

Taurean Cats tend to retreat in the face of violence. The Bull is normally a combative type. But Cats are so invariably squeamish that the Bull's heavy belligerence can never temper it enough. As a result, the Taurus/Cat will be the sort of parent or sibling who ex-plains each interdiction, reasons with family members endlessly about why we have to do this because it's the way civilized people do this and why we cannot possibly allow ourselves to be seen do-ing that because it's not attractive or graceful or pleasant.

If yon have a Taurus child born Cat, turn the classical music up louder and buy a harpsichord kit. These children adore music. They love to dream. They are happiest in peaceful and pastoral surround-ings. They are not fighters. You won't get anywhere with them by strict disciplinary tactics. Sit them down quietly and explain. Oth-erwise you might mar their gentle little psyches forever.

Profession

The work life of a Taurus/Cat person is often characterized by a swift and impressive upward swing when the person is between twenty-five and forty. These years are the ones in which the Taurus/Cat can still believe and has not yet been hurt or disappointed or discouraged by the roiling big bad world.

After the age of forty or forty-five, this person may seem to have run plum out of gas. This slowdown is the result of two important factors in the life of a Taurus/Cat. First, he's been disappointed and has shrugged off too many sullying experiences and wants an end to it. Secondly, because he is careful and cautious with spending and saving, he can afford to sit back and relax away from the madding crowd he hates so fervently.

As a boss, this person is respectable and even a bit sanctimonious at times, with his eternal good examples. As an employee this subject is almost a saint. He won't want to stay late at the office much, as his home beckons more strongly than money or advancement. But he will be both industrious and dutiful.

Taurus/Cat should choose from artistic or glamour careers for the most success: set designer, singer, actor, cabinetmaker, piano tuner, diplomat, landscape architect, jeweler, potter, inventor.

Famous Taurus/Cat/Rabbits:

Alley Mills, Andrea Anders, Andy Murray, Candice King, Christina Hendricks, Christopher Cross, Dale Earnhardt, David Beckham, Dr. Benjamin Spock, Dulé Hill, Emily Bergl, Enrique Iglesias, Harvey Keitel, Hunter Parrish, Jacques Lanzmann, Jean-Paul Belmondo, Jet Li, Johnny Galecki, José Arthur, Judy Collins, Michel Gondry, Natasha Richardson, Orson Welles, Rebeca Andrade, Robert Zemeckis, Robin Bartlett, Stephanie Corneliussen, Tony Danza, Vanessa Williams, William Moseley.

TAURUS
QUALITIES
ARDOR, DETERMINATION, INDUSTRY,
PATIENCE, LOGIC, SENSUALITY
QUIRKS
LANGUOR, PREJUDICE, INTRACTABILITY,
GLUTTONY, COMPLACENCY, JEALOUSY
Motto: *"I have"*
Elements: *Earth, Venus, Fixed*

--

DRAGON
QUALITIES
STRENGTH, SUCCESS, GOOD HEALTH,
ENTHUSIASM, PLUCK, SENTIMENTALITY
QUIRKS
RIGIDITY, MISTRUST, DISSATISFACTION,
INFATUATION, BRAGGADOCIO, VOLUBILITY
Motto: *"I Preside"*
Elements: *Positive Wood, Yang*

Might and bite come together here, giving us a powerhouse of brutal energy and excessive adroitness. Nobody will ever tell yon that they "just couldn't care less" about a Taurus/ Dragon. People either adore Taurus Dragons or they detest them!

Wood and earth. Two organic elements. On the one hand, this native exudes down-to the-ground good sense, but on the other he is tempestuously foolish and selfishly attention-getting. Taurus and Dragon form an unforgettable couple.

Strong opinions characterize people born under this pair of signs. "I should think" or "I would suppose" is here replaced by "It is!" and "You're wrong!" and "Two and two are not four!" and "That's that!"

This person is competent. At an early age he will head out of the nest, forage around the world in a thousand different jobs, pursuits and causes. Then, just when you think he's about to become a bona fide lifetime failure, Taurus/Dragon gets it together, comes back to his home town, is instantly hired in the top job in the business of his or her choice, and within two years he has been promoted to president.

The Taurus/Dragon is haughty. He blusters, "Why should I apply myself until I am good and ready?" Conceited? Yes. But the thing is, people born under these two signs generally end up getting what they want. They are so blatantly determined and industrious (and moreover are not shy about admitting it) that others can't help it. They are impressed.

Taurus/Dragons are plucky. When you meet one you'll see what I mean. They've always done things nobody else has tried, like running off to a foreign country where a revolution is going on or dancing topless in a bikini on a bistro table in Saudi Arabia where even the female dogs and cats wear veils. Taurus/Dragons are daring to a fault.

It is not uncommon for the Taurus/Dragon's travels and derring-do to be financed by somebody more settled than he—an ex-spouse or a parent or even just an old friend. Scruples are not a Taurus/Dragon affliction. So long as the money keeps rolling, he or she does not care where it comes from. As far as the Taurus/Dragon is concerned, his own immediate cause surpasses in value all others. When he's tired of it, when he's had it with helping starving Bedouins and wants to take a break, Taurus/Dragon might rush out and spend his last dinar on a bunch of new clothes. Then, he quickly telegraphs home to Kalamazoo for airfare.

There is a kind of mute force present in the Taurus/Dragon's nature. Rather than being the exclusively vocal fire breather most Dragons are, this Dragon tends for the most part to seem quiet. Except, of course, if provoked. And being of such strong and unshakable opinions, Taurus/Dragons are always provoked. "What do you mean by that?" seems a harmless question, doesn't it? Well, try asking it of a Taurus/Dragon

sometime. Then stand back. Horns and scales quiver, a roaring sound emanates from the chest, then—thar she blows! You would do well to remain seated or the enraged Taurus/Dragon will blow you over with his hot shower of protestations.

It's a bit off-putting, I admit. Taurus/Dragons cannot really know everything. Yet, no matter what we do to counter them, they go on believing that what they think and do is right and proper and the best. Taurus/Dragons love a good fight. When they storm the Bastille of your defenses, they are not only defending their cherished ideas, Taurus/Dragons are cruising for a good old-fashioned row. They'll throw themselves into a scrap with more verve than practically any other sign. No blind rages either. Low blows and hair-pulling allowed.

Love

Of course this Taurus born in a Dragon year is most sentimental. No matter how pushy and aggressive this person seems, if you scratch the surface you'll discover a substance not unlike swan's down, in great quantity. Taurus/Dragons are serious lovers. They admire and adulate their mates. Once they have found the person they will love for a long, long time, Taurus/Dragons are capable of remaining utterly faithful to said mate.

The Dragon is interested in love and in having romance in his life. But I'd venture he is actually more interested in his own advancement in the world. In other words, Taurus/Dragons are not known for their grandiose, torrid extramarital love affairs. But they are often known for their jealousy and excessive need for attention from lovers and mistresses.

I know a Taurus/Dragon lady who repeatedly kept her lover up all night "discussing" their relationship. Not long ago, she boasted to me of a trick she once played on him after a night-long row. "At six a.m., he just turned over and went to sleep on me," she explained. "He always gets up at seven to go to work."

"He must have been very tired," I opined. Poor guy needed at least one hour's sleep.

"So do you know what I did?" said the Dragon lady. "I went in the kitchen and got a rope. And I tied all four doors in his bedroom together by their handles. Then I brought the rope over and lashed his sleeping form to his bed."

Aghast, I asked her how she could do such a terrible thing to someone she loved,

"I wanted to talk some more. I knew that if I didn't tie him down as soon as he woke up he'd leave. Then, I jumped on the bed and shook him awake," she told me with a twinkly smile of pride.

"What happened then?" I was very curious by now.

"He talked to me," she declared, as though there was no other solution. "I didn't let him go to work until eleven-thirty."

And they're still together. Isn't that amazing?

Compatibilities

The beautiful trouble with Dragons is that they get along with hordes of other signs, other tough Taurean Dragons not excepted. You will find possibles among Cancer, Virgo and Capricorn/Rat and Monkey subjects. You will also be turned on for life by the sleek Virgo born in Snake. You won't have any trouble cohabiting with Pisces/Roosters, Rats or Monkeys. If I were you, though, I'd give Leo and Scorpio/Oxen and Dogs the slip. You need to preserve all your fight for your own advancement. Don't mingle intimacy with friendship where Aquarius/Oxen and Dogs are concerned, either.

Home and Family

Despite his penchant for globetrotting and excitement, the Taurus/Dragon usually makes an excellent parent. His family preoccupies him no little and he wants them to love, honor and obey him. In return, he provides well, bringing home plenty of bacon for the gang.

Remember, this person is a Dragon. And Dragon is the most secretly affectionate of Chinese animal signs. Emotional attachments stir this subject deeply. Taurus/Dragon will take every move his or her child makes personally. If the kid gets good marks, then Taurus/Dragon pats himself on the back and thinks, "My child is a genius." (Accent on the my.) Or conversely, if the Taurean Dragon's son is a juvenile delinquent who robs banks, the parent will take it badly, feel personally responsible and not spare the rod.

The Taurus/Dragon child will be boisterous. The need for attention that comes with the Taurus/Dragon territory may shock an unsuspecting parent. The child must be channeled early on into activities that require the energy to be applied. Positive behavior must be encouraged. This child's parent will often be weary from applauding. A Dragon born in Taurus is a uniquely talented performer. Let this child follow his instincts. If you don't, he will follow them anyway.

Profession

Taurus/Dragons are both overachievers and malcontents. No matter whether they take up whether it's social work or sculpture, teaching or medicine, these subjects are Hell-bent to succeed. They often rise to the top of the ladder. They make testy employees whose aim it is to take over the store. On their way to the best position in the company, they may whine a lot: The water cooler is too far from their desk. Or the sun shines in their window at the wrong time of day. Or maybe the salary is too low or the working conditions too rigorous. Whatever their job, Taurus/Dragons air their grievances—abundantly. Nobody can ever expect to really get along with a Taurus/Dragon in work situations. Instead, they put up with him, admire and revere him. Taurean Dragons won't have it any other way.

Ideal professions for the Taurus born Dragon are: Advertising executive, artist (all kinds), athlete, movie star, radio or TV personality, psychiatrist, college professor.

Famous Taurus/Dragons:

Adele, Al Pacino, Ana de Armas, Anna Kalata, Anna Vergelskaya, Burt Young, Carrie Henn, Charles Aznavour, Christine Baranski, Christoph Sanders., Darius McCrary, Djimon Hounsou, Edouard Molinaro, Frances Fisher, Gregg Henry, Hosni Mubarak, James L. Brooks, Jean Gabin, Jennifer Capriati, Johannes Brahms, Lady Helen Taylor, Lars Mikkelsen, Lee Majors, Mary McDonnell, Melissa Gilbert, Nikki Reed, Peter Benchley, Renaud, Rick Nelson, Robbie Amell, Robert Zemeckis, Sage Stallone, Sally Hawkins, Salvador Dali, Sara Paxton, Shirley Temple, Shohreh Aghdashloo, Sigmund Freud, Stan Mikita, Yannick Noah, Yehudi Menuhin.

TAURUS
QUALITIES
ARDOR, DETERMINATION, INDUSTRY,
PATIENCE, LOGIC, SENSUALITY
QUIRKS
LANGUOR, PREJUDICE, INTRACTABILITY,
GLUTTONY, COMPLACENCY, JEALOUSY
Motto: *"I have"*
Elements: *Earth, Venus, Fixed*

--

SNAKE
QUALITIES
INTUITION, ATTRACTIVENESS, DISCRETION,
SAGACITY, CLAIRVOYANCE, COMPASSION
QUIRKS
DISSIMULATION, EXTRAVAGANCE,
LAZINESS, CUPIDITY, PRESUMPTION,
EXCLUSIVENESS
Motto: *"I sense"*
Elements: *Negative, Fire, Yin*

This is the most natural of Snakes. As Snake people often display cosmic leanings and cleave to the other worldly, the presence of Taurus grounds them. This Snake will be intuitive as usual, and wonderfully discreet. But the Taurus part of the character will lend earthiness.

There is a definite talent here for acquisition. Snakes like money and often come by it with more ease than others. They covet luxury, too, and revel in comfort. The Taurus is similar in that what he gets, he keeps.

Art and beauty hold much for the Taurean Snake. He not only wants to participate in its creation (and he might very well); the Taurus/Snake wants to bathe in a totally artistic ambience. The Taurus/Snake's sense of luxury is not like, say, the Pig's desire for live-in opulence and gluttonous wealth. Taurean Snakes are more drawn to serious beauty than they are to ostentatious display.

Like all natives of the Snake sign, the Taurus/Snake will spend his life in full battle with his archenemy: laziness. As Taureans frequently suffer from languorousness, are stubborn and sometimes eat rather too much, imagine what the Snake's lassitude can wreak on this person's waistline.

Like all Snakes, this native will possess a special brand of beauty. Snakes are always wonderful to look at. But Taurean Snakes have added solidity and will be less translucent and coldly gorgeous than other Snakes.

This Taurean will be a procrastinator. He or she will start and stop the same task a hundred times before finally completing it down to the last detail. It's not that Taurean Snakes are hesitant or lack self-confidence. But this person wants to take his time about getting to the end of everything—from lovemaking to basket weaving. He's not a plodder. He's a "fit and starter."

People born in Snake years under the sign of Taurus appear straight-faced. They strike one as a mite too serious. But surprisingly, the Taurean Snake character is capable of gigantic feats of silliness. I know one Taurus/Snake woman who regularly causes a dinner party of six or eight guests to collapse in a helpless heap of laughter by her zany antics. It is a common miscalculation to find these subjects forbidding.

Dissimulation is always a problem for Snakes. The Taurus logic and true patience may temper this bad habit but it will still surface from time to time anyway. Snakes tell fibs—even to themselves. It may even be part of the reason they operate slowly when confronted with inevitable conflict. They are capable of telling themselves that whatever is happening is not really happening at all.

Jealousy will crop up here, too. Taureans are jealous beasts. Snakes have a hard time with faithfulness. The very combination presents obvious problems. Why do I stay with Jack? Because Jack is mine. Why do I cheat on Jack? Because I love to seduce. Why do I go back to Jack? Because Jack is mine.

Love

As a lover or mate this person will be so attractive that you will want to spoil him or her to death. My advice? Don't. The Taurean Snake will take care of that on his or her own. Fact is, natives of Snake and Taurus both need to have a structure in their lives in order to accomplish anything. If you love one of these characters, help put some starch in his sails. Bring some order into the kitchen, and sharpen those tools she left lying out in the rain. Hang up the clothes you find scattered everywhere, and lay down the law about self-discipline. It's the biggest favor you can do for this slightly indolent, slippery character.

In turn, the Taurean Snake will hold you in high regard, listen to your woes and give sound advice on all of your problems, keep the larder and the library filled with exciting exotica and, in short, seduce you anew every day.

Compatibilities

Normally you get along with Cancer, Virgo, Capricorn and Pisces in the form of Oxen, Dragons and Roosters. You need stability but are magnetized by folly. Watch out for headstrong Leo/Tigers and Pigs. And don't get caught up in either Scorpio or Aquarius/Tiger's catchy refrains. Keep your cool in the face of these enchanters or the result could be disastrous.

Home and Family

For this person surroundings are ultra-important. She will want to call in the finest decorators and finish the bedroom doors in Chinese red lacquer. He will insist on creamy leather couches and tufted armchairs from England. These souls are the epitome of plush. Theirs will be a home in which you can flop in style.

Security means a great deal to this person's ultimate happiness. A family may not be quick in coming (procrastination rears its head) but when it does, the Taurus/Snake will not make light of it. As a parent, Taurus/Snake is generally reliable and sensible as well as sensitive.

The child Taurus/Snake should be nurtured and never pushed. He or she will react badly to any attempt by aggressive parents to steer a course he or she has not chosen personally. Taurus/Snake kids will have a silly streak that can be fun, but then again it might not always amuse the parents to have a clown around the dinner table. Taurus/Snake may be a rather taciturn child, keeping much to himself, taking solitary walks and knowing how to play alone in his room. Do not jolt.

Profession

Taking risks is not this subject's forte. He is serious about gain and not one to fritter or gamble money. As a result, you will usually find Taurus/Snake in surefire professions where earning power is high and the promise of retirement in the not-too-distant future certain. His talents lie in intellectual areas or in the classical professions.

As a boss, the Taurus/Snake may not be too terrific because he is slow about making decisions. Taurean Snakes are not adept at delegating authority, preferring to keep most of it for themselves and only issuing permits to those they deem worthy. But as an employee, providing he is well remunerated and his occasional pranks don't get in the way of progress, the Taurean Snake might make a handsome and useful addition to any work environment.

Jobs that might suit the Taurus/Snake personality are: professor, artist, librarian, lawyer, doctor, and all other classical professions right on down through to pharmacist. Then too, these people make excellent designers, stunning performers and remarkable precision engineers.

Famous Taurus/Snakes:

Adrian Pasdar, Amy Hill, Anastasia Baranova, Audrey Hepburn, Behati Prinsloo, Danièle Darrieux, Emily Rios, Eric Bogosian, Henry Fonda, I.M. Pei, James Russo, John Cena, Kal Penn, Kevin James, Kristen Taekman, Lari White, Leslie Hope, Lindsey Shaw, Luann de Lesseps, Lynn Collins, Lynn Whitfield, Matt Czuchry, Melanie Lynskey, Nora Arnezeder, Nora Ephron, Paige Turco, Pierce Brosnan, Richie Valens, Tom Welling.

TAURUS
QUALITIES
ARDOR, DETERMINATION, INDUSTRY,
PATIENCE, LOGIC, SENSUALITY
QUIRKS
LANGUOR, PREJUDICE, INTRACTABILITY,
GLUTTONY, COMPLACENCY, JEALOUSY
Motto: *"I have"*
Elements: *Earth, Venus, Fixed*

--

HORSE
QUALITIES
PERSUASIVENESS, UNSCRUPULOUSNESS,
POPULARITY, STYLE, DEXTERITY,
ACCOMPLISHMENT
QUIRKS
SELFISHNESS, AUTONOMY, REBELLION,
HASTE, ANXIETY, PRAGMATISM
Motto: *"I demand"*
Elements: *Positive Fire, Yang*

G reedy for dominion over others, the Taurus/Horse wants to play the *beau rôle* in all of life's dramas. The Horse is a prancer and even when housed in the mind and body of the drudge-tolerant Taurus, that old pony will kick up his heels, show who's boss and even occasionally throw his rider—just to keep the record straight.

There is frequently much talent apparent early in the life of Taurean Horses. They may be prodigies in music or art or even in sports or intellectual pursuits. I wouldn't be surprised if those kids who win international competitions at age six include many Taurus/Horses among them. The Taurus/Horse child's personality is obedient and well-behaved, diligent and ambitious in the first part of his life. Parental urging is heeded by the Taurean born Horse child. This kid practices his piano.

But somewhere in the melee of adolescence, when the first inter-minglings with peers begins, the genius in Taurean Horses becomes compromised by social life, by the demands of a "normal" existence. Not that the clever Taurean Horse can ever really fit in. He cannot. He is different, separate by virtue of both his specialness and his bit-terness at not being chosen for a Nobel Prize at age thirteen. Tau-rus/Horses find satisfaction in greatness. Otherwise they are grumpy because nobody recognizes how brilliant they really are.

Growing up is a comedown to a lot of Taurean Horses. It was great when Mom and Pop applauded every breath and your fifth-grade teacher told you that you had natural gifts unlike any she'd ever seen. But being an adult is a terrible drag. You have to go out there and prove yourself, fight your way among people far less tal-ented than yourself who, by some fluke, advance more quickly than you do.

So let me give you some advice, Taurus/Horse. It's true that you surely have more talent and ability than most. You are a marvelous human being. But you are socially lazy. You don't want to make that extra effort to ring up somebody who needs a smile, to go call on the sick grandmother or the guy who said he'd give you a con-tract. You don't want mere action. You want privileges. And I'm sorry to break this to you, Taurus/Horse, but privilege evolves from the whole experience of getting to the top. If you back out before you begin it won't happen for you for long. There will always be some less talented, more humble or wily person who comes along and pulls the magic carpet out from under you.

Nobody can say that Taurus/Horses are not conscientious work-ers. They are always the first ones at the office and the last to go home at night. Taurus/Horses are materialistic and love to own beautiful things. They tend to show off their wealth and dress in rather colorful yet conservative clothes. They are far from dull. They have plenty to talk about. Taurean Horses are responsible and respectable people. They grow more discreet and have better man-ners as they get older and move away from the childish self-image of prodigy who can do anything and get away with it because of superlative talent.

Actually, the Taurus/Horse, with all the brilliance given him at birth, is more of an instinctive being than he is an intellectual. He can think but he would rather operate on hunches. He can reflect but he'd rather play music—or even baseball! This person needs much understanding from his entourage—patience, good humor and solicitude.

Love

How, you may ask, can this egomaniacal semi-genius stop preening long enough to love anyone? Well, the fact is that love is the only area in which the Taurus/Horse does not deem him- or herself automatically superior. Taurean Horses are excessively susceptible to love affairs. They are capable of giving up everything for the sake of gaining the affections of the person they fancy. Taurus/Horse people care enormously about their public image and worry about what others think of them. Therefore, discretion is an important factor in the Taurus/Horse's love life. He doesn't particularly enjoy bandying his romantic business around. He or she will hardly be the type to hold hands or kiss in public.

The Taurus/Horse needs someone in his or her life who is willing to hover in the wings while he or she performs. I don't, however, recommend anyone too long-suffering and self-sacrificial. The Taurus/Horse doesn't want to be fawned over. Usually he or she has had enough of that in youth.

So give your Taurean Horse a challenge. Tempt him or her to come off his self-imposed pedestal. Drag your Taurus/Horse victim to parties and get him involved in social work. Otherwise he may turn into a stay-at-home misanthrope who feels misunderstood and complains a lot. Taurean Horses need to be jollied up, tickled and taught to laugh—especially at themselves.

Compatibilities

You'll get on with Cancer, Virgo and Capricorn/Tigers, Roosters and Sheep. You'll feel superior to them in one way, yet they know how to stand up to your sometimes magnified self-image. Pisces/Tigers confront well, too, so you may find yourself entrapped by one. But the Pisces/Sheep is the one you would really die to catch. Good luck. Rats, above all of the Scorpio and Aquarian families will not do. Make yourself scarce for Leo/Monkeys, Aquarius/Oxen and Pigs, and give Scorpio/Pigs a pass, too.

Home and Family

The Taurean Horse's home will be his castle. No place is better suited to his temperament and no place on the outside makes him feel comfortable. In fact, I would venture that all Taureans born in Horse years are at their very best in their own very personal surroundings.

As a parent, the Taurean Horse may at first be thrown off guard by his children's innocence. He wonders, "What do these little people really want from me?" Nothing but love? How terrific! A family life of their very own is the best way for Taurus/Horses to take their minds off themselves.

As a child, the Taurean Horse will be almost too good to be true. You will be amazed at his abilities and want to send him to Hollywood or Harvard. You will find this little person's behavior exemplary and you will love the little darling to pieces. One word of advice: Take it easy on the kid! Don't push too hard, and keep the applause to a minimum or his head will grow too big for his social life. Encourage his talents but don't forget to prepare him for the real world.

Profession

Sometimes, of course, the Taurean Horse is so gifted that he begins an artistic or art-related career very young and sticks to it. But we know that in the lives of kids who start out very early, there is many a slip 'twixt the high school stage and the Oscar. The wise Taurean Horse goes to university or pursues some kind of practical studies parallel to his creative pursuit. He makes a very demanding boss. As an employee, the Taurus/Horse is generally much appreciated by superiors fur his rigorous attention to detail and his real desire for advancement.

Taurean Horse can choose almost any artistic career if they can take the heat that goes with it. Otherwise there are many art-related fields such as production or communications. And why not law? Or advertising? All areas where one needs practicality and poise will do.

Famous Taurus/Horses:

Amadeo Giannini, Andrea Tafi, Barbra Streisand, Daniel Franzese, David Keith, Deborah Kara Unger, Dev Patel, Ella Fitzgerald, Janet Jackson, Jasper Johns, Jeffrey Dean Morgan, Jerry Seinfeld, John Pankow, Johnny Logan, Kurt Godel, Laetitia Casta, Leven Rambin, Luke Kleintank, Malin Akerman, Martha Graham, Matthew Davis, Michael Moore, Mike Wallace, Pablo Schreiber, Pat Summerall, Paul Mazursky, Pennel Roberts, Polly Walker, Stana Katic, Stephen Baldwin, Thomas Brodie-Sangster, Ulysses S. Grant, Vladimir Lenin, Yui Hashimoto.

TAURUS
QUALITIES
ARDOR, DETERMINATION, INDUSTRY,
PATIENCE, LOGIC, SENSUALITY
QUIRKS
LANGUOR, PREJUDICE, INTRACTABILITY,
GLUTTONY, COMPLACENCY, JEALOUSY
Motto: *"I have"*
Elements: *Earth, Venus, Fixed*

--

SHEEP
QUALITIES
INVENTION, LACK OF FORESIGHT,
PERSEVERANCE, WHIMSY, GOOD MANNERS,
IMPRACTICALITY
QUIRKS
PARASITISM, SENSITIVITY,
TARDINESS, PESSIMISM, TASTE, WORRY
Motto: *"I depend"*
Elements: *Negative, Fire, Yin*

This person is, by turns, a taciturn pixie, an industrious nitwit and a brilliant dreamer. Great genius often visits people born Taurus/Sheep. And, if properly handled, this inner spark or enormous creative ability can take them far in both worldly and personal development. But without optimum growing conditions, this subject will spend his or her life seeming to putter about, half-finishing projects and partly realizing dreams.

Essentially, the Taurus/Sheep struggles his whole life long with a yearning for security that comes from without. The Taurus character is slow but solid—even stodgy at times. Taureans are down-to-earth, acquisitive and sensual. Taurus likes order and thrives on certain sameness that others might deem monotony. But the Sheep nature is evanescent, shifting and spasmodic. Sheep excel by fits and starts.

Visualize the nimble mountain Sheep propelled by a fierce effort up a steep incline. A great impressive leap gets the Sheep sure-footedly to an inaccessible peak. Here comes Taurus. And what does Taurus do to the flighty Sheep? He causes him to sit down, look around, examine a few of the wild flowers underfoot, admire himself in a nearby pool and even set up camp on that peak until some new impetus comes along to force his next gigantic push.

Taurus and Sheep are complementary signs. Slowness and surefootedness work well together. So do logic and invention. Patience goes well with perseverance. There are parts of this character that assure us a totally calm human being. And most Taurus/Sheep do possess composure.

Behind the scenes, however, we find determination opposed to lack of foresight, languor as against intractability. These contrary traits are constantly at battle. Repeatedly, for concrete earthly reasons to be sure, Taurus/Sheep's spirit is invaded by his inner contradictions. This makes him by turns pessimistic and anxious. The personality develops flaws of near Mephistophelian proportions.

How does all of this apply to the Taurus/Sheep's daily life? Well, I've known my share of Taureans born in Sheep years. And they all give in to periods of self-doubt, frustration and even violence.

Taurus/Sheep are viscerally attracted to what is beautiful. They have more discerning good taste in one hoof than you or I have in our whole bodies. Normally the Taurus/Sheep builds, creates, invents, interprets and decorates. And, when not actively engaged in said activities, this person backs off from society, takes refuge in pastoral surroundings and plots his next stroke of genius.

The iffy part or this portrait only arises when Taurus/Sheep are hindered from implementing their brilliant moves. Financial considerations bore Taurus/Sheep. They are usually nigh unto incapable of turning their creations into ready cash. They lack drive and they anger easily when pushed. If anybody, and I mean anybody, should so much as dare to cast a shadow on their parade, Taurus/ Sheep surrender. Then, they seethe. They don't give up. Their dreams are still intact. But the interfering party, he who hurls the wrench into Taurus/Sheep's works, will not go unpunished. Revenge – even violence—is not out of the question.

Taurus/Sheep cannot discuss their frustrations. They are not the whimpering "feel sorry for me" type. And they aren't excessively articulate either. So, Taurus/Sheep are either peaceful or else they are out there swinging. They have their own timetables and their own personal aesthetic. Don't get in the way of either and the Taurus/Sheep will be happy to spend the rest of his/her life eating off your plate.

Love

To hear jilted Taurus/Sheep talk you would think all of their various "exes" (wives, husbands, companions) were but a pack of thieves, strumpets and pimps. Taurus/Sheep likes to be loved—and cared for. He needs enormous security and is not very apt at providing same. He also needs praise. But he can't give very much of that either. Taurean Sheep simply have to be loved for the part-time jollies they can give. They have little staying power in love. They fly off the handle at the slightest forgotten birthday or wedding anniversary. They attach importance to roses and Valentines, but they might just forget your cat in the refrigerator overnight. For serious mates, Taurus/Sheep are exasperating.

And Taurus/Sheep need serious mates. They cannot function in a couple where they have to wear the trousers, bring home the bacon or bathe the baby. Taurus/Sheep can—and only just—create. They have no sense of time, no memory for anything more important than their mate's credit card numbers and they refuse to see the reason to change.

If you are prepared to be strong and tough and police the everyday life of some adorable but violent and wacky artiste, run out and lasso yourself a Taurus/Sheep. I'm sure there are lots of them going to waste. Taurus/Sheep is an inertia worshiper. Yours is probably just sitting there prettily, waiting to be discovered in a long-defunct Hollywood drugstore.

Compatibilities

You'll like Pisces/Pigs and Horses. You'll be charmed by Virgo/Cats, and entranced by the cultivated Virgo/Pig. Capricorns and Cancers, both Monkeys and Horses, will please you, too. Your best bet is found among Capricorn/Monkeys, but they are very much in demand so you will need to hurry. Don't take up with Leo/Oxen or Dogs. Keep your distance from Scorpio/Tigers and Oxen and run when you see an Aquarius in a Dog or a Tiger costume.

Home and Family

The home situation is dependent upon whom Taurus/Sheep can depend. If the family unit is solid and the central pivotal force provides a fertile and comfortable ambience for the subject to evolve in, Taurus/Sheep will make a delightfully blissful parent.

Taurean Sheep love to play, to gambol hither and yon over hill and dale, to frolic with their children and show them how to appreciate life's finer things. You may find Taurus/Sheep in the basement fashioning a slick new toy for the baby or in the kitchen frosting cupcakes with perfect little faces, each different and each precisely the likeness of a family member.

Of course, you must also expect that the toy may not be finished until baby is of voting age and those cupcakes may be stale by the time all the expert facial decorations are complete. Somebody has got to push this Sheep up those basement stairs, or out of the kitchen and into the dining room with the dessert. Whenever you meet up with this character, look for the person holding the cattle prod just inches away.

As children, Taurus/Sheep must be patiently encouraged to pick up toys, to complete homework projects, to follow through on tennis serves, to check the temperature before going out in a frigid world wearing only a T-shirt. A careful parent is in order. This child will of course be charming and a wizard with his hands. This talented kid needs discipline, a firm but loving hand that slowly, imperceptibly loosens the rope that tethers the child to home. There is probably a form of genius here. But it will remain a lazy prisoner if left un-nurtured.

Taurus/Sheep are perfect grist for the mills of stage mothers the world over. But I wouldn't count too heavily on this person's professional orientation taking him or her much further than the front door. Unless—and this is crucial—others who have noted the genius are willing to sacrifice their own notoriety, give up their own personal ambition for the sake of their prodigy's success.

Profession

The advice I can give to Taurus/Sheep is slim. I don't pretend to know how to alter this person's tendency to indolence without using force. I am, as you know by now, of the Sherman tank school of human dynamics. "If you don't feel like doing something, do it anyway," is my motto. This theory doesn't work with Taurus/Sheep. What does work? Maybe lots of affection, warmth, coziness and endurance, encouragement and blind unquestioning faith in Taurus/Sheep's work. I'd say that Taurus/Sheep who spy that mountain peak from way far away at age fifteen or less and consciously undertake to conquer that peak by age forty are way ahead of Taurus/Sheep who do not find their challenge early. Taurus/Sheep must surround themselves with richness and approval, sound advisers and steel-nerved allies. Such foresight is, however, not native to the Taurus/Sheep. Will somebody please give this creature a shove off the starting block?

Ideal professions for the Taurus/Sheep are: Genius, movie star, artist (all kinds) and diva.

Famous Taurus/Sheep:

Aleisha Allen, Ana Gasteyer, Bérénice Marlohe, Bill Paxton, Chow Yun-Fat, Debra Winger, Eva Peron, Frank Dillane, Freddie Boath, Honoré de Balzac, Jacques Dutronc, Jaime King, James McAvoy, Joey Graceffa, Kari Wuhrer, Kate Mulgrew, Katharine Hepburn, King Willem-Alexander of the Netherlands, Laurence Olivier, Leslie Jordan, Madhuri Dixit, Philippe Séguin, Prince Carl Philip of Sweden, Princess Charlotte, Robert Morse, Rosario Dawson, Rudolph Valentino, Sheryl Lee, Teresa Brewer, Tim McGraw, Vincent Kartheiser, Willie Mays.

TAURUS
QUALITIES
ARDOR, DETERMINATION, INDUSTRY,
PATIENCE, LOGIC, SENSUALITY
QUIRKS
LANGUOR, PREJUDICE, INTRACTABILITY,
GLUTTONY, COMPLACENCY, JEALOUSY
Motto: *"I have"*
Elements: *Earth, Venus, Fixed*

--

MONKEY
QUALITIES
IMPROVISATION, CUNNING, STABILITY,
SELF-INVOLVEMENT, WIT, OPPORTUNISM
QUIRKS
DECEIT, RUSE, LOQUACITY,
LEADERS, SILLINESS, ZEAL
Motto: *"I plan"*
Elements: *Positive, metal, Yang*

Here is one Monkey whose ruse and trickery are satisfied to remain in the wings for a lifetime. Taurus settles the busy, agile Monkey character. This is a fortuitous combination of signs.

Taurus/Monkeys are stable. Their equilibrium sticks out all over them. Capable of emotional highs and lows like everybody else, the Taurus/Monkey sets himself apart by dealing with trauma better than most. Beset by loss or tragedy, this creature remains buoyant through it all. Of course he will be aggrieved by the death of someone near. Naturally, he will pine for the lost loved one. Certainly, the Taurus/Monkey is able to sob along with the best of us. But he will also be among the first to rise from a wet pillow, place his feet squarely on the floor and decide to design better days for himself.

I am not describing, however, the jack-in-the-box resilience or the Rooster, who never gets too involved in the first place and therefore digs himself out faster. Taurus/Monkey is, after all, Taurean. He feels things profoundly and is devoted to his emotional attachments. But Taurus/Monkeys are sensible. They know instinctively when to give in. They are not afraid to surrender and start over when no alternative presents itself. Taurus/Monkeys are savvy.

Monkeys born in Taurus will be realistic people. They are not given to vapid dreaming or empty longings for things or experiences they can never have.

Taurus/Monkeys are temperate, take their methodical time about accomplishing tasks and don't settle for slapdash results. Others to whom the Taurus/Monkey has promised favor, a ride to the PTA meeting or a loan, can count on this subject never to let them down. Taurus/Monkeys will either categorically say, "No, I can't," or "Yes I'd be glad to," with a smile. And if, for some reason beyond his control, a Taurus/Monkey cannot come across with the goods, he will simply and in due time call or write or holler to apologize.

The equilibrium of people born under this marriage of signs is their single most important virtue. When you feel all right about yourself vis-à-vis the world, nothing actually can stand in the way of your happiness. Taurus/Monkeys rarely doubt themselves. Oh, they may have private moments of panic. But you'll never see a Taurus/Monkey dragging himself along whimpering about how miserable he feels inside. Instead, he will take pains to exhibit his best side, to inspire confidence in others and rarely, if ever, to place blame for his own shortcomings on colleagues or cohorts.

The Taurus/Monkey knows his own strength. Therefore, if a noisy Leo/Dragon or pushy Aries/Ox wants the limelight, Taurus/Monkey doesn't mind sitting behind the curtain feeding the boss his lines. Taurus/Monkey leadership abilities are obvious. But he doesn't need to sit on the throne to be happy using them.

Taurean Monkeys are kind, too. They go out of their way to lend a hand, cheer up a sick friend, or jolly up a grump. But with this, despite their basic generosity of spirit, Taurus/Monkeys personify independence. They need no company for activities such as going to movies or concerts, traveling, eating, dancing, and so on. It's not that Taurus/Monkeys do not adore company. But so at one are they with their own rhythms, they don't require a second opinion or even a sounding board in order to know what they enjoy in life. So if you need a Taurus/Monkey, you can call on him for help. But when you don't write SOS in the sky or jiggle the Taurus/Monkey's chain, he may just be off by himself on a bike hike around Eastern Europe.

It seems we can find no failing in this monster of stability. Yet, people do complain about Taurus/Monkeys. What they say is that Monkeys born Taurean possess such a hearty measure of self-confidence and pep that by comparison, others may feel like just so many slouches. And it's true. The Taurus/Monkey only offends by reflection. His character is so sterling, his integrity so dear, that others feel small next to him.

Taurus/Monkeys are modest too. So we cannot even accuse them of bravado. They're bright and funny, good listeners and dexterous in the extreme. Taurus/Monkeys are devoted and uncomplicated. But don't ever try to corner one. You won't be able to fence him in. Don't expect him to hang around and mope if rejected or disobliged. This character is all of a piece. Therein lies his unbeatable force.

Love

Faithfulness, as we all know, is relative. Everyone has a slightly different point of view and interpretation of what it means to be constant in love. To a Taurus/Monkey, faithfulness in relationships is directly connected to loyalty, friendship and dedication. This person is certainly adept at loving others. Yet, he will never get involved in any long-term love affair or marriage that threatens to compromise his autonomy. For Taurus/Monkeys, mutual respect and freedom are synonymous with love.

I have never known a Taurus/Monkey whose passion for another human being crippled him. To a Monkey born in Taurus, incapacity is death. If he feels a weakness approaching his knees and can practically hear the butterflies flapping about his stomach, the Taurus/Monkey will be gone in a wink, pleasantly and preferably without harsh words. The Taurus/Monkey is likely to want a longstanding life commitment in love. But the concessions incumbent upon such a commitment may daunt him. The prospect of long dull evenings around the glowing hearth will discourage the Taurus/ Monkey from early marriage. And by time he gets around to accepting a love alliance that is sure to cramp his style, the Taurus/Monkey may consider himself too old and set in his ways to actually implement it.

There is something of the eternal child in his character. He's charming but he is also elusive. Taurus/Monkey is a footloose soul who frequently imagines himself in settled loving care. But very often he ends up like Peter Pan left behind by Wendy and the Boys to fend for himself in Never-Never Land.

Compatibilities

Normally you should be compatible with Cancer, Virgo, Capricorn and Pisces/Dragons. Dragons and Monkeys respect each other a lot. You also get along with Rats of the Cancer, Virgo and Capricorn persuasions. I'd advise you to look into the possibility of a lifetime Pisces/Rat, too. They are sweet and strong-minded at the same time. I cannot see why you are not allowed a Scorpio/Tiger, but the odds are astrologically against longevity in such relationships. Scorpio/Snakes and Aquarius/Dragons are also forbidden territory. Forget Leo/Ox, Tiger and Horse people. They are too egocentric for you.

Home and Family

Taurus/Monkeys (if they ever get around to it) make excellent parents. They are serious and caring. Also, they have a childlike quality themselves and so are amusing and playful with their kids. And of course they always provide.

As siblings, aunts and uncles and cousins, Taureans born in Monkey years are dy- no – mite! The element of liberal movement implied in such platonic relationships appeals to the Taurus/Monkey. He'll bring his nephew the most extraordinary toys and take his favorite cousins on trips to faraway places. He'll gladly offer his participation in family projects or build a new swimming pool for his little sister Sara's suburban ranch house.

In order to develop a healthy Taurus/Monkey child, parents must try to allow him freedom to evolve in his own private space. Taurus/Monkey children may go off on their own too often to please a clinging parent. They will definitely leave any suffocating family atmosphere at the earliest possible moment. To ensure this person's happiness as an adult, he must always be given choices and never be forced to struggle against excessive authority. And no matter what you do as the parents of this bubbly, capable achiever, he will soon be off into the world to seek his fortune.

Profession

Taurus/Monkeys like to spend money. They therefore usually know how to earn it. As I have already said, these people are industrious and willing to pitch in and help out in almost all situations. These traits do not hinder the Taurus/Monkey's progress in career pursuits.

Taurus/Monkeys are affable, too. They enjoy meeting new people, exchanging ideas with them and learning new methods of doing things. Sales and public relations are suitable jobs for Taurus/Monkeys, as are positions in journalism or medicine. Most important, of course, is that the career choice allow for mobility. The Taurus/Monkey may, for example make a terrific photographer. But if he is obliged to sit in a dinky office somewhere taking pictures of babies with topknots in a cold white studio, all his talent will drain out before he gets a chance to apply himself. He hates to be confined. But put this energetic photographer on location in the thickest fray of the fashion or advertising world and hear that shutter click gaily away.

Uppermost in orienting a person born in Taurus/Monkey is the acquisition of a sound liberal education. The idle Taurus/Monkey mind is never a happy one. There are few fields in which he will not excel and he is especially drawn to those that excite his curiosity. Once he has a bit of knowledge on a subject that interests him, the Taurus/Monkey can study on his own, research and assimilate for a long time without further tutelage.

Famous Taurus/Monkeys:

Adrian Scarborough, Aidan Gillen, Alexander Ludwig, Amy Ryan, Anouk Aimée, Ashley Rickards, Bob Saget, Catherine Tate, Channing Tatum, Christine Bravo, Christine Ockrent, Ellie Kemper, Elvire Popesco, Harry Truman, J.M. Barrie, Jack Gleeson, Jack Quaid, Jeffrey Donovan, Jill Clayburgh, Jordana Brewster, Kelly Killoren Bensimon, Kevin McNally, Lars von Trier, Leonardo da Vinci, Mary Robinson, Michel Audiard, Olivia Culpo, Paige O'Hara, Pia Zadora, Pope John Paul II, Rafaela Silva, Sam Heughan, Sam Smith, Sugar Ray Leonard, Timothy Olyphant, Traci Lords, Wendy Crewson.

TAURUS
QUALITIES
ARDOR, DETERMINATION, INDUSTRY,
PATIENCE, LOGIC, SENSUALITY
QUIRKS
LANGUOR, PREJUDICE, INTRACTABILITY,
GLUTTONY, COMPLACENCY, JEALOUSY
Motto: *"I have"*
Elements: *Earth, Venus, Fixed*

--

ROOSTER
QUALITIES
RESILIENCE, ENTHUSIASM, CANDOR,
CONSERVATISM, CHIC, HUMOR
QUIRKS
COCKINESS, BOASTFULNESS, BLIND FAITH,
PEDANTRY, BOSSINESS, DISSIPATION
Motto: *"I overcome"*
Elements: *Negative, Metal, Yin*

Great wisdom and authority characterize the Taurean born in Rooster years. This person will he self-possessed in the extreme. Taurus endows him with unshakable determination. Rooster lends enthusiasm and blind faith. From an early age, the Taurus/Rooster exhibits a tendency to dominate. Taurus/Roosters are, however, not usually political leaders. These folks do not ever try to get elected to office by popular vote, cheered at the football game for their team spirit or even hailed as the "best mom or dad in the world" by their kids. Taurus/Rooster is quite simply, fearlessly and naturally prominent.

Preeminence does not have to mean tyranny. Taurus/Rooster is not interested in running the lives or careers or the spiritual lives of others for the sake of wielding power. Yet, because of their exceptional mettle, Taurean Roosters are often found in high places. Water seeks its own level. Even if one wanted to, it would be impossible to relegate this feisty person to an inferior rank. Subordination does not just make Taurus/Roosters crazy and neurotic and angry the way it might a Taurus/Ox. Submission just doesn't fit Taurus/ Roosters. Subjugation and Taurus/Rooster form an impossible juxtaposition that simply cannot exist.

Because Taurus/Roosters possess natural (not artificial, remember) power, they come by compassion easily. You will note among the Taurean Roosters of your acquaintance that in dicey situations they invariably take the side of the underdog against unfair authoritarian practices. Taurus/Rooster wants to help out people he feels are less suited for dealing with this complex life. A Taurus/Rooster can always be counted on to stick up for the little guy, back the downtrodden and tout the advantages of hiring the handicapped.

Now, due to this penchant for favoring the ill-used and rising up against the bullies of the world, Taurean/Roosters sometimes lose themselves in personal causes or vendettas in the name of another, less fortunate soul. What starts out as pity or charity can wax into passion. If he doesn't watch out, before he knows it, the Taurus/ Rooster is locked into a very unhealthy love relationship. Underdogs have a funny way of secretly wishing to be masters. Within the confines of a love affair or even a friendship, secrets will out. I have known some Taurus/Roosters, basically outwardly dominant people, whose wills have been broken by an underdog/bully. The strong are perhaps ineffably attracted to the weak. Sympathy is a lovely sentiment. But beware, Taurus/Rooster, don't let yourself be buffaloed by simpering ne'er-do-wells. Of course you should help people in need. But try not to let them slip between your sheets.

In personal style, Taurus/Roosters typify what I like best about the countryside. Earthiness, solidity, purity, sensuality and generosity. Taurus/Rooster is gifted for maintaining order in nature's chaos. And this person's character provides just the proper amount of steely agility to carry his coherent projects into effect.

Taurus/Roosters may have an eating problem. I've never known a skinny one. The Taurean tinge of gluttony combined with Rooster's enthusiastic adventurousness naturally makes for a certain Epicureanism. Taurus/Roosters are conscientious people, so they know how to diet and discipline themselves. But the leaning is toward the good—maybe just a smidgen too good—life.

Taurean/Roosters are substantial people. Despite all appearances (a certain cockiness and garish dress habits), these people are deeply, densely, irremediably conservative. And they are often very, very bright. For a Taurus/Rooster to skip the first four grades nr primary school and enter Harvard at age twelve is practically status quo. And it isn't just their intelligence that pushes them either. Taurus/Roosters don't particularly need social chitchat and are not upset if they don't fit in with groups. As they are intrinsically head and shoulders above others, their precocious successes, gained in a thoroughly independent fashion, are many.

Rooster's resilience is compromised in Taureans born under its influence. The Taurus is an emotional reservoir. Feelings embed themselves so profoundly under their sensitive skins that even being born a bouncy Rooster can't save them from occasional periods of frightening gloom. Loss, separation, partings and even just change really jar Taurus/Roosters. They ruminate and scratch about in the dirt and sulk and weep and brood. Only time heals the wounds Taurus/Rooster feels so achingly. Time and affection—and plenty of serious hard work.

Love

Although Taurus/Roosters are serious as a rule and not attracted to frivolity, their choice of love partners often hints at the contrary. Roosters born Taurus like to be amused. Their lives are serious enough as it is. They feel they want some levity in a partner. You will often see a strong Taurus/Rooster whose companion is a limp-wristed wisp of a thing who doesn't stop blabbing and smiles a lot. "What does she see in that boob?" you may wonder. Fun. Hilarity. Enjoyment. Pleasure, Silliness. Lightheartedness. Joy. All the elements which are missing from the Taurus/Rooster's solemn nature.

Taurus/Roosters are faithful, to a point. They are not the syrupy falling about, I-can't-live-without-you types who promise undying physical exclusivity. No. The Taurus/Rooster is above that. But involvements and emotional attachments do grab the Taurus/Rooster's heartstrings and are not readily dislodged. His passions run deep. Should a Taurus/Rooster err a bit while away on a business trip, you can be sure that she'll come home just as in love with her lifetime partner as when she got on the airplane last Tuesday. These people are not given to abandonment of true affection.

Should you love a Taurus/Rooster, you must be careful not to weigh too heavily on their seemingly unflinching souls. These people appear more emotionally tough than they really are. If you see a black cloud float in and hover over your Taurus/Roosters head, engendering a week-long silent sulk, you must be brave. Get the best food and drink around. Have a candlelight dinner ready when Taurus/Rooster arrives and wait till he's just a wee bit tipsy. Then talk. And talk fast. Ask what's wrong. Insist. Show your compassion. Be amusing. Wear your heart on your sleeve. Taurus/Roosters need to cry too. But they don't like to admit it. It's up to you to bring out their emotions – and the Kleenex box.

Compatibilities

Your greatest affinities are with Cancer, Virgo and Capricorn people born in Ox, Dragon or Snake years. You'll also find Pisces alluring in their Ox or Snake form. Don't dally with Leo/Cats or Leo/Roosters. Their vanities clash with your own. Aquarius and Scorpio/Dogs and Cats are not your favorite house pets either. Too much competition for authority.

Home and Family

In all matters pertaining to what is serious and profound, the Taurean Rooster is a champ. Family life, with all of its intricately braided emotional patterns and tics, pleases old Taurus/Rooster right down to the ground. The more kids the merrier. The more parties and birthdays and bar mitzvahs and weddings they can throw, the happier they'll be. Taurus/Roosters like to be entertained, cajoled, brought along to enjoying themselves. They make a perfect audience for all manner of family skits and shenanigans.

As a sibling, cousin, aunt or uncle, Taurus/Rooster is also right up there with the best. As Taurus/Roosters take duty seriously. they never forget to phone an aging relative or remember to celebrate Mother's Day for their maiden aunt's sake. They are likewise disappointed in family members who don't accept their offerings of affection and aid. Taurus/Roosters are bossy people. I wouldn't want to have a Taurus/Rooster mother-in-law.

Taurus/Rooster children are strong-minded. Tough but adorable. Resilient but sentimental. To do right by one of these very special kids, the parent should try to provide an atmosphere of learning, growing, building and knowing. The Taurus/Rooster child's seemingly independent spirit requires far more cuddling and nurturing than he or she lets on. Always tuck them in at bedtime, read them stories, nuzzle their necks and remind them how much they are loved.

Profession

There is nothing a Taurus/Rooster cannot do—except be relegated to subordinate positions. All jobs where authority is needed will suit this character's needs. The Taurus/Rooster can also run his or her own business without any trouble whatsoever. Law, medicine, scholarly pursuits—all of these will work. The Taurus/Rooster is a capable sort.

And not only is this character able, he is gifted for earning a living. I don't think he is the type to end up rich. Taurus/Roosters don't much care about wealth. They like to be comfortable. But they're not interested in money for its own sake. But work is the Taurus/Rooster's friend. He loves to perform well in whatever he does. As failure cannot be taken lightly by such a Spartan soul as Taurus/Rooster, he usually doesn't allow himself to go under. Circumstances can, however, get beyond his control. And when they do, Taurus/Rooster tries desperately to re-create order to stem the tide of inevitability. His efforts are valiant.

You can trust the failed Taurus/Rooster to struggle back up the ladder to find a new, way to get ahead and satisfy his need for prowess. Nothing really daunts this person forever. But the uphill trudge will be both long and hard. We are not exactly dealing with a butterfly.

Suitable careers for Taurean born Roosters are: Writer, leader, musician, actor, journalist, real estate magnate.

Famous Taurus/Roosters:

Adrian Scarborough, Amy Ryan, Andrei Sakharov, Annie Dillard, Bjorn Ulvaeus, Bob Saget, Cate Blanchett, Catherine of Russia, Catherine Tate, Craig David, Daniel Gélin, Danielle Fishel, Debbie Ryan, Ellie Kemper, Felipe Massa, Jeffrey Donovan, Jessica Alba, Jordana Brewster, Joseph Morgan, Kevin McNally, Lady Gabriella Windsor, Lars von Trier, Miranda Cosgrove, Otto Klemperer, Paige O'Hara, Peter Townshend, Rachel Platten, Renee Zellweger, Rod McKuen, Rory McCann, Sam Heughan, Timothy Olyphant, Traci Lords, Wendy Crewson.

TAURUS
QUALITIES
ARDOR, DETERMINATION, INDUSTRY,
PATIENCE, LOGIC, SENSUALITY
QUIRKS
LANGUOR, PREJUDICE, INTRACTABILITY,
GLUTTONY, COMPLACENCY, JEALOUSY
Motto: *"I have"*
Elements: *Earth, Venus, Fixed*

--

DOG
QUALITIES
CONSTANCY, UNSOCIABILITY,
RESPECTABILITY, SELF-RIGHTEOUSNESS,
INTELLIGENCE, TACTLESSNESS
QUIRKS
UNEASINESS, CRITICISM, DUTY,
CYNICISM, HEROISM, MORALITY
Motto: *"I worry"*
Elements: *Positive, Metal, Yang*

Here is a dutiful combination gifted for performances of all kinds and cursed by a surfeit of uneasiness, which easily translates into dissatisfaction. Let me explain. Taureans born in Dog years tend to complain a lot. They find fault with much of what life offers, As for what life doesn't offer—they feel it should. Taurus/Dogs have an overdeveloped sense of injustice. They cannot understand why it seems as if the cards are always stacked against them. Why are others so lucky? Why do things seem to just fall into their laps? Why don't wonderful lucky things happen to me? grumbles the dissatisfied Taurus/Dog.

Childlike appeal and apparent innocence of all that is tawdry and crooked make the Taurean Dog a lovable and dear companion. He's interested in and capable of many different pursuits. He usually has a talent for amusing crowds and is willing and able to take on great responsibilities. Despite his inborn talent for determination and respectability, for industry and even heroism, the Taurus/Dog suffers from a painful lack of self-confidence. He is never, from childhood forward, quite sure of himself. Often, because of this insecurity, the Taurus/Dog settles for remaining in the wings of life for the whole or his childhood and adolescence. Then, by the time he is old enough to answer his cue and leap onto center stage, Taurus/Dog may not feel quite ready yet. He'll hang back, find excuses for delaying his one-man show and, if he not careful to find the right partner who pushes and prods and loves and cares enough to shove the Taurus/Dog out there, the Taurus/Dog may find himself at retirement age standing hangdog in the same wings of life wondering whatever happened to his cue.

This person is a natural-born worry wart He's also extremely perfection conscious and wants things to be done right and go well and come out flawless. If they don't, he will be the first to blame not only himself but also to scold those who surround him. "Why don't you take things more seriously?" wonders Taurus/Dog to his light-hearted friend or mate or child. "Why can't you see how important this is?" he may chide.

When the Taurus/Dog does succeed in a big way, he may tend toward smugness. He feels he has worked harder than others to get where he is. He knows that some people might have cheated or tricked to get places in life. But not the Taurean Dog. Never! Taurean Dogs are the first to consider themselves "good" people who always do things "right." Struggle and huff and puff and bark and growl and sweat. Then, when they do win fame or fortune or the approval of their entourage, Taurus/Dogs are capable of opining, "I deserve this. I work harder than anybody else. It's about time somebody recognized my enormous talent."

You see, life really is not easy for Taurus/Dogs. Because of their own reticent attitude, they often are left out, overworked, and misunderstood.

They are more conscientious than lots of other folks. And they are sensitive in the extreme. Couple this sensitivity with a native tendency to jealousy and possessiveness and you come up with a mighty testy character. You may see the Taurean Dog as inexcusably self-involved. But don't think for one minute that lie perceives himself as anything less than Albert Schweitzer—caring, loving, giving, warmhearted, kind, indulgent.

Taurus/Dogs do take up causes and care a lot about the little guy. They are liberal-hearted and willing to go far to help out the less fortunate. This person can persevere in what seems to be hopeless situations. His loving and caring capacity is very, very strong.

Usually, these people are generous and willing literally to give you the shirt off their backs. They are sweet-natured underneath all that ill-tempered blather and dither. Taurus/Dogs are the kinds of dogs who growl a lot when they first meet you and who, before you know it, have jumped into your lap and are licking your face all over. They need encouragement and plenty of applause.

Love

The doubting Dog nature coupled with the plodding and stubborn yet possessively ardent Taurus personality provides us with a constant, faithful and sincerely devoted lover. No mountain is too high to climb, no river too wide to wade across for the sake of this person's love object. In relationships, the Taurus/Dog always feels that he is the one who gives the most. And he likes it that way.

What Taurean Dog people sometimes fail to take into consideration is that in order to be able to love them back with the identical fervor they throw into each affair, their partner must be possessed of abnormally superior powers of tickle. To be the full-time lover of a snappy and grave Taurus/Dog, you have to be a stand-up comic, a Saint-Bernard and a clown. The successful mate for Taurus/Dogs is able to find humor in all aspects of things. Otherwise, what with the natural Taurean Dog pessimism turned up full volume for life, the household ambience may amount to something akin to a cemetery's. Bottom line: if you love a Taurus/Dog, always keep 'em laughing.

Compatibilities

Love will blossom between you and Cancer, Virgo, Capricorn and Pisces/Cats, Horses and Tigers. Blends like the above suit your testy and essentially pessimistic nature. You need to be buoyed, optimized and occasionally booted in the rear end, too. But not by Leo, Scorpio or Aquarius/Tigers, Dragons or Sheep. Their motives may not be wholly altruistic. Yours usually are.

Home and Family

The Taurus/Dog will not make a great fuss about his surroundings. He usually likes things efficient and warmly colored. But whether or not he has the latest in designer furnishings is of little consequence. Rather than fussing about the latest or the best in modern or antique design, the Taurus/Dog will want things personalized his way. He may move the furniture around in a hotel room or tack up magazine pictures on the walls of a rented vacation flat. He likes things to be quaint and cozy and comfortable. He eschews plastics.

The Taurus/Dog's family, even though it is often a source of immense disappointment to him from the beginning of his life, ranks high on his popularity meter. Where there is a need for devotion and duty and a call for duty and reliability, you can always count on the services of this loyal cohort. Where his children are concerned, he will be both careful and serious. He may be a tiny bit strict with kids, but it's only because he wants them to be happier than he ever was and the Taurus/Dog firmly believes that self-restraint is one of the secrets of happiness. You watch. If a Taurus/Dog ever dares to indulge himself in any debauchery at all, the guilt and self-recrimination are shattering to witness. He wants to be thought of as above reproach.

The Taurus/Dog child will strike you as rather solemn at first. He is not easy to know and requires lots of cheering up and jollying along. This child can be counted on to obey and to try to do things the way parents wish. If you have such a kid, look for his own personal passion very early on and force him to overcome shyness and trepidation, so that later on he will have fewer chances to moan about what he missed. Get him out of the shadows at a young age.

Profession

There is little the Taurus/Dog cannot accomplish, He is usually both talented and willing to work. He may prove slower to achieve than others, but the fine results will always be worth the extra time he spends. Dogs born in Taurus will be both reliable and concerned about the impression made on colleagues and clients. As he may be a touch awkward socially, the Taurean Dog must be careful to surround himself with outgoing and gregarious colleagues. Taurus/Dogs are good at detail, and although not exactly influenceable, they are definitely open to new ideas and always ready to try out more modern methods.

As an employee, the Taurus/Dog will be loyal and forthright. From time to time he may prove a shade argumentative over niggling little points. But on the whole Taurean Dogs take care to see a job well done. As bosses, Taurus/Dogs enjoy a good reputation among their workers. The Taurean Dog, remember, is a fair person and, even if a tiny bit grouchy sometimes, is overall a kindly sort who doesn't mind sharing the less pleasant tasks with his colleagues. If cheated or tricked in business deals, the Taurus/Dog may grow bitter. He doesn't take kindly to con jobs. So, if you were thinking of trying to hoodwink a Taurus/Dog, remember that his bite is almost as harsh as his bark,

I can see Taurean Dogs in all sorts of jobs. They might be physicists or city planners or own and operate a newspaper store or bookstore. Show business and politics alike present the Taurus/Dog with opportunities to use his talents well. He'll be very fulfilled as a teacher or in any rural job requiring attention to ecological concerns.

Famous Taurus/Dogs:
Alexandra Breckenridge, Andre Agassi, Arletty, Caspar Lee, Cassidy Freeman, Cher, Daniil Kvyat, Georges Moustaki, Giancarlo Esposito, Golda Meir, Harry Shum Jr., Jacqueline Laurita, Jamie Dornan, Jane Wiedlin, Jason Lee, Joanna Lumley, Jonathan Jackson, King Carl Gustaf of Sweden, Kirsten Dunst, Lenin, Master P. Michel Poniatowski, Melania Trump, Michelle Pfeiffer, Rebecca Hall, Rob Riggle, Samantha Mathis, Scott Bairstow, Serge Reggiani, Shirley MacLaine, Socrates, Tina Fey, Tom Daley, Uma Thurman, Yannis Xenakis.

TAURUS
QUALITIES
ARDOR, DETERMINATION, INDUSTRY,
PATIENCE, LOGIC, SENSUALITY
QUIRKS
LANGUOR, PREJUDICE, INTRACTABILITY,
GLUTTONY, COMPLACENCY, JEALOUSY
Motto: *"I have"*
Elements: *Earth, Venus, Fixed*

--

PIG
QUALITIES
SCRUPULOUSNESS, GALLANTRY, SINCERITY,
VOLUPTUOUSNESS, CULTURE, HONESTY
QUIRKS
CREDULITY, WRATH, HESITATION,
MATERIALISM, GOURMANDISM, PIGHEADEDNESS
Motto: *"I civilize"*
Elements: *Negative Water, Yin*

You are likely to find one of these subjects among the "beautiful people." Taureans born in Pig years, albeit rather rustic in certain ways, are attracted to the upper levels of society. Material wealth will serve to embellish the opulent life of the Taurean/Pig. He enjoys both riches and position and, frankly. never accepts less than what he feels is his absolute due (lots). This person is also quite bossy. He needs to have his own way. He will cooperate. But only if he gets to be the "Mommy."

The types of activities that can be undertaken by a Taurus/Pig are myriad. No task or chore is too difficult for his brute force. No fine detailed work with needle, brush or knife defies his deftness. This is a big sign, both generous and loving in the extreme, hardworking and very down-to-earth.

The Taurean born Pig may not have a sparkling youth or a smooth, harmonious adolescence. But when he grows up, the Taurus/Pig deliberately sets out to find his lost chords, to put order and concord back into his tumultuous lire. Methodically and with great thought and care, the Taurus/Pig finds the people with whom he will share his life, takes great pains to protect and make them comfortable in luxurious surroundings, and then grippingly, fervently, solidly loves them.

Taurus/Pigs are very often handsome people whose grace, despite the avoirdupois that both Bull and Porky summon in the mind's eye, is lovely to watch. They are tough and dense people. But Taurus/Pigs are rarely severe or unkind, cruel or unfair to others. They truly like their fellow man and are seldom, if ever, thoroughly disgruntled.

Combine the logic and patience of the Taurus with the scrupulous sincerity of the Pig and you have a limpid, sterling character. This person will readily share his material wealth, and draw up and carry out huge serious projects. And his word is as good as law—better. He honors his contracts and is fraught with terrible self-doubt and worry if for some reason he cannot.

Because the Taurus/Pig is essentially such a pure soul, always willing to give ears and tail to cooperate with others, it follows that sometimes he is also extremely influenceable. I mean, if a Taurus/Pig believes in somebody, buys someone's act all the way, then his faith and loyalty to that person will be unshakable. If, unfortunately, the "someone" in question is a rotten egg and drags the poor good-hearted Taurus/Pig into treachery and crime, it will be the moral and emotional undoing of our hero.

Taurean Pigs don't like to be rude to others. But if they are pushed too far, they will read their tormentor the riot act in no uncertain terms. Like all Pigs, this one puts up with a lot. But when they are pushed to the limit and have been taken advantage of one time too many, Taurus/Pigs charge full steam ahead into the fray, vituperating like wet hens. Trust me, nobody wants to be told off by an enraged Taurean born in a Pig year.

Powerful these people are. And impenetrable as well. They love company and are always the ones who shop and cook and make lovely dinners where people remember having such a roaring good time. But when they are working or just thinking, you need a power-driven crowbar to enter their concentration aura. This ability to persevere alone, nibbling slowly every day at a huge amount of work, is what gives the Taurus/Pig his ticket to success. Everything this person does is tinged with victory.

Love

When it comes to knowing how to love, romance, tenderness, loyalty and depth of feeling are true qualities. Taurus/Pigs have them all. They are really all-or-nothing love bugs with a unique taste for the finest that sensuality has to offer. These types adore food and don't even mind tippling a bit. Their homes are invariably comfortable and richly appointed. The entire ambience speaks of occasions for amorous activity. Large bedrooms, draped in velvets, and tinted lampshades entice the loved one into a nest whence he or she is not likely to exit intact.

Taurean Pigs crave beauty and comfort. They require a lot of chatting and foreplay, appreciate lavish gifts and elegant parties. Don't invite a Taurus/Pig to come and stay with you in a hut or a tent. These subjects really hate to rough it. Give a Taurus/Pig a luxurious villa on the French Riviera or a sprawling palazzo in Tuscany. Invite him to stay on a huge ranch in Texas. But don't ask a Taurus/Pig to love you unless you're willing and able to help provide at least one of the above.

You will need to arm yourself with patience, too. Taurus/Pigs get things done but they love to take their time. If they are busy playing a piano sonata when they're supposed to be at an appointment, Taurus/Pigs will finish the music first. Taurus/Pigs are also mild people. They don't go for exaggerated, mawkish knight-in shining-armor behavior. Never serenade a Taurus/Pig under his window or swashbuckle around him.

He'll only laugh and you may never get to see that cozy nest I was talking about earlier. Be cool. And intelligent. And funny.

Compatibilities

Pursue a Capricorn or Cancer/Cat, Dragon or Sheep for the purposes of happiness ever after. For some hanky-panky you might be amused by a bout with a sexy Virgo or Pisces/Sheep character. Your sensitivities match up perfectly. But if you want some future with your sensuality, stick with Cats and Dragons of the Cancer, Virgo, Capricorn or Pisces persuasion. Both Chinese signs are capable of true complicity with you. Don't waste any time on Leo/Snakes or Monkeys. Steer around Scorpio/Tigers, Roosters and Dogs. Whatever yon do, don't go getting involved with Aquarius/Snakes, Roosters or Monkeys.

Home and Family

The call of duty is music to the ears of Taureans born Pig, Relatives are always welcome at their homes, family reunions are often held in their backyards, and when cousin Sara gets married it's usually good old Taurus/Pig who throws the reception at his place. Taurus/Pigs faithfully phone their aging parents and listen to hours of woeful tales with an indulgent smile on their lips.

As parents themselves, Taurus/Pigs may be incidentally bossy, but they are not very authoritarian. They like to think they are giving leeway to their kids, room to grow and imagine and learn about art and culture. Taurus/Pigs are themselves very artistic people. The thought that their child might feel constrained or restricted by stodgy teachers or dumb rules irks the Taurus/Pig. He'll be the first parent to summarily remove his kid from any stuffy environment where the child is unhappy.

Taurus/Pig children are rich in spirit. They don't mind sharing their games or letting other kids borrow their bikes. But little Taureans born in Pig years often insist on having their own way. Their angers are few but when they arise they amount to real bite-the-rug tantrums. This child needs a comfortable and secure environment in which to develop his artistic side. Take him to museums and the ballet, shower him with affection and don't be shy of encouraging self-discipline. He will respect rigor as long as it is combined with true caring.

Profession

This person will be talented for professions requiring diligence, strength, artistic appreciation and a sense of team spirit. Taurus/ Pigs are not loners. They crave company and like to feel as though they "belong" where they work.

As a coworker, the Taurus/Pig will probably strike others as slightly on the demanding side. He is stubborn and when an idea sticks in his brain, he doesn't let go of it easily. I feel sorry for anyone who tries to take his position away or one-up the Taurus/Pig in a chain of command. This person has a natural penchant for surpassing others.

Appropriate jobs for the Taurus/Pig are: executive, museum curator, artist, university administrator or professor, art dealer, antiques expert, giant of industry or even politician.

Famous Taurus/Pigs:

Adrianne Palicki, Amber Tamblyn, Bridget Moynahan, Catherine Mary Stewart. , David Boreanaz, Domhnall Gleeson, Elyes Gabel, Eric Mabius, Fred Astaire, Gabourey Sidibe, Geneva Carr, Gigi Hadid, Guy de Cars, Henry Cavill, James Buchanan, Jamie Luner, Johan Cruyff, Jonathan Dekker, Laurent Cabrol, Luciano Benneton, Mare Winningham, Maureen O'Sullivan, Megan Boone, Missy

Franklin, Oliver Cromwell, Patrick Bruel, Queen Maxima of the Netherlands, Sofia Coppola, Victoria Rowell, Ving Rhames, Vladimir Nabokov, William Randolph Hearst.

GEMINI
QUALITIES
QUICK-WITTEDNESS, PERSPICACITY,
FLEXIBILITY, VERSATILITY,
PERFORMANCE, DEXTERITY
QUIRKS
IMPATIENCE, GLIBNESS,
INCONSTANCY, SELF-DECEPTION,
SUPERFICIALITY, INDECISIVENESS
Motto: *"I think"*
Elements: *Air, Mercury, Mutable*

--

RAT
QUALITIES
NERVOUSNESS, INFLUENCE,
ACQUISITIVENESS, THIRST FOR POWER,
INTELLECTUAL SKILL, CHARISMA
QUIRKS
APPEAL, VERBOSITY, THRIFT,
SOCIABILITY, GUILE, MEDDLING
Motto: *"I rule"*
Elements: *Positive Water, Yang*

A shooting star of infinite genius and practically no end of tales to tell, your average Gemini/Rat flits amiably around the room at any and all gatherings, charming and bright, delighted and delightful. Catch me if you can.

And the fact is you can. But you must first discover Gemini/Rat's secret password. The key to the Gemini/Rat's most guarded intimacy is "I." This character observes the world through an almost impenetrable haze of ego.

Geminis born in Rat years blend the flittery-fluttery Gemini spirit

181

with the Rat's excessive nervousness. Both signs thrive on motion. Just think of it! A butterfly with a jet engine inside, moving all the time, busy at applying talents he doesn't even know he has.

The Gemini/Rat is a generous person. He likes to give away anything and everything. He wants to make people laugh and cry or in any case react to him, respond to his dynamism and admire his marvelous ways. He's a born doer and always feels that whatever he's created or earned can be replaced. Gemini/Rat knows instinctively that there will always be another novelty waiting in line inside his head.

Perseverance is another pair of socks altogether. Gemini/Rats can only really learn to stick to a single place or long-term chore if there is the absolute certainty of gain. For money, this Rat will perform nightly at the same spot. But don't forget to give him top billing. If suitably rewarded, he'll stay on for as long as the show can run.

There is a whimsicality about the Gemini/Rat that lightens the sometimes heavy atmosphere surrounding other Rat characters. Geminis love to show off. The Rat Gemini is no exception and because he is at the same time active in the extreme and full of Rat drive, he is capable of great theatricality. His sales acumen is such that he might sell stray dogs to the ASPCA.

Where Gemini/Rats are long on dazzle, they are acutely short on decision-making. They're never really sure if they want to do this or that. "Well, maybe, I'll see what's going on when Tuesday rolls around I'll call you. No, look, I'll think about it. I'm not really all that sure . . ." and on and on. Gemini/Rats are just plain capricious.

The solution to this personality's major dilemma is for him or her to find the right partner who knows just how much rope to issue every morning so that this nutcase doesn't go and hang him- or herself during the day. A nice, solid sort who knows how to put his or her own ego in a back pocket, allow the Gemini/Rat to zip around basking in his or her own ego and still rein in the little darling when night falls. This person is a handful and a half. But worth it.

Love

Inconstancy is a Gemini fault. The Rat brings skill, a desire to "make it" in the world and to earn power as well as silver and applause. Though steadiness is not innate in this subject, it can be learned. If a Gemini/Rat needs his mate to assist him or her toward the power/money goal, the relationship is likely to go a long way.

Beware of Gemini/Rat seduction routines. These folks will say absolutely anything to beguile. From the jump they want control. It's never a heavy or ponderous sort of domination. Rather, the Gemini/Rat controls by whim. He wants to be taken to the theater on his birthday. But no. Perhaps he'd rather take flying lessons. It's uncertainties like this that can baffle an unsuspecting partner and eventually lead to annihilation of confidence.

If you love one of these restless people, give the Gemini/Rat plenty of space in which to play at being "me." Take up one or more outside activities. Go bowling and teach yourself how not to cling. Cloying sentimentality drives the Gemini/Rat to distraction. He may not mind having a loving and admiring full-time partner. But he or she will despise being leaned on.

Compatibilities
There's an Aries, Leo, Libra or Aquarius in your future. Make sure you choose him or her from among the Dragon or Monkey crew. Don't hang around with Virgo, Scorpio, Sagittarius or Pisces/Cats. You don't seem to think alike. Erase Horses from your mind altogether, and prefer the solid Aries/Ox or, for some diversion, why not invite a Libra/Tiger to lunch?

Home and Family
This person will live in comfortable surroundings, but he or she will not necessarily be the one who designed them. Most certainly Gemini/Rats will not have stitched up the draperies or painted the baseboards by hand. Gemini/Rat is the idea man in all his pursuits.

Gemini/Rat will depend largely on his mate to raise the children. He is not the type of self-sacrificing angel who struggles to get custody and then deprives himself his whole life long just to raise his kids on his own The main thrust of the Gemini/Rat parent-child rapport will be what the old Gemini/Rat parent can teach to offspring and how much he can amuse them, cajoling them with sales talks on early bedtimes and fun methods of eating their spinach. The Gemini/Rat, like all Rat parents, will be protective of family members and the family name.

As a kid this person will be tremendous fun to have around, always smiling and gurgling, even from the start. As long as you lay on the attention, Gemini/Rat babies will chortle their way to adulthood without a single sulk. But woe unto the busy parent who hasn't time for Junior. This kid will think up myriad ways to get attention—and keep it. Watch out for hypochondria and trumped-up excuses. This child needs lots of affection and a firm hand.

Profession
The talents of this character lie in his ability to communicate. Gemini/Rats are monsters of perspicacity and quick-wittedness. Their ability to see a situation is their special individual streak of genius. I

cannot say your average Gemini/Rat has tenacity because he doesn't. One big weakness in this person's makeup is his tendency to blame others for what he does wrong or bungles.

As a boss, this person is too easygoing. He'll let his employees get away with too much. But because like all Rats he's a Rat first and a Gemini second, this person will know enough to associate himself with steadier people than he. Gemini/Rats usually succeed through a sound partnership. As an employee, this person will be hard to handle, detached, lighthearted. No amount of yelling and screaming will change that. Gemini/Rats hate taking orders.

Jobs that suit this person are: politician, TV producer, realtor, ad person, entrepreneur, actor or actress, tour guide or chef.

Famous Gemini/Rats:

Alexia Umansky, Andrea Casraghi, Angelo Assumpção, Archie Panjabi, Bob Champion, Chris Elliott, Claude Brasseur, Doug Jones, George Bush Sr., Joe Giudice, John Cheever, John Gallagher Jr., Karl Urban, Kodi Smit-McPhee, Kristin Scott Thomas, Laverne Cox, Leslie Hendrix, Mary McCarthy, Normani Hamilton, Paul Dano, Phillip Van Dyke, Robin Tunney, Thomas Haden Church, Thomas Hardy, Tom Holland, Torrey DeVitto, Tracy Grimshaw, Wentworth Miller.

GEMINI
QUALITIES
QUICK-WITTEDNESS, PERSPICACITY,
FLEXIBILITY, VERSATILITY,
PERFORMANCE, DEXTERITY
QUIRKS
IMPATIENCE, GLIBNESS,
INCONSTANCY, SELF-DECEPTION,
SUPERFICIALITY, INDECISIVENESS
Motto: *"I think"*
Elements: *Air, Mercury, Mutable*

--

OX
QUALITIES
STUBBORNNESS, STRENGTH OF PURPOSE,
ELOQUENCE, STANDOFFISHNESS, INNOVATION,
VINDICTIVENESS
QUIRKS
INTEGRITY, BIGOTRY, PLODDING,
DILIGENCE, BIAS, STABILITY
Motto: *"I preserve"*
Elements: *Negative Water, Yin*

Ox is a boon to the Gemini's blithe spirit. This is a settling-down Gemini, a family sort of Gemini with eyes for the good life. A Gemini born Ox will always go forward, albeit more deliberately and ponderously than other Geminis, toward goals big and small. This Gemini is a thinker, yes. But he's not guilty of leaping from thought number one to idea number thirty-three and back to thought number one in two seconds flat. Concentration is possible and great work may even be accomplished.

This creature can be amazingly unlike what he seems. Gemini/0x, like all Oxen, seems really rather dull. But wait till he starts talking.

Wait till she begins telling you the story of her latest car accident and how she ran away from home when she was sixteen because her father beat her and her mother drank. And watch how positively transfixed you will be when your favorite Gemini/Ox recounts the tale of his youngest son who went to university in England and met a girl who practiced witchcraft. You will not blink the whole time. Pick up a Gemini/Ox and you won't be able to put him or her down. These folks are real page-turners.

Gemini/Oxen are wry, too. They are not the kind of rollicking funny people who tell jokes and try to make you laugh. Instead, they manage to inject humor into their accounts of this or that event so that you hardly know it's there. You are smiling and keeping your ears cocked for more. No pokes in the ribs. Just a steady stream of wit.

The Ox is often a loner and this one is no exception. The time he spends alone will be the time he enjoys the most. As loquacious and eloquent as he can be, the Gemini/Ox is nonetheless a rock of personal inner strength. He likes his pleasures simple and his ideals healthy. It's all right to have lofty dreams, but if they are unrealizable, the Gemini/Ox is not interested. "Yes. I would enjoy having a castle in Spain. But as I lave a large house in the United States that takes lots of care and upkeep, and three children to send through college, it doesn't look as if I'll ever have one," says the sensible Gemini/Ox.

The Gemini/Ox prefers the intimate dinner party with close friends to the giant open house where fifty people a minute float by in gossamer and tails. This is essentially a country person whose tastes and needs are easily satisfied by the generosity of Mother Earth. Yes, she will go thirty miles out of the way to buy the right kind of smoked ham. But the Gemini/Ox doesn't see that kind of detour as luxury. She's a person who requires quality and finds it difficult to accept second best.

Demanding? Indeed! I would say that this Gemini is just that. He wants things right. He does not mind waiting but he hates clutter and waste and drivel. He's impatient with flibbertigibbets and has no time for fools. Gemini/Oxen may even be accused of choosiness and a certain degree of name-dropping snobbery. Whom you know seems to the Gemini/Ox almost as important as what you know.

Love

For the Gemini/Ox there are two kinds of love. There is family love. And there is sexual love. Otherwise there isn't any love. The Gemini/Ox is a worker. He may claim not to be as diligent as he appears. But basically his goal is personal accomplishment. He's not interested in romance. He's interested in results.

The above often causes the domestic love life of the Gemini/Ox to be somewhat sterile, if not to say positively chilly. Yet, the Gemini/Ox is a busy and serious seeker of the favors of the opposite sex. It's an odd mix. On one side, Gemini/Oxen are stay-at-home family types who don't seem the least sex-oriented. On the other they run after everything that moves. The Gemini/Ox is an armchair Lothario.

If you should have the misfortune to fall in love with such a character, I would suggest you learn early how to turn the other cheek. This person will either choose you for home loving or for sexual loving. Never the twain. And should you have been the one chosen for home loving, don't you dare get out of line. Oxen never forget.

Compatibilities

You are fond of Aries/Rats, Snakes and Roosters too. You and the sexy Leo/Snake or the efficacious Rat born in Leo can also cut the mustard together. A gentle Libra/Rat or Rooster might do the trick for you as well. And don't forget that Aquarius/Rat, Snake and Rooster can make you swoon. I don't advise you to attempt long-standing relationships with Virgo, Capricorn, Sagittarius or Pisces of either the Tiger or Sheep families. You won't exactly adore Monkeys born in Pisces, either.

Home and Family

Here is where the Gemini/Ox's heart (if he has one at all) really lies. The environment of Gemini/Ox people is, to say the least, cozy. The furniture, the kitchen appliances, the basement setup, the garage and the cars that go in it, the yard and the gardens and the woods and the whole bloody works come from the most authentic, the best and the finest craftsmen. It has all been put together with care and is maintained like a well-run ship.

For all his diligence, this person enjoys doing nothing. He doesn't mind sitting around twiddling his thumbs so long as the cars are freshly waxed and the maid is in the kitchen getting together a feast. This person makes a fabulous parent. There is no area of his child's life that doesn't interest him intensely.

The Gemini/Ox child may appear too quiet. The "good baby", "model child" act is frequent with these kids. Don't worry, your Gemini Ox child will get up to plenty of mischief by the time he or she is an adult. Be patient and give this little one plenty of time alone. You won't make him participate no matter how hard you try. It's just not his thing. He likes himself and his cronies. That's it.

Profession

Responsibility suits the Gemini/Ox down to the ground. He is capable of great hardheartedness and brilliant strokes of sarcasm designed to break the heart of a glacier. What the Gemini/Ox wants to do, he or she wants to do and will do. He's a deep thinker and an effective doer. He doesn't let sentiment get in the way of his actions.

As a boss the Gemini/Ox is unreasonable. She wants things done the day before yesterday and each job must be performed to perfection. Yet, she is indulgent with those who cooperate. She is even open-handed. But she doesn't want any flak. As an employee this person won't be very happy. The Gemini/Ox is really better off on her own in some kind of authority position where it's up to her if the sun shines today or tomorrow. It s better for everybody concerned if this person gets to be the Mommy. Otherwise she goes home. She might even sniffle a bit at how misunderstood she has been. The Gemini/Ox can be quite a baby when it comes to having her own way.

Famous Gemini/Oxen:

Boy George, Carey Mulligan, Celina Jade, Colleen McCullough, Dave Franco, Eddie Cibrian, Heidi Klum, Henri Tisot, Jean d'Ormesson, Juliette Lewis, Keesha Sharp, Kiran Bedi, Lana Del Rey, Lea Thompson, Leander Paes, Lionel Richie, Madison Kocian, Marc Pickering, Melissa Etheridge, Michael J. Fox, Neil Patrick Harris, Pierre Salinger, Rochelle Okoye, Roman Reigns, Sam Harris, Susannah Fielding, Tao Okamoto, Tom Wlaschiha, Waylon Jennings, William Butler Yeats, William Styron.

GEMINI
QUALITIES
QUICK-WITTEDNESS, PERSPICACITY,
FLEXIBILITY, VERSATILITY,
PERFORMANCE, DEXTERITY
QUIRKS
IMPATIENCE, GLIBNESS,
INCONSTANCY, SELF-DECEPTION,
SUPERFICIALITY, INDECISIVENESS
Motto: *"I think"*
Elements: *Air, Mercury, Mutable*

--

TIGER
QUALITIES
FERVOR, BRAVERY, MAGNETISM,
GOOD LUCK, BENEVOLENCE, AUTHORITY
QUIRKS
IMPETUOSITY, HOTHEADEDNESS,
DISOBEDIENCE, SWAGGER, INTEMPERANCE,
ITINERANCY
Motto: *"I Watch"*
Elements: *Positive Wood, Yang*

This impetuous person needs good brakes. When you combine hotheadedness with mercurial tendencies, you get some very smart dynamite. The pep and seductiveness of this character has a sort of generous pussycat congeniality to top it off. It's pretty delectable to behold. But it's very difficult to hang on to.

As Gemini never stops darting from pillar to post, philosophy to news flash, project to love affair, the character is already injected with a large dose of blast-off fuel. To add to the instability, along lopes our old friend the tawny Tiger, whose basic idea of himself is that he is extraordinary, ought to be chosen king of the jungle right now if not sooner and would you please move over so he can sit down on that throne? Charm, magnetism and natural authority added to all that Gemini mutability make a sort of benevolent speed demon.

Gemini/Tigers are forever getting themselves into emotional hot water. Their desire to be considered both winning and wonderful drive them to wish to perform great deeds. But it just isn't enough to devise dreams. Somebody has to stick around when they come to punch the ticket. Gemini/Tigers have a sort of whirling dervish effect going all the time. Their restlessness sticks out of them like tiny inverted arrows all over their skins which say, "Look at me. I'm the Gemini/Tiger. Am I not marvelous? Do I not impress you with my looks, my brains, my very tawniness?"

Yes. Okay. Sit down now. And for heaven's sake, think! No. Not that kind of flitting-about thinking, real sound planning type of thinking. Where do you really want to go? What is your main goal? How can you avoid all these interim meaningless goals to which you are repeatedly drawn? Gemini/Tiger, you'd get stuck hanging on a bus strap if there was someone watching you who seemed transported by your aura. Three stops later you might remember where you were headed. But then, because you are so ... adventurous, you might not even care where you were going, stay on the bus and follow it to your next chosen destiny. You are not stupid. But you are sometimes too zany for words.

Bad things can happen to people who don't pay attention to the doughnut and watch only the hole in the middle. And Tigers who are born in Gemini are some of the best targets for ill fates. They are not tied down to the earth by any reality other than the moment, the breakthrough, the jackpot, the fabulous party, the sexy guy in the aisle seat, the dame in red.

Of course Geminis born Tiger are smashingly attractive. One is automatically magnetized by their seductive manners and sizzling charm. But eventually, if they don't settle themselves early into routines that channel their energies and instruct their explosive minds, Gemini/Tigers can become very angry at life. When you are so naturally appealing, it's easy to float along on your appeal. But then what? What happens when you hit a snag in life? What happens when your mate leaves you or your child falls ill or your job is eliminated? What then, Tiger/Gemini? Where will you go and whom will you charm? The Fates?

No. You can only go on so long casting about from place to place, moving from relationship to relationship. Life will eventually catch up with you. Then you'll have to face the music and you may even have to face yourself—alone. I know it's not your favorite idea. But then, you know very well that you have always avoided introspection. But if you did take time to think ahead and apply one or two of your many talents, you would be able to move mountains. You know you are strong. But you are also lazy. You prefer to bask in seduction. That, you are aware, Gemini/Tiger, is silly.

Love

The Gemini/Tiger's biggest stumbling block in romantic affairs is getting involved with people whose adoration the Gemini/Tiger does not really return. He finds their worship of the very ground he walks on irresistible. Yes, it is egotistical. But not intentionally so. If reminded of this trait, the Gemini/Tiger will humbly agree that she's not really wild about Jerry, but Jerry loves her so much that it would break his heart if... Well, the "if" inevitably occurs. And then Jerry is left to inhabit the populous past of the Gemini/Tiger siren.

The Gemini/Tiger needs to be given lots of room. He or she will like to be taken to restaurants and shown off at elegant receptions and spas of all sorts. He will often tell silly stories that you have heard a hundred times before. Either get earplugs or bite your tongue. He does not want you to get into the act by venturing, "No, dear, it wasn't Tuesday when Maria forgot your pants at the cleaners. It was ..." I would give you more advice on how to hang on to one of these flying saucers, but I don't really think anything will work. They are pretty much alone in life's crowd and their fate belongs exclusively to them.

Compatibilities

You'll find happiness with a number of signs. Among them are Aries/Dogs and Horses, Leo Dogs or Horses, too, and Librans born either Dog or Horse. In Aquarius you'll be most attracted to the Dragons, but perceptive Aquarius/Dog won't disappoint you. You are better off losing Virgo and Scorpio/Snakes, Tigers and Monkeys in the crowd. As for Sagittarians, you should abstain from Horses, Cats and Sheep of that sort. Don't take up with a Pisces/Snake. They're too slippery for your clumsy big paws.

Home and Family

Regulation home life coupled with family life and all of its daily habits and chores does not match up very well with the Gemini/ Tiger's desire for movement and experience. They often have very dramatic interiors draped with laces and furbelows, or padded in wall-to-ceiling carpets with remote control lights and mirror effects. Gemini/Tigers can be incredibly theatrical.

As parents they are very loving and warmhearted. They encourage their offspring to do whatever appeals to them and will go to great lengths to see that their kid is properly educated. Gemini/Tigers get along well with kids, too. They are extremely spontaneous people. You will often see a Gemini/Tiger parent actually "playing" with children. They are not bored by the company of little people and of course enjoy any extra attention they can get.

The Gemini/Tiger child will need strict control over his penchant for zigzagging. If you as the mother or father of this being can manage to gently urge some degree of self-discipline, this creature may have a better chance of making some kind of normal life. Lessons, regular bed times and hours to brush teeth, telephone curfews and the like are important. If you have the patience, your Gemini/Tiger child has the talent.

Profession

Fast and energetic, the Gemini/Tiger is born with the ability to adapt to new situations in a trice. This person lives his or her life quickly and gets on to his next goal without much ado about the previous one.

Unusual destiny is the best part of being Gemini/Tiger. As a boss he's hopeless. As an employee too. This person is an original. He cannot be expected to arrive on time and leave at a certain hour. He hates routine and will perform much in the way of mental and physical gymnastics to escape from it. Gemini/Tiger is always succeeding when he least expects to. From out of nowhere flashes luck.

Gemini/Tigers are best employed at jobs they have thought up for themselves. They take kindly to freedom of movement. Give them a paper bagful of delicious-smelling soaps to go around selling and they will have them all bought up in an hour. The Gemini/Tiger is a remarkable communicator. Trouble is, on the way back to bring you the proceeds, Gemini/Tiger may stop off at the leather goods store and purchase a nicer bag for himself so that next time he goes out selling he'll be more attractive. It's a dilemma.

Famous Gemini/Tigers:

Alanis Morissette, Ally Sheedy, Arnold Vosloo, Ashley Olsen, Barbara McClintock, Bobcat Goldthwait, Daniel von Bargen, Dee Dee Bridgewater, Diego Hypolito, Fairuza Balk, Gina Gershon, Gregory Harrison, Joanna Gleason, Kat Dennings, Kathy Baker, Lio, Maggie Siff, Mahesh Bhupathi, Marie Avgeropoulos, Marilyn

Monroe, Marlene King, Mary-Kate Olsen, Miles Davis, Molly Ephraim, Oona Chaplin, Richard Madden, Sean Gunn, Sebastian Koch, Seth Rollins, Shia LaBeouf, Sonia Braga, Sonya Walger, Suzi Quatro, Yuri Andropov.

GEMINI
QUALITIES
QUICK-WITTEDNESS, PERSPICACITY,
FLEXIBILITY, VERSATILITY,
PERFORMANCE, DEXTERITY
QUIRKS
IMPATIENCE, GLIBNESS,
INCONSTANCY, SELF-DECEPTION,
SUPERFICIALITY, INDECISIVENESS
Motto: *"I think"*
Elements: *Air, Mercury, Mutable*

--

CAT/RABBIT
QUALITIES
TACT, FINESSE, VIRTUE,
PRUDENCE, LONGEVITY, AMBITION,
QUIRKS
SECRETIVENESS, SQUEAMISHNESS,
PEDANTRY, DILETTANTISM,
HYPOCHONDRIA, COMPLEXITY
Motto: *"I Retreat"*
Elements: *Negative, Wood, Yin*

C at and Gemini make strange bedfellows. The discreet, prudent, careful Cat character infused with Gemini's mercurial pizzazz gives me pause to ponder how in the world such a person might achieve self-knowledge and control. I mean, look at the problem. Geminis are all sizzle and snap. Cats, on the other hand, tend to gentility, caution, comfort. To me it seems the busy Gemini rushing about tilting at a huge variety of windmills must, when born in Cat years, from time to time feel himself suddenly leapt upon—surprise!—by his feline-nature mate whose padded feet dart out sharp claws to remind the Gemini, "Take it easy. Go slow. Back off. Sit still. Don't grab. Hang back. Beware." Mild schizophrenia.

Superficially this person will give the impression of flitting gaily from flower to flower, of a certain lack of seriousness and of an odd off-center disorganization. But the surface portrait is all wrong. Underneath, the Gemini/Cat is steady, watches every move of those around him, and has a more perfectly ordered inner life than Einstein at the height of his intellectual powers. Agility is the weapon, flexibility is the ammunition, brains the soldier. Gemini/Cat is his own personal army of sinew and muscle camouflaged under cuddly purrs and fur.

The Gemini/Cat's is an unflinching territorial imperialism: He will invite you to his home, open up his guest room, and even offer you lots to drink. But the Gemini/Cat will never give you the key to his private cupboard where he keeps the microfilm. You will never get beyond the door that leads to the study where a Gemini/Cat operates his personal business. The fortress is beautifully kept, every stone in place and the locks all polished to a blinding sheen. Don't try to get in. Take what hospitality the cheerful Gemini/Cat is willing to give. But unless you relish wearing long sleeves to cover the gouges on your arms for the rest of your life, I suggest you stay out of his filing cabinets.

In this person, the Gemini indecisiveness is just about canceled out by the Cat's careful consideration. Once a Gemini/Cat has given due thought to a project, he no longer hesitates or dawdles as to its execution. When they want something, these folks are efficient and know how to zero in on the jugular.

Where performance is concerned, Gemini/Cats are right up there with the stars. Geminis are attracted to all aspects of theater. But for the most part Geminis like to act! They are born performers whose greatest kick in life comes from interpreting roles and inducing thrills or applause from their audiences. The Gemini/Cat is no exception. He takes great pains to please his public, amuse the gallery and remain in character while on stage. Watch a Gemini/Cat give a dinner or cocktail party. From the moment they arrive the guests are all smiles, nodding and listening attentively to the Gemini/Cat's gripping tales and adventures.

This Gemini is nervous as a cat. Complexity blesses both Cats and Geminis from birth. These are not simple people whose pleasures roll in as uncomplicatedly as the waves on a beach. Oh no. The Gemini/Cat has a Byzantine set of senses. The choices he makes, from foods to clothing to habitat to friends to jobs, are never the obvious ones. Gemini/Cats stalk their options, circle them and test their reactions, walk away and reflect, come back and test again. Then they may deign to make a firm choice. And that vigilant selection may very well forecast the home, or style of mate, of the Gemini/Cat's choosing.

In Gemini/Cats you may notice a certain false sense of assurance. These people are given to imagining themselves a cut above the rest of us. Gemini/Cats tend to snobbishness and may be accused of name-dropping, too. This person is conservative. Sometimes, his reactions may strike us as puritanical or Spartan. But one must remember that Cats, no matter when they are born, are not naturally quarrelsome. They avoid conflict. The Gemini is a good talker, but when he's born a Cat that talent can only be used for communication—never for battle. The most important goals in this person's life are comfort and freedom from confrontation. The Gemini/Cat will do anything to insure those ends.

Love

For Gemini/Cats love is never just a game. These serious-minded yet garrulous people hate anxiety. A broken heart or home can so upset a Gemini/Cat's fragile nervous structure that he may never rise from his coiled-up shadow in front of the blazing hearth. Single Gemini/Cats are always looking for the partner who will be willing to dare where he cannot, to lash out when he won't, and to confront where he is incapable.

In exchange for the services of a loving, protecting partner, Gemini/Cat offers charm, comforts, coziness, reason and culture. Gemini/Cat is a traditional soul. He will prefer tall windows with curtains to naked picture-sized panes. He's private and warmhearted. But the Gemini side is not exactly compassionate. His understanding of others is limited to polite nods and even an occasional "tsk." But he's not the person to run to when you're in danger or ready to leap out a window. This person does not make a good mate for the troubled and tortured soul. He feels that he is complicated enough himself and will shy away from hitching up with someone who might possibly turn up the heat under an already sizzling network of frayed nerve endings.

If you love a Gemini/Cat, then you must accept solving you problems and even undertaking to sort out some of his. You must be ready to block outside influences and bar the door to trouble. The Gemini/Cat can definitely take care of himself. But his equilibrium can be abetted by coupling with another, less jumpy and more optimistic person than he.

Compatibilities

Aries and Libra/Sheep, Dog or Pig subjects will enhance your existence with their ready sensitivities attuned to yours. You'll also have crushes on Leo/Dogs and Pigs and Aquarius/Sheep and Pigs. No Virgo/Rats or Roosters for you. Nor do I suggest Sagittarius/Tigers or Pisces/Dragons or Roosters. Too cocky and pushy for you.

Home and Family

Don't expect a Gemini/Cat to pop out seven kids in seven years and enjoy hanging out in the laundry room for the rest of his life. This person is anything but hardy. Of course he can marry and make a good home and even have one or two children. But the need for repose and calm is great here. The turbulent household is not prescribed for the Gemini/Cat's family life.

Rather, a large dose of refinement, plenty of genteel celebrations for observing birthdays and holidays, and well-behaved children are sure to appeal to the Gemini/Cat person. For him a family is a place to find calm and to escape from the hard-edged world outside. The Gemini/Cat hardly wants a daughter or son who brings in five teenage friends every afternoon to practice rock music in the living room. Not on your nine lives! If you meet a Gemini/Cat parent who informs you, "My daughter Nellie is studying medicine in Boston," you can be sure you are talking to a happy Gemini/Cat.

Gemini/Cat kids are likable, reasonable and peace-loving. They require understanding from parents, and must be encouraged to develop their minds. They can be talked into sports so long as the game has some tradition behind it. You can send a Gemini/Cat to tennis camp, but don't expect him to become a bleached-haired Windsurfer who wears an earring in his nose. The Gemini/Cat could well adore being allowed to stay with grandparents, cajoled and spoiled and comforted.

Profession

This is not your average run-of-the-mill hard-nosed businessman. Gemini/Cats know how to engineer schemes and attend to the inner workings of plans. They even manage very well executing the plotting of others and usually get positive results from same. But what Gemini/Cats don't particularly know how to do is invent devious plots for themselves. In this way they are truly handicapped in commerce. As we all know, negotiation requires a certain degree of ruse and guile. It's not that the Gemini/Cat doesn't possess large quantities of both. It's more that he'd rather not have to use his talent for deviousness. Negotiation can lead to conflict and we know how Gemini/Cats feel about conflict.

So not being a businessman or merchant type, the Gemini/Cat will do well to choose careers requiring contemplative behavior, performing, persuasion and execution. The Gemini/Cat should choose to do business without the business. He can sell things, for example, or draw up documents, or stage-manage a theater or become a movie director. Gemini/Cat make excellent lawyers or real estate agents, researchers and scientists. As long as they don't choose a branch of any of the above professions that requires head-on collision with coworkers, the Gemini/Cat will be safe and secure. In fact, the marriage of Cat and Gemini gives us a sign gifted in security, talented in performance and adept at all variety of refinement

Famous Gemini/Cat/Rabbits:
Abbey Lee, Abby Elliott, Alessandra Torresani, Allen Iverson, Andrew McFarlane, Angelina Jolie, Bella Heathcote, Bob Hope, Bray Wyatt, David Koepp, Elizabeth Reaser, Helen Hunt, Hugh Dancy, Jason Isaacs, Jeanne Tripplehorn, Joe Piscopo, Johnny Depp, Kate Magowan, Kendrick Lamar, Lauryn Hill, Lily-Rose Depp, Margaret Drabble, Marguerite Yourcenar, Mel B, Meredith Hagner, Michelle Keegan, Mike Myers, Nicki Aycox, Queen Victoria, Rebecca Breeds, Richard Thomas, Russell Brand, Sally Ride, Stellan Skarsgård, Stephen Tobolowsky, Theo Rossi, Tim DeKay.

GEMINI
QUALITIES
QUICK-WITTEDNESS, PERSPICACITY,
FLEXIBILITY, VERSATILITY,
PERFORMANCE, DEXTERITY
QUIRKS
IMPATIENCE, GLIBNESS,
INCONSTANCY, SELF-DECEPTION,
SUPERFICIALITY, INDECISIVENESS
Motto: *"I think"*
Elements: *Air, Mercury, Mutable*

--

DRAGON
QUALITIES
STRENGTH, SUCCESS, GOOD HEALTH,
ENTHUSIASM, PLUCK, SENTIMENTALITY
QUIRKS
RIGIDITY, MISTRUST, DISSATISFACTION,
INFATUATION, BRAGGADOCIO, VOLUBILITY
Motto: *"I Preside"*
Elements: *Positive Wood, Yang*

The active, aerated Gemini mind couples brilliantly with our friend the dashing Dragon. Here you meet up with unforgettable characters in the strictest sense of the world "character." Gemini/Dragons are exciting and bewitching. They have élan to burn and charm galore. Gemini/Dragons personify panache. But don't count on them to perform any mental gymnastic that requires more than ten minutes' concentration.

Gemini/Dragons are sprinters. The hot fire of novelty burns brightly and excites this subject to create great dreams and formulate giant plans. But the Gemini/Dragon is easily bored. He wants the living room to be painted a beautiful creamy white by the time the guests arrive this weekend. But he cannot stop practicing his golf swing long enough to go to the hardware store to buy the paint.

So, what Gemini/Dragon people are famous for is their aptness at hiring people to do their work for them. Gemini/Dragons are "idea men." And indeed they can fish new notions out of their bag of tricks as fast as we can say "paintbrush." They can rally groups and dispense all their ingenious schemes and methods of getting things done—but Gemini/Dragons will not fill out so much as one form or make a single telephone call on their own. They don't consider dirty work part of their job.

Of course these people have so much personal magnetism and charm—and push!—that they scarcely need much else. Their bravura really does squeak them through. Their self-belief is uncanny. They are rocks of strength and wit. Yet, the loss of a loved one, a business failure or a romantic breakup can cause them to be horribly shaken. And when that happens, watch out! A hurt Gemini/Dragon flails and emotes more savagely and vociferously than a herd of wounded moose. Weep? I never saw anybody weep so much in my life. Rail against fate? It's the Gemini/Dragon's specialty: "Nobody loves me. I've been wronged. Everybody hates me" ought to be the Gemini/Dragon theme song.

Gemini/Dragons intimidate others. As Geminis, they of course enjoy performing. Early on, they learn that it's possible to impress others by playing "grump" or "hard-hearted" or even "gangster" roles. The Gemini/Dragons I know behave like scary monsters upon first encounter. They present themselves in a condescending fashion that really makes people stand back and wonder what they might be about to say or do.

Fact is, Gemini/Dragons are only paper dragons. You can push one over with one puff of reason or snipe. But you have to dare to puff. And Gemini/Dragon plays his Dragon part so convincingly that you probably won't even believe me when I tell you that you can make him fall pit apart if you find the path to his gooey roasted marshmallow heart. Try tears or complaining. If that doesn't work, lie down and pretend that you are so ill you might pass away in the night. Gemini/Dragons melt at sight of weakness in those they love. It makes them fear they might have to do the loved one's work for him or her, or lose their audience.

In social situations, the Gemini/Dragon is often impossible. I remember seeing a favorite Gemini/Dragon of mine slam away from a party because nobody was paying attention to his jokes. And worse, if a Gemini/Dragon feels threatened in any way, if a person he meets appears more exciting than he, he may say or do the most outrageous crazy things—like turn the coffee table upside down with the coffee still on it—just for attention. Gemini/Dragons are naughty. And that's the way they like it.

Despite the aura of pizzazz and pride that radiates from Gemini/Dragons, their tendency to scold and most of all to unfavorably compare their successes to yours, the Gemini/Dragon is anything but a real meanie. Geminis born Dragon are truly loving, warm-hearted souls who hug their children a lot. But they have a way, a manner, a carriage that puts others off. It's only a front, a façade—but what a cover!

In small doses, Gemini/Dragons make super friends. They are usually amusing (when they are not horrid) and always game for a party or an evening out. In my experience with Gemini/Dragons, they will only cut up or carry on like madmen if you stop paying full attention to them for half a second. Should such a situation arise, I suggest you simply turn on your heel and walk away, pretending you never saw the Gemini/Dragon person before and wouldn't know him if you tripped over him. Solitude is the Gemini/Dragon's number one enemy.

Love

Although most Gemini/Dragons may appear trivial and flighty, they are most decidedly not either frivolous or trifling about love. For these people there is no such thing as lukewarm sentiment. Gemini/Dragons adore their partners down to the last toenail paring. They will do anything to prove their loyalty to a loved one. In return, they demand a brand of exclusivity that is not only out of style but is nigh unto impossible. Gemini/Dragon dialogue goes like this: "Don't read that book! You may fall in love with the main character. I don't want you going to that movie. It might give you funny ideas about traveling. I don't want you to travel. Stay here. Stay with me and love me and listen to me and hold my head in your lap and comfort me."

If you love a Gemini/Dragon (and as a past lover of Gemini/ Dragons I attest to the pure thrill of same), be there for him or her. Wait for him to come home, or better still invite lots of people in so your Gemini/Dragon can perform, crowd-please and entertain. As mate or companion of one of these people, it is your job to help him exhibit his talents. You will best serve his purposes by showing him off, giving him the guarantee of your undying passion and keeping your sense of humor for the rough spots.

And rough spots there will be. Gemini/Dragons are not classically faithful. They are passionate, fervent, avid and vocal lovers. They usually have a life partner to whom they cling with unreal ardor. But, Gemini/Dragons are flirts. They cannot help themselves. They go around at parties kissing and hugging and enticing the guests. Young or old, beautiful or plain, exciting or dull, everybody has to be tested, teased, stroked and talked to by Gemini/Dragon. If this sort of public promiscuity doesn't always terminate in successive affairs, it looks as if it will—which may be worse for the lover who cares about appearances. But then if you cared about appearances, you wouldn't be with a wicked old Gemini/Dragon the first place, would you now?

Compatibilities

The Aries/Rat, Monkey and Pig are all capable of improving your dazzling self-image and maintaining your lifelong interest. Leo/Rats, Tigers and Monkeys will also beckon you, but watch out! They are short on naiveté and you may have trouble fooling them. A nice Libra or Aquarius/Rat would suit you, and a Libra/Monkey would be perfect. Brush off all advances by Virgo/Oxen. They are tar too stodgy for your flashy tastes. You won't want to take up with Scorpio, Sagittarius or Pisces/Dogs or Oxen.

Home and Family

In the Gemini/Dragon character there is lots of room for children, parents and cousins and aunts and uncles and siblings. This is a big-hearted person whose generosity is as broad-based as his huge sphere of influence at parties. No family member (who doesn't try to upstage the Gemini/Dragon) will go unnoticed or uncared for so long as the Gemini/Dragon is around. This person is a protector of the weak, a Popeye character who rescues helpless females from the arms of bounders and cads. So long as any person in the ken of a Gemini/Dragon is in need, he can count on the Gemini/Dragon to find ways to sort him out.

Despite his kindness, the Gemini/Dragon will be a demanding parent. The offspring of a Gemini/Dragon will tell you that their mom or dad really made them toe the line. Gemini/Dragons don't accept any back talk or sulking from their kids. But they don't necessarily want their kids to achieve a high position in life. The Gemini/Dragon is afraid of having his show stolen, remember? Well, a child who becomes a bigger star than his parent is a threat to the Gemini/Dragon.

Gemini/Dragon children are exhaustingly adorable. They chatter interminably and test your patience with their endless displays of bravado. They love celebrations and are willing to perform anything from magic tricks to skits to baton exhibitions for the guests. They require attention and affection from parents—especially if they have been hurt or rejected outside the home. Failure to please on any level can wound a Gemini/Dragon child deeply. He must be reasoned with and made to understand the necessity of hard work and application to study. He cannot get by on his charms forever.

Profession

The wherewithal for real solid success is present in the Gemini/Dragon character. He is capable and has true vital energy to spend on all manner of projects and jobs. Gemini/Dragons are attractive, too, and people enjoy being around them—for a few minutes at a time. On first glance a Gemini/Dragon seems the incarnation of success.

There is, however, a rub. Gemini/Dragons are sprinters. Their initial performances are always perfect. Their three-month trial period always goes off like a charm. Their first deal is always a huge boon to the company's accounts. Everybody in the office adores the new Gemini/Dragon on the fifth floor. But wait. Give the Gemini/ Dragon on five a chance to settle in. Watch how he or she behaves at the first office Christmas party. Notice how cheeky the Gemini/ Dragon has become with his superiors. Watch the boss's facial expression as the Gemini/Dragon expounds an inside secret to non classified folk. Over the long run Gemini/Dragons just don't hold to their courses. They fall out of character after about a year or so on any given task. They veer and swerve and sometimes get themselves fired for misbehaving.

For this reason, Gemini/Dragons are best employed by themselves in businesses requiring lots of contact with the public. Sales or public relations, owning restaurants or bars or even performing in general sorts of country-doctor medical careers will appeal to the versatile Gemini/Dragon. This character can be in a thousand places at once and keep track of everything in all of them. Staying put and delving deeply into any one subject or task is beyond the Gemini/Dragon's pale.

Famous Gemini/Dragons:

Amber Marshall, Annie Cordy, Ben Daniels, Carol Kane, Cillian Murphy, Claire Holt, Cole Porter, Colin Farrell, Courteney Cox, David Morrissey, Dayo Okeniyi, Dick Vitale, Erinn Hayes, Ernesto "Che" Guevara, Fabienne Thibeault, Francis Crick, Isabella Rossellini, James Brown, Jean-Marie Le Pen, John Goodman, Jonathan Nolan, Kara Killmer, Kathleen Turner, Laurie Hernandez, Lenny Kravitz, Liam Neeson, Lindsay Davenport, Mae Whitman, Mariette Hartley, Mark Sheppard, Mary Cassat, Michael Cera, Nancy Sinatra, Nathan Parsons., Omri Katz, Orhan Pamuk, Parker Stevenson, Ralph Bellamy, Ray Stevenson, Rick Riordan, Scott Adkins, Sybil Danning, Tom Jones, Virginia Hey, Willow Shields.

GEMINI
QUALITIES
QUICK-WITTEDNESS, PERSPICACITY,
FLEXIBILITY, VERSATILITY,
PERFORMANCE, DEXTERITY
QUIRKS
IMPATIENCE, GLIBNESS,
INCONSTANCY, SELF-DECEPTION,
SUPERFICIALITY, INDECISIVENESS
Motto: *"I think"*
Elements: *Air, Mercury, Mutable*

--

SNAKE
QUALITIES
INTUITION, ATTRACTIVENESS, DISCRETION,
SAGACITY, CLAIRVOYANCE, COMPASSION
QUIRKS
DISSIMULATION, EXTRAVAGANCE,
LAZINESS, CUPIDITY, PRESUMPTION,
EXCLUSIVENESS
Motto: *"I sense"*
Elements: *Negative, Fire, Yin*

A paradoxical character is the Gemini/Snake. If he can get a good grip on the specialness that is his natural endowment from birth, this person is qualified for true greatness. The Gemini/Snake is a thinker. Imagine the lucky combination of reflection and intuition! The marriage of the two signs is fortuitous indeed.

But this heady mixture of influences is a veritable minefield of pitfalls as well. People born in Gemini/Snake are sitting ducks for both Byzantine self-delusion and rank laziness. Every single day of their lives these people must bite the bullet and grit their pretty teeth just to get out of bed in the morning. Invertebrate inertia, fueled by an oddly sunny despair, pushes Gemini/Snakes earthward and very often just won't let up.

Maybe this yellow jaundice of the spirit comes from too much intuitive knowledge of the perils and disappointments each Gemini Snake sees ahead. It is as if this person sensed how deeply he affects the world when he really tries and for that reason simply desists before he begins. It's inevitable that this combination of signs give us a performing Snake, the actor or actress with the overdeveloped brain, the show business personality with the weighty intellectual baggage, the irresistibly cheery political figure with heartbreak written across his smile. The Gemini/Snake's hereditary dice are loaded.

So the Gemini/Snake suffers from excessive foresight. Before anything happens to him, he knows it's about to occur. While it's happening, he's relatively excited about it. But when it's over, he's convinced that maybe it wasn't worth the trouble and it might have been more fun to have a vacation instead.

Gemini/Snakes have to discipline themselves to engage in far-reaching and complex pursuits. They must always bite off more than it seems hey can chew? The Gemini/Snake needs not only challenge, but he needs to develop an inner bulldozer to push him into things—encourage him to slither along and accept the cheers and notoriety that are his natural rewards—as well as his neurosis.

Like every self-respecting Snake, this person loves to be rich. Money and the gathering of wealth can become a driving force in the Gemini/Snake's life. Trouble is, he is too smart to be too rich. Though he may enjoy opulence and be most comfortable in silken sheets, the Gemini/Snake finds the touch of the shekel distasteful and will seek ways to avoid it.

When I think of the Gemini/Snake, an image of a lovely furry caterpillar creeps into my mind's eye. The pace is the same, to be sure—as is the promise. When you see a caterpillar, you know there will one day be a butterfly, ephemeral perhaps but so glorious and so fantastic that its beauty leaves an indelible mark on your life. Temporary permanence is the personification of the paradoxical Gemini/Snake .

This person will surely prove to be fragile of health and testy to live with. There's so much going on inside this creature that frequently he cannot be bothered seeing to day-to-day material necessities. He wants to use his mind to soar off in twenty mental directions at once, to invent some new philosophy, to change the world, to inspire his fellow man. Why do you persist in asking him to scrub the floor when you know full well that he cannot, does not, will not ever care one way or the other if that stupid floor gets itself scrubbed or not? The Gemini/Snake is above it all. Really.

The bright witty company of Gemini/Snakes gives us all great pleasure. These subjects are never boring. Their agile minds follow every train of thought and dart from flower to flower doing justice to each and every one. You can talk with this fellow for hours, jabber, chat and hash and rehash till you come up with a whole new way of looking at something.

Gemini/Snakes are inspiring and thoughtful of others. They are persuasive, seductive and remarkable in every way. If this person can begin a task, conquer his latent sloth and dive into a real personal project he will always be a natural winner. Nose to grindstone and one eye in the cleanest, most truthful mirror available—then onward and forever upward he will fly.

Love

First of all, everybody falls in love with Gemini/Snakes. They are usually beautiful to look at. They smell nice and have pretty, fragile, tern natures. They are intelligent and funny and compassionate. Yes. Everybody loves a Gemini/Snake.

For the Gemini/Snake himself, this general acclaim and adulation causes no tiny amount of emotional disturbance. Just as those around him are one by one tumbling at his feet, he is likewise attracted too. Gemini/Snakes tend to promiscuity—and it isn't even their own fault. Who could resist all those fawning fans? Not I.

As a life partner the Gemini/Snake requires a patient understanding soul mate. This person cannot interact with clumsy or incompetent companions. Solemnity and gloom are also out of the question. Gemini/Snakes have enough trouble getting themselves out of their pajamas and into the car without having to assist someone else in doing likewise. Gemini/Snakes can inspire others. But they will not force-feed them.

The prizes that fall as though by magic into the hands of Gemini/Snakes will be shared and showered on their mates as well. The Gemini/Snake needs love from one reliable and respectable person on whom he can count and whom he trusts forevermore. If you can provide this sort of unflinching adoration and will yourself promise perfect exclusivity, Gemini/Snake can make you very, very happy. But if you feel you can be shaken by infidelity, or that you might envy or compete with this character, stay away. You'll only be hurt. The Gemini/Snake rules.

Compatibilities

You will automatically be drawn to Aries and Aquarius, both Roosters and Oxen. Leo/Dragons and Oxen please you, too, and so do Libra/Dogs and their Ox brothers and sisters. You are not really suited to Virgos, especially Tigers and Pigs. Nor will you find happiness with Sagittarius/Tigers or Pigs or Pisces/Tigers or their Monkey counterparts. Take my advice. Steer clear of Scorpios, especially the Tigerish kind.

Home and Family

This temperamental soul is hardly your average family man. As a sibling or cousin or aunt, this person will inspire much respect. But as a parent the Gemini/Snake has some trouble getting down to his kids' level, crawling around on all fours making googly sounds and playing hide-and-seek. I would say that if this person decides to have children, he should also decide to hire a nanny. He's not the cuddly, lovable, huggable bear type at all.

Children born in Gemini/Snake will seem wise beyond their years. They may cause some parents to be disconcerted by their early grasp of abstract concepts. Don't worry. It's normal. This child will always be smart—even brilliant—in school. But he will most likely also favor lying abed till all hours on weekend mornings, then by three in the afternoon hanging about the house like a slug reading mature books and being charming. It's in his nature. You cannot really do much for this self-possessed child's future plan except to instill in him a sense of the work ethic and its utter necessity to successful living.

He cannot be treated aggressively but he can be gently rolled uphill by loving and intelligent parents. He probably won't get on too well with siblings. Don't worry about it. It's his nature to be exclusive about affections. He doesn't need to share his toys in order to learn how to become President of the United States or head of IBM.

Profession

These people always arrive at some form of success in life. They are naturally superior thinkers and although not hard-hitting world beaters of the classical rough-and-ready type, Gemini/Snakes usually manage to find some degree of equilibrium in their work life.

They make excellent teachers and philosophers, doctors and lawyers, writers and even politicians. Gemini/Snakes are magnetic and can learn anything well. They will require an extensive education and their hobbies will probably all have to do with reading and assimilating knowledge. They even do crossword puzzles with a special intellectual knitting of brows.

Artist or businessman, rich and famous or not, the Gemini/Snake is always caught between wanting to fit in and longing to opt out. Of course he is ambitious and wants to get somewhere in life. But wouldn't it be easier to just stay home and dream about how he will get there, read tomes on the subject dearest to his heart and occupy the chaise longue?

Famous Gemini/Snakes:
AJ Styles, Alfred Molina., Anne Frank, Beverly Sills, Bob Dylan, Brooke Shields, Chick Corea, Christopher Mintz-Plasse, Danielle Harris, Danny Elfman, Elizabeth Hurley, Emilio Sanchez, Eric Christian Olsen, Frank Grillo, Imogen Poots, Jean Paul Sartre, John C. Reilly, John Fitzgerald Kennedy, Johny Paybeck, Kanye West, Kim Dickens, Lana Wachowski, Liza Weil, Lucy Hale, Mallory Jansen, Mary Albert, Melissa McBride, Nell Campbell, Paul Winfield, Riley Keough, Sadie Frost, Sarah Wayne Callies, Stacy Keach, Sullivan Stapleton, Tanya Burr, Tim Allen, Xi Jinping, Zachary Quinto.

GEMINI
QUALITIES
QUICK-WITTEDNESS, PERSPICACITY,
FLEXIBILITY, VERSATILITY,
PERFORMANCE, DEXTERITY
QUIRKS
IMPATIENCE, GLIBNESS,
INCONSTANCY, SELF-DECEPTION,
SUPERFICIALITY, INDECISIVENESS
Motto: *"I think"*
Elements: *Air, Mercury, Mutable*

--

HORSE
QUALITIES
PERSUASIVENESS, UNSCRUPULOUSNESS,
POPULARITY, STYLE, DEXTERITY,
ACCOMPLISHMENT
QUIRKS
SELFISHNESS, AUTONOMY, REBELLION,
HASTE, ANXIETY, PRAGMATISM
Motto: *"I demand"*
Elements: *Positive Fire, Yang*

The Horse's strut measured against the Gemini mutability gives us a multitalented person whose own worst enemy is himself. There's a nagging little gremlin wringing his hands inside the head of this character who says, "I don't have to take this garbage! I don't have to put up with this nonsense! I want my freedom. I want my soul back."

Well, of course we all know that our soul is never our own. But the Gemini/Horse works very hard to disprove that. He wants to be different, unusual, better than everybody else, cleverer, sexier, better dressed, and most of all, coolest. Yes, the Gemini/Horse wants desperately to be considered cool, one of the gang, a terrific fellow.

Not that Gemini/Horses cannot stick to their work. They can. Normally they choose a career that interests them and go ahead with that forever. They are often talented in music or graphic arts and are always in some very important way involved in theatrical endeavors. Gemini/Horses are circus horses. Instead of walking, they prance.

The Gemini/Horse, like most Horses, usually leaves home at an early age, takes up a line of work that appeals to him, and then proceeds to pass rough stage after stage of shifts and changes within that particular job slot. If he's a musician, he doesn't just join a band and play for weddings and bar mitzvahs for the rest of his life. No. The Gemini/Horse may join a band and play with it while the sun is shining on that band's head. Then when it looks like the going may get rough because somebody broke a rule or an instrument, the Gemini/Horse doesn't stick around. He moves off. And may the devil take the hindmost.

Horses born in Gemini enjoy amusing jokes and will go to great lengths to do so. They tell jokes or get up to crazy antics, pull pranks (do magic tricks just to get you to pay attention and applaud. It is my humble opinion that the average Gemini/Horse who is not in some way controlled by an authority figure can really get very out of hand in the performance department. They are so easily turned into spoiled brats through over-admiring parents, friends and fans that it's wise not to chortle too loudly or encourage them unless they really are doing their best.

This person will be very quick-witted. You'll have to get up bright and early in the morning to beat him to the punch. Repartee is second nature to him. Gemini/Horses are hale fellows with plenty of down-to-earth vitality, always ready to go clamming or sailing or windsurfing or to take a hike. These two qualities, quickness and hardiness, make Gemini/Horses excellent companions.

The Horse's selfishness has to be accommodated somewhere in this portrait. I'm sorry to divulge it, but this person is a monster of self-involvement. As gregarious and outgoing as he may seem, the Gemini/Horse really never sees things from any other point of view than his own. Sympathy is not his strong suit. Yet, oddly, this person can be a professional nurturer. Gemini/Horses can enjoy taking care of people as hobby. They even seem to need to protect and watch over others. But they do it out of a conscientious sense of charity and not out of a feeling of pity or compassion.

Gemini/Horses are fearless and undertake long-term jobs and projects that would make you or me grow pale. In this way their capacity for selfish pursuit of goals helps out. They can go ahead with something that others have never dared to try without flinching because they are gifted with enormous self-belief.

Love

The word "infatuate" comes immediately to mind. People say this Horse is not constant in love. People claim he requires change for his emotions to experience the thrills he covets. Yet, they don't take the trouble to find out that deep down this apparently shallow person is searching for some ideal in which he wants desperately to believe. He wishes that others were nicer, more giving, understanding, generous and kind. Gemini/Horse Subjects cannot tolerate cynicism in others. They're looking for the "right" man or woman to come along who will have no faults and who will give years of devoted service.

To properly love a Gemini/Horse, you must appreciate his jack-of-all-trades-master-of-none side. You must know how to appear kindly and charitable even when it seems impossible. You must be devoted to Gemini/Horse and to his causes. And you have to like theatrics. Scenes. Tantrums. Rages. This Horse has a very short fuse, but his little contretemps usually don't last long. The remedy is apathy. Ignore him for three seconds. Leave him alone and he'll calm down.

Compatibilities

Leo and Aquarian Dogs and Tigers appeal to your immodest self-image. but you can also get along with Aries/Sheep and/or Tigers and live with a creative Libra/Sheep subject too. Don't mingle with Virgo or Scorpio/Oxen or even conceive of hitching up with a fiery Sagittarian Ox. You want top billing and they hate competition. Virgo, Pisces and Sagittarius/ Rats are out as well, as is the opulence-loving Pisces/Pig.

Home and Family

The Horse's home is extremely important to him or her if only as a place to run away from. Gemini/Horses are the slam-out-of-the-house-in-a-fury types. For this reason, the home of a Gemini/Horse must be rock strong. He must be able to come back repeatedly to a comfortable, neat, orderly and well-run place where he can lay his weary head and moan about how *triste* the world out there really is.

He or she will favor brightly-colored furniture but despite the chromatic exaggerations, the style of Gemini/Horse's abode will probably stick close to the traditional. In other words, this person will not live in a skyscraper but rather in a townhouse, which he may then decorate in sunshine shades of cadmium yellows and lime green.

This person is almost overly painstaking as a parent. The investment of self in others strikes this essentially ego-oriented subject as earthshakingly nerve-wracking. A Gemini/Horse mother or father will want to "do right" by his kids, for his kids and not for the gallery. If any love bond is capable of extruding selflessness from the selfish, it is surely the parent/child relationship. You will marvel at the devotion of Gemini/Horses to their own issue. Not so gushing are they with regard to their own parents and siblings. It's not the same. Gemini/Horse likes to think it really is he or she who created his or her child. Nonsense.

Gemini/Horse children will tend to be showoffy. They can be accused of clowning around in school and are sometimes said to be rabble rousers on the playground. It is true that this child will need early training and discipline, as persevering at tasks he doesn't absolutely love doing is difficult for the Gemini/Horse child. He'd so much rather be out playing.

Profession

Gemini/Horses are scatty people. When not deeply involved in one or another flaming project or personal mission, they flitter and languish. Their basis is self. But their urge is other. This conflict produces a personality that is capable of immense push over a brief period. Motivated by his sense of other, the Gemini/Horse will struggle uphill in champion style. But lo, his mind wanders to his own problems, and the suddenly distracted Gemini/Horse sits down and turns into a mule.

So his trump card in a work situation will be to have the luxury of attacking new projects all the time. It's best for Gemini/Horses to work for people whom they respect greatly and who are known to keep them in line. They make excellent bosses but need a sidekick or helper to pick up the daily thread of activity.

Theater, circus, dance, cinema, all entertainment-related jobs suit this subject. He or she can be anything from a choreographer to a stagehand; as long as the theater is in there somewhere, the Gemini/Horse will thrive.

Famous Gemini/Horses:
Aaron Taylor-Johnson, Allison Schmitt, Ashley Laurence, Bachendri Pal, Chris Colfer, Clint Eastwood, Dennis Haysbert, Dominic Cooper, Edward Woodward, Eric Cantona, Gena Rowlands, Ginnifer Goodwin, Harvey Feirstein, Harvey Milk, Helena

Bonham-Carter, Iggy Azalea, Igor Stravinsky, Ilan Ramon, Jason Patric, Jim Belushi, Josephine Baker, Josh McDermitt, Julianna Margulies, Kathleen Turner, Laura Silverman, Lauren Socha, Lisa Edelstein, Margaret Bourke-White, Paul McCartney, Robert Pastorelli, Robin Lord Taylor, Samuel West, Sophie Lowe, Tom McCarthy, Traylor Howard, Tristin Mays, Will Patton, Zoe Saldana.

GEMINI
QUALITIES
QUICK-WITTEDNESS, PERSPICACITY,
FLEXIBILITY, VERSATILITY,
PERFORMANCE, DEXTERITY
QUIRKS
IMPATIENCE, GLIBNESS,
INCONSTANCY, SELF-DECEPTION,
SUPERFICIALITY, INDECISIVENESS
Motto: *"I think"*
Elements: *Air, Mercury, Mutable*

--

SHEEP
QUALITIES
INVENTION, LACK OF FORESIGHT,
PERSEVERANCE, WHIMSY, GOOD MANNERS,
IMPRACTICALITY
QUIRKS
PARASITISM, SENSITIVITY,
TARDINESS, PESSIMISM, TASTE, WORRY
Motto: *"I depend"*
Elements: *Negative, Fire, Yin*

The Gemini/Sheep is either a firefly who flits about in others' lives out of sheer caprice or a tired pessimist who denigrates and disagrees with the world at large. Or perhaps he's the eternally disillusioned but charming critic whose longing for perfection (in others, of course) leads him to drop acerbic comments as though they were rose petals. The Gemini/Sheep is a bit of all of these things. And... he or she is mighty attractive too!

You won't find many Sheep running around loose. Sheep need

other people. All Sheep require both company and guiding forces. Gemini is the mercurial sign: quick, volatile, fickle. So put these together. Dependency and fickleness. Like being a smiling, chubby baby who's looking around for a change from his dull parents and leaps into the arms of almost anybody who passes his stroller in the street.

Gemini/Sheep are decidedly bright and usually extremely, bitingly, observantly funny. They have a capacity for laughing at themselves. Somehow, Gemini/Sheep are so disconnected from the concrete that they must be very tuned in to the instinctual. They can see a hunch coming at thirty miles.

The Sheep born in Gemini is gifted in things artistic. He will be good with his hands and truly know how to handle a wide variety of materials. Gemini/Sheep are able to be content and carry on with artisanal projects or craft hobbies (which they truly love) only when they feel safe. Tie a Gemini/Sheep on a crowded, trafficky boulevard sidewalk and you will be able to fetch him there three hours later to remove him directly to the mental institution. This person functions best in security.

Sheep/Geminis like to gossip. They are curious about everyone they meet. "Does he have a girlfriend? Is she really a dress designer? Did he have a car accident and kill his dog or was it his wife?" Sheep/Geminis want to know your story and that of everybody you know or hear of talk to them about. They don't often give out information on themselves unless asked, however. They are not exactly secretive. They are guarded. They know what they do with the information they glean about other's private lives, so for obvious reasons they are not quick to share their own.

One very nice thing about these people is their ability to use language. They are extremely, delicately and tersely eloquent. They "must have kissed the Blarney stone," as my Irish mother would say. Gemini/Sheep are good at foreign languages too. They imitate well, and as they have highly sensitive hearing, they pick up nuances easily.

"Devotion" is a word I like to think of as applicable to the Gemini/Sheep. As an adult this person may seem to you to be dragging a traveling circus of family, family's family, friends of family's family, and friends around with him all the time. These Sheep not only like to be around other people, they must have company.

They also like to watch people enjoy themselves. They are uncomfortable with sorrow. It's as though sadness were a personal insult to Gemini/Sheep. They don't want anything to do with it.

As Sheep go, the Gemini/Sheep is rather less pessimistic than others. He does have a kind of jaundiced view of other people and how they live their lives. He likes to put down other people of whom he doesn't approve or whom he finds silly or ridiculous. He doesn't really care what other people do. He is not judgmental. But he likes to poke around in their dirty laundry and guffaw if he finds something untoward.

Love

I seem to write only about unfaithfulness in love. I confess it is beginning to weigh on my spirit. But never mind. Sheep/Geminis are about as faithful as Jezebel and care about this flaw in their characters even less. The Gemini/Sheep is a person who wants to live one-on-one with another You will rarely, if ever, find a confirmed bachelor Gemini/Sheep. But somewhere, somehow, someone else invariably comes along. The plumber. The baker. That handsome young man with the pretty teeth. Or that lovely girl who works at the supermarket. Well, they can't help it. It's part of their charm.

If you love a Gemini/Sheep, remember to make it appear that you're holding things together. Act as if you are the strong one. The devotion you will receive in return will well outweigh the pain of petty jealousies elicited by the above-mentioned peccadilloes. Gemini/Sheep make great partners for people who want to go out into the world and stomp about getting successful. Gemini/Sheep will never stand in the way of an ambitious partner.

The only advice I would give here is to remember that to love a Gemini/Sheep is to be willing to stand watch over his tendency to indolence. As he or she cares a lot about what his loved one thinks of him and desires his mate's respect, your firm hand will never be ignored and will even be secretly appreciated. It's a job. But Gemini/Sheep give lots of fantasy and fun in return.

Compatibilities

I can see you playing house with a nice Aries/Cat or Libra/Horse or Pig. Aquarius/Cats and Pigs and Leo/Horses turn you on, too. You are happiest with steady but not rigid types, so climb a telephone pole if you see Virgo or Scorpio/Ox coming. Keep away from Virgo, Sagittarius and Pisces/Dogs and Tigers. They are too pessimistic and easily exasperated by your flights of fancy.

Home and Family

This is the location of Gemini/Sheep's heart. He or she may not necessarily spend all his time there, but the fact of a home is of primary importance to this subject's existence. He likes to come home, go home, be home, receive in his home, be sick at home, give birth at home and die at home. And he would rather go home than go fishing.

Gemini/Sheep likes the warmth and coziness of a family home where each person has his own room and everybody gets together to eat around the same table for a whole lifetime. Gemini/Sheep wants to be the center of others' lives. Parenting comes naturally to this subject. He or she will not only give love and sacrifice for their offspring but they will be attentive to their kids—in both negative and positive ways—until they die. They have uncanny patience for "A spoonful for Uncle Louie now. And a spoonful for Daddy," etc.

The Gemini/Sheep child will be first and foremost a love bug. He or she will nestle and snuggle and hop into lap after lap as long as the lap owner is cuddly and warm. This kid will also be a first-rate communicator and will probably be gifted in the lively arts. Of course he or she needs lots of parental loving control and supervision for everything from lessons to choice of companions. The Gemini/Sheep is easily influenced. He could fall in with the wrong crowd.

Profession

Again, as this subject is Gemini and also a talented and artistic Sheep, this person can aim at any career connected with entertainment. There are few fields involving meeting the public in which he cannot succeed.

The Gemini/Sheep may complain about his boss a lot away from work but he makes a terrific, interesting and devoted employee. His talent for dependency will steer him clear of most positions of authority. Gemini/Sheep not only doesn't make a good boss, he doesn't want to be boss. As a star performer this person will be quite content. He doesn't mind being prodded and is not terribly dependent on applause.

Basically this person is quite easy-going about work, and it always shows in the gracious way he goes about his chores.

Some suitable careers for Gemini/Sheep are: TV personality, painter, diplomat, actor or actress, critic.

Famous Gemini/Sheep:

Anna Torv, Arthur Conan Doyle, Brooke Shields, Brooke Smith, Carrie Preston, Carroll Baker, Chris Pratt, Cilla Black, Dana Ashbrook, Dana Carvey, Elizabeth Wettlaufer, Emily Ratajkowski, Frances O'Connor, Guy Lux, Hervé Alphand, James Ransone, Jesy Nelson, Jian Ghomeshi, John Maynard Keyes, John Wayne, Johnny Hallyday, Joyce Meyer, Julianna Rose Mauriello, Julie Hagerty.,

Kathryn Prescott, Laurie Metcalf, Maggie Q, Marla Gibbs, Martin Landau, Mia Sara, Monica Keena, Morena Baccarin, Nicole Kidman, Nikki Runeckles, Olympia Dukakis, Paul Giamatti, Pauline Kael, Poppy Drayton, Rachel Carson, Richard Schiff, Ron Livingston, Sandrine Bonnaire, Sarah Ramos, Willa Holland, William Forsythe.

GEMINI
QUALITIES
QUICK-WITTEDNESS, PERSPICACITY,
FLEXIBILITY, VERSATILITY,
PERFORMANCE, DEXTERITY
QUIRKS
IMPATIENCE, GLIBNESS,
INCONSTANCY, SELF-DECEPTION,
SUPERFICIALITY, INDECISIVENESS
Motto: *"I think"*
Elements: *Air, Mercury, Mutable*

--

MONKEY
QUALITIES
IMPROVISATION, CUNNING, STABILITY,
SELF-INVOLVEMENT, WIT, OPPORTUNISM
QUIRKS
DECEIT, RUSE, LOQUACITY,
LEADERS, SILLINESS, ZEAL
Motto: *"I plan"*
Elements: *Positive, metal, Yang*

M onkeys and Geminis resemble each other, I always used to say. When I consider the energy level of this New Astrology sign, it's as though someone took twelve Monkeys, piled them on top of a dozen sets of twins, tailed a couple of Rolls-Royce jet engines and then let 'er rip. These people never cease moving. In fact, I wonder if Gemini/Monkeys ever sleep. Gemini/Monkeys love to talk. They need to perform, and even, I afraid, to show off. For this reason, Gemini/Monkeys enjoy entertaining and watching others have a good time. They plan giant festivals and feasts complete with hand-opened oysters and lobsters flown in from the farthest reaches of the earth.

A Gemini/Monkey bash is a guaranteed jolly time for all, your all-time unforgettable pig-out of a lifetime, your best party memory ever— until of course next week, when Gemini/Monkey will be throwing a far more sedate party. This time he's only inviting seventy very select friends. "We will begin at six with a wine-tasting. I've brought in a sommelier from the *Tour d'Argent*. After that there'll the balloon rides. We have to do that before it gets dark. ..." The attractions are endless. Gemini/Monkey excess knows no frontiers. If you have a Gemini/Monkey for a friend you'll never be bored again.

With all of this apparent folderol comes the best aptitude of all— genius. Yes. Gemini/Monkeys are always brilliant. Not only do they have active, vivid minds, that can make quantum leaps in a single bound. Gemini/Monkeys have wildly creative spirits. They are always on to some new breakthrough idea that will revolutionize the horse-racing industry—and they may not even be vaguely connected to horses. But one day were watching a horse race and it popped into their heads that if such and such were so and so, then maybe the races wouldn't have to be thus and such. Gemini/ Monkeys are addicted to improvisational living. They hate to do the same thing twice in the same way, and therefore spend time imagining new solutions.

There's a bit of the snob in our friend the Gemini/Monkey too. As he enjoys everything bigger and better and grander and smarter, a touch of class, he feels, never hurt anybody. You can count on the Gemini/Monkey to have at least one fast car in his garage, an elegant brand of dog and an equally chic and very proper mate. The accoutrements are part of the show—and with Gemini/Monkeys the show is life itself.

Don't think Gemini/Monkeys are as light-headed as they are light-hearted. These are self-reliant, responsible independents who are not averse to buckling to a hard day at the office or a heavy single-handed spring cleaning. They know how to do such a variety of different tasks at once that watching them work is akin to viewing a master juggler in the center ring. Gemini/Monkey can delegate authority well. And he doesn't belie being bossy in order to get people to work for him.

This person is a born iconoclast. Rules, he thinks, are made to be broken, flouted, torn up and written anew. Smashing idols is to the Gemini/Monkey only the first step in true progress. If he can't prove that a fusty old rule is dull and simple-minded by mere logic and a bit of persuasion, then he will make short work of testing that brittle old law. Don't ever tell a Gemini/Monkey not to ride his bike in a hospital corridor or you will soon see him cruising down the hall in Ward III.

The rule-breaking this subject gets up to can cause him some trouble. He is not a crook or a criminal. But he could very well be called a troublemaker by higher-ups. Generally his genius saves him from destruction by those too serious to see beyond their own belly-button. They know he's impossible. But he's so necessary to their cause that won't let him go. Exile is one tactic used in trying to discipline the Gemini/Monkey. But no matter which remote boondock they banish him to, the Gemini/Monkey will come up giggling and raring to try his skill at some new implausible scheme.

Love

This is no ordinary lover. The Gemini/Monkey is a demanding and insistent gourmet of affection. He needs constant attention and will stop at nothing to have the spotlight permanently turned his way. It is this person's ingenious charm that eventually seduces those he courts with such craft. How would you respond if your beau placed a diamond ring in the bottom of your bubbling champagne glass? How would you like to be presented with a shiny red sports car just because you caught the Gemini/Monkey's eye at a dinner party? The bigger, the better. All's fair in love—and in war? Well, Gemini/Monkeys don't take well to amorous conflict. They like their romance clear-cut and without ghosts.

Loving a Gemini/Monkey is not particularly complicated, though. You simply have to be willing to spend your whole life standing blind-folded on the very tip of a very springy diving board with a strong wind blowing from behind. That's all. Just stand there and quake. Of course you also have to do all the dirty work because Genius is too busy blowing up balloons for the party to remember to wash the dishes. But never mind, what you get in return is full-time nonstop fun and games. If you like show biz, the Gemini/Monkey is definitely your kind of mate.

If you have a Gemini/Monkey in your life and feel a lot like shooting him or her from time to time, I can certainly understand. The Gemini born in a Monkey year is an exhausting challenge to the sedate people he often chooses to love. Yet, there is so much joy in the best moments spent with this dynamo of imagination that all I can advise is—great, unflagging patience. If a Gemini/Monkey loves you, hold on tight. You're in for the ride of the century.

Compatibilities

Why don't you take up with a Libra/Rat or Dragon? Your senses of humor match well. Aries/Dragons and Monkeys are good for you too, as are Leo/Rats and Aquarius/Dragons. You'll fail miserably if you try to woo a Virgo/Tiger or Snake, a Sagittarian Ox, Snake or Dog. Worse still would be the spotlight-grabbing Capricorn/Snake. You want all the attention, remember?

Home and Family

Gemini/Monkeys like to have all sorts of different homes. They dream of living in the mountains part of the year, in the tropics another, and then again in Rome or Milan or why not Morocco? Wherever they go, Gemini/Monkeys are quick to settle in, claim the loveliest hut for their own and set about inviting a zillion people in for a smorgasbord.

Although they are fond of luxury and class, Gemini/Monkeys cannot be accused of trying to impress with their wealth. To them, an environment should bespeak the understated elegance of a fine leather easy chair and expensive lived-in carpets six inches thick.

As a parent, the Gemini/Monkey is extremely serious. He may have many children and will love them and tend to them with equal kindness and understanding. He doesn't, however, like being misused, and reacts badly to any relative, child or otherwise, who tries to dupe or trick him. The Gemini/Monkey possesses enormous guile himself. But he tends not to apply it to cheating those he loves. He's a fabulous friend, faithful and out-on-a-limb involved with his old pals and cronies. He never forgets people with whom he's had fun.

The Gemini/Monkey child is a handful. Hyperactivity is not unusual in these kids. They must be directed and disciplined into applying talents and using up each day's energy that day. Otherwise, they may keep you up all night. Sports, music lessons, clubs and--most of all—theatrical experiences will both please and excite the Gemini/Monkey child. Keep the never-a-dull-moment Gemini/Monkey busy and I guarantee you your child will be happy. Pay attention to him when he has achieved. But don't give him too much free applause.

Profession

This person is gifted in very serious, intricate and difficult roles in life. He can be anything from a cancer research specialist to a high-minded theatrical director. But this person thrives on change, variation and diversification. Truly, the Gemini/Monkey is the most mutable of all the mutable signs. No matter what he does it must involve the opportunity to invent, to innovate, to create new methods and points of view. He is vibrant and full of mercurial mental motion. He must never be stuck in a dull office or forced to work in a bank or any confining place. The Gemini/Monkey cannot tolerate isolation. He likes space and requires company and attention from coworkers.

As a boss or director of operations, this person will manage very well. People are attracted to the antics of the Gemini/Monkey and if he is careful to surround himself with a loving audience, he will never have to use force or coercion to see that work is done. Even at his silliest, even when he's rolling around laughing at fate and the damned rules, the Gemini/Monkey still inspires admiration and respect in his "subjects."

Famous Gemini/Monkeys:
Alain Souchon, Ben Feldman, Ben Lurie, Bill Burr, Bjorn Borg, Brian Benben, D.J. Cotrona, Daryl Sabara, Disha Patani, DJ Scratch, Duchess of Windsor, Gregg Sulkin, Helen O'Connell, Ian Fleming, James Patrick Stuart, John Ortiz, Jon Glaser, Kate Upton, Keith David, Kim Walker, Kylie Minogue, Lauren Lee Smith, Lisa Hartman, Lisa Niemi, Lucien Laviscount, Manuel Blanco, Marquis de Sade, Mike Dopud, Nazanin Boniadi, Paul Gauguin, Peggy Lee, Pierre Daninos, Prince Alois of Liechtenstein, Robert Rodriguez, Sarah Parish, Scott Wolf, Sibel Kekilli, Tika Sumpter, Venus Williams, Yasmine Bleeth, Yves Robert.

GEMINI
QUALITIES
QUICK-WITTEDNESS, PERSPICACITY,
FLEXIBILITY, VERSATILITY,
PERFORMANCE, DEXTERITY
QUIRKS
IMPATIENCE, GLIBNESS,
INCONSTANCY, SELF-DECEPTION,
SUPERFICIALITY, INDECISIVENESS
Motto: *"I think"*
Elements: *Air, Mercury, Mutable*

--

ROOSTER
QUALITIES
RESILIENCE, ENTHUSIASM, CANDOR,
CONSERVATISM, CHIC, HUMOR
QUIRKS
COCKINESS, BOASTFULNESS, BLIND FAITH,
PEDANTRY, BOSSINESS, DISSIPATION
Motto: *"I overcome"*
Elements: *Negative, Metal, Yin*

The performing Gemini is herein blessed with a complement of the Rooster persuasion, who loves to swagger and swash-buckle, wears finery with aplomb and carries it all off as though he'd been born in a backstage wardrobe trunk. Gemini/Roosters, as actors or teachers or doctors or show business personalities, have it all over their competition. Talent? Yes. These people do have a certain amount of interpretive skill. But their strongest card is resilience. This Gemini/Rooster is a walking trampoline. Nothing, not illness, not rejection, not sorrow or self-pity, can keep this good man down.

Gemini/Roosters are very bossy people. They feel that their way is truly the best and most efficient way to get things done. So why should they not share their efficiency with you? They have a gentle way, an airy Gemini method of pushing others around. But they nevertheless do think of life as a giant chess board on which those they love or work with must be manipulated so as to ensure that the Gemini/Rooster will win.

It's not unpleasant to be a pawn in the Gemini/Rooster's game, that is, as long as you accept your role fully from the outset. With a Gemini/Rooster around the house, if you are feeling lazy or non-combative, you can just lie back and wait till he or she gives one of those claps of the hands meaning "Up and at 'em!" Even then, when you leap to your feet, you really only have to be ready to walk through your lines. The Gemini/Rooster will take care of the decor, the music, the food and everything else.

Gemini/Roosters are usually very attractive people. Their dignified carriage and equally lofty self-image cause others to notice them in public places, pick up on their vibes and sometimes actually be drawn to them physically without knowing why.

These people are also very charitable and willing to help others out—even if it is only on their terms. The Gemini/Rooster is attracted by helpless small things such as puppies and orphans and stray kittens. As his own opinion of himself is rarely, if ever, diminished by setbacks or run-ins with adversity, he enjoys the luxury of being willing to share this well-being with those less fortunate than he. Mind you, the Rooster is a rigorous person and adds starch to the Gemini's normally floppy sails. He may take in strays, but he will not sit back and let those same strays destroy themselves or become spoiled. Gemini/Rooster is a demanding benefactor.

Emotionally, this person has a tendency to fragility. I am not suggesting that he's lily-livered or even weak. Not by a mile. But the Gemini/Rooster, like all Roosters only more so, repeatedly falls victim to life's craggy peaks and chasms. His whole existence will resemble the most rapid and rickety, scary and thrilling roller coaster ride. From fame and fortune he can plummet overnight to ignominy and drink. Conversely, from sloth and dissipation, this fellow can trundle himself to his feet, tuck a flower behind his ear and become an overnight success as a flamenco dancer. The "weakness" I spoke of is the alluring temptation to let it all slide and/or think, "What the hell? Who cares?" He doesn't lack enthusiasm. But sometimes the Gemini/Rooster lacks staying power.

There is a spiritual element to this person's nature that cannot be ignored either. The combination of the meteoric and sometimes even celestial Gemini with the blindly faithful Rooster can give us a true religious fanatic, a holy roller who believes in and performs for his deity. Who else could be running this zany amusement park life?

Dame Fortune is fickle in a Gemini/Rooster's life. Now you see her. Now you don't. But no matter how many times Lady Luck hurts him and then deserts him, the Gemini/Rooster will rise again. He likes adventure anyway. And he learns young to watch out for flying shreds of bad karma.

Love

Despite the myriad ups and downs to which the Gemini/Rooster is subjected and the sheer volume of events he finds along his busy way, this subject is an amazingly constant lover. I know a very famous and sexy lady named Jane Russell (Gemini/Rooster 1921), who has, for a movie star sex symbol whose breasts are more famous than Everest, had the most un-Hollywood love life you can imagine. First, at eighteen, when she was discovered by Howard Hughes and starred in the racy Outlaw, Jane was in love with her high school sweetheart. Even after becoming world-famous and rich in the bargain, Jane would spend weekends at home going to the beach with her football-hero boyfriend.

Later, this same football hero (Bob Waterfield, Leo/Monkey 1920) became famous in his own right. But Jane did not marry him for any other reason than true love. Through thick and thin, Jane stayed married to BW for 23 years! In Hollywood! Later on, she did divorce and remarry, but this time as well she has been married for the longest time to her husband, John, the ex-Army officer Texan and tough guy. She's mad about him. And it seem to be mutual.

The Gemini/Rooster may not appear to be the long-haul marrying kind. But if properly handled he or she can give many years of excellent service. Gemini/Roosters need someone strong as a mate. They must have met their mental match before they can really settle down. Gemini Roosters don't fall for weak people. But sometimes the weaker types do fall for them. As they are flatterable in the extreme, Gemini/Roosters can be drawn into temporary relationships with inferiors. But they never last. If you love a Gemini/Rooster, get ready to scrap your way to happiness

Compatibilities

You have everything to gain from relationships with Aries or Libra/Snakes. You'll also benefit from love affairs with Leo/Dragons (power houses) and be fascinated by Aquarius/Oxen. You are a versatile sort and need to be challenged. Stay clear of Virgo, Sagittarius, Capricorn and Pisces/Cats. They hate conflict. You thrive on it. Sagittarius and Pisces/ Roosters are out for you, too, as are Sagittarius/Pigs and Pisces/Dogs.

Home and Family

Here is where the Gemini/Rooster wavers and finally falls down. He loves his family, adores his kids, needs personalized top-of-the-line decoration in his house, but Gemini/Roosters don't exactly love staying home. They wouldn't mind being able to pick up their whole kaboodle and move with them from hotel room to vaudeville stage and back every night. But when that's impossible, the old Gemini/Rooster has to pick up and take off anyway.

Kids are important to this subject. He is, after all, an impressionable interpretive type. He is able to absorb much from the attitudes and activities of his kids. Moreover, the Gemini/Rooster often serves as the core of his extended family. Cousins and uncles and parents depend on the Gemini/Rooster's ability to organize and get things together for reunions and fun fests. They may even be willing to follow their mystical leader far and wide, just so they don't have to take care of organizing themselves.

If you have a Gemini child born in a Rooster year, you ought to encourage him to not only create projects and invent new ideas, but to learn how to carry through with them. You will not be sorry if you encourage the streak of interpretive ability in this child. He may be capable of great performances later on. Mind you, as a child, the Gemini/Rooster is not really a ham or overly theatrical. He may only be interested in his friends and playing a little sandlot ball or jumping rope. But as this child matures he will require outlets for his performing talents. Don't neglect the applause meter—you'll be needing it.

Profession

From a career point of view this person is talented in all things requiring organizational skills, precision, authority, performance and even service. He is critical and able to discern and define what suits what and who should go with whom.

As an employee the Rooster born in Gemini will be obedient and acquiescent so long as he feels he has been given leeway and has dominion over at least one or two other souls in the office. No Rooster makes a good flunky. And the Gemini is no exception. He doesn't mind fixing coffee for the gang in the accounts department so along as he gets to choose the brand, the color of the cups and the hour at which coffee breaks are to be taken. Not that the Gemini/Rooster causes dissension in groups Instead, by thinking faster and acting sooner, he will maneuver him; into a position of mild power so that he doesn't have to take orders from anyone he doesn't respect.

Gemini/Roosters have quick minds. They can, of course, be actors or theatrical or movie directors and producers. They can also find outlets for their talents in decorating, engineering, architecture and/or sales.

Famous Gemini/Roosters:

Adrienne Barbeau, Alex McGregor, Amy Schumer, Anna Kournikova, Anne Heche, Anne Murray, Chris Evans, Danielle Chuchran, David Sutcliffe, Errol Flynn, Errol Garner, Hoku Hu, Ice Cube (O'Shea Jackson Sr.), Jerzy Kozinski, Joan Collins, Jon Gries, Jonathan Bennett, Jordan Fry, Judge Reinhold., Larisa Oleynik, Maika Monroe, Michael Kelly, Natalie Portman, Peter Dinklage, Prince Philip Duke of Edinburgh, Sean Berdy, T.D. Jakes, T.J. Miller, Ted Levine, Teri Polo.

GEMINI
QUALITIES
QUICK-WITTEDNESS, PERSPICACITY,
FLEXIBILITY, VERSATILITY,
PERFORMANCE, DEXTERITY
QUIRKS
IMPATIENCE, GLIBNESS,
INCONSTANCY, SELF-DECEPTION,
SUPERFICIALITY, INDECISIVENESS
Motto: *"I think"*
Elements: *Air, Mercury, Mutable*

--

DOG
QUALITIES
CONSTANCY, UNSOCIABILITY,
RESPECTABILITY, SELF-RIGHTEOUSNESS,
INTELLIGENCE, TACTLESSNESS
QUIRKS
UNEASINESS, CRITICISM, DUTY,
CYNICISM, HEROISM, MORALITY
Motto: *"I worry"*
Elements: *Positive, Metal, Yang*

This is the one Dog subject who escapes the knitted brow and ready bark of many Dog characters. The Gemini's sociability lends exactly the right amount of levity to the disquieted Dog's nature. The Gemini/Dog is a bouncy person with many talents and aptitudes who needs, above everything, to adhere faithfully to the rules. Otherwise, if a Gemini/Dog swerves off course, tests authority and tries to get by with less than true hard work and grit, or tries to cheat his way to success, disaster will ensue.

Altruism is the Dog's special quarter. We know that people born in Dog years are forever taking up causes and joining crusades for the sake of their fellow human beings. Dogs are good people. The addition of lighthearted Gemini, with his talent for the verbal and ability to amuse and even show off, to the steady, hard-working and worried Dog person's life is a mixed godsend. Either this Dog will spend too much of himself on the woes of the world and of others, or if, alas, he has allowed the Gemini superficiality to run away with him, he may not give a pig's whistle about others.

If the latter is true, the Gemini/Dog will be impossible, lumbering, pushy, fast-talking, self-involved, self-pitying and most of all heartbreakingly adorable. More commonly, if the Gemini/Dog has had a fine upstanding education and been sent to schools where he has had to toe the line and also been loved by solid-citizen parents, this subject is both amusing and noble, a show-off and a sweetheart, a worker and a dear who will spend his last dime to see someone he loves smile through a mist of tears.

Activity is essential to the Gemini/Dog. He practically never stays home and knits by the fire. Rather, he'll take you to a movie and then get a little dinner together for some intimates, then perhaps you'll play cards, and after that he'll take you on a midnight walk down by the river so you can watch the fish jump in the moonlight. Meanwhile he will break your eardrums talking, recounting endless funny experiences and offering opinion after opinion about this, that, and the other. Gemini/Dogs make fabulous traveling companions. They remember every detail, getting the tickets, bringing the thermos and tipping the waiter.

Unusual things attract the Gemini/Dog. He's always seeking some weirdo bedroom set that used to belong to Greta Garbo when she played in Grand Hotel, or searching through heaps of junk for that one rhinestone clip to polish up and take to his sister for a present.

This person is shocked by any sort of force or vulgarity. He may have fought bravely in a war but as a civilian he doesn't want anything to do with power or strength for its own sake. You won't find this person front row center at a prize fight. More likely you will find him fascinated by art and beauty, animals, nature and traditional paintings, music and literature.

I have a Gemini/Dog friend who was robbed some years back. His stash of antiques was sorely diminished by this intrusion. This sort of violation is a blow for anyone. But for my Gemini/Dog friend, having his house broken and entered while he was out amounted to rape. That was all there was to it. For months, for hours on end and even now if the subject of theft ever arises, Jean-Charles launches into his robbery speech. "How could anybody? What did I do to deserve it? I don't understand I wouldn't think of . . ." True. Gemini/Dog, you wouldn't dream of committing such a heinous crime against humanity. You're just too nice for such crummy low tricks. But the world is not like that. What else car I say to you after I have said one thousand times that I am sorry it happened to—of all people—you?

These subjects are usually very efficient and like things kept neat around them. They work best in orderly surroundings and dislike finding that the tool they keep in a certain spot has been moved. These Dogs are the jolly jump-up kind. Even their occasional scowls don't mean much. In the long run, they're faithful and lovable, cheerful and optimistic. They are also spendthrift and wasteful. Why? Because they are horribly, stupidly generous.

A certain childlike quality stays with the Gemini/Dog long after childhood is through. Imagine a forty-year-old woman curling up on your lap and licking your face. These people have a bit of that. While the intention is good, the action isn't always appreciated. As they are quick to give affection and easily swayed by those about whom they care, Gemini/Dogs can be misused by others who will abuse their good natures and take advantage of their talents. A wise Gemini/Dog is a circumspect Gemini/Dog. Wait, think, don't jump up on that pretty lady's skirt!

Love

"How do I love thee? Let me count the ways." A Gemini/Dog in love is a poet, a minstrel, a swain and a bit of a fool as well. When this person falls for someone, bells ring, lights flash and cherubs are requested to tune up too. Geminis born in Dog years are very romantic, believe implicitly in their love object's purity of soul and will stop at nothing to entice said object into their kennel.

As a mate, the Gemini/Dog needs someone solid. He is airy and will fly in impractical directions or be influenced by nefarious people. A stable and plain-thinking, slightly cynical mate is in order. If you love tradition, and enjoy being led around by your companion, helped over stiles and lifted across rills, choose a Gemini/Dog. These folks are not merely mannerly and gallant either. They often find great solutions to complex technical problems and maintain a very lofty conversational level. But your average Gemini/Dog does talk far too much and has to be told firmly, "Get down, Spot!" from time to time. If you love this character, buy yourself some ear muffs and settle back for a real down-home Dog's life.

Compatibilities

Aries, Leo and Aquarius/Horses will cheer you up and know how to love you properly. Leo and Libra/Cats are fine as well. Or why not take up with a nice Libra or Aquarius/Tiger person, or Virgo, Sagittarius, Capricorn and Pisces/Sheep and Dragons. You need real, deep, loyal love, not virtuosity.

Home and Family

Gemini/Dogs are more likely to be found living permanently in the country than in any roiling metropolis of this world. These subjects tire quickly of the metallic polluting rat race of the town. They like activity and are good spectators and even performers, but they need calm, a bit of greenery, and contact with the rhythms of nature in order to cool out and find their own natural pace again. Their homes will, in any case, be full of beautiful objects and well designed for comfort and convenience

Children? Well, for Gemini/Dogs the parent/child authority figure vs. victim is a tough one. Gemini/Dogs are performing circus animals They want to amuse and please and can only love people by adoring them. Clamping down on a kid's privileges is not exactly the Gemini/Dog's favorite sport. He'd rather not have to hurt anybody's feelings—ever. So parenting is difficult for this subject and in many cases I would even say to be excluded. If the other parent is willing to do all the shouting and reminding, then the Gemini/Dog is capable certainly of being, in name at least, a parent. But he won't get involved in the heavy discipline.

Gemini/Dog kids are serious and fun at the same time. They usually like to please their parents and do all they can to be charming and helpful around the house. They need a firm hand only insofar as they may tend to disperse their energies in too many directions at once. Don't ever slap or spank a Gemini/Dog child. He will not understand how you can love and hit him at the same time.

I'm not suggesting you allow him free run of his whims. But should you need to discipline or punish this child, you should use a firm but gentle method such as putting him in a chair in the corner or, if he's old enough, simple logic. These children are somehow too babyish and at the same time almost too grown up in some ways. They will have a disquieting serious side.

Profession

Artistic professions suit this subject. He can be a film director or a successful antique dealer, a fine interior decorator or a heartbreakingly emotional performer. You see, there is this quality about Gemini/Dogs that I'll call appeal. It's a kind of halo of attractiveness that is irresistible to sentimental people. The Gemini/Dog, even at his worst and most repetitively verbose and invasive, can make a grown man weep with his sob stories, can cause your heart to go pitty-pat with compassion with his mere expression.

So show business, if he can take the heat of dealing with sharks and ruthlessness, is a natural niche. By the same token, this person would make a fabulous trial lawyer or fund raiser for a charity. Truth is, this Gemini/Dog person must be inspired in order to carry on with any given job. He doesn't mind slogging and drudgery in an office so long as it's for a reason in which he believes. Providing he has this belief in his work, the person will make a cheerful and malleable employee.

The Gemini/Dog will have pronounced difficulty being boss. He does not like force, remember? Nor can he accept being hated or even mildly disliked by others. He should choose an independent career or else accept being hired on by someone more asbestos-hearted than he.

Famous Gemini/Dogs:
Alexa Davalos, Alice Englert, Aly Raisman, Amelia Warner, Anne Sylvestre, Annette Bening, Arthur Darvill, Artie Schaw, Benjamin Walker, Cayden Boyd, Chantal Goya, Clifton Collins Jr., Donald Trump, E.G. Marshall, Esmé Bianco, Gilda Radner, Guy Bedos, Helen Baxendale, Ivana Baquero, Jacques Cousteau, Jamie Kennedy, Jewel Staite, Jonathan Tucker, Joseph Fiennes, Judy Garland, Kelli Williams, Lea DeLaria, Leah Remini, Lorelei Linklater, Margaret Colin, Missy Peregrym, Mouloudji, Naomi Campbell, Prince William, Rainer Fassbinder, Robert Cummings, Scatman Crothers, Suzie Plakson, Ted McGinley, Will Forte.

GEMINI
QUALITIES
QUICK-WITTEDNESS, PERSPICACITY,
FLEXIBILITY, VERSATILITY,
PERFORMANCE, DEXTERITY
QUIRKS
IMPATIENCE, GLIBNESS,
INCONSTANCY, SELF-DECEPTION,
SUPERFICIALITY, INDECISIVENESS
Motto: *"I think"*
Elements: *Air, Mercury, Mutable*

--

PIG
QUALITIES
SCRUPULOUSNESS, GALLANTRY, SINCERITY,
VOLUPTUOUSNESS, CULTURE, HONESTY
QUIRKS
CREDULITY, WRATH, HESITATION,
MATERIALISM, GOURMANDISM, PIGHEADEDNESS
Motto: *"I civilize"*
Elements: *Negative Water, Yin*

The Gemini born in a Pig year boasts the double blessing of versatility and scrupulousness. Pigs, as we already know, seek riches and know how to cultivate the best in life. But they can sometimes be a bit sluggish too, and quite stubborn in their own peculiar way. The mercurial Gemini adds levity to the good Pig's dowdy nature, buoys up his occasional spells of dark wrath and lends action to this character's existence.

You will note in Gemini/Pigs that they can seem to be as busy as queens during a drone strike, traveling hither and thither, darting at flower after flower in an effort to get everything done at once. Then again, you'll find them sprawled on a silken divan eating bonbons from *Fauchon*, positively languishing in affluent sloth. Gemini is double-faced and despite the solidity that Pig brings to this person, he cannot escape the need to feel free to dash off in at least two directions on any subject or in any situation.

This last quality endows Gemini/Pigs with an uncanny gift for rapid problem-solving. Their quick Gemini brains flash and sprint around the whole issue at hand and then they simply sit Piggy down and figure it out. Gemini/Pigs are often "big" people. They grow their own enterprises out of nothing, and don't need the help of others to succeed. If one door doesn't answer, Gemini/Pig simply knocks on another. And he always finds a way.

Like everyone else, the Gemini/Pig has the faults of his virtues. As a Pig subject he will always have difficulty learning to say "no" —especially in emotional circumstances. But on the other hand, because he doesn't wax negative easily, the Gemini/Pig is not one to be told "no" either. He emanates positivity in all exterior aspects of life. He's a go-ahead guy with an open smile and a ready nod of approval. Gemini/Pigs are careful, even cautious, in business and money matters. But they are so enchantingly charming that you hardly notice that killer clause they slipped into your contract—until, of course, it's too late.

Gemini/Pigs enjoy all matters concerning culture. They visit museums and listen to great music and attend opera openings. They keep up on all the newest films and dance programs. I'd say they are culture vultures of the first water and interesting companions for it. Often, you will find that Gemini/Pigs have a secret charity or help out a poor family who want to send their kids to college. Albeit Gemini/Pig may sometimes seem light of heart with his ready crinkly smile and his cheery round face, this person is profoundly serious and well-meaning. He is also usually funny and exhibits a wry, knowing wit.

The Gemini/Pig never entertains small ideas. He is always ready to go out and change the world. He repeatedly dreams up huge international deals and stalks the necessary prey with deft sure-footedness. His way is gentle and fanciful too.

Eating may be a problem. The Gemini/Pig often travels in his business life and has great difficulty resisting champagne and caviar in the first-class section (where he invariably rides). Too, he is not much of a homebody and so falls often into the busy person's trap of eating prepared foods from specialty shops. Who could resist that brownie or cheese cake from the Golden Palate Food Shoppe? Not our Gemini/Piggy—particularly if the goody is expensive.

Gemini/Pigs want to be noticed and know how to go about getting attention. They are more emotional than they look and can be sorrowful and despairing over loss or hurt. They are, above all, oriented toward achievement. Gemini/Pigs are not interested in failure and usually stay far away from it.

Love

Of the three circles, family, business and love, the one that baffles the Gemini/Pig most is the latter. Gemini/Pigs are forever falling in love with the wrong person. What they can give is so enormous and so fulfilling and so complete and amusing that they frequently make the mistake of thinking that the person they choose as a mate can be quite attractively empty-headed so long as he or she is presentable and socially acceptable. Gemini/Pig is perfectly strong enough for two people. So why bother to go looking for trouble by marrying or living with one's intellectual equal?

This attitude on the part of Gemini/Pig causes him untold pain. After the first blush of excitement wears off this socially acceptable and presentable relationship, Gemini/Pig (because he is such an honest person as well) up and finds himself bored. Now what? Well, Gemini/Pigs have been known to be unfaithful. But they are also very often and verbosely dissatisfied with their love lives. "Why is he or she so crazy? What have I done to him/her? Where did she/he get the idea I was trying to run away?"

If you love a Gemini/Pig, be smart. That's right. Keep your wits honed to a razor edge and don't let anything get past you. But try to look dumb—or at least fetchingly dense. The Gemini/Pig needs to feel as though his mind is superior—but he hates to be bored.

You're quite right. The strategy I suggest is sheer hypocrisy. Don't worry. Gemini/Pig probably knows you're only pulling his leg, but he's also aware that your acquiescence is precisely what he needs in order to feel good about himself. Don't ever cheat on a Gemini/Pig unless you want your head in a vise.

Compatibilities

Aries, Libra and Aquarius/Cat subjects will purr you to sleep in your country retreat and never hanker after the city's clamor. Leo and Aquarius/Sheep like your bank account and give you great creative thrills. A gentle but strong Libra/Ox will bring you happiness too. By now you know enough to avoid Virgo and Sagittarius/Monkeys. But I'm not so sure you know how to resist the pull of a Pisces/Rooster. Above all, don't get too involved with either Virgo, Scorpio or Pisces/Snakes. You'll be tempted, but don't say I didn't warn you if you find yourself wearing a boa constrictor for a noose.

Home and Family

This part of the Gemini/Pig's life practically always goes well. Gemini/Pig involves himself willingly and with ease in everything that has to do with nurturing, taking care of and loving his family. Mother and father are as important as mate and children. Brothers and sisters and cousins alike, the Gemini/Pig adores them one and all. He is masterful when it comes to dealing with the dicey problems that arise out of family squabbles or childhood traumas.

At home you will find Gemini/Pigs living in conditions of advanced *luxe*. They like silks and satins and thick carpets and gilt. In town they favor large rooms: walls buckling inward from the weight of multitudes of paintings, tables wilting under antique vases filled with lavish bouquets and high ceilings from which hang chandeliers under which Louis XIV would have been proud to have breakfast. It is Plush City around the Gemini/Pig's townhouse.

In the country he will have heavy rustic seventeenth-century furniture and tapestries. "Baronial," "palatial," "villa," and "chateau" are terms essential to the Gemini/Pig decorating vocabulary.

The Gemini/Pig child will be loving and curious—and bossy. His busy intelligence may unnerve the placid or overly relaxed parent who would rather read a book than talk to him. This kid will not let up till his position in the parent's critical affections and respect has been earned. There is not too much need here for sloppy fawning or hovering. Gemini/Pigs can take care of themselves. But they do need attention and contact.

Profession

The Gemini/Pig is a born winner. He has both managerial and organizational talent. He doesn't mind working on his own or taking on huge responsibilities. He is capable of chicanery, but prefers to keep things on the up and up. As a merchant, the Gemini/Pig drives a very hard bargain and never comes out of any deal scathed.

There is little this subject cannot undertake. First of all he can sell anything from real estate to roller skates. He's a brilliant subject for art dealing or international antique sales. The Gemini/Pig might also try owning a chain of restaurants or going into the entrepreneurial side of show business.

Another good bet for a career for Gemini/Pigs would be advertising account executive. The bargaining capacity marries well with this person's quick creative side. As Gemini/Pigs are not afraid to espouse strong opinions, they might be good at political activities or even, because of their taste for discretion, diplomacy. Whatever they choose, it ought not to be piddling. Teensy jobs and routine get on this person's nerves and ultimately stultify his active spirit.

Famous Gemini/Pigs:

Adrian Paul, Aidan Turner, Amanda Pays, Bernard Clavel, Blaise Pascal, Blake Woodruff, Christo, Eileen Davidson., Françoise Sagan, Henry Kissinger, Hubert H. Humphrey, Hugh Laurie, Idina Menzel, Jake Busey, Jean Moulin, Joel Tobeck, John Franklin, John Ross Bowie, Joseph Schooling, Josh Lucas, Leelee Sobieski, Mark Wahlberg, Megalyn Echikunwoke, Michael Malarkey, Mike Pence, Nathan Morris, Nick Cassavetes, Noah Wyle, Paul Bettany, Prince Rainier of Monaco, Rachael Blake, Rupert Everett, Salman Rushdie, Sarah Dugdale, Sterling Beaumon, Sylvia Hoeks, Taylor Armstrong, Thomas Mann, Torrance Coombs, Troye Sivan, Tupac Shakur, Vincent Price.

CANCER
QUALITIES
IMAGINATION, INSIGHT, TENACITY,
AFFECTION, CARING, CAUTION
QUIRKS
AVARICE, IRRITABILITY, DESPONDENCY,
POSSESSIVENESS, MOODINESS,
HYPERSENSITIVITY
Motto: *"I feel"*
Elements: *Water, Moon, Cardinal*

--

RAT
QUALITIES
NERVOUSNESS, INFLUENCE,
ACQUISITIVENESS, THIRST FOR POWER,
INTELLECTUAL SKILL, CHARISMA
QUIRKS
APPEAL, VERBOSITY, THRIFT,
SOCIABILITY, GUILE, MEDDLING
Motto: *"I rule"*
Elements: *Positive Water, Yang*

Because he is born a Rat, the Cancer/Rat naturally lives by his wits. But as he is also a moon child and hence tends to drown in his own emotions this person's behavior wavers. The Cancer/Rat, we say, is a "private" person. He likes to crawl into his cubbyhole in the tower where he studies life and writes about interior subjects. But just when you think the Cancer/Rat has hidden away for good, will only venture out for the odd crust of bread and seems to be surviving on coffee and water up there in that tomblike turret, an invitation arrives at your door requesting the honor of your company at a huge reception complete with great groaning boards of food and gaiety and sociability to boot. Who is your host or hostess but your favorite recluse, the Cancer/Rat.

Be he a writer or a carpenter, a musician or a head nurse, this character will always be sure to have plenty of evidence of material wealth around him. *Objets d'art* and antiques abound where the Rat/Cancer lives. Books crowd the shelves, first editions and comic books and the latest jazz reviews, everything counts—especially if it has words on it. Cancer/Rats adore the written word.

This subject is likely to favor a singular elegance in his dress habits. He wishes to stand above the fashionable crowd, to exhibit his individuality through his manner of dress. Even his coiffure will cry: "Me! Look at me! How different I can be!!"

Cancer/Rats like society, but they need to stand apart from banality. They resist mediocrity in every choice they make, whether it be friends or lovers, houses or cars, trips or vacation spots. Not that Cancer/Rats go after the popular "best" or the trammeled idea of what is superior. Rather, they seek their own brand of excellence, and once they have found it, adhere to it like super glue.

Charm is part of the Cancer/Rat's panoply of qualities, too. He is not your average Don Juan or Lothario though. He won't sidle around trying to get cozy with you just for the fun of it. Cancer/Rats try to be appealing in spurts. They will invite you to a play or take you to lunch just to be agreeable and pleasant. But the Rat/Cancer charm is subtle. It can even be a little off-putting. You are never quite sure if the Cancer/Rat is going to smile or snap. You cannot tell whether he's in pain or just looks that way and is instead on the verge of a huge guffaw. The charm of Rat/Cancer is inscrutable.

Like all Rats, this Cancer/Rat is talkative. Unlike, say, an Aries or Leo/Rat, however, this Rat subject will enjoy talking about his feelings. "Do you think he really likes me? Can you tell if I am getting the right vibes? I'm so sad, happy, miserable, pained, ecstatic, joyful bored, annoyed. . . ." If you like this character and want to have him as a friend, you must polish up all of your listening devices. Not only does this person restoke his furnaces in company that he knows how to assemble to this end, but he'll drub your ears until they fall off in order to figure out vocally what his next step ought to be. There is no question about it, this person thinks on his feet. And remember, don't try to be the star. When you are at a Cancer/Rat party, you are a mere guest on "The Cancer/Rat Show."

Creativity abounds in the people born under the signs of Cancer and Rat. The obvious depth of Cancer emotion coupled with the

Rat's tendency to ferret out information infuses this person with a natural talent for writing stories. Too, as the Cancer/Rat possesses this excessive need to expound his feelings and rehash his emotions and ideas, writing books or poems or songs is the perfect therapy for him. Cancer/Rat is a private soul trapped in the body of a public personality.

A curiosity about justice and doing the "right thing" by others causes people born in Cancer/Rat to expend a lot of energy in litigious activity. Not that Cancer/Rats grow suddenly furious and want to get revenge on enemies, but they feel that fair is fair in life and will go to the fore to help a friend in legal trouble or to sort out the truth in a complex dossier. This tendency to want to see that justice is done can sometimes be a form of meddling. I have had a couple of winning, voluble, loyal Cancer/Rat friends who, because they thought my current beau was being unfair me or was behaving in a "macho" fashion, literally edged the unsuspecting gentlemen out of my life. In one case, I think the relationship would have died its own death soon enough. But in the other case, I really wasn't finished with loving the poor fellow. But my Cancer/Rat friend deemed him unworthy of me. And she chucked him out. Really.

Love

A fascinating subject to love. In romantic situations, Cancer/Rat is always miles ahead of his mate, calculating and feeling, intuiting and sensing, what should happen next. His goal in love is never to be bored, to maintain his passionate sentiment at a pitch difficult to achieve even at age seventeen. For these ends, the Cancer/Rat is known to be deliberately fugitive, hard-to-get, maverick and elusive. As we already know, he is secretive. When you do notice him from time to time, sleeping next to you as though he hadn't been gone for ten days (and you don't dare ask where), it seems such a blessing, a miracle, that you just accept and get on with it.

The Cancer/Rat is not necessarily unfaithful. He may not have gone away for ten days with anyone but himself. But he does usually have many successive lovers and at least a few mates in his busy life.

If you love a Cancer/Rat and want to hang on for a while, I suggest you practice examining his face for signs of retreat , bad temper, dreaminess and /or lust. When you learn to read your Cancer/ Rat's cryptic facial features, you will have won half the battle. Don't try keep him down on the farm. Don't fence him in. Don't smother him with marshmallow kisses. But do provide a secure and safe environment (complete with ivory tower) for his personal development, give him expensive presents, and above all, clean out your ears. You'll be needing them.

Compatibilities

You are extremely love-oriented. Partners suitable for you will be readily found among Taurus, Virgo, Scorpio and Pisces subjects. Prefer Oxen and Monkeys. They understand your brand of subtle power play. You clash with Horses, especially Aries, Libra and Capricorn/Horses. Don't be flattered by the attention of Aquarian, Libra or Capricorn/Cats. They are not patient with your nervous (and sometimes gloomy) nature.

Home and Family

You won't find this person happy living in a hovel. The Cancer/Rat's surroundings will be luxurious and original. The normal plenty of any Rat's pantry will be redoubled by the inclusion in his sign of the hoarding, acquisitive Cancer. Cancer/Rats are noted for their chic, well-appointed homes, where the dining room is the center of activity. Family dinners and gatherings are essential to this character's equilibrium. His kin come first. And to defend them, the Cancer/Rat would kill.

As a parent, the Cancer/Rat is strict, possessive and grasping. At first, he loves willingly and without question all of his children equally. Then as time passes and the children begin to take on individualities and express their own desires, the Cancer/Rat will be guilty of some favoritism. He may unconsciously choose to favor the child who needs him most, the kid who can't make it without Mom or Dad's help. Cancer/Rats don't particularly admire independence (from them) in their kids. A strong-minded child who disagrees with his Cancer/Rat parent should leave home early to escape tyranny. The Cancer/Rat feels he must protect his offspring. To do so, he sometimes meddles in their lives.

A Cancer/Rat child will surprise you by turns with his seeming solitary ways and his perfect sociability. The loner side of his nature should be encouraged, as this often difficult and testy-natured child will grow into his own skin best if he has time to do so at his own speed in his own place. Try not to force him to share his toys or his room with a sibling. The Cancer/Rat child is an independent sort.

Profession

It's difficult for me to imagine any Cancer/Rat who is not a writer. I have four close Cancer/Rat friends and they are all writers. Moreover, among the famous Cancer/Rats I found are both Antoine de Saint-Exupéry and George Sand. The Cancer/Rat career dice seem to be loaded in favor of the pen.

I don't see this watery creature as an executive or even a whistling happy worker bee. There's so much emotion to be expressed, so much heart over head in this subject, that I can best imagine him or her in artistic or art-related fields. Of course, as an independent, this person could surely choose dentistry or medicine or law as a career. He certainly has the intellectual wherewithal. Politics and government jobs are out. The Cancer/Rat hates witnessing corruption. If he works in an office he will rail at all in-office inequities. And he won't stick around very long if he feels these same injustices are about to be wreaked on him. The Cancer/Rat is quick-tempered and a mite snooty when attacked.

The Cancer/Rat is a hard worker. But he will not be pushed or bossed. Jobs requiring solitude or independence will work for him. Even commerce—if he owns his own store—can serve him well. He should, however, steer clear of careers that require plodding and day-to-day hypocrisy. He cannot hack phony smiles and insincere pats on the back.

Famous Cancer/Rats:

Alan Turing, Aubrey Plaza, Benz Antoine, John Elway, Kathy Bates, Khloe Kardashian, Lauren Jauregui, Lord Louis Mountbatten, Prince Dasho Jigyel Ugyen Wangchuck, Rachael Taylor, Rosalind Halstead, Sam Claflin, Sami Zayn, Sidney Lumet, Sofia Vergara, Sven Lõhmus, Zinedine Zidane.

CANCER
QUALITIES
IMAGINATION, INSIGHT, TENACITY,
AFFECTION, CARING, CAUTION
QUIRKS
AVARICE, IRRITABILITY, DESPONDENCY,
POSSESSIVENESS, MOODINESS,
HYPERSENSITIVITY
Motto: *"I feel"*
Elements: *Water, Moon, Cardinal*

--

OX
QUALITIES
STUBBORNNESS, STRENGTH OF PURPOSE,
ELOQUENCE, STANDOFFISHNESS, INNOVATION,
VINDICTIVENESS
QUIRKS
INTEGRITY, BIGOTRY, PLODDING,
DILIGENCE, BIAS, STABILITY
Motto: *"I preserve"*
Elements: *Negative Water, Yin*

It is no coincidence that many, many famous and respected artists of all sorts were born under the twin signs of Cancer and Ox. Here is the personification of determination. The profound sensitivity of Cancer coupled with the Ox's down-to-earth strength of purpose creates in this creature an emotional forcefulness unparalleled anywhere else in the new zodiac. This person always tries harder.

The Ox side of this subject's character endows him or her with formidable powers of tenacity and innovation. Cancer gives even more creativity and adds a hefty dose of feeling to the cocktail. These folks go after what they want with acute single-mindedness. For a Cancer/Ox a task is a chore is a rule is a religion! What must be accomplished must be, and there are no two ways about it, no shortcuts, and no tricky escape routes.

Cancerian Oxen hate to fail. Neither do they like to be told what to do or when or how to do it. They are a law unto themselves. They admit it. Yes. They are bossy and smothering and overly possessive. If you don't like that, then you will have to take your business elsewhere.

The great size of the Cancer/Ox's achievement is equal to his feeling for those he loves and those who have shown him loyalty. With these people he will share generously. But woe unto Cancer/Ox's enemies. Woe and begone. The Cancerian born Ox has no room in his spirit for self-doubt. If anyone tries to worm his or her way underneath the Cancer/ Ox's self-confident shield, the Cancer/Ox will quite simply eliminate them. Cancer/Ox is unforgiving and vengeful.

When you encounter such a character, naturally you know you have met someone extraordinary. Cancerian Oxen radiate a dense golden light of superiority. They know how to be alone. They know how to take their time. They know how to study hard. They know enough to get a good night's rest before a big event. They are exasperatingly perfect, and it is for this reason (and not only because of their talent) that they succeed at what they do.

The Cancer/Ox's brain is nothing to be sneezed at either. These folks are bright. They don't miss a trick and "never lose sight of the north," as the French are wont to say. But Cancerian/Oxen are not the intellectuals of the twin zodiacs. Far from it. They are too watery to be strictly gray-matter-oriented. No. The Cancerian Ox is an instinctual being who operates out of grit and endurance. He knows from the beginning that the shortest distance between two goals is straight ahead, and so he applies himself and goes there. Simple, *n'est-ce pas?*

This person will strike you at first as a beaming, jolly type. He or she seems to proceed through life as though it were all a chuckle. They never let on that anything might be even vaguely wrong. Don't be fooled. The Cancer/Ox is far less expansive in real life than he or she appears upon first meeting. In fact, they do not enjoy crowds and they only tolerate groups if they have summoned the group for a meeting or a family dinner. Cancerian Oxen are body snobs. They like to be left alone.

Love

For Cancerian Oxen, love is their own private premise. They live for their love and very often stay with the same loved one for life. Cancer/Ox is gifted in love the way he or she is gifted in success. Long-lasting and serious love affairs and marriages take patience and courage and much compromise. The stubborn Cancer/Ox knows surprisingly well how to compromise in matters of feeling. Romance and caring for others is what Cancer/Ox considers his reward for all his grueling hard work. He hangs on in the most perilous of marital storms.

Don't, however, expect daily bouquets or champagne with every meal. The Cancer/Ox is first of all a sensible being who wants to get somewhere in the realm of the real world. Yes, he or she definitely wants to be number one in your life, too. But don't underestimate the Cancer/Ox powers of concentration on the concrete. If he needs to finish a job or concoct a new scheme, ardent passions can be abstracted and even forgotten for a time. Emotions and sex interest this subject only insofar as they don't hinder his progress.

Compatibilities

Strength and mood are your bywords. You seek both in a helpmate. How about a feisty self-sufficient Taurus/Rooster or even a Virgo or Pisces of the rugged Rooster family? Or you might take up with a Virgo, Scorpio or Pisces/Rat person for easy compatibility. Rats protect you from the outside world and are complicit in spending (or hoarding) your gains. Scorpio and Pisces/Snakes make your heart beat faster, too. No Aries or Libra/Sheep for you moonchild Ox. Sheep in general exasperate you with their airy fairy notions. You will no doubt be fascinated by Tigers. But hands off! Tigers compete with you. Besides, they move too fast and confuse the issue with their undue speed. Capricorn/Dragons are pretty to look at and lucky in love – but not with Cancer/Oxen.

Home and Family

This character's snug surroundings promise to welcome the most desolate pilgrim to come in out of the cold. It's always pretty at Cancer/Ox's place. There's a sense is of solidity and coziness together. Overstuffed sofas and traditional tables and comfortable armchairs around a roaring fireplace lend harmony to the Cancer/Ox's headquarters.

This character will love children—all children. He may even take in strays and adopt orphans. He's a nurturer, remember. His or her attitude toward kids is that they should be happy but respectful, comfortable but willing to work for their comforts. The Cancerian

Ox doesn't give a his hard-earned money for the sake of a sweet smile or flattering remark. The same holds true for his family. "I love you, but I can only do so on my own terms."

You may find the Cancer/Ox child slow to react and rather more deliberate than other, more active kids. The Cancer/Ox child doesn't do much clowning or cutting up unless he knows well in advance that his act has been perfected. He likes to be good at things. So he waits till he's polished them before he shows them off to others.

Profession

One doesn't have to look far to find your nearest Cancer/Ox's professional talents. By the time they reach adulthood they will surely have a sound idea of what they want to do. They are definitely more artistically savvy than they are financial or scientific. There are two water signs at work here. Both of them are tough, persevering money-earners.

Where are the weaknesses? Well, this subject's strength can also be his own worst enemy. Somewhere along the line, because of a categorical refusal to behave frivolously, they are going to miss out on some of the fun that "normal" people get themselves involved in. Also, if by some fluke they should fall into some light-headed scheme or other, they will suffer far more from its unfortunate results than will people who don't take life so bloody seriously. If you are looking for servitude or subordination, don't employ a Cancer/Ox. But if you are interested in perfection, professionalism to the nth degree, hire a Cancer born in an Ox year. You won't be disappointed.

Famous Cancer/Oxen:

Ashley Tisdale, Barbara Cartland, Bill Cosby, David Hockney, Diana Princess of Wales, Gerald R. Ford, Henry David Thoreau, Iain Glen, Jacques Delors, Jean Cocteau, Lionel Jospin, Malala Yousafzai, Meryl Streep, Michael Phelps, Monica Lewinsky, Nico Rosberg, Nicole Johnson, Peter Paul Rubens, Prince Haakon of Norway, Queen Sonja of Norway, Rubens, Tom Stoppard

CANCER
QUALITIES
IMAGINATION, INSIGHT, TENACITY,
AFFECTION, CARING, CAUTION
QUIRKS
AVARICE, IRRITABILITY, DESPONDENCY,
POSSESSIVENESS, MOODINESS,
HYPERSENSITIVITY
Motto: *"I feel"*
Elements: *Water, Moon, Cardinal*

--

TIGER
QUALITIES
FERVOR, BRAVERY, MAGNETISM,
GOOD LUCK, BENEVOLENCE, AUTHORITY
QUIRKS
IMPETUOSITY, HOTHEADEDNESS,
DISOBEDIENCE, SWAGGER, INTEMPERANCE,
ITINERANCY
Motto: *"I Watch"*
Elements: *Positive Wood, Yang*

Tiger people are essentially combative. Cancers are sensitive, moody and susceptible to melancholy. "Roar!" says the Tiger inside the Cancer's sulky self. "I want my independence!" Or: "Give me some laughs!" Or "Send me some conflict!"

Cancer and Tiger are a strange, almost comical combo. There is, of course, a lot of true sentiment running around wild here. In fact, their worst enemy is loss of confidence and surrender to a dissolute and rudderless existence. Tigers are restless people who need to learn moderation. It is paramount to their survival. These brilliant subjects, you may recall, are in constant danger of being suddenly snuffed out—often as the result of their own excessiveness. Tigers need good counsel, advice, wisdom and common sense. Cancer is, for the most part, a sensible sign. But Cancers can drown in their own sensitivity. It's a treacherous combination.

We are, of course, all capable of self-betrayal. We can all be duped sooner or later by our sentiments. But here, with the Cancer and the Tiger together, there is a dicey penchant for self-delusion. Hale and hearty go-get-'em Tigers scarcely ever look before they leap unless they have some brilliant lieutenant standing next to them saying, "Watch out, boss! Take it slow, sir! You may feel differently tomorrow, chief!" The Cancer, with his moodiness and tendency to sulk or brood, is hardly the snappy lieutenant type, is he now?

So the best thing to say to this character is "Watch out!" Take life by steps. Get yourself organized and stick to routines. Structure your life or have someone structure it for you. You will not enjoy this discipline. But it will advance you. And you will enjoy the advancement.

"Eccentricity" is an apt word to describe Cancer/Tigers. These people are capable of living a wholly bohemian life. But that would be a mistake.

Cancer is too much of a bourgeois sign to follow in the nutty footsteps of the headstrong Tiger. Better to follow the moon child and go for the traditional home sweet home.

Everyone will enjoy knowing this person. He's generally cheerful (except when he gives in to his Canceresque melancholy) and amusing. He's a romantic, a dreamer who would change the world, make everybody nicer and more honest, a sentimental sort who longs for peace of mind and just about never achieves it.

Why? Well, the Cancer/Tiger is a mighty creative figure. New ideas and exotic places, people and pursuits attract him. Just when he or she appears settled and secure, bam! He's off to new and more hair-raising adventures. You see, the Cancer/Tiger not only enjoys seeking out the unusual, but he likes to be noticed for having done so. The Cancer/Tiger is a preener and a proud fellow when it comes to receiving praise for accomplishment. Praise, in fact, brings out the best in this subject and should not be rationed in his regard. He won't get a big head over it. Rather, it will urge the Cancer/Tiger on to bigger and better breakthroughs and conquests.

The Cancer/Tiger needs a lot of room to roam. Small spaces rub his back hairs the wrong way. He needs latitude and despite his home-loving nature on the one hand, this Cancer needs change. Even if he only moves the furniture around every other day, he likes to feel himself challenged by new environments.

Love

Unlucky in love in the early part of his life, this person's true emotional direction takes quite a while to develop. He or she will be very attractive to potential sex partners. Some important creative time can be lost here because of shilly-shallying with impromptu love affairs that rarely work out over the long run.

If you love a Cancer/Tiger, look up to him or her. Admiration and respect are what turn them on. The Cancer/Tiger needs to shine. He's not a show-off, though. He's really quite discreet. But he likes to be viewed from his best angle. Flatter him. And most of all, cuddle this lummox.

The Cancerian Tiger is very jealous. He hates having his spotlight so much as tiptoed into by someone else. He will fight very hard if he's attacked but is not the type to be aggressive in domestic situations. Don't compete with your Cancer/Tiger lover. Instead, do your own thing and let him do his. Be ready for affection at all times. And don't meddle in this person's private business,

Compatibilities

Tigerish Cancer that you are, you'll find Taurus, Virgo and Scorpio/Dogs beguiling. You may flip for Scorpio and/or Pisces/ Dragons and Horses. And of course you find the cultured Pisces/Pig irresistible. Don't trifle with Aries, Libra or Capricorn/Monkeys. Stay away from Aries and Libra/Snakes and eighty-six all lubricious thoughts about Aries and Libra/Oxen. Don't set your heart on a Libra/Sheep either. They are even more temperamental than you.

Home and Family

This area of the Cancer/Tiger's life is rife with push-me-pull-you-ism. Where the Cancer is home-loving, the Tiger is a wanderer. Where the Cancer is moody and emotional, the Tiger is optimistic. The decor alone will be schizophrenic. Clashing colors and arcane styles abound.

Of course the Cancer/Tiger is a natural parent. He or she loves his home and in it he sees family as part and parcel of the picture. The Tigerish side of this person's character, his spirit of adventure and his tendency to dream, will enchant children. This person is likely to be the "pal" kind of parent whom kids like to hang out with. There will be a certain amount of discipline around the Cancer/ Tiger's house, but remember his bohemian side—a little mess makes a house look more lived in, now doesn't it?

Cancer/Tiger kids are strivers and achievers. But in order to get places they must be taught very early the value of rigor and self control. The marginal side of the character can be the undoing of a child later on in life. So from the start he must be encouraged to give in to routine. Small daily chores and regularity in meal and bedtimes will help this little person to focus his future.

Profession

This character is only partially after gain. Material wealth is of some importance in his scheme of things. But (and this is a big but), because he's a Tiger, this Cancer's grabby side will be noticeably diminished. He may be the type who invents a wondrous new process, but when it comes to marketing it, he'll seem to chicken out. He'll back down in the face of the kind of long term involvement necessary for real advancement. He wants a BMW. He might even love to drive around in a Rolls-Royce. But if he takes the time to earn the means and then to protect the means thereafter, he fears he will be bored and that some other new wondrous processes will go undiscovered as a result. So Tiger/Cancers tend to live for what they can invent in life.

Of course this approach is good when you are the boss of the enterprise. If you hire the right people, you can stay in your crazy quilt lair and create your head off while your loving staff picks up the paperwork. It's less desirable for an employee not to carry through on his serves. So, if possible, this subject should work for himself.

Famous Cancer/Tigers:

Amanda Donohue, Anthony Edwards, Deirdre Shannon, Diana Rigg, Dierdre Lovejoy, Donald Faison, Drake Bell, Elisabeth Kübler-Ross, Franka Potente, George Windsor (Earl of St Andrews), Jaden Smith, Jake McDorman, Jeff Cohen, Joel Edgerton, Jules Mazarin, Kaitlin Cullum., Larsa Pipsen, Lindsay Lohan, Matthew Couch, Richard Rodgers, Sam Claftin, Thomas Gibson, Tom Cruise, Tom Kenny, Wyatt Russell.

CANCER
QUALITIES
IMAGINATION, INSIGHT, TENACITY,
AFFECTION, CARING, CAUTION
QUIRKS
AVARICE, IRRITABILITY, DESPONDENCY,
POSSESSIVENESS, MOODINESS,
HYPERSENSITIVITY
Motto: *"I feel"*
Elements: *Water, Moon, Cardinal*

--

CAT/RABBIT
QUALITIES
TACT, FINESSE, VIRTUE,
PRUDENCE, LONGEVITY, AMBITION,
QUIRKS
SECRETIVENESS, SQUEAMISHNESS,
PEDANTRY, DILETTANTISM,
HYPOCHONDRIA, COMPLEXITY
Motto: *"I Retreat"*
Elements: *Negative, Wood, Yin*

A startling combination of the home-loving and the home-loving, if the Cancer/Cat didn't have to go out and make a living, he indeed might opt to never leave the comfort of his perfectly decorated, carefully appointed and cozily efficient house. To a Cancer born a Cat, the center of his universe is his hearth. If he has any enemies, they will only be able to really wound the Cancer/Cat where it hurts if they attack his epicenter—the home.

Don't get the idea that this person is a recluse. On the contrary, once he gets to know you, Cancer/Cat is a veritable bundle of amiability and chitchat. He lights up when he sees you and launches into a bevy of subjects to please you. Often, this person talks of things to come, dreams and future plans of castles (always castles or manor houses or mansions) in Spain or Normandy or in the lush green dank of Ireland. For Cancer/Cats there is always glory or brilliance - and contentment! Ahead.

I know a few Cancer/Cats. They are the epitome of comfort, always inviting you right in to sit and have coffee or uncorking the kind of wine you like. And they invariably recount stories again and again about the day when their great Aunt Tillie, who is ninety-eight and a half, will pass away and their own life will become nirvana. "And don't think I've always lived like this," says the Cancer/Cat. "Why, in 1965 alone I spent over half what my poor husband earns today on help. Yes, I had maids. I was a lady!" You never really know if the past opulence and future inheritances actually exist. But finally, it's not important. It is a matter of total indifference because wherever the Cancer/Cat is, in whatever tiny cove he runs aground, this character creates instant chintz curtains, comfy armchairs, a long generous table covered with pretty, tasty foods, and an aura of greeting and welcome that nobody could resist. Spartans, beware. This Cancer/Cat could draw you into his fur-lined lair and cause you to renounce your faith in frugality.

Cancer/Cats are dependable, too. And trustworthy. You can leave them your keys, your kids, your dog and your wife or husband and expect to return months later and find everybody sitting around drinking cocoa and playing Scrabble. No hanky-panky will have gone on behind your back. Cancer/Cats are honorable and virtuous people.

If pushed to the extreme, virtue has the bad habit of becoming self-righteousness or even pedantry. Cancer/Cats have to watch out for this tendency. They can wax a bit sanctimonious from time to time. Cancer/Cats can be guilty of impatience with those less "worthy" than themselves. This minor fault can grow into a real pain in the *derrière* if the Cancer/Cat feels cornered or threatened. Remember, Cancer/Cats are both crabs and felines. Superficially, they don't represent any real physical horror or menace. But in both creatures there is the real, ever-present and close-to-the-surface possibility of claws! Be nice with Cancer/Cats. Don't cross them or try to take their new vacuum cleaner away. These folks can be vicious when irked.

Cancers like to acquire things. Cats like to polish and refine things. Put them together and you have an antique dealer, or worse—a collector. These people collect stuff, hoard material goods and build up stocks of finery the likes of which would turn Sotheby's or Christies green with jealousy. If you have a Cancer/Cat relative who has no other heir beside yourself, he may not look like a good prospect for a huge legacy with his modest attitudes, but in the attic this guy has more wealth than there are stars in the sky. Careful, cautious, prudent, ambitious, avaricious and secretive. Don't forget that covert part of this character's nature. He may strike you as sentimental and even self-pitying and sometimes maudlin, but take my advice: Stroke the pretty Cancer/Cat's fur the right way—you may live not to regret it.

Love

In love with love. I have that jotted in my Cancer/Cat notes. And it's true. Cancer/Cats are invariably, unchangingly and impressively in love. Not infatuated or having a crush on someone. The Cancer/Cat is not interested in short-lived intimacies. He wants a home. He wants a family. He wants pretty furniture and authentic oak floors and baptisms and weddings complete with lilies and roses and champagne and chamber music. The Cancer/Cat is an ardent, squishy, soft and delicious love bug—with taste and discernment thrown in for good measure.

The Cancer/Cat needs a solid and faithful partner to accompany him through the vaulted halls of his home life. And one helpmate will suffice. The Cancer/Cat may have some jaunty adventures in promiscuity when young or at loose ends. But this is not a person who can live with a series of one-night stands. Cancer/Cats needs your love, all of it, unconditionally and forever. In return you will receive more than anybody's share of security and illusion, dreams and cups of warm milky tea, cakes, and even a tiny drop of the finest claret from time to time. If you are lucky enough to fall into the clutches of a moonish Cancerian Cat, lie back and enjoy it. But don't forget to take out the garbage, wash the windows, get the spare room ready for Grandma and pick up the gold mirror from the refinisher at five o'clock. You'll be happy. But boy! Will you ever be busy.

Divorce or separation, breakups of all kinds will devastate the Cancer/Cat. No one perceives a broken home as more of a personal failure than the Cancer/Cat. He takes full blame. After a broken heart, the Cancer/Cat broods and sulks and licks his wounds for a long, long time. No rebound flings for this person. But just wait. When finally the Cancer/ Cat locates his next true-blue soul mate, he backs off a little, crouches and then-pounce! You're hooked for life. Do not try to escape. It's useless.

Compatibilities

Taurus, Virgo, Scorpio and Pisces catch your fancy. They are all capable of hunkering down in the coziness of you for life. You'll particularly enjoy romance with Sheep, Dogs and Pigs of the above sign groups. I don't see you taking up with either Aries, Libra or Capricorn/Tigers, Dragons or Roosters. Too businesslike. You need gentility and a home-loving type to maintain both security and interest.

Home and Family

I've already described the Cancer/Cat's ideal as home. You will be surprised at the number of times you will find him in when you phone this subject. You will marvel at the degree of order that reigns in this persons house. Life is always busily going forward and yet there is room for a smile, a little gab session, a brief gossip over the back fence. And the reason for this cauldron of household efficiency and good cheer? The Cancer/Cat is always chez *lui*.

The Cancer/Cat is a tireless parent, generous and loving, warm-hearted and forgiving. But he's also quite demanding of his kids. He is himself a tactful and discreet person with a bent for culture and exorbitant dreams of refinement.

It will therefore not do at all for a Cancer/Cat to have undisciplined, ill-kempt or clumsy, vulgar children. All of this person's kids will respect and admire their Cancer/Cat parent. The Cancer/Cat is capable of great sacrifice for the sake of his kids—but he doesn't let them forget it either.

A Cancer/Cat child must be made to feel warm and secure. He may not seem the most outgoing kid at first. But when he feels really snug, then you will start to notice those crinkly smiles he's to become so famous for.

Surround him with culture. He will be capable of absorbing all variety of artistic endeavor. Don't make him play football if he doesn't want to. He's a refinement freak. Not necessarily athletic-tough, but not necessarily a black belt in karate or an Olympic figure skater.

Profession

Obviously, this home-lover can be a marvelous homemaker. Leave this person home all day and he'll never be idle or bored. The framework of home life is sufficient to keep Cancer/Cats even-tempered and equilibrated for a long while.

If, however, this person ever gets out of the house, he is talented in medicine, teaching, picture framing or printing, curative and restorative jobs.

The Cancer/Cat makes an excellent, reliable and loyal employee. He can get along well with coworkers because he knows he ought to—not necessarily because he likes them or thinks they are fun to gab with in the cafeteria at lunch time. But the Cancer/Cat is a sensible creature. He knows which side his bread's buttered on. He'd prefer to have a nice small cozy office with a door that shuts (he cares less for a window than a door) and locks to exclude untoward influences. As a boss, the Cancer/Cat will be efficient and just. He may not be liked by his employees because he seems a mite on the snooty side for their taste. But never mind. He gets the job done.

Famous Cancer/Cat/Rabbits:

50 Cent, Anjelica Huston, Cheryl Ladd, Cheyenne Jackson, Claude Sarraute, Ed Westwick, Geoffrey Rush, George Michael, Gina Lollobrigida, Huey Lewis, Jesse Ventura, Joe Dempsie, Joey Rive, Julia Duffy, Lionel Messi, Lisa Rinna, Neil Simon, Phoebe Cates, Ralf Schumacher, Robin Williams, Saül Bellow, Sebastian Vettel, Tobey Maguire, Yann Martel.

CANCER
QUALITIES
IMAGINATION, INSIGHT, TENACITY,
AFFECTION, CARING, CAUTION
QUIRKS
AVARICE, IRRITABILITY, DESPONDENCY,
POSSESSIVENESS, MOODINESS,
HYPERSENSITIVITY
Motto: *"I feel"*
Elements: *Water, Moon, Cardinal*

--

DRAGON
QUALITIES
STRENGTH, SUCCESS, GOOD HEALTH,
ENTHUSIASM, PLUCK, SENTIMENTALITY
QUIRKS
RIGIDITY, MISTRUST, DISSATISFACTION,
INFATUATION, BRAGGADOCIO, VOLUBILITY
Motto: *"I Preside"*
Elements: *Positive Wood, Yang*

Great emotional vitality is the foundation of this astonishing character's personality. The Cancer/Dragon is born with all of Cancer's profound ability to feel life in every aspect. Too, this subject is endowed with the Dragonish pluck and fire we all know and love so well. So we have here a forceful and dauntlessly enthusiastic character. Cancer's eternal black moods will be lightened by the Dragon's phoenix-like ability to rise from the ashes of his own immolation by his natural pep and vigor. Dragon's unwieldy braggadocio will be tempered by Cancer's good sense and dignity.

Cancer/Dragon is almost boyish in the variety of charm he exudes. He's got just a *soupçon* of a twinkle in a very sensual glance. Bedroom eyes with a skylight. Cancer wants to keep this subject home. Dragon longs to race out and beat the world at any game in town. This creates a natural inner conflict. Who decides the issues? What breaks the camel's back every time? Sentimentality. This Cancer/Dragon subject is terminally sentimental. With this sentimental side, of course, comes a tendency to be hypersensitive. The Cancer is the only Dragon who will cry at weddings and faint at baptisms and bar mitzvahs. They know how to mix feelings with theater. "It's alarming how charming . . ." and so on.

The impression one gets when encountering this person for the first time is one of great strength of character and giant capability. "Gosh!" you say to yourself. "This woman looks as if she eats elephant meat for breakfast." Thing is, if you get to know her, you'll see that this power rarely exploited. Cancer/Dragons have muscle. But they don't like to have to use it.

Though not often classically attractive, this person will enjoy much success with the opposite sex. Much of the Dragonish fire is doused by Cancer's watery side making this character steamy rather than just sexy. The Dragon/Cancer, then, is less obviously pushy and egotistical. This is a toned-down Dragon. A spiffed-up Cancer.

Cancer/Dragons are curious people and often go traveling and bring back reports or trophies from their wanderings. This person knows how and where to apply the dynamic energy he owns, and makes an interesting—though perhaps a mite too talky for my taste—companion. Dragon/Cancers are idealistic, too. They'd like to change the world—or at least try.

The Cancer born Dragon will be drawn to things artistic and will probably be something of a culture vulture. He or she will enjoy appearing in public places well turned out and *suffisant*. Cancer/Dragon is a sign of strength without the disadvantages that often go along with domination.

Love

In romance as in life in general, the Cancer/Dragon will operate mostly out of energetic sentiment and fiery sensuality. It's a turbulent mix at best. "I feel for this and love that and adore her and hate him and am passionate about everyone and what's worse, I am outrageously attractive." Oh, you poor little waif! You mustn't feel so guilty. Don't put your charm back in your pocket. Get out there and wow 'em with your pizzazz! But be careful. Remember how sentimental you are. This world of admiring strangers is mined with pit-falls for people like you.

You see, for a Dragon to be even the least bit discreet and digni-fied, reserved and genteel, he has to be a Cancer. This person will be adorably humble on the outside but oozing with Dragonish mag-netism, which he'll never be able to completely hide. For this rea-son I would not take bets on his fidelity. If you love a Cancer/ Dra-gon, stay home by the phone and keep your little black book well filled with alternatives.

Compatibilities

Taurus, Scorpio and Pisces/Monkeys tease you and entrance you, sweet Cancer/Dragon. You may also find happiness with a Scorpio or Pisces/Rat. You love Snakes for their innate beauty, so why not try a Taurus or Pisces/Snake? But beware! Snakes love to tell fibs. And when you're in love, you can easily be duped. Taurus/Pigs and their Rooster brothers and sisters can also turn up your volume. Don't try coupling with an Aries, Libra or Capricorn/Dog, a Capri-corn or Libra/Ox. And don't even think about marrying any kind of Cat.

Home and Family

This person is a Cancer. So he will have a comfortable and rea-sonably sane home life. But as he is also a Dragon and wont to show off, I'd say the house will be large and imposing, the gardens well tended and the *luxe* apparent. Cancerian Dragons do not know how to keep their zip zippered. You will not be unimpressed.

As a parent the Cancer/Dragon's a doll. He will love his kids to pieces and adore showing them off to relatives and to the world at large. He'll offer them security and in return he will expect obedi-ence and manners. He or she will also revel in performing for the kids. (If your father or mother is a Cancer/Dragon, I suggest you laugh at their jokes.)

The Cancer/Dragon child will be sweet-natured and quick of wit. You shouldn't have too many problems with him or her provided there are many outlets for all the energy they are born with. They should be trained at many different disciplines, as they are capable and diligent learners whose aim is to please. He or she will proba-bly have an interest in theater.

Profession

This person is a born leader. He or she needs much education and should seek knowledge from an early age. Their natural curiosity will prepare them for studies of an advanced nature. Cancer is dili-gent and persevering. The adult Cancer/Dragon has real talent for jobs requiring personal authority. He's strong-minded. But he is not stubborn. He's dutiful. But he's not Pollyanna.

So, as a boss, this person will be both strict and lenient. The trick is always to know just how much of which. If Cancer/Dragon runs into a snag, he can feel his way to the best solution. I have my doubts about Cancer/Dragon's abilities as an employee. These people really hate playing second fiddle and may sulk if subordinated. Lots of college diplomas should help Cancer/Dragons start out near the top.

Jobs suited to this mix are: preacher, actress, adventurer/writer; journalist, restaurant owner, TV personality, international lawyer.

Famous Cancer/Dragons:

Alex Trebbek, Andrea Glass, Benedict Cumberbatch, Bernard Buffet, Craig Charles, Diane Kruger Don Imus, Elie Saab, Haile Selassie, Helen Keller, Jacques Chancel, Jean-Baptiste-Camille Corot, Jean-Luc Delarue, Kristen Welker, Olivia de Havilland, Pablo Neruda, Patricia Stewart, Pearl Buck, Ringo Starr, Steven R. McQueen, Vinessa Shaw.

CANCER
QUALITIES
IMAGINATION, INSIGHT, TENACITY,
AFFECTION, CARING, CAUTION
QUIRKS
AVARICE, IRRITABILITY, DESPONDENCY,
POSSESSIVENESS, MOODINESS,
HYPERSENSITIVITY
Motto: *"I feel"*
Elements: *Water, Moon, Cardinal*

--

SNAKE
QUALITIES
INTUITION, ATTRACTIVENESS, DISCRETION,
SAGACITY, CLAIRVOYANCE, COMPASSION
QUIRKS
DISSIMULATION, EXTRAVAGANCE,
LAZINESS, CUPIDITY, PRESUMPTION,
EXCLUSIVENESS
Motto: *"I sense"*
Elements: *Negative, Fire ,Yin*

As Cancers go, the Snake type is more independent of ponderous emotional fetters than his kin. He's familial to be sure, and even clinging—after all, he is both Snake and Cancer! But the Cancer born a Snake, unlike certain other Cancers we all know and love, recognizes his own weaknesses, comprehends his black moods and, because of his cool-headed sagacity, usually manages to slither out of the lunatic doldrums for which Cancers can be so famous.

As Snakes go, the Cancer/Snake will be less cold-blooded than other serpents. Cancer's brooding soulfulness and profound affectivity lend the Snake a blanket, caress his cold exterior and warm the heart into something close to affability. Snakes can be really cool customers. They wiggle and squirm their way in and out of every variety of situation and are clever as snakes at turning most circumstances to their favor. In the Cancerian Snake, this tendency to want the leading role in all of life's movies is tempered by common sense and natural reserve.

All Snakes are created fabulators. But some are more prevaricating than others. Cancer/Snakes are among the least slippery of serpents. They might not bamboozle their grandmothers just to make themselves look good. Nonetheless, even the sensible Cancer/Snake is capable of rank dissimulation and tells ingenious and Byzantine fibs. He can't help it. He believes his own fantasies. Fibbing, after all, is part of the challenge of seduction and capture. And all Cancer/Snakes want to be thought of as captivating, charming, beautiful to behold, better than their neighbors and taller and handsomer and better dressed than anybody anywhere ever. Attractiveness is inborn and crucially important to this creature.

These folks are not above name-dropping and label-flaunting. Picture the splendid home-loving Cancerian/Snake seated on his designer couch, wearing his designer jeans. His tanned and braceleted arms embrace a brood of beautiful towheads in designer frocks and Bermuda shorts Behind his head, a Picasso. At his feet, a giant Pyrenees hound found only in the furthest darkest caves of Andorra. Everybody knows these huge beasts eat at least one small cow every day, are *très, très à la mode* and fetch a fortune. Never mind. The image is the message with Cancer/Snakes. No matter the cost or the travail involved, count on your friendly neighborhood Cancer/Snake to own the most chic and fashionable of everything. .

Incidentally, if you don't live in an upper-echelon neighborhood you may never meet one of these gorgeous creatures. If they can help it, Cancerian Snakes don't hang out in scruffy sections. They may come from poverty, but they are determined not to stay there for long. Up and over they go, attending the "right" schools and rubbing shoulders with the "in" crowd, marrying the one person in the whole gang who is sure to become famous and rich. Cancer/Snakes don't only like comfort, they think they invented it.

These people love to entertain, too. Once they have achieved a modicum of security and know a few of the "top" people, count on the Cancer/Snake to throw some of the most lavish and well-attended parties in town. Of course Cancer/Snakes will have catered food and a pair of bartenders, set a team of servants to work shucking the oysters, and then will circulate. The way he sees it, the Cancer/Snake cannot very well move about among his guests, charm the pants off the chancellor of Germany whose press secretary promised he'd put in an appearance, inveigle the secretary of the art museum to give him a private showing of the new upcoming work of the younger artists and serve drinks at the same time—or can he? Well, it doesn't really matter, because he won't. Cancer/Snakes like to be waited on. And as long as they can afford slaves they will be sure to have them.

These people are extremely artistic. They have a way of embellishing everything that comes their way. And Cancer/Snakes are also wise and can be of good counsel. They are super intuitive, really can project themselves into other people's skins and will think long and hard about someone's dilemma before dispensing a single word of their sage advice.

Cancer/Snakes are fun-loving too. They are always up there dancing till dawn with the heartiest of the youngsters, looking fabulous and enjoying being the envy of all present. And don't put it past a Cancer/Snake to be "that woman who stripped to her undies last week at the posh club over in Soho." Cancerian Snakes have a naughty streak. They like to be considered a mite outrageous or exotic.

Love

Possessive? Exclusive? Demanding? Intractable? You got it—the Cancer/ Snake is all of these and much, much more. The Cancer/ Snake is so attractive and sexy and lovely to watch move that people may gather just to watch him or her enter a public place. These people have the market cornered on slink.

Underneath the slink is an amazing amount of good-scouted, good-hearted fellowship and an enormous caring for friends and lovers alike. The Cancer/Snake will not be faithful. But he or she will always be seductive and alluring. Even if he's carrying on a roaring affair with the German minister's secretary, the Cancerian Snake will always attend to his or her mate as though he or she were the ruler of Germany itself.

If you love a Cancerian Snake, get ready to make a lot of money, spend it all and then go out and make some more. As the mate of this exciting person, you will luxuriate in perfectly glorious surroundings and have scads of very decorous friends and acquaintances to whom you can complain that your Cancer/Snake companion is too attractive to other men and women and you wish you had married a nice solid Taurus/Dog. In order to get the best out of life with a Cancer/Snake, you have to be able to fall down laughing, ooohhh and aaahhh when he comes down the stairs dressed to kill, and enjoy cooking your own meals and eating them alone by the fireside while Cancer/Snake is out rounding up some new sculptures to beautify your existence.

Compatibilities

You get a charge out of Roosters. Your best shots with them will be found among Taurus, Virgo, Scorpio and Pisces. The same goes for Oxen in all those categories. You're not thrilled by Aries or Capricorn/Tigers or Monkeys. Leave Pigs alone. I know they are usually naïve and often have lots of money; and you have plenty of guile for both of you and excel at spending money. But, let's face it. You don't always have Piggy's best interests at heart.

Home and Family

Cancer/Snake's main home will be located, it goes without saying, in the best possible quarter of the closest metropolis to heaven. But then there is, of course, the house in the country. This little manse is likely to want to be situated right in the heart of the most celebrated verdant horse and dog-breeding territory, not too far from the first paradise we mentioned. Then, you have to have a place at the beach. That'll be located on the prettiest seashore available at the highest price, please. And don't forget the little *mas* in the south of France—or was it Tuscany? Well, wherever, it won't be long before the Cancer/Snake invests in some opulent, trendy foreign real estate.

Inside these homes will live masses of children and dogs and cats and house guests and maids and nannies—well, you name it, it lives at the Cancer/Snake's house. You see, with all their elegance and *savoir vivre*, Cancer/Snakes love pets and kids and guinea pigs and horses etc. Cancer/ Snakes are really incredibly dear, sweet people. They really don't mind if your Doberman jumps up on their new St Laurent tweed skirt.

If you have a Cancer/Snake child, you must be careful to provide him or her with lots of security and plenty of animals to love. As is true with all Snakes, it's probably best for the exclusive Cancer/ Snake child to be an only child, or at least the baby of the family. Cancer/Snake kids are bright in school and work hard to get ahead. They usually don't cause their parents many problems and carry on with their lives quite independently of the parents' intervention. These little people are very affectionate. You must always tuck them in warmly and kiss them goodnight.

Profession

In the early part of his life, the Cancer/Snake, like all his serpent brothers and sisters, will try to wriggle out of chores and tasks. And just because he's a Cancer doesn't mean that he won't have to fight the great battle against sloth that is native to all Snake subjects. But as adulthood approaches and the Cancer/Snake grows more and more independent of parental security, he will note that riches and work are irremediably intertwined. Then his true Cancer nature will take over. He'll still be on the sit-around-and-look-beautiful side of a lazy Sunday afternoon. But the grown-up Cancer/Snake can be counted on to pitch in when there's a need for a second shoulder at the wheel.

Talented in everything related to beauty and the home, this person can succeed at decoration, architecture, graphic design of all kinds, fashion or advertising. Gifted in deception, persevering and supremely intuitive, Cancer/Snakes might also choose law—even politics—as a life's work. This character is more cerebral than manual but might employ his talents well in some light labor such as landscape gardening. Cancer/Snakes can very satisfactorily hold dominion over others. They do not have to abuse power because their authority is so natural that people rarely question it. As an employee, the Cancer/Snake might tend to be a little on the snooty know-it-all side. I'm not sure I'd hire one to do a menial job of any sort.

Famous Cancer/Snakes:

Alain Krivine, Andrew Wyeth, Ashley Montagu, Brock Lesnar, Christiane Rochefort, Craig Handley, Crown Princess Victoria of Sweden, Daniel Radcliffe, Daniel Ricciardo, David Henrie, Hannah Murray, Henri Salvador, Kathryn Erbe, Keegan Allen, Liv Tyler, Martha Reeves, Matthew Lewis, Milo Ventimiglia., Peter Maas, Prince George, Twyla Tharp, Vicki Carr.

CANCER
QUALITIES
IMAGINATION, INSIGHT, TENACITY,
AFFECTION, CARING, CAUTION
QUIRKS
AVARICE, IRRITABILITY, DESPONDENCY,
POSSESSIVENESS, MOODINESS,
HYPERSENSITIVITY
Motto: *"I feel"*
Elements: *Water, Moon, Cardinal*

--

HORSE
QUALITIES
PERSUASIVENESS, UNSCRUPULOUSNESS,
POPULARITY, STYLE, DEXTERITY,
ACCOMPLISHMENT
QUIRKS
SELFISHNESS, AUTONOMY, REBELLION,
HASTE, ANXIETY, PRAGMATISM
Motto: *"I demand"*
Elements: *Positive Fire, Yang*

The Horse, you may recall, is able to give himself up to a romantic passion and chuck everything—including his self-respect—for the sake of love. Cancer/Horses are, with their Scorpio counterparts, about the most self sacrificing. Love and its vicissitudes, the preservation of a home and kids and pets and insurance policies and telephone bills, can all be capable taken in hand by the Cancer/Horse. When questioned as to why he continues to struggle so hard and so seemingly alone without compassion or cooperation, the Cancer/Horse merely smiles. "It's for Janet. I love her."

The impression given by the Cancerian Horse is one of noble strength and calm. One gets the feeling with these people that you could set off a Roman candle under their chair and they would hold their ground and nod knowingly. "Oh, someone has played a trick on me." Where most of us would be circling the room screaming, "War! Help! War!" the Cancer/Horse will just get up and fetch us another cup of coffee. He's willing and ever so able and kind. Very little in the way of surprise can really perturb him.

The Cancer/Horse's appearance is always conservative, too. Navy blues and beiges in good-quality lambswools and flannels. Sensible but chic leathers and only the strict minimum of gold jewelry—a watch, an antique brooch or ring. No frills on this person's exterior.

Inside, however, there lives a certain baroqueness of spirit. Lots goes on at once inside this person's mind. Cancer/Horses carry an inner compass around with them. They study it before diving into foolhardy schemes and they keep it pointed in the direction of common sense and good measure at all times.

Do these people have any faults? Oh, sure. There are no good nor bad signs, remember? With the ability he has to indulge himself in sacrificial acts for the sake of others and/or for the sake of a loved one, this person can naturally be very seriously hurt and embittered. Sometimes the love object might prefer his Cancer/Horse let up on the devotion pedal. There is such a thing as too much abjection. If you take the Cancer/Horse's self-denial trip away from him, you remove his raison d'être. This can cast him down, and one begins to hear phrases like, "I don't know what I'm going to do about Sara Jane. She's drinking too much. She carouses too late. I'm really worried. I think she'll leave me." The cry of the professional victim rings out in the night.

Why doesn't he try drinking himself, or walking out on her? Why can he not just leap the quantum here and show Sara Jane who's boss? Because he's a Cancer/Horse, that's why. It's his pleasure to be the lover, the adulator, the admirer. He wants nothing to do with bravado if he has to hurt the one he loves to show it.

Don't worry about the Cancer/Horse, though. He's always the downtrodden sorry-looking mate who has put the house, the building where wifey's office is and the children and pets and cars in his name. This person owns an uncanny practicality. He or she doesn't miss a trick—and is not above a little sleight of hand of his own—to ensure his future, of course, and that of his loved ones.

This person is anything but stingy. He is in fact very generous of spirit and of pocket. But he is careful and cautious and so sure of what he wants that sometimes he just has to steal it. He's long-suffering and can withstand much discord and zaniness from partners and colleagues. He's a sort of rock of strength. But unlike, say, the sort of brute-force strength of an Ox or a Leo, the Cancer/Horse is a subtle emotional powerhouse whose mind simply never sits still.

Usually Cancer/Horses are very manual and capable of building things for their home. They might, for example, get involved in a hobby where artistic handwork is needed. Their product will rarely be avant-garde and abstract. The Cancer/Horse's artistic abilities are quotidian, not pedestrian but of the day-to-day, concerning people in slices of normal life, how they interact and what their joys and sorrows comprise.

There is a dangerous capacity for gloom here. The Cancer/Horse is perhaps the least selfish of Horses, but nonetheless he prefers to have it his way. Now, when the tables start to turn or even sometimes a glimmer of resistance appears on this Horse's horizon, he can sink to depths of depression from which it isn't simple to emerge. The despair may not even be apparent to those around the Cancer/Horse. He may ritually and pragmatically go through his daily paces without ever so much as heaving a sigh to hint that he's sliding towards emotional oblivion. Then, one day, his car crashes into a pole or he cuts off his index finger while chopping vegetables. Then (and only then) we notice that our Cancer/Horse hero has slid into a deep depression. The buildup of pain over taxes, loss of a loved one, moving house etc. will be slow and mute. Hardly noticeable. But the blues can last a long time. The answer? Seek professional help.

Love

Love is what makes the Cancer/Horse's world go round. He finds out very young that what he's looking for is to shower his excessive tenderness and affection on someone worthy and wonderful whom he can love for the rest of his natural life with a burning and excessive passion. But... he often marries late.

What frequently happens to the Cancer/Horse as he strides forth bearing this unreal mission in his huge heart and plunks it in the lap of somebody he thinks is deserving, is that the other person, the one he loves so much, is not at all on his wavelength. "Sure, I love you. Now would you mind if I got down off this wobbly pedestal?" says the loved one. After all, being loved so earnestly and graspingly can be truly annoying. If you are constantly revered as though you were some kind of household movie star, you may quickly tire of the role you've been given. It is not always easy to live up to other people's ideals. In his or her youth, there will be many sentimental disappointments for our Cancer/Horse.

If you love a Cancer/Horse and want to be the ever-after love of his life, then put on your dancing shoes. Really. If he loves you and adores your style and has chosen you above all others for the rest of his life till death do you part, you can retire from searching for emotional stability. The Cancer/Horse provides. You, as the loved one, need only to execute the steps of the daily dances with elegance and charm.

Compatibilities

Taurus, Virgo, Scorpio and Pisces are possibles for you in their Tiger, Sheep and sometimes Dog incarnations. Actually, you might not fare perfectly well with the snappish Virgo/Dog or the slightly pessimistic Pisces pooch. So for Dog partners, prefer Taureans and Scorpions. Aries, Libra and Capricorn/Rats are your archenemies. You're not mad for Aries or Libra/Oxen either. Don't fall in love with an Aries or Capricorn/Pig, please. Your natures are too divergent for lifelong harmony to ensue.

Home and Family

The Cancer/Horse's home will always be a friendly place, lived-in but not messy, cluttered but never sloppy. You can slouch on a Cancer/Horse's couch even if it did cost four thousand dollars more than any other couch in the store because the fabric was hand-woven by Hopi Indians. Cancer/Horses are hospitable and enjoy company. They love to gossip and chat and hash over ideas. When life is going well they are homey and cheery people. You can get your own beer out of the fridge and drink it from the bottle. Or they'll serve it to you in a crystal goblet—name your poison. When they are feeling their oats, Cancer/Horses love to play host. But when they are sad or down in the dumps, they retreat and you can forget going to the fridge for a beer because there won't be any in there.

As parents these people are, of course, extremely possessive and emotionally involved. Their kids, like their loved one, must be seen to be happy and stable and well educated and sensible and practical and and and...The Cancer/Horse is so entangled in his own web of exigencies regarding those he cares for that he leaves himself open for frequent disappointment. His kids sometimes just cannot measure up. They may want to escape the nest at a young age because of pressure they cannot bear coming from the Cancer/Horse parent.

As a relative or pal, this person is an angel. He doesn't invest himself all that much in outsiders but willingly shares his jolly hearth with those he likes, inviting people he fancies to come, stay, hang out and feel comfortable. After a few weeks, he will wish his guests gone. But telling them to leave will be extremely difficult as he enjoys the role of nice guy almost more than he hates having his guests sleeping all over the living room floor.

A Cancer/Horse child will need lots of security but must also be taught not to idealize teachers, school chums and others. He will begin early trying to invest people he likes with his own high standards. This should be discouraged and logic employed as soon as he knows how to reason. A classical education won't hurt the Cancer/Horse either. He takes readily to discipline and as a practical soul will want to succeed and please parents and teachers alike. In adolescence, he or she may go through a rebellious stage. Leave him alone. He'll come around. The Cancer/Horse is not capable of long-term alienation from those he cares about. He'll straighten out when he's ready. Patience.

Profession

There are few jobs that this person cannot undertake. He is both intelligent and skilled manually. He will always want to provide well for his family and give his kids a good start in life. Too, as he enjoys entertaining and having guests, he doesn't mind spending money. Therefore, he need to make quite a lot. But as we know, Horses are workers. They can outwork almost anyone except the Ox, who works for pleasure. Being a Cancer compounds this work penchant and endows him with a fine sense of artistry as well.

He'll be an excellent employee and an even better boss. Of course his tactic in bossing people is teaching by example. If he, the president of the company, can clean out the toilets, then why does the secretary hesitate to do so? He'll empty wastebaskets and stay up all night doing accounts just to show that he is working as hard as—if not harder than—anybody else in the whole office.

Career choices for the Cancer/Horse might be restaurant owner, professor, doctor, diplomat, cabinetmaker, builder, sculptor, entrepreneur or all of the above at the same time. This person is able to do almost any job, but I advise him to steer clear of jobs requiring abject solitude. He likes people too much to sit alone for days and days writing poetry, for example.

Famous Cancer/Horses:

Angela Merkel, Ann Landers, Claude Chabrol, Claudia Wells, Eddy Mitchell, H. Ross Perot, Ingmar Bergman, John Cusack, Josh Hartnett, Karen Black, Margot Robbie, Matthew Fox, Nelson Mandela, Nicole Scherzinger, Pierre Sabbagh, Polly Bergen, Prince Michael of Kent, Rembrandt, Robert Evans, The Duke of Windsor, Topher Grace.

CANCER
QUALITIES
IMAGINATION, INSIGHT, TENACITY,
AFFECTION, CARING, CAUTION
QUIRKS
AVARICE, IRRITABILITY, DESPONDENCY,
POSSESSIVENESS, MOODINESS,
HYPERSENSITIVITY
Motto: *"I feel"*
Elements: *Water, Moon, Cardinal*

--

SHEEP
QUALITIES
INVENTION, LACK OF FORESIGHT,
PERSEVERANCE, WHIMSY, GOOD MANNERS,
IMPRACTICALITY
QUIRKS
PARASITISM, SENSITIVITY,
TARDINESS, PESSIMISM, TASTE, WORRY
Motto: *"I depend"*
Elements: *Negative, Fire, Yin*

I like this sign. My father was a Cancer/Sheep. When I think about his personal kind of serious whimsy, tears well up. My dad was not only Cancer and Sheep, he was the perfect Cancer/Sheep! To start with, these people are adorable. They combine all the fancy-free laugh-a-minute capriciousness of the Sheep with the steady, tenacious and loving Cancer character. It's a great marriage. Nuttiness and lead.

Cancer/Sheep people bruise easily. They want to be solid citizens and go about their work taking care to see that things are in order and hoping that in the bargain everybody will be happy. They sincerely want everybody to have a good time, be honest and fair and hail-fellow-well-met. But the Cancer/Sheep is too naively earnest. He should know better, he's been through some terrible disappointments in his time, but the Cancerian Sheep persists in believing in Santa Claus.

Of course he doesn't really get to age thirty and still expect the Easter Bunny to hide colored eggs in his shoes. But practically. The Cancer/Sheep is a huge fun-loving kid trapped in the body of a grownup. Responsibility troubles his every waking hour. Accounts and repairs and loans and insurance policies cloud his widely innocent eyes. "Why do I have to do all this boring stuff?" whines the Sheep inside this large innocent kid. "Because you're a big person now and you have to make money for your family and provide for their educations," grumbles a voice inside the Cancer side of this subject's dual nature. The two priorities, giggle and grab, are constantly at war inside this person's many headaches. .

As a result of his built-in Cancerian striving for a solid home life, this Sheep character may decide at a young age that he wants nothing to do with poverty. He dreams, in fact, of making lots of money, striking it rich, making a bundle. Why? Because what he really wants to do is lie down in the pretty fresh-smelling grass and watch the clouds roll by. He's tired. But he works steadfastly till dawn on a scheme that will surely make him that killing. He's worn out. But he'll drive a thousand miles anyway just to see this guy about a deal who might just be the one guy who could put the Cancer/Sheep over the top. By the time this person is forty, he's worn out from trying to get to a point in his life where he can relax. Does he give up? Will he surrender the wheel to someone younger and craftier than him? Nope. He'll kill himself if he has to, but he's going for broke. So he bets everything on yet another scheme and works and slaves and stays up late, perhaps only to fail at that scheme too.

What the Cancer/Sheep longs to live in luxury's lap with the person he adores. He would like to travel, see the world and learn about exotic lands. But he can't. He's in too big a hurry to get to work.

I know a Cancerian Sheep who has a restaurant. To begin with, this person has that same cuteness I was talking about earlier. Secondly, typically, she is always working. And although she's exhausted, I never see her just sprawled on a chair in her restaurant at the end of a busy lunch time head in hands, wishing it were all over and she could just lock the door and go to sleep. Instead, she's up washing dishes and talking to stragglers and gossiping with regulars about this new movie or that play. This woman never sits down. She is constantly on her feet, pushing the rock of daily meals for ungrateful humans up that old hill. Of course she dreams of holidays and sunshine and lying about in the green fields of Elysium. But she never does. Even when this Cancer/Sheep goes on holiday she works: (1) at getting thin in a fat farm spa, (2) at learning about Egyptian culture, (3) at making jams and jellies to serve in her restaurant. It's true. I've seen this woman take off on a three-day vacation in order to slave over a hot stove. Is she looking for the pot of gold at the end of the rainbow? I don't think so. I think she's working toward leisure that she knows she will never have. Meanwhile, it's very attractive and the food is great.

With Cancer/Sheep the fare is always important, as is the style in which it is served up. My father always insisted on mother dragging out Limoges and crystal glasses and sterling silver utensils on any and all occasions. "Festive," he called it. And festive it was.

Cancer/Sheep love a party. They enjoy socializing and drinking and eating too much. They also get a big kick out of seeing old friends and cronies they may not have seen for a long time. Cancer/Sheep are lovingly sentimental and tenaciously fond of their many loyal friends.

Love

He may not know much about how to make a fortune, but the Cancer/Sheep knows everything about love. He's devoted and caring. And the Cancer/Sheep is amusing, fun to be with and inventive in the extreme when it comes to making up fun things to do. He'll take you to all the best plays and movies. He'll want to be up on what's going on, who is winning the Oscars and what star to watch rising in the dance or operatic world. Cancer/Sheep love their mates and companions deeply and without reserve. They take emotion seriously and never trifle with people's feelings.

If you love a Cancer/Sheep, you must strive to bolster him (or her). Every day, make him believe that he is the center of your universe, the star of his own show and the darling of the social set in which you run. Read Kafka. He was a Cancerian Sheep. You'll get this idea very clearly through The Metamorphosis. "I'm a weirdo" is typical of the way Cancer/Sheep perceive themselves. So show him that he's not your only multicolored fancy, but that his devotion is all that counts to you at any time. Requited love is the Cancerian Sheep's special domain. He needs security and he needs to feel loved—nay, worshiped! Then he can be pushed out into the world early so he'll have a head start.

Compatibilities

For your best partner possibilities, choose from among Taurus, Virgo and Scorpio/Horse people. Or maybe you'd like a Taurus, Scorpio or Pisces/Cat. If not, you can get on famously with any of the Taurus, Virgo, Scorpio or Pisces/Pigs. Don't frequent Aries, Libra or Capricorn/Dog subjects. The Dog is only good for you in small doses – as a friend or a colleague at work. Aries and Capricorn/Oxen too seem too rigid for your gentle nature. And I certainly don't advise you to take up with too many Tigers.

Home and Family

I've never known a Cancer born Sheep who didn't care desperately for his siblings, his cousins and aunts and uncles and of course his children and his children's children. You see, the Cancer/Sheep is not really terribly connected to this earth. He's a tiny bit of a flit wit. He forgets to remember to pay the school tuition. And he really didn't mean to but he neglected to bring home those sheets you needed for the guests who are arriving tonight. But he did remember to bring you a bottle of *Moët et Chandon* and some of your favorite munchies. To have a family is to be plugged in to the mainstream. The Cancer/Sheep depends on his family and on its demands to keep himself from flying off into space.

The Cancer/Sheep is a bit of a snob about interior design.. His surroundings will always be in good taste. He cares a lot about what people think of him. His status again is something that can attach him to terra firma. As can his authority. And watch out for the domination crises native to this sign. The Cancer/Sheep is a natural sap. His very epidermis is like finest velvet and cannot be grazed without bruising. So, as he is Cancer and not some lighthearted la-di-da sign, when he is confronted with a weighty problem that appears to be out of proportion to his squeamishness, he starts to assert himself. I called it bullying when I was a kid. It's really Sheepying. And it's a pain in the rear end. As a parent the Cancer/Sheep is kind and loving, but he's bound and determined to be boss.

Profession

Cancer/Sheep don't have foresight about money matters. They love to spread what money they have around, lavishing presents and entertainment on loved ones and investing in impressive models of automobile. But they hate to pay bills. They don't want to save up for a washing machine. They want that machine now. So they are big on credit plans of all sorts, and can borrow themselves into debt far beyond their means.

Were I to advise a Cancer/Sheep about a career choice, I think I'd suggest a "glamour" job. Fashion coordinator or advertising artist or Beverly Hills hairdresser would do. But I know very well that my advice would be met with a groan. Cancer/Sheep don't want to be just plain employed. They want to be enterprising and do it themselves. Of course, they have great difficulty organizing their own business or shop, because they hate to plan further than the end of next week and may just get in a stock of champagne when they need nuts and bolts. So, perhaps it's more realistic to offer the Cancer/Sheep more free-wheeling choices such as novelist, journalist, movie star or tycoon.

Famous Cancer/Sheep:
Adrienne King, Alice Munro, Amelie Mauresmo, Andrew Divoff, Buckminster Fuller, Busy Phillips, Cindy Lauper, Dan Howell, David Steele, Eve Hewson, Franz Kafka, Iris Murdoch, Isabelle Adjani, Jade Barbosa, Jimmy Smits, Karen Cheryl, Leslie Caron, Lino Ventura, Lyle Brocato, Madylin Sweeten, Pamela Anderson, Terri Ivens, Travis Fimmel, Will Ferrell, Willem Dafoe.

CANCER
QUALITIES
IMAGINATION, INSIGHT, TENACITY,
AFFECTION, CARING, CAUTION
QUIRKS
AVARICE, IRRITABILITY, DESPONDENCY,
POSSESSIVENESS, MOODINESS,
HYPERSENSITIVITY
Motto: *"I feel"*
Elements: *Water, Moon, Cardinal*

--

MONKEY
QUALITIES
IMPROVISATION, CUNNING, STABILITY,
SELF-INVOLVEMENT, WIT, OPPORTUNISM
QUIRKS
DECEIT, RUSE, LOQUACITY,
LEADERS, SILLINESS, ZEAL
Motto: *"I plan"*
Elements: *Positive, metal, Yang*

Cancer/Monkey—the emotional planner. This person is forever awake to new concepts and possible avenues. He's always on his toes. Even in the middle of the night, this variety of Cancer is raring to find out who makes the kinds of candles that exactly replicate church candles from Poland in the eighteenth century. Like all Monkeys, the Cancer/Monkey is a problem-solver. He can not only see a situation for what it is—as he is coldly objective when necessary—but he can see through cloudy dilemmas and for that reason come quickly to the end of them. The Cancer/Monkey lets very little grass grow under his feet.

There is, in this tasteful creature whose interests range from obscure Amazonia to collecting various types of bus tickets used throughout the world, an inclination to social-climb. This penchant doesn't always show itself in the classic manner. That is, you won't see a Cancer/Monkey sidling up to Mrs. Snootyboot just to cop an invite to her next ball. The Cancer/Monkey is far from subtle about his desire for social recognition. He will come at it from his job success, for example. First, he will see to it that he is the best known in his field of endeavor. Then, of course, everyone will want to know him and he'll begin being invited to all the right parties.

The Cancer/Monkey is a calculating creature who leaves few stones unturned in his quest for success in his job. But there is one thing that can hold him back. It's called sentiment. The Cancer/Monkey may be a ruseful and cunning Monkey—but he is irredeemably a caring and possessive, hypersensitive Cancer as well. Caring, although he does it supremely well, is the Cancer/Monkey's nemesis. If, for example, his loved one doesn't want to live in a big city and he is well known as a crackerjack big-city planner, the Cancer/Monkey may concede the boondocks to his beloved. He may not be perfectly happy there because his employ is limited and he needs to feel useful and busy and even top-drawer about his work. But when he loves, the Cancer/Monkey does so with such brainless enthusiasm, wearing his heart not only on his sleeve but all over his face too, that there's no cure for what he's got.

The moods and grumps and blues that can overcome Cancer/Monkeys are of epic proportion. He doesn't take well to criticism because he really wants to do his best at all times and be right on the button and never err or stray like a lost sheep. Any emotional or career setback can do this person in for a week of gloom, insomnia and even a bit of drinking or other unhealthy indulgences.

Whatever he does, the Cancer/Monkey will be clever with money. He makes save investments, wise moves on the financial chess board, and is in fact a bit of a wealth wizard. He's not really the type of person to become gigantically, sickeningly, wallowingly rich, but the Cancer/Monkey is a prosperous person. He always has a little bit more than enough.

The Cancer/Monkey is sure to be talented in the arts. Whether connoisseur or practitioner, this person strives for an frequently attains excellence in creative fields. The Cancer/Monkey is talented, of course. But he is also gifted with that magical Monkey wit and sense of improvisation. He thinks well on his feet and even emotes effectively as he's working.

The Cancer/Monkey does not require thirty days' notice to accept an offer to a dinner party. He knows right away when you ring him up if he's busy or whether you have interesting parties and exciting guests. He also knows if he's tired or feeling ill and should avoid late nights and rich foods. The Cancer/Monkey is a monster of good sense and profound yet controlled emotions.

Cancer/Monkeys have excellent manners. Ladies first and hats off in the elevator and may I carry your briefcase, sir? This willingness to serve might be interpreted as obsequiousness or even seen as an effort to seduce—it's definitely the latter. Cancer/Monkeys love to be liked—and they prefer to be loved. And I mean loved. These creatures are sexual in the extreme and masters of monkey business in all of its most rococo and baroque forms. Cancer/Monkeys love their homes—but oh, you kid!

Love

Promiscuity is such an ugly term. Let me just say that the Cancer/ Monkey exhibits a certain prodigality in his sexploits. Cancer/ Monkeys like to make love. They are curious about sex and would do a lot more of it than just breakfast, lunch and dinner, plus midnight snacks, if they had the physical wherewithal.

As they are also quite possessive and conscientious people, Cancer/Monkeys .suffer from their own frequent and urgent desires. They are secretly afraid that their regular partner with whom they are madly in love and also want to make love to every fifteen minutes might somehow be exactly like them. This would he tragic as Cancer/Monkeys hate to be wronged in the classical sense. They get angry and can be quite feisty when irked.

I don't mean to say that Cancer/Monkeys don't know how to love their mates. On the contrary, Cancer/Monkeys arc geniuses at adoring their mates—all of them! Gifts. Trips. Candlelight dinners. Fur coats. You name it, honey, and you've got it

Now if you want to be the mate of one of these densely talented and interesting people, you have to play their game. I mean by this that you must show your loyalty and devotion to them by being a little bit difficult, spoiled or even nagging (this keeps them un their toes and they like it that way). You should try to be the type of person who earns the Cancer/Monkey's respect, as ultimately he's interested in souls far more than in the multitudes of bodies he knows too well. If you show courage and more fortitude and rectitude, the Cancer/Monkey will buy you a house on the moon (if you ask nicely).

Compatibilities

Cancers marry well with Taurus. Virgo, Scorpio and Pisces. As a Monkey type you will be well advised to pick a Dragon or a Rat from within those four occidental classifications. If 1 were you I would circumvent Libra/Oxen. They are a teensy bit too competitive with you. Aries, Libra and Capricorn/Dogs are out, too, as are Aries and Capricorn/Horses. Stay away from Aries/Pigs, too.

Home and Family

As a relative, this person is a champion of responsibility. He will go very far out of his way to prove filial devotion. He's generous to nephews and nieces and caring about his parents" needs. As a sibling, I'm not so sure. This person tends to think he's risen above the level whence he came and may, upon the death of his own parents, decide to see less of his sisters and brothers than before. He likes them. But he feels superior to them.

Sacrifice for the sake of the kids is not difficult for the Cancer/ Monkey. But he doesn't realty want those finger marks on his seventeenth century parchment lampshades, so would you mind putting the kids bad in their rooms? Having children cramps the Cancer/ Monkey's style. If he has really a lot of money, then he will probably have plenty of kids and nannies and boarding schools. If not, he will be out a lot, or locked in his study, or holed up in the bedroom reading. He will take his kids on outings and spend time helping them with studies. But the turmoil—the basic round-the-clock bustle of kids—gets on his nerves. The Cancer/Monkey is really too sensitive to put up with people barging in at all hours and eating out of his bowl. He will be authoritarian in a semiserious way.

The Cancer/Monkey child is all sensitivity and very little guile. It is only by attending the school of hard knocks that he grows wary and opportunistic. He must be protected against all variety of cruelty (school, parental or other) and watched for signs of allergies or other nervous disorders. He is extremely talented and needs security in which to develop his gifts.

Profession

Career choices here are varied. The Cancer/Monkey is naturally endowed with every sort of ability. He can be an artist or write about art. He has talent for everything from ballet to war. He's zealous, and wily, and power-hungry too. A clever tactician, this fellow will rise to great heights in his chosen field by means of strategic moves and lots of overtime.

The Cancer/Monkey will not, however, usually get to be number one in his professional life. His fatal flaw is sensitivity. He feels too deeply and will always hesitate before committing the one horrid crime necessary to his supreme achievement. He can very well accept being second in command because he doesn't really want to have to take the low blows that bosses have to accept. But in command he will be anyway. In work situations where there are colleagues and coworkers to deal with, the Cancer/Monkey may not be very well liked. He's tough—on himself and on others. And he seems to float so easily to almost the top of the heap that he creates jealousies.

This person can be painter, musician, poet or the like. But he can also be a successful doctor or lawyer, antique or art dealer, journalist or advertising executive. He'd be good at investment banking too. The theater or cinema? Somewhat talented but a bit too social-conscious to become a real star.

Famous Cancer/Monkeys:
Alexander Dinelaris Jr., Amália Rodriguez, Amadeo Modigliani, Amy Vanderbilt, Artnesa Krasniqi, Billie Catherine Lourd, Billy Crudup, Calvin Coolidge, David Brinkley, Douglas Booth, Eric Strecht, Isaac Stern, Julius Caesar, Lord Byron, Michael Weatherly, Michel Polnareff, Michelle Kwan, Nelson Rockefeller, Salvador Allende, Selena Gomez, Yul Brynner.

CANCER
QUALITIES
IMAGINATION, INSIGHT, TENACITY,
AFFECTION, CARING, CAUTION
QUIRKS
AVARICE, IRRITABILITY, DESPONDENCY,
POSSESSIVENESS, MOODINESS,
HYPERSENSITIVITY
Motto: *"I feel"*
Elements: *Water, Moon, Cardinal*

--

ROOSTER
QUALITIES
RESILIENCE, ENTHUSIASM, CANDOR,
CONSERVATISM, CHIC, HUMOR
QUIRKS
COCKINESS, BOASTFULNESS, BLIND FAITH,
PEDANTRY, BOSSINESS, DISSIPATION
Motto: *"I overcome"*
Elements: *Negative, Metal, Yin*

Don't look to this warmhearted person for forgiveness. There is lots of deep Cancerian tenderness here. But there is also a great chunk of Rooster abrasiveness. This subject is a closet position-seeker and, despite his jolly—even rotund—appearance, carries vengeance to its drastic conclusion every time. You may find him or her open and even charming at first. But probe a bit. Or try living next door to one of these folks. It can be a trial by fire.

The outgoing side of this person's nature wants to be of assistance to others. He or she will show newcomers the ropes and volunteer to hand out programs at church on Sunday. But hold on. Isn't that pleasant chubby woman over there the one who snapped at little Jimmy in the supermarket the other day? Yep. You guessed it. The Cancerian Rooster has an irritable, cranky side. It's as though all the up-front heartiness had a dark and sinister lining. The Cancer/Rooster is strength personified. He or she will always have enormous energy and a gargantuan capacity for endurance in work. Never forget that this person has probably worked harder and struggled longer uphill than most to achieve whatever position he or she has in life. He is not going to relinquish such hard-earned gain to some fly-by-night smarty pants.

Cancer/Roosters are amusing people. They like to laugh and to make others chuckle with their stories of home and pets and kids. They are very hard-working and give out advice (even when it isn't asked for) willingly. They always present themselves well. They know how to make the best of whatever looks nature has given them and are natty dressers as well.

They are indefatigably willing to work overtime and lend a hand during lunch hour. But every supplementary second the Cancer/Rooster gives to the cause or contributes to the order, whether he knows it or not, is designed to help him stay in position.

Because of this clutching need for getting and keeping a foothold (both of these creatures have pinching claw mechanisms), the Rooster Crab has little time for minor distractions. (He is impatient with frivolity and deplores wasted time or goods.) Too, any situation in life, be it professional or romantic, will burst and collapse when too tightly squeezed.

This is exactly what happens in the life of Cancer/Roosters. The Cancer side grabs and claws and gets. But one day the Rooster gets a little too cocky, and boom! Down he tumbles. It takes a while, but Cancer/Rooster always stumbles to his feet and eventually toddles off to start clawing and grabbing again.

Cancer/Rooster is not a disastrous sign. It's moody but it's also both prolific and efficient. This person will be self-styled, original and interesting—especially in familiar surroundings. He's sharp-tongued and hyper-critical of those he feels he can daunt. And he's both loving and giving at the same time. He's not afraid of change – as long as he initiates the change himself.

Love

In love relationships the Cancer/Rooster is both constant and sure. He does not cotton to the variations of approach necessary in order to be one who sleeps around, and therefore chooses to remain faithful. In fact, personal serenity is essential to this person's equilibrium. While his work life vacillates vastly and his public life is often chockablock with activity, he prefers a quiet, traditional sort of home life.

If you love a Cancer/Rooster, prepare to learn how to cook. These people live to eat—and drink—and they enjoy receiving guests, whom they entertain lavishly right down to the last crystal liqueur glass. They are tender-hearted, too. You will have to tolerate their numerous pets and their desire for hordes of children. In return the Cancer/Rooster gives allegiance to home. He's not the most imaginative lover in the world. But he's there and you'll always know it.

Compatibilities

The Taurean born Horse gets under your skin in a pleasant fashion. Otherwise you get on with Oxen, Dragons and Snakes of the Virgo, Scorpio and Pisces persuasions. Taurus/Snakes, with their uncanny intuition, enchant you. Restrain yourself in the presence of Aries, Libra and Capricorn/Cats. Don't try to build a life with an Aries or Capricorn/Dog. Eschew the Libra/Rooster.

Home and Family

The center of any Cancerian's life is at home. The Rooster is able to leave home rather readily and as a rule doesn't care too much for dandling babies or chucking toddlers under their chins. But in this subject the Cancer side wins out. Cancer/Roosters love their homes. They busy their practical Roosterish minds and nimble fingers with projects and plans for new wings and roof-raisings. They reorganize the kitchen cupboards twice a week and herd the animals through their respective molts and shots and flea-powderings. These people are talented at homemaking. Their decor will be cozy but practical and—I would venture—neat as a pin.

The Cancer/Rooster parent is a kind of saint, giving to and loving kids, yet knowing instinctively how to make them behave. These parents can be harsh and vindictive. But underneath that tough exterior they are adoringly kind.

As a kid, the Cancer/Rooster will be serious and hard-driving for acceptance in his peer group. He will be crushed if he doesn't win and keep first place in sports or grades or whatever area he excels in. He will be a sensitive child whose sharp tongue could get him into some trouble in school. You can expect this child to appreciate all he or she is given in the way of affection and material things. Try to get this little person to talk about himself. It's not his strong suit, but it could make the difference between happiness and sorrow in his future. He must learn to expand and become flexible.

Profession

This person will shine in jobs that require precision and tenacity. The Cancer/Rooster is an effective human being. He does not seek to indulge himself in frippery. He wants to apply his mettle to some serious pursuits and he doesn't like to search without result.

As a boss, I should think this person insufferable. Holding on to hard-won power with fierce talons makes the Cancer/Rooster testy and leads to some very feisty, prima donna behavior. There's a goody-goody streak in this subject that makes him tend to want to lord it over others. Better if he or she takes a secondary post with a nice title on the door.

Suitable jobs for Cancer/Roosters are: scientist, executive secretary, restaurateur, TV producer, dentist, shop owner.

Famous Cancer/Roosters:

Ally Brooke, Ariana Grande, Ayelet Zurer, Carly Simon, Claudio Abbado, Clive Standin, Fran Kranx, François Reichenbach, Jake LaMotta, Jamie Thomas King, John Glenn, Joseph Papp, Josh Holloway, Katia Granoff, Michael Huisman, Nancy Reagan, Perrie Edwards, Princess Alexia of the Netherlands, Rick Husband, Robyn Weigert, Stavros Niarchos, Taylor Kinney.

CANCER
QUALITIES
IMAGINATION, INSIGHT, TENACITY,
AFFECTION, CARING, CAUTION
QUIRKS
AVARICE, IRRITABILITY, DESPONDENCY,
POSSESSIVENESS, MOODINESS,
HYPERSENSITIVITY
Motto: *"I feel"*
Elements: *Water, Moon, Cardinal*

--

DOG
QUALITIES
CONSTANCY, UNSOCIABILITY,
RESPECTABILITY, SELF-RIGHTEOUSNESS,
INTELLIGENCE, TACTLESSNESS
QUIRKS
UNEASINESS, CRITICISM, DUTY,
CYNICISM, HEROISM, MORALITY
Motto: *"I worry"*
Elements: *Positive, Metal, Yang*

Omnipresent in the native of this sign is "feeling." Emotions run both deep and high in this sensitive—even touchy—character. Cancer/Dogs seem to carry a blinking sensor-beam radar system on their very skins. Everything affects them and affects them profoundly. A word, a glance or—god forbid—a harsh remark can dissolve these susceptible souls into a heap of nervous prostration in a wink. Cancer/Dogs are born to be artistic. Touched by the magic wand of aestheticism, these people need protection from the big bad world and its vicissitudes. They are born innocently sensitive and long to be able to remain so all the days of their lives.

Despite their hyper receptivity to stimuli from the outside, Cancer/Dog people do get on in life. They secure jobs and have children and take care of business in a serious and competent manner. Cancer/Dogs get involved in complex and difficult schemes and are always attracted to the most baroque of problems, which they set about solving with quiet grace.

The most intricate circumstances, in all their complexity and labyrinthine turns, do not daunt this patient, serious character one bit. Cancer/Dogs are the people who burn midnight oil, smoke too many cigarettes and worry through dense thickets of ideas and plans till they sort out a brilliant solution. Even the least of Cancer/ Dogs will be drawn to improving on life's scenery. Dogs born in Cancer love to garden and redecorate and plan buildings and books and paintings and musical compositions. They are both creatively and technically gifted.

Worry is their main hobby. Cancerian Dogs fret over any and everything that comes along. They panic and grow anxious at the least missed appointment or deadline. They agonize over the exhibition of their works and stay awake nights gnawing at themselves over whether or not the woman in the department store who sold them the paint brushes was lying when she said the brushes were real sable. Cancer/Dogs can fuss over what seems to less testy creatures minor and petty detail. For a Cancer/ Dog the air he breathes is rife with menace. He's careful about absolutely every part of his existence. But no matter how cautious he tries to be, life persists in surprising him.

As a result of his excessively wary approach, the Cancer/Dog sometimes gives the impression of being painted into his own corner. Is he afraid of his own shadow? Is he a little paranoid? To tell you the truth, I think he is. The average Cancer/Dog person has one finger on the panic button at all times—and it shows. "Did I turn off the gas? Fill out the tax form? Send in the check? Get the oil checked?" Their minds churn with preoccupation over doing "the right thing".

Being on the qui vive all the time does not, however, stop this person from being entirely reasonable and enormously just in his dealings with others. If he believes in someone he will go to the limits of his ability to bring succor to them. His capacity for empathy is enormous and his sixth sense about what is right and meet in any given situation is always accurate.

The Cancer/Dog is a giver, too. He's generous and kindly and because he wants very much for others to measure up to the heights of self-sacrifice of which he himself is capable, he is adorably encouraging to the people he loves. Patient and gentle and good, the Cancer/Dog makes an ideal partner. If he is involved with others, whether in business or in some artistic project. he is never after the fame or the glory of success for himself. Cancer/Dogs merely want to get on with making something wonderful happen. They are anything but egomaniacal, but because they place beauty and rectitude so high on their list of priorities, their goals may seem selfish or demanding.

Fact is, Dogs born in Cancer are not really of this world. Left to their own devices, they would probably manage very well to set themselves comfortably up in a cave somewhere, get themselves some books and papers and invite along some pets to love them—and maybe a mate to admire—and keep themselves busy till the cows come home with many useful and beautiful pursuits.

Love

The special province of Cancer/Dog people is their uncanny ability to love others. Although harmony won't necessarily invest their every affair, you can be sure that the Cancer/Dog half of any couple is the one who is making the most real effort to keep things on an even keel. A snappish person, the Cancer/Dog is often on edge and seems cranky when he's really just insecure about something. His need for true affection and tenderness is imperative to his very physical health. Love really does make this person's world go round.

The Cancer/Dog cannot live well without loving. He must have an object for his bottomless well of emotion. Without somebody to shower with indulgence and admiration, the Cancer/Dog will be tempted to give up, lie down and waste away. He must be loyal and faithful to another soul and he desperately needs to feel awful if he dares betray said lover. Cancer/Dogs thrive on the emotional tension between themselves and the other in any love relationship. Without the daily thrill of feeling love for someone, they skulk about looking whipped and sorrowful.

If you love a Cancerian Dog person, you must arm yourself with patience. There will be two big problems involved in maintaining a loving rapport. On the one hand, your Cancer/Dog sweetheart will seem thoroughly unavailable at times and reluctant to step down from his creativity cloud. And on the other, this lovable bundle of feelings will seem to cling to you until you choke. With Cancer/Dogs it's all or nothing.

Compatibilities

You will get along with Taurus, Virgo and Pisces/Cats. Taurus, Scorpio and Virgo/Tigers are strong favorites as well. Horses born in Scorpio might irritate you, but almost any other Horse will be a good bet. You admire the Horse's capacity for hard work and self abnegation. Aries, Libra and/or Capricorn/Dragons and Sheep unnerve you. As for Aries/Pigs—forget it! They are creative. But they want to be boss. And everybody knows that's your job.

Home and Family

Of course, this esthetically-oriented person will invariably abide in loveliness. Surroundings are essential to the Cancer anyway. Cancers of all persuasions need to make homes and are born with the nesting instinct. This particular Cancer subject, whose dogged pursuit of the aesthetic know no frontiers, will automatically want to evolve in a safe and secure—as well as beautiful and well-designed—ambience.

The Cancer/Dog's family is everything to him. But, as I said earlier, sometimes he seems absent or distant from his natural emotional ties. The truth is, no matter what the Cancer/Dog is preoccupied by, he's always most at ease and feels best in his skin when there are family member about. He may be writing the greatest novel of all time or painting masterpiece in his hermetically sealed studio, but Cancer/Dog is listening for the friendly noises of family life below stairs. The smells and sound of everyday existence keep the Cancer/Dog's feet on the ground. As parent he is dutiful and kindly.

As a child, this person is hypersensitive and emotionally fragile. All brands of loving attention are in order. He doesn't require applause so much as he does tenderness, direction and sincerity from parents and siblings. The Cancer/Dog child needs to be understood and his creative side seeks indulgence. Lessons of all sorts, encouragement, slow patience teaching and plenty of hand-knit afghans to curl up in front of the fire with will ensure the stable future of this gentle talent.

Profession

The life's work of Cancer/Dogs is cut out for them at birth. Learning how to apply sensitivity and creative talents to life in a modern world is as large a chunk as anyone can be expected to bite off. Directing and molding talent into workable forms will take a lot of this person's time and energy He cannot be expected to work in a bank or to take orders in a hamburger joint. He will not be fulfilled by any impersonal work. Embellishing life is what he does best.

Were I to hire a Cancer/Dog, I would never worry that he'd be late for work or forget to add up a column of figures. These people are hyper conscientious. So I would let me Cancer/Dog employee make his own schedule and encourage him to work weekends and take off during the week if it pleased him. Cancer/Dogs know the value of money and are careful to maintain their accounts and keep their debts to a minimum. Not only do they make excellent workers in areas where their creativity is challenged, but they can even be bosses—and good ones—provided the area in which they're called upon to exert authority is an attractive one where their talents are used to the fullest extent. They can direct operations on a building site, as long as the building is the Louvre or the Taj Mahal or a cathedral on top of a mountain. To be worthwhile, life must be beautiful. We already know that Cancer/Dogs make excellent artists of all varieties. They can also try dealing in antiques or paintings or even agenting for painters or owning an art gallery. Cancer/Dogs make good commercial artists, too, and building and home decoration is one of their obvious career field specialties.

Famous Cancer/Dogs:

Alexander Calder, Chris O'Donnell, Claude Debussy, Connor Jessup., Erin Moriarty, Estee Lauder, Fiona Shaw, George W. Bush, Giorgio Armani, Gloria Stuart, Hilarie Burton, Hussein (Crown Prince of Jordan), Jared Padalecki, Jean Anouilh, Justin Chambers, Lily Rabe, Lizzy Capalan, Marcel Proust, Nick Offerman, Paul Thomas Anderson, Paul Wesley, Pierre Cardin, Priyanka Chopra, Sylvester Stallone, Toby Kebbell, William Hanna.

CANCER
QUALITIES
IMAGINATION, INSIGHT, TENACITY,
AFFECTION, CARING, CAUTION
QUIRKS
AVARICE, IRRITABILITY, DESPONDENCY,
POSSESSIVENESS, MOODINESS,
HYPERSENSITIVITY
Motto: *"I feel"*
Elements: *Water, Moon, Cardinal*

--

PIG
QUALITIES
SCRUPULOUSNESS, GALLANTRY, SINCERITY,
VOLUPTUOUSNESS, CULTURE, HONESTY
QUIRKS
CREDULITY, WRATH, HESITATION,
MATERIALISM, GOURMANDISM, PIGHEADEDNESS
Motto: *"I civilize"*
Elements: *Negative Water, Yin*

The self-starter of all time, this person could live on a desert island and rise at dawn, say his prayers, prepare his tea, wash up, go to the rock that serves as the office, slave for fourteen straight hours, come back to his grass shack, prepare himself a huge feast, eat it, say his prayers, lie down under the palm tree and start again the next morning. Integrity is a word invented to describe Cancer/Pigs. They are whole, complete unto themselves, and require little other than fawning admiration, unflinching affection and obedient devotion from others. That's an exaggeration. Cancer/Pigs are utterly generous and charitable in the extreme. But they do like things their way and generally one way or the other see to it that the wheels turn in the direction they dictate.

The Cancer/Pig is home- and luxury-loving. Perhaps the most opulent of all Pigs in the New Zodiac, the Cancerian Pig often accumulates wealth through the purchase of art objects and real property. Then, he finds ways to turn his wealth into more wealth. He, of all acquisitive Cancers, is the most conserving of riches. You can give a Cancer/Pig five dollars and come back in twenty years to claim your million. That also is hyperbole. But seriously, this Cancer/Pig fellow is an ace at making money and making it stick. He's an art freak of the first water. No exhibit escapes his notice. No rising young sculptor gets away without selling him a bronze. The Cancer/Pig not only knows how to appreciate art, but he is truly fascinated by its conservation and perpetuation.

There is an odd dichotomy within the Cancer/Pig personality structure. On the one hand this character must be on his guard against all variety of excess. He is tempted by all manner of extravagance. The flip side of this unhealthy pull to overindulge is excessive self-denial. As the Cancerian Pig sees in his deepest soul an exorbitant capacity for letting his hair down too far, his reaction is frequently to cultivate a strict personal policy of austerity: No fun. None at all. Never go outside and play. Stay in and study. Never buy yourself pretty clothes or indulge in beautiful foods. Just keep busy and accumulate and acquire and save and preserve.

Feeling is for other folks. Obviously this Spartan philosophy is nothing more than self-indulgence in reverse. It's a problem for Cancer/Pigs. They must learn to moderate and seek balance in both directions.

Shows of force on the part of Cancer/Pigs are frequent and impressive. The scowl. The glare of intent. The tightening of the lips. It can be scary. But it isn't real. That copse of bushy eyebrows is only there for effect. The Cancer/Pig is really a darling, a charitable, warmhearted and obsessively giving person. He is rigorous and gives the impression of severity. But he's really always laughing inside himself and mostly he's dreaming up new schemes to be able to live his life exactly as he pleases.

Oh, you may scold and deride him, but the Cancer/Pig will barrel on ahead with his plans and his hefty donations and generous contributions, his rushings about to art shows and oriental rug exhibits. He hears you—his ear is far from deaf to your supplications—but he does not heed you, and never will.

Tenacity is this person's real trump card. Nothing short of serious physical or mental illness can keep a Cancer/Pig down. He holds on for dear life to his ideals and his ways. He believes fervently and goes stubbornly beyond reason in his religion. His politics are clear-cut and no-nonsense, buckle down and button up, starch in the sails. As far as the Cancer/Pig is concerned, what's wrong with this world is that nobody has any tenets to live by anymore. Where is the old morality? Where are the good old days? Who stole the stiff upper lips of an entire generation? He cannot understand it. The Cancer/Pig does not know why people don't just stop all this shilly-shallying and get on with the work of the world. Then, he thinks, they would have time for fun and games and relaxation when they get old.

Modern life disappoints the pure-hearted Cancer/Pig. If he can struggle so unceasingly against the forces of evil and never even be discouraged, why doesn't everybody else do likewise? Because they're lazy, Piggie. And self-seeking and mediocre. But we can't say that about you, can we?

Love

The Cancer/Pig's capacity for true, pure, unmitigated love is enormous. His talent for perversion is about equal. The numerous excesses at play within the scrupulously emotional Cancer/Pig can wreak havoc on his nervous system and indeed sour him on romantic love and its complexities forever.

This person is sensitive in the extreme, traditional and dutiful. There is no apparent reason for him not to have the most satisfying of sexual and sentimental lives. But there's always the Cancer/Pig peculiarity regarding self-denial and restriction of pleasure. Just as he's about to settle down to enjoy himself for a few minutes, the Good Fairy sweeps into his bedroom asking, "Will this act lead to others, more debauched and less positive? Will I end up on skid row if I take a drink? Will I explode into a million shatters if I make love?" One does not get very far in a love affair with such nagging thoughts riding around upstairs.

So love is complicated for Cancer/Pigs. It's too much and at the same time it is so precious little that the Cancer/Pig disdains it as weakness.

If you love a Cancer/Pig, seduce him. Woo him. Court and badger him into loving you back. Be they tempting gargantuan dinners or Spartan repasts, meals work quite well on these reluctant subjects. Flowers please them, too. But a basket of fresh blueberries, a newborn puppy or a just-out-of-the-oven loaf of crunchy bread would probably work better. Cancer/Pigs are inexorably drawn to earthy down-home seduction routines.

Compatibilities

You fancy the solid yet slightly mad Taurus/Tiger and his talented Sheep counterpart. You will also be well matched with a Virgo, Scorpio or Pisces/Cat or Sheep subject. Taurus/Rat is always right there to protect you from your own severity, too. Don't hitch your wagon to an Aries or Libra/Monkey. Capricorn/ Roosters are also a no-no. All Snakes will enchant you. Leave them alone. They spend more money than you can ever earn. And when the money source dries up, the Snake slithers out the back door, carrying the family silver.

Home and Family

Cancer/Pigs were meant for this area of life. They adore their cousins and their cousins' kids and their cousins' cousins' kids. Cancer/Pigs are forever out there buying presents for godchildren and their own children and the neighbor's little boy who is sick in bed. Cancer/Pigs are naturally charitable and giving of their riches. But what makes the Cancer/Pig person so generous to children or to those less sophisticated than himself is innocence. The Cancer/Pig admires innocence and will always regard it as a virtue.

In family matters the Cancer/Pig can become too controlling of others. There is so much real domestic devotion here that family members who are adored and solicited by this magnanimously loving relative may actually feel smothered. Too much is too much—it may be considered meddlesome.

The Cancer/Pig's surroundings will be, to say the least, opulent. If he doesn't live in a wondrous huge house with lots of wall space and high-ceilinged rooms, where will the Cancer/Pig keep that art collection?

It may seem improbable to you, but I dare say the average annual income figures of Cancer/Pig subjects are among the highest in the world. Their tastes are classical and their homes always imposing and grand.

Too quiet and reserved to be completely comfortable as a child, this colossus of feeling and culture will prove a diligent student. His room should be lined with books, and traditional artwork made available to his discerning eye. Don't try to jolly him into behaving like a cheerful little imp who giggles all the time. It just plain will not work. This is a serious and mild-mannered little kid who, if crossed or too often teased, may burn a hole through you with his glare. His anger is terrific. But, thank Zeus, infrequent. Sulking may be a problem. Don't spank. Reason. And hug.

Profession

One quick look at this forbidding person and you just know that he's destined for greatness. Thing is, the Cancer/Pig is not one to go searching for admiration or applause. Instead, in his own imposing and stolidly graceful manner, he goes forward—always forward—never back. The Cancer/Pig doesn't know what it's like not to have his own way. To him, there is no other way. And the annoying thing is he is mostly right! Going about things as they ought to be gone about and you will be amazed at the result. For a Cancer/Pig right is might.

For a Cancer/Pig career, the first choice is monarch. The next is pope, and the third might be zillionaire. But seriously, this subject should first be educated till he can't see the letters on the pages anymore. Then he should be let loose on the business or artistic world (or both). Whatever he does, it will be excellent and admirable, serious and heartfelt. The Cancer/Pig makes a wonderful boss because he finds it difficult to imagine holding any lowly position. The Cancer/Pig doesn't mind doing menial work. Oh no. He'll get in there and scrub out the stalls with the best of 'em. But he prefers to give the order to clean out those stables. I cannot imagine him taking orders from any but an Ox.

Famous Cancer/Pigs:

Camilla Duchess of Cornwall, Carlos Santana, Charlotte Gainsbourg, Cheryl Cole, Corey Feldman, Dalai Lama, Donald Sutherland, Erika Jayne, Ernest Hemingway, Federico Garcia Lorca, Georges Pompidou, Georgie Henley, Ginger Rogers, Henry VIII, Hume Cronyn, John D. Rockefeller, Jordyn Wieber, Juan Trippe, Kristi Yamaguchi, Kurt Warner, Laurent Terzieff, Marc Chagall, Marcel Achard, Robert Knepper.

LEO
QUALITIES
NOBILITY, POWER, LOYALTY,
PHILANTHROPY, WARMTH, PROTECTION
QUIRKS
ARROGANCE, SELF-SATISFACTION,
VANITY, TYRANNY, PROMISCUITY,
IMMODESTY
Motto: *"I will"*
Elements: *Fire, Sun, Fixed*

--

RAT
QUALITIES
NERVOUSNESS, INFLUENCE,
ACQUISITIVENESS, THIRST FOR POWER,
INTELLECTUAL SKILL, CHARISMA
QUIRKS
APPEAL, VERBOSITY, THRIFT,
SOCIABILITY, GUILE, MEDDLING
Motto: *"I rule"*
Elements: *Positive Water, Yang*

The cinematic image that comes to mind when I ponder the combination of Leo and Rat is of Gene Kelly, umbrella in hand, dancing through teeming rain and singin' his heart out. Leo/Rats have it all over everybody else in the capacity for conjuring sunshine. They can make a party out of a thunderstorm more lavishly and efficiently than you can imagine possible. Leo/Rats' attributes are many, their faults serious but few.

When he is loved and properly admired, the Leo/Rat strides through life as though he were going to consume its every facet before noon. He is active and exudes uncommon self-confidence. He has his own rhythm and knows how to pace his every activity so it fits into his jam-packed day. Leo/Rats can take an early breakfast with the queen, spend the morning pep-talking a group of sumo wrestlers and hurry back home to have lunch with their kids. Afternoons can be spent in a flurry of efficiency, getting letters off to the hospital steering committee (of which, of course, Leo/Rat is chairperson) and chatting with the mayor about that new housing project he's thinking of funding. In between letters and phone calls and visits with dignitaries, Leo/Rat might be doodling a spiffy design for the new wing on his house in the country or listing possible names for his new horse. After work he'll hurry to a conference with his kids' teachers and then homeward to dress for the opera, which he attends with rigorous regularity as he does the subscription symphonic series and the appearance of every new film and theatrical effort around. The Leo/Rat ability to accomplish a wide variety of effective deeds in his life is astounding.

Leo/Rats are usually not poor for long. They know how to measure their guile into neat level spoonfuls and dish it out where needed for the making of money. They are extravagant but sensible people. With their hard-earned riches, Leo/Rats are generous and even philanthropic. But they won't go around giving money to bums and do-nothings just for the sake of charity. Leo/Rats prefer to help out promising young painters or musicians than just proffer money aimlessly. The marriage of Leo's natural strength and the Rat's desire for power is unbeatable in business and cultural activities. This person will always be a leader, in the vanguard of human endeavor and serious about the wielding of influence, of which he will probably have masses.

The donation of concrete ideas and the exertion of indomitable will for the sake of furthering great civilizing causes is not to be taken lightly. A Leo/Rat who feels he has been let down by cohorts or associates in his drive for power over evil or famine or poverty will be a portrait of despair. Leo/Rats believe fervently in the potential of friends and colleagues for true trust. Leo/Rat considers his partners long and hard before allowing himself to become their allies. If they disappoint him by virtue of their mediocrity or even lukewarm sentiments, the Leo/Rat takes it as a personal failure. When Leo/Rats fall, they fall hard and hit rock bottom with a deafening clunk. Climbing back up means humbling oneself. And humility is not easy for Leo/Rats. They need to be in control, on top of things. They will be saved by engaging in new and more challenging activities. Not by going into a rest home.

The main talent of Leo/Rats is enterprise. They know how to confront challenge better than many other people. They attack every new obstacle as though it were nothing more than a bigger and better seesaw which will swing them higher into the air and thus improve their lot. Every sport or dance or new wave of trendy jazz that comes their way is examined and understood and conquered and embraced by the Leo/Rats. Show him a camel and he will show you how to ride a camel. Leo/Rat is a natural teacher and shines brightly with achievement when his pupils catch on.

Leo/Rats are cranky when confused. He likes to choose which row his entire party will sit in at the movies and prefers to drive than to be driven in automobiles. The Leo/Rat's bearing is aristocratic and his personal magnetism unparalleled. But he hates to lose. If he does, you'll hear about it.

Love

As Leo/Rat people have a lot to give, they tend to seek partners whose dimensions permit the gracious reception of hordes of expressions of their devotion. If a Leo/Rat loves somebody deeply and fondly and tenderly, it is very often irrevocably forever. The Leo/Rat is so busy getting places and, once he is there, staying there, that he doesn't really like to make time for dalliance. He prefers to use his extraordinary imagination to maintain an existing passion than to go out seeking new ones that may only disappoint or deceive him. As I said before, the Leo/Rat invests himself in his relationships, both public and private. He cannot abide disloyalty.

If you love a Leo/Rat and he/she loves you back, you had better hustle to find ways to amuse and entertain this active monster mind. You can expect shortness of temper and loud yawns of utter boredom to emanate from any Leo/Rat person forced to be idle for half a minute. If he sits down, don't think he's going to stay down. He's just waiting for you to fire the starting gun and up and out he will be in a flash. Loving one of these people means expending both energy and emotion. You cannot be only partially in love with a Leo/Rat. He or she will make scenes and cause you untold horrors if you exhibit hesitations about the relationship's solidity. Be confident. Otherwise . . . well, I'd rather not discuss it. For Leo/Rats there is no such thing as "otherwise."

Compatibilities

You get on with bunches of types. Your best bet is an Ox subject chosen from among Gemini, Libra, Capricorn or Sagittarius subjects. Other allies can be found for you in the Dragon family—especially Gemini, Libra, Sagittarius and Capricorn/Dragons. Aries,

Gemini, Libra and Capricorn/ Monkeys are fun for you too. You are indeed popular. But give wide berth to the haunts of Horses in general and, in particular, flee the likes of Taurus, Scorpio or Aquarius/Horses. Don't go getting yourself involved with either a Scorpio or an Aquarius/Cat. Cats and Rats????

Home and Family

The Leo/Rat is a provider. Going out into the world and fetching back stores and stores full of wares, which will then be stocked and stashed and displayed on shelves, in cupboards and in closets, is one main pleasure of the Leo/Rat. Moreover, Leo/Rat likes to protect his family from harm and cold and shelter them in sumptuous surroundings. You won't see a Leo/Rat dragging back to his hovel from a hard day at the mine, and greeting his worn-looking wife and sooty kids with a grunt. Never. This person wants to be greeted at the door of his chateau after a busy, energetic day in the outside world by a bejeweled, intelligent and witty mate who has just spoken to the president and the first lady about an intimate dinner they'll share next Wednesday in Leo/Rat's red room. And the children? Preferably Nobel Prize winners who closely resemble Cindy Crawford or Leonardo DiCaprio and speak fourteen languages at age three. In their quest for excellence, Leo/Rats set no limits.

The Leo/Rat child will be demanding and bright. He or she needs lots of very top-drawer education and careful cultural guidance. Don't be surprised by this kid's interest in absolutely everything that has to do with power. Leo/Rats are not interested in namby-pamby activities, and will only seek to achieve in areas where stardom is the objective.

Profession

As enterprise and attack are the chief talents of the Leo/Rat, it's obvious that this person can expect to gain glories in managerial and entrepreneurial fields. If money is available, the Leo/Rat can start his own business and run with it to the end of his life. But if he is not wealthy and has to start at the bottom, the Leo/Rat will always distinguish himself by his tireless energy and innovation in work situations. No boss worth his salt would not promote this masterful character to head of the department, chief of operations or vice president in charge of presidents. To attempt to keep a Leo/Rat down is folly. This person will always seek to rise above and get ahead of his coworkers. He will only prove a good employee if his specialness is recognized and intelligently utilized. I can't think of anything more annoying than a nervous, energetic Leo/Rat in a lazy snap job—disgruntled? Oh, my.

This sign's inborn desire to assist his fellows and exert beneficent power qualifies Leo/Rat for all political positions—especially president. He may also make a fine professor whose sideline is writing books and making speeches around the world on his pet subject. Of course the Leo/Rat will make an excellent owner of any type of business and could even be a very successful gentleman farmer on a grand scale. He won't be too handy at manual tasks. He prefers to be in a position to pay people to fix things for him.

Famous Leo/Rats:
Angie Harmon, Antonio Banderas, Ato Essandoh, Ben Affleck, Charles Malik Whitfield., David Duchovny, Elizabeth Berkley, Eve Torres, Geri Halliwell, Gina Rodriguez, Jacinda Barrett, James Baldwin, Jason O'Mara, John David Washington, Kenny Wormald, Kyle Schmid, Leon Uris, Mark Costanzo, Marlon Wayans, Mata Hari, Matthew Del Negro, Maya Rudolph, Melissa Ponzio, Paul Cernat, Ryan Eggold, Ryan Lochte, Sean Penn, Simone Manuel, Taylor Schilling, Timothy Hutton, Wil Wheaton, Yves St. Laurent.

LEO
QUALITIES
NOBILITY, POWER, LOYALTY,
PHILANTHROPY, WARMTH, PROTECTION
QUIRKS
ARROGANCE, SELF-SATISFACTION,
VANITY, TYRANNY, PROMISCUITY,
IMMODESTY
Motto: *"I will"*
Elements: *Fire, Sun, Fixed*

--

OX
QUALITIES
STUBBORNNESS, STRENGTH OF PURPOSE,
ELOQUENCE, STANDOFFISHNESS, INNOVATION,
VINDICTIVENESS
QUIRKS
INTEGRITY, BIGOTRY, PLODDING,
DILIGENCE, BIAS, STABILITY
Motto: *"I preserve"*
Elements: *Negative Water, Yin*

Leadership and dominion combine here to create an unforgettably forceful personality type. The tone of rapport with Leo/Oxen never feels quite intimate or cozy enough. One wonders if there is really a heart beating inside their dense ribcages or whether they are propelled by some remote control device in their garage. This assessment of the indifferent attitude that the Leo/Ox emanates is perhaps harsh, or may seem unfair. But the Leo/Ox is so austere in manner that it's difficult not to imagine him as obdurately insensitive.

Leo/Oxen get places. They never cease pushing and advancing and arriving at goal upon goal despite hurdle after hurdle. We usually admire the Leo/Oxen that we meet and we cannot help but admit that they are amazing: strong, courageous and, most of all, effective. Leo/Oxen take the reins in every situation and when they are onto a project or idea, they never let up until they have mastered it.

These people are opportunists and do not hesitate before the dark wall of the devil. They plunge through fire and never flee conflict.

Normally, Leo/Oxen don't talk very much. Around the house or office, they come off as strong but silent, even stodgy personages. It's always obvious that Leo/Ox feels himself individual and separate from the group. And if he involves himself at all in any group endeavor or communion, he must have center stage, do all the talking, crack all the jokes and generally hold forth. Now, all of a sudden, in company with a captive audience, the Leo/Ox becomes gregarious. When he is listened to, the Leo/Ox is an orator, a performer, a fabulous synthesizer of information and a raconteur par excellence.

Leo/Oxen are "know-it-all" types and rarely let anyone get a word in edgewise when they speak. They are not too curious about others' opinions or reflections on their views. Leo/Oxen is the personification of the Father Knows Best approach. He is the first and final judge of what is suitable and intelligent. If you have a different opinion, keep it. When there is a Leo/Ox in the room, everybody present is on his show. He is intransigently, tenaciously and arrogantly there. You are mere decoration.

The Leo/Ox character seeks permanence and longs for solidity in both personal and public ways. He is as earthy as they come and seems to need to sop up warmth from the outside, to hold on tight to love and marriage and dreams of home and family for dear life. Yes, he is successful and unbeatably strong. But it can get lonely inside that autocratic head. And the Leo/Ox needs somebody else to turn on the heat. He can build and make and do anything at all humanly possible—except simple tenderness. Expressions of affection are not given to the Leo/Ox, and when you get to know them well, you realize that what's lacking weighs them down.

These people have great minds and good memories. In fact, they have trouble forgetting—and forgiving. Humility escapes them. If they goof, they don't want it to show. Failure is not acceptable.. If someone near to their heart disappoints them, they don't just pass it off as unfortunate or even sad. They take it as a personal affront to their dignity. And they cannot, will not, humble themselves to retrieve lost love.

Although this person is brilliant at order and runs a tight ship, his life will be missing a certain spontaneity. He prefers plans and schedules to the impromptu gathering or hurry-up picnic in the park. He's rigidly concerned about his image and maintaining same vis-à-vis his subjects. This, of course, cuts down on the Leo/Ox's jolly times. He's active and busy and energetic in the extreme. But the Leo/Ox is nonetheless ponderous and somehow, despite the velocity of his life, leadenly slow.

Love

For the Ox, romantic love is frequently reduced to the common denominator of sexuality. The Leo is, however, armed by the sun with inner glowing heat. A Leo/Ox will not be cold in bed nor will he reject the idea of sentiment or sweetness. But he will find it difficult to engage in the frolicsome aspect of love. He cannot forget to take everything seriously.

What the Leo/Ox needs as a mate or lover is someone whose sense of permanence helps get the fun together for him. Leo/Oxen are so exaggeratedly sensible that they need to be tickled and teased and learn to accept being jollied up and cheered along by a perfectly adoring and sweet-natured partner.

The real victory in fact, over the Leo/Ox's dense murk of gravity, is to make him laugh, loosen up and enjoy. If you love an Ox born in Leo, you will surely admire him as well. But that is the easy part. Get him to join a roller-skating club or do yoga. Relax him and limber up the stiff-old-geezer part of his nature. He'll love you for it and he will never let you down—so long as you obey his every order and don't get out of hand.

Compatibilities

Green light for Rats, Snakes and Roosters of the Aries, Gemini, Libra, Sagittarius and Capricorn class. Scorpio and Taurus/Dragons are off limits for you, as well as Scorpio and Aquarius/Tigers. Taurus/Monkeys annoy you with their eternal antics. And Sheep? You eat Sheep for breakfast.

Home and Family

The Leo/Ox's home environment will be orderly and impressive. He has always just redecorated and built new closets and bookshelves and had walls removed so that his huge dining table will be better accommodated. Leo/Oxen are big eaters and can learn to be good cooks. They work very hard and need a study or office in their house as well as outside. All will be designed for order and planned to the last butter knife and fish fork for efficient and clean-cut living.

As for his relationships with family and siblings, the Leo/Ox will of course, as always, take all ties and kinships seriously. If he gives a dinner party and doesn't invite his cousins and nieces and nephews, then he'll give them a special party of their own the next week. Leo/Oxen are authoritarian but they like to be thought of as fair and just, too.

Woe unto the child of a Leo/Ox who doesn't toe the mark, work well in school, follow in his mother or father's well-established social pattern, and do as he is told and not what he wishes with his life. The Leo/Ox gives everything to his kids. He provides them with an array of activities and high-minded outings and holidays and clothes and glut of every possible sort. Leo/Ox is an able and sure-footed family person. But he's also positively dictatorial. If the spoiled kid with all the toys and clubs and sports doesn't do what Mama Leo/Ox or Papa Leo/Ox demands, he is exiled.

Leo/Ox kids are impressively self-contained. They want to be allowed to remain separate from the kiddie nucleus and will try to order younger brothers and sisters around. The best environment for a Leo/Ox child is among his peers, where he may find other people of similar strength and sovereignty to learn from. He needs to be taught humility and the value of lightness and frivolity. But he doesn't learn those qualities easily.

Profession

The Leo/Ox character requires enormous challenge just to get through the day. He is not interested in crazy new notions or zany schemes. He wants to work and achieve and get on with his career. He must be cajoled and coaxed to want to have fun. Mind you, when inspired, Leo/Oxen can be very amusing. They have an uncanny ability to satirize. But their aura is stodgy. And they struggle and plod and drudge toward every performance.

Now, you cannot very well put a person like this behind a counter in a five and dime. He'll take over the whole joint in ten seconds, replace the manager and rearrange the working schedule. Leo/Oxen cannot possibly be asked to perform subordinate roles in their professional lives. Hence, they need to be independent. They must have a sound education and prepare themselves for their work from an early age. They will always rise to the top of any career organization—slowly perhaps, but intensely and certainly. Bossing is the Leo/Ox's mission in life.

Career possibilities for the Leo/Ox are best selling novelist, Noble Prize winning journalist, president in charge of presidents, king, queen, pope, Dalai Lama, imam or, at the least, chancellor of the exchequer. Another possibility is film director, or any job where a combination of talent for story-telling and dictatorial management is required.

Famous Leo/Oxen:

Anna Kendrick, Barack Obama, Caroline Manzo, Cristin Milioti, Dinah Jane Hansen , Dustin Hoffman, Emily Kinney, Glenn Plummer, Honor Blackman, Janet McTeer, Kate Beckinsale, Kathryn Hahn, Kevin McKidd, Kristen Wiig, Kylie Jenner, Laura Haddock, Lauren Tom, Laurence Fishburne, Louis Armstrong, Maggie Wheeler, Menachem Begin, Michael Ealy, Mikis Theodorakis, Molly Hagan, Napoleon, Oscar Peterson, Rebecca Staab, Robert Hirsch, Robert Redford, Russell Baker, Shantel VanSanten, Stephen Dorff, Susan Olsen, Vera Farmiga, Woody Harrelson.

LEO
QUALITIES
NOBILITY, POWER, LOYALTY,
PHILANTHROPY, WARMTH, PROTECTION
QUIRKS
ARROGANCE, SELF-SATISFACTION,
VANITY, TYRANNY, PROMISCUITY,
IMMODESTY
Motto: *"I will"*
Elements: *Fire, Sun, Fixed*

--

TIGER
QUALITIES
FERVOR, BRAVERY, MAGNETISM,
GOOD LUCK, BENEVOLENCE, AUTHORITY
QUIRKS
IMPETUOSITY, HOTHEADEDNESS,
DISOBEDIENCE, SWAGGER, INTEMPERANCE,
ITINERANCY
Motto: *"I Watch"*
Elements: *Positive Wood, Yang*

The old Tiger admonition: "Seek temperance before it's too late". fits the Leo brand of Tiger to a T (as in Tiger). If moderation were to be ignored in this borderline arrogant character, the result would be: haughtiness in dissipation, disobedient self-satisfaction, swaggering tyranny. This is a tricky combination. The fate of an intemperate Leo/Tiger could be disastrous.

Throughout his life this subject will feel utterly superior to everything and everybody around him. As a result of his built-in superiority complex, the Leo/Tiger will have difficulty making and keeping friends. Why? Maybe other people just don't understand how lonely it feels to be the king of the mountain.

Because this person imagines himself a head taller than his fellows, it is impossible for him not to affect a royal bearing. What happens, as he feels a sense of near embarrassment at being so terrific, is that the Leo/Tiger may come off as a snob. His idea of himself is too big to get through the door. So in company he exhibits a kind of phony simplicity, which unfortunately shows. Leo/Tigers try to be appealing, kittenish and even cute. But it doesn't work. Everybody sees through that air of boyishness. For this reason some people think the Leo/Tiger is insincere. Nothing could be further from the truth. He is merely a tad shy about feeling so magnificent.

Leo/Tigers are gutsy. In adversity they have the courage of ten Lions and as many Tigers, all leaders of the pack. They can laugh all the way through illness, exile, sorrow and loss, and still keep their pride posted like a neon sign that flashes HOPE in the densest darknesses that befall them. Theirs is not a bouncy Rooster or Aries resiliency. The Leo/Tiger's pick-me-up takes the form of a long prowl, watching, psyching out the enemy, slinking through underbrush on padded feet, circling the field hundreds of times waiting for the propitious time for comeback. Then, pounce! They are on their feet and off and running again as though nothing had happened. No migraines. No backaches. Just the panacea of all Tiger ills—movement. As long as the Leo/Tiger doesn't have to sit in one place waiting for time to heal his wounds, he can get through anything—he can even defy death so long as nobody hobbles his chunky tough legs.

Leo/Tiger people, by the way, are always beautiful to behold. It's their carriage and poise that gives them the edge in any gathering. They tend toward classical dress and actually don't fuss much about what they wear as long as it doesn't get in the way of their actions. Often, they also have that luscious leonine mane of light hair we all long to touch.

This person has a very hard time accepting second place. For example, you may see him dash for the front passenger seat in the car, then catch himself and defer to his grandmother who is, after all, eighty-seven. It's not the discomfort of the back seat that bothers the Leo/Tiger. It's the social significance and the sinking feeling of not being up there in front where it's happening and whence he might even, although he may not be the driver here, exert some control. His lucidity and sense of humor about himself will develop with time, and after thirty-five the Leo/Tiger should mellow into quite a balanced person—providing his head is not irrevocably swollen by years of parental and peer group kow-tows.

Love

Sentiment is not an easy part of the Leo/Tiger's life. For a start, his natural pride puts people off. The Leo/Tiger's inner sense of how exceptional he can be and how fabulous he intends to make his life one day may keep him from settling down to one person, making a family and building a home. You see, the Leo/Tiger cannot envisage himself attached to anyone who is not at least equal to him both in power and stature. In so doing, the Leo/Tiger limits his chances for marriage and family life. He does not, however, deprive himself of sexual adventures, wherein he doesn't much care whether the partner is equal to him so long as he looks up to him and sighs a lot.

Should you find yourself in love with one of these benevolent despots, don't ever appear weaker than he. Even if you feel like sobbing, keep your dukes up. This person is impassioned by strength, excited by force and turned on by aggressivity. Keep this Cat on his toes!

Compatibilities

Aries, Gemini, Sagittarius and Capricorn enhance your existence. Choose among Dragon, Horse and Dog signs. That's not so many to choose from, but then, you are not the easiest person in the world to please, are you now? Taurus, Scorpio or Aquarius/Monkeys are out of the question for your lifestyle, as are both Taurus and Aquarius/Oxen. Taurus and Scorpio/Snakes don't make it for you one bit, and don't even entertain the thought of a Cat partner. Cats are not confrontational. But they are subtler than you – and they know how to win by sheer stealth

Home and Family

The Leo/Tiger will probably live in a comfortable but utilitarian home. This person favors authenticity in furnishings and may own only one beautiful antique, which he will proudly display and cleverly place among his other, less expensive, pieces. The Leo/Tiger has an excellent sense of quality and enjoys refinement, but he cannot really be bothered seeking material perfection. He likes to think of himself as a swashbuckler who has no real home, but rather rides the perilous range saving little Native American kids from the rigors of public school education. Heroism and bourgeoiserie don't go together.

This person is devoted to his family. As long as he is free to race about the earth and busy himself outside the home (if he has one), he will delight in the company of his children, cousins and siblings alike.

Leo/Tiger kids need parental control and lucid reminders that they are not little gods. They will of course have great presence as children, and the temptation is to spoil them rotten and applaud their every blink. Teach them to look in the mirror. Encourage them to try and fit themselves into their own reflection. "There, Johnny. No. Be tinier. Squinch yourself up. That's it. Now you're normal. Your superiority complex hardly shows."

Profession

Talented at managerial jobs, the Leo/Tiger, because of his quest for humility, may not want to boss others. Leo/Tigers like to be left alone to evolve at their own particular pace. They don't fancy milling about offices with bunches of co-workers and supervisors breathing down their necks. So independent careers are the wisest choices for these people.

The Leo/Tiger is a bit of a "cause" person too. He will always find injustices in the world that annoy him and push him toward good deeds. You may find him at the head of charity or socially benevolent organizations. Leo/Tigers are good speakers. They can be teachers or choose sales as a career. They might be excellent actors or singers, too. And the Leo/Tiger may well be gifted in art and follow a calling as a painter or sculptor.

Famous Leo/Tigers:

Alexandra Chando, Amy Adams, Anne Princess Royal, Carlos Pratts, Chris Messina, Danielle Staub, Elliott Ehlers, Emilia Fox, Emily Brontë, Eric Hoffer, Ever Carradine, Gary Larson, Hilary Swank, Jackie Cruz, Josh Radnor, Manuel Valls, Megan Park, Michael Shannon, Misha Collins, Monica Raymund, Natalie Wood, Natasha Henstridge, Nolan Gerard Funk, Peyton List, Shawn Mendes, Shawn Pyfrom, Suzanne Collins, Usain Bolt, Winston E Scott, Wunmi Mosaku.

LEO
QUALITIES
NOBILITY, POWER, LOYALTY,
PHILANTHROPY, WARMTH, PROTECTION
QUIRKS
ARROGANCE, SELF-SATISFACTION,
VANITY, TYRANNY, PROMISCUITY,
IMMODESTY
Motto: *"I will"*
Elements: *Fire, Sun, Fixed*

--

CAT/RABBIT
QUALITIES
TACT, FINESSE, VIRTUE,
PRUDENCE, LONGEVITY, AMBITION,
QUIRKS
SECRETIVENESS, SQUEAMISHNESS,
PEDANTRY, DILETTANTISM,
HYPOCHONDRIA, COMPLEXITY
Motto: *"I Retreat"*
Elements: *Negative, Wood, Yin*

This person is so nimble and quick-witted that to know him is to wonder where he went. The Leo/Cat is a double feline with all the evasiveness and slink that such a combination implies. Regal and independent, refined and endowed with Leo's noble generosity, this sort of person has the wherewithal for greatness. Yet. Leo/Cats rarely seek power or celebrity. Mostly they are content to sit home and listen to their money crinkle. The single character trait that prevents Leo/Cat from forging a public image is squeamishness. This person doesn't want to see the seamier side or life. He wants no part of bloodshed, conflict, confrontation or enmity. He is after a busy yet peaceful existence.

Being Leo, this subject naturally demands a lot of attention. He likes to be admired. And he prefers to be right. The Leo/Cat retains his leonine right to pomp and vanity, yet he never thrusts his superiority in anyone's face. The Leo/Cat is a mild-mannered egomaniac. He never forces his high opinion of himself. No matter if you don't think he's wonderful, he does.

You can trust this creature's judgment. Leo/Cats have a sixth sense about tricky situations. They sniff out other people's troubles and lend true assistance to friends in times of need.

Despite this diagnostic gift, Leo/Cats are rarely embroiled in human complexities. Their hunch tells them when something's about to go awry and they rapidly move in the opposite direction. Leo/ Cats eschew muddy waters. They seek clarity in all rapports. Job descriptions are important to them. They must know where they stand in relationships. Whichever way the cookie crumbles, the Leo/Cat doesn't want any crumbs on his side of the bed.

The Leo/Cat is supremely able. He's willing and participates—so long as he gets some of the best lines—amiably. He is also capable of fathoming the need for humility and so can learn how to play second fiddle if need be. If they don't offer him the position of top dog, the Leo/Cat will take a graceful step backward, the better to pounce next time.

I think Leo/Cat skirts the spotlight's glare out of a sense of self-preservation. If double cat signs have eighteen lives, it's probably because they know how to stay out of the line of fire.

This Leo is prudent and munificent, wily and wise. He creeps upon Lady Luck when she isn't looking. Leo/Cats are loophole leapers. They never use their elbows.

Love

As the Leo/Cat is extremely popular among members of the other sex, he or she will have some difficulty fending off admirers. The character of Leo/Cat is somewhat intense and may give the (false) impression of lust. Actually this person's main interest in choosing a partner is the other person's ability to fit into Leo/Cat's well-ordered universe. He's more careful than passionate.

If you love a Leo/Cat, never be guilty of vulgarity of any kind. These people deplore shabbiness. Show your taste for refinement. Point up your love of hearth and home. This character's main pleasures center around what happens in his or her living room. Be a good sport and whatever you do, don't whine! Leo/Cats have no patience with snivelers. Learn how to blink your eyes admiringly and don't expect any kudos—just lots of good sound Leo/Cat advice and admonitions about how mindful one should be of everything from drafts to overdrafts.

Compatibilities

You will be attracted to Aries, Libra and Capricorn/Sheep and Pigs. You find Sagittarius/Pigs cute, too. Don't be surprised if you wake up next to a Dog for the rest or your days. You are enchanted by Dog people born in Gemini, Libra or Sagittarius. They seem so "involved," which appeals to your sense of altruism. Not so for Taurus, Scorpio or Aquarius/Rats, Tigers and Roosters. You are not exactly crazy about Scorpio/Dragons or Taurus/Cats either.

Home and Family

The Leo/Cat is certain to want elegance in his or her surroundings. Fine antiques of real value will furnish a solid house, which is most likely paid for. There can be a touch of exhibitionist grandeur in this subject's taste center. It's characteristic but not serious.

As a parent this person will be loving and demanding of hard work and respect from offspring. Leo/Cats don't: usually allow their kids to indulge in folderol. For Leo/Cats, the place for frivolity is on vacation; otherwise, it's shoulder to the wheel.

Leo/Kittens are smart little buggers who keep their own counsel and usually only clutter up their parents' lives with their diplomas and honors. They can be cheeky though, as they are always right. And they can even be rebellious if, God forbid, they are horn into a noisy, vituperative family group. Leo/Cats don't like noise unless they make it—and they don't do that very often. This child needs his or her own space in which to rest in peace between exams and piano lessons, ballet classes and computer courses. He or she is probably very pretty to look at.

Profession

Not many tasks escape the skill of the Leo/Cat. Be it manual or intellectual, the work is the objective in itself. This person will enjoy what he or she chooses as a career. Whatever he or she does, the result is likely to be brilliant. Leo/Cat likes to shine and be adored by fellow workers, be they subordinates or equals.

It's very hard for a Leo/Cat not to be boss. But unlike certain Leos this one is able to accept retiring jobs or at least not go mad it he doesn't get this or that promotion. The Leo/Cat boss will be slightly patronizing but tries to be fair. There is, however, no doubt the show Is Leo/Cat's personal trip and all employees are paid guests. An obedient servant, the Leo/Cat will only be subservient when he has no other choice.

Jobs best suited to the Leo/Cat personality are: antique dealer, doctor, jeweler, attorney, teacher, philosopher, veterinarian, artist.

Famous Leo/Cat/Rabbits:

Alex Rodriguez, Alicia Witt, Annie Parisse, Carole Radziwill, Casey Affleck, Charlize Theron, Clara Bow, Cody Kasch, Coolio, Dan Fogelberg, Donnie Yen, Emmanuelle Béart, Fidel Castro, Genesis Rodriguez, Isiah Washington, Ivry Gitliss, James Buckley, Jay North, Jemima West, John Carroll Lynch, John Stamos, Jon Gruden, Kaitlin Olson, Katie Leung, Lisa Ann Walter, Lisa Kudrow, Lynda Carter, Mara Wilson, Mark Strong, Michael Welch, Mika Boorem, Patrice Laffont, Peter Bogdanovich, Queen Noor of Jordan, Ring Lardner, Rodrigo Santoro, Sam Underwood, Taika Waititi, Whitney Houston.

LEO
QUALITIES
NOBILITY, POWER, LOYALTY,
PHILANTHROPY, WARMTH, PROTECTION
QUIRKS
ARROGANCE, SELF-SATISFACTION,
VANITY, TYRANNY, PROMISCUITY,
IMMODESTY
Motto: *"I will"*
Elements: *Fire, Sun, Fixed*

--

DRAGON
QUALITIES
STRENGTH, SUCCESS, GOOD HEALTH,
ENTHUSIASM, PLUCK, SENTIMENTALITY
QUIRKS
RIGIDITY, MISTRUST, DISSATISFACTION,
INFATUATION, BRAGGADOCIO, VOLUBILITY
Motto: *"I Preside"*
Elements: *Positive Wood, Yang*

My notes on this combination proclaim: "A total egomaniac with a heart of gold." Is that what we are to think of Leo/Dragons? Are they truly so self-centered as to deserve the hyperbolic appellation of "egomaniac"? Yes. They are. But I mean it as a compliment.

It is not given to everyone to be born superior to her or his fellows. And, as I have repeated at least three times in this book alone, no sign is better than another. There is no such thing. But Leo/Dragons are damned lofty creatures whose act is so together and whose health and courage and true sense of "noblesse oblige" are

315

so well developed that one is almost tempted to say all signs are equal but some are more equal than others.

Don't go guessing that the love of my life is a Leo/Dragon and that's why I'm carrying on like this. It's not my style at all (much to my own chagrin) to hang out with these monarchical types. I'm a Tiger. These people would have me for breakfast. No. I'm not in love with a Leo/Dragon. But I have always thought that if I'd had a choice of signs to be "when I grow up," I'd choose Leo/Dragon. It's so ... so pompous and magnificent, and ever so nice as well.

Leo is the magnanimous Dragon. The fair and just Dragon. The loyal, powerful and protective Dragon. It is this Dragon who best personifies what Dragons are all about. Fire. Sunshine. Noise. Expertise and self-confidence. And in a funny way this is the one sign that allows for Leo's magnanimity to outweigh his immodest side.

Leos are good-hearted and emanate warmth and like to share their wealth. Dragons can be purely selfish. But they are hopelessly sentimental. The combination is just right for give and take because where the Leo might be too generous the Dragon side steps in and says "Nope. Not thirty tons of jellybeans for the kids at the orphanage. Oh well, go ahead. Yes, give them three tons." And when the Dragon gets a little stingy, his Leo angel comes along and says, "You should be ashamed of yourself. Give that poor widow a bunch of money and hurry up about it!" Leo/Dragon is a mix that works.

The integrity and true nobility of Leo are precisely the qualities lacking in many Dragon subjects. The Dragon's mistrust calms the Leo's tendency to believe in himself just a smidgen too much. Also, Dragon brings Leo good health and a kind of sizzling vitality that is sometimes lacking in the slightly languorous Leo.

This subject is so sentimental that it amounts to a weakness. He cannot tolerate the knowledge of personal tragedy. He skips over the articles in the newspaper about battered children and squashed dogs. He's so soft-hearted that he's almost squeamish. But he is dutiful, too. He will take the reins and come to the fore if the tragedy happens in his own realm or family. Otherwise he'd rather not discuss the story about the boy locked in a closet for ten years. He's too sympathetic to the boy's plight.

Unusual longevity is often awarded the Leo/Dragon. They are extremely vain, so the desire to stay better-looking longer may urge them to watch what they ingest. And this is a sign whose subjects take care of themselves in order to better take care of others. Moreover, they are always so busy with huge, complicated, earth-shaking projects that growing old is nigh unto impossible—they don't have the time to be decrepit. As well, remember that Dragon people are awarded exceptional good health at birth.

Love

This area of the Leo/Dragon's life is frequently bumpy, to say the least. Look at it this way: These people are rightly convinced of their superiority from the jump. They rarely hesitate or take stock before deciding what to do. They just seem to know what they want and go after it. The Leo/Dragon rules. It's his fate by virtue of his title.

As Leo/Dragon is blatantly aware of his innate mission to surpass others, he's a handful as a lover or mistress, spouse or companion. You will be but an "accessory" and although you may achieve the rank of necessary accessory you will nonetheless remain superfluous to his survival.

To love this person properly you must accept living in his shadow, which will loom over your whole existence, protecting and shading you from overexposure to the world. If you like competition, stay away from this person—unless, of course, you are also a Leo/Dragon.

Compatibilities

You are "in like with" Aries, Gemini, Libra, Sagittarius and Capricorn. From among these occidental signs you do well to choose Monkeys, Roosters and Snakes. The Monkey assists but doesn't compete. The Rooster firms up your plans and carries them through. The Snake is so beautiful that he or she doesn't need to do much of anything but accompany you to functions and remain attractively quiet.. Aries and Sagittarius/Rats will do as well. Taurus, Scorpio and Aquarius/Oxen and all manner of disquiet Dog are too dour and may attempt to impose rigor where you need it least.

Home and Family

Leo/Dragon's home is his stronghold. He may well build a very tall wall around it too, with or without moat, depending on his means. You are invited at any time to visit or to stay awhile. Leo/Dragons are hospitable in the extreme. Besides, they like having as many subjects around the palace as they can. They tend to like precious antiques and objects made of gold. Why are we not surprised?

Parenting will attract the Leo/Dragon. They often have several children from several difficult unions. But they do not neglect any of their children or spouses. They think it would be nice if everybody sort of lived together. These people are serious about their kids' welfare and insist that they study and eat properly, be in the house on time and do chores when asked without sulking. Leo/ Dragon mothers are not usually smotherers. They rule with an iron hand but they love intensely, too.

A Leo/Dragon child will automatically make the most of his life. There is little you have to do except put up with him. He will certainly be a noisy and demanding child. Pay no attention or, if you'd rather, spoil him rotten. It won't change anything anyway. This kid is unflinchingly sure of what life has to offer and doesn't need much advice.

Profession

Sorry, Leo/Dragon, but the job market for benevolent despots is filled to the teeth right now. I'd suggest you try forming your own country. But seriously, the Leo/Dragon has talents for almost anything. He can be a computer expert or a baseball player, a journalist or a novelist, an actor or a designer. Whatever he or she chooses to do, it is likely it will be done well. Failure kills Leo/Dragons off like flies. They normally don't allow for it. But when it happens, they succumb. The fire goes out and the Grim Reaper knocks insistently.

As an employer Leo/Dragon is all the things I promised earlier and then some. He or she should prove to be fair, just and despotic. Kind underneath all the abrasive personality traits. And , despite the Dragon's occasional tendency to limit spending, generous. I can't think of Leo/Dragons as employees, but I suppose they have to start somewhere. Likely they will be a pain in the neck until they get to be boss and take your job away from you.

Famous Leo/Dragons:

Andrew Wilson, Craig Bierko, Debi Mazar, Deng Xiaoping, Francia Raisa, George Bernard Shaw, Jessica Capshaw, Jill St. John, Karlheinz Stockhausen, Kevin G. Schmidt, Laura Fraser, Laura Wiggins, Leah Pipes, Lori Loughlin, Martin Sheen, Mary-Louise Parker, Mats Wilander, Parker Young, Patrick Swayze, Phil Proctor, Rumer Willis, Sam Worthington, Sandra Bullock, Sebastian Roché, Stanley Kubrick, Tyson Fury, Valérie Harper, Vicky Leandros, Vivica A. Fox,

LEO
QUALITIES
NOBILITY, POWER, LOYALTY,
PHILANTHROPY, WARMTH, PROTECTION
QUIRKS
ARROGANCE, SELF-SATISFACTION,
VANITY, TYRANNY, PROMISCUITY,
IMMODESTY
Motto: *"I will"*
Elements: *Fire, Sun, Fixed*

--

SNAKE
QUALITIES
INTUITION, ATTRACTIVENESS, DISCRETION,
SAGACITY, CLAIRVOYANCE, COMPASSION
QUIRKS
DISSIMULATION, EXTRAVAGANCE,
LAZINESS, CUPIDITY, PRESUMPTION,
EXCLUSIVENESS
Motto: *"I sense"*
Elements: *Negative, Fire, Yin*

The Snake born in Leo is always right. Even if he's wrong. He is nonetheless absolutely certain that he knows best. And frequently, especially for himself and in order to achieve his own ends, the Leo/Snake is not far off. Wisdom and clairvoyance are part of the Snake legacy. But the addition of Leo to the cool-headed Snake character, although it lends some sunshine and warmth, also deals this character a hand loaded with vanity. Now the already extravagant and presumptuous Snake has to carry around excess baggage in the form of a swollen skull that just doesn't quit.

Then too, there is the question of Leo will. The pushiness quotient is rising. And we also have to consider the Snake's inherent laziness. And his tendency to dissimulate and pinch pennies. Are you beginning to get the picture? Can you see why the Leo/Snake is always—infuriatingly—right?

Of course anybody who is so indubitably right has to go very often far wrong. Extremes operate that way. But as they say in French, and I paraphrase, No matter how high up you may be sitting, it is wise to remember you are only sitting on your derrière. Accepting his own pride as occasional foolishness or humbling himself long enough to accept aid or assistance is simply beyond the Leo/Snake. He is one of those people who always gives you an indulgent laugh and snaps, "Don't be so naive! I know what I'm doing." Shortly after you have turned tail and left the overconfident Leo/Snake teetering at the edge of his favorite precipice, you hear the thud. He's not one to complain.

Leo/Snakes invariably arrive at the summits they climb to by means of their attractiveness and charm. These people are not even charming on purpose. They exude, breathe, ooze attraction. When you meet one, be prepared for a metallic "ping" sound to go off in your head. Even if you were not thinking of paying attention to them, Leo/Snakes, by their very presence in the same room with you, will mutely and coldly demand attention.

As you get to know them, Leo/Snakes will loosen up and warm to your personality. They need friendship and are loyal to their pals—especially their old cronies. But they will never, no matter how well you know them, allow you the luxury of giving them advice. They will dish out hours of "you should do this and you must try that" but our Leo/Snake wants none of that nonsense from you. How could you, poor dear, know anything about what they should do? Fact is, this refusal to accept counsel is often their undoing. Leo/ Snakes have been known to go under because they wouldn't listen to reason.

Deep down, Leo/Snakes entertain thoughts of grand charitable gestures and acts of philanthropy. They really think that one day they will make some kind of huge contribution that will cure social ills or help the starving poor. But the day rarely arrives when they actually do much more than adopt a war orphan or cut the ribbon to open the local playground. They don't mean to be remiss, but Leo/ Snakes get too Leo/Snake caught up in their own personal tragedies and losses (of which, poor things, they have more than their share) to really see that their grand good deeds get done. Too, they are a little more indolent than they ought to be and fairly self-involved. None of the above makes it easy to do much more than write a check for the United Fund.

The Leo/Snake cannot live happily without bushels of finery. Even the poorest Leo/Snake will always be wearing the latest net stockings, sporting an ivory cigarette holder and blinking out at the world from behind a tiny jet veil. The Leo/Snake has natural class and style. Even ugly Leo/Snakes are beautiful. It's the way they stand there with that come hither look in their eye that makes Leo/Snake people irresistible. Too, when they can (and they usually get to where they can in a big way), Leo/Snakes shower themselves with little gifties and accessories from Tiffany and Cartier and Van Cleef. These are the mysterious people you are always wondering about who keep posh jewelers like Harry Winston in business.

Never underestimate the Leo/Snake's capacity for drugs either. There is a dangerous tendency here to delight in consciousness-altering substances. It could be that the Leo/Snake is seeking solace from his cold, cold natural habitat. But this tendency must be watched, and watched closely.

Love

Here is the Leo/Snake's own private quarter. His life will be a veritable merry-go-round of love. He may have lots of affairs and a few marriages and divorces. But that is not what I mean to imply. I mean that the Leo/Snake personality distinguishes itself from others because of its beloved character. Leo/Snake people are always famous loved ones. They incite and inspire great love the way Juliet or Isolde or some great mythical character like Ulysses can. Leo/Snakes are the world's greatest "lovees." They seem to attract a partner out of nowhere, hold on to him with stranglehold tenacity and will until the person is limp from worshiping his love object, and then—sometimes, not always—they slough the poor creature off into oblivion again.

Now by this I do not mean that Leo/Snakes are any more promiscuous than other Snakes (which isn't saying much, I know, but fair is fair). It's just that they are the most loved of all our notoriously lovable Snakes.

If you love a Snake, hand in your key to the Chastity Belt Club, rush out and become president of General Motors so you can support the Leo/Snake's voracious acquisitive instincts and, above all, join a gym. You will never cease to adore your Leo/Snake partner and he or she will probably know that. But my advice to someone who wants to keep any rapacious Leo/Snake under control is to make yourself unavailable. Take an occasional "business" trip. Make the Leo/Snake wonder what you're up to—for a change.

Compatibilities

I love my wife, but oh you Snake! Gemini, Libra, Sagittarius and

Capricorn/Oxen will follow you anywhere you want to go. The same goes for Aries, Libra and Capricorn/Dragons. Sagittarius and Capricorn/Roosters are wild about you, too. Face it. You're gorgeous! Even Libra/Roosters fall flat for your charms. Nix on Taurus, Scorpio and Aquarius/Tigers and Pigs. All Tigers are too speedy and impetuous for your languid pace. And Pigs may be fair game, but you tend to treat their innocence unfairly.

Home and Family

Get out the address and phone number of your favorite domestic service agency and have it tattooed on your wrist. Leo/Snakes need luxury, and they need lots of it! To enter a Leo/Snake home is to finally understand the meaning of the word "palatial." Leo/Snakes were invented to lounge, to look good in negligees and smoking jackets, to be promised anything and given designer everything.

Leo/Snakes are born recipients. They like to entertain and be offered champagne and flowers, introduced to myriad prospective husbands and coddled and cuddled by their guests. Their surroundings are, of course, ultra-important. And always impeccable—providing the maid didn't take a sick day.

The average Leo/Snake probably gives birth to three-quarters of a child per lifetime. Parenting is not their thing. I mean, picture a glacially gorgeous, pristine princess in a floaty peach peignoir feeding strained spinach to a gurgling infant. It's absurd. A Yorkshire? Maybe. But not a real live squawking, puking baby! Mind you, when these people do manage to hatch a couple of kids they make serious and intelligent parents. It's not really in the cards, but when it comes along baby is adored. Leo/Snakes don't hate children. But they are a mite on the fragile side where emotions are concerned and the traumas of raising children can actually bring on migraines, depressions and anxiety attacks.

Also, Leo/Snakes are bright. They are among the most intellectual of signs. So a lot of the time they are too busy reading to get down to the business of baby-making.

Leo/Snake kids show right from the jump that they are not willing to take any nonsense about doing dirty work around the house or pitching in to run the vacuum cleaner after school. They may offer to find themselves a rich man who will pay for you to have help. But normally, Leo/Snake kids like to do two things: strut their stuff and do their homework. Their health is a bit shaky. Take them often to good doctors. And tickle them once in a while. Leo/Snake children take themselves too seriously.

Profession

Leo/Snakes might be able to work providing the work was cerebral in nature and could be accomplished from the unusual vantage point of a chaise longue. Leo/Snakes are industrious, but only with their brains. They are most decidedly not movers and shakers. I can't see a Leo/Snake rushing about carrying pots of bubbling fondue to a catering job, or even running an office full of cackling cuties. The Leo/Snake is high-strung and wired for brilliance. He's a loner, and if he accomplishes anything spectacular, it shows.

This is one employee you would never be able to convince to work in the stock room or accept having an office without a window. If you have a Leo/Snake employee, watch your job. You may be in serious danger of being supplanted by your hired hand. Even so, Leo/Snakes don't make excellent bosses. They can't be bothered bossing people around ...in a designer negligee?

Standing up to the strong-willed Leo/Snake in any professional capacity will be difficult. He could make a super lawyer or sales person. But your average Leo/Snake would rather know a lot about a lot and then become a famous movie star—it's prettier than being a lawyer.

Famous Leo/Snakes:

Alexander Fleming, Benjamin Harrison, Callum Blue, Cecil B. De Mille, Claudia Christian, Courtney Gains, David Crosby, Dito Montiel, Dorothy Parker, Doug Liman, Edward Furlong, Embeth Davidtz, Gracie Allen, Hisanobu Watanabe, Hughes Aufray, Illeana Douglas, J.K. Rowling, Jackie Kennedy Onassis, Jaime Pressly, James Tupper, Javier Botet, Jeremy Piven, Jonathan Rhys Meyers, Kenneth E. Hagin, Kevin Dillon, Kyra Sedgwick, Lindsay Sloane, Mae West, Natalie Delon, Paul Anka, Peter Bogdanovich, Peter Krause, Robert Mitchum, Sam Mendes, Sandra Ng, Sara Martins, Slobodon Milosevic, Viola Davis.

LEO
QUALITIES
NOBILITY, POWER, LOYALTY,
PHILANTHROPY, WARMTH, PROTECTION
QUIRKS
ARROGANCE, SELF-SATISFACTION,
VANITY, TYRANNY, PROMISCUITY,
IMMODESTY
Motto: *"I will"*
Elements: *Fire, Sun, Fixed*

--

HORSE
QUALITIES
PERSUASIVENESS, UNSCRUPULOUSNESS,
POPULARITY, STYLE, DEXTERITY,
ACCOMPLISHMENT
QUIRKS
SELFISHNESS, AUTONOMY, REBELLION,
HASTE, ANXIETY, PRAGMATISM
Motto: *"I demand"*
Elements: *Positive Fire, Yang*

This good-natured steed rides high among his fellows and practically always passes muster with flying colors. The Leo/Horse is a winner. He knows no obstacle too high nor does he fear adversity. This person wants more than anything in life to get there, to surpass himself in all areas of endeavor, and to do so in an atmosphere of good cheer. The Horse born Leo is not a sulker. His dauntless Leo side permits the normal fear of failure that haunts every Horse subject alive to retreat almost into oblivion.

Once the Leo/Horse knows what he wants, he bridles himself to the phone, makes appointments, goes to meet the bankers, saddles himself with the regulation loans and starts painting the walls of his new shop or office. Leo/Horse is a doer.

Of course, being of sunny disposition and a solid citizen is not quite enough to ensure instant victory. Nor can all the elbow grease in the universe guarantee success. But Leo/Horse doesn't know that. Leo/Horse thinks that if you do something, it automatically becomes viable. This is where our heroes occasionally fall and break a limb or two. And this is why the Leo/Horse is so frequently baffled and disappointed. How could those collaborators, with whom he made such a fair and just and effective deal, try to trick him? Why did that shoplifter steal from her shop? She seemed such a nice woman, such a good customer. The Leo/Horse shakes his/her head in confusion. "Why would anybody want to do me in? I'm so nice. I work hard. I'm not lazy. Poor little me."

Now in some people, this variety of disappointment leads to depression and even surrender. Not with the Leo/Horse. The Leo/Horse hates setbacks, despises failure, deplores trickery (unless he's the magician, that is).When confronted with any of these misfortunes he responds quite simply in kind. He gives back what he gets—in spades! He never goes looking for trouble, but should it befall him, the Leo/Horse is a tough and pitiless adversary. Scruples be damned. For Leo/Horses wrong is wrong and right is very definitely might.

This person suffers from a prickly ego. He cannot accept criticism gracefully and will resist vigorously any hint of judgment from others. He is an analytical person so he has his opinions. Yet, the Leo/Horse refrains from openly judging others. He doesn't want anybody meddling in his business and usually returns the favor by keeping his nose utterly clean.

He is, however, given to sounding off at a moment's notice. At parties or family gatherings it is often the Leo/Horse who feels a sudden obligation to address the company. Frankly, these people tend to be bombastic and even somewhat preachy at times.

But Leo/Horse is also a charitable sort. Perhaps the act of giving to those less fortunate is a kind of penance for feeling so good about himself. He will often head committees for the eradication of some human evil, campaign for the PTA's building fund bake sale or even give the first hundred dollars toward the church mortgage-burning party. The Leo/Horse enjoys being philanthropic—especially when it shows.

Their physical makeup is usually rather impressive. Leo/Horse men are dashing and elegant, even foppish at times. And Leo/Horse women practically live for grooming themselves. They are always pulled together with just the right black silk scarf to go with those pretty jet earrings. These people care enormously about how they look. They exercise and jog and try to eat the right foods and, as a result, are tremendously attractive.

Love

The Horse is generally a passionate creature, full of dash and vigor. Leo is no slouch in the ardor department either. The combination sign will be both extra hot-blooded and super-seductive. Trouble is, Horses can be very unscrupulous in love. They cannot see the other person's viewpoint, remember? Missing a date or forgetting to come home for a few days at a time, going out into the woods alone and letting you sit home worried sick that your Leo/Horse has been eaten by a bear—all of the above seem perfectly natural to the Leo/Horse. "Yes, of course I love you. I came home, didn't I?" This speech after three or four days' absence is a common Leo/Horse response.

Leo/Horse either takes love in this rather cavalier fashion or the Leo/Horse falls disastrously, madly, head over hooves in love and gives up everything for the sake of passion. Nothing matters then but the love object and the love object's whims. This is a foible of all Horse characters but the Leo/Horse with his built-in vanity and self-satisfaction is even more likely to fall victim to these extreme fevers of love. Either way, if you love a Leo/Horse, put on your safety belt and dig in your heels. You're in for more than a trot through the park.

Compatibilities

Aries, Gemini, Libra, Sagittarius and Capricorn/Tigers are your natural born darlings. Ditto for Dogs born in these same western signs. You will fall for Aries and Capricorn/Sheep in a jiffy, too. No dice with Taurus, Scorpio or Aquarius/Rats and Monkeys. These last are unlucky for you and will attempt to thwart your progress.

Home and Family

Horses like to create beautiful and comfortable environments. They are not drawn to opulence nor do they indulge in *luxe* for its own sake. The Horse is always down-to-the-ground practical. For the Leo/Horse, a house ought first off to function efficiently. The decor will be snappy but conservative. Each detail will be seen to. The Horse born Leo is not one to tolerate leaky faucets. Will the Leo/Horse repair his own plumbing? Only in an emergency.

As a parent this person will shine. He is not overtly authoritarian but rather lovingly domineering. It just wouldn't do to behave badly. The Leo/Horse believes in what is meet and right. He or she communicates with kids and enjoys spending time with them, reading or playing games together.

The Leo/Horse child will want to be given lots of attention and will require (although this child hardly ever asks for it) huge amounts of affectionate cuddling. He or she will be sunny and a pleasure to have around the house. Usually these children exhibit their talents early in life. They will be excellent subjects for participation in school programs and enjoy digging into large-scale homework projects.

Profession
This subject can (and will) do almost anything. There are aptitudes here in large quantities that await the Leo/Horse's indomitable will and practicality, his sense of application and his flashy ardor. He plays to win and he often does. Give this person an office and a telephone and before you can say jackrabbit he'll have something going for himself. This person is thoroughly unafraid of success.

As the Leo/Horse finds authority despicable and will not tolerate so much as a sigh of criticism in his presence, you will usually find him in positions of authority himself. He doesn't mind rules as long as he's the one making them. Because he lacks in subtlety what he possesses in brilliance, this subject can be his or her own worst enemy in business situations or group work. The Leo/Horse is something of a blurter.

Leo/Horses make excellent employees for people who don't feel like bossing very much. Their self-image helps get them from step A to step B without running to ask the supervisor whether they should color the page green or blue. Leo/Horses are naturally grand. They present well. Give them the jobs requiring poise and flair. They won't disappoint you. Sales, public relations, advertising, receptionist, merchant.

Famous Leo/Horses:
Adelaide Kane, Aldous Huxley, Alex Grossman, Andy Samberg, Colin Cunningham, Dave Pearson, Daveigh Chase, David Halliday, David Scott Morgan, Dean Cain, Don Ho, Elvis Costello, François Hollande, Frank Gifford, Halle Berry, Hugo Rafael, Indiana Evan, James Cameron, James Corden, Jason Watkins, Jay McGuiness, Jennifer Lawrence, Jerry Garcia, John Huston, Jonathan Silverman, Kerry Fox, Kobe Bryant, Lucas Till, Marisa Miller, Michelle Borth, Neil Armstrong, Nick Sandow, Percy Bysshe Shelley, Philo Farns-

worth, Richard Steven Horvitz, Robert Culp, Robert Goddard, Sam J. Jones, Ted Hughes, Thomas Sowell, Tommy Dewey, Vera Miles.

LEO
QUALITIES
NOBILITY, POWER, LOYALTY,
PHILANTHROPY, WARMTH, PROTECTION
QUIRKS
ARROGANCE, SELF-SATISFACTION,
VANITY, TYRANNY, PROMISCUITY,
IMMODESTY
Motto: *"I will"*
Elements: *Fire, Sun, Fixed*

--

SHEEP
QUALITIES
INVENTION, LACK OF FORESIGHT,
PERSEVERANCE, WHIMSY, GOOD MANNERS,
IMPRACTICALITY
QUIRKS
PARASITISM, SENSITIVITY,
TARDINESS, PESSIMISM, TASTE, WORRY
Motto: *"I depend"*
Elements: *Negative, Fire, Yin*

This Lion has the ephemeral spirit of an artist and the ambition of two Napoleon Bonapartes. It is just this mix of sensitivity and resolve that makes for the Leo/Sheep's uncanny ability, despite fuzzy appearances and general lunacy, to arrive smack in the middle of the spotlight. Leo/Sheep are blessed with the one thing most Sheep people lack—common sense.

Of course a Sheep is a Sheep and this one is not so exceptional as to escape the handicap native to all Sheep subjects and often responsible for their undoing: lack of foresight. Sheep often have little or no sense of consequence. The Sheep lives for the moment, in this instant, at the very split second of now. Hence, should his aims become realities, he frequently simply stands there watching them slip by. Sheep can't hang on to anything for long. It's almost as though they didn't want to.

Leo's brilliance will couple nicely with the Sheep's imaginative nature. These people have both the drive and the incisiveness necessary for all variety of artistic endeavor. Leo/Sheep, however, hate criticism and usually pretend to ignore it by going right ahead and doing what they were criticized for. They don't hesitate to use others for their own aggrandizement and in this way can be called (once again) dependent. Their successes are often those of the character who is catapulted into a position of power or celebrity by virtue of someone else's diligence. It is the very malleability of the Sheep and the Leo's natural pizzazz that allow for this phenomenon. The Leo/Sheep is definitely not your average hard-driving, workaholic drudge.

Sheep are always hovering somewhere about three feet over their own heads watching the world go by. Leos, in another, more pompous way, do likewise. Leos sometimes puff up so much they can't see their shoes after a time. This makes for a heady combination, to say the least. You may find this subject lofty and even distant. Ring twice. And if he doesn't answer, lean on the bell.

Opportunism is written all over this sign. The Sheep is not often really with us. But when he is, he's sharp and aware of the slightest nuance. Leo dominates. Leo watches out. Leo protects. And when the Sheep side of this Leo gives him the cue to pounce on a chance for advancement—whoosh! He's the king of the world.

Unless, however, The Leo/Sheep uses his head for something besides a hat rack, he may be a short-lived king indeed. Leo/Sheep need to surrender their decision-making to wise men and women whose advice they should both seek and heed. Their unfortunate characteristic of forgetting about tomorrow will always undermine their strength unless they are carefully and intelligently made mindful of the dangers ahead.

Leo/Sheep are daredevils. They often strike out on their own when young and attempt to gain notoriety by shocking people who are more conservative than they. They are a little bit bombastic, too, and their enthusiasm for the sound of their own voices can rarely be quelled.

Love

If dependency there is (and dependency there will no doubt be), it shows up in the Leo/Sheep's love life. With Leo to push from behind, the Sheep is more than able to conquer a loved one. But the Leo/Sheep's will to prevail will generally screech to a halt right there. Sort of "Aha! Now I've got you!" Suddenly the gleam leaves the greedy eye and the Sheep character falls into a swoon and sighs (subtly at first), "Take care of me, you big brute." Leo/Sheep may be able to provide the initial push, but subsequently the hero vanishes, to be replaced by a nonvenomous but nonetheless debilitating emotional parasite.

Leo/Sheep are damned attractive, however, so don't be surprised if you find yourself hitched to one. If so, don't panic. With the proper care and feeding, your Leo born a Sheep can become anything you desire. Her imagination is vast and zany, his motives anything but self-interested.

Leo/Sheep is made of material out of which you can mold a great human being. But you have to do the fashioning. As the mate of a Leo/Sheep, you are Dr. Frankenstein. Give your dreamy monster lots of room—and plenty of money. He'll take you places you never imagined existed.

Compatibilities

Aries, Gemini, Sagittarius and Capricorn/Pigs are your best bets for long-term mates. They know how to protect you discreetly so you can get on with your creative efforts. Libra, Sagittarius and Capricorn/Horses give you lots of courage too. Capricorn and Libra/Cats adore you, and the feeling is usually mutual. Taurus, Scorpio and Aquarius/Oxen and Dogs are definitely not your types. Your eternal quest for living in the moment exasperates them.

Home and Family

This person's house may be situated in a place he or she did not grow up. The Leo/Sheep, so easily carried away and so hasty in his youth, is frequently an expatriate or at least prefers to live where his family is not. Leo/Sheep like to create their own individualistic environments. They are not comfortable living in fusty or traditional spaces. They like lots of room. They require security in the form of comfort and elegance and prefer to evolve in zen-like spaces devoid of clutter. Most Sheep are skillful with their hands. They love to build and shape their surroundings themselves. Their tastes are strictly theirs, recognizable by their sheer originality.

Leo/Sheep parents are sincere and warmhearted with their offspring. Enjoying children is no hardship for the childlike soul of the Sheep. And with Leo to add punch, this person will know how to reserve his indulgences for special occasions.

The Leo/Sheep child is a love and a half. Sunny and imaginative, proud and yet self-effacing. He or she needs exposure to all things artistic. Give your Leo/Sheep a daily bath in beauty and drown him or her in secure-making billings and cooings. This exceptional kid is fun to have around.

Profession

The Leo/Sheep, like most Sheep, indeed, is gifted in things creative. He's a wizard at imitation, poetry, dance and music. He can probably paint and draw, too. Moreover, this person is malleable and willingly adapts his style to the desires of his public. He's energetic. But he's not stubborn.

As a boss, this person might get carried away with his own zany ideas unless he has a strict board of directors keeping him in line. As an employee, he'll want to hold a high position but he won't necessarily try to take over the whole office. He needs wealth, so he'll be drawn to careers that promise great booty. Ideally, this person should work alone with only his closest friends and relatives to prod him.

Suitable professions for Leo/Sheep are: artist (all sorts), interpreter, public personality,

Famous Leo/Sheep:

Adewale Akinnuoye-Agbaje, Alun Davies, Andy Warhol, B.J. Novak, Benito Mussolini, Billy Bob Thornton, Brent Sexton., Carrie-Anne Moss, Charlotte Lewis, Coco Chanel, Dominique Lapierre, Edward Trevelyan, Eric Johnson, Evangeline Lilly, Geraldine Chaplin, Jacob Dalton, Jason Momoa, Jason Statham, Jason Statham, Jean-Claude Killy, Jennifer Finnigan, Jerry Van Dyke, JoAnna Garcia Swisher, Joe Rogan , Matt LeBlanc, Michel Déon, Mick Jagger, Peter Gallagher, Peter Hermann, Philip Seymour Hoffman, Prince Gabriel of Belgium, Robert De Niro, Rose Byrne, Satya Nadella, Ty Burrell, Wayne Knight, William Goldman, Willie Shoemaker.

LEO
QUALITIES
NOBILITY, POWER, LOYALTY,
PHILANTHROPY, WARMTH, PROTECTION
QUIRKS
ARROGANCE, SELF-SATISFACTION,
VANITY, TYRANNY, PROMISCUITY,
IMMODESTY
Motto: *"I will"*
Elements: *Fire, Sun, Fixed*

--

MONKEY
QUALITIES
IMPROVISATION, CUNNING, STABILITY,
SELF-INVOLVEMENT, WIT, OPPORTUNISM
QUIRKS
DECEIT, RUSE, LOQUACITY,
LEADERS, SILLINESS, ZEAL
Motto: *"I plan"*
Elements: *Positive, metal, Yang*

The noble and magical Leo/Monkey is one beast you will never tire of learning about. This character has a heart of pure gold, a sterling silver tongue and a mind like a steel trap. He can tickle your funny bone. He will move you to tears. And if you hang around with him long enough, he may even drive you to drink. He's a powerful little devil.

For a Leo, the Monkey born under the sign of the king of beasts is actually quite a lamb. Oh, he has that impenetrable haughty bearing for which Leos are famous. But by his association with the steady nimble-minded Monkey, this Leo avoids the main Leo pitfall of megalomania. The Leo/Monkey's ego doesn't always need to be petted and stroked and acclaimed. Yes, he still wants to be admired and once in a while can be caught preening for effect. But the Leo/Monkey, although deserving of much praise, knows a great deal about abnegation, kindness and altruism.

The Leo/Monkey has remarkably few illusions about his own shortcomings Of course, like everybody else, this character commits errors and even has glaring faults. But you can tell a Leo/Monkey, "Don't you think you're being a little huffy about the way you want your vegetable cooked tonight?" And surprise! He doesn't stomp out of the room or crack his newspaper at you. Instead he may very well simply say, "Yes, you're right. I was being a jerk about that." *Fini!* Let's not say another word about it. You have to admit this ability to face unpleasant truths about oneself puts the Leo/Monkey in a special, almost unreal, category by himself.

So the Leo/Monkey is sensitive and objective. But he is nobody's fool. He is not willing to take a lot of vapid flak or listen to senseless nagging. Nor does he like to do dirty work, be anyone else's slave or bow low before his colleagues or mates. The Leo/Monkey is a full time card-carrying Leo. But as he is also a Monkey, he's cooler than Leos usually are. He is gentler, and what's more, the Leo/Monkey is a model of stability and pluck.

Actually, the Leo/Monkey is more courageous for others than for himself. He doesn't tolerate seeing those he loves hurt or mistreated. Although he is not particularly aggressive, when it comes to defending a friend he will lay his life on the line. Leo/Monkeys identify with strength. They admire people who stick up for their rights and who dare to buck the system. But they don't want to take the rap for any wrongdoing. And they definitely don't need to be in the spotlight. As a result, they are not usually the ones found rotting in prisons for revolution's sake. Yet, Leo/Monkeys are great crusaders for the causes of those they look up to.

Leo/Monkeys are very attractive. They often have simian features and a short stocky build. They like to be clean and fresh but are not mad about perfumes or cosmetics. Leo/Monkeys always exhibit a certain lucid optimism about life. They know it's not perfect but while it's happening, they feel one should be having a good time. They have moods, but their ill humor never lasts long. In their relationships with others, Leo/Mon-keys strictly avoid the use of force or loud tones. They are reasonable people with an impish teasing streak.

Leo/Monkeys are curious about everything and most of all about everyone they meet. They love to speculate about people's motives.

They usually have a wide variety of acquaintances from all walks of life. But gregarious as they are, Leo/Monkeys make very few lifelong close friends. They are quite objective about people and never idealize newcomers. Leo/Monkeys are loath to trust others. If you have one for a friend, hang on to him. You won't get many of this caliber, believe me.

This person will be talented for just plain living. However, he is not noted for being careful with material things and tends to be messy about the house. Philosophy interests him. New ways of doing things capture his fancy. A Leo/Monkey will call you up from Alaska to Louisiana if he thinks he has found a better mousetrap. He loves solving problems, sorting out chaos, and most of all the Leo/Monkey enjoys watching those he loves smile big broad happy smiles. If a Leo/Monkey loves you, your joy is his pleasure.

Love

It is only in romantic affairs that the Leo/Monkey ever has to trip over his unwieldy ego. Leo/Monkeys are possessive and jealous. They may seem playful and eschew what they term "middle-class values," but Leo/Monkeys don't like anybody trespassing on their sentimental property. Here is the one place you daren't say, "Darling, don't you think you are being a little huffy, the way you marched me out of that restaurant because that nice man spoke to me?" A Monkey/Leo in love is a perfect fool. I know Leo/Monkey women who, when they have to leave their lovers for a weekend, call them once an hour the whole time they're gone to be sure they are still in there. It's weird and out of character with this normally sensible soul, but there you have it. Leo/Monkey's emotional attachment is of the Gothic novel variety.

Now if you happen to love one of these people, let me give you some friendly advice. Don't smother them. Don't crowd them. Don't nag them. But do protect and advise them. Hover a bit and play nicey nice with Leo/Monkeys. They need petting and hugs. They need to be reassured that you belong to them and only to them. Leo/Monkeys also require that you not be lazy or indolent. They are capable of relaxing but they really respect hard work. Your backbreaking struggle for achievement will turn them on. If they see you working and trying hard to make it, they will be inspired to do likewise. If not, if you sit back on your heels and watch the world go by, your industrious Leo/Monkey will be silently but deeply disappointed. He may even try to belittle you or even to get rid of you altogether. Leo/Monkeys are patient. But they know their own patience limits. Don't push them. You'll be sorry.

Compatibilities

Go for a Gemini, Libra, Sagittarius or Capricorn/Rat. Aries, Gemini, Sagittarius and Capricorn/Dragons are good for you, too. You won't cut much ice with a Scorpio or Aquarius/Snake subject. Taurus and Aquarius/Horses don't appreciate your sense of humor, nor can you get much of a rise out of a Taurean born in a Pig year. I do however advise you take up with Tigers. I know that the Chinese sages claim that the Monkey is the Tiger's enemy. I have not found that to be true in western culture. Monkeys make excellent lieutenants. And Tigers, God knows, need wily sidekicks.

Home and Family

Here's one person you can count on for full family involvement. If the Leo/Monkey has kids he will pitch right in and wipe bottoms and dry tears and spoon pablum with the same enthusiasm and good humor he brings to other parts of life. There's something childlike about the Leo/Monkey's wide-eyed approach anyway. He's reliable and serious about the important things like hard work and play. But the Leo/Monkey is not a stickler for neatness or a bossy disciplinarian. Leo/Monkey parents use magic instead of authority to get things out of their children.

The homes of these people will be innovative and peculiarly decorated. The Leo/Monkey designs his spaces for comfort in living. They appreciate a certain amount of ease in their day-to-day lives. But they are not materialistic, nor are they gain-oriented. Nor do they care to impress. As far as the Leo/Monkey is concerned, all that's necessary for a cozy environment are clever practicality and the addition of his favorite funky found objects. The overall effect is eclectic and sunny (and sometimes quite messy as well).

If you are lucky enough to have a Leo/Monkey child, you must treat him with great care and respect. Of course one treats all kids this way; but in the case of the Leo/Monkey child he must not be talked down to or babied. He will want a straight deal from his parents, a sound education and plenty of loyalty. He needs affection much more than he lets on. Cuddle this child. Joke with him and tell him jokes. But most of all—love the little monkey.

Profession

The Leo/Monkey is high-minded. He enjoys the study of metaphysics and can be attracted to the spiritual life as well. There is a poet living inside this impish character. Yet Leo/Monkeys like to apply their artistry to real life. They are down-to-earth. In this way Leo/Monkey is a strange mix. Yet it's an interesting one, because it allows for all variety of endeavor and doesn't limit the Leo/Monkey person to one career or even one type of profession. He usually likes sports and works hard to keep his body in shape.

This person's versatility will recommend him for any job from sports coach to tour guide, from copywriter to social worker or secretary of the army. There is almost no job—except galley slave—to which this person is not suited. He might be a photographer or architect. The Leo/Monkey works well alone and carries on in work situations with a rare sort of diligent separateness. He doesn't require a leader and would actually rather not have to be one. The policing of other people's lives is against his humanitarian principles so he would prefer to leave the bossing to the bossy. He hates to clean up. So we can forget garbage collector as a possible career choice.

Famous Leo/Monkeys:
Alexandre Dumas fils, Anna Gunn, April Bowlby, Bella Abzug, Carla Delevingne, Catherine Bell, Charles Bukowski, Charli XCX (Charlotte Emma Aitchison), Cliff Curtis, Cole Sprouse, Debra Messing, Demi Lovato, Dominique Swain, Dylan Sprouse, Edgar Faure, Eric Bana, Gillian Anderson, Helen McCrory, Henri Cartier-Bresson, Karlie Kloss, Kristin Chenoweth, Laura Leighton, Louis Pauwels, Maggie Lawson, Maureen O'Hara, Merritt Weaver, Michèle Bernier, Monique Ganderton, Nadia Bjorlin, Olivia Williams, Rachel Miner, Ray Bradbury, RJ Mitte, Shawn Levy, Sophie Winkleman, Sylvie Vartan, Terry Crews.

LEO
QUALITIES
NOBILITY, POWER, LOYALTY,
PHILANTHROPY, WARMTH, PROTECTION
QUIRKS
ARROGANCE, SELF-SATISFACTION,
VANITY, TYRANNY, PROMISCUITY,
IMMODESTY
Motto: *"I will"*
Elements: *Fire, Sun, Fixed*

--

ROOSTER
QUALITIES
RESILIENCE, ENTHUSIASM, CANDOR,
CONSERVATISM, CHIC, HUMOR
QUIRKS
COCKINESS, BOASTFULNESS, BLIND FAITH,
PEDANTRY, BOSSINESS, DISSIPATION
Motto: *"I overcome"*
Elements: *Negative, Metal, Yin*

The Rooster's many talents will invest this Leo subject with a wealth of choices unavailable to the usual "me first" Leo person. Conversely, Roosters will benefit by being born with the noble, generous, magnanimous Leo aura. Where one of these signs is strong, the other tends to be lacking. Complementary indeed.

Leo/Roosters seem to require considerable means. Without money, the Leo/Rooster becomes moody, morose—or even worse, he may take drugs or involve himself in other treacherous debaucheries. This person is almost insanely proud. The health of his self-image depends entirely on which facade he can create for himself to believe in. Once the self-image is projected on Leo/Rooster's inner screen and its reflection pleases him, he proceeds to project it outward. He is far less spontaneous than he appears.

The wiry physical makeup of Leo/Roosters is part and parcel of their indomitable strength. These people suffer ups and downs of epic proportion. They swoop and glide and fly higher than their loftiest dreams. Then, all of a sudden-thwack!—Leo/Roosters plummet back to terra firma with a vengeance. And, miracle! they get to their feet, brush off their fine coats, pat their coiffures and strut away to discover new runways. Like old bantam roosters, Leo/ Roosters are resilient, sinewy and tough.

Sometimes Leo/Roosters overdose on pride. Either they get to thinking about how terrific they are or else they get to griping because they are so terrific and nobody seems to notice. Either way, when they are in one of their haughtiness fits, Leo/Roosters can be impossible to be around. They swagger and hold forth and try to get everybody's attention. A cocky Leo/Rooster can be a real pain in the ass.

Attacks of Leo/Rooster self-importance don't last long. Life, in its inimitable wisdom, takes care of that straightaway. Baby gets sick and has to be rushed to hospital. Leo/Rooster to the rescue! Mama's had another of her attacks. Run get Leo/Rooster! She'll know what to do. It's amazing to watch Leo/Roosters, who always give the appearance of not giving a hoot, in tight spots and emergencies. Their behavior is exemplary.

The Leo/Rooster is a dandy. Clothes and everything to do with the pageantry of la toilette appeal to the Leo/Rooster's elevated elegance quotient. He never goes out of the house looking scruffy if he can help it; there's always that little scarf or pin or hair ornament that sets off the studiedly casual look Leo/Roosters like to affect.

I have a lovely Leo/Rooster pal who suffers untold misery because he is color-blind. Imagine the handicap! He can only differentiate yellows and purples. The rest of the world's spectrum looks a dull series of olives and drabs, like a carpet of shaded camouflage fabric. Luckily, this fellow has married a brilliant designer. Evenings, before retiring, his wife sets out his clothes for the next day. He chooses whether he wants sport shirts or dress, flannel or twill. But his wife chooses the colors that will harmonize when the outfit is worn. Once a beautiful woman said to him, "You have a very distinctive way of dressing." With native cockiness, my friend answered, "Thank you. My wife dresses me." "Well, she certainly makes sure that nobody else ever gives you a second look," said the pretty lady. "That purple tie with those canary yellow trousers!

Wow." Suddenly my pal recalled that his wife had left to visit her mother for a few days and that morning he had chosen his own ensemble in the only colors he can recognize. He blushed. Bright purple.

All Leo/Roosters have scads of friends. When people like a Leo/Rooster, they stick by him through thick and thin. And as there is bound to be too much thin and not enough thick in the course of a Leo/Rooster's turbulent life, the type of friends who cultivate Leo/Roosters are of the fast friends variety. Leo/Roosters are funny and interesting. They are clever and talented and unflinchingly able to start over. New projects and dreams are the stuff of their busy lives. Yet they are afraid of danger. And they should be. It's everywhere in their speedy lives. They need to seek temperance and surround themselves with loyal allies who will go to bat for them when they are in trouble (which they sometimes are). Leo/Roosters are lovable and warmhearted and wise.

Love

The Leo/Rooster lover prides himself on his passions. If ever there was a devoted soul in long-term love relationships, it's the Leo/Rooster. If he has chosen a mate, then it is usually for life, for a home and children, an organic garden, and hatchback, pickup and power Rototiller. Leo/Roosters are such wells of ability, able to make music out of cacophony and flowers from weeds, that monogamy doesn't really bore them all that much. There are so many more interesting things to do than cheat on your mate. So why bother?

If you love a Leo/Rooster, you had better begin accumulating patience. These people have enormous mood and temperament swings. They sometimes tunnel under the bedclothes for days groaning about how wronged they've been, and how they haven't the courage to tunnel back out, and would you please just turn on the gas jets and lock the door behind you when you leave? Or they may go around the house (out of nowhere, mind you) lighting candles and setting out flowers and turning on fabulous music in a spirit of joy that you were sure had left them forever during their last siege with depression. Up and down. That's how these folks are. You can like it or lump it. And if you like it, you'll be sure to love it.

Leo/Rooster needs to be cared for and most of all to be listened to and understood. If you can get the food together and keep things on an even keel around the house, a Leo/Rooster mate will provide years of faithful—and funny, amusing, jolly—service.

Compatibilities

The Ox, the Snake and the Dragon woo and win you with ease. You need to be brought along, cajoled and encouraged. Be careful to look for your steady date among Aries, Libra, Sagittarius and Capricorn people of the above animal signs. Taurus, Scorpio and Aquarius people don't really know where to look for the tenderness button you wear behind your left ear. Keep away from Cats and Roosters of those Occidental categories. And don't hang around with Aquarius/Dogs much, either.

Home and Family

The Leo/Rooster rules the roost with panache. He is a serious householder. Although he may often seem preoccupied by outside influences and personal depths no one but himself would dare try to plumb, the Leo/Rooster nature is a home-loving one. Even so, he likes adventure and is capable of saying glibly, the way Roman Polanski (Leo/Rooster 1933) did, "Wherever I hang my hat is my home." And even though Leo/Roosters love to travel and see new places and excite their own bottomless curiosity with adventures of all kinds, they always get nostalgic for home. Leo/Roosters are fake wanderers. They love their hearths and long for security.

The Leo/Rooster home is frequently very beautifully done up. It is sure to be comfortable and in good—even conservative—taste. Leo/Roosters demand a certain order around the household. They make excellent serious parents and yet are not terribly interested in diapers or baby bottles. The Leo/Rooster's favorite age in children is adolescence, when they can be really talked to and exchanged with on an almost adult level.

If you have a Leo/Rooster child, remember that he or she will be interested early on in everything to do with clothes and appearances. Spectacle, too, attracts the cocky Leo/Rooster. He or she will dream of performing. Encourage skits or give this kid drama lessons at a young age. Also, you can be sure he or she is bright. Good schools with high standards are in order.

Profession

Success does not come easily to Leo/Roosters. The early part of their adult life is frequently fraught with repeated failures, which give the impression each time, by their very magnitude, that they will sink the Leo/Rooster—and his navy too. Losses and illness, discouragement and discord, bad luck and accident are all very much present in the early Leo/Rooster life.

If this character can grit his teeth and bear it through the fiery hell of the first part of his professional life, his destiny will probably be grand. From birth the lucky winner of unusual fates, the Leo/Rooster you knew at thirty, who nearly ended up alcoholic because of the loss of one of her children in a freak accident, may well be, at forty, the president of the town bank, a teetotaler and a model citizen at that.

Leo/Rooster is of course a leader type. But I wouldn't say that Leo/Rooster adores being boss. Setting the pace for projects or trends is the Leo/Rooster way of leading. He would prefer to teach rather than to pontificate. Leo/Roosters like to do things. They undertake huge enterprises that would cow the rest of us and, by the time you blink an eye, they're finished and onto the next huge undertaking. Leo/Roosters are talented and they know how to get places in the world. But they always need someone by their side to hold their hand through the darkest nights of Roosterish gloom. They don't mind working alone—may even prefer it to tandem or group activities. But they need a dedicated cheering section. For this reason they are usually best working at jobs that allow for personal application to lead to success: film director, writer, politician, prospector, musician, journalist, ski instructor.

Famous Leo/Roosters:

Abigail Spencer, Alex Haley, Alexis Arquette, Allison Stoner, Ben Barnes, Bradley McIntosh, Cameron Monaghan, Carole Bouquet, Cassi Thompson., Charlotte McKinney, Christian Slater, D.B. Woodside, Donnie Wahlberg, Edward Norton, Elizabeth Gillies, Fernando Alonso, Francesca Eastwood, Gene Roddenberry, Ginni Rometty, Helen Mirren, Jacqueline Susann, Jennifer Lopez, Jerry Falwell, Jesse Williams, Jim Courier, Lynn Cohen, Maia Mitchell, Matthew Perry, Meghan Markle, Melanie Griffith, Nana Visitor, Nathan Jones, Roger Federer, Roman Polanski, Ross Marquand, Simon Baker, Summer Glau, Taylor Momsen, Timothy Omundson, Triple H (Paul Michael Levesque).

LEO
QUALITIES
NOBILITY, POWER, LOYALTY,
PHILANTHROPY, WARMTH, PROTECTION
QUIRKS
ARROGANCE, SELF-SATISFACTION,
VANITY, TYRANNY, PROMISCUITY,
IMMODESTY
Motto: *"I will"*
Elements: *Fire, Sun, Fixed*

--

DOG
QUALITIES
CONSTANCY, UNSOCIABILITY,
RESPECTABILITY, SELF-RIGHTEOUSNESS,
INTELLIGENCE, TACTLESSNESS
QUIRKS
UNEASINESS, CRITICISM, DUTY,
CYNICISM, HEROISM, MORALITY
Motto: *"I worry"*
Elements: *Positive, Metal, Yang*

All the Dog's respectability, heroism and undying constancy shot through with Leo loyalty, nobility and philanthropy find us confronted here with one of the most frankly earnest people ever born. So indulgent is this character with those he loves that if one of his friends committed a cold-blooded act of horror before his very eyes, the Leo/Dog would deny he saw it. He would find an excuse for the person. He would bake cake upon cake with files inside. He'd spring for the bail, the fines, the lawyers. And when finally, through his devoted efforts, his friend the criminal is set free again, Leo/Dog will find him a vacation spot, encourage his friend to invite whom he wants along and pick up the tab for that, too. Leo/Dogs are incorrigibly caring.

For the above reasons, no matter what happens to these people, they are rarely really disappointed. They see life from the beginning as a kind of natural hell on earth crawling with injustices and wrong-doings of all sorts, which they are bound to bark at and try to chase away. Let's face it, Leo/Dogs are not overly optimistic. But pessimism doesn't destroy their enormous capacity for belief. In certain other Dog people there is a tendency to crawl under the chair and stay there till the strife is over, cowering and growling when anything threatens to beckon them emerge. But not the Leo/ Dog. Leo/Dogs seem to be able to take enormous punishment from the vagaries of their lives and still come up smiling, scrapping and facing up to responsibility, perched jauntily on their chairs wearing an expression of utter candor and warmth.

I know some Leo/Dog people. The gentlemen of this persuasion that I have met can be, without qualification, called "ladies men". Ditto the female Leo/Dogs. Five and six or seven consecutive (or simultaneous) affairs that would make a sex-crazed Hollywood star look like a nun. Real hot numbers are these Leo/Dog people. They just plain like sex. But even more important they love passion. They need excitement, and to them romantic involvement is synonymous with excitement. And naughtiness adds spice to their kicks.

The Leo/Dog is noted for his ability to work long and hard at many different and difficult pursuits. No Leo/Dog ever imagined that success comes easily and that he ought to have been promoted over somebody less capable. He makes it his business to advance through his life with rigor and pep. Leo/Dogs are not dreamers. They are doers.

Leo/Dogs hate to hurry. They prefer to find themselves in situations where one is encouraged to take one's time. They are deliberate and careful. They don't want to be achievers just for the sake of achieving. If they get someplace in life, Leo/Dogs want that place to have been earned by the sweat of their brows. They have a talent for concocting far-reaching plans and may thus be accused of moving too slowly in emergencies.

Leo/Dogs are on their guard much of the time, and they can be very feisty. There is a definite tendency here to pick fights. The Leo/Dog cannot leave details alone. He notices the fact that you said last week you'd be buying chicken, and then you came home with a turkey. And Leo/Dog disapproval is enough to make anyone feel like a criminal. But rest assured, it doesn't last long. As quickly as the desire to rip at you arises, it retreats. A mere smile will melt the Leo/Dog's kind heart and if you actually weep or even snivel while he's growling at you, he'll take you out to dinner to make up for it.

As the Leo/Dog performs many good deeds, he is particularly sensitive to receiving favors. Do a Leo/Dog a service of any kind, lend him money, give him a key chain—anything—and he will be sure to return your gesture. But he is also showing you how he feels the world ought to be. He is stating his policy by setting an example. It's a terribly nice, subtle method of trying to set the world right. But, of course, it doesn't always work.

Leo/Dogs, unlike most Leos, are modest to a fault. They don't want applause and they don't care about remuneration. They don't need anything but love and respect from other people. And even if they don't get either, they remain steadfastly loyal, fair and tolerant.

A sentimental type, the Leo/Dog cannot be swayed from his affections by reason or logic. He feels things strongly and is not afraid to turn his emotions into actions. He's pleasantly naughty and makes a terrific friend.

Love

As I've already pointed out, the Dog born Leo is a lover of love. This person will not feel the need to be physically faithful to a mate. But his moral and spiritual connection will be above reproach. This person would defend the best interests of her husband if he were an axe murderer, child molester and wife beater. She believed in him once and she will go on believing in him always.

Even when Leo/Dogs have various subsequent sexual affairs, they remain loyal in spirit. They never interrupt friendships willingly. Once they care, they care irremediably and forever, without reserve.

In order to love a Leo/Dog properly, you must understand the testy pride with which you are dealing. Leo/Dogs are ostensibly modest people. They never prance (unless they're drunk) much. But inside their noble stalwart hearts lives a tiny shrinking violet on an enormous ego trip. The Leo/Dog doesn't often let the violet show. Nor do we much notice he even has an ego. But you, the lover or mistress or wife or husband of this monster of modesty, you must learn to know the violet and how to care for its fragile petals. You must learn how to stroke the ego just right so that hardly anybody notices. Then, you'll be the favorite pet of the Leo/Dog forever.

Compatibilities

You suffer from testiness and occasional disquiet (not to mention paranoia). Stay close to Aries, Gemini, Libra, Sagittarius and Capricorn people born in Cat or Tiger years. Gemini/Horses are nice for you, too. You'll be less satisfied with a Taurus, Scorpio or Aquarius/ Dragon or Sheep. You don't need to be reminded that the world is a terrible place full of woes and perils. You just want to live with some pleasant, cheerful soul who boosts morale and provides suffi- cient applause. Try hooking up with a sexy Pig subject (Scorpio for example). The Pig's delight in all things sensual may help keep your eye from wandering too far afield too often.

Home and Family

Don't go looking for luxury at the Leo/Dog's house. To this person a house is only a place to live. Usually, the Leo/Dog's house looks used and comfortable. The books might be strewn around a little and the dishes left unwashed for a few hours. But basically the Leo/Dog likes order. Underneath the slight mess will rule a definite statement of neatness. Opulence is of little importance to the Leo/ Dog.

The Leo/Dog is a marvelous family member. As a responsible person he can be counted on to go fetch the kids at the movies and pick up sister's little friends at the skating rink. He's a good fellow about parties too, and enjoys entertaining and being entertained. But be forewarned: Leo/Dogs aren't very funny. Don't encourage them to tell jokes. And they worry. Constantly and earnestly and without restraint. Encourage the Leo/Dog in all areas that require responsibility. Don't hesitate to ask him to get up with the baby at three in the morning. He won't mind and eventually may even make a religion of it. Don't be afraid to ask him for money either. Leo/Dogs are generous people (I didn't say spendthrift).

The Leo/Dog child may seem sullen and withdrawn to you at first. His reserve is simply his way of checking you out and casing the joint before joining the fun and participating in real life. He needs lots of real down-home affection and jollying up. He also needs to be taught not to sulk. He will be a bright but pokey child. Don't try to hurry him. He likes to linger over his food, his math, his toys. He's careful, remember?

Profession

Leo/Dogs are talented in all sorts of intricate work that requires analysis and logic, pondering and planning. They are capable of working alone and survive very well in jobs where no human inter- action is necessary. They are terminally industrious and will always try to do a job properly.

As a boss, the Leo/Dog will be fair and put up with many she- nanigans from his employees. Actually, now that I think of it, one doesn't see many of these people in regular day-to-day boss posi- tions. They either get somewhere in their lives on their own steam and at their own speed, or else they remain in the ranks. Often they hold important positions in those ranks. But Leo/Dogs are not on any power trips and they don't really like policing others. So expect them to be either pillars or invisible within office situations. Otherwise, outside the normal routine of working for others, Leo/Dogs can excel at personal causes, be political or sociological innovators and even shine in show business or in literary or artistic work. They make good loners.

Engineering and science are natural fields for Leo/Dogs. They may also choose to pursue other careers where their humanitarian talents will be put to good use. Otherwise, I advise solo jobs of all sorts that don't put too much pressure on the Leo/Dog to adhere to strict rules he may deem stupid and unnecessary.

Famous Leo/Dogs:

Abbie Cornish, Alain Robbe-Grillet, Angela Bassett, Anna Paquin, Anthony Anderson, Bill Clinton, Cam Gigandet, Charisma Carpenter, Christopher Nolan, Elisabeth Moss, Forrest Landis, Herbert C. Hoover, Israel Broussard, Jacqueline Emerson, James Gunn, Jennifer Lopez, Kelvin Harrison Jr., Kevin Cadogan, Kevin Smith, Laurent Fabius, Lesley Ann Warren, M. Night Shyamalan, Madeleine Stowe, Madonna, Malcolm Jamal-Warner, Martin Starr, Micheline Presle, Nikolaj Coster-Waldau, Norman Lear, Norman Schwartzkopf, Paul Wesley, River Phoenix, Sebastian Stan, Taissa Farmiga, Thomas Lennon, Yvonne Strahovski.

LEO
QUALITIES
NOBILITY, POWER, LOYALTY,
PHILANTHROPY, WARMTH, PROTECTION
QUIRKS
ARROGANCE, SELF-SATISFACTION,
VANITY, TYRANNY, PROMISCUITY,
IMMODESTY
Motto: *"I will"*
Elements: *Fire, Sun, Fixed*

--

PIG
QUALITIES
SCRUPULOUSNESS, GALLANTRY, SINCERITY,
VOLUPTUOUSNESS, CULTURE, HONESTY
QUIRKS
CREDULITY, WRATH, HESITATION,
MATERIALISM, GOURMANDISM, PIGHEADEDNESS
Motto: *"I civilize"*
Elements: *Negative Water, Yin*

This fiery and conscientious soul will always leave you laughing. Even in the most tragic circumstances, when the chips are down and Leo/Pigs seem to have reached an emotional nadir, from out the shivering bundle of despair will shine one little quip, one last pun or smart remark to bring a smile to your lips. Leo/Pigs cannot help it. They're funny people. It must be the Leo sun shining on the Pig's sincerity meter. Or else it s the Pig's honesty infused with Leo's philanthropic side. Whatever causes it, this person's sense of fun will be capital.

Excess is the lurking temptress for Leo/Pigs. Not only do they love to make wry jokes, but Leo/Pigs adore everything sensual in great gobs and bunches. Food, sex, ease, work, love, comfort, conversation and luxury. Do these people ever like to wallow in *luxe!* Opulence is the very stuff of their lives. They need gorgeous, sumptuous, scrumptious surroundings; and they are willing to work hard to get them. They like to fetch home their foodstuffs from the best shops and open markets. Their clothes are always "Oh, this old rag" from Yves Saint-Laurent's most recent collection, in which, despite his eternal uphill struggle against midsection spread, your average Leo/Pig looks positively stunning. How else can I say it? Leo/Pigs have class.

They also frequently have a lot of loot. They are generous and sharing, magnanimous and hospitable. They'd give you the silken Christian Dior shirt off their backs. And the next day they would show up in a little cashmere number from Givenchy. So openhanded are Leo/Pigs that they are sometimes accused of wastefulness. What saves them from this last, however, is their major preoccupation with security, home, hearth and the well-being of loved ones. Leo/Pigs look out for their own, are reliable and responsible and exude a special shimmering sort of brightness and warmth that is very convincing. When you are in the company of a Leo/Pig who is paying attention to you, you feel that you are the only person in the whole world, that their happiness depends on your next breath and that you are indeed just what the doctor ordered for your Leo/Pig interlocutor. "I've missed you so, my sweetheart," my Leo/Pig friend Monique always tells me. Now, I am sure that this woman hasn't really thought about me in weeks. She's busy and active and beloved and sought after by her friends and family. But the way she tells me, "My little *chou chou*, I'm so happy you called," well, I don't know about you—but I melt.

The magnetism of Leo/Pigs very often ensures their career success, too. Leo/Pigs hardly ever have trouble getting jobs and keeping them. They are willing and able, and so amusing, too. But they feel that climbing, scratching and clawing their ways to the proverbial top is beneath their dignity. If Leo/Pigs really "make it big" in a public way, it's always thanks to their careful hard work and sterling abilities.

In adversity the Leo/Pig is courage personified. Of course, no self-respecting Leo/Pig would agree with that. "I'm not brave," he will tell you. "I'm nothing better than a jellyfish when it comes to grinning and bearing it." The Leo/Pig is not only courageous but he is also modest. He doesn't want praise and applause. Now, now, none of that clamor please. Quiet down! But secretly he needs to be hailed and looked up to and admired. He may be a pure-of-heart gallant and honest Pig. But he's still a vain old Leo underneath.

Love

When it comes to affection, the virtue of the Pig enhances the warmhearted Leo side of this character. Albeit Leo has a tendency to gad about preening, and from time to time harking to the enticing sirens; here the Pig's reserve and discretion do come to the fore. This subject may be a gadfly, even a shade promiscuous, but he will never be indiscreet. You won't receive an invitation to an exposition of his infidelities. Such things are, for the Leo/Pig, to be kept under one's (very chic) hat.

One-on-one the Leo/Pig requires an unflinchingly faithful and loyal lover. As he may have many setbacks and moments of discouragement in his life, the Leo/Pig also needs to choose a mate who can portage him and his wry sense of humor from safe harbor over some of the rougher patches of jungle and onward to the next haven. Leo/Pigs take love seriously and are deeply affected by its implications. They are responsible people. It follows that they don't take other people's feelings any more lightly than they do their own.

If you love a Leo/Pig, be prepared to exhibit qualities of intelligent devotion and sobriety. Should your Leo/Pig binge out on a whole smoked salmon and a kilo of Russian caviar at one sitting, he wants you to call him to order. "Hey, what's this suicide I see going on around here?" is a safe line. Or, "You seem to be hell-bent on ending up in the hospital." Keep it light. Leo/Pigs don't like to feel they are being policed. But they do favor mates who promise to keep them on the straight and narrow. Buy an ornate medieval lock with a golden key and install it on the refrigerator door. Leo/Pigs favor the traditional in decor.

Compatibilities

As humor (the blacker the better) beguiles them, you will do best with Aries, Gemini, Libra, Sagittarius or Capricorn/Oxen, Cats and Sheep. You like to be comfortable and warm but you don't want to be smothered, so steer clear of Snakes—especially Aries, Taurus, Scorpio and Aquarius/Snakes. For you, happiness is a Gemini/Dog who knows how to cook.

Home and Family

And they will stop at nothing to see themselves ensconced in surroundings of good taste. The Leo/Pig is always the person with the prettiest garden, the most enormous prize roses and the vacation plan so luxuriously unusual and lavish as to make your eyes water with envy. You see, Leo/ Pigs spend a lot of time on luxury. They cannot lie down in a bed that by day does not wear velvet and by night antique satins and laces. Oh, I don't mean that if pushed they cannot be good sports. But mostly, no. It's not a good idea to take your Leo/Pig brother to a rock concert in the park in the rain. He's not going to like freezing his duff off just for a shred of the strains of "Yah Yah Baybee" wafting over the ether. He'd much rather be home in his leather armchair listening to his high-quality stereo set and drinking a glass of champagne.

In family matters, the Leo/Pig is both serious and sardonic. He has an individual way of dealing with disappointment with mates or kids or in-laws. He bypasses his hurt feelings with humor. "Well, Judith never did like *foie gras,*" says the Leo/Pig about his daughter, who has just failed her final exams. Yes. Leo/Pig is disappointed. But he's also ever prepared for others to be less than sincere, not quite so gallant nor so loyal as he. He doesn't have a superiority complex. He's really superior. (At least that's how it feels to be a Leo/Pig—or so I'm told.)

If you have a Leo/Pig child, don't leave him alone to grow up willy-nilly and hope for the best. True, he will seem extraordinary right from the cradle. He'll be reserved and profound—a deep thinker. He may seem slow. And he surely is exceptional. But the Leo/Pig child needs desperately to be guided, gently prodded and shown how to apply his talents. Otherwise, when he grows up, if he hasn't developed his abilities, he may fail miserably. Only a Leo/ Pig can fail so dramatically which only makes him feel more inadequate. Yes. He knows he's funny. But for the Leo/Pig with his lofty goals and serious sense of duty, funny is not enough. He wants to shine in all his endeavors.

The Leo/Pig is gifted from birth with standards so high, for himself first and foremost, that he must achieve a high degree of excellence in his field or else give up (long before anyone else would). The Leo/Pig deplores mediocrity. So go heavy on the music lessons and enroll him in the poshest, most academically rigorous private schools. Junior Leo/Pigs need (and love) good training.

Profession

A Leo/Pig friend of mine always tells me that his burning ambition was nipped in the bud very early on in life by an inner-directed cold shower of laziness. He claims to be so lazy that no serious project ever really tempts him for more than five minutes. Of course, I know this person's achievements are many, and projects that would daunt Lindbergh and Amelia Earhart, Jacques Cousteau and Superman, are but meager deeds to this talented Leo/Pig character.

The lack of belief in self, shall I say, or the bitterness based on repeated disappointment in coworkers or superiors (the Leo/Pig would call them "inferiors"), may cause the honest and credulous Leo/Pig to give up before he begins. As I have already said, this subject will not stoop to conquer. Either they give him that super promotion because of his merits, or they can eat cake.

A happy Leo/Pig is one whose talents flower due to some curious turn of fate or wise choice of colleagues or mates. The Leo/Pig can work wonders in the proper ambience of emotional security, encouragement, free expression and hunger for money.

Famous Leo/Pigs:
Alfred Hitchcock, Alice Evans, Amy Forsyth, Andrew Garfield, Anne-Marie Peysson, Arnold Schwarzenegger, Ashley Johnson, Cantinflas, Carl Jung, Chris Hemsworth, Christine Taylor, Greta Gerwig, Henry Ford, Jacob Vargas, Jeff Gordon, John C. McGinley, Jonathan Ke Quan, Justin Theroux, Kevin Spacey, Laura Breckenridge, Liana Liberato, Lucille Ball, Lulu Antariksa, Mamie Gummer, Marcia Gay Harden, Merrin Dungey, Mila Kunis, Mirjana Puhar, Parker McKenna Posey, Pete Sampras, Ray Wise, Richard Armitage, Richard Griffiths, Rosanna Arquette, Sally Struthers, Tammin Sursok, Teanna Trump, Tom Green, Yvette Nicole Brown.

VIRGO
QUALITIES
LUCIDITY, DISCRIMINATION, COURTESY,
PRACTICALITY, SERVICE, DECORUM
QUIRKS
NIT-PICKING, NEGATIVISM, SNOBBERY,
METICULOUSNESS, CRANKINESS, RESERVE
Motto: *"I analyze"*
Elements: *Earth, Mercury, Mutable*

--

RAT
QUALITIES
NERVOUSNESS, INFLUENCE,
ACQUISITIVENESS, THIRST FOR POWER,
INTELLECTUAL SKILL, CHARISMA
QUIRKS
APPEAL, VERBOSITY, THRIFT,
SOCIABILITY, GUILE, MEDDLING
Motto: *"I rule"*
Elements: *Positive Water, Yang*

A peppy, analytical person will be born of these two strong signs. Without the bulldozer punch of some of the other forceful New Astrological signs, the Virgo/Rat goes about his business craftily and with both system and industry. The Rat's aggressiveness is tempered here by Virgo's methodical intelligence. Virgo/Rats are neither hotheaded nor foolish—except in love.

The thing about Virgo/Rats that sets them above the madding crowd is their total independence of pressure from without. They do what is necessary when they feel it propitious and will not suffer to be hurried or cornered by associates or adversaries. "Wait." The

Virgo/Rat will hold up his hand in an important meeting. "Let me think." And reflect he will—for as long as it takes to dredge what information he needs out of his own head. This character works best alone and needs no straight men or canned laughter to propel him to perform.

As Virgo/Rats deal so resolutely from within their own sphere of influence, it is sometimes difficult for them to listen or heed advice or opinions from others. They seem to absorb information perfectly while it is being spewed at them. Then, surprise! They have not assimilated the facts as they were emitted. They have instead fed some facts into the data bank in their own inner world in their personal, private, meticulously exact language. In doing so, the Virgo/Rat is capable of sapping all the emotional punch from another person's idea before the idea has a chance to take its first breath.

Of course this coin has a reverse side. Overly windy and impulsive people can be skillfully assisted by the likes of Virgo/Rats. The staid and sinuous thought processes of the Virgo born in a Rat year can sort the feeling from the fact in seconds flat. Go crying and weeping to a nice Virgo/Rat person sometime and watch his style. "Now sit down. Calm yourself. Collect your thoughts. What was it again?" they may say cannily. By the time you look up from your sopping handkerchief, the Virgo/Rat is on the telephone. It usually turns out he had begun calling your enemy's number before you got through your first gasp. He doesn't need to hear all the gory details. He sifts through rapidly, and click, he's got the fellow on the line.

There is something of a Popeye quality in this deep-thinking dynamo, too. The idea of rescuing people in distress is tempting and so easy for the Virgo/Rat that he doesn't see why he shouldn't just pop a can of spinach and dive into the fray. I have Virgo/Rat friends who seem to prosper on the trouble that others can cause for them. They marry problems, they hatch problems and they fall in love with their problems' problems. Virgo/Rats' upheavals have upheavals. But they just keep going ahead at their own mild-mannered pace, getting to their office on time, calling the psychiatrist for their daughter's husband, and then getting the firemen on the phone about their cousin the arsonist's most recent caper, and after that they write a letter to the police about their wife or husband's little knife incident.

You'd think they would explode from the complexities of other people's lives. But no. They find it perfectly normal that their forty-five-year-old sister-in-law just found out she was illegitimate and had a nervous breakdown in Macy's. They dash out to buy another straitjacket.

Virgos and Rats both take kinship and friendship very seriously. They never forget an old pal, and would literally give you the shirt off their backs if you needed it. If someone they care about deprives a Virgo/Rat of his friendship for any reason whatsoever, he is stunned and shocked. As a benefactor, he cannot understand why people he has helped and admired would jilt him. Trouble is, he can sometimes be so blindly preoccupied with his bevy of pet nutcases that it exasperates his friends. This he cannot understand. And it wounds his spirit deeply.

Love

Where hearts are concerned, lucidity is not the Virgo/Rat's strong suit. Although he may be a genius at scrutinizing a contract for a pal who just got a role in a film and is worried he'll be ripped off, Virgo/Rat cannot be even slightly objective about his personal life. He loves people with irrational passion. And I am sorry to say that he idealizes them too. As Virgo/Rat is such a straight-up guy, he thinks everybody else is just as direct-dealing and fair as he is. Of course Virgo/Rats have the most devastatingly bad luck in love affairs because they cannot see the forest for the trees. People pull more wool over Virgo/Rat's eyes in love affairs than is produced in all of Australia.

Yet, the Virgo/Rat needs love desperately and will travel far and wide to locate just the right person to fall in love with. I know a Virgo/Rat woman who, at forty, left her wealthy Protestant minister husband in a gossipy small town in the South, took her five children under the age of twelve and moved to India to follow the love of her life. India? "Why not?" says the impassioned Virgo/Rat. "I loved him, didn't I?"

If you love a Virgo/Rat, do him or her a favor: Don't make life easy for them. Be complicated. Make scenes and cause rows and burn down the living room once in a while. But—and this is the big but with Virgo/Rats—always be sweet. Virgo/Rats are always a bit stiff. They are bowled over by sweetness and docility. They like nice people, and really don't care how you act as long as you stay as sweet as you are.

Compatibilities

I can see you felicitous next to an Ox, a Monkey or a Dragon of the Taurus, Cancer, Scorpio or Capricorn schools. I'm not quite so sure about those Scorpio/Dragons, however. They are fairly dashing and dauntless and you usually prefer to do the dashing and daunting. If I were you I would avoid Gemini, Libra, Sagittarius and Pisces born in either Cat years. Please don't marry a Horse or any color, shape or size whatsoever. Horses and Rats are initially attracted to each other, but long term the two signs do battle and someone—usually the Rat—gets hurt. Rats are sentimental and home-loving, protective and caring. Yet, it's no secret, they want the power in relationships. Horses can be loving and caring too. But they are more pragmatic and proud and do not give up power without a fight. Result? Constant wrangling.

Home and Family

A model of family responsibility, the Virgo/Rat likes to take care of others, give them everything he has and allow them whimsy and fantasy galore. But oddly, with all of this apparent indulgence, Virgo/Rats want the rules to be obeyed. They are not like cops. Virgo/Rats don't go goose-stepping around laying down the law. But they themselves respect the rights of others and behave in a mannerly and orderly fashion. They would never be able to comprehend a child or spouse or even a parent who did not do as much. The Golden Rule describes the way Virgo/Rats treat their families. Some kids take advantage of this good-natured fair play attitude and walk all over their Virgo/Rat parents by not playing the game. I'm not mentioning any names but some kids need a good boot in the bottom.

The Rat/Virgo's home will be a haven for everybody he loves to come and visit, sit around the fire, chat and gas and natter on till all hours. As he is a sensualist and appreciates fine wines and foods, he will share them with you as though there were no tomorrow. "Here. Try this *Ro-manee-Conti.* No? You'd rather have *Gevrey-Chambertin?* Hang on, I've got just the bottle for you." You'll never see such sumptuousness laid on anywhere but in the festive Virgo/Rat's dining room. Too, as he is both a careful Virgo and a hoarding Rat, this character will be the best friend you want to know during food shortages. This person stocks up on everything. You should see my Virgo/Rat friend Irma's pantry. She never buys one of anything in the supermarket. Dog food for years to come. The dog will be dead by the time she uses it all up.

Virgo/Rat children may seem too quiet and reserved to be healthy. But it isn't so. Virgo/Rats enjoy behaving well. You cannot keep them still for long, though, as they need to move about a lot and are curious about all matters. But they can be taught almost any skill with their hands, and usually enjoy refined tastes in everything from food to music at a young age. These children need a neat place to grow in. Try not to force them to share with a messy sibling. It won't teach them anything and will only further fray their fragile little nerve endings.

Profession

This person is a gifted analyst. His talents lie in areas requiring research and a systematic approach. He is able to act quickly but does not like to make rapid or ill-considered decisions. Virgo/Rats are especially talented in fields where they have the opportunity to help other people achieve their ends. They enjoy being privy to the inside dope in any situation and can keep secrets—except about their personal lives.

Virgo/Rats are not terribly flexible people. They are often disquieted and restless. All careers that require dealing with the public are wise choices. But Virgo/Rats will probably not take well to vapid or empty-headed jobs. They don't mind doing menial or routine jobs and are capable of enormous patience for poring over accounts and densely worded documents. As a boss, a Virgo/Rat would be ideal for a hard-working, cheerful employee. But if he has to use a cattle prod to get his workers moving, he'll simply fire them. Virgo/ Rats do not suffer inefficiency in themselves or anybody else. Virgo/Rats make fabulous employees themselves. They may be just a bit on the rigid side in their outlook. But better rigidity than sloppiness, *n'est-ce pas?*

Career opportunities for Virgo/Rats will be found in these fields: psychoanalysis, agenting (all sorts), real estate development, business administration, medicine, entertainment

Famous Virgo/Rats:

Cal Ripken Jr., Callum Keith Rennie, Cameron Diaz, Claude Pepper, Colin Firth, Damon Wayans, Daniele Hypólito, David James Elliot, Gene Kelly, George RR Martin, Hugh Grant, Idris Elba, Joan Jett, Joseph Kennedy Sr., Lauren Bacall, Leo Tolstoy, Lisa Vanderpump, Maurice Chevalier, Melissa Leo, Prince Harry, Queen Letizia of Spain, Todd English, Zendaya.

VIRGO
QUALITIES
LUCIDITY, DISCRIMINATION, COURTESY,
PRACTICALITY, SERVICE, DECORUM
QUIRKS
NIT-PICKING, NEGATIVISM, SNOBBERY,
METICULOUSNESS, CRANKINESS, RESERVE
Motto: *"I analyze"*
Elements: *Earth, Mercury, Mutable*

--

OX
QUALITIES
STUBBORNNESS, STRENGTH OF PURPOSE,
ELOQUENCE, STANDOFFISHNESS, INNOVATION,
VINDICTIVENESS
QUIRKS
INTEGRITY, BIGOTRY, PLODDING,
DILIGENCE, BIAS, STABILITY
Motto: *"I preserve"*
Elements: *Negative Water, Yin*

"Nothing worthwhile ever comes easily," says the plodding model of human rectitude who is Virgo and Ox. An air of the ascetic emanates from this stolid character. He is deliberate. He is careful. He is meticulous. He is diligent, classical, traditionalist and sincere. And he never hangs out with anyone who is not at least some of the above. Virgo/Ox needs to rule his life single-handedly. He asks help of no one but his own people. These he has either hatched himself or chosen as friends and colleagues after much sorting and weeding out over the years.

All variety of criticism can be directed at this subject. He is such a caricature of his stodgy self that we could spend paragraphs on his foibles. But that would be too easy. You can see for yourself that of all the characteristics of both the Virgo and Ox signs, there are only a couple of really feathery qualities. This person is at best both courteous and innovative—that's it for the jolly side, folks. As for solemnity, this person is a past master.

What saves this character from sinking under his own natural weight is his sense of lucidity and of course his unbeatable eloquence. This person is well spoken and makes a near religion out of fastidiousness in manner and in deed. He doesn't believe in doing things the easy way or in using shortcut methods. The Virgo/Ox firmly espouses the idea that what is right is inalienably and immutably right. Black is black and white, white. Do not attempt to clutter up his mind with nuance.

You can trust this person with your house, your life, your husband, wife, children and pets. Virgo/Oxen pride themselves on their respectability. They are reliable and efficient. They are also, in a sort of severe and crisp way, loving. They are loyal and honest. They can be tempted by ruses, although this is rare, and involvement in any crooked scheme will be their undoing. They cannot live with a bad conscience. These folks need to keep a clean slate inside their heads. With them it's all or nothing. If they got caught with their hand in the kitty, they'd probably commit hari-kari.

Virgo/Oxen are better at achieving success through hard work than almost anybody else. They are some of the world's most addicted workaholics. Virgo/Oxen are not interested in airy cocktail conversation and they eschew small talk. Some people think they are rather too unsociable. But it's their way. They will talk if they want to tell you a story and they'll do so brilliantly. Then they clam up. In other words, Virgo/Oxen are not funny off the set.

The Virgo/Ox resists change. If tasks are done one way, and have been done like that for a long, long time, and he or she has learned the skill of handling said task with characteristic artisanal perfection, then this person sees no reason to alter his way. He may innovate and develop something that turns out to be foolproof. But he will test it for ten years before he'll attempt to commercialize his scheme. He's conservative and thrives on both zeal and exertion. When it comes to endurance, to perseverance and steady toiling, the Virgo/Ox wins the race.

Love

Constancy is the Virgo/Ox's middle name. He is essentially a practical sort and so usually falls in love with someone who will be useful as well as, say, decorative or sexy or brilliant. One of the Virgo/Ox's most out-standing traits is his discrimination. These people are mighty choosy about whom they frequent, and seek, above all, a sense of probity and industry in friendship. Ephemeral passionate love affairs are too messy for straight-arrow Virgo/ Oxen.

If you find yourself attracted to this hulking nit-picker with the full pocketbook, show him your calloused hands and tell him how you had to milk the cows all by yourself in the cold barn when you were five years old. Give him plenty to admire you for. Then try to resign yourself to being just as dutifully hard-working as he for the rest of your days. Virgo/Oxen don't want just a pretty face as a mate. Industriousness, they feel, is about the best quality a spouse can offer.

Compatibilities

Harmony can be found, especially if you go looking for it, among Taurus, Cancer, Scorpio or Capricorn people. In Taurus you will particularly enjoy the company of Snakes and Dragons. The Cancers in your life will probably be Horses and Dogs. Same goes for Scorpios and Capricorns—Horses and Dogs all the way. Don't go marrying any Gemini/Dragons, Horses or Sheep. Refrain from associating with Sagittarius/Sheep and Tigers. And whatever you do, don't take up with Pisces of the last two animal categories. Too wishy washy new-agey oogah boogah spiritual for your down-to-earth workaday tastes.

Home and Family

This person's surroundings will be traditional and comfortable to a point. He is not one to buy plush squishy armchairs or pouts made of satins and silks. He wants things to be both practical and sturdily handsome.

Above all, he likes his environment to be efficient for family living. Luxuries? Well, they can come later. I know a Virgo/Ox who is building his wife her first new kitchen in fifty years of marriage. She's been patient, he tells me.

If your mother or father is a Virgo/Ox, you know by know that when you grew up you were supposed to be either exactly what they were or, at the very outside eccentricity, a doctor or lawyer. Virgo/Oxen sacrifice materially for their families. In return they expect Junior and little Sukey to toe the mark and follow in their footsteps. In families, the Virgo/Ox runs the show, wears the pants and holds the purse strings.

The Virgo/Ox child will be a stubborn and deliberate sort. There is no jollying him or her along. Just make sure they learn how to perform some skill or enter some serious line of work that challenges their enormous capacity for effort. Tire them out daily with sports and chores and homework. This kid is basically structure-oriented and cannot tolerate inactivity for long.

Profession

This subject favors quiet environments without benefit of the city's clanging or rush. He or she is talented in the countryside's demands. Remnants of the gentleman farmer or the elegant provincial wife live very near the surface of Virgo/Ox's soul. He's thorough and accurate, conscientious and aboveboard. Moreover, the Virgo/Ox is endowed with a sharp intelligence that will ensure that whatever job he chooses gets done right.

As a boss, this person is terrific. Virgo/Oxen can and do dictate, make rules and see that they are carried out. They know how to delegate workloads and are not afraid of disciplinary measures. They are often good businesspeople and they know how to live economically. The same holds true if this person is employed. He is not afraid of discipline, nor is he too proud to obey when necessary. The natural Virgo/Ox authority is not ego-based. This person can take orders as well as give them.

Some suitable professions for the Virgo born Ox are: market analyst, artisan, dog trainer, athlete, cattle rancher, farmer.

Famous Virgo/Oxen:

Lafayette, Peter Sellers, Robert Bresson, Ben Blue, Billy Ray Cyrus, Dan Marino, Eric Stoltz, Henri Krasucki, Jennifer Tilly, Julien Green, Mylène Farmer, Philippe Labro, Scott Baio, Vincent Trintignant, Ally Walker, Nancy Travis, James Gandolfini, Joanne Whalley, Jared Harris, James Marsden, Andrew Lincoln, Rose McGowan, Shannon Elizabeth, Madeline Zima, Amy Manson, Alyssa Diaz.

VIRGO
QUALITIES
LUCIDITY, DISCRIMINATION, COURTESY,
PRACTICALITY, SERVICE, DECORUM
QUIRKS
NIT-PICKING, NEGATIVISM, SNOBBERY,
METICULOUSNESS, CRANKINESS, RESERVE
Motto: *"I analyze"*
Elements: *Earth, Mercury, Mutable*

--

TIGER
QUALITIES
FERVOR, BRAVERY, MAGNETISM,
GOOD LUCK, BENEVOLENCE, AUTHORITY
QUIRKS
IMPETUOSITY, HOTHEADEDNESS,
DISOBEDIENCE, SWAGGER, INTEMPERANCE,
ITINERANCY
Motto: *"I Watch"*
Elements: *Positive Wood, Yang*

The Virgo/Tiger is a tough cookie with a heart of gold. Virgo/Tigers don't let anything get past them. They notice and calculate and tot up and plan and analyze and then... they pounce. It's an unbeatable combination for the person himself to live with, but maybe it's a little bit on the cranky, know-it-all side for those who have to live with him. Redeeming qualities? Plenty.

Virgo as an added ingredient to Tiger restricts the Tiger's impetuousness, turns the Tiger's tongue around three times before letting him blurt out his foolhardy schemes, and truly molds the Tiger's normally sprawling, messy existence into something quite wonderful.

First of all, the Virgo/Tiger is a dutiful slave. No amount of work daunts this unflinchingly industrious person. Whatever the task, no matter how many there will be for lunch or dinner, or how many stops he has to make along the way to let Junior out to pee or give sister some air, the Virgo/Tiger performs admirably.

Now all of this unstinting driving and cooking and cleaning and welcoming and more driving and cooking and cleaning are not done without complaint. The Virgo/Tiger may be a slave. But he is not a willing slave. Rather, he is bound by duty, imprisoned by his sense of obligation and tied down by his fervent belief in what is right. He will go to that goddamned office every morning on foot and without a sigh for thirty years if need be, without ever missing a day. But woe unto the dependent who doesn't appreciate what that sensible Virgo/Tiger goes through for his sake. Virgo/Tigers make wonderful allies. And they make indomitable enemies as well. They never forgive.

You see, normally Virgos don't mind being serious. It's part of their lot. But here, the Tiger comes loping along with that silly grin pasted on his chops and entices the darkest side of Virgo, summons him to prankishness and movement. If the Virgo/Tiger is sensible and doesn't go off the Tiger's deep end, he may have a terrific life. Tigers are not at all like Virgos. But they do understand them. So, properly handled, the Tiger lends a bouncy note or je ne sais quoi to what could be a stodgy Virgo life.

There will be a definite streak of charity here, and the ability to perceive the problems of others as his own. Virgo/Tigers are good advisers. They are strappingly sensible and wise. Too, they can be meddlesome and don't hesitate to upbraid their friends for peccadilloes the size of your pinkie nail. They're meticulous and fussy about what they eat, and with whom they spend time, and whether or not those items are up to their rather exaggerated standards. Virgo/Tigers are not quite bossy. They're pushy. But not authoritarian.

You often find Virgo/Tigers in conservative places. They are fond of museums and warm to the mystery of archeological digs. They move a lot and don't mind wandering and travel. But they like to make the most of whatever they are doing and therefore tend not to be mobile just for the sake of being mobile.

This variety of Tiger will be a snob. Tigers already have a pretty high opinion of self. Virgos are lucid about their own limitations, but they like to feel they know the "right" people. It can become annoying to be constantly reminded by a Virgo/Tiger host who so-and-so is rather than just being allowed to get to know him or her. Yet this name-dropping habit is native to the Virgo/Tiger, who sometimes seems more concerned about who people are in society than who they really are in their hearts

The Virgo/Tiger boasts a fine bearing and, although not classi-cally beautiful, seems to know how to make the best of whatever looks he was born with. Here again, it pays to be objective about one's appearance. Objectivity is the Virgo/Tiger's specialty. He may try to fool you. But he never fools himself about anything.

There is a lot of innate cheer in the Virgo/Tiger, too. They like to have fun, make others laugh, cut up and play. They are often good at sports and are dead serious about their tennis or golf or squash. Virgo/Tigers put a lot of effort into making their lives swell places to live in. They share well and truly enjoy providing others with joy. Thcy won't ask for much applause, either. They're just doing their best, which is always impressively better than the best of other, less dutiful souls.

Love

A more honorable life partner, upstanding in the extreme and a reliable organizer of everything—including sentiment—one could not even dream of. But don't count on the Virgo/Tiger for lascivi-ous roll-in-the-hay voluptuousness. Virgo/Tigers enjoy lovemaking and throw themselves into it as vigorously as they do their cooking and driving and jogging. But the trouble is, while they are engaged in the lustier pleasures, Virgo/Tigers may give you the eerie im-pression that they are worried about that cake they slipped into the oven just before the wooing began, Is it falling or rising? Virgo/T igers can't help it. They just have to be useful.

If you love a Virgo/Tiger and want to please him or her, I suggest you make every effort to be a respectable and even hugely impor-tant person in society. Virgo/Tigers are interested in position. They are turned on by people they can admire and look up to. Lazy or just so-so achievers bring out the picky Virgo side of Virgo/Tigers. They may become lifelong grumps, embittered by association with someone they love but don't respect. And although the Virgo/Tiger will do anything to keep up appearances, you will be able to tell if the respect is evaporating when you and your favorite Virgo/Tiger are finally nose to nose between the sheets. For this character it's all or nothing. No maybes.

Compatibilities

You are attracted to Capricorns. There's something similar in your dry, dense approach to the way Capricorn/Horses and Dogs behave. You will get on. Taurus, Cancer and Scorpio/Horses and Dogs make excellent choices for you as well. You're too fiery for the stolid Aries/Ox and you are not laid back enough for old Gemini/Sheep. Gemini, Sagittarius and Pisces/Snakes and Monkeys will not do.

Home and Family

The Virgo/Tiger's home will favor a traditional decorating scheme. As this person cleaves to whatever is stable and real, he generally enjoys surrounding himself with antiques and treasures of veritable value and status. In choosing colors, he tends toward yellows and turquoises. Virgo/Tigers like to liven up their environment with comfortable prettiness. Flowers will be part of their weekly budget, and exotic teas and jams will please them.

Family, if the busy Virgo/Tiger ever gets around to having one, holds the paramount place in this subject's life. Lots of children are probably not in the cards. Noisy brats crashing about the Virgo/ Tigers' cushioned salons and bashing into their flower vases do not fit into their ideal picture of family bliss. Yet, if they do have a child or two, they will be devoted and special parents whose every action is intended to ensure the happiness and future of little Junior or Missy. As for their parents, Virgo/Tigers are responsible about calling Mother on her birthday and taking Dad to the doctor for a checkup, but they will not allow meddling in their own lives and practically never actually cohabit with their parents after they reach maturity.

Virgo/Tiger children make wonderful house pets. They can be counted on to keep their rooms clean and run errands and wash dishes. They may, however, display picky nervousness and be mildly cranky at times. They will probably study well, but not for long. The establishment of a home and family at an early age is the natural outgrowth of this person's serious and self-reliant nature. He likes to establish himself on his own and free himself from dependence.

Profession

The Virgo/Tiger's earthy, energetic self will lend itself to any career requiring both mobility and responsibility. It will not do, however, to expose this security-conscious soul to excesses of free enterprise or unplanned projects. Virgo/Tigers are a bit on the hotheaded side and can be impetuous. But they will probably reserve their impulsivity for sound, sane actions within an established framework. You won't find many Virgo/Tigers rushing off to become mercenaries or saving lepers in Africa, either. They enjoy comfort and ease and do not mind creating and maintaining it for themselves and loved ones.

The Virgo/Tiger is not uncharitable, and might be happy as a church or Red Cross volunteer. Also, you will find Virgo/Tigers among solid business professionals such as controllers and investment bankers. Too, as the Virgo/Tiger treasures his neat little nest and cares about his social image, he will make a fine houseperson whose daily job it is to see that those who live with him evolve successfully. Virgo/Tigers usually like staying home and preparing elegant dinner parties too. The creativity of this person is often applied in areas related to decoration or style.

Famous Virgo/Tigers:
Alfie Allen, Armie Hammer, Bill Murray, Cathy Guisewaite, Cheri Oteri, David Fincher, Elliott Gould, Emmy Rossum, Ian Harding, Jimmy Fallon, Joan Lunden, Karl Lagerfeld, Lea Michele, Lea Michele, Molly Tarlov, Narendra Modi, Paul Feig, Rob Morrow, Ryan Phillippe, Sofia Richie, Willie DeVille.

VIRGO
QUALITIES
LUCIDITY, DISCRIMINATION, COURTESY,
PRACTICALITY, SERVICE, DECORUM
QUIRKS
NIT-PICKING, NEGATIVISM, SNOBBERY,
METICULOUSNESS, CRANKINESS, RESERVE
Motto: *"I analyze"*
Elements: *Earth, Mercury, Mutable*

--

CAT/RABBIT
QUALITIES
TACT, FINESSE, VIRTUE,
PRUDENCE, LONGEVITY, AMBITION,
QUIRKS
SECRETIVENESS, SQUEAMISHNESS,
PEDANTRY, DILETTANTISM,
HYPOCHONDRIA, COMPLEXITY
Motto: *"I Retreat"*
Elements: *Negative, Wood, Yin*

Virgo/Cat is the picture of caution. His first portrait can only be painted after many years of slow and deliberate development. You will never hear him complain, nor will you notice him creeping up on you. This person is sagaciously circumspect, stays out of the way of danger and will even throw away what is most important to him just to keep the peace and dodge conflict.

With all of this, the Cat born Virgo is often obliged to be alone. He likes his home, feet up next to the hearth, books to read, dense silence to keep him company. This image is only possible if the door is armored, the windows equipped with alarm systems and the wall around the property ten feet thick. Cats born Virgo don't want nobody messing' with them. These people have difficulty communicating. They would rather work or build or restore or putter with a project than just sit around shooting the breeze. Small talk not only bores them, it positively frightens them. Chitchat all seems so glassy and insubstantial. Those petty remarks and gossipings that people find amusing make Virgo/Cat feel uneasy. Why aren't these folks busy with some more edifying pursuit? he asks himself.

I'm not suggesting that Cats born Virgo are goody-goodies or Polyannas. Not a bit. These people do not parade themselves as models of good behavior. Their exemplary deportment comes quite naturally to them. They are not obliged to force themselves to be virtuous, nor do they scoff at those who aren't. Virgo/Cats are supremely tolerant of others and know how to put up with their eccentricities and faults.

The Virgo/Cat is genuinely preoccupied with advancement and, in his or her own quiet way, seeks only to achieve progress and find the ideal environment that he knows intrinsically is right for him. Virgo/Cats are motivated by duty and spurred forward by the search for an ideal world wherein everyone would leave the noble Virgo/Cat to his own devices. He will pull with the masses, so long as the end result includes his own peace of mind.

Because of an innate difficulty with human contact, this person may seem aloof and even tyrannical. He or she will require feats of performance from associates. The Virgo/Cat asks as much, if not more, of himself. Why then shouldn't his colleagues strive to match his efforts?

The Virgo/Cat is often accused of social climbing. This stems from his desire for refinement and his need to cleave to what is traditional. He is fussy about manners and frets over social faux pas. He prefers not to take big risks and yet, when called upon to act in an emergency, can prove heroically courageous. Routine doesn't annoy the Virgo/Cat. Nor does a certain subjugation, so long as said slavery protects him or her from accident. Virgo/Cats deplore unforeseen occurrences and balk at change.

Love

This person's love life will have two very distinct parts. In his or her youth, the Virgo/Cat will probably get involved with kinky or zany types. In youth this character likes to wallow in a bit of human mud. During this time of experimentation he may well fall madly in love with some oddball. But this "nut' love period is, I fear, very short-lived. What this person is ultimately looking for is not a laugh a minute or a glamorous life in the spotlight. Before age thirty, Virgo/Cats usually dive for cover from early romantic errors. They often surface years later as the wife of some oil magnate or the very safety married owner of a shoe store in Topeka.

They do, however, have a soft spot for the unfortunate. Virgo/Cats sometimes get their virtue mixed up with their sense of sacrifice. Then they may fall prey to relationships that turn them into unwilling slaves for the rest of their lives. If you care about a Virgo/Cat, do yourself and him or her a big favor—learn to leave him in peace. Don't talk to this character unless it is absolutely necessary. Don't hover around your Virgo/Cat's chair or buzz in his ear. Turn the TV off forever and go to your room and read until dinnertime. For this delicately strung human instrument, heaven is tranquility.

Compatibilities

Oh how you get on with Taurus, Cancer, Scorpio and Capricorn/Pigs! All of these hearth-dwellers to the manor born are capable of giving you happiness. You are also welcome to try Taurus, Scorpio and Capricorn/Sheep and Dogs. You get on especially well with Taurus/Cats, too. I don't advise Gemini, Sagittarius or Pisces/ Roosters for you. They are far too elastic to fit into your cautious lifestyle. Gemini and Sagittarius/Rats are out, as are Pisces/ Dragons.

Home and Family

In addition to all the locks and bolts and alarm systems, this person's home will be discreetly furnished with antique *objets d'art* designed to grow gracefully older along with their owner. Virgo/Cats like beige and old gold. They are attracted to ivories and off-whites in their decor. They cling to culture and tradition in everything from soup to nuts—including the kitchen sink.

This person will make an intellectually responsible parent. He or she will surely spend time trotting Jason and Sarah to museums and seeing to it they are taught old nursery rhymes. Of course Virgo/Cats provide. They are superlative wage-earners and believe in the nuclear family as the salvation of the future. I wouldn't mind being this person's child at all. It would certainly be comfy and safe.

This child will be fearful and squeamish. Virgo/Cats are born with a ponderous respect for danger and must be cajoled into acts of daring. They don't take kindly to change, so try not to have a Virgo/Cat child if you plan a divorce. This kid needs order and routine more than almost any other sign.

Profession

As Virgo/Cats require security and seek to set their wealth safely aside forever, they are good at all jobs that earn them a decent, steady income. Of course, Virgo/Cats don't always achieve fame or even succeed at amassing the fortune they covet because they are scaredy-cats. As we all know, the jackpot lands most often in the lap of the one who dares take a chance. Virgo/Cats can't. They will work and even slave efficiently and earnestly. But they will never venture out on a limb.

In positions of authority these people tend toward rigor and severity infused with a kind of unspoken understanding of their own superiority. They are, in fact, paragons of patronizingness. They like to think they are caring for their employees, providing for their families and financing their whims. It's annoying. But effective.

The Virgo/Cat employee is a model worker. He is so virtuous and honorable that he never gets fired—much to his detriment, I fear. These folks have been known to stay in the same dumb, slavish, steady job all their lives for sheer terror of not finding another.

Careers suitable to the Virgo/Cat are: museum curator, librarian, archivist, market analyst, travel agent, diplomat, gardener, decorator, musician.

Famous Virgo/Cat/Rabbits:

Blake Lively, Cassandra (Elvira) Peterson, Claudette Colbert, Danielle Panabaker, Emma Kenney, Evan Rachel Wood, Ingrid Bergman, Jack Lange, Jason Sudeikis, Jorge Branco de Sampaio (Portugal), Julie Kavner, Margaret Sanger, Mark Harmon, Memphis Slim, Michael Chiklis, Michael Keaton, Mireille Enos, Steven Downs, Timothy Bottoms, Tom Felton, Tyler Hoechlin, Van Morisson, Wiz Khalifa.

VIRGO
QUALITIES
LUCIDITY, DISCRIMINATION, COURTESY,
PRACTICALITY, SERVICE, DECORUM
QUIRKS
NIT-PICKING, NEGATIVISM, SNOBBERY,
METICULOUSNESS, CRANKINESS, RESERVE
Motto: *"I analyze"*
Elements: *Earth, Mercury, Mutable*
--

DRAGON
QUALITIES
STRENGTH, SUCCESS, GOOD HEALTH,
ENTHUSIASM, PLUCK, SENTIMENTALITY
QUIRKS
RIGIDITY, MISTRUST, DISSATISFACTION,
INFATUATION, BRAGGADOCIO, VOLUBILITY
Motto: *"I Preside"*
Elements: *Positive Wood, Yang*

The Virgo/Dragon couples Virgo decorum with Dragon sizzle. This Dragon is hard-edged. He has enough spunk and perseverance to take a dare to walk across Australia – solo! He always maintains a coy Virgo reserve in order to keep Dragonish taste for fresh blood under dignified wraps. If you're looking for performance, it's a hard to beat combination. The fiery Dragonesque soul is tempered by Virgo's taste for social grace. Virgo/ Dragon is ambitious and has a mind like a platinum bear trap.

In this discriminating character there is not as much braggadocio and volubility as in other Dragons. Yet, when this person is angry (which is frequently), fireworks invariably occur. The marriage of Dragon to Virgo, with all of their possible complementary traits, is just a shade too self-interested to be called harmonious. Virgo/Dragons are picky and strong-willed. They carry a harsh and vituperative tongue around in their heads. The general atmosphere is not exactly cozy.

Although this person starts out life bursting with sentimentality and tenderheartedness, adulthood brings disenchantment. The result is a jaded, blasé and sometimes even dangerous grownup.

Driving volition is an important Dragon/Virgo personality trait. This person goes at life with a burning zeal that borders on fanaticism. There is, of course, much success out there for such determined people. But there are also a lot of dead bodies in their wakes. What Dragon/Virgo wants, Dragon/Virgo gets.

These subjects can be thoroughly attractive. They carry themselves with a certain arrogance and they know how to dress. They are born with good health and stay in shape to preserve that state. This person wants to "make it" in life, to beat out his competition, to take the world title in his field, and nothing will stand in his way. Except his terrible temper.

Virgo/Dragons are stompers and fumers and fussers and screamers. They are furious about one-third of the time—at their families, at their bosses and at themselves. They despise failure, and even hate themselves for a tiny booboo or goof such as hitting their finger with a hammer. Such tempestuous behavior, of course, repels people who might be able to really care for this alluring demon. Virgo/Dragons are their own worst enemies. They are sassy and they don't know how to remain invisible.

There isn't much room for small talk with this resolute soul. He or she will prefer getting immediately to the nitty-gritty. Poetry is hardly the Virgo/Dragon's favorite entertainment. He likes competition sports and war, business deals and starring roles. Forget the gingerbread. Just give him a hunk of raw meat to chew on.

Seriously, this person is lucky to possess inordinate self-confidence. He will always keep a clear head. He can be counted on to finish what he starts and he is not often a disappointment to colleagues and partners. Virgo/Dragons demand their share in life, and they most often get it.

Love

The personal lives of Virgo/Dragons don't prove so felicitous. Of course, this person is constantly pursued by members of the opposite gender because he or she will reek of sex appeal and mystique.

But unfortunately this person is more fascinated by his career and his social effect than by intimacy with one person.

If you love one of these feisty creatures, you'll have to enjoy standing on the sidelines, smiling and cheering your Virgo/Dragon to victory. He or she will insist on your cooperation in their act. Life with a Virgo/ Dragon is never a two-way street. In short, there is much to admire and not all that much to hug.

Compatibilities

In general you favor Rats, but Taurus and Capricorn/Rats are your most vulnerable targets for romance. Taurus and Cancer/ Roosters keep you quite busy too, as do Taurus, Cancer and Capricorn/ Monkeys. You will be floored by the sexy Scorpio/ Snake. Gemini, Sagittarius and Pisces/Dogs, with their constant hesitations and doubts, irritate you. Oxen both Sagittarius and Pisces, are your most notorious foes. Steer a wide berth.

Home and Family

The decor will be stark and striking. The whole scheme of things in the Virgo/Dragon's environment is severe and in excellent taste. His choice of furniture is generally conservative in line and not too comfortable. One must not lie down nor lean too far into idleness. You are welcome but don't linger, is the Virgo/Dragon's motto.

It takes the Virgo/Dragon quite a while to get around to having a family. Often he will decide on children later rather than sooner in married life. Virgo/Dragons make responsible yet demanding and disciplinary parents. When they pass middle age, they tend to revert to their original sentimentality, too. Dragons born in Virgo are the kind of people who mellow with age. They make indulgent grandparents, compensating for all the rigidity of their middle years.

The Virgo/Dragon child will toe the mark in school. Here is the president-of-the-class type who has an eye for the glittering prizes in store. He may be vulnerable, too, and easily hurt. Don't worry, he'll toughen up as he goes along. But as a little person the Virgo/ Dragon needs a lot of attentive protection. You will certainly have reason to be proud of your baby Virgo/Dragon. But if you are not, don't worry. He'll be proud enough for both of you.

Profession

The Dragon born Virgo is happiest and most fulfilled by his or her work. This person is talented in every type of career that permits personal promotion and an eventual rise to the top of the heap. Virgo/Dragons are more restrained than most Dragons. This person's eye never strays from the ball and when he connects, it's home-run time. Virgo/Dragons make peppy, fire-eating bosses. They will attempt to be fair so long as you don't get in their way. Then—well, they feel "all's fair in love and war," and will act accordingly. These people make very competent employees, whose main concern is getting praise for getting the job done. This can be exciting and a relief for an overworked employer. However, the Virgo/ Dragon will always try to leapfrog his superiors and in some way or other scramble his or her way to the best job in the house.

Careers suitable to the Virgo/Dragon are: politician, theatrical or film director, judge, stockbroker, entrepreneur, athlete.

Famous Virgo/Dragons:

Brian de Palma, Carice van Houten, Evan Ross, Hans Hartung, Jamie Kaler, Jimmy Connors, Josh Bernthal, Keanu Reeves, Kim Richards, Linda Gray, Matt Roth, Max George, Merlin Olsen, Nelson Ascencio, Oliver Hudson, Paul Williams, Pauline Collins, Raquel Welch, Régis Debray, Rosie Perez, Rossy de Palma, Rupert Grint, Steven R. Monroe.

VIRGO
QUALITIES
LUCIDITY, DISCRIMINATION, COURTESY,
PRACTICALITY, SERVICE, DECORUM
QUIRKS
NIT-PICKING, NEGATIVISM, SNOBBERY,
METICULOUSNESS, CRANKINESS, RESERVE
Motto: *"I analyze"*
Elements: *Earth, Mercury, Mutable*

--

SNAKE
QUALITIES
INTUITION, ATTRACTIVENESS, DISCRETION,
SAGACITY, CLAIRVOYANCE, COMPASSION
QUIRKS
DISSIMULATION, EXTRAVAGANCE,
LAZINESS, CUPIDITY, PRESUMPTION,
EXCLUSIVENESS
Motto: *"I sense"*
Elements: *Negative, Fire, Yin*

Analysis and intuition are two essential elements in the personality of a Virgo/Snake. This Virgo is both emotional and attractive. He is endowed with wisdom and depth of understanding. He may appear serious and even grave. The tongue, you will notice, however, is conveniently stored inside the cheek. This person's strength is that he is not really of the world. Virgo/Snakes exist outside of the mundane and always wear a secret smile.

Nothing is too technically complex for this subject's intellect and perception. Nor are metaphysical problems beyond his reach. We are dealing here with a monster of attraction and appeal whose flat-out—almost cold—sensuality will warm the blood of even the most reserved observer. Virgo/Snakes are calculating. They always need to know where they are headed. Before they undertake a project they want every element worked out in minute detail. Virgo/Snakes are capable of magnificent insincerity.

I'd say that the Virgo/Snake is introverted yet avidly interested in others. His motive behind this gregariousness is simply his need for admirers. Of these he always has more than his share. He is a long-lasting friend with the ability to listen and to cheer. It's not that Virgo/Snakes are innately funny. They have crinkly-eyed charm that is irresistibly amusing.

This person is remarkably combative for a Snake character. He's quite a scrapper when crossed, and involves himself in monumental tongue-lashings and verbal conflict to spare his pride. Virgo/Snake simply does not tolerate being toyed with. He is dignified and insists on remaining thus. If, however, he sees that the joke is irrevocably on him, this person is capable of laughing at himself. A breakthrough for the sometimes too proud Snake.

These natives seem oblivious to aging and stress. They slither through their daily rounds with a rare sort of detachment from almost every problem encountered. They insist on stability and expect to maintain equilibrium in their personal lives. They never make useless trouble.

Laziness is the Virgo/Snake's enemy. Yes. Even the efficient Virgo can be tempted by the Snake's tendency to sloth. From time to time his analytical side will assess the situation and you'll marvel to see him rise like a spinning top from his sagging sofa and shift into whirlwind activity. This is a capable soul. But if the sun is shining and the livin' is easy, he can grow sluggish. Gourmet food will tempt him too. Virgo/Snakes should avoid waist-expanding foods and keep up a steady exercise routine.

Most striking of all the Virgo/Snake's characteristics is his open-mindedness. This person is always ready for new experiences. He is willing to try anything once, and makes a good companion for someone who likes adventure.

There is a critical side to this subject as well. But since Snake people are disposed to sagacity and they intuit rather than puzzle things out with logic, Virgo nit-picking and fault-finding is kept to a minimum. Gossip, however, pleases the Virgo/Snake, and although he is discreet and never meddles in the affairs of others unless invited, he can frequently be caught in merry derision of the garish color of his neighbor's new car.

Virgo/Snakes are also bossy. Or rather, they rule. Period. Their methods of expressing authority consist of silent pressures and the application of well-defined rules without excessive rant. They care a lot about those they dominate, and can usually convince themselves that their despotism is benevolent. Don't count on getting the best of this class-act person. He's got it all figured out and he knows precisely how to keep it that way.

Love

The Virgo/Snake's love picture is a tiny bit smudgy. You see, Snakes tend to slink in and out of a variety of love affairs throughout their lives. Virgos are rather more constant, yet they are sensuous as well. The tendency is toward slip-sliding away. Virgo/Snake makes the transition from passion to camaraderie smoothly. He remains friends with his "exes."

If you love a Virgo/Snake, you will be so mad for him or her that the very idea of "handling" will not occur to you. But the way to deal with this person, happily, is simply not to try. Don't manipulate him. He doesn't take kindly to machinations behind his back. Don't make fun of him. He'll take offense. Respect him and accept the dense soul that belongs to all natives of this sign. Admire the intellect but don't, for heaven's sake, fawn!

Compatibilities

You are turned on by Oxen and Roosters. If I were you I would stick with those born in Taurus, Scorpio and Capricorn. Don't shed your skin over Gemini, Sagittarius or Pisces/Tigers. Take no for an answer from a Gemini/Monkey. Whatever you do, don't get tangled up in a plot to marry a Pig. It could be detrimental to your health and will certainly be disastrous to the Pig's.

Home and Family

Virgo/Snakes tend to enjoy their freedom and covet being unencumbered. Their surroundings are not of much importance to them, as they are so often on the road. They do like comfort, so you'll see a few easy chairs scattered about and there'll be plenty of good vittles in the larder. But Virgo/Snakes are not homebody types.

If this person does become a parent, he or she will probably indulge the children in whims of all sorts, letting well enough alone and hoping for the best. The Virgo/Snake is autocratic but he's not domineering or interested in policing lives. This parent will have fun with his kids, as he likes a good laugh and can readily join a group of any age for a few giggles.

The Virgo/Snake child will be beautiful to look at and carries himself with that dignified coldness I spoke of earlier. He will probably like parties and astonish you and his teachers with his intellectual skill. There is not much you can do to spoil such a child, as his very presence will demand just the amount of attention he feels he deserves. There is no place in this child's life for parental sarcasm. It enrages him.

Profession

Mostly industrious, the Virgo/Snake only occasionally slides into a laziness rut. He's gifted in things technical from childhood and will know how to build models and fiddle with handiwork projects requiring great attention to detail. This, coupled with his exceptional native intelligence, gives Virgo/Snake a definite edge in all scientific areas and in careers requiring mathematical skill. Cultural activities also attract the Virgo born in a Snake year. The arts, in general, will be tempting as a profession.

As a boss, Virgo/Snake will personify the expression "noblesse oblige." He's so naturally ahead of the game that to question his authority would be silly. He's probably fair and just because he is particularly altruistic. In any case, efficiency will be the rule. This person makes a dutiful and happy addition to any work group. Virgo/Snake employees are both responsible and capable of handling delegated work. They are also able to work alone at jobs requiring precision and application of self-discipline. Virgo/Snakes usually work to live and not the opposite. They like to spend money, so they work for it. But they are not driven by any Protestant work ethic. They adore tropical vacation spots where their chilly nature can absorb the Sun's healing rays.

Careers that suit this subject are: computer programmer, research scientist, economist, copy editor, engineer, architect, auditor.

Famous Virgo/Snakes:

Andy Martinez Jr., Bernie Sanders, Bronwyn Reed, Caterina Murino, Charles Esten, Charlie Sheen, Cheryl Hines, Claude Nougaro, Elena Delle Donne, Fiona Apple, Goethe, Greta Garbo, Hugh Mitchell, Jesse James, Jessica Brown Findlay, Jessica Mitford, Kat Graham, Kyle Chandler, Larry Collins, Marisa Ramirez, Otis Redding, Rhys Ward., Robin Leach, Sunita Williams, Tom Hardy, Valtteri Bottas, William H. Taft, Yasser Arafat.

VIRGO
QUALITIES
LUCIDITY, DISCRIMINATION, COURTESY,
PRACTICALITY, SERVICE, DECORUM
QUIRKS
NIT-PICKING, NEGATIVISM, SNOBBERY,
METICULOUSNESS, CRANKINESS, RESERVE
Motto: *"I analyze"*
Elements: *Earth, Mercury, Mutable*

--

HORSE
QUALITIES
PERSUASIVENESS, UNSCRUPULOUSNESS,
POPULARITY, STYLE, DEXTERITY,
ACCOMPLISHMENT
QUIRKS
SELFISHNESS, AUTONOMY, REBELLION,
HASTE, ANXIETY, PRAGMATISM
Motto: *"I demand"*
Elements: *Positive Fire, Yang*

The marriage of Virgo and Horse is one both lofty and elegant. Horses are self-motivated strivers, doers of grand deeds and sometimes—with all of their parading—a mite foolish and overly passionate. The Virgo, as we all know by now, is reserved. He takes care never to go outside the lines in the coloring book of life. Virgo is tasteful and a bit of a nit-picker to boot.

Do you begin to see what I see? Here you have all the talent and prance of the Horse character, tempered just so by Virgo's reticence and discrimination. And in the other direction we get, perhaps even more glaringly, a Virgo whose reserve is peeled away just far enough so that he knows precisely how to reach the masses. You see, some Virgos really suffer from their retiring natures. They are often unable to suffer contact with just anybody. We say they are discriminating. Some might more callously remark that they are fussy and persnickety, choosy and difficult. Horse comes along in this sign and gives the fusty old Virgo a kick in his bony derriere— just what the Virgo needed to feel good about himself again. A healthy measure of that Horsey self-possession and the Virgo born Horse is off and running.

Normally Horses are accused of selfishness and are known to be excessive in their dress. But the Virgo/Horse person is drier, more metallic than most, and for that reason more conservatively got up. Your Virgo/Horse will be heartbreakingly attractive to look at. This person has the kind of stately charm that appeals to everybody from grandma to the pooch.

The Virgo/Horse is immensely talented, too. Imagination here is tamed but not smothered. Creativity is controlled. Rebelliousness is quelled by Virgo's sense of duty and social decorum. The merits of Virgo/Horse are many. He can drive himself. He can innovate. He can teach. And this character can perform brilliantly.

One or two small details: Virgo/Horses tend to be conceited. The Horse personality already suffers from inflated self-image. Virgo's snobbery doesn't help. This person is a social climber who canters rather than climbs. Secondly, the Virgo born Horse is rankly pragmatic. Whatever serves to move this person from one point to the next will be acceptable behavior as far as he's concerned, even if he has to trample an underling or two on the way to the executive lavatory. Virgo/Horses are fairly unscrupulous about gain and achievement. They are thorough and damn good workers. But they like to hog the spotlight.

With this, the Virgo born Horse is also charitable. He is an espouser of causes and enjoys being seen as a person who cares about others. All in all, the Virgo/Horse is well balanced and understands his role in life, knows how to keep his nose clean and doesn't throw his weight around. This person is affable. People honestly enjoy his or her company and respect his opinions. In short, this subject is a solid entity and declares as much without false modesty. He's enthusiastic and deserving of admiration.

Love

Sex appeal is hardly a sufficient term to attribute to the Virgo/ Horse's seductive self. People virtually fall at this character's discreetly shod feet. Naturally, he knows how amiably appealing he is. The Virgo/Horse is gifted for romance and is remarkably creative sexually. In fact, this person appears dignified and a mite dry. But in bed, he or she is sweetness personified.

If you love one of these characters you might as well know right away that you are not alone in your passion. Virgo/Horses tend to flirt and are given to "running around". They want and even need a sound and serious homey relationship in the background, but when they go on those little trips alone well, who could resist? Certainly not the beautiful Virgo/Horse.

Compatibilities

The Virgo in you inclines most naturally to Taurus, Cancer, Scorpio and Capricorn subjects. From among their ranks don't hesitate to choose Dogs or Tigers. Your emotions dovetail perfectly with both Scorpio and Cancer/Sheep. You won't find easy harmony with Gemini, Sagittarius or Pisces/Rats. Nor will it be a snap to reach an understanding with Pisces/Monkey persons. Stick to liking people who like you back.

Home and Family

The Virgo/Horse is definitely a shade on the bourgeois side. He or she will want a home with perfect proportions and the finest furnishings. If he can afford them, the Virgo/Horse will have servants. But he will be friendly with his slaves. And the parties and fêtes he throws promise to be written up in (at least) Vogue.

The Virgo/Horse is an enthusiastic parent who enjoys doing things with his or her kids. This parent will insist that his or her children stay in line and especially that they show good performance in school. As this character is glaringly attractive, kids will sort of "fall in love" with a Virgo/Horse parent and admire her almost too adoringly. The Virgo/Horse mother or father should be careful never to condescend to the children.

As a kid, this person is a joy to parents. Virgo/Horse kids demand a lot of attention. But they are so cute that not even the cruelest wicked stepmother or father can resist their wiles. Early on in the Virgo/Horse's life his talents should be assessed and catered to. This youngster is special and will need training and discipline to help him or her toward a successful starring role in adult life.

Profession

Virgo/Horses are gifted for public life. They have the innate ability to charm thousands and can think of new methods of keeping their audience spellbound every three seconds. Virgo/Horse is also creative and is able to slave long hours over an artistic project. Whatever this character chooses to do, he will make it his business to do it better than other people. He has no time for failure, which, should it befall him, he knows he could not easily survive.

As a boss, this person is demanding and strict. He wants things done right. But he is also able to accomplish any chore, no matter how lowly, by himself. This means that his employees will either work hard and respect him or they will have to quit. As an employee, the Virgo/Horse is serious and driving. He wants to get ahead and knows that by hook or by crook he will. He's able to accept servitude so long as he sees a light at the end of the tunnel and knows he will excel on the other end.

Careers suitable to this subject are: public relations, TV or entertainment personality, artist, realtor, publisher, politician, composer, journalist.

Famous Virgo/Horses:
Adam Sandler, Alan Jay Lerner, Anthony Mackie, Ben Gazzara, Charlie Boorman. , Clayton Norcross, David Bamber, Denise Fabre, Don Wilson, Elvis Costello, Grant Wilson, Kobe Bryant, Leonard Bernstein, Leonor Fini, Lupe Ontiveros, Mark Lindsay Chapman, Michale Emerson, Michel Drucker, Paul Bulcke, Reed Birney, Salma Hayek, Sean Connery, Shinzo Abe, Takao Doi, Toby Jones, Vera Miles, Werner Herzog, Wes Bentley.

VIRGO
QUALITIES
LUCIDITY, DISCRIMINATION, COURTESY,
PRACTICALITY, SERVICE, DECORUM
QUIRKS
NIT-PICKING, NEGATIVISM, SNOBBERY,
METICULOUSNESS, CRANKINESS, RESERVE
Motto: *"I analyze"*
Elements: *Earth, Mercury, Mutable*

--

SHEEP
QUALITIES
INVENTION, LACK OF FORESIGHT,
PERSEVERANCE, WHIMSY, GOOD MANNERS,
IMPRACTICALITY
QUIRKS
PARASITISM, SENSITIVITY,
TARDINESS, PESSIMISM, TASTE, WORRY
Motto: *"I depend"*
Elements: *Negative, Fire, Yin*

The combination of the purity and crackle of Virgo with Sheep dependency and love of luxury make for a rather uncertain personality type. This person's sturdy Virgo side wants to come across as a serious and efficacious worker. He bolsters his image so as to better believe in himself. But the languor-loving Sheep invariably comes gamboling along and tips Virgo's rigidity right over. What we get then is a person with very strong opinions who is easily influenced and prey to those more crafty and less gullible than himself.

Virgo/Sheep comment on absolutely everything they encounter. "It's horribly hot in here. The pictures are hanging crooked. The cars emit too much exhaust for my taste. That hairdo looks revolting on you. Why do you wear those kinds of shoes? They make your legs look so fat." And on and on.

Sometimes their chatter can be pleasant, however. If they are feeling insecure, they are less likely to deride. These people need to graze in fertile fields, hold steady jobs and be protected—both privately, by a strong mate or family, and publicly, by the system.

This character is also wont to show off. He's not so much a clown as he is a tad snooty and know-it-all pedantic. Of course, once you get to be his friend, you realize that all those snazzy antics and exotic toilettes are merely part of the same act I mentioned above. The Virgo/Sheep is insecure. Wardrobe-flaunting and name-dropping are just two of the myriad ways he or she tries to protect herself from the arrows of those stronger or more meretricious.

Finally, let's just say it. This person is an eccentric. Ideally, he or she lives in a countrified cozy environment that is paid for by someone else. In the best of instances the Virgo/Sheep is obliged only to do his work and come home to put up his feet and enjoy. Not only is he quirky and a little bit balmy too, he is as a rule exceptionally talented in the work he has chosen. He puts tons of imagination into whatever he is employed at and it really does wear him out. This person is not nearly so strong as he appears. He needs a lot of propping.

There will be much dexterity in the hands of Virgo/Sheep. You may find them sitting up all night finishing the new upholstery on their love-seat, or trimming Christmas trees with ornaments saved up over thirty years, balancing on ladders and risking their lives so that the result will be aesthetically perfect. Virgo/Sheep are meticulous and artistic. They are best utilized and most comfortable in their homes and studios. Society's demands are almost too much for their delicate nervous structure. The big bad world makes these people crabby.

What with Virgo's clear-cut lucidity and the Sheep's bent for pessimism, this native will have quite a struggle against negativism and prejudice in his or her life. He wonders why everybody can't see what he sees. "Can't you tell that that girl over there is pregnant?" "Didn't you notice that Jim was sulking?" This person is the victim of his own glaring sensitivity. He is well advised to seek a secure field of endeavor and a canny partner from the jump.

Love

The ideal love life for a Virgo/Sheep is coupledom. But Virgo/ Sheep, with his tendency to be haughty and her huffy personal opinions, doesn't always hold on to such a relationship for long. He is capricious and he flits from whim to whim with a self-assuredness that throws off even the most perceptive admirer. This person must humble himself to accept his real dependent nature before he can truly find happiness in a one-on-one long-lasting affair or marriage.

If you are the lover of one of these delicately balanced creatures, I advise you to be firm and sure of yourself before undertaking any major emotional investment. The Virgo/Sheep's insecurities are such that without even meaning to, he or she can undermine friends' and lovers' confidence. There's a push-me-pull-you effect at work here. Virgo/Sheep criticizes his or her mate in a deprecatory way. The mate then doubts himself, which makes the Virgo/ Sheep feel even less secure. His bastion of strength, his strong and sturdy mate, has wavered. Vicious circle department. Watch out.

Compatibilities

Taurus, Cancer, Scorpio and Capricorn are mostly trustworthy working people so they appeal to your sense of congruity in romantic situations. Your top choices will come from among Cat and Pig subjects born in the above-mentioned signs. You'll also find effective partners in Cancer and Scorpio/Horse characters. I advise against Gemini, Sagittarius and Pisces from either Ox or Dog families. Pisces/Tigers may seduce you, but your patience will fast run out. They cannot protect you sufficiently to suit your needs.

Home and Family

The Virgo/Sheep's home will be decorated in a tasteful and individualistic manner. He or she favors elegant fabrics—lovely velvet draperies and damask napery both please and reassure the Virgo/ Sheep. He wants to receive people in style, and is often a smashing host or hostess.

As a parent this person will vacillate between bossiness and total indulgence of his children. He is not happy providing security for others. Being a breadwinner is very rough on the Virgo/Sheep, and in the long run it takes its toll in stability. He is, of course, especially gifted in relating to children as he is a bit of a child himself. Some Virgo/Sheep never marry or have children but remain close to their aging parents, who provide a comfortable security blanket.

The Virgo/Sheep child will be adorably affectionate and willing to perform and participate in all things childish, poetic and romantic. In fact, childhood is the best place for Virgo/Sheep to shine. So long as they have a stimulating environment, these kids feel good about themselves. Don't ask them to be world-beaters. Give them lots of artistic chances. You won't be disappointed.

Profession

On his own, the Virgo/Sheep will be drawn to steady jobs and professions. He can communicate well and is often involved in a career that requires speaking to groups. The Virgo/Sheep is a blindly prejudiced person whose opinions are staunchly his own. He can perform well in jobs where he is appreciated for his unusual outlook and his ability to work around the clock for the betterment of the system.

As a boss this person is hopeless. He's either huffy and sarcastic or he is a melted marshmallow in the hands of his employees. He does, however, make an enthusiastic employee who seeks favor through hard work and the application of his own individuality in areas of personal interest.

Some professions suitable for this character are: sociologist, theater designer, midwife, landscape gardener, artist, craftsman, sculptor, tailor/seamstress or decorator.

Famous Virgo/Sheep:

Aaron Paul, Alison Lohman, Anne Bancroft, Carter Jenkins, Dylan O'Brien, Faith Hill, George Wallace, Harry Connick Jr., Jacob Young, Jean-Claude Killy, Jeana Keough, Joe Sugg, Larry Hagman, Leslie Jones, Louis CK, Malik Yoba, Noémie Lenoir, Sanne Wevers, Skandar Keynes, Spencer Locke, Tamra Judge, Tom Hollander, Walter Reuther, William Carlos Williams.

VIRGO
QUALITIES
LUCIDITY, DISCRIMINATION, COURTESY,
PRACTICALITY, SERVICE, DECORUM
QUIRKS
NIT-PICKING, NEGATIVISM, SNOBBERY,
METICULOUSNESS, CRANKINESS, RESERVE
Motto: *"I analyze"*
Elements: *Earth, Mercury, Mutable*

--

MONKEY
QUALITIES
IMPROVISATION, CUNNING, STABILITY,
SELF-INVOLVEMENT, WIT, OPPORTUNISM
QUIRKS
DECEIT, RUSE, LOQUACITY,
LEADERS, SILLINESS, ZEAL
Motto: *"I plan"*
Elements: *Positive, metal, Yang*

The Virgo born Monkey carries himself like a prince. Women of this sign are elegantly stunning and give off the kind of superior vibes equaled only by the wicked queen in Disney's Snow White. Nonetheless, Virgo/Monkeys never have it easy. They must nibble away at all aspects of their lives, from childhood onward, in order to enjoy even a measure of success.

Virgos tend to want to surround themselves with "important" people. Snobbism makes Virgos feel secure. Monkeys, however, are rarely concerned with superficiality unless it serves a practical use. If it is in Monkey's interest to drop a name or attend a boring cocktail party, he'll do it gladly. But mostly Monkeys can take or leave the top drawer and the executive lounge crowd.

This disparity within the Virgo/Monkey's character can cause no end of struggles. On the one hand Virgo feels he ought to go over and talk to Herr Bigshot. But Monkey is hungry. He'd prefer to go straight to the buffet without the benefit of Herr Bigshot's boring prattle. Monkey says, "What do I care about that creep?"

What emerges here is a power-stricken, nervous personality type. Virgo/Monkey wants to control his own life and the lives of others. But circumstances often force him to relinquish that power before he's had a chance to really put it in place. This leads to great disappointment. And then to a certain self-pity and blame-laying. "If nobody will stick by me, I shall go into my tower and consult the magic mirror," wails the disillusioned Virgo/Monkey. "At least it loves me."

Virgo/Monkeys have quite a good sense of what is right for others and don't mind meddling in others' business enough to let them know it. Their assessments of other people's dilemmas are often accurate. Too, Virgo/Monkeys are charitable and love doing for the less fortunate. They are generous and will even splash cash on those who need it. Trouble here is, Virgo/Monkey takes all of his favors back in compliments, fawning and even sycophancy. Bottom line? Virgo/Monkeys are selfishly altruistic.

The basic Virgo/Monkey temperament is one of wiry and dry authority. They are acquisitive and grasping both of material things and of people. You are right to think that their need to possess is merely a hedge against their insecurity. Virgo/Monkeys are meticulous and work their fingers to the bone. They are lucid and capable of profound human understanding. They make sound investments. They are hospitable. But they are desperate for dominion and will stop at nothing to keep it.

Virgo makes for intelligence, Monkey for cunning. Virgo is reserved. Monkey is outgoing and cheerful. This person is always torn apart from within about which of his qualities he should apply in a given situation. Pickiness often wins out.

Love

In love relationships the Virgo/Monkey is perfectly serious. He's also an arch romantic. He wants to get and to keep his loved one. He will court and seduce in many clever and winning ways. But remember, this person has a weak spot. He has to possess completely what he loves. It gets a little close in the room after a while with Virgo/Monkey entwined enticingly around the neck of his amour.

If you love a Monkey born in Virgo, give her the impression that she is the only person in the universe beside yourself. Live as a united couple in complicity against the world. Sacrifice your own way of life to hers. The Virgo/Monkey will in turn see that you are comfy and warm, well fed and entertained. But she may also lock the door to the tower and throw away the key.

Compatibilities

Meeting of the minds for you with Taurus, Cancer and Scorpio/Rats and Dragons. You truly admire them. They know how to reciprocate. Capricorns of those two animal signs also interest you. They sense your love of purity and respect your integrity. I warn you not to wax too ardent over Gemini, Sagittarius or Pisces/Tigers. You risk being wounded in action. Gemini and Sagittarius/Pigs aren't tolerant of your antics. Pisces/Snakes are too flashy and Sagittarius/Oxen too fervent.

Home and Family

I've never seen a Virgo/Monkey's home that wasn't a veritable showplace of expensiveness and tradition. The same insecurity that reigns in this person's personal life rules his decor. He will have done much of the work himself, painting and scraping and plastering and finishing this and that tiny detail by hand. From cuisine to carpentry, he's a deft craftsman when he sets to anything.

As a parent, Virgo/Monkey's possessiveness streak rears its nasty nose, of course. Virgo/Monkey parents are like feudal lords. "This is my house" is one of their favorites. But don't get any funny ideas about leaving home. The Virgo/Monkey parent will devise a multitude of schemes to retrieve a prodigal child. Mostly, though, they never have to bother because their kids wouldn't dare err or stray.

Little Virgo/Monkeys will be scared of a lot of things. The dark, crowds and nightmares are the enemy. This child wants to be surrounded with comfort and tenderness, shown compassion and given much to be secure about.

Profession

The Virgo/Monkey has lots of talent for minutiae. He's able to be on time and never miss a day's work. This person's work life is a study in perfectionism. He's not only practical, but he's cautious and ambitious as well.

The Virgo/Monkey makes a very diligent employee. As a boss, this person is something else. Of course he or she will want to be in command. He or she may secretly want his name on the cover larger than yours, and in gilt letters. Virgo/Monkey is a demanding and methodical sign full of savvy about money and accumulating wealth. He doesn't like to give up one centimeter of popularity or power. This grabbiness can be his or her undoing.

Good jobs for Virgo/Monkeys are: trouble-shooter, philanthropist, script girl, entrepreneur, administrator.

Famous Virgo/Monkeys:

Ben Savage, Blake Jenner, Camille Grammer, Chad Stahelski, Charlie (Bird) Parker, Chris Pine, Connor Franta, Craig Claiborne, Cynthia Watros, Eve Angeli, Guy Ritchie, Jack Warden, Jacqueline Bisset, Jessica Henwisk, John DiMaggio, John Fields, Julia Sawalha, June Foray, Lara Pulver, Lyndon Johnson, Macaulay Culkin, Max Greenfield, Maxwell Perkins, Michelle Williams, Michelle Williams, Mickey Rooney, Paul F. Tompkins, Rachael Ray, William Saroyan.

VIRGO
QUALITIES
LUCIDITY, DISCRIMINATION, COURTESY,
PRACTICALITY, SERVICE, DECORUM
QUIRKS
NIT-PICKING, NEGATIVISM, SNOBBERY,
METICULOUSNESS, CRANKINESS, RESERVE
Motto: *"I analyze"*
Elements: *Earth, Mercury, Mutable*

--

ROOSTER
QUALITIES
RESILIENCE, ENTHUSIASM, CANDOR,
CONSERVATISM, CHIC, HUMOR
QUIRKS
COCKINESS, BOASTFULNESS, BLIND FAITH,
PEDANTRY, BOSSINESS, DISSIPATION
Motto: *"I overcome"*
Elements: *Negative, Metal, Yin*

This brand of Rooster keeps coming back for more and rising victorious from even the most murky miasma, or else he dies trying. Virgo and Rooster are signs of determination and pluck. There is a truckload of perseverance here. These people are drivers whose love of detail and acuity for fact-gathering make them useful to society as well as to themselves.

Virgo/Roosters are conscious of their social position. If it is money they lacked as youngsters, then they will go hell-bent after money as adults. If they suffered for lack of class, they will become class-crazy adults whose quest for good taste and refinement and "doing the right thing" will about choke you. They are never uncertain about where they fit and to which stratum they have been relegated. It bothers Virgo/Roosters if they are not considered top drawer.

Virgo/Roosters are talented in all intellectual pursuits. They can learn and retain obscure facts, eccentric verb forms and mathematical formulae in a trice. With this ability comes natural cunning. They quickly learn the ropes in any new situation, and on no matter what level, the Virgo/Rooster will always make sure his cronies are the leaders of their pack. Virgo/Roosters understand discretion. They know how to keep their counsel on touchy or classified subjects. They are crafty and not above subterfuge.

Although the Virgo/Rooster is a shade on the old-fashioned side, he can never be accused of conformism. He's definitely an individualist and will not be among those stay-at-home people who sacrifice their own advancement to please their parents or families. Whatever the Virgo/Rooster wants is for himself. He is not unduly altruistic nor is he likely to lean toward liberal politics. These folks are self-propelled.

They can however, for the sake of friendship, take on jobs and do favors that would daunt anyone less devoted. The Virgo/Rooster wants to be liked and will go to great lengths to ensure his own popularity. Too, this person is usually very amiable and makes a marvelous addition to one's entourage. Virgo/Roosters like to travel, and come back to tell all about their experiences. They enjoy music and theater and will recount endless hours of entertaining tales of performances. They are savvy critics too, and can be called upon to advise about anything from coiffure to love affairs.

The most precious of the Virgo/Rooster's innate gifts is his remarkable inner discipline. These people will rise at six to study their Russian grammar before taking a long run in the woods with their dog, then go back to bone up on a little calculus before catching the bus to go to work. They are inner-directed and they are bold. I wouldn't exactly say they are fearless, but they are certainly able to allay anxiety better than most of us.

Love

Romance is a problem for Virgo/Roosters. Their natural desire to shine above everyone else is usually controlled in social situations. They know well how to be flexible and shift gears in order to be liked. But in order to be loved . . . well, the Virgo/Rooster is exceedingly inflexible about romance. He wants everything amorous to be on his own terms and prefers being admired to admiring. He likes to impress his paramours and perhaps even frighten them a bit. Sadistic? Maybe just a tad.

If you love a Virgo/Rooster you had best prepare for a whirlwind lifestyle. This person is a mover and a shaker. If he or she decides to drag you along on his forays into the world of social acceptance, then hold on to your hat. But if, and this is a very big if, your Virgo/Rooster leaves you at home, then you'll have to learn how to play solitaire, because this creature is always out somewhere. If you like loneliness and don't mind weighty telephone bills (she is in Peru this week, remember?), catch yourself a Virgo/Rooster. They will keep you in conversation if not in diamonds and furs.

Compatibilities

Stay close to the Snake population when choosing a mate or love partner. You'll be particularly happy with Taurus, Cancer, Scorpio or even Capricorn/Snakes. The package is important to your ego and Snakes understand packaging. You can't go wrong with a steady Taurus or Capricorn/Ox, and the scrupulous Capricorn/ Dragon is just what you need to inspire you to greater heights. Don't pick a Gemini, Sagittarius or Pisces/Cat. Stay away from Sagittarius/Roosters, who are too like you on the one hand and too, too different on the other. Don't marry a Pisces/Dog. Their bite is worse than their bark.

Home and Family

The Virgo/Rooster's home is a messy museum or at least a lived-in library reading room. There are half-read books all over the place. These usually coexist pacifically with deep armchairs and sofas and pre-Columbian sculpture and half-opened crates. "Put that down on the piano. Or no. Here. Put it on top of the sitar I got in New Delhi last week."

As a rule, Virgo/Roosters don't have a lot of children. They are partial to individualism. At best they are able to tolerate the mild disruption of a cat or small dog. The prospect of having in-laws and Sundays at Grandma's with little Betsy and Bill is probably more folksiness than they will want to handle. The Virgo/Rooster is egocentric and quite sufficient unto himself.

As a child he will amaze you by his skill at memorizing things. The Virgo/Rooster kid is the one who recites a whole scene from Shakespeare before he can understand the words. He or she is likely to be talented in the arts but to find the artist's simple life lacking in fascination and so abandon that early. Virgo/Rooster kids need company and are socially ambitious.

Profession

"One day I shall have a beautiful house on a hill with walls of books and easy access to the city and a season ticket to the opera and a fabulous lover who accompanies me everywhere but who never gets in my way." This is the dream life of the Virgo/Rooster. Inherent in this tableau is, of course, money.

Although he or she can perform even the most workaday of grinds in a seeming trice, the Virgo/Rooster is never happy in the clutches of a "dumb job." Virgo/Roosters want theater and drama in their professions. They long for danger and adventure and challenge in their work. As an employee, he will be forever dreaming of better, more exciting times. As an employer, likewise. This person can do everything but mostly prefers to do precisely as he pleases.

Careers for Virgo/Roosters are: anthropologist, explorer, society journalist, film director, undercover agent.

Famous Virgo/Roosters:

Alexis Bledel, Alfie Deyes, Arthur Mariano, Ben Bradlee, Beyoncé Gloria Estefan, Bing Bing Fan, Boyd Holbrook, Cardinal Richelieu, Chad Michael Murray, Chandra Wilson, D. H. Lawrence, Elia Kazan, Franz Beckenbauer, Hélène Lazareff, Itzhak Perlman, Jack Black, Jason Priestly, Jonathan Schaech, Jonathan Taylor Thomas, Keke Palmer, Liam Payne, Michel Jobert, Niall Horan, Noah Taylor, Patrick Adams, Patrick Schwarzenegger, Rachel Bilson, Tyler Perry.

VIRGO
QUALITIES
LUCIDITY, DISCRIMINATION, COURTESY,
PRACTICALITY, SERVICE, DECORUM
QUIRKS
NIT-PICKING, NEGATIVISM, SNOBBERY,
METICULOUSNESS, CRANKINESS, RESERVE
Motto: *"I analyze"*
Elements: *Earth, Mercury, Mutable*

--

DOG
QUALITIES
CONSTANCY, UNSOCIABILITY,
RESPECTABILITY, SELF-RIGHTEOUSNESS,
INTELLIGENCE, TACTLESSNESS
QUIRKS
UNEASINESS, CRITICISM, DUTY,
CYNICISM, HEROISM, MORALITY
Motto: *"I worry"*
Elements: *Positive, Metal, Yang*

K indness and bite combine in the Virgo/Dog character. No matter how crabby this person may seem at times, a vigil light of sweetness burns brightly from behind his eyes. Virgo/Dogs may try to hide their vulnerability under a cloak of sophistication and worldliness. But beneath the veneer is a surface as sensitive and soft as purest down.

Virgo/Dogs are reliable people. They believe in righteousness and practice good works. They do nothing haphazardly and leave very little to chance. You can always call on a Virgo/Dog for assistance.

You can always ask him for a dime. Consult anyone who has a Virgo/Dog friend and they will corroborate what I claim. They may not always be smiley. But they are ever obliging, willing to lend a hand and serious about their responsibilities.

This person will be calculating and able to amass fortunes through sheer hard work and dutiful application of elbow grease. He is thorough and even a smidgen on the compulsive side. But never mind. You cannot trust everybody in life or you know where you will end up, don't you? Virgo/Dogs sense danger and are always on guard against evil. Underhanded or slightly batty schemes don't appeal to them. They watch every penny, but they are remarkably generous too. Virgo/Dogs take care of their own, and then some.

Dogs born in Virgo are not solitary types. They enjoy the company of people they trust and love. They like to feel that they are the center of a warm group of "good" folks and will go to great lengths to prove their loyalty and test that of others.

Whatever they do, you can be sure it is in good faith, although you have to keep an eye on their overly naive attempts at righting wrongs too wrong ever to be retrievable. Sign their petition. They mean no harm.

The Virgo/Dog is generally conservative. He is not one to go looking for a free lunch. As he believes in hard work and is clever about burying his bones in the right gardens, he doesn't see why others should expect a free ride from life or society. His generosity does not extend to people who don't show industry and grit.

The combination of the worried Dog sign with the meticulous, analytical Virgo can cause this person plenty of anxiety. He or she will pick every situation to pieces and ulcerate over petty (sometimes meaningless) details. This clutching behavior can put the Virgo/Dog into a sort of limbo spot whence he finds progress impossible. It is then that he needs his friends to jog him out of the fear paralysis with real, concrete solutions. He's amenable to advice and heeds those he feels are wiser.

The Virgo/Dog's biggest handicap is his inability to refuse help to those weaker or less fortunate than himself. He's excessively honorable and often allows himself to be hoodwinked by tricksters and bounders. When this happens he is deeply hurt and can acquire a kind of beaten dog look that takes him a while to shake off. Duplicity makes the Virgo/Dog angry, too. Watch out for this temper. You have never seen white rage till you've watched a mad Virgo/Dog in action. When really provoked, they totally lose control.

Love

The Virgo/Dog is circumspect about his love relationships. He doesn't usually dash about seeking favors and attentions he didn't deserve in the first place. Rather, the Virgo/Dog decides when he wishes to marry, does so and stays that way in more or less peace and quiet forever. Oh, he can be snappy and harsh-tongued sometimes. But he's able to ride out storms because he has the courage of his convictions.

If you love such a person, you must keep the atmosphere jolly and try to make him or her laugh a lot. The Virgo/Dog loves to giggle and be silly and has a finely honed sense of humor. But as he is also fretful and preoccupied with duty, he sometimes needs to be drawn out encouraged to enjoy. If your Virgo/Dog loves you back, you are a lucky person indeed. He will never let you down.

Compatibilities

You are innately charmed by Taurus, Scorpio and Capricorn people. In those categories you will find yourself most at home with Tigers. Cancer, Capricorn and Scorpio/Cats tickle your fancy as well. They are all quite calm—and they are smart! Scorpio and Capricorn/Horses also provide you with much long-lived pleasure and well-deserved encouragement. I don't vote for Gemini, Sagittarius and Pisces/Sheep for you; and I most solemnly counsel you to avoid taking up with Pisces or Sagittarian Dragons.

Home and Family

Unlike the Ox or Cancer, who loves home just because it's there, Virgo/Dog loves his home because he made it himself. Most Virgo/Dogs have carefully molded their surroundings alone, have built themselves and their families a way of life of which they are proud and have logged hours and hours of sacrifice in the name of home. The furnishings will be spare and efficient, perhaps even a mite stark, but that vigil light of sweetness is always there in the form of a hand-crocheted afghan or a cozy hot water bottle. Virgo/Dog keeps his life together himself.

As a parent there's no question this person is both sane and healthy. He takes all responsibility seriously. And he actually sits down and helps with the homework, and stays up and bakes the cookies. Kids who have Virgo/Dog parents have to keep up appearances and behave impeccably to outsiders. But at home they can relax and feel good about themselves. Their Virgo/Dog parent could try to be just a tad less critical. But all in all, parenting is a fine job for these folks.

Virgo/Dog children would do well to be born the eldest of their families. They carry off that role with aplomb. They don't hate bossing their siblings and they sincerely do not mind helping parents out. In fact, the average Virgo/Dog child surprises adults with his precocious maturity. Whether you like it or not, this child will worry and require plenty of reassurance. Nightmares come with the territory.

Profession

Duty-bound, the Virgo/Dog is able to engage himself in a wide variety of jobs requiring attention to detail and the application of intellect to the practical aspects of a job. He will surely excel at the mechanics of his or her profession. If he has difficulty in succeeding, it is sometimes due to his excessive indulgence of others in work situations. If his coworkers are lazy and shiftless, the Virgo/ Dog may not say anything, but instead do the extra work himself. This exhausts him and puts his nerves and his career in jeopardy.

I cannot imagine a fairer or more just boss. This character is able to mete out exactly the doses of work each subordinate needs, follow through on their progress and distribute judicious pats on heads where needed. As an employee, the same holds true. He's a virtuous person, sometimes cranky and tempestuous, but never dishonest or wicked.

Some of the careers I think best suited to the Virgo/Dog character are: psychiatrist, musician, nursery school teacher, engineer, computer expert, professor, humanitarian.

Famous Virgo/Dogs:

Andrea Bocceli, Aviva Drescher, Barry Gibb, Christian Jules Leblanc., Claudia Schiffer, Debbie Gibson, Howard Zinn, Ione Skye, Jean-Louis Barrault, Jennifer Tilly, Joan Jett, Julia Nickson, Kate Millet, Lenny Henry, Leonard Cohen, Michael Jackson, Michèle Alliot-Marie, Mother Teresa, Natalie Dormer, Queen Rania of Jordan, Rene Levesque, Roxann Dawson, Scott Patterson, Sophia Loren, Steve Guttenberg, Tim Burton, Wendy Jo Sperber.

VIRGO
QUALITIES
LUCIDITY, DISCRIMINATION, COURTESY,
PRACTICALITY, SERVICE, DECORUM
QUIRKS
NIT-PICKING, NEGATIVISM, SNOBBERY,
METICULOUSNESS, CRANKINESS, RESERVE
Motto: *"I analyze"*
Elements: *Earth, Mercury, Mutable*

--

PIG
QUALITIES
SCRUPULOUSNESS, GALLANTRY, SINCERITY,
VOLUPTUOUSNESS, CULTURE, HONESTY
QUIRKS
CREDULITY, WRATH, HESITATION,
MATERIALISM, GOURMANDISM, PIGHEADEDNESS
Motto: *"I civilize"*
Elements: *Negative Water, Yin*

To merge Virgo with Pig in a human character is tantamount to displaying pearls on an ivory satin quilt. The purity-of-spirit quotient is almost too high. It's lagniappe. Naive and industrious, sensual and sensible, methodical and meticulous, Virgo/Pigs are good guys with a capital G.

For the Virgo/Pig, wickedness doesn't really exist. They really don't think that base, low, crafty, evil souls are dancing about our ears at all times in all climes. Virgo/Pig is born believing in the noble savage. To him, all people, animals and even inanimate objects are basically right and honorable. They may err. Oh yes, people or animals may stray from the path of righteousness. But it is always the fault of society. Virgo/Pig finds excuses for every individual's most reprehensible behavior.

You see, Virgo/Pigs are themselves so pure of mind and so whole in spirit that they cannot tell when others are bad. They do not see the boy stealing from his mother's purse. They instantly transform the thief into a victim whom they want to help. If that boy were their son, he wouldn't have to commit crimes. He would be educated and cultured and have only lofty notions worthy of the son of a Virgo/Pig.

We may see this approach as naive. We may be tempted to call the Virgo/Pig haughtily credulous, and say he allows the wool to be pulled over his eyes. But the fact is that evil must be called to the Virgo/Pig's attention. As a result, he is frequently the victim of deception.

This person is a practical sort. There is little he or she cannot fashion by hand. No manual task is too complex. Art, be it the appreciation of beautiful works or their very creation, is second nature to this sensitive character. Virgo/Pig is one New Astrology sign that just about guarantees some involvement in the arts.

On first meeting, this person may give the impression of near gypsy bohemianism. There is something of the poet in the eye and the way of dress of these people. Yet, when you get to know Virgo/ Pigs you will realize that all the paint-stained smocks and frowsy hairstyles in the world cannot cover up the essential Virgo/ Pig need for and insistence on lavishness. Here is the complete artiste, circles under eyes, drawn and fragile-looking, nervous and ever so shy, who has just had her kitchen remodeled to the tune of half your next year's earnings. If Virgo/Pig doesn't have opulence, he's miserable. Art is nice but gold keeps the wolf from the door.

Virgo/Pigs, then, hate what is corrupt but covet what corruption can acquire. The variance causes a mild schizophrenia. They claim to want a simple country life. Yet they are forever hankering after a Picasso. They seem to care only for the essential, and yet long for the luxurious. Virgo/Pigs are sometimes so clean-cut that they may be secretly attracted to naughtiness. When they least appear to be, you can be certain Virgo/Pigs are up to something—discreetly, that is.

Love

Loyalty and love go well together. This person will be irreproachably devoted to a loved one or a friend. In turn, the Virgo/ Pig demands as much from those he loves. He is capable of protracted personal sacrifice in the effort to preserve a relationship and will stop at nothing to seduce someone he finds irresistible. Gifts and services of all variety are offered in the name of love.

Beware the Virgo/Pig's wrath! Anger is rare in a subject so giving and forgiving by nature. But when the Virgo/Pig's saturation point has been reached, when she cannot take another disappointment and has truly had her faith trampled by careless or traitorous scallywags, white blind rage is not even adequate to describe the reaction. Virgo/Pig is capable of turning her back on people forever. An angry Virgo/Pig considers his enemies (and they are few) dead. If you love a Virgo/Pig, pay him or her obeisance. If you'd like to keep a Virgo/Pig, you must never so much as hint at betrayal.

Compatibilities

An out of the ordinary partner for you would be the Aries/Ox. You are a solid sort who requires luxury. Aries/Ox will provide. Otherwise, the standard catch for you will be found amongst Taurus, Cancer, Scorpio and Capricorn/Cats and Sheep, nature-loving and tranquil souls. A Taurus/Tiger or Pig might do the trick, too. I'd keep away from Gemini, Sagittarius and Pisces/Snakes. They are opulence symbols, it's true. But they enjoy squeezing Piggies just a bit too tightly for the Pig's own good. You won't have much luck with Gemini or Pisces/Monkeys. Forget about that Pisces/Dragon you met last week.

Home and Family

Virgo/Pigs like their comfort. They always live in pleasant surroundings and are attracted by the real thing in home furnishings. Antiques and lovely paintings will come before gourmet pleasures in this subject's life. Yet, of all the Pig natives, this one is perhaps the most ascetic. He won't be fat and the decor will not be cluttered or baroque. Clean lines and few good (very good) things.

Parenting is a natural outlet for virtue. Virgo/Pigs are experts at virtue. They are the parents who hand-sew the angel costumes for the Christmas pageant, stand in the freezing snow applauding their kid's skiing tumbles, and never forget to sign the homework and make appointments for their kids' regular six-month dental check-ups. Duty-bound, this parent will also make his or her children behave, teach them good manners and punish them when they get out of line. Serious, dutiful and able.

If you have a Virgo/Pig child, you will wonder why God has so blessed you. Your child will be prim and bright. He will have a fine sense of discretion at an early age and an unfailing eye for detail. This child won't know how to express his affections easily, and benefits from imposed cuddling. Artistic one and all, these little people ought to begin creative writing or painting lessons early on.

Profession

The Virgo/Pig will be able to do almost any job well—except those requiring advanced scientific knowledge. This person is mostly artistic. Science bores him. As he will certainly know how to spend money lavishly, he is likely to know how to earn it as well. Virgo/Pigs work hard and are innately industrious.

The Virgo/Pig will make an excellent boss whose employees will like and respect him for his ability to set examples. He is not above performing any and all chores personally. As an employee, this person will be reliable and remain above suspicion. He or she will always be seeking a higher position, as no matter where he fits in the chain of command he would rather be higher. Virgo/Pigs also work extremely well alone.

Some careers for these scrupulous people are: nun, priest, set designer, musician, writer, painter, curator, archivist.

Famous Virgo/Pigs:

Alexis Petridis, Alfonso Freeman, Any Poehler, Brian Thompson, Carla Gugino, Frej Larsson, Haviland Morris, Henry Thomas, Jada Pinckett Smith, John Hawkes, John Head, Jorge Luis Borges, Joseph Mazzello, Josh Charles, Ken Kesey, Lance Armstrong, Maggie Grace, Martin Freeman, Patrick Poivre d'Arvor, Pippa Middleton, Rebecca De Mornay, Robert Benchley, Sean Brosnan, Stacey Nelkin, Stephen King, Zoe Kazan.

LIBRA
QUALITIES
JUSTICE, AESTHETICS, CHARM,
GENTILITY, EQUILIBRIUM, IDEALISM,
QUIRKS
QUARRELSOMENESS, MANIPULATION,
PROCRASTINATION, SELF-INDULGENCE,
INDECISION, TALKATIVENESS
Motto: *"I balance"*
Elements: *Air, Venus, Cardinal*

--

RAT
QUALITIES
NERVOUSNESS, INFLUENCE,
ACQUISITIVENESS, THIRST FOR POWER,
INTELLECTUAL SKILL, CHARISMA
QUIRKS
APPEAL, VERBOSITY, THRIFT,
SOCIABILITY, GUILE, MEDDLING
Motto: *"I rule"*
Elements: *Positive Water, Yang*

A gifted combination, to say the least. Libra/Rat lives in a perpetual state of hopefulness. Libra/Rat wants to break the bank at Monte Carlo, star in a play on Broadway and... write a bestseller. Further, they'd like to beget—or better still, be—the president of the United States. And when she is finished with those incidentals, she would like to take time out to win the Nobel Prize.

Libra/Rats are almost self-destructively ambitious. They cannot leave the quest for supremacy alone. As their truest gifts lie within the realms of poetry and fancy, the usual Rat pursuit of power—that is, power over others—rarely, if ever, enters their tense little claws. These people are also extremely gabby and exhaustingly communicative. They want to tell it all, all the time and in the most excruciating detail.

It's easy to enjoy a Libra/Rat's company. They are affable and open. They are curious about others and show quick compassion for their interlocutors' problems and sorrows. Libra/Rat is a fascinating sign. These subjects intrigue and plot and gossip their whole lives away. They behave in a convoluted and complex fashion. They are both avaricious and generous. They like to have money so they can give it away to those they deem worthy. They are idealistic and extreme.

Libra/Rats want to dominate. Yet they are not nasty or authoritarian people. Their method of controlling others is unusual. Libra/ Rats control through sweetness. They endear themselves through their apparent guilelessness to those they admire and seek

the company of. By this enticing means, the Libra/Rat manages to become indispensable to those who love him or her. Once you have a Libra/Rat as a friend you will have no end of real companionship. But neither will you be alone—ever again.

Librans and Rats both tend to talk out their inner feelings as a method of problem solving. Neither sign is violent. Neither personality suffers from stodginess. As a result, there is a quality of lightness that surrounds this character, of amiability and an almost childlike candor. Thing is, the attitude is just that. The overt sincerity we encounter in this person is a bit of an act. Libra/Rats pretend to be simple folk. They come on plainspoken and "How dee do." But watch out. Before you know it you'll be outmaneuvered by this wily bundle of sunshine.

Libra/Rat is painfully sensitive to others and is therefore capable of inspiring an audience to follow his high-blown ideals. Librans born in Rat years have a remarkable memory for detail and a giant capacity for creation. Both Rat and Libra are deeply rooted in tradition. Customs and religion die hard in the minds of these exacting creatures.

For a feisty Rat person to be born under the aesthetic sign of Libra is indeed a blessing. Libra's gentility tames the Rat's occasional harshness. The oft-prejudiced Rat personality benefits from Libra's sense of justice and picks up subtlety in the bargain. The combination certainly doesn't want for maneuvering tactics, nor does it lack charisma.

Love

The Libra/Rat takes his or her feelings very seriously. Emotion is, to the Libra/Rat, a commodity that he or she dispenses with great care and discrimination. Once he has taken to a sweetheart, the plot very definitely thickens. Romance is not something to be trifled with where Libra/Rat is concerned. Moreover, he is never unfaithful to love itself—only to his lover or mistress.

If you have fallen in love one of these crafty beauties, I suggest you invest in some velvet gloves. "Handle With Care" is stamped all over the tenderness center of Libra/Rat. This is a vocal lover. He or she will come on strong. The initial impact will surely be noteworthy. You cannot ignore this effervescent character. Like fine champagne, this person requires a little stirring up to get rid of the excess bubbly. Then, sip slowly and enjoy.

Compatibilities

You are fatally attracted by Geminis, Leos, Sagittarians and Aquarians. Narrow the field of choice from among these signs to Monkey people. They not only appeal to you but they have something to offer you in return. You like Dragons and Oxen, so choose them, if you prefer, from the same sign groups as the Monkeys. Leo/ Dragons are a bit much for your delicate equilibrium, so leave that one alone if you can. I don't believe you can be happy forever with an Aries, Cancer or Capricorn/Horse—or any other Horse subject, for that matter. Cats born in Cancer or Capricorn are too fearful to stand by you in times of trouble.

Home and Family

Nobody loves a cozy atmosphere like a Libran born Rat. Thing is, this person is not expert at creating said ambience and needs a homier soul to get furnishings and decor together. If it were up to the Rat/Libra, he would call in a decorator and have him build everything from some grandiose Rat/Libra-inspired plan. He's not much of a putterer, this Rat. And he isn't really drawn to things noncerebral, like model building model airplanes or fixing lawnmowers. This person's home is only as beautiful as his decorator is talented. He doesn't see the point of getting his hands dirty with do-it-yourself projects like painting ceiling and plastering walls.

As a parent this person is reliable and responsible, warm-hearted and sincere, communicative in the extreme and not all that lenient. Libra/Rats want their kids to excel at everything. They take their children's victories (and their failures) personally. Rat/Libras are essentially social parents and love being part of everything their children do. From the PTA bake sale to the Little League picnic committee, you can count on a Libra/Rat parent to be there with bells on.

The Libra/Rat child is a hypersensitive chatterbox. He or she will probably respond ticklishly to criticism and have a hard time accepting disapproval from parents or teachers. Personality is a definite plus in Libra/Rat kids, so of course they will be popular among their peers. Encourage this child to read. Words delight the Libra/Rat and may indeed furnish him with a sound future métier.

Profession

To stem the flow of words emanating from the Libra/Rat is to cruelly hinder his or her development. Libra/Rats think aloud. They are supremely talented in all work involving communication, persuasion and sociability. They can be both meddling and quarrelsome and need occasional squelching from superiors to stay in line. Libra/Rat is a dickerer over prices and understands the value of a shckcl. He or she is idealistic about career matters. Libra/Rats don't see themselves as any small potatoes. They're intellectual as well as dynamic.

Rats born in Libra make less partial bosses than one might think. Libra loosens the Rat's tight grip on his underlings, making him more altruistic and diplomatic. Oh, yes. He does blab a lot. But then better a blathering boss than the old strong silent mean type. If you aim to employ this fellow gainfully, you'd better make sure he works in a closet without telephones. He is very easily distracted by communication with co- workers and can be the king of the water cooler crowd. Libra/Rat is, however, efficient and well worth his weight in phone bill when it comes to telephone skills.

Good career choices for Libra/Rat are: writer, advertising executive, teacher, composer, salesperson, journalist, entertainer, switchboard operator, psychologist, preacher.

Famous Libra/Rats:

Avril Lavigne, Bella Hadid, Charlton Heston, Claudia Black, Eminem, Erin Daniels, Eugene O'Neill, Gwyneth Paltrow, Helen Hayes, Hiroyuki Sanada, Jean Piat, Jean-Claude Van Damme, Jim Henson, Jimmy Carter, Joelle Carter, Kurt Cole, Lotte Lenya, Marcello Mastroianni, Meghan King Edmonds, Melody Thornton., Nicola Bryant, Nicole Croisille, Olivia Newton John, Rob Marshall, Saffron Burrows, Stephen Bechtel, T.S. Eliot, Thomas Wolfe, Truman Capote.

LIBRA
QUALITIES
JUSTICE, AESTHETICS, CHARM,
GENTILITY, EQUILIBRIUM, IDEALISM,
QUIRKS
QUARRELSOMENESS, MANIPULATION,
PROCRASTINATION, SELF-INDULGENCE,
INDECISION, TALKATIVENESS
Motto: *"I balance"*
Elements: *Air, Venus, Cardinal*

--

OX
QUALITIES
STUBBORNNESS, STRENGTH OF PURPOSE,
ELOQUENCE, STANDOFFISHNESS, INNOVATION,
VINDICTIVENESS
QUIRKS
INTEGRITY, BIGOTRY, PLODDING,
DILIGENCE, BIAS, STABILITY
Motto: *"I preserve"*
Elements: *Negative Water, Yin*

Beauty and the Beast. This subject is a veritable storm of contradiction. Every detail must be perfect, every line straight and every flaw concealed. Weakness must be routed. Sloth eradicated. Yet, under this foil of faultlessness, Libra/Ox hides a secret. On the strict surface, Libra/Ox is efficiency and power, example and security. Underneath? An anthill of conflicting emotions. Purity charms this sterling character. He claims not to want any messes about. He protests he needs calm and cannot live in turmoil, Yet, Libra/Oxen are forever getting themselves involved in emotional scrapes. Even though they seem to be above it all, they take in strays. They seek out madness. They are magnetized by complexity.

Librans born in Ox years are basically gentle people. They are addicted to beauty and cannot resist following this penchant. Their dream is perfection in life design. Clean, well-mannered children and pets. Lovely surroundings. Soft music playing in the background. Sumptuous haute cuisine, overflowing Louis XV dining tables, a sensible, fascinating mate who does Libra/Ox proud in the world at large, and even well-behaved in-laws.

But Libra/Oxen also fear that just as they have achieved this precious house of cards, tied up their own prettily wrapped package, the slightest breeze will certainly come along and destroy it.

Disappointment is the enemy of Libra/Oxen. They are constantly finding others less impeccable than they would like. They are often deceived by those they love, and yet, time and again they come back for more. If certain configurations repeatedly disillusion us, we ought to avoid those patterns. But the Libra/Ox refuses. Stubbornly, and with no apparent sense of what has gone before or what is to come, Libra/Ox wakes up after monstrous bouts with chagrin and disenchantment, staggers to his feet and starts all over again. This time it will be different, hopes the earnest Libra/Ox. And this time is always exactly the same. Only the sets change.

Libra/Ox people make eloquent raconteurs. When a Libra/Ox tells you the tales of his repeated woes and how he has been battered and buffeted by life and friends and family, you are riveted to your seat. What? This calm, unassuming, ingenuous and simple sort has been involved in such weirdness? Such baroque emotions have lived in that homespun person's heart? Frankly, when you see a Libra/Ox in all of his or her glorious homeliness, you can only wonder where all the complexity fits in.

Libra/Ox, it goes without saying, is a family-dependent person. He or she will not be much of a party-goer or social butterfly. Libra/Ox prefers home (and all of its relatively manageable embroilments) to the scatty and unclean outside world. Sometimes, if you're lucky, this Ox (because he is born Libra) will have acquired a certain distance from his own emotions. Then, with the natural eloquence given him or her at birth, this character can become exceedingly humorous.

These folks know how to use words wisely. Libra is naturally talkative but not always artful. Ox, on the contrary, doesn't say much but what he says is usually skillfully articulated What results in the Libra/Ox personality is sometimes known as the "gift of gab"—a real talent for entertaining with words.

Love

The province of romance in this person's existence is densely populated, to say the least. If you consider the variety and disparity of emotional influences alive in this subject's spirit, you will begin to comprehend just how overgrown is the sentimental acreage behind his superficially stolid facade. This native is deceptively frolicsome as a love partner. Inside, he or she is a roiling cauldron of emotional hang-ups and demands. In love situations, Libra/Ox is both quarrelsome and manipulative.

One of the compensations for the difficulties of cohabitation with the Libra/Ox is that you will always be guaranteed a safe and secure home. Moreover, should you wish to, you are allowed to appear to be thoroughly insane. Libra/Ox will love you more for your eccentricities, your oddball beliefs and your own complex miseries. Remember, however, that the Libra/Ox's stability is only skin deep. Act crazy if you want. But keep your head about you. The Libra/Ox, in his lust for experience, may be needing a wise second opinion.

Compatibilities

Your natural partners usually live in Gemini, Leo, Sagittarius and Aquarius. Snakes born in these signs are wise choices for you. You also get on with Rats born in Leo, Sagittarius and Aquarius. Gemini and Sagittarius/Roosters suit you well, as do Roosters born in both Leo and Aquarius. There now, you have quite a wide choice, don't you? But beware! Aries, Cancer and Capricorn/Tigers don't inspire you with their flashy causes. Nor do Cancer/Dragons, Horses and Monkeys.

Home and Family

"United we stand, divided we fall" should be the Libra/Ox's motto. This person's devotion to the unit, the cause, the order, the system and of course the family is exemplary. As head of a household he's at his most content. Libra/Ox likes to think of himself as the most benevolent, generous and philanthropic despot who ever lived on this earth. You, as a card-carrying member of his clan, should be honored to have him as your leader. Yawn.

I've already mentioned the secret furbelows that this person prefers in his home decor. No matter how roughly countrified his home may appear, this person will have a "lace curtain" mentality. He likes frippery and his tastes run to the gaudy. Nowhere, in fact, is the Libra/Ox schizophrenia so obvious as in his home. The heavy and cumbersome is always side by side with the frivolous. That's Libra/Ox: a porcelain teacup in a heavy ceramic saucer.

As parents these people are demanding and loving. They cling to rigid standards and yet indulge their kids emotionally. The Libra/Ox child will be both dutiful and fanciful. This kid needs security and a sense of teamwork. He or she will respond well to schoolwork, as such a child is always looking for stability and order. Don't be surprised by your Libra/Ox child's solemnity. On the other hand, don't be shocked by this kid's desire to tie bows on the Doberman's ears. They like things pretty.

Profession

Librans born in Ox years tend to achieve in the outside world. They have a taste for regular hours and can adhere to strict schedules, meet deadlines with ease and deliver the goods where work is concerned. They are diligent and (exceptional for Oxen) very cooperative. Libran Ox people are even diplomatic. They nit-pick a lot but are endowed with extraordinary strength and won't hesitate to take on the toughest jobs in any work situation.

I'm not sure I'd like to have a Libra/Ox boss. They are such models of good behavior on the surface that I should always feel diminished by comparison. Libra/Ox rules by example. This person is also a model employee. He doesn't balk at even the least gratifying tasks. Moreover, when he's on his way up, he's always willing to put in overtime. He'll be stubborn. But essentially he wants to cooperate.

You can impress him by your own irreproachable behavior. Some good careers for Libra/Oxen are: writer, preacher, newscaster, educator, antique dealer, social worker.

Famous Libra/Oxen:

Alberto Giacometti, Alex McCord, Art Buchwald, Bella Thorne, Benjamin Netanyahu (Israel), Bruce Springsteen, Cassandra Jean, Chester Alan Arthur, Deontay Wilder, Ed Sullivan, Emerald Fennell, Enrico Fermi, Eric Stoltz, Gore Vidal, Heather Locklear, J.P. Elkabach, Jessica Lucas, Jodi Benson, Julienne Davis, Lena Headey, Margaret Thatcher, Mario Lopez, Max Irons, Pedro Almodovar, Verstappen, Michelle Trachtenberg, Never Campbell, Sheila Kelley, Sigourney Weaver, Steve Young, Talulah Riley, Temple Fielding, Wynton Marsalis.

LIBRA
QUALITIES
JUSTICE, AESTHETICS, CHARM,
GENTILITY, EQUILIBRIUM, IDEALISM,
QUIRKS
QUARRELSOMENESS, MANIPULATION,
PROCRASTINATION, SELF-INDULGENCE,
INDECISION, TALKATIVENESS
Motto: *"I balance"*
Elements: *Air, Venus, Cardinal*

--

TIGER
QUALITIES
FERVOR, BRAVERY, MAGNETISM,
GOOD LUCK, BENEVOLENCE, AUTHORITY
QUIRKS
IMPETUOSITY, HOTHEADEDNESS,
DISOBEDIENCE, SWAGGER, INTEMPERANCE,
ITINERANCY
Motto: *"I Watch"*
Elements: *Positive Wood, Yang*

An original if there ever was one, the Libra/Tiger is unforget-tably winning. This person wants to impress and please you. You may react coldly, but more likely you will warm to the Tiger-ish Libran charisma and want to know more—much more—about him. Attractive? My gawd. These people emit personal magnetism rays that dance all over their countenances. Libra/Tiger seems per-petually on the brink of bursting out laughing. It's adorable. It's fascinating. And it is mighty perilous for the heartstrings.

In its raw state, personal magnetism doesn't pay the rent. There is not a lot for which you can barter a pound of intangible cuteness. But somehow these people charm the very pants off the world, invite respect and recruit followers with a mere snap of their fingers. I am not, decidedly not, suggesting that the Libra/Tiger is a phony. He doesn't flit about picking up groupies on a whim. The Libra/Tiger understands the value of a hard day's work and is willing to put in his time on all manner of projects. But the most arresting quality that this native possesses is self-assured magic. It will take him or her very far.

Libra/Tigers have a finely developed sense of justice and care deeply about doing good. They are, however, exceedingly irreverent. Systems and social conventions, outdated traditions and even up-to-date laws strike the Libra/Tiger as inapplicable to a person of his lofty stature. Libra/Tiger feels as though by virtue of his own natural superiority, he knows best for himself and for those he advises and leads. He is almost incapable of acquiescing to play by the rules, but is luckily endowed with just enough

Libran balance to keep him (most of the time) out of jail.

In a way, for a Libra to be born Tiger is troublesome. Libra is attracted to the "feminine" in life. He or she aims at drawing the beauty out of every encounter and is, on principle, a peace-seeker. As we already know, Tigers don't care about peace. Tigers care about truth. Tigers care about ideals. Tigers care about Tigers. This causes some basic disparity in the Libra/Tiger nature. That silly Tiger whose need for security is nil and who couldn't care less about social graces or bother with frills living inside the genteel Libra's head drives the Libra to distraction.

But distracted this subject does not remain for long. Libra/Tiger is dauntless in her search for a place in the sun, a name for herself, a star in the heavens of renown. This person's stabs at fame and fortune are many. And she often succeeds brilliantly at what she's set out to do. She is hotheaded and sometimes even foolish. But Libra/Tigers have a spark of refinement and a nose for the elegant that serves to scrape them off the woodwork and back into the good graces of whomever their hotheadedness has offended.

The Libra/Tiger's specialty is the stroke of genius. Whether it be in the realm of global politics or the more mundane business of throwing a Sunday brunch in honor of nothing more sophisticated than a family birthday, this person has an unbeatable touch. It's charismatic, yes. But it's also intelligent. Libra/Tiger has innate brilliance in his sign. Nothing he puts his hand to will be ordinary. It can be very wicked. But it will never be banal.

Love

Librans born in Tiger years make excellent mates. They are sufficiently sexual, but they are not dependent on sex for their equilibrium and are therefore one step ahead of the rest of the pack. For a Tiger this person is sweet-natured and sentimental. He's vulnerable, too, so don't go being harsh with this darling. The presence of this dashing person always lends enchantment to romance. They are rash and argumentative. But they are fun to fight with.

If you have the good luck to know one of these delectable creatures or even to be in love with one, I envy you. Libra/Tigers are among the world's swaggerers. They know how to dress. They carry off everything they try with panache and aplomb. They swashbuckle. If you want to keep this person in your home, you must provide him with permanent opportunities for creating a splash. This person wants notoriety in his own circle and even in a cosmic way. You will best please him or her by staying out of the path, never making disobliging comments and secretly, skillfully, advising your loved one to keep his or her mouthiness in check.

Compatibilities

You'll love a Gemini, Leo, Sagittarius or Aquarius born in Horse or Dog years. The harmonies flow naturally with them. Dragons from Sagittarius and Aquarius also hit the spot. You're better off without Aries, Cancer or Capricorn/Cats. You'll have trouble getting along with Aries/Snakes. Capricorn and Cancer/Oxen as well as Sheep are taboo.

Home and Family

Dear, dear. What can I say? The Libra/Tiger is a terrible spendthrift about the house. This impulsive charmer adorns his surroundings in an expensive and lavish fashion. "Change those ordinary-looking doorknobs. Get me a golden molding on that picture frame. Put up this embossed satin wallpaper imported from Thailand, and don't forget to allow for at least enough hot water for my three baths per day." Oh, my. It's so luxuriously efficient around the Tiger/Libra house.

As a parent the Libra/Tiger is caring. He or she will be thoughtful with regard to children and enjoy providing the guidance they require. The Libra/Tiger seduces kids like a parental Pied Piper. There's a spirit of cooperation and fairness about the parent-child relationship. Libra/Tiger may not always be available to watch over every detail. But when he or she is around, the time spent with kids is quality time.

Profession
Without hesitation I can say that Libra/Tigers are willing to pitch in and work. They are not shy of dirtying their hands and rarely complain of fatigue. These people are wiry and resistant. They have natural grace and don't hesitate to use their charms for personal betterment. They are not concerned with social climbing unless the "right" people prove somehow useful to them. Tiger/Libras are leaders and don't like to follow. They need a wise staff of advisers, as their weakness is haste.

Of course this person will want to be boss. You would have a hard time persuading him otherwise. As a boss, this character is surprisingly impartial and congenial. Tigers born Libra are fair and square, idealistic even, about how they treat others. They often take unpopular stands and will exact utter loyalty from underlings and associates alike.

As an employee or subordinate, the Libra/Tiger is circumspect and knows how to wait his turn to be boss. He will never accept a subordinate position in life. If he is obliged to, he will simply pine away.

Some career choices for Libra/Tigers are: head of government, clothes designer, decorator, revolutionary, speechwriter, adventurer, philosopher, playwright, entertainer, fundraiser.

Famous Libra/Tigers:
Amandla Stenberg, Ayatollah Khomenei, Bib Odenkirk, Chester A. Arthur, Chuck Berry, Danièle Delorme, Durga McBroom, Dwight D. Eisenhower, Esai Morales, Evil Knievel, Groucho Marx, Howard Rollins, John Coltrane, Mary McFadden, Melissa Sue Anderson, Michel Foucault, Oscar Wilde, Ray Kroc, Rimbaud, Romy Schneider, Rutherford Hayes, Susan Anton, Thor Heyerdahl, Tom Petty, Tommy Lee, Tyler Blackburn, Valéry Giscard d'Estaing.

LIBRA
QUALITIES
JUSTICE, AESTHETICS, CHARM,
GENTILITY, EQUILIBRIUM, IDEALISM,
QUIRKS
QUARRELSOMENESS, MANIPULATION,
PROCRASTINATION, SELF-INDULGENCE,
INDECISION, TALKATIVENESS
Motto: *"I balance"*
Elements: *Air, Venus, Cardinal*

--

CAT/RABBIT
QUALITIES
TACT, FINESSE, VIRTUE,
PRUDENCE, LONGEVITY, AMBITION,
QUIRKS
SECRETIVENESS, SQUEAMISHNESS,
PEDANTRY, DILETTANTISM,
HYPOCHONDRIA, COMPLEXITY
Motto: *"I Retreat"*
Elements: *Negative, Wood, Yin*

Tasteful, gracious living is the aim of the character born in the double sign of aesthetic appreciation. Librans born in Cat years are stay-at-home, suspicious, squeamish souls. They trust with great difficulty. Libra's discretion about passing quick judgments becomes, in this subject, a near refusal to judge anything or anyone. Libra/Cats hesitate so long before making decisions or committing themselves that they frequently lose their prey.

"Oh, wouldn't he or she make a wonderful mate for So-and-so?" is a question often asked about the Libra/Cat. Outwardly, the calm and delicate, sensible and graceful person we describe here seems

415

to have the makings of a perfect mate. But image is not always reality. Don't forget that when they encounter conflict, Cats slide away. They hate to be confronted. They never attack head on. They simply disappear.

Libra/Cat is the worst kind of slip-slider. He or she will never be held down—not even to a fight! Moreover, the act of hitching their wagon to an ideal or to another human being is practically beyond them. Libra/Cats are the epitome of bewildered indecision. And what's more, they like it that way.

In a very young person, constant vacillation is acceptable. People, these days, seem to spend quite a number of their youthful years "finding" themselves. At thirty, if you haven't found yourself, you might safely deduce that you were not there in the first place, and simply carry on as before. Libra/Cats sometimes die looking for themselves—at age eighty! These people hem and haw. Nothing is ever quite good enough for their refined tastes. So they frequently just stay where they are (even if it's still at home with mother) for want of the pluck to decide to change anything.

Libra/Cat is not stubborn. But if challenged by an emergency decision, he may grow cranky and bad-tempered or deliberately give the impression of somber seriousness so that nobody will call on him. His or her intimate involvement in human interaction is minimal. Yet, because of a very busy social calendar, the Libra/Cat may give just the opposite idea of himself.

Libra/Cats love to entertain. They will go to parties if they are sure to meet celebrities (and name-drop a bit, I might add) or talk animatedly with people who they feel can help them or even just amuse them. But when they leave the party and go home, they draw tight the shutters and crawl down into the safety of home. They cherish their domestic comfort and safeguard it carefully. Libra/Cats are unconscious victims of their need for security. A bohemian lifestyle terrifies them. Lack of certainty freaks them out. No matter how avant-garde a Libra/Cat ever appears, rest assured it's only skin-deep. Libra/Cat is an inveterate bourgeois.

Love

Romantic entanglements delight this tasteful and graceful creature. He or she will often be "in love." Libra/Cats are pleasant and make sweet companions who like to laugh and find beauty everywhere. Like all Librans, the Libra/Cat talks about his love too. They are tender, generous and passionate lovers. But they will have difficulty staying with one person. Are they fickle? Not really. Just indecisive.

If you love a Libra/Cat, the last thing you should do is try to move in with him. You must court them and tease them, giving back some of the medicine they dish out. Don't always be available to them or fawn over their good looks. They need to do the chasing. Keep the ball of yarn just out of reach and watch the Libra/Cat jump for it. The only way to keep a Libra/Cat content is to keep him or her guessing.

Compatibilities

Your closest affinities will be found among Gemini, Leo, Sagittarius and Aquarius people. Within this large family of souls you should look for a Sheep, a Dog or a Pig to associate yourself with for romantic purposes. You are not so compatible with Aries/Oxen. You plainly do not get along with Cancer or Capricorn Roosters or Rats. Don't be in a hurry to marry. Take your time. Before getting engaged, ask everybody you know and trust (not your mother) to have a chat with your choice of life partner. If they think he or she will be good for you, your marriage has a chance to succeed.

Home and Family

The home environment of a Libra/Cat will be refined and traditional, even rich-looking. He favors velvets and satins, stone or marble houses, and furnishes his life in a decorating scheme that allows him to wallow in the "feminine." Big, foam-filled bathtubs, and bouquets of cabbage roses on the wallpaper. Thick carpet up to the tub's rim and comfy robes kept warm at the bathside. And remember, Libra/Cat is not trying to impress anyone but himself.

This person, if he or she ever settles down, will make an okay parent. I say "okay" because parenting is messy and requires plenty of regular confrontation. Fighting is not the Libra/Cat's province at all. This subject will do well with the sweet parts of parenting and eschew the disciplining and mess. Not that Libra/Cat's intentions are not honorable. He or she loves children. But they are so turbulent, aren't they?

The Libra/Cat child will be happiest as an only child. He needs peace and quiet and will shy away from sibling rivalries. If he is the eldest, he can take charge and make sense out of that. Otherwise he'll suffer at the hands of rough and tumble brothers and sisters. Give the Libra/Cat child a refined atmosphere in which to evolve and feel secure. When he comes of age, you will practically have to pry him loose from the nest with a crowbar. If staying home is too comfy, he'll likely never leave.

Profession

Don't expect this person to go rushing out to start his own business, build it into a multimillion-dollar concern and fight his way into the best circles. Libra/Cats are best suited for jobs that allow them to stay at home and work independently. Because of their natural amiability and great strength of character (inside that frail shell is a Mack truck!) they leave an indelible personal impression wherever they go. If a Libra/Cat has to be boss, he will do what he can to slough the real domination off onto someone harsher than himself. He or she will be the sort of boss who hires a "whip" to do the dirty work of seeing that the slaves tote those barges.

Libra/Cat prefers to remain behind the scenes and willingly acts as the brains of any operation. This person has trouble being an employee, too. Libra/Cats don't take direction as gracefully as, for example, they circulate at parties. Their neck hairs bristle when they are treated unfairly or asked to participate in something they see as vulgar or futile. They make a pretty picture, but ought not to be required to "do windows."

Some excellent career choices for Libra/Cats are: bookstore owner, diplomat, translator/interpreter, piano tuner, interior decorator, museum curator, actor/actress (classical theater), writer.

Famous Libra/Cat/Rabbits:
Arthur Miller, Bob Geldof, Brian Boitano, Elisabeth Shue, Flávia Saraiva, George C. Scott, Glen Powell, Guillermo Del Toro, Günter Grass, John Cougar Mellencamp, Karen Allen, Kate Winslet, Leo Burnett, Marion Jones, Mark Hamill, Monica Bellucci, Nell Tiger Free, Pam Dawber, Paul Hogan, Peter Finch, Ralph Lauren, Roger Moore, Sean Lennon, Sting, Tatyana Alekseyeva, Taylor Hicks, Vladimir Horowitz, Zac Efron.

LIBRA
QUALITIES
JUSTICE, AESTHETICS, CHARM,
GENTILITY, EQUILIBRIUM, IDEALISM,
QUIRKS
QUARRELSOMENESS, MANIPULATION,
PROCRASTINATION, SELF-INDULGENCE,
INDECISION, TALKATIVENESS
Motto: *"I balance"*
Elements: *Air, Venus, Cardinal*

--

DRAGON
QUALITIES
STRENGTH, SUCCESS, GOOD HEALTH,
ENTHUSIASM, PLUCK, SENTIMENTALITY
QUIRKS
RIGIDITY, MISTRUST, DISSATISFACTION,
INFATUATION, BRAGGADOCIO, VOLUBILITY
Motto: *"I Preside"*
Elements: *Positive Wood, Yang*

The Libra/Dragon is not just anybody. Librans are born manipulators. Dragons tend to be suspicious. Librans seek equilibrium in all matters. Dragons seek to be heard and seen. Neither sign is particularly taciturn. The match is stormy. But despite the tempestuous nature of the Libra/Dragon, he or she will be gifted in carving out unusual destinies.

Many Librans, because they are naturally discreet and seek balance, will know how to put their personality in their pocket—if only for the purpose of not making waves. But here, along comes the thrilling Dragon. Dragons are noisy and know it all. They want to compete and they want to win. I have the impression that in this sign, Libra spends a lot of energy trying to convince his Dragonish volubility to retreat back inside that pocket. And (if you know one of these powerhouses, you will understand what I mean) they don't very often succeed.

Dragons born in Libra get places in life. No matter where they begin, you can be certain they don't end up at square one. These people know the meaning of the adage that you get out of life exactly what you put in. They contribute to their own lives' successes; they make something of themselves and they are not afraid of putting their pride on the line in order to achieve goals.

Libra/Dragon is a creative sign. But even more it is an interpretive sign. People born under this pair of signs combine discernment and energy, idealism and pluck, talkativeness and boastfulness. But never mind. These ebullient folks take us on fabulous trips through their own exciting, imaginative new worlds. They benefit from the unique distinction of self-worship with apparent impunity. Life, for the Libra/Dragon, is there exclusively for his use and pleasure. He has few scruples about taking what he needs and walking away from the rest. His ego is in terrific shape.

Libra/Dragons never give up. They are not dull, hardworking long- sufferers. Oh no. They are brilliant and even fanatical. And when I say they don't give up, I mean they don't even recognize opposition. For the Libra/Dragon, opposition isn't really there. Obstacles melt before them. One wonders, is it magic? And I reply, yes. There is a form of sorcery at work in the Libra/Dragon character. He is self-directed and quite oblivious to the needs of the crowd or the trends of the market. But somehow he knows what to do to please the crowd and to hit that market spot on. He plays hunches—and he wins.

As the center of attention, the Libra/Dragon personality ticks over like a charm. No problem as long as the spotlight is on him. He will expand and amuse and ape and strut and breathe fire endlessly so long as you are tuned in to his channel. Libra/Dragons are even kindly and sentimental and tender-hearted when their egos are being satisfied. But watch out. Don't ever let this person feel that you're about to switch stations. He or she can be real nasty when wronged.

Love

The Libra/Dragon's love life is a patchwork of ups and downs until, after much experimentation, he or she finds the mate of his or her dreams. You see, Libra/Dragons need a built-in audience of one. They have to keep a permanent sounding board around the house. Passion is important to them. But adulation is perhaps more so. Libra/Dragons like to be worshiped. Anything short of homage will leave Libra/Dragon lukewarm.

If you want one of these special little numbers around your house for all time, you've got your hands full. You will definitely save on entertainment costs. You won't need TVs or radios or videos or stereos. Libra/Dragon is the whole show by himself. Your job? Be sensible for your Libra/Dragon. Don't let him or her go too far off the deep end. If you have trouble with him, try pulling on his heartstrings. It's the only method I know of to control this attractive beast's pretentiousness.

Compatibilities

Rats born in Gemini, Leo, Sagittarius or Aquarius will turn you on. You also enjoy harmony with Gemini, Leo and Aquarius/ Monkey people. Leo and Sagittarius/Roosters are good for you, as are lovely Leo/Snake folks. Don't promote any long-standing relationships with Aries, Cancer or Capricorn/Cats or Dogs. And whatever you do, don't get mixed up with a Cancer/Ox. Too stodgy and emotional.

Home and Family

Physically, this person may not be all that smashingly attractive. But he will surround himself with beauty and he will know exactly how he wants his home to be decorated, his clothes to look, his image to project itself on the world. He may choose exotic or exciting furnishings, since he likes to impress. But whatever decor he chooses, its purpose will be to set off the Libra/Dragon to his or her best advantage. Librans born in Dragon years are good at parenting. They like to be looked up to by their offspring. Because of their exceptional view of self and their desire to shine at any cost, Libra/ Dragons sometimes have difficulty getting on with their older kids. They don't handle contradiction well. And there is nothing more contradictory than an adolescent child.

Childlessness is common among Libra/Dragons. Many of these complex people, for both personal and professional reasons, prefer not to bother having a family.

Profession

Here is where the Libra/Dragon can really shine. The Libra/ Dragon loves his or her career more than anything. Here is where the magic and pizzazz really have a chance to glow. At work, be it a shop or a restaurant, a TV program or a factory production line, when Dragon shows up with Libra in tow, the curtain opens to reveal the great, the one and only—move over world—here comes the king! I don't see this person employed as an underling for long. The patience and rigor factors are extremely low in Libra/Dragons.

But as a boss, this fellow can be quite loving and warm-hearted. The Libra/Dragon is fervently enthusiastic about himself and his projects and his way of looking at the world. But he's not a mean person. He's not a tough guy. Libra/Dragon wants everything his way, but then his way is, of course, the best way, *n'est-ce pas?*

Some promising careers for this character are: TV personality, general, entrepreneur, public figure (politician for example), airline pilot, shop owner, musician, entertainer, evangelist.

Famous Libra/Dragons:

A$AP Rocky (Rakim Mayers), Alicia Vikander, Angie Dickinson, Anthony Delon, Jeanane Garofalo, Candice Swanepoel, Christopher Reeve, Elie Wiesel, Glen Powell, Graham Greene, Imran Khan, Jacques Chazot, Jeff Goldblum, Jimmy Breslin, John Lennon, Kathryn Edwards, Kevin Durant, Lilly Singh (||Superwoman||), Mesut Özil, Nietzsche, Olivia Jordan Thomas, Pelé, Rex Reed, Sarah Bernhardt, Vladimir Putin.

LIBRA
QUALITIES
JUSTICE, AESTHETICS, CHARM,
GENTILITY, EQUILIBRIUM, IDEALISM,
QUIRKS
QUARRELSOMENESS, MANIPULATION,
PROCRASTINATION, SELF-INDULGENCE,
INDECISION, TALKATIVENESS
Motto: *"I balance"*
Elements: *Air, Venus, Cardinal*

--

SNAKE
QUALITIES
INTUITION, ATTRACTIVENESS, DISCRETION,
SAGACITY, CLAIRVOYANCE, COMPASSION
QUIRKS
DISSIMULATION, EXTRAVAGANCE,
LAZINESS, CUPIDITY, PRESUMPTION,
EXCLUSIVENESS
Motto: *"I sense"*
Elements: *Negative ,Fire, Yin*

Magnetism personified. The Libra born in a Snake year will, above all, attract. This combination is a mostly happy one. People born under this sign may be less so. This is because they are not only irresistible; they are also stubborn and willful. They want things done their way, and like to order others around subtly. Often, things are done for them, their way, by willing lackeys. These people have charisma to burn.

Libran Snakes rule others through emotion. They are capable of sensing exactly what another needs from them. They are remarkably perceptive and even have a gift for the supernatural. Librans born in Snake years know how to exalt an audience with their cool, reasonable yet emphatically sentimental discourse. These people are born to serve as shepherds of human flocks, moralizers and brotherhood mongers.

There is a Saint Valentine quality about the Libra born Snake person. A lacy, heart- shaped, whimsical yet meaningful self that always shines through. I'd say that this sign is more "feminine" than masculine in flavor. Libra/Snakes indulge in finery. They like to "mother" others. And they embody a kind of exemplary passivity that lends a quality of femaleness to their characters. They are not wont to go after power over their fellows unless it is requested of them by followers. In fact, Libra/Snakes have to contend with laziness, luxuriating, dissipation and wanton pleasure-seeking. They are given to excess and must do everyday battle with a monumental delight in languor.

Their fatal flaw in all of this is, of course, their inability to escape their own seductiveness. Eventually, after years of watching people fall at his or her feet in admiration, the Libra/Snake gets the picture and usually becomes a pace-setter of some sort. Taking up causes is, in the case of Libran Snakes, always performed in the most graceful and non-violent way. Libra/Snake wants to reason with danger, to talk over differences, to discuss the peace arrangements. Then he will make a touching speech on the subject, and more people will collapse at his feet. Libra/Snake doesn't have to overpower. All he has to do is attract.

One quality that the Libra/Snake possesses and frequently uses in his or her profession is humanitarianism. The Libra side of this person's character wants justice for all. The Snake is kindness itself, always compassionate and understanding, willing to lend an ear or a shoulder to cry on. The two signs together create a being of enormous altruism, who is not afraid to do something about hunger or poverty or injustice. The rosters of international relief organizations are loaded with the names of Libra/Snakes who care about their fellow man enough to spend their time and money to help out.

Not that the Libra/Snake is basically generous. He is not. This person might even be slightly guarded about spending money on necessities. Yet, when he feels the urge, he indulges in an expensive bibelot or adorns himself with some golden gadgetry or other. Libra/Snake is a sneaky spender and is not above a fib or two about how much baubles really cost.

Love

Does the Libra/Snake know anything else? These subjects are all love and sensuality, sexiness and grand romance. Of course, they are too gorgeous to be forever faithful to one person. But they are definitely devoted mates in every other way. Too, Libra/Snakes, for all of their beauty and languor, can be a lot of fun. They are mischievous, a little zany, and they know how to laugh at themselves.

If you are attracted to one of these miracles of charm, I suggest you adopt his or her ideals immediately. You will be needing all the patience and pacifism you can get when your Libra/Snake goes off on a tour of African hunger areas without you, leaving you home to keep the kids alive. You will need great personal fortitude and lots of dignity to walk beside your beloved Libra/Snake. Keep your nose in the air and don't give that adoring crowd the time of day.

Compatibilities

Roosters are high on your priority list. Try sticking to those Roosters born in Gemini, Leo, Sagittarius and Aquarius. Leo, Sagittarius and Aquarius/Oxen make swell bedfellows for you too. Aries and Capricorn/Monkeys get on your nerves. Cancer and Capricorn/Pigs are too critically scrupulous for your slightly slippery attitudes to jibe with theirs. And Cancer/Tigers are so moody and jumpy as to drive you up a wall.

Home and Family

Count on the Libra born in Snake years to furnish his or her environment in plush fabrics and line the walls with precious *objets d'art.* This person is a lover of luxury and, despite his sackcloth and ashes pitch, adores comforts and hates to live without them. You will be welcome at the Libra/Snake's home, too. Feel free to drop in any time. There's always enough room for a few more uninvited guests.

The Libra/Snake will want to have lots of children. This character enjoys caretaking and protecting others. He or she may, for this reason, mollycoddle a bit too much and hover anxiously over his sleeping bambinos. But when they awaken they will be in for a good time. Libra/Snake parents bedazzle their kids the same way they enchant everyone else. However, these parents tend to preach. Their sermonizing must be quelled. Moralizing sets kids' teeth on edge.

As a child this person will be delightfully winning and have a kind of funny grownup wisdom in speech. Too much material spoiling is not good for this sensitive child. He or she must be taught the value of basics. Nature hikes and camping trips will remove some of that city glitter from his eyes. I highly recommend sports and scouts. This child can be subject to psychosomatic allergies if he or she is not regularly brought firmly to earth by routine and security.

Profession

By nature, the Libra/Snake is a leader of men. But he or she is non-competitive and wants no part of belligerence. The gift here is attractiveness. People willingly revere this subject, hang on his every word and long to be like him or her. Misused, this talent can, of course, be extremely dangerous. But as the Libra/Snake is not so power-hungry as he is willing to take the reins if they are given him, there is less danger here than may be feared.

The Libra/Snake does not take well to subordination. It's not that he or she cannot understand the need for humility, but that the underling station annoys them. They know they can run the show, so they wonder why somebody doesn't just hang a sign on their door saying "Boss." But they don't misuse power as a rule, and are as conscientious as those who work with them. Libra/Snakes make excellent partners for less charismatic people who know how to do earthly things like add and subtract and pay their taxes. Libra/ Snakes want top billing but don't rankle at sharing the profits.

Some good career choices for the Libra/Snake are: spiritual leader, model, actor, singer, talk show host, executive officer, newscaster, politician.

Famous Libra/Snakes:

Aimee Teagarden, Alfred Nobel, Anne Rice, Anthony Joshua, Bill Nunn, Brie Larson, Chris Penn, Chubby Checker, Clea Duvall, Dakota Johnson, David Morse, Emma Rigby, Jesse Jackson, Joel David Moore, Kathy Wakile, Kiele Sanchez, Laura Regan, Lenni James, Leore Hayon, Linda McCartney, Mahatma Gandhi, Matt Bomer, Mia Wasikowska, Paul Simon, Pia Wurtzbach, Pierre Bellemare, Rebecca Pidgeon, Sam Witwer, Sean Patrick Flanery, Thelonious Monk, Tony Shalhoub, Valerie Golino.

LIBRA
QUALITIES
JUSTICE, AESTHETICS, CHARM,
GENTILITY, EQUILIBRIUM, IDEALISM,
QUIRKS
QUARRELSOMENESS, MANIPULATION,
PROCRASTINATION, SELF-INDULGENCE,
INDECISION, TALKATIVENESS
Motto: *"I balance"*
Elements: *Air, Venus, Cardinal*

--

HORSE
QUALITIES
PERSUASIVENESS, UNSCRUPULOUSNESS,
POPULARITY, STYLE, DEXTERITY,
ACCOMPLISHMENT
QUIRKS
SELFISHNESS, AUTONOMY, REBELLION,
HASTE, ANXIETY, PRAGMATISM
Motto: *"I demand"*
Elements: *Positive Fire, Yang*

For a Horse character this person born in gracious Libra will be genteel and dignified. Horses are sometimes rebellious and hardheaded. Libra practically never is. Libra wants peace and knows how to go after equilibrium. In this sign, Libra climbs on to the Horse's back and hangs on for dear life until she has tamed the selfish stallion into a better, more civilized person.

When joined to Libra, the Horse personality gets to keep many of his worldly goods. He retains full interest in his elegance and style. He hangs on tight to popularity and has the market cornered on idealism. Libra lends Horse refined taste. Moreover, in hitching his wagon to Libra, the Horse doesn't have to give up one iota of his fancy. You know how Horses only like to do what they want when they want to ? Well, Libra doesn't mind that. In fact, Libra encourages this quality, as she knows that with her well-developed sense of measure the Horse will never totally buck the system.

This blend of signs often hatches excellent talkers. The Horse has a commanding presence. He or she will captivate audiences with poise and self-assuredness. Libra adds charm and a touch of the aesthetic to this popular image. The Libra born Horse can be an impressive performer.

Horses born in Libra often experience the phenomenon of unusual destiny. This obviously has to do with their gift for being in the right place at the right time. The Libra/Horse is very mobile and is concerned with self-advancement. The combination of good luck and a nose for connections makes this person a fine candidate for sudden, unexpected fame or fortune.

No Horse character is ever lazy. But Libran Horses will be slightly less hectic than their counterparts in other signs. They know how to relax and slow down for the sake of gain or improvement and are not so preoccupied with the pragmatic as most Horses. The Libra/Horse is an exalted type of person, whose opinions and stances are fiery and willful. You will not forget meeting up with one. And, as they are extremely sociable, you may very well encounter one at a party this very evening. Parties and gatherings, receptions and meetings play a large role in this person's life.

The Libra/Horse is, above all, a convincing person. He is persuasive and eloquent. He is not very compassionate or sentimental. But he can be carried away by the fervor of an ideal. There is poetry in the soul of this effective human being and it shows on his dignified, tasteful surface. He can be unscrupulous for self-interest's sake, and if he's trying to talk you into one of his plans he will never take no for an answer.

The Horse born in Libra seeks justice for all and favor for himself. He usually achieves autonomy and is not above creating a scandal to get it. The Libra/Horse is an oddball, and often invents or performs some outrageous deed to shock more conventional souls. But never mind. This person does not suffer from self-doubt, but goes straight for the jugular—ever so elegantly.

Love

Passion is more important than tenderness in the life of a Libra/Horse. He or she will be attracted by ideals in another person, or by some characteristic besides appearance—like money, for example. Libra/Horses are not quite so rapacious as most Libras, but they nonetheless like to take a room by storm. They are sensuous and given to flirting.

Loving someone born in Libra/Horse can present complications. This person is something of an island unto him- or herself. They are not too dependent on the image of a relationship and will seek in a partner the capacity for self-sacrifice that Libra/Horse lacks. If you love one of these creatures, get ready to spend a good part of your time combing that luxuriant mane and rubbing down your beautiful steed. The Libra/Horse is a primper and a preener.

Compatibilities

Seek a life partner from among Tiger people born in Gemini, Leo, Sagittarius or Aquarius. Flings can turn into much more when dabbled in with either a Gemini or a Leo/Sheep. Sagittarius and Aquarius/Dogs make earnest companions for you. I don't advise you to dally with Rats born in Aries, Cancer or Capricorn. Discourage passes from eager Capricorn/Sheep too.

Home and Family

Here the Libra/Horse will really go for broke. This native wants a handsome home atmosphere where he or she can receive platoons of friends and associates. The sofas will be velvet and the drapes heavy and probably burgundy or soft brown. Libra/Horse is a luxury-lover extraordinaire. He will also be sure to own every last device to enhance the household's appearance. The lights will all be on dimmer switches and the flowers freshly arranged by the person who comes in for just that purpose. Libra/Horse spares no expense when it comes to impressing his audience. He deplores vulgarity and does not take kindly to guests who show up in tattered blue jeans. Flair's the thing.

There will be a distance between this character and his or her offspring. The Horse born in Libra may feel some competition from children. He or she will require help in raising kids as the Libra/Horse is frequently out or too busy doing something personal to care for them. Actually I think the average Libra/Horse gets on best with his or her kids when the kids start being grownups. Then, when the petulant childishness has begun to fade, the child will become more acceptable to the tasteful Libra/Horse.

As a child this person will show great promise and impress adults with his apparent ease in acquiring social graces. There is rebelliousness in the young Libran born Horse that wanes when the child matures and sees that tempestuousness will not get her where she wants to go. This kid can be funny and quirky—a sort of odd man out with his cronies. Yet the Libra/Horse will always be well liked and admired. No matter what you do as his parent, this child will eventually go his own way.

Profession

As this person is both argumentative and persuasive, he or she will excel at all jobs requiring verbal skill and conviction. Moreover, the Libra/Horse is elegantly well dressed and presents a fine image to the world. His or her weakness will stem from an unwillingness to play the game for the sake of keeping the peace. Libra/Horses care less about peace than they do about their own advancement. They will only be cooperative if compromise in no way impedes their progress.

Depending on the situation, this person can either shine at dispensing authority or at taking orders. The only prerequisite, as far as the Libra/Horse is concerned, is personal interest. If being the boss gets Libra/Horse to the top, then he'll gladly accept an executive post. Otherwise, you can keep your lofty titles. All the Libra/ Horse really wants from a job is upward mobility-and, of course, money.

Careers accessible to Libran Horses are: city planner, landscape architect, gossip columnist, critic, merchant, publicist, actor, restaurant owner, decorator, teacher.

Famous Libra/Horses:

Ang Lee, Anthony Mackie, Bai Ling, Britt Ekland, Cassandra Freeman, David Cameron, Dmitri Shostakovitch, Eric Charden, Hafiz al-Assade (Syria), Harold Pinter, Jodi Lyn O'Keefe, Jon Favreau, Jonathan Lipnicki, Karen Parsons, Leopold Senghor, Lola Kirke, Lorrain Bracco, Luke Perry, Michael Dudikoff, Penny Marshall, Philippe Noiret, Richard Harris, Rita Hayworth, Roberto Bonanomi, Rutherford B. Hayes, Samantha Barks, Scott Bakula, Shannyn Sossaman, Trevor Donovan, Will Estes.

LIBRA
QUALITIES
JUSTICE, AESTHETICS, CHARM,
GENTILITY, EQUILIBRIUM, IDEALISM,
QUIRKS
QUARRELSOMENESS, MANIPULATION,
PROCRASTINATION, SELF-INDULGENCE,
INDECISION, TALKATIVENESS
Motto: *"I balance"*
Elements: *Air, Venus, Cardinal*

--

SHEEP
QUALITIES
INVENTION, LACK OF FORESIGHT,
PERSEVERANCE, WHIMSY, GOOD MANNERS,
IMPRACTICALITY
QUIRKS
PARASITISM, SENSITIVITY,
TARDINESS, PESSIMISM, TASTE, WORRY
Motto: *"I depend"*
Elements: *Negative, Fire, Yin*

O stensibly a dependent lover of beauty and equilibrium, this person claims to need a peaceful environment, but we know better. Librans born in Sheep years are testy and quarrelsome people. They love an argument, a good old heated discussion, a challenge. The Libra/Sheep requires the regard of his peers. He likes to be looked at, contemplated, taken seriously and admired. To this end, the Libra/Sheep will do almost anything—once.

With Libra and Sheep under the same roof, people born in this sign will be doubly attracted to elegance and finesse. They truly prefer to furnish their lives with ornate classics and line their walls with books than to spend time and money on trendy wardrobes or spiffy automobiles. These characters can be social climbers. As such, they prefer to climb culturally rather than merely be included in the annals of society, party-giving or going. Libra/Sheep are a bit light-headed. But they are not superficial.

There is great creativity in the Libra/Sheep nature. This person, provided the ambience is secure and safe, can invent and imagine all manner of craft and artistry. I would not say this subject is a gifted artist in the Picasso sense. But there is, inside the Libra/Sheep head, a kaleidoscopic imagination. The Libra/Sheep leaps from idea to idea with a special rapid grace all his own. He understands the labyrinthine. He comprehends complexity, and is superbly talented at all sorts of communication.

One of the Sheep/Libra's handicaps is his unwillingness to believe in self. I say unwillingness rather than inability because the phenomenon is more a refusal than a lack. "I can't. Who cares? Who wants to listen to little old me? It's not really important. Never mind." That's the kind of talk you hear from non-directed Librans born in Sheep years.

You see, Librans born in Sheep years are extremely sensitive. In their youth they are often drawn to strong, stable types whose very presence seems to promise to shore up their courage. Then, after a while, when the weirdo Libra/Sheep sees just what a high price he must pay to be "normal" and "stable," when he grasps the useless, boring sameness of a life without creation or experiment, he bolts. But this bolting seems to Libra/Sheep a terribly cowardly act. He is disappointed in normalcy. But he blames his disappointment on his own unwillingness to "go straight." This, once again, makes him lose confidence in himself. As he never had masses of self-belief in the first place, this makes him less effective, and a vicious circle effect sets in.

Libra/Sheep are excessive. They are vulnerable to addiction. They are ambitious and fashion-conscious. They are inventive and talented in all sorts of glamour-related pursuits. The trouble with Libra/Sheep, besides their intermittent lack of self-assurance, is that they tend to disperse their energies in too many flittings about. They are easily distracted. They must learn to settle on one idea and push it through to its logical conclusion. And they must seek the wisdom of those more thoughtful and sagacious than they. It is by heeding good advice and not flying off the handle till the wood is all chopped that Librans born in Sheep years will succeed.

Love

Romance is one area in which the Libra/Sheep feels comfortable and capable. This person is gifted for sentimental rapport. He or she will revel in the trappings of love: the candlelight dinners and the trips to tropical islands, the banter and, of course, the sex. Libra/Sheep are very pretty people, sort of frail looking and fey. They always dress to suit their looks and have a finely developed nose for style. They will depend entirely on their relationships with their mates. Living alone is out of the question. These people thrive on tenderness and offer top drawer companionship to a mate.

If you love a Libra/Sheep, you must first win his or her favors through clever and aesthetic courtship methods. Your Libra born Sheep is fatally attractive. You will not be the only one seeking his or her affections. Be unusual. The Libra/Sheep cleaves to the arcane and is fascinated by the strange. Ordinary workaday people only attract the Libra/Sheep in his very first blush of youthful naiveté.

Compatibilities

You have a propensity for cohabitation with Cat people. You'll want to choose from Cats born in Gemini, Leo, Sagittarius and Aquarius. There are plenty of Horse subjects out there for your pleasure, too. Try sticking to Gemini, Sagittarius or Aquarius/ Horses. They have the necessary earning power to keep you in style. Leo and Aquarius/Pigs also enjoy high standards of living. Aries, Cancer and Capricorn/Dogs are out of the running, as are Cancer and Capricorn/Oxen.

Home and Family

The Libra/Sheep is not terribly concerned with decoration. He will be happiest in a messy, intellectual sort of decor with deep worn velvet or leather armchairs and generous working surfaces. He's not overly conscious of how his or her interior strikes others. He wants it to be comfortable first and beautiful later. Libra/Sheep enjoy the haphazardness of the "lived-in" look.

These people make conscientious parents who want the best in culture for their children. Occasionally Libra/Sheep seem to be overwhelmed by their children and even a bit bamboozled by them. They don't like to discipline their kids. But neither can they tolerate being a punching bag for little Johnny or Mary. Often, they allow trouble to build up before stepping in to do something about it. This avant-garde childrearing method leads to its share of yelling.

Libra/Sheep kids are too sweet for words. They are loving and enchanting little people whose beauty alone is enough to make you want to squeeze them. My advice? Don't. Libra/Sheep children, like their adult counterparts, are not as fragile as they look. They hate to be treated like dumbbells. These bright people gobble education. The best schools are in order.

Profession

Libra/Sheep are not independent people. They must be surrounded by aides-de-camp or buoyed by a well-constructed system in order to achieve their goals. They are talented and innovative. Libra/Sheep have natural poise and are mannerly and dress tastefully. They are especially gifted for complex creative work requiring a sense of true invention. Libra/Sheep are easily discouraged and can very quickly be overcome by the prospect of having too much on their plates. One dish at a time is the method best suited to the advancement of their artistic natures.

Jobs that best suit Libra/Sheep are: freelance illustrator, poet, fashion journalist, scriptwriter, homemaker, graphic artist, musician.

Famous Libra/Sheep:

Anita Ekberg, Anthony Newley, Barbara Walters, Caitriona Balfe, Catherine Deneuve, Charlotte Spencer, Chevy Chase, Chris O'Dowd, Christopher Gerse, Deni Villeneuve, Desmond Tutu, Dilip Shanghvi, Doris Lessing, Franz Liszt, Guy Pearce, John Le Carré, Julez Roy, Julio Iglesias, Kate Walsh, Kimi Räikkönen, Kristanna Loken, Lech Walesa, Leigh-Anne Pinnock, Mickey Mantle, Miguel de Cervantes, Pierre Trudeau, Stacy Keibler, Yo-Yo Ma.

LIBRA
QUALITIES
JUSTICE, AESTHETICS, CHARM,
GENTILITY, EQUILIBRIUM, IDEALISM,
QUIRKS
QUARRELSOMENESS, MANIPULATION,
PROCRASTINATION, SELF-INDULGENCE,
INDECISION, TALKATIVENESS

Motto: *"I balance"*
Elements: *Air, Venus, Cardinal*

--

MONKEY
QUALITIES
IMPROVISATION, CUNNING, STABILITY,
SELF-INVOLVEMENT, WIT, OPPORTUNISM
QUIRKS
DECEIT, RUSE, LOQUACITY,
LEADERS, SILLINESS, ZEAL

Motto: *"I plan"*
Elements: *Positive, metal, Yang*

This combination of signs can talk his or her way in or out of just about any paper bag. The Libra/Monkey's strength lies in his brilliant manipulation of words and ideas to fit situations both commercial and artistic. Librans born Monkey are gentle con artists whose characteristic eloquence and gift of gab make them thrilling company.

The Libra side of this person's nature will want to live life as a couple and will be attracted to early marriage. Adding Monkey traits to the jabbery Libra's chart infuses it with an increased need for communication—and even a certain desire for healthy conflict.

The Libra/Monkey combo is not restful. These people are attracted to motion for its own sake. Sometimes they need to forget what they have just seen and travel on to new territories in order to soak up some joyful or at least different vibrations.

The Libra born Monkey is manipulative. He or she will not be above exploitation of others. The Libra/Monkey sees the world as his playpen. He doesn't see why he should not extract sentiment in favor of gain. After all, whatever shenanigans the Monkey born Libra is up to, he will be the first to assure both you and himself that he has the best interests of everyone concerned at heart. Libra/Monkey is not a parasite. He is active and energetic, has sharper than average intelligence and can be wittily clever.

There is a freewheeling aspect to the Libra/Monkey personality. This person exudes boyishness and carries a twinkle around in his eye that intimates that he has caught his entire entourage with their hands in the cookie jar. Libran Monkeys don't go around policing the world. They are intuitive and feel both personal and social changes very strongly. Often, you will find Libra/Monkeys in the vanguard of an artistic or political movement.

Life is sometimes just too much for the Libra/Monkey's heightened sensitivities to bear. This character can be drawn to inducing euphoria and ingesting consciousness-altering substances. He doesn't always feel strong enough, combative enough—although he is obviously smart enough, by a long shot—to meet a challenge.

Not that Libra/Monkeys are weak. Far from it! But they can lack self-assurance and hesitate before steamrolling a competitor. They don't mind winning through guile or shiftiness. But they really prefer not to confront adversity head on. Might, where the Libra/Monkey is concerned, is never right. He prefers satire as a weapon. He'd rather use humor or even just his brains to outdistance opposition. The Libra/Monkey is skilled at dealing with his audience. He has dignity and a biting repartee. His talents are many and he can rise to great heights in any area he chooses because of his willingness to adapt, to bend and change with the current. This person is the antithesis of stubborn. Although he can be discouraged and may indulge in temporary surrender, the Libra/Monkey is flexible and even-tempered.

Love
In romantic endeavors as in more prosaic pursuits, the Libra born Monkey can be deceptively self-interested. Mostly, though, as the couple is of paramount importance in this person's life, the interests of maintaining that relationship will take precedence over all others.

Libra/Monkeys are sentimental, and even when they take unfair advantage of another's love for them, they remain devotedly attached. What Libra/Monkeys are looking for in love affairs or marriages is a balance between two people whose mutual passion and interdependency can create a symbiosis. As Libra/Monkey takes, so he or she will give in return.

Should you be enamored of a Libra/Monkey, you can rest assured he or she will make of your rapport an idealistic mission in search of lifelong equilibrium. Their hopes are so high, in fact, that it can put quite a bit of wearying responsibility on their better halves. The Libra/Monkey wants to be the stable element in your couple, which will give you the chance to go ahead and be about as loony as you like. Don't worry, Libra/Monkey will provide emotionally.

Compatibilities

There might be a Dragon in your future. If so, he or she will best be chosen from among Gemini, Leo, Sagittarius or Aquarius subjects. You will also get on with Leo, Sagittarius and Aquarius/Rats. The vibes are not perfect between you and Aries or Cancer/Horses. Ditto for Cancer or Capricorn/Tigers. Cancer/Pigs and Capricorn/Oxen are just plain too rigid for your lithe and changeable nature to enjoy for long.

Home and Family

The Libra/Monkey's home is where he hangs his hat. He likes beauty and luxury but doesn't necessarily need a mammoth homestead to prove to himself that he has roots. Libra/Monkeys are rooted in the moment. It seems to be enough for them. They are not nomads or hobos. But if they do have a lovely home, its purpose will more likely be to please others than to lend security.

The Libra/Monkey makes a sincere and loving parent. One thing he or she regrets in the first place is having had to grow up and become serious and stodgy and adult. So this person will be the kind who plays with kids, and takes them to amusement parks, and accompanies them on roller coaster rides. Libra/Monkeys will expect their children to be imaginative and encourage them in creative areas.

Libra/Monkey kids are sweet little things. They have a ready smile and are always willing to go along with Auntie Linda or leap into the unsuspecting arms of Uncle Oscar. They are both gregarious and sunny. Of course, they must be watched for naughtiness. These kids are mischief-makers of the first water. They are always up to something. Also, they tend to jabber your ear off. Give them lots of good education so at least when they grow up they'll have something interesting to jabber about.

Profession

The Monkey born Libra boasts an aristocratic bearing. We know by now that he or she also possesses the ability to talk—at length. There is, as well, a talent for adapting words to ideas. The Libran Monkey makes an excellent colleague or partner, and handles exterior relations better than any other Monkey signs. The Libra/ Monkey boss figure will not be terrifying at all, but rather will impress by his loquacity and razor-sharp mind. People respect the Libran/Monkey for his noble touch and acuity about world affairs or social developments.

Profitable ways to employ the Libra/Monkey's services: Either leave him or her entirely alone in a windowless room, thereby enforcing concentration, or send him or her on the road selling—anything! But make sure they meet their daily quota. Libra/ Monkeys have a sorry tendency to disperse their energies in vapid chitchat.

Any career is suitable for Libra/Monkey if it guarantees movement and social contact: realtor, actor, professor, insurance salesman, speechwriter, legal aide, social worker, public relations, advertising "idea" person.

Famous Libra/Monkeys:

Ben Whishaw, Buster Keaton, David Haye, Diane Dufresne, Eleanor Roosevelt, Emily Procter, F. Scott Fitzgerald, Glenn Gould, Grace Johnston, Henri de Verneuil, Hugh Jackman, Jacques Sallebert, Jacques Tati, Jana Novotna, John Kenneth Galbraith, Josh Hutcherson, Julie McNiven, Kaci Fennell, Kevin Magnussen, Kim Kardashian, Mario Puzo, Martina Hingis, Martina Navratilova, Montgomerey Clift, Naomi Watts, Ray Charles, Sam Mikulak, Theresa May, Timothy Leary, Walter Matthau, Will Smith, William Conrad, Zachary Levi.

LIBRA
QUALITIES
JUSTICE, AESTHETICS, CHARM,
GENTILITY, EQUILIBRIUM, IDEALISM,
QUIRKS
QUARRELSOMENESS, MANIPULATION,
PROCRASTINATION, SELF-INDULGENCE,
INDECISION, TALKATIVENESS
Motto: *"I balance"*
Elements: *Air, Venus, Cardinal*

--

ROOSTER
QUALITIES
RESILIENCE, ENTHUSIASM, CANDOR,
CONSERVATISM, CHIC, HUMOR
QUIRKS
COCKINESS, BOASTFULNESS, BLIND FAITH,
PEDANTRY, BOSSINESS, DISSIPATION
Motto: *"I overcome"*
Elements: *Negative, Metal, Yin*

Libra/Rooster lives a life full of chasms of despair followed by summits of felicity. And thank Zeus for Libra's sense of equilibrium. Libra lends poetry to the Rooster's cocky strictness and tickles his conservatism, even prodding it into the occasional flight of fancy. Also, Libra tempers the Rooster's tendency to over-react. For a Rooster, this person will be gentle and might even qualify as "calm."

What does Rooster, then, give to our friend Libra in exchange? Plenty. For one, Rooster's earthiness and enthusiasm lift the lid off Libra's occasional self-indulgence. "Come on now, Libra old girl, you've got to work. You cannot just lie there in your satin sheets reading confession magazines. Up and at 'em. There's a new toy out in the kitchen, a fascinating event on the front porch, a terrific person to meet on the sidewalk," urges the eager Rooster. Rooster's resilience plays an interesting role in the Libra/Rooster personality. As we already know, Libra does not take stands. He or she is not hastily judgmental. The Rooster's life is constantly being saved at the last minute by his innate ability to accept and undergo upheaval that would kill anyone less bouncy. These two qualities are highly complementary and give Libra/Rooster an edge when it comes to some of the sharper turns on the highway of life. Rooster knows how to brush off the experience without a blink, and Libra doesn't judge him for having done so. This person has few, if any, regrets.

Rooster brings rigor and energy to the Libra subject and his candor lightens Libra's sometimes unnecessarily feisty speech. To Rooster, Libra lends an air of relaxed attractiveness often missing from the bossy and cocky Rooster image. Libra/Rooster is mild-mannered, tweedily clad, and appears to have no axe to grind. The image is appealing. Roosters born in Libra are popular with peers. There is something of the quiet know- it-all here. The smarty pants attitude.

This person can be accused of self-complacency. The impression is: "I'm right because I'm me." It can be a bore. This Rooster does not exhaust himself at workaday jobs.. He likes to shine, be brilliant and knock 'em dead in a single performance. Reruns don't interest the Libra/Rooster. He'd rather you would suggest a new endeavor or ask him to perform one of his works in progress. This person is a hive of novelty. He does not lack for surprises.

All in all, this Rooster is talented and sensitive enough to create both poetry and music. He or she can take artistic careers far. They have stick-to-itiveness and they can present their material in a winning (Libran) manner. They are slightly conflictual and seem to take pleasure in philosophical tugs of war. It's just as well; it gets the job done.

Love
The Libra/Rooster wants to respect as well as love his or partner. He has enormous devotion and faith to offer. But he does not want to give it away foolishly. Rooster usually settles on one love object and is able to maintain interest in a single mate for life. Not all Roosters are so lucky. But the Libra side of this one gives him extra sensitivity.

If you love one of these Librans, you must be very happy. Libra/ Rooster is a person you can look up to, admire and feel sweet about as well. Libra/Roosters appreciate tenderness and know how to receive affection. They may seem a bit preoccupied with their eternal artistic flights of fancy. Don't worry. If they said they loved you, they mean it. If not, you'd better look elsewhere. This person is unbudgeable in the fidelity department.

Compatibilities

I see you happiest with an Ox or Snake character. The atmosphere will be best if you take care to select your partners from Oxen and Snakes born in Gemini, Leo, Sagittarius or Aquarius. Discriminate. Don't be too tempted by Aries/Pigs, Cancer/Roosters and Capricorn/Cats. Each in his or her own way is too emotionally unstable to give you what you really need—cool headedness and tranquility.

Home and Family

The Libra/Rooster does not wish to show off with his posh decorating scheme. This person is an outside man or woman. He likes his place of habitation to be well appointed, but he doesn't want to pound the nails or sew up the curtains himself. Libra/Rooster feels a closer involvement in his or her cerebral work than in any manual labor, no matter how lofty. If the house is practical and traditionally furnished, Libra/Rooster will be content with it.

This person's parenting talents will be limited to guidance and a rather distant sort of sunny affection. Libra/Roosters do not wish to wipe bottoms. They'd rather hire a nanny. Libra/Roosters are not exactly family types anyway. They enjoy being part of a couple. But they don't really have time for running the PTA or selling cookies for the Girl Scouts.

The Libra/Rooster child will be active and loving. He or she needs much cultural input at a young age. The fine sensitivity of this child will want stimulating. Nature and all of its joys have a calming effect on the Libra/Rooster child. He will be an odd mix of activity and repose. No matter how you parent this kid, he'll be okay. But the more attention you pay to his intellectual development the better.

Profession

Gifted in all things poetic, this person has a real chance to apply his artistic skills in life and to achieve public acclaim. Normally Libra turns away from the natural conflicts that haunt the shadows of notoriety. But here, Rooster comes along and struts through the curtain to sing you a little song while you are figuring out the complexities of a contract. Libra coupled with Rooster is a combination almost destined for some degree of fame. This is not your everyday run-of-the-mill human being.

In order to utilize Libra/Rooster's capacity for artistic endeavor, he or she must (and almost always does) begin work at a young age. He can try to fit into some system or even invent his own. But within either of these he must feel he's being treated with deference. If the Libra/Rooster's opinions are not heard, he is not pleased. You might think he'd make a good boss. But I think, paradoxically, that he'd rather not have to direct anyone. He really wants to be free, to create, to react, to invent, to expound.

Libra/Roosters make resigned employees. They understand the need for working at a paying job. But they'd really rather not. They want to be active. On their own terms.

Some good career choices for the Libra/Rooster might be: naturalist, singer, poet, screenwriter, TV producer, photographer, critic.

Famous Libra/Roosters:
Al Capp, Barbara Palvin, Catherine Zeta Jones, Charles Merrill, Deborah Kerr, Dominique Moceanu, Dylan Neal, Geneviève Dorman, Georges Brassens, Giuseppe Verdi, Gwen Stefani, James Whitmore, Jesse Helms, Jim McKay, Karine Quentrec Eagle, Louis Aragon, Manu Bennett, Serena Williams, Tom Poston, Wendi McLendon-Covey, William Faulkner, Yves Montand, Zach Galifianakis, Zachery Bryan.

LIBRA
QUALITIES
JUSTICE, AESTHETICS, CHARM,
GENTILITY, EQUILIBRIUM, IDEALISM,
QUIRKS
QUARRELSOMENESS, MANIPULATION,
PROCRASTINATION, SELF-INDULGENCE,
INDECISION, TALKATIVENESS
Motto: *"I balance"*
Elements: *Air, Venus, Cardinal*

--

DOG
QUALITIES
CONSTANCY, UNSOCIABILITY,
RESPECTABILITY, SELF-RIGHTEOUSNESS,
INTELLIGENCE, TACTLESSNESS
QUIRKS
UNEASINESS, CRITICISM, DUTY,
CYNICISM, HEROISM, MORALITY
Motto: *"I worry"*
Elements: *Positive, Metal, Yang*

An altruist. A worrywart. An idealist. A complainer. An aesthete. A scientist. A handyman. A bon vivant. Need I say more? Of course I must. I have a book to write here.

Libra/Dogs are dignified and brilliant. They possess innate humanitarianism and are soft-hearted in the best possible way. You will always be able to get sympathy from a Libra/Dog. He will help you, cheer you along and applaud your courage. He's a great friend, a super associate and a bundle of nerves. Libra is able to sort out any of life's conflicts through diplomacy and impartiality. In fact, one of the most annoying things about Libras is their refusal to take unpopular stands. They can always see both sides.

Dogs are not unlike this. They don't favor conflict unless it's absolutely unavoidable self-defense. So when you put the two signs together you get a very pacific and merciful creature who wouldn't hurt a flea—unless, of course, he feels personally threatened. When that happens, get out the muzzle!

Libra/Dogs gripe a lot. They complain about how bad life is and how many evil bounders are wallowing about in the world stealing from poor people and hurting the handicapped. They carp and they are wont to snap as well. Of course their bark is ever so much worse than their bite. But nonetheless, life with Libra/Dog can be trying.

Librans born in Dog years always try to settle differences through compromise. They understand that you don't want to eat your soup because you hate onions. There are plenty of reasons to hate onions, heaven knows. When I was a child I didn't exactly love onions myself. And it's true that my mother forced me to eat them. I sure didn't like that. So I can see how you would hesitate. Where you or I might say, "Eat your damned soup and be glad you have something to eat!," inspiring tears and even indigestion, Libra/Dog will trot all around the issue in such a compassionate way that it'll be Thursday by the time his victim eats his soup.

Of course Libra/Dogs get walked all over by unscrupulous blackguards. They take unheard-of flak from family and friends who never hesitate to use and abuse their hospitality and services. They are just too darned nice. They know it. They feel it. Then, when they are up to their necks in sycophants and hangers-on, they start to bitch. But by this time nobody can hear the Libra/Dog's complaints. By now everyone is so used to his self-sacrificing act that his pleas for help fall on deaf ears.

Does he gain circumspection by this means? Not on your life he doesn't. The Libra/Dog always sticks to his beliefs and adheres to his causes with a fervor and zeal like nobody else's. No matter how tense the family holidays were last year, she will always say, "Of course you can come for Christmas. Bring the kids."

Libra/Dogs are dexterous with their hands. They make models and build furniture, draw up charts and know how to grow things. They are kindly and home-loving. But they can be snappish and dry, hesitant and moody, too.

Love

Libra/Dogs are choosy about their love partners. As much as they don't mind peopling their social life with ne'er-do-wells and unfortunates, Librans born in Dog years take meticulous care not to choose an unworthy partner. They are gifted in love relationships, but they are also afraid of excessive intimacy. They don't like to take criticism as much as they like to dish it out. Cohabitation is not their forte.

If you love a Libra/Dog, be patient. Learn how to wait (years!) for him or her to make a decision about settling down. Show how helpful you can be and agree with all of Libra/Dog's humanitarian schemes. Don't be afraid to leave him or her alone. Libra/Dogs know very well how to amuse themselves by puttering. Don't cling. Wait.

Compatibilities

Be wary and settle on a magnanimously magnetic yet understanding Tiger. Choose him or her from among those born in Gemini, Sagittarius or Aquarius. You can get on well with Cats born in Gemini, Leo or Aquarius, too. And you will blend in perfectly with the exciting lifestyles of Leo and Sagittarius/Horses. Gemini/ Snakes are cute, too. And you will admire their cheerful incisiveness. Dragons are most definitely out, especially if they were born in Aries, Cancer or Capricorn. You don't have much affinity for Cancer or Capricorn/Sheep. A Cancer born in a Monkey year will get on your already testy nerves.

Home and Family

The Libra/Dog will be happiest in the country. The city and its harshness grate on his delicate nervous system. The interior of his home will be neat and orderly. His tastes will run to the slick and modern. Yet his favorite colors will be earthy reds and yellows.

The Libra/Dog parent is self-sacrificial. But then Libra/Dogs usually marry late (if at all) and seldom have children. They are loving and kind to their kids if they do have them. But they are also very critical and can be sarcastic. They know how to provide for their kids and they like the cozy atmosphere of family life.

Little Libra/Dogs will be charmers. Everybody in the whole neighborhood will like this tot. He or she will be smiley and outgoing, sincere and a mite outspoken. Don't put early achievements past this little Libra/Dog. This kid may be tops in his nursery school class and stay up there for his whole career. Duty and responsibility come early to this character. Tickle him or her for at least one minute a day.

Profession

Members of this sign are talented in jobs that require technical skill, human understanding or the chance to please their fellow man. Libra/Dogs like nature and animals. They care about social order, and are interested in politics and the law. This person is a bit of a poet, too. His force is his kindness. His weakness is his kindness, too.

People like their Libra/Dog bosses. There is always a spirit of democracy and camaraderie around the office when a Libra/Dog is running the show. Also, employees respect this person's humane notions and will work hard to come up to the Libra/Dog's high standards. It's easy for the Libra/Dog to be an employee. He is never a person with something to prove or with a mission to get ahead of others or beat out the competition. He or she just wants a pleasant, safe and sane existence.

Libra/Dogs are capable of lifelong routine jobs as a means to the ideal they are always searching for in their private lives. Some careers that will suit this character are: veterinarian, social worker, doctor, midwife, animal trainer, landscape gardener, research scientist, Internet wizard.

Famous Libra/Dogs:

Aliya Mustafina, Amy Jo Johnson, Anna Camp, Brendan Meyer, Brigitte Bardot, Charles Dance, Charles Ives, Dan Stevens, David Ben-Gurion, Erik Von Detten, George Gershwin, Halsey, Ian Thorpe, Jansen Panettiere, Jodelle Ferland, John Wooden, Josie Bissett, Kelly Ripa, Kirk Cameron, Lacey Chabert, Lil Wayne, Mary Kate Malat, Matt Damon, Michael Madsen, Michael Paré, Nana Mouscouri, Sheri Moon Zombie, Subrahmanyan Chandrashekhar, Susan Sarandon, Tim Robbins, Viggo Mortensen.

LIBRA
QUALITIES
JUSTICE, AESTHETICS, CHARM,
GENTILITY, EQUILIBRIUM, IDEALISM,
QUIRKS
QUARRELSOMENESS, MANIPULATION,
PROCRASTINATION, SELF-INDULGENCE,
INDECISION, TALKATIVENESS
Motto: *"I balance"*
Elements: *Air, Venus, Cardinal*

--

PIG
QUALITIES
SCRUPULOUSNESS, GALLANTRY, SINCERITY,
VOLUPTUOUSNESS, CULTURE, HONESTY
QUIRKS
CREDULITY, WRATH, HESITATION,
MATERIALISM, GOURMANDISM, PIGHEADEDNESS
Motto: *"I civilize"*
Elements: *Negative Water, Yin*

L oving is what the Libra/Pig does best. This person is devoted, exclusive, jealous and loyal to a fault. Nothing really counts much in the Libran Pig's life except the relationship he or she has with a mate. All activity centers around the bond that Libra/Pig has created with someone else. Householding, money, children, hobbies, friendships—you name it—will be relegated to second place. The marriage (or love affair) is the sun. It governs every gesture, every effort, and every joy and sorrow.

Libra requires loveliness in order to survive. Pigs need riches. Libra is able to create her own beauty and longs to be free to admire it in a peaceful ambiance. Pigs also enjoy peaceful surroundings. They are enslaved to cultural pursuits of all manner and variety.

They thrive on opulence. If the Libra/Pig has his "druthers," he'll live comfortably ensconced in a luxurious love affair for all of his days.

The Libra/Pig's goal, although it may not always appear so, is to feel spoiled. This person languishes in dreams of magnificence and glut. She may secretly wish she were a movie star or at least a fairy princess or a queen. The mundane workaday routine at which Libra/Pig excels is but a secret stepping stone to that place where, when his ship comes in, all squalor and discord will be transformed into gaiety and charm, enjoyment, excess, gentility and voluptuousness. People in the Libra/Pig's dream world will anoint him with oils and tender him gifts of untold worth and antiquity. He will lie about eating rich, fattening foods and testing the quality of all the wines in the kingdom.

It is important here to note that the Libra/Pig perceives everything through a haze of his above-described secret dream world, and because of this is truly handicapped when it comes to dealing with bland drudgery. He can go through the motions of routine and seem surprisingly efficient at dull tasks. But Libra/Pig is not really there. He or she is waiting for the next moment of romantic exaltation to occur. The dishes and the floor-scrubbing will get done. But Libra/Pig's soul is elsewhere.

Many of the Libra/Pig's dreams never come true. He or she will not really be an effective world-beating type. The word "talented" comes to mind. Libra/Pig is very adept at creative pursuits. But the rocky road to realization of projects often discourages the fragile soul of the artistic Libra/Pig before he accomplishes the project. His or her mind may overshoot the goal, leap ahead of the finishing line, and the project, of course, bogs down en route.

What arises, then, is anger, bitterness and quarrelsomeness. When too many dreams are dashed, when too many hopes have been scrapped, resentment builds up. Many Libra/Pigs die resenting the whole human race for its inability to comprehend what they were getting at in the first place.

The best thing Libra/Pigs can do is settle down with someone who adores them for their pacific tastes and ability to add grace to any hovel. The Libra/Pig's strongest suits are his charm, his capacity for blind, tireless love and his sensuality. If he insists on ruling, then he ought to do so from the wings of a safe and pleasant house in the country whence he does not often venture into the fracas of metropolitan life. Libra/Pig needs equilibrium and reacts badly to all outside resistance to his whims.

Love

At the risk of redundancy, I remark here that the Libra/Pig's best shot is in the love department. He is able to give of himself in personal interchange and shared complicity better than most other human beings. Libra/Pig is self-sacrificial where his or her mate is concerned. The pleasure of Libra/Pig's life is mostly derived vicariously through the achievements of those he loves. As for himself? Well, he can't really decide what his preferences are. He probably doesn't want much more than love, comfort and a few stabs at an artistic hobby or two.

If you love one of these people, you already know that they are willing (although sometimes a tad resistant at first) to give up everything of their own for the sake of your happiness and advancement. What you must give in return is, however, no mean compensation. Libra/Pig wants luxury, comfort, and utter and complete devotion. Don't fail him. You'll pay dearly.

Compatibilities

Your romantic leanings predispose you to getting on with Cats and Sheep. You appreciate their discretion. Try to commit yourself to a Gemini, Sagittarius, Leo or Aquarius/Cat or Sheep lover. Snakes in general are proscribed for Pigs, and your worst choices would come from Aries, Cancer or Capricorn-born Serpents. You don't get along with Capricorn/Monkeys, either. Too cerebral and not funky enough for your sensual streak. Dragons? Maybe. A sweetie-pie Cancer or a noble-spirited Capricorn/Dragon could enhance your existence.

Home and Family

The home of a Libra/Pig will be a showplace of comfortable luxury. One thing these people know how to do is contribute beauty to any environment in which they live. They will always prefer the ornate to the practical, the majestic to the humble. A lot of the time, their tastes are expensively out-of-reach which doesn't help in the bitterness department.

Libra/Pig parents may have a tendency to feel that children only run a close second to their mates. They are dutiful toward their offspring. But they often give more attention and affection to their partners. Still, children round out the happy picture for Libra/Pigs and so they are essential to their well-being. The children of these sweet, giving people can ask almost any service of their Libra/Pig parent. It's impossible for Libra/Pigs to say "no," especially to a dish of ice cream or an extra helping of dessert.

Profession

The Libra/Pig native is always interested in social advancement. But again, this progress translates best only insofar as it applies to the union in which the Libra/Pig is involved. Love first. Achievement later. Social betterment only within the realm of the couple. The Libra/Pig is mightily talented and certainly adept at all manner of undertaking. But he won't go it alone. Libra/Pig will get involved professionally if said career improves the lot of the alliance that he or she has chosen as lifestyle.

This person makes a hesitant boss. As he is not attracted to domination or interested in taking charge of others, he finds supervising painful and nerve-wracking. The Libra/Pig would probably rather be bossed than be a boss. As an employee he is responsible and industrious so long as his romantic life is functioning smoothly. If he or she has a row with hubby or wife, the day will surely be ruined and a black cloud of uncertainty will hang over the Libra/Pig's head. For Librans born in Pig years everything that matters involves what belongs to him or her, what he or she cares for and loves. The rest is gingerbread.

Libra/Pigs excel at everything having to do with the home. They make good homemakers, wonderful farmers and chefs , restaurateurs and wine growers.

Famous Libra/Pigs:

Billy Bush, Chen Ti, Cheryl Tiegs, Chris Kirkpatrick, Emmanuelle Laborit, Felicity Jones, France Gall, Ireland Baldwin, Jacques Manière, Jenna Elfman, Jesse Eisenberg, Julie Andrews, Julien Clerc, Kevin Richardson, Kira Reed Lorsch, Le Corbusier, Luciano Pavarotti, Melina Mercouri, Michel Oliver, Prince Edward Duke of Kent, Rebecca Ferguson, Sacha Baron-Cohen, Sarah Duchess of York, Sasha Lane, Shawn Andrews, Spencer Grammer, Tessa Thompson, Vaughn Monroe, William Brent.

SCORPIO
QUALITIES
DEDICATION, SOVEREIGNTY, MAGNETISM,
INSPIRATION, TENDERNESS, DISCIPLINE
QUIRKS
MERCILESSNESS, FANATICISM, REVENGE,
SADISM, SUSPICION, INTRANSIGENCE
Motto: *"I create"*
Elements: *Water, Mars, Fixed*

--

RAT
QUALITIES
NERVOUSNESS, INFLUENCE,
ACQUISITIVENESS, THIRST FOR POWER,
INTELLECTUAL SKILL, CHARISMA
QUIRKS
APPEAL, VERBOSITY, THRIFT,
SOCIABILITY, GUILE, MEDDLING
Motto: *"I rule"*
Elements: *Positive Water, Yang*

A sharp-tongued magpie if ever there was one, the Scorpio born in a Rat year will be chatty and cutting. This person is generally lithe and agile as well as quick-spirited. He or she will probably enjoy all manner of graceful sport and prove able at competitive games.

The Scorpio/Rat is an amiable fellow. People like him or her straightaway and never guess that behind the ready smile is a rare drive for power. He does not necessarily want to rule others, but he does want to hold a potent place in whatever area he has chosen as his own.

The Scorpio/Rat has a strong character. He is not namby-pamby and knows precisely what he wants out of life. With the sneaky old Scorpio to temper his aggressiveness, this person will be more reserved than the average Rat. He will surely enjoy receiving visitors and entertaining them generously. The Scorpio/Rat is often gregarious for his own interests, but his charm is that he does not hide this fact. He's not afraid to admit that he's out for himself and those he loves and that he intends to protect them by any means available.

One of the most striking traits of this person's character is his vision and sense of the future. He is an excellent critic of things both artistic and political, and seems to have a sixth sense about what will be popular and well liked in years to come. The Scorpio/Rat is more than intelligent.

He is wily and clever and full of guile. If he puts this cunning to good use as a creator or protector, the Scorpio/Rat's fate will be felicitous. He's a caring and understanding creature and can do much good for humankind. If, however, he is tempted by underhandedness, disaster may strike. The Scorpio/Rat is more vulnerable to disapproval than he seems.

This is basically a noble nature that on the whole wants no ill to befall others. He is both nervous and suspicious, so he worries a lot and may suffer from anxiety attacks. He is magnetic and projects a pleasant presence. He will not take kindly to the meddling of others but can be accused of meddlesomeness himself. Scorpio/Rat enjoys judging others and is adept at pinning them down to fine points or nailing them on delicate subjects. This person can make himself very unpopular with adversaries if he is not ever so careful on whom he passes his hasty judgments

The creative side of Scorpio/Rat is frequently scotched by his need to compete and win. He does not handle failure well. He or she can be leveled by setbacks and will give up anything and move to the country if the establishment gets in the way.

Finally, the Scorpio/Rat is quite sufficient unto himself. Although he persists in wanting to shine against the foil of competition and to triumph over those he considers his opponents, if he will learn to sit back and take stock, to quiet down and examine his problems calmly, he may be surprised to note that he does not need to pit himself against the opposition in order to prove his worth. It's obvious anyway.

Love

The Scorpio/Rat is a hatcher of complex romantic plots. He or she will not be attracted for long to any fly-by-night lover. Scorpios born Rat must find the person they finally settle down with exceptional. They are extremely sensual and preoccupied by passion early in their lives. Yet as they know themselves to be tempted by conquest, they often decide to marry homebody types whose very seriousness keeps the Scorpio/Rat on the straight and narrow. You may not often hear about the spouses of these busy, sometimes treacherous, souls. That's because the ideal Scorpio/Rat mate keeps the home fires burning.

If you love a Scorpio/Rat, you must arm yourself with a bludgeoning ability to defend yourself. Scorpio/Rat is a harsh and demanding critic. He is nothing short of a perfectionist when it comes to relationships, mulling over every detail to verify the sentiment's purity. This person is competitive, too, and may be rapaciously jealous. If he or she is capable of running around, then you, too, must be guilty. It's an odd turn of mind, but it's the Scorpio/Rat's specialty.

Compatibilities

You can probably walk hand in hand forever with Cancer, Virgo and Pisces/Ox subjects. Another one of your prospects might be the Cancer, Capricorn or Pisces/Dragon, along with Cancer, Virgo and Capricorn/Monkeys. All of the above love to listen to your late night worries. A less willing ear will be lent by Taurus, Leo or Aquarius/Horse. Be sure to keep your distance from Taurus and Aquarius/Cats.

Home and Family

Rats born in Scorpio are strong-willed. They like their surroundings to say something about them, show off their achievements, be identifiably theirs and no one else's. Many Scorpio/Rat interiors are sleekly ultramodern.

This subject is forward-thinking and always imagines herself in the avant-garde. Too, Rats born in Scorpio are creative and will tend to display their works to best advantage at home.

The Scorpio/Rat parent is reliable and protective of the brood. This person never forgets to be prepared for any eventuality or emergency. As kids are the soul of the impromptu, the spontaneous Scorpio/Rat is often Johnny-on-the-spot when Junior needs a map of Venus for school the next day and it's already past midnight. Scorpio/Rats are affectionate and communicative with their offspring.

A Scorpio/Rat child will be alert and ready with friendly smiles from the cradle. This kid is a charmer. He wants attention from parents and teachers, neighbors and his peers. He knows how to go after approval through achievement. He or she is bound to be very powerful among peers or else busy seeking power. These natives compete mercilessly all their lives for first place. They need parental encouragement to go after the things they are interested in.

Profession

The Scorpio/Rat's ideal profession is vociferous critic. He is expert at picking apart situations that need decorticating. He or she can be canny at law or excellent at diagnosing diseases, troubleshooting in industry or entertainment, or inventing things that demand minute attention to detail. He is of sunny disposition but will be acquisitive and hungry for power.

You can hire the Scorpio/Rat, but his or her eye will be on the throne from the jump. Scorpio/Rats prefer first place to subordination and they usually don't have undue qualms about reaching goals. They train or learn how till they've got the whole system down pat and then Bingo! They're running the company. Machination is the stuff of the Scorpio/Rat's life

As a boss, the Scorpio/Rat will be demanding and protective, patronizing even. As he or she is very effective at any level and can handle any and all the jobs at hand, the same kind of behavior will be expected from underlings.

Some careers that fit this competitive person's nature are: fashion journalist, insurance salesman, inventor, athlete, performer, critic or politician

Famous Scorpio/Rats:
Aaron Copeland, Auguste Rodin, B. D. Wong, Brandi Glanville, Claude Monet, Dick Cavett, Diego Maradona, Eric Dane, Fernando Valenzuela, Finn Whitrock, Hailey Baldwin, , Jena Malone, Jonny Lee Miller, Josh Duhamel, Katy Perry, Kyla Ross, Margaret Mitchell, Missy Pyle, Prince Charles, Rebecca Romijn, RuPaul, Scarlett Johansson, Stanley Tucci, Thandi Newton, Tye Sheridan.

SCORPIO
QUALITIES
DEDICATION, SOVEREIGNTY, MAGNETISM,
INSPIRATION, TENDERNESS, DISCIPLINE
QUIRKS
MERCILESSNESS, FANATICISM, REVENGE,
SADISM, SUSPICION, INTRANSIGENCE
Motto: *"I create"*
Elements: *Water, Mars, Fixed*

--

OX
QUALITIES
STUBBORNNESS, STRENGTH OF PURPOSE,
ELOQUENCE, STANDOFFISHNESS, INNOVATION,
VINDICTIVENESS
QUIRKS
INTEGRITY, BIGOTRY, PLODDING,
DILIGENCE, BIAS, STABILITY
Motto: *"I preserve"*
Elements: *Negative Water, Yin*

A whiz kid with a crazy streak is the Scorpio born in Ox years. Oxen are deliberate, plain people who, as a rule, stodge their way to success come hell or high water. They are slow and they are thorough. Scorpios are very tricky and fanatical, mistrustful and magnetic. They veer all over the place in order to attain goals that the Ox heads for, horns lowered, steady as you plod. Put these two signs together and you get a kind of zippy Kremlin or a slightly kooky Sherman tank.

Scorpio/Oxen are uncanny. They seem to know instinctively how to elbow their way through a crowd without so much as grazing the sleeve of opposition. These people are always on their way somewhere. Their dust makes Challenger look like a third-class railway carriage in Darjeeling. Not that the Scorpio/Ox is in a hurry—oh no. He is simply ruthlessly and sadistically determined to get where he's going, which in this case is always to the top of the profession where there are the highest salaries and the most glory and seniority and hoopla.

A curious facet of this person's character is the unspoken superiority he or she carries around. There is never any question about who's boss in groups when Scorpio/Ox is present. You see, this person is equipped with both the natural sovereignty of Scorpio and the strength of purpose of Oxen. Decisions, he feels, should be made without any consideration for sentiment. Scorpio/Oxen can understand the need for emotion, and indeed store up their share of lunatic experience in a lifetime. But they don't usually allow their passions to interfere with progress. If they do, they know full well that their goose will be cooked.

Of course, Scorpio/Oxen are domineering. They have to rule others. But they are pleasant about their ability to take over in any situation and have the gift of gab necessary to put their message across with charm. These people are often quite humorous and know how to make others laugh. They are not terrific at laughing at themselves, however, as their egos are quite a lot stronger than their self-awareness.

Because of their apparent ease of success, Scorpio/Oxen are enviable. People become easily jealous of them and often try to hinder their progress by violent or underhanded means. But not to worry. Scorpio/Ox is a tough customer. He does not give up territory willingly. He drives a very hard bargain. He is a wicked adversary and a devoted friend. Scorpio/Oxen are self-centered people whose heavy step can be felt across continents, and who don't hesitate to make big (surfer-variety) waves in order to ensure themselves smooth sailing.

No Scorpio is more vengeful than the Scorpio/Ox. He never forgets a wrong done to him by another, and will recall a debt, whether moral or financial, after decades of silent fury. He doesn't like mollycoddling and is never guilty of indulging others. Fools? Either he makes use of them, or "Off with their heads!" Because of his or her insistence on taking perilously stubborn stands and living fast, madcap lives, Scorpio/Oxen are often in mortal danger.

Love

As the Scorpio/Ox is attractive as well as powerful, he or she will have many admirers. Among these, they will be likely to choose a mate for malleability and beauty rather than for smarts. Scorpio/Oxen are not really too interested in intellectual exchange with a lover but are rather fascinated by the thunder and lightning storms of angry outbursts, rows, separations, and breakdowns. They get their kicks from emotional crises which are hardly ever of their own making.

It's a pretty risky business being the mate or even the casual lover of one of these impressive maniacs. They are passionate and sexy. But they are also always right, always on top and always slightly cuckoo. It's nice cuckoo. But cuckoo, nonetheless. If I were to be attracted to a Scorpio/Ox, I'd think twice before tying any permanent knot. The Scorpio born Ox can be a right rascal and a bit of a tramp to boot.

Compatibilities

Rats agree with you—especially from the Cancer, Virgo, Capricorn and Pisces families. Roosters are winner mates for you, too. Choose from Cancer, Capricorn or Pisces. Snakes will wrap you in happiness if they belong to Cancer, Virgo or Capricorn. Not so happy will be relationships with Gemini, Taurus, Leo and Aquarius/ Sheep. Disappointments aplenty await you with Taurus and Gemini/Dragons. Your sullen moods will not mix with Taurus/ Monkeys, Gemini/Horses or Aquarius/Tigers.

Home and Family

The Scorpio side of this person may make him or her a little outrageous, but his or her choice of lifestyle, due to the stolid Ox's penchant for domesticity, will be far more earthy than his personality indicates. The Scorpio/Ox will enjoy a gracious country life and be attracted by quiet, plush surroundings. He will be sure to have limelight installed in all the rooms of his ponderous great mansion.

The family life of this hefty creature will depend on whomever he has the intelligence to hitch up with. As Scorpio/Ox is often out in the world being a whiz kid, he must either keep a dedicated staff at home to look after details such as children and pets, or else travel with family in tow. The busy life inherent in this sign often demands mobility. Scorpio/Ox will be a devoted parent and maintain communication with his or her kids long after they have left the nest.

Profession

Power professions are those that attract the Scorpio/Ox. But his eloquence will also attract him or her to all aspects of performance. This person is an acting genius born. He can also lead crowds to giant deeds and even to revolution. He's a shade too crazy to be entrusted with military force. Besides, he prefers laughter to aggression.

Careers that might suit this person are: performer, entertainer, actor or actress, political leader, teacher, writer, film director, theatrical director, communications expert, comic.

Famous Scorpio/Oxen:

Aishwarya Rai, Andre Malraux, Ben Aldrich. , Ben Aldridge, Caitlyn Jenner, Dylan McDermott, Gabrielle Union, Gary Valentine, Janet Montgomery, Jawaharlal Nehru, Johnny Carson, Jonathan Winters, K.D. Lang, Larry Mullins Jr., Lee Strasberg, Lily Aldridge, Mariel Hemingway, Meg Ryan, Olivia Taylor Dudley, Paul Ford, Peter Jackson, Radha Mitchell, Ralph Macchio, Richard Burton, Robert Kennedy, Seth MacFarlane, Troian Bellisario, Troian Bellisario, Vivien Leigh.

SCORPIO
QUALITIES
DEDICATION, SOVEREIGNTY, MAGNETISM,
INSPIRATION, TENDERNESS, DISCIPLINE
QUIRKS
MERCILESSNESS, FANATICISM, REVENGE,
SADISM, SUSPICION, INTRANSIGENCE
Motto: *"I create"*
Elements: *Water, Mars, Fixed*

--

TIGER
QUALITIES
FERVOR, BRAVERY, MAGNETISM,
GOOD LUCK, BENEVOLENCE, AUTHORITY
QUIRKS
IMPETUOSITY, HOTHEADEDNESS,
DISOBEDIENCE, SWAGGER, INTEMPERANCE,
ITINERANCY
Motto: *"I Watch"*
Elements: *Positive Wood, Yang*

At the risk of being accused of vest pocket autobiography, I confess that this sign is my very own. Moreover, I like my sign and have many friends of the same persuasion. Forgive me if I wax sentimental in this portrait.

First off, I'll tell you that all Scorpio/Tigers are excessive. They do everything to extreme. They never take life as it comes, but rather race out and try to head it off at the pass. They are constantly in dangerous situations, where they have plunked themselves deliberately. They never take their time and plan every detail, or write lists to be sure that every last mothball gets accounted for in the winter clothes. These people are hasty and hotheaded and really honestly quite mad. I call Scorpio/Tigers "blitz" people. They come screeching up to every new experience, gobble, slurp, inhale, consume, build, make, bake, scrape, paint, fix—and they're off to the next challenge. Scorpios born in Tiger years are always trying to get three lives out of one.

The combination of Scorpio's dark magnetism and Tiger's swaggering charm makes this subject fairly fascinating to other people. This translates into Scorpio/Tigers being quite popular among their peers. People look up to this character and Scorpio/Tiger loves to be looked up to, told how wonderful he is and, in return for admiration and approval, goes to great lengths to continue to be wonderful so that the applause never dies down.

Scorpio/Tigers are egomaniacal. But they're nice about it. These headstrong characters are automatic leaders. But they are not exactly crazy about being leaders. Scorpio/Tigers know how to do a lot of different things and tend to be jacks-of-all-trades. The dream of this contrary soul, then, is to do one thing well. Scorpio/Tiger is a proud person. But he rankles at his own tendency toward pride and is constantly kicking himself in the derrière, saying, "Be more humble. Don't get carried away. Shrink your head to normal size." And worst of all, Scorpio/Tigers are fighters. They are ferocious and even dangerous as adversaries. They can be both rancorous and bloodthirsty. But they hate being so mean. They long to be nicer.

Now that you understand the basic Tiger/Scorpio schizophrenia, I will tell you what they need to do so as not to die young: Scorpio/Tigers must gain wisdom at an early age. This wisdom will not come from within. It will always be delivered by an outside source. Scorpio/Tigers must keep their floppy little ears clean and listen carefully to the wise people in their hectic lives. Spunk they have. Sagacity they don't. When this person finally learns reason and temperance, he can move any mountain he comes upon with a single switch of his tail. Without common sense and measure this person is a goner.

Once the Scorpio/Tiger has assimilated level-headedness as a way of life he or she can go very far indeed. These people boast a certain brilliance, possess panache to burn and are competent in the extreme. There is nothing you cannot entrust to them. They are self-starters, pushy but congenial, and they'll battle to the death with injustice. Scorpio/Tigers hate rules unless they make them themselves. They always think they know best. They are hotheaded, jealous and ruthless when crossed. They don't mind brute force but they hate trickery. Scorpio/Tigers stalk dishonesty in the dark of night. They thrive on victory and just about never admit defeat.

Love

This person doesn't find true love in two weeks. First of all, he or she lives a tumultuous life, full of adventure and change. Without change, the Scorpio/Tiger would turn to drink or drugs. He does not necessarily want to switch partners, and I would even say the Scorpio/Tiger is a faithful type, but he likes to change scenery, alter his habits, move the furniture around in his life. When and if he finds someone to follow this restless prowling, Scorpio/Tiger can settle on a mate. He's very sexual and can even be kittenish in the bedroom.

If you love a Scorpio/Tiger and wish to remain near him forever, you must first be respectable. Scorpio/Tigers want to be the crazies in the family. They don't want any competition in the cuckoo department. Moreover, this subject has to feel admiration for the one he loves. Otherwise he loses interest. So be your own person, be thoughtful and wise. Do not, I repeat, do not cling, lean or fawn. All of the above cause Scorpio/Tigers to lose their lunch.

Compatibilities

Bliss might arise from complicity with you and Cancer, Virgo, Capricorn or Pisces/Horses. You'll be barking up the right tree if you choose a Dog partner from the same western astrological signs. Pisces/Dragon's fire will light up your life. Discord, on the other hand, will ensue if you take up with Aries, Taurus or Aquarius/Sheep. Taurus/Snake, Monkey and Pig could cause you inner turmoil. You will surely quibble with Gemini/Tigers. Money will be an issue with Aquarius/Oxen.

Home and Family

This person's home will be a palace of funk and whimsy. Scorpio/Tiger is interested in decoration only insofar as it expresses his personality. He moves into a house and guts it, turns it inside out, raises or lowers beams to suit his habits, adds a room for his hobbies, puts in a wall-to-wall dishwasher so he can store up his dirty dishes for weeks. Scorpio/Tigers don't care to impress anybody, and will arrange their environment to suit themselves and those they love—period!

The Scorpio/Tiger parent is loving but strict. He doesn't want little Mary or Betty to grow up to be unruly like him. Actually, what Scorpio/Tigers want from their kids is that the kids not need them. Scorpio/Tigers are very private at home and are not eager about helping with homework or putting up Christmas trees. They are sincere parents who care a great deal about their kids but who would prefer not to have to care for them. Nose wiping grates on their nerves.

Little Scorpio/Tigers are defiant and a bit odd. They don't join in much with the other kids and they always have a thousand projects going at once. They are naturally rebellious, and may think up some doozies to bedevil their parents. They need to be left alone except when they are on the brink of committing some major booboo—which is often.

Profession

If this person has found temperance and buckled under to reason, there is no career closed to him. He is clever and wily, strong and reliable, capable and trustworthy. Trouble is, it usually takes about ten extra years in the young life of this reckless character for him or her to settle down. He likes to test careers, try new projects, join different groups and travel before he is ready to zero in on one in particular. You'll never meet a Scorpio/Tiger who tells you he always wanted to be a baker and went to baking school at age twelve and here he is at forty still baking bread. No way. Scorpio/Tigers have usually tried at least a hundred different jobs by the time they are forty.

If I were to employ a Scorpio/Tiger, I would keep a close eye on his method of doing things. These people don't like rules, remember? They tend to make up their own. Let a Scorpio/Tiger loose in your office and you may find your filing system totally reorganized before morning. They are efficient and obedient—but only to a point.

As a boss, the Scorpio/Tiger is loving and tough. These people command respect easily, and as they don't like bossiness, they try to turn their orders into suggestions. They are not above cleaning latrines, either, as they like to teach by example. They also work well alone.

Some fitting careers for Scorpio/Tigers are: preacher, prospector, psychiatrist, politician, traveling salesman, personnel manager, publicist, journalist, editor, mercenary, leader.

Famous Scorpio/Tigers:

Cary Elwes, Charles de Gaulle, Chloe Sevigny, Colleen Ballinger, Demi Moore, Drake, Dylan Thomas, Italia Ricci, Jane Pauley, Jean Seberg, Jeanne Kirkpatrick, Joaquin Phoenix, Jodie Foster, John Candy, Josh Peck, Kathleen Rose Perkins, Laura San Giacomo, Leonardo DiCaprio, Leslie Bibb, Markie Post, Matthew Rhys, Michael Gaston, Mohammed, Nolan Gould, Pete Townshend, Sania Mirza, Ted Turner, Turgenev.

SCORPIO
QUALITIES
DEDICATION, SOVEREIGNTY, MAGNETISM,
INSPIRATION, TENDERNESS, DISCIPLINE
QUIRKS
MERCILESSNESS, FANATICISM, REVENGE,
SADISM, SUSPICION, INTRANSIGENCE
Motto: *"I create"*
Elements: *Water, Mars, Fixed*

--

CAT/RABBIT
QUALITIES
TACT, FINESSE, VIRTUE,
PRUDENCE, LONGEVITY, AMBITION,
QUIRKS
SECRETIVENESS, SQUEAMISHNESS,
PEDANTRY, DILETTANTISM,
HYPOCHONDRIA, COMPLEXITY
Motto: *"I Retreat"*
Elements: *Negative, Wood, Yin*

An imposing figure is the Scorpio/Cat. He is respectable, able to earn and keep his money, and he commands respect from peers. On the outside he is calm and refined. On the inside there's a blazing fire of intent.

Scorpio/Cat means what he says and says only what he means. He's thought it all through beforehand and believes fervently in whatever theories or precepts he is advancing.

People are inspired by this person's presence. He has poise and handles tricky situations with aplomb, knowing just how to defuse potentially angry crowds and reckless madmen. The Scorpio side of this person's nature understands darkness and has a thorough knowledge of what causes fear. The Cat brings him steady-as-you-go tact and finesse.

The combination is unbeatably self-assured. Scorpio tempers the Cat's squeamishness and gives him the courage to face adversity. The cautious Cat shuts down the Scorpio's sadism, increasing his capacity for compassion.

The outward appearance of this humanitarian soul, then, is dignity personified. Inwardly he may be shuddering with fright at the prospect of what he has undertaken. But never mind. Stage fright is only a passing state of mind. And when Scorpio/Cat finds him or herself in front of the audience, not a hair out of place, not a whisker atwitch, the effect is powerful.

The Scorpio/Cat knows how to make a silk purse from a sow's ear. He can drag himself up from nothing, bounce back from illness or poverty and sally forth to real success without blinking an eye. This person is a dreamer of impossible dreams and can, quietly and without undue commotion, make his visions into realities.

The Scorpio born Cat is a natural performer too. He is comfortable before a group of people to whom he is delivering a message or teaching a concept. He is not very flexible, however, and can sometimes be accused of bigotry or narrow-mindedness. He believes so fervently in his ideas that he never wants to give them up. He cherishes what he has espoused in the way of creed, and sticks closely to its tenets.

The Scorpio/Cat usually has a good sense of humor. Cats are circumspect and tend to watch the world from a privileged position, hovering about three feet above everybody's head. Scorpios keep a well-honed tongue in their heads and are ever ready with a sharp crack. The combination can be unbearably acid and satirical.

The secretive or private side of this character is slightly overdeveloped. Scorpio lends suspicion to the Cat's already stealthy and reticent nature. It won't do to try and jolly this person out of his private moods. He does not take kindly to criticism, feeling that he is alone the judge of what's best for him. Scorpio/Cat can be admirable, but also haughty and sometimes pompous.

Love

Love, to the Scorpio born Cat, is a matter of great import. As this person generally has a mission or cause to accomplish in life, he cannot permit himself the luxury of lots of petty superficial affairs. He may err from his solid marriage or stray occasionally from the mate he has chosen, but such peccadilloes will be handled with tact and delicacy. Scorpio/Cats are looking for a mate who will ensure the management of day-to-day events in order that he or she might get on with the serious business of living.

If you love a Scorpio/Cat, it is probably because you first admired him. The natural progression with these impressive creatures is from one kind of worship to another, more intimate type. As they are rather strict about their ideas of how you should appear as their mate and cohort, you will need to be adaptable and ready to fit into a mold to please society.

Compatibilities

Your honeymoons will most likely be shared with Cancer, Virgo, Capricorn or Pisces/Sheep, Dogs and Pigs. Their love of nature and the good life will help to calm your occasional emotional qualms. Irreconcilable differences exist between you and Taurus, Leo and Aquarius/Roosters. The Leo/Rat will give you trouble too.

Home and Family

Here the Scorpio/Cat is the ruler. All things homelike must revolve about the leader and his or her needs. The main room in the house might well be Scorpio/Cat's office. The rest will be comfortable and refined in the extreme. But the center of the home for this very "central" person will be decorated to suit his taste. Each individual child may have his or her own color scheme, and yet there will always be the sense that the careful Scorpio/Cat has supervised it all. Clashes are not allowed. Harmony is the objective.

The Scorpio/Cat is a reliable and responsible, if a bit too authoritarian, parent. Rules are unspoken but they are nonetheless laws to be adhered to closely and with respect. The Scorpio/Cat has very likely brought herself to a certain social position through hard work and diligence. She will not tolerate disobedience or bad examples from her kids. Scorpio/Cats like to save face.

As children, these people will be secretive and enjoy playing alone. They will seek audiences for their plans and theories as soon as they are old enough to read and formulate schemes themselves. They like security but are able to overcome upsets gracefully and philosophically. They can be cheeky. It's best to reason rather than spank. They cannot abide violence.

Profession

It's fairly obvious to me that these people are made for responsible jobs. They truly enjoy taking care of others and seeing to the well-being of a group. They are serious people whose no-nonsense approach is much appreciated by employers. As they can be haughty and even persnickety and viper-tongued, it's not easy to be employed by them. They have an attitude of "I'm only doing this for your own good," which can be trying.

Good careers for these people are: astrologer, musician, psychiatrist, research scientist, preacher, tour guide, teacher.

Famous Scorpio/Cat/Rabbits:

Amelia Rose Blaire, Cleopatra Coleman, Dermot Mulroney, Evelyn Waugh, Gilbert Bécaud, Grace Slick, Harry Hamlin, Hugh Bonneville, Jake Abel, James A. Garfield, James K. Polk, Jayne Kennedy, Jimmi Simpson, John Adams, Lauren Holly, Lou Ferrigno, Maria Thayer, Marie Curie, Marla Maples, Martin Luther, Mary Hart, Melanie Liburd, Michael Beach, Ming-Na-Wen, Patrick Sabatier, Rachele Brooke Smith, Roland Barthes, Rosy Varte, Sushmita Sen, Tara Reid, Tatum O'Neal, Terry Ferrell, Tom Cavanagh, Tove Lo.

SCORPIO
QUALITIES
DEDICATION, SOVEREIGNTY, MAGNETISM,
INSPIRATION, TENDERNESS, DISCIPLINE
QUIRKS
MERCILESSNESS, FANATICISM, REVENGE,
SADISM, SUSPICION, INTRANSIGENCE
Motto: *"I create"*
Elements: *Water, Mars, Fixed*

--

DRAGON
QUALITIES
STRENGTH, SUCCESS, GOOD HEALTH,
ENTHUSIASM, PLUCK, SENTIMENTALITY
QUIRKS
RIGIDITY, MISTRUST, DISSATISFACTION,
INFATUATION, BRAGGADOCIO, VOLUBILITY
Motto: *"I Preside"*
Elements: *Positive Wood, Yang*

When you add Dragon to Scorpio and mix well to blend, the batter thickens. Scorpio lends mystery and ruthlessness to an already plucky and boastful Dragon nature. Add a dash of swagger and some good old Scorpio vengeance and jealousy and you will concoct yourself a mighty baroque human being. This dish is spicy and copious.

Seriously, the Scorpio/Dragon is a Dragon's Dragon and a Scorpio's Scorpio. All of the characteristics of each sign are magnified by their amalgamation. This person is ambitious. She will have masses of personal charm and will know how to go after what she wants. They see no reason why they cannot be head of the world if they so choose.

Scorpio/Dragon holds his scaly green head up so high that he can peer directly over the mountain at the lush green valley of his success. Often, however, his eyes are bigger than his stomach. The mountain he must cross presents him with innumerable insuperables. Trudging from obstacle to obstacle with your pride in your front paws can be discouraging. Scorpio/Dragons have been known to give up. But mostly they bounce back and, like the phoenix, rise from the ashes of their own funeral pyre to strike again.

Scorpio/Dragons come on strong, and have gigantic reserves of courage and cunning. They want to get places in life. They are combative and charming. But their giant pitfall is that they want to be paid homage as well.

Modern life is difficult for these haughty creatures. The Scorpio born Dragon has a hard time with moderation. He is drawn to excess and self-indulgence and has a tough time resisting the dissipation of his or her talents. Magnetism is indeed a fabulous trump card in the game of life. But it is not quite sufficient to ensure either success or happiness. Some warmth, pith and density must be incorporated very early on in the preparative stages of this person's life. He must not get carried away from basics and then one day find himself standing naked and frightened atop his mountain— alone! The Scorpio/Dragon may seem invincible, but he's still a Dragon and he's sentimental. Deep down he weeps over stories about lost dogs. He's a pushover and a soft touch. Perhaps that's why he seems stone-facedly to have no sense of humor. He doesn't want to show his hand.

Scorpios born in Dragon years are strongly individualistic. They have plenty of imagination and can think up a hundred new schemes a minute. People automatically like them and even agree to take them in and feed them and care for them because of their unusualness. Thing is, the Scorpio/Dragon is not always cooperative and sometimes gets asked to leave after only a few days. Why? Because in their struggle for singularity, these people often alienate the very plain folks they need most by snubbing them or simply ignoring their needs. It doesn't hurt a Scorpio/Dragon to help with the dishes. But it somehow doesn't occur to him or her that such lowly tasks exist. I'm not suggesting that the Scorpio/Dragon is a snob. He's just oblivious to simplicity.

Love

You cannot expect this passionate fanatic to cool his ardor anywhere—especially in the bedroom. The Scorpio/Dragon is adorable and knows how tempting he seems to potential lovers and mistresses. But sometimes, just to be perverse, he will be faithful in the extreme to a single and wonderful person who knows just how to applaud the Scorpio/Dragon while twisting his earlobe to make him behave.

Scorpio/Dragons like to think they are sexually free. If you love one of these interesting and irresistible characters, I advise you to give her lots of space to roam about, lots of liberty and the distinct impression you couldn't care less whom she gets involved with. Such a casual attitude will keep her close to home. Your apparent indifference will serve as a challenge to her. Scorpio/Dragons are predictably jealous.

Compatibilities

Snuggle up to a Virgo, Capricorn or Pisces/Ox or Monkey. Cancer, Capricorn and Pisces from the Tiger group are your second marriage signs. Cancer/Rat and Pisces/Rat are both terrific in bed. Cancer and Virgo/Roosters turn you on as well. And the luxury-loving Cancer/Snake is one of your surest matches made in heaven. Dragons get along with practically everybody except the Leo and Aquarius/Ox, the Taurus and the Leo/Cat, and Taurus, Leo and Aquarius/Dog.

Home and Family

The Scorpio/Dragon likes a comfortable home, but he's not one to putter about clipping the hedges and evening out the flowerbeds. Scorpio/Dragons don't see the need for excessive nit-picking in decoration. They like clean lines and surfaces on which to work and/or receive their multitudes of guests. They impress as much with their presence as with their interior, so they often don't make much of the latter.

The Scorpio/Dragon parent is patently crazy about his or her kids. These are proud people, remember. They set great store by their kids and are proud of what their kids achieve. They love unconditionally, yet expect great deeds. The Scorpio/Dragon parent knows how to play with kids and will invent games and spend time with the little ones. He can also be a grabby parent. I would not, for example, want to have a Scorpio/Dragon mother-in-law.

The Scorpio/Dragon child is indestructibly perky. You will want to take him or her home with you. They smile and giggle and coo and sing little songs to charm and win attention. They can be sulky, too. But nonetheless you will be hard put not to spoil this little tyke. If you resist the temptation to shower him or her with admiration and worship, this kid will have a chance to learn humility. A measure of modesty learned early on will be money in the bank for this prideful darling.

Profession

The Scorpio/Dragon career is often pockmarked with mini failures. I don't want to sound discouraging, but the Scorpio/Dragon person has more fervor than he does perseverance, and sometimes expects too much in return for the effort exerted. In order to prosper, this person must first learn to hold his emotional tongue and not consider anything gained until all the bets are in. He will benefit from a solid classical education, against which he will probably rebel. Find that person who knows how to twist earlobes so lovingly and put him or her on the case.

This subject wants power over others. It does not, however come easily. Conferring authority on one so self-enraptured is tricky and dangerous. As a boss, this person could be perfectly heinous. As an employee with an impressive title, the Scorpio/Dragon and his co-workers are better off.

Watch him or her for streaks of lording it over others. Keep the Scorpio/Dragon busy and insist he apply his fine imagination to getting concrete results. A happy Scorpio/Dragon is an occupied one.

Careers that might suit this heady personality are: TV performer, politician, fashion designer, public relations officer, mercenary, undercover agent, entrepreneur, gossip columnist, religious leader.

Famous Scorpio/Dragons:

Alistair Brammel, Analeigh Tipton, Annie Potts, Calista Flockhart, Chad Lindberg, Devon Murray, Elke Sommer, Emma Stone, Famke Janssen, Francois Mitterrand, Jamie Campbell Bower, Janel Parrish, Jim Cummings, Laura Harris, Logan Marshall-Green, Partick Warburton, Piper Perabo, Roberto Benigni, Roseanne Barr, Ryan Reynolds, Sam Page, Sam Waterston, Siva Kaneswaran, Trevor Einhorn, Walter Cronkite, Wiley Wiggins, Willow Smith.

SCORPIO
QUALITIES
DEDICATION, SOVEREIGNTY, MAGNETISM,
INSPIRATION, TENDERNESS, DISCIPLINE
QUIRKS
MERCILESSNESS, FANATICISM, REVENGE,
SADISM, SUSPICION, INTRANSIGENCE
Motto: *"I create"*
Elements: *Water, Mars, Fixed*

--

SNAKE
QUALITIES
INTUITION, ATTRACTIVENESS, DISCRETION,
SAGACITY, CLAIRVOYANCE, COMPASSION
QUIRKS
DISSIMULATION, EXTRAVAGANCE,
LAZINESS, CUPIDITY, PRESUMPTION,
EXCLUSIVENESS
Motto: *"I sense"*
Elements: *Negative, Fire, Yin*

To a Scorpio/Snake, life without beauty and luxury, tenderness, compassion, admiration and extravagance is not worth living. This person is sensitive in the extreme and, for a cool-handed Snake, remarkably warm-hearted and loving. People appreciate this character for a certain innate nobility, which is both unquestionable and very comforting. Scorpios are already very sensual people with a tendency to introspect and suspect. To add the Snake characteristics of sagacity, clairvoyance and intuition certainly doesn't diminish the philosophical side of Scorpio's nature. This person is deep-thinking, sometimes even tormented.

There will necessarily exist in Scorpio/Snake's makeup a flamboyance and attention to wardrobe that sets him or her apart from the rest of us. You will never see a shabbily dressed Scorpio/Snake. They may be said to push personal appearance to the limit. Their manner of getting themselves up might even be called "costuming." They are invariably arrayed in finery so unusual as to be stunning, and fit only for their type of personality.

This person has a native ability to intuit the needs and desires of others. He or she is able to understand nuances that escape even the most discerning audience. Scorpios born in Snake years have a kind of special genius for picking up hints and following hunches that takes them very far in a worldly way. It may be something as simple as guessing the direction a stock will take or foreseeing the need for a certain market in commodities or goods. Scorpio/Snakes are not often poor.

The variety of superiority that the Scorpio born Snake possesses is of near cosmic proportions. You cannot encounter a Scorpio/Snake and come away from said meeting without a vivid picture in your mind's eye.

Snakes born Scorpio may not impress you favorably, but they always impress you. You see, they embody a sort of arrogance that, I suppose, arises from the fact that they have easy success in life, are lucky with money and generally suffer only from emotional pain that they inflict on themselves. Scorpio/Snakes preen a lot and keep their noses in the air. The effect is not "Look at me!" the way it might be with a Dragon or even a Rat personality. Rather, Scorpio/Snakes command attention. The unspoken charisma is just there.

As you might have already guessed, the Scorpio/Snake's ego fares well. There is a very healthy sense of self here. But Scorpio/Snakes don't let their ego get too far ahead of their inner logic. They strike a careful balance between reality and dreams. Oh, they are capable of lying. The famous Snake powers of dissimulation are very active in this subject. But Scorpio/Snakes don't often lie to themselves. They like to maintain a cool head no matter what cloud tempts them to climb on for a joyride.

Scorpio/Snakes are jealous people. They want to keep everything—especially power—for themselves and their loved ones. They don't like to share the spotlight and they make no bones about it. As Snakes go, the Scorpio is not too lazy, either. He's so avid for gain and attention that his ambition keeps him moving. Fact is, he doesn't have to make much effort to succeed. It comes naturally.

Love

Everybody wants to love a Scorpio/Snake. These characters are so untouchably gorgeous and unutterably cool that they can literally be said to attract everyone. But don't worry. The Scorpio/Snake is choosy about whom he takes up with. Often, this person takes a mate he or she can manipulate and even enslave.

If you love a Scorpio/Snake, join the club. Get in line. Queue up. Really, if you are attracted to such a person, it's no surprise. It's not even your fault. If you like being outshone in public, take up with one of these stars. You had best enjoy staying home and burning those fires because Scorpio/Snake will be out slaloming through the admiring hordes whether you like it or not.

Compatibilities

You and the Dragon are fast friends. Choose yours from out of the Virgo, Capricorn and Pisces lot. There are four Roosters who love your company. They are Cancer, Virgo, Capricorn and Pisces/Roosters. Accept no substitutes. And then there's a Cancer/Ox. And that's about it for affinities. Less advantageous are alliances with Taurus, Leo and Aquarius/Monkeys. Taurus and Leo/Tigers are not quite perfect for you, either. If you care about your self-respect, avoid Taurus and Gemini/Pigs.

Home and Family

The Scorpio/Snake home will be large and impressively decorated. Silks and brocades abound. The last little pickle fork will have been hand-fashioned of vermeil. *Luxe* ain't the word. Posh is more like it. The Scorpio/Snake resides in a decor comparable to his stature and opinion of herself.

The Scorpio/Snake parent is serious but likes to be quite indulgent with little ones. He or she will spoil children materially but demand that they appear like ladies and gentlemen for company. There can be a problem of jealousy here. Scorpio/Snakes don't take kindly to competition for attention. If the kids are too charming, Mom or Pop might freak. The house should perhaps be outfitted with wall-to-wall spotlights.

These kids will be, first of all, extraordinarily attractive. They will probably have to be protected from admirers and taught that there is more to life than being an eye-catcher. They will also tend to fib. Don't wash their mouths out with soap. Show them instead that you have seen through them. Scorpio/Snake kids operate best when parents are firm but loving. Don't be seduced by this wily beauty. He or she needs you, the parent, to represent truth.

Profession

This person is mostly creative. He or she will take to all activity wherein the spirit of invention is useful and applicable. Scorpio/ Snakes might work well alone but can fit into the system, provided the system recognizes their superiority and remunerates it accordingly.

Bossing suits the Scorpio/Snake best. He will be a reluctant subordinate. If he is the boss, you can expect him to be democratic and understanding of his workers. He likes to have power, but is not one to wield it unless crossed or pushed. Then, watch out. Scorpio/Snakes are ruthless and attack their enemies pitilessly. Competition? Never heard of it.

Natural careers for this super Snake are: king, queen, movie star, pope, and so on. But in reality, if they have to actually work at jobs, they might like to try: modeling, acting, advertising, or stocks and bonds. They make terrific artists, too.

Famous Scorpio/Snakes:

Aiden Ehrenreich, Art Garfunkel, Brittany Murphy, Eliza Taylor, Frances Conroy, Francisco Barreto, Fyodor Dostoevsky, Grace Kelly, Helen Reddy, Henri Gault, Indira Gandhi, Jamie Gertz, Jean Tardieu, Juliet Mills, Madeleine Robinson, Mads Mikkelsen, Marilyn French, Nastia Liukin, Pablo Picasso, Patrick Sébastien, Princess Elisabeth of Belgium, Scoot McNairy, Sean Murray, Shah Rukh Khan, Taron Egerton, Tom Fogerty, Tyga.

SCORPIO
QUALITIES
DEDICATION, SOVEREIGNTY, MAGNETISM,
INSPIRATION, TENDERNESS, DISCIPLINE
QUIRKS
MERCILESSNESS, FANATICISM, REVENGE,
SADISM, SUSPICION, INTRANSIGENCE
Motto: *"I create"*
Elements: *Water, Mars, Fixed*

--

HORSE
QUALITIES
PERSUASIVENESS, UNSCRUPULOUSNESS,
POPULARITY, STYLE, DEXTERITY,
ACCOMPLISHMENT
QUIRKS
SELFISHNESS, AUTONOMY, REBELLION,
HASTE, ANXIETY, PRAGMATISM
Motto: *"I demand"*
Elements: *Positive Fire, Yang*

This jaunty creature embodies most of the positive traits of the signs it combines. Scorpio/Horses are magnetic. And they are popular. They are disciplined and accomplished. They are persuasive and inspired, dedicated and fashionable. Scorpios born in Horse years are both independent and autonomous. There is little to prevent these folks from succeeding in a world class way.

This character has the vision and perspicacity of Scorpio and knows how to couple it with the Horse's natural vitality. He will take on projects that would cow anyone less competent, and carry them to their logical ends with remarkable facility. The Scorpio/Horse is a doer of impossible deeds. Success is written all over whatever he touches. He's not afraid of work and he's got some of the most unbelievably fanciful notions you ever heard of.

This bent for fantasy can sometimes be his undoing. The Scorpio born Horse does not fit in well with his peers. He is popular and admired, but people don't understand him very well. He's too different. He's too odd to make others feel completely comfortable about him. Scorpio/Horse is, moreover, unafraid of popular opinion and carries on with his fancy ideas no matter what or who tries to get in his way. He's not cruel. Just ruthlessly determined to get where he is going.

Scorpio/Horse takes no detours, either. Nor does he beat around the bush. He says what he thinks needs saying and then he sits calmly watching the fireworks. He is the voice of truth. He proclaims outrageous verity with apparent impunity. Once you know this person and understand how extraordinarily individualistic he really is, you expect the satirical banter, which can also make you crack up laughing.

The Scorpio/Horse has a rather difficult time getting started in life. He is easily affected by his surroundings, and if his family life is not perfectly peaceful, he can suffer undue guilt feelings. He's an anxious sort, and so sensitive to what is going on around him that he feels responsible and may retreat into his shell as a child. As a young adult he will search hard to find his true path. Once he gets past thirty, nothing can stop him. He's a winner, an eccentric, and quite a deep thinker as well.

Scorpio/Horses likes to dress up in fanciful garb. They are drawn to the conservative but find adding a rhinestone clip or splashy tie irresistible. He likes to present well and is overly concerned about physical attributes, both in himself and others. He cares if he's going bald. She worries if she notices a wrinkle.

This person will have excellent skill with things manual. He or she may build rooms or restore old houses or design wallpapers or knit shawls with weird patterns in them. Scorpio/Horse is, in fact, a bit of a bohemian by nature, and does not hesitate to flout convention or commit acts that "shock" society. Scorpio/Horses are compassionate and will help out those less fortunate than themselves. They are not comfortable with money. They are, by turns, stupidly spendthrift and stingy.

Love

The love life of Scorpio/Horse people is rarely based on undying passion. Scorpio/Horses, like all other horses, are practical above and beyond everything. They choose mates for their convenience and comfort. They take lovers if they need to enjoy the odd fling. But inside their marriages they appear staid and perfectionist.

Have you a Scorpio/Horse mistress or lover? If so, you already know that she or he is totally weird and wonderful. There is depth and charm in this character. You will be entertained and amused. The Scorpio/Horse likes sports and enjoys games. You will love him or her best by standing by in times of crisis and otherwise staying out of his or her way. The Scorpio/Horse needs a helpmate in the truest sense. He would like to do it all himself and certainly could—but he'd rather have a nice sidekick.

Compatibilities

If you meet up with a tawny Tiger or graceful Sheep, you'll probably fall for the Cancer, Virgo, Capricorn or Pisces variety. The Virgo and Pisces/Dogs, despite their apparent disquietude, appeal to your sense of caring. Rats never get on with Horses. Be particularly wary of Taurus, Gemini, Leo and Aquarius/Horses, especially when it comes to matters of the home. Aquarius/Cat is the last person on Earth you should hang around with.

Home and Family

Scorpio/Horse is meticulous about his interior. He wants it just right and comfortable as well as beautiful. He likes things orderly but is not maniacal about cleanliness. Mostly, Scorpio/Horse is conscientious about his surroundings, and if they are pleasant it is because he made them that way.

As a parent, this person can be accused of fanaticism. Scorpio/ Horses adore their kids. They live for their offspring and they do far too much for them. They give their kids everything any kid could want, and more. They spend time with them and they play with them. Scorpio/Horses should have scads of children. They are really good at it.

These children are cuddly and wise, sensitive and sensible. If a parent says "You can't have that today, dear," the Scorpio/Horse child, reasonable beyond his years, will invariably say, "All right. I can always have it another time." These kids are loving and easy to raise. They go it alone for most of their lives, and ask little more than love and feeding. They spend much time on their own, and like to be allowed to do crafts and pursue hobbies.

Profession

Gifted for achievement, the Scorpio born Horse mutely proclaims from the moment he is born, "I demand to create." It is a motto that suits him down to the ground. He will carry off all professions with aplomb but will be best suited to artistic ones.

As an employee, the Scorpio/Horse may prove unruly. He hates routine. He can adjust to workday habits, but he prefers to do things on his own time and in his own personal way.

I see the Scorpio/Horse best suited for leadership or even for independent solitary work. He is always champing at the bit to get his project done. He needs little prodding.

There is no reason Scorpios born in Horse years cannot be bosses. But I expect they would have difficulty delegating authority and might tend to do rather too much of the work themselves.

Suitable careers for this character are: undercover agent, lawyer, medical researcher, entrepreneur, chef, choreographer, singer, city planner, graphic artist, film producer, actor.

Famous Scorpio/Horses:
Teddy Roosevelt, Daniel Barenboim, Jacques Faizant, Martin Scorsese, Nestor Almendros, Serge Lama, Aleksander Kwasniewski (Poland), Billy Graham, Sophie Marceau, Tom Ellis, Gretchen Rossi, Michael K. Williams, Rachel McAdams, Zahn McClarnon, David Schwimmer, Michael Kenneth Williams, Gwendoline Christie, Tom Ellis, Zoë Bell, Kirby Bliss Blanton, Carlson Young, Jean-Luc Bilodeau, Alison Doody.

SCORPIO
QUALITIES
DEDICATION, SOVEREIGNTY, MAGNETISM,
INSPIRATION, TENDERNESS, DISCIPLINE
QUIRKS
MERCILESSNESS, FANATICISM, REVENGE,
SADISM, SUSPICION, INTRANSIGENCE
Motto: *"I create"*
Elements: *Water, Mars, Fixed*

--

SHEEP
QUALITIES
INVENTION, LACK OF FORESIGHT,
PERSEVERANCE, WHIMSY, GOOD MANNERS,
IMPRACTICALITY
QUIRKS
PARASITISM, SENSITIVITY,
TARDINESS, PESSIMISM, TASTE, WORRY
Motto: *"I depend"*
Elements: *Negative, Fire, Yin*

By combining creativity with dependency, you might think we would come up with a sort of brilliant layabout genius. Yet Scorpios born in Sheep years are busily inventive and perhaps the least lazy of all Sheep subjects.

Nonetheless, Scorpio/Sheep tend to live off the endeavors of others. By this, I certainly don't mean that they refuse to work on their own. Far from it. But their choice of work is invariably dependent on a structure coming from without. They are not disciplined people and should not attempt to be. They simply must recognize that

479

their genius overrides their need for order. Then, they can set about getting their lives structured by outside forces. This force can take the form of a marriage, a business, a child or two, a project, a course of study or even a lover or mistress.

But whatever the structure, you can be certain it does not come from within the scatty Scorpio/Sheep himself. Inside, the Scorpio/Sheep is a roiling cauldron of invention, new ideas, schemes, plans and dreams—some of them realizable and many of them totally off-the-wall useless.

You see, the Scorpio/Sheep is the opposite of practical. He is eccentric and erratic. He has spurts of genius and is truly gifted for artistic endeavor. But he is also hyperidealistic about his projects. He wants his plans followed (by others of course) to the letter. He operates largely for the sake of his own gain. He wants the glory and the returns. This makes him, despite his good intentions, an unwitting user.

Scorpio/Sheep are interested in absolutely everything. They like to be aware of all news and up to date on styles, and they follow the careers of new artists with zeal. They are even a tiny bit snobbish intellectually, and they are blatant know-it-alls. There is no subject upon which this person will not attempt to expound. "Do you know why the traffic pattern in Schiphol Airport was altered?" Nope. "Because the people who come to Holland from Malaysia . . ." and on and on. You don't have to talk at all in tête-à-têtes with Scorpio/Sheep. Just sit there with your ears open. They'll tell you everything you need to know, and then some.

To the naked eye this person may appear fragile and delicate, as though he or she might not survive a brisk wind. Yet inside the frail, brittle shell is a person of gorilla strength. The eccentric dress and the bizarre behavior are meant to throw you off, to make you think there isn't really a Scorpio in there at all. Don't be fooled. Scorpio/Sheep is no stranger to the use of force. He feels that he already understand all the alternatives (and he frequently does). So more often than not, he will opt for the head-on collision rather than lollygagging or dithering on about which direction to take.

Too, under the guise of expansive generosity, adopting poor relations, and jettisoning silver dollars at bums on the street, these people are avid for the last penny in transactions of all sorts. They like to think of themselves as philanthropic. But they are actually quite unashamedly miserly.

The beauty of Scorpio/Sheep is his or her rainbow of curiosity. This person wants to know how to play the piano and dance the tango, ride horses and program computers. He's earnestly attracted to cultural events and enjoys great talent of his own. If he can find the necessary structure, his innumerable talents can blossom. Without it, he may become dissipated and disillusioned.

Love

Here is one of the chances for structure from outside. Often, Scorpio/Sheep find themselves a hardy, clever, stronger partner who lays down certain subtle rules and regulations so that Scorpio/Sheep can get on with his busy life. In the same way that the Scorpio/Sheep's appearance of fragility will serve as a cover for him or her, this mate may not come across as strong. "Patricia's sick. We can't go out tonight." "John is depressed. Sorry I can't give you a hand with that piano." In truth, both Patricia and John can run rings around you and me—move that piano, tote that barge, lift that bale —but Scorpio/Sheep likes us to think otherwise.

If you love one of these people, get ready for a lifelong struggle. Scorpio/Sheep like nothing better than a good fight. They are strong-willed and quite unabashedly selfish. They are, however, fascinating, interesting, and extremely faithful to their partners. You win some, you lose some.

Compatibilities

A fine kinship exists between you and the Cancer, Virgo, Capricorn and Pisces/Pig family. Go for it. Or else follow your inclination toward Cats and take up with a Virgo, Capricorn or Pisces feline. Virgo and Pisces/Horses can both form a harmonious intimacy with your character. I'd like to see you with a subtly forceful Snake. But not a Leo or Pisces/Snake. There may be some animosity between you and Taurus or Aquarius/Oxen. You also have a slight aversion to the Leo/Dog, and you're not exactly crazy about Aquarius/Tigers either.

Home and Family

The interior of the Scorpio/Sheep household is often impressive. These folks love beautiful things and do not disdain luxury. Their homes will be cleverly decorated and just a tad bohemian or artsy. They are not much in the kitchen, so that area may be naked. But check out the pile of art magazines on the hand-hewn coffee table, the little Giacometti in the corner, that Picasso etching over the harpsichord. Bliss, *n'est-ce pas*?

Parenting is something these people claim to be very interested in. I've never been so sure. They definitely require the affection they get from children and they also enjoy returning same. But they are not really very wise about their kids' tricks. They let themselves (and their guests) be walked over by Junior's robot tanks and Sissy's performing hamsters. It's quite a mess in the kids' rooms and Dad or Mom Scorpio/Sheep would even like it to be a bit worse, if you please. They are cheerful parents. But indulgent.

Scorpio/Sheep kids are smashingly cute. They love being the only child. They like to be taught new things and be taken on trips and to museums and the like by adults. In fact, they thrive on adult attention and make terrific little companions for maiden aunts. These children require occasional rigor to prevent spoiling.

Profession

With the proper education and the right dose of discipline as a child, this person can train for a serious profession like sculpture or medicine or film editing or direction or creative writing, or more than one of those. The touche-à-tout aspect of the Scorpio/Sheep character can be a giant trump card. But getting him or her to stick to one art long enough to make anything of it is the problem. They function well in office situations as long as they get all the attention and can innovate their heads off.

As a boss, this person will be lovable, and most often bankrupt—or at least he says he is. I have always noticed that Scorpio/Sheep hide their wealth from their employees. So expect to enjoy working for a Scorpio/Sheep, but don't expect to get rich doing so. As employees, Scorpio/Sheep work hard (even round the clock if necessary) in an erratic kind of way. They get the job done. They want lots of praise.

Some good career choices for Scorpio/Sheep are: singer, poet, commercial artist, painter, sculptor, interior decorator, movie director, hairdresser, dance instructor, psychologist, plastic surgeon or jazz musician.

Famous Scorpio/Sheep:
Annie Girardot, Bill Gates, Boris Becker, Daisy McCrackin., Dan Rather, David Guetta, Ike Turner, Indra Nooyi, Joni Mitchell, Julia Roberts, Katherine Kelly, Kris Jenner, Lisa Bonnet, Mark Ruffalo, Mike Nichols, Morley Safer, Nate Parker, Olga Kurylenko, Roland Emerich, Rufus Sewell, Salvador Adamo, Shailene Woodley, Steve Zahn, The Shah of Iran, Whoopi Goldberg, Yves Brayer.

SCORPIO
QUALITIES
DEDICATION, SOVEREIGNTY, MAGNETISM,
INSPIRATION, TENDERNESS, DISCIPLINE
QUIRKS
MERCILESSNESS, FANATICISM, REVENGE,
SADISM, SUSPICION, INTRANSIGENCE
Motto: *"I create"*
Elements: *Water, Mars, Fixed*

--

MONKEY
QUALITIES
IMPROVISATION, CUNNING, STABILITY,
SELF-INVOLVEMENT, WIT, OPPORTUNISM
QUIRKS
DECEIT, RUSE, LOQUACITY,
LEADERS, SILLINESS, ZEAL
Motto: *"I plan"*
Elements: *Positive, metal, Yang*

Combining plotting and creativity can cause some human fire-works. The Scorpio born in a Monkey year will bear all the the earmarks of the complex Scorpio nature. He will be crafty and enigmatic and harsh-tongued and strong. Yet he will seek to muffle those darker characteristics by pretending jauntiness and affecting a slightly silly attitude at times. Monkey and Scorpio can sometimes be—but only sometimes—allies. They are both tricky, ruseful and capable of leadership. At other times, however, these two signs are at odds. Monkeys are sometimes deceitful but they pretend they are only kidding around. Scorpio is hardly ever just fooling around. Scorpio means business. Monkeys are builders. Scorpios can be destroyers. Monkeys are zealous, Scorpios jealous.

So inner discord is no stranger to the Scorpio born Monkey. There is a veritable storm of conflicting emotion at play inside this person's pretty little cranium. "Should I just lie back and let someone else do the work and consider myself the brains behind this operation?" asks the devious Scorpio of his Monkey conscience. "Or..." pipes up the Monkey, fair and square, "how about if I not only think up the plan, but I go and do it, too, and everybody will see what an industrious little worker I am." Either way the work gets accomplished, the plan is hatched and the battle done. But the method may leave a bitter taste in our hero's mouth.

He's often dissatisfied by his own imperfections. He'd like to be able to gaze long and hard into the mirror and say, "I am an accomplished something-or-other and I am proud of it." Instead, his reflection often comes back a disappointing mosaic of "maybe next time," and "if only," and "try harder." This shattered view is unpleasant to the Scorpio/Monkey. Yet he is hard put to fight his dualities fiercely enough to focus the image.

The Scorpio/Monkey is quick-witted and lively. Tying him down will not change his basic desire to come and go at will, to detour if he wants and to find his proper path by attempting many divergent ones. He is basically self-interested, wants recognition for his achievements alone, and finds sharing the burdens of less capable and imaginative souls untenable. The Monkey will lead. He will shine, and he will triumph. But first he has to get that temptress Scorpio out of his system.

The Monkey born Scorpio aspires to great heights of creativity. He is capable of undertaking and accomplishing projects of real complexity and import. The Monkey alone is a remarkably temperate soul. So the Scorpio side of this character gives inspiration and draws him into wilder territories than most Monkey people ever frequent.

At first he may balk and feel slightly tipsy from the journey and the rarefied air. But wait until he gets his little Monkey paws busy; this person adapts instantly to new circumstances once he's found a project to zero in on.

You may find this creature slightly bumptious and too talkative for your taste. Some Scorpio/Monkeys seem to have a scratched phonograph inside their heads and will endlessly repeat stories you have already heard a hundred times before. They need to be reminded of their hyperblabbiness. Fortunately, they take criticism with a smile. For Scorpios these people are practically without sulk.

They may be anxious and wracked with self-doubt. But Scorpio/ Monkeys will prevail. It's in their nature.

Love

This person is no ordinary super sexy Scorpio. He or she is also an erotically active Monkey. The combination of the two very sexual signs makes for an energetic if somewhat preoccupied lover. The Scorpio/Monkey wants to be exalted, exhilarated and excited. He or she will have no time for lukewarm affairs and is mainly interested in long-term and long-winded love matches.

It is not as important to admire the Scorpio/Monkey as it is to remember that his or her sexual needs take precedence over almost anything else. Some people say that sex tires them, wears them out and drains them. Not the Scorpio/Monkey. For him, sexual activity imparts self-confidence, builds his sometimes worried ego and energizes his creativity center. If you love such an eager beaver, don't underestimate his or her needs in bed or you may be sitting home by the phone doing crossword puzzles while the Scorpio/Monkey races about thrill-seeking. Don't ever tie this person down. Urge him or her to take trips without you. Often the illusion of freedom is enough to keep the Scorpio/Monkey down on the farm forever.

Compatibilities

If you take up with a Rat born in Cancer, Virgo, Capricorn or Pisces, count your blessings. Cancer, Capricorn and Pisces/Dragons create an atmosphere of well-being that impresses you. Taurus and Leo/Tigers might hold you back and keep you from making decisions. Then too, there are Leo/Horses and Leo/Pigs who get in your way. Aquarius/Oxen and Sheep test the limits of your patience.

Home and Family

The Monkey born Scorpio would rather have three funky houses than one palace. He's one of the roving kind. His walls will be plastered with souvenirs and mementos of travels and vacations in exotic places. His piano usually has the cover sawed off and he may drive a perfectly frightful car. For this person, chic is definitely out. Monkey/Scorpio considers that decor should be functional and personalized.

All Scorpio/Monkeys should have kids. There's a Peter Pan quality in this character. The Scorpio/Monkey likes to teach his or her children and to delight them with jokes and join in their pranks. The Monkey born Scorpio also feels lightness and innocence emanating from children, and this attracts and fascinates him. He may try to be authoritarian, but he'll probably giggle right in the middle of his somber lecture on table manners.

The Scorpio/Monkey child will be troubled if he or she doesn't succeed right away in life. There is great sensitivity here, and emotion takes longer to grow up than does intellect. The best advice I can give the parent of this child is: Leave him or her alone until a definite direction can be discerned. Then, leap at the chance to allow your Scorpio/Monkey to learn everything she will need to know about what interests her. This kid needs encouragement, freedom of action and a sterling example to follow.

Profession

The Scorpio/Monkey's talents often lie in creative areas, but he or she is also capable of excellent interpretive work. They can be good storytellers, as they like to talk and have orderly intellects. This person works best in small groups, where his or her artistic qualities are appreciated and implemented by the other members of the group. Again, in the profession chosen, this person must have the impression of leeway or breadth of action in order best to utilize talent. They can be short-tempered when pushed on deadlines or anxious about the success of the project.

Frankly, I don't think the Scorpio/Monkey wants to be boss. This person seeks, above all, an independent means to work on what interests him most. Being in a position of authority imposes strictures on the Scorpio/Monkey that he considers more of a prison than a privilege. He can be a diligent employee so long as he is not forced into excessive routine or the compromise of ideas. You'll find this person most happily employed doing his or her own thing. The Scorpio/Monkey is an original. Fitting in is not one of his goals.

Some appropriate careers for Scorpio/Monkeys are: photographer, musician, roadie, florist, potter, choreographer, boat-builder, sound engineer, historian.

Famous Scorpio/Monkeys:
Alistair Cooke, Ben Foster, Casey Wilson, Eddie Kaye Thomas, Esther Rolle, Gustaf Skarsgård, Isaac Hanson, James Kilpatrick, Jan Vermeer, Kelly Rutherford, Kocheril Raman Narayanan (India), Lexi Ainsworth, Louis Malle, Mehcad Brooks, Nathan Kress, Owen Wilson, Parker Posey, Petula Clark, Ryan Gosling, Sam Rockwell, Sidse Babette Knudsen, Stan Musial, Tammy Lauren.

SCORPIO
QUALITIES
DEDICATION, SOVEREIGNTY, MAGNETISM,
INSPIRATION, TENDERNESS, DISCIPLINE
QUIRKS
MERCILESSNESS, FANATICISM, REVENGE,
SADISM, SUSPICION, INTRANSIGENCE
Motto: *"I create"*
Elements: *Water, Mars, Fixed*

--

ROOSTER
QUALITIES
RESILIENCE, ENTHUSIASM, CANDOR,
CONSERVATISM, CHIC, HUMOR
QUIRKS
COCKINESS, BOASTFULNESS, BLIND FAITH,
PEDANTRY, BOSSINESS, DISSIPATION
Motto: *"I overcome"*
Elements: *Negative, Metal, Yin*

A steely ardor for living characterizes this combination. Scorpio, always mysterious and secretive, here encounters cockiness, bravura, and a love of what is exterior and apparent. Instead of causing conflict, the mélange engenders a simmering synergy and a kind of What Makes Sammy Run? dispatch.

Talent is no stranger to the Rooster born a Scorpio. This person usually has bushels of skills. Scorpio/Roosters are idealists and, because of the crossing of Scorpio's determination with the Rooster's resilience, will suffer less from setbacks than many other people. The Scorpio/Rooster's story is invariably one of climbing precipitous summits followed by full fanny slides back down. The craggy chasms in which you sometimes find Scorpio/Roosters flailing about seem not to ruffle their feathers. It's amazing how they bounce back from sorrow, divorce, loss and human bankruptcies of all sorts. These people seem fragile, almost brittle at times. But they are really solid and strong.

This subject wishes to appear supple and relaxed—cool—if you must. But scratch the surface of a Scorpio/Rooster and you will find instead a rare brand of rigid conservatism. The playboy or girl with the ready grin and the big fancy car is really not spendthrift or promiscuous in the least.

Scorpios are sexy people. But the Rooster/Scorpio, although he puts up a good front, is not so sensual as he would have you think. He's a bit of a frustrated Scorpio, who talks a big story but is not all that crazy about using his or her own precious body for lowly physical pleasures.

These people are direct. They blurt their desires and needs. They talk a lot and they keep a steady stream of complaints going as well. The Scorpio/Rooster sometimes feels victimized by others. He or she may gripe and blame more than is necessary. That sad tale about how Jimmy left you to marry Francine because she was such a siren is indeed regrettable. But weren't you partly responsible? Are you sure, Scorpio/Rooster, that Jimmy didn't have his reasons? Were you not a bit quick to anger? Did you not ask for the moon and only give peanuts in return? Were you not excessively nervous and jittery at times? Come on, Scorpio/Rooster, 'fess up. You tend to feel overly sorry for yourself.

There is a streak of old-maidishness in the talented Scorpio/ Rooster. She likes everything in its place and has a place for everything. He is picky and has enormous respect for promptitude. This confirmed-bachelor trait is not always negative, however. The Scorpio/ Rooster adheres swimmingly to routine, and can run rings around laziness. The marriage of these two very particular signs makes this native choosy, persnickety even, but it also gives him faultless taste and pushes him out of bed in the morning.

Roosters born in Scorpio are self-starters. They can drudge their way through all sorts of laborious mires and come up laughing. They are pretty near invincible, and if they do get discouraged, they fight depression by getting busy. Scorpios born in Rooster years personify the rugged individualist who, despite his eccentricities, manages to stay firmly put in the system.

Love

Talk about ups and downs! The Scorpio/Rooster's love life looks like the terrain in a war zone after a heavy bomb strike. These people are perfectionists. They are even Utopian. The muddy waters of casual passionate love affairs truly disturb their delicate senses. What does the Scorpio/Rooster want out of love? Permanency. Coziness. Everlasting fidelity. A marriage that works and keeps working—a love affair forever. It's a big order, especially nowadays. As a result, many Scorpio/Roosters don't stay involved too long. They see the weensiest flaw in a relationship as a gaping rent. And they leave. The Scorpio/Rooster does not want an imperfect love life. So sometimes he prefers to have none at all. He'd rather live in isolation than deal with murk.

Should you find yourself in love with a Scorpio/Rooster, behave. If you want to get and keep one of these punctilious creatures, it's up to you to get your act together so he or she can admire and adore you. Once you have caught the Scorpio/Rooster, you will have to accept living according to some very scrupulous patterns that inevitably belong to this person's existence. If he or she gets up at 3:00 A.M. to work on a diary, then you will probably be well advised to arrange your schedule accordingly.

Scorpio/Roosters like things to run their way. In return they give utter devotion and ruthless protection. They will fight for your rights as well as for theirs. But don't ever betray them. Scorpio/ Roosters do not forgive. They leave.

Compatibilities

Snakes in their infinite wisdom and attractiveness appeal to your highly developed sense of good taste and decorum. Cancer, Virgo, Capricorn and Pisces will be the best Snakes for you. Both Capricorn and Pisces/Oxen please you by their loving kindness. Capricorn and Pisces/Dragons have a certain consideration for your sensitivities. You find them irresistible. On the dark side, it is doubtful you can cohabit with Taurus/Pigs. The Leo/Cat and Rooster are definitely not your style. Don't even try to relate to Aquarius/Rats. You don't agree on much.

Home and Family

The homes of Scorpio/Roosters are epic places filled with authentic antiques and perfect wiring systems, and they boast every appliance ever seen by man. There may be a billiard room, too. The Scorpio/ Rooster is a gay blade type, loves entertaining, and lives to be admired. He'll let you drink his whiskey and eat all his pound cake as long as you remember to tell him how much you enjoyed his last TV show.

The Scorpio/Rooster is a loving and careful parent. He or she remembers everybody's birthday and brings in circus acts and magicians for little Molly's party. He or she will be the kind of parent who wants the kids to enjoy themselves while they are young.

Scorpio/Roosters sometimes miss having children because of their hesitation to marry unless they find the perfect mate. But if they don't have a family, they will regret it. Kids, with all their spontaneity and natural mirth, offer this rather stiff person the opportunity to relax with impunity.

The Scorpio/Rooster child will be easy to raise. He or she will probably excel in subjects requiring exactitude and accuracy. Also, this person will be popular with friends and favored by aunts and uncles for his or her fine academic performances. This girl or boy will no doubt enjoy sports, too, and do well in those athletic endeavors that smack of class and elegance, such as fencing, tennis and horseback riding.

Profession

Gifts abound in the nature of the Scorpio/Rooster. He or she will be good at many different jobs. They like to undertake vast projects that demand personal involvement and self-discipline. Versatility and perseverance is the special province of the Scorpio/Rooster. She may be able to speak three languages. He will have won several medals for tennis tournaments and be a crackerjack painter, too. Scorpio/Rooster likes to surmount difficulty and only gets into a situation if he or she thinks it's a winner.

Either "Employee" or "Boss" etched in the glass on their office doors will mean the same thing: Boss. This Scorpio doesn't take orders gracefully unless he covets the job of the person giving the orders. He or she is a natural stickler and will drive him- or herself as hard as anybody. Scorpio/Roosters are also concretely creative. They come up with new ideas and carry them out.

Some appropriate careers for Scorpio/Roosters are: editor, photographer, auditor, TV producer, advertising executive, buyer, actor, actress, market analyst, linguist.

Famous Scorpio/Roosters:
Andrea Riseborough, Anni-Frid Lyngstad, Bill Mauldin, Bojana Novakovic, Brett Kelly, Brian Keith, Charles Bronson, Dolph Lundgren, Ellen Pompeo, Ezra Pound, George Patton, Gerard Butler, Goldie Hawn, James Jones, Katharine Hepburn, Lucky Luciano, Matthew McConaughey, Nasim Pedrad, Neil Young, Princess Leonor of Spain, Rodney Dangerfield, Vanessa Bayer.

SCORPIO
QUALITIES
DEDICATION, SOVEREIGNTY, MAGNETISM,
INSPIRATION, TENDERNESS, DISCIPLINE
QUIRKS
MERCILESSNESS, FANATICISM, REVENGE,
SADISM, SUSPICION, INTRANSIGENCE
Motto: *"I create"*
Elements: *Water, Mars, Fixed*

--

DOG
QUALITIES
CONSTANCY, UNSOCIABILITY,
RESPECTABILITY, SELF-RIGHTEOUSNESS,
INTELLIGENCE, TACTLESSNESS
QUIRKS
UNEASINESS, CRITICISM, DUTY,
CYNICISM, HEROISM, MORALITY
Motto: *"I worry"*
Elements: *Positive, Metal, Yang*

The convoluted emotional swamp that personifies Scorpio comes a cropper when it meets up with the frank, open, direct and altruistic Dog character. The basic Dog self, the worrier, the doubting and tender-hearted champion, will at first be utterly flummoxed to be born a Scorpio. "A Scorpio?" wonders the baby Dog. "What's that?"

Of course there are positive similarities between the two signs. Both Scorpio and Dog are dedicated and devoted people. Scorpio lends fire to this dedication, and adds open jealousy to the picture should this devotion be betrayed. Both Dogs and Scorpios like to

491

advance strong opinions. Dog is a shade more know-it-all than the secretive Scorpio. But the Scorpio can be quite a talker. What's more, Dogs do a lot of nipping and snapping. With the Scorpio's viper tongue to dispatch the Dog's verbal snipes, you can see that this is not a person who minces words.

So the Scorpio/Dog character is acerbic and sarcastic. At the same time he or she will also be very nice and full of brotherly love in caring about others. If riled (and that is not difficult with this edgy, disquiet soul), the Scorpio/Dog will bite. These subjects can be scrappers, and although they are rarely actually physical, they can be mightily sadistic in their commentary. Let's say that the Scorpio/Dog uses his tongue and his wits to battle his way through life.

Scorpio/Dogs are analytical and begin longing to change the world while still very young. They are judgmental. They find compromise almost impossible. They are not naturally friendly and outgoing, tail-wagging Dogs. Scorpio/Dogs go straight to the heart of the matter. They are easily hurt. But by the time they reach thirty, they have usually resigned themselves to their dissatisfied nature. Then their Scorpio side comes to the fore and they begin to make public their critical and sarcastic natures.

Resignation in the case of Scorpio/Dogs is an asset. It allows them to laugh not only at the world but at themselves. Age gives them the necessary perspective for becoming funny, witty satirists.

There is a quality of sweetness in this mad Dog's character, too. You can always tell, despite the acid remarks and the dry witty comments, that underneath shines a light of human understanding and genuine good will. The Scorpio/Dog means no harm. He loves humanity. That's why he tears it to shreds, to get a better look at its inner workings so that maybe he or she can do something about it. There is no question that the Scorpio/Dog wants to do good.

But, as we all know, where there is much good, evil is never far away. Evil stalks the good man, tempting him and testing his probity. Scorpio is a temptress of the first water. "Come on. Put your hand in the till. Nobody will ever know. Don't worry so much. Just take the bracelet...." Scorpio/Dogs suffer deeply at the hands of this Jezebel Beelzebub. They must use all their strength to resist devoting so much as a wink to the devil. Laughter, they find, is an excellent antidote to evil.

Love

I love them all. Scorpio/Dogs are tender-hearted, nervous sweethearts whom you would like to comfort and soothe. Of course, all the balm in the world won't shut the eyes of this perspicacious hound. Nor will it quiet his caustic tongue. What this person wants in a lover is a companion. He wants somebody to respect, who doesn't grovel at his feet, and who keeps his or her part of the bargain one hundred percent of the way. No free rides. And should he be disappointed in love once, he won't want to take another chance. Scorpio/Dogs require gentle persuasion to accept happiness in love.

As this person is always nit-picking and hunting for the flaws in a relationship, if you love one you must be as even-tempered as possible. Swathe yourself in layers of down quilts to resist the arrows of your loved one's sharp wits and don't—I repeat, do not be defensive. Pretend you don't hear them. They'll be deflected by your indifference.

Compatibilities

You are well disposed to harmony with Tigers born in Cancer, Virgo, Capricorn and Pisces. Cancer, Capricorn and Pisces/Cats and Horses know how to appreciate your special tolerance and merciful understanding. Conversely, Gemini and Aquarius/Dragons get on your none-too-steady nerves. Your trustworthy self will not find the Taurus/Rooster or Pig a satisfactory subject for faithfulness. You're tempted by, but must not approach, the Aquarius/Sheep.

Home and Family

At home the Scorpio/Dog feels less threatened by wickedness. Here he will try to create an environment of pipe-and-slippers comfort. The Scorpio/Dog doesn't much bother with frippery or furbelow, but rather she will want others simply to feel welcome at her place. There will surely be a fireplace and lots of books at the Scorpio/Dog's house. But you probably won't see any apparent gold. It's all hidden under the mattresses (or in a Swiss bank).

The Scorpio/Dog parent idolizes his or her kids. Kids, for this idealist, represent hope for the future. Kids are untainted by sordid reality. This parent will take great pains with the education and guidance of his or her children. The Scorpio/Dog earnestly believes he or she can alter the course of a life through early training. This person has many regrets about his own childhood and wants to make amends.

The Scorpio/Dog child will not be chubby or roly-poly huggable. You are more likely to find him or her rather bony and sinewy. The kid will have many dreams about the future, and a wise parent would feed those dreams by keeping the child in touch with nature and goodness at all times. The Scorpio/Dog's brutal sensitivity can easily turn to vinegar if too much reality is allowed to assail him before he is old enough to fight his own battles. So protect your Scorpio/Dog child. And try to teach him how to laugh at himself.

Profession

Jobs, for the Scorpio/Dog character, ought to put his capacity for analysis and criticism to good use. By the time Scorpio/Dog reaches adulthood, he will be ready to apply himself to trying to put some order into the social chaos he sees so clearly. This person can put the finger on trouble in a trice.

The Scorpio/Dog is not so much bossy as he is snappish. Authority, as such, doesn't grab him. This creature needs liberty of action in her work and should not be tied down to the routine of domination, or any other routine, for that matter. Too much sameness will remove the challenge that Scorpio/Dog lives for. She will certainly be a reliable employee, but time clocks and nagging office managers will alienate her. As Scorpio/Dogs are naturally industrious, you can be certain this subject will do everything not to be unemployed.

Some careers for Scorpio/Dogs will be: writer, city planner, recording engineer, troubleshooter, photographer, humorist, undercover agent, journalist, psychiatrist, social worker.

Famous Scorpio/Dogs:

Anne Hathaway, Bethenny Frankel, Carl Sagan, Chris Jericho, Damon Wayans Jr., David Stockman, Ethan Hawke, Georges Bizet, Jacques Loussier, Jamie Lee Curtis, Javy Lopez, Justin Chatwin, Kurt Vonnegut, Laura Bush, Magritte, Nadine Trintignant, Pete Wilson, Raymond Devos, Rosemary DeCamp, Sally Field, Sean P. Diddy Combs, Tonya Harding, Voltaire.

SCORPIO
QUALITIES
DEDICATION, SOVEREIGNTY, MAGNETISM,
INSPIRATION, TENDERNESS, DISCIPLINE
QUIRKS
MERCILESSNESS, FANATICISM, REVENGE,
SADISM, SUSPICION, INTRANSIGENCE
Motto: *"I create"*
Elements: *Water, Mars, Fixed*

--

PIG
QUALITIES
SCRUPULOUSNESS, GALLANTRY, SINCERITY,
VOLUPTUOUSNESS, CULTURE, HONESTY
QUIRKS
CREDULITY, WRATH, HESITATION,
MATERIALISM, GOURMANDISM, PIGHEADEDNESS
Motto: *"I civilize"*
Elements: *Negative Water, Yin*

In his book Animal Farm, George Orwell writes in jest that "all pigs are created equal... but some are more equal than others." The Scorpio/Pig possesses natural magnificence. He's duskier than most. Scorpio has just what the doctor ordered to remedy that silly piggie credulity: suspicion. It's a good match. This person will surely go a long way in life. Moreover, he or she will be cheered along by many admiring companions.

Often, Scorpios born in Pig years are exceptionally good-looking. They have an enigmatic quality that other more direct Pigs would envy. What's more, Scorpio/Pigs know how to dress. Both signs have a taste for the sensually appealing. Watch for elegant décolletages and spiffy smoking jackets.

I'd rather not have to say it, but our friend the Scorpio born Pig can be both mouthy and pushy. This guy knows what he wants and never hesitates to play the squeaky wheel in order to get it. He can be loud and boisterous. He loves jokes and off-color stories. The Scorpio born Pig is lusty. In his younger years he can be accused of sowing rather more than his share of wild oats.

The reason for his aggressive dynamism is Scorpio/Pig's raw ambition. These people don't like to be poor. They struggle very hard in order to impose their ideas in work situations. They are not afraid to ring up the director of the Metropolitan Museum of Art in New York from some obscure boondock to say that they are the best painter in Illinois—maybe in the whole world—and they think the curator should give them a one-man show. Oddly, sometimes these forward tactics work, and work very well. In any case, the Scorpio/Pig will try anything once in order to advance his own interest.

The Scorpio/Pig is less pure than other Pigs. He or she will know how to flimflam and will be tempted to do so for the basest material ends. Unfortunately, the Pig character is deeply affected by improbity. A touch of dishonesty can be disastrous for a Scorpio/Pig. He does not bounce back from crooked deals. He does not handle guilt very well. Best the Scorpio/Pig stay away from trickery. If he asks for trouble, he usually gets it.

Every gesture of the Scorpio/Pig, even if it is an invitation or a kindness, is self-interested. This person is not evil, but he is very desirous of getting where he wants to be. He's ruthless, in fact. His parties may be spectacular and his gifts lavish. But there will always be a tinge of egotism connected to them. Maybe he needs a phone number for car repair or perhaps you know a guy who might hire his daughter. Scorpio/Pigs cannot seem to give just for the sake of giving.

This person's capacity for self-righteous anger is monumental. Scorpio has never been noted for self-control. But a Scorpio born in a Pig year—my dear! If you happen to see one of these creatures winding up for a rip-roaring tantrum, batten the hatches and run for your life. Scorpio/Pig anger is murderous—but infrequent.

All in all, the Scorpio/Pig is quite a jolly, attractive sort. He is strong-willed, loving and able to compromise—for gain. He hates to lose and rarely does. He can be narrow-minded and conservative, but he's fun to be with and knows how to cut a mean figure in public.

Love

In all areas where the Scorpio born Pig performs, he does his best. But he is a tinge on the selfish side. And he or she will be demanding. Thing is, these people are very bright and funny. They are also pretty to look at. They adore sex and everything that goes before it and after it. They're demonically fetching. They will love deeply and exclusively.

Should you be enchanted by one of these Scorpios, I would suggest that you never arouse their jealousy. Like their rages, their attacks of green-eyed monsterism are epic. Scorpio/Pigs like to be adored and hate being taken for granted. They play with the emotions of whomever they are with, but they cannot accept being toyed with in their turn. It's a ticklish route being in love with a Scorpio/Pig. Ask Louis XVI: Marie Antoinette was one of these characters.

Compatibilities

Your well-meaning spirit will oblige the Cancer, Virgo, Capricorn and Pisces/Sheep. You empathize easily with Cancer, Virgo and Pisces/Cats. They are home-loving, and seek refinement the way you do. Try to resist the attractive Taurus and Leo/Snakes. They might misuse your philanthropy. Taurus/Horses may buckle under the yoke of marriage to such as you. I advise you to control your enthusiasm about Aquarius/Monkeys.

Home and Family

Decor in the Scorpio/Pig's life is a must. Home is one of the outward and visible signs of his achievement. The prospect of building a real home where each room, each objet d'art and every last cranny will bespeak the person who inhabits it is delightful to the domesticated Scorpio/Pig. The furniture will usually be traditional, the monogrammed linens ironed fresh and fashioned from finest imported fabrics. The Scorpio/Pig makes much of his or her home. He is handy and clever and skillful at building and decorating. Scorpio/Pigs love to throw lavish receptions and invite all the "right" people.

Parenting also pleases the Scorpio/Pig. He or she will most likely be bossy and even domineering as a parent. But they will love their kids with a passion. For the Scorpio/Pig, each offspring represents another feather in his cap. This is a proud and demanding parent who compensates for being overly authoritarian by dispensing impressive amounts of tenderness and loving care to children. The Scorpio/Pig spends time with kids, but has a bit of trouble accepting adolescents. His self-assurance is threatened by the questioning attitude of teenagers. He wants to be obeyed—and never disapproved of.

The Scorpio/Pig child is a pleasure. First of all, he or she will surely be beautiful. Secondly, these kids have enormous giggling capabilities and love to wallow in the lushness of childhood's joys. Take your Scorpio/Pig child to the country and let him skinny-dip. He will enjoy lolling in the tall grass after his swim. Infrequent (but impressive) tantrums aside, this is a sweet child who asks little more of his young life than loving parents and a safe home.

Profession

This person's job will be the vehicle by which he rises to success. The Scorpio/Pig person is not interested in modest wages and life-long security. He cares about getting to the top, having lots of money and living in opulent surroundings. He's a driver and a doer. Early in his career this person will have some difficulty obtaining top-level positions. He will represent a threat to other executives and his angry side can also cause problems. When the Scorpio/Pig learns to tone down and cool it with the ambition act, people will be less anxious about according him jobs involving authority. In any case, by middle age, these people are usually rich. It comes with the territory.

Bossy. Yes. But humane all the same, and so creative that sometimes the bossiness is understandable. Scorpio/Pig wants to get things done. He's impatient and can be rowdy. Whether boss, employee or independent worker, this person will have success or die trying.

Some fitting careers for Scorpio/Pig are: painter, actor, actress, cattle rancher, restaurant owner/caterer, interior decorator, stockbroker, politician.

Famous Scorpio/Pigs:

Adam DeVine, Adam Driver, Alain Delon, Anthony Rapp, Bethany Mota, Chiang Kai-Shek, Eugene Ormandy, Hillary Clinton, Jean Cazenave, Joel McHale, Katie McGrath, Kendall Jenner, Kevin Kline, King Hussein (Jordan), Leo Baekeland, Madison McLaughlin, Mahalia Jackson, Marie Antoinette, Nadine Gordimer, Richard Dreyfuss, Rosemarie Dewitt, Roy Rogers, Snoop Dog, Viva Bianca, Walton Goggins, Winona Ryder.

SAGITTARIUS
QUALITIES
CHEERFULNESS, OPENHANDEDNESS,
SOLICITUDE, VALOR, HONOR, REASON
QUIRKS
OUTSPOKENNESS, RECKLESSNESS,
BAD MANNERS, VACILLATION,
CARELESSNESS, CONTRADICTION
Motto: *"I see"*
Elements: *Fire, Jupiter, Mutable*

--

RAT
QUALITIES
NERVOUSNESS, INFLUENCE,
ACQUISITIVENESS, THIRST FOR POWER,
INTELLECTUAL SKILL, CHARISMA
QUIRKS
APPEAL, VERBOSITY, THRIFT,
SOCIABILITY, GUILE, MEDDLING
Motto: *"I rule"*
Elements: *Positive Water, Yang*

The marriage of Sagittarius to Rat brings us a healthy and vivacious person full of energy and abustle with activity. The Sagittarius born Rat just about never sits still. This person likes groups and is always surrounded by guests, friends and family alike. Less charm-conscious than many Rat subjects, the Sagittarian is impatient to achieve but is not concerned about what others think of him. He or she presents a candid self-image without frills or pretense. If you like that sort of thing, you will enjoy this dynamic Sagittarian's company. If you are not attracted by his or her simplicity and directness, then you don't have to come around. It's all the same to Sagittarius/Rat.

He has no time to please dissenters.

Despite being a super host or hostess and the best group animator in any crowd, this person is oddly impenetrable and reserved. The Sagittarius/Rat is not the life of the party, laugh-a-minute type. Rather, the Rat born in Sagittarius transcends the show-offy, stand-up comedian type of party thrower. This person draws people together not out of a need to be surrounded but out of a desire to see others happy, to watch them amuse themselves and to observe their interactions. The Sagittarius/Rat is the first to run to get the wine and to offer you the best chair in the house. Be comfortable. Enjoy.

In the same concerned way, the Sagittarius/Rat is a protector of loved ones. This person has the natural on-top-of-the-world quality necessary to boost the morale of ten disquieted Dogs or nervous nellies. Not that Sagittarius/Rats spend hours stroking their pals and family members, but there is something reassuring about the presence of this guiding-light creature. One always has the feeling the Sagittarius/Rat won't forget to turn out the lights before going to bed and will be sure to lock the gate.

The people born under the dual signs of Sagittarius and Rat are opportunistic for themselves and for their loved ones. They are quick to see the worth of a situation or the use of a new person or thing. In an emergency, they act rapidly and intelligently, keeping a cool head despite their feverish action. They know how to take apart a problem and put it back together so it works. They leap at the occasion to take advantage of a stroke of luck.

Sagittarian Rats are gamblers with life. They barrel ahead when they feel the time is ripe, and they very often reap huge benefits because they have followed their nose. If you are ever in doubt about a new acquaintance's honesty or mettle, ask a Sagittarius/Rat to have a look. They know how to pick a winner.

This person is an inveterate traveler. He or she may leave home at a young age to wander, to seek a new place to settle, to find his or her own level upon which to be free to move unhampered by social convention or fusty family ties. The Sagittarian Rat has an incisive mind and is talented for rendering the human comedy in artistic ways. Such people will have the wherewithal to become leaders in charitable causes, as they feel deeply for those less fortunate than themselves. Sagittarius/Rats can make lots of money, but they are not good managers of wealth. They tend to be spendthrift and overly generous in the wrong places.

Love

In love situations this person is idealistic. Sagittarian Rats are easily disappointed in romance and may never marry. Because of their basic mistrust of all of society's demands, these people tend to shy from shoes-under-the- bed security and snug-as-a-bug-in-a-rug cliché relationships. They are fascinated by the exotic and so invested with adventure and wanderlust as to be difficult to match with a suitable life partner.

Should your affections lean to the Sagittarius/Rat and you have fallen under his or her inimitable spell, I advise you to buy a couple of seats on an airplane to Hong Kong or the Seychelles and invite your sweet Sagittarian Rat along for the ride. You may never unstick him or her from the palm trees and rickshaw lifestyle. But then you can always set up shop in a foreign land so as to be closer to your freewheeling Sagittarius/Rat and his/her projects. Don't settle in too deeply, though this person likes to keep moving. Who knows? Maybe next year you'll be moving to the Costa del Sol.

Compatibilities

Reciprocity with Aries, Leo, Libra and Aquarius/Dragons is easy for you. You can form close ties with them and you approve of their snappy approach. Leo, Libra and Aquarius/Monkeys and Oxen suit you just fine. You are wildly attracted by Libra/Sheep. Tensions will arise between you and Gemini, Virgo and Pisces/ Horses and Cats.

Home and Family

The Rat born in Sagittarius lives in authentic luxury. He or she will be big on paintings by the latest artists and sculpted furniture from Italy or Sweden. The Sagittarius/Rat never sacrifices comfort for luxury, however. His or her aim will always be to provide and protect family and create an ambience where huge receptions feel natural and right. Sagittarius/Rats don't mind having help in their palaces, either. They will be as nice to the service personnel as they are to their own family. This person is naturally not a snob.

With children, as with anyone who needs their help or attention, Sagittarian Rats are cleverly care-conscious. They never hover or fret over their kids. But these kind, outspoken parents never let their kids out of their minds for a minute. They are gentle and loving but they are also firm. A kid whose parent is a Sagittarius/Rat will never forget to say "Hello" to company and stand up when adults enter the room.

The Sagittarius/Rat child is likely to spread his toys and influence around a good bit even before he's out of diapers. This little tyke cannot stand to be confined, and will learn early to climb out of playpens and over high railings. The travel bug sets in early with these curious and active souls. Field trips and vacations to untrodden lands will occupy these youngsters till they are old enough to fly alone. Watch out for signs of rebellion in early adolescence. This child cannot exist in hypocritical surroundings. If there is too much unspoken tension around the home, this kid may try to pack his teddy bears and leave at age seven. Cards on the table time.

Profession

Attributes such as those of the Sagittarius/Rat are rare. This person's ability to zero in on human situations and make truth out of a single notion or vision is not common. He or she will be best utilized and happiest in peripatetic fields involving decision-making. Sagittarius/Rats are both perseverant and brave. Adventurous jobs appeal to their need for freedom.

The Sagittarius/Rat boss doesn't want power over others unless he gets truth with it. If accused of wielding blind authority, this person will find the situation intolerable. Although usually not hotheaded, Sagittarius/Rat is capable of summarily firing an employee for groveling and sniveling. He wants contact. Not obeisance.

This person is not a contented employee. He or she is always trying to get to the boss stage. They will be efficient and dutiful but never stay underlings for long. As independents these subjects work admirably well toward success.

Some professions that might please the Sagittarius/Rat are: journalist, ski instructor, sociologist, newscaster, social worker, ambulance driver, volcano explorer, geologist, sportswriter, personnel manager, lawyer, veterinarian.

Famous Sagittarius/Rats:

Abbie Hoffman, Alan Ritchson, Alyssa Milano, Amanda Wyss, Amy Grant, Brian Baumgartner, Carlo Ponti, Cathy Moriarty, Daryl Hannah, Eugene Ionesco, Franklin Pierce, Frederic Tuten, Jackson Rathbone, Jason Mantzoukas, John F. Kennedy Jr, Julianne Moore, Kenneth Branagh, Kenneth Copeland, Lou Rawls, Mary Elizabeth Winstead, Michel Tournier, Miranda Hart, Poorna Jagannathan, Pope Francis, Reiko Aylesworth, Samuel L. Jackson, Sarah Rafferty, Shannon Woodward, Stuart Townsend, Theo James, Thierry Mugler, Tip O'Neill, Toulouse-Lautrec, Vanessa Paradis, Willis Carrier.

SAGITTARIUS
QUALITIES
CHEERFULNESS, OPENHANDEDNESS,
SOLICITUDE, VALOR, HONOR, REASON
QUIRKS
OUTSPOKENNESS, RECKLESSNESS,
BAD MANNERS, VACILLATION,
CARELESSNESS, CONTRADICTION
Motto: *"I see"*
Elements: *Fire, Jupiter, Mutable*

--

OX
QUALITIES
STUBBORNNESS, STRENGTH OF PURPOSE,
ELOQUENCE, STANDOFFISHNESS, INNOVATION,
VINDICTIVENESS
QUIRKS
INTEGRITY, BIGOTRY, PLODDING,
DILIGENCE, BIAS, STABILITY
Motto: *"I preserve"*
Elements: *Negative Water, Yin*

Oxen can really accomplish a lot in life. But Sagittarius/Oxen can do more. These folks are dynamos. They are both fiery and placid. They are eloquent beyond belief. They are direct, humanistic, open-handed and strong. What's more, Sagittarians born in Ox years are ambitious for power, influence, control and prestige. They don't despise money, either.

Foresight and reason blend here, making the Sagittarius/Ox a different kind of Ox from other, more deliberate or belligerent types. This Ox is born with flair, chutzpah, style, pizzazz, charm and appeal. What they go after in life, they get. To them, success is simplicity itself. They cannot imagine failure, don't know what color it is and wouldn't recognize it if it rushed up and brained them. For the Sagittarian Ox, life is achievement. You start out small and you work hard and you get where you have always wanted to be. Any questions?

"Well, dear Sag/Ox, I do wonder why you manage to 'make it' so frequently while others of us lag behind, bring up the rear and/or positively flunk? How is it your roster of famous brave men and good women looks longer than everybody else's?" asks the Good Fairy. "Everything is relative," answers the Sagittarius/Ox. It's true. Sagittarians born in Ox years are irretrievably stolid, stuck-up and standoffish. They are impeccably idealistic and invincibly brash. They are not afraid of anything or anyone. They charge at life like an army of foot soldiers on a steady diet of Kale and Tofu. But they are not race-around speedy. Sagittarius/Oxen are merely serious practitioners of the science of self-promotion and narrow-minded, unswerving belief in the strong-arm method of winning.

Fiery and steadfast, courageous and reckless, the Sagittarius/Ox can lead anything from a Dixieland band to an empire with good cheer and nose-in-the-air aplomb. Hitler was not a Sagittarian. Hitler wanted to kill a lot. Sagittarians like to do good in the world, help others and improve mankind. They eschew murder. And they are not shy of pain. Sagittarius/Oxen are danger-loving and will take outrageous chances to get where they care to go. They risk life and limb without blinking an eyelid for the sake of their cause or their "ism." They are not solely self-interested, though, and I have to hand it to this brand of Sagittarian—they sacrifice much comfort and security to advance their causes. Sagittarius/Oxen all have different notions of what the betterment of humanity means. But they all go after it equally hungrily. Sagittarian Oxen can have very roughshod ways and don't hesitate to air unpopular grassroots opinions. Or else they exhibit similarly uncharming conservatism. Either way, the goal is the same: Get there no matter how many little guys you have to intimidate to do so. No. The Sagittarian Ox doesn't walk over dead bodies to get where he wants to be. He works people till they drop from exhaustion. Then he covers them sweetly with a bonny blue blanket and moves on.

Love

The Sagittarius/Ox is usually married. Or perhaps I should say he or she is unusually married. These folks often exhibit fervent fidelity in love relationships. I mean they advertise their love for their mate. They tell you how wonderful old Marsha is and what a terrific doctor Sam has learned to be and how Jim is going to save the world. It can be very flattering for both the Sagittarian Ox and the husband or wife. Otherwise I am not sure the Sagittarius/Ox would do it. These tough customers are just a wee bit on the public side—not show-offy unless they have something to say, but they always have plenty to say.

If you love a Sagittarius/Ox and he or she doesn't return your love, you will be fiercely unhappy. This person would be very hard to lose. But should you still have a chance to nab this super good catch, before wedlock sets in I advise you to make it your business to understand working on a team of which you are decidedly not the coach. Learn how to track Ox footprints through the desert in the summer. You'll be needing all the breadcrumbs you can stash.

Compatibilities

Your favorite people live among the Leo, Libra and Aquarius/Rat and Snake people. A bond of communication exists between you and Aquarius/Roosters as well. Don't try to interdepend with Dragons. You have the most difficulty with Gemini, Leo, Virgo and Pisces types. Gemini and Virgo/Monkeys exasperate you. So do Gemini/Horses, Gemini and Virgo/Sheep, and Pisces/Tigers.

Home and Family

Like everything else in their busy lives, the Sagittarian Ox's home is a showplace of efficiency, good cheer and personality. No matter who lives there, the house (or houses) is definitely a statement of the Sagittarius/Ox's preferences, tastes and attitudes. If she likes sailing, the living room will have portholes instead of windows. If he's into archery, duck!

Parenting comes naturally to this leader type. Sagittarius/Ox does everything effectively, so why not raise a couple of children, too? Why not indeed? This person should be understanding and compassionate, but he or she may be intransigent with kids and impatient with shilly-shalliers. He will surely be sincere and dutiful. Also, Sagittarius/Oxen tell a mean story. Kids like stories.

You won't believe how tremendous this child's ambition is. He or she will probably do well in school (unless somebody higher up tries to thwart him or her), shine on committees and run the baked goods sales and the fundraisers. At home, this child may be very inward and spend much time reading. He or she will definitely be sports-minded. Competition delights the Sagittarius/Ox—even if he's only competing against himself.

Profession

This character is hell-bent to get somewhere in his or her professional life. Although business is not of primary concern to this struggler, he or she will probably make bezillions. This nature is so all-encompassing and "into" life and projects and adventures and details that he cannot let even one insignificant bank statement error past him without straightening it out. They are avid for security, but that's not the point. The real moral thrust of Sagittarius/Ox is the "shepherd" complex. They take care of everything and everybody, needed or not. And Sagittarius/Ox gets to keep half.

Boss. Definitely power post. The will to dominate is king in the makeup of the Sagittarius/Ox. Naturally, nobody will come close to this person's excellence in group situations, so if they don't get elected or chosen for the job of director, they'll simply take it. Being employed as subaltern doesn't even graze the subconscious of this hearty monster. Working alone, he or she will have factory force.

Jobs that suit the Sagittarius/Ox are: star, best-selling author, race car driver, famous anything, cartoonist, scientist, historian, president, pope, king, queen, emperor, head nurse, Mother Superior, prefect of discipline, God, pilot.

Famous Sagittarius/Oxen:
Alain Chapel, Alexander Godunov, Alfonso Cuarón, Alison Pill, Amanda Seyfried, Bill Nighy, Danielle Nicolet, Dean Ambrose, Don Johnson, Frankie Muniz, Gary Hart, Holly Marie Combs, Jacques Dessange, Jane Fonda, Jean Marais, Jean Mermoz, Jean Sibelius, Jeff Bridges, Jeremy Northam, Joe Lando Jr., Kaley Cuoco, Kim Delaney, László Cseh, Margaret Meade, Monica Seles, Nancy Meyers, Nia Peeples, Nick Beggs, Peter Facinelli, Raven-Symoné, Rian Johnson, Sammy Davis, Scott Cohen, Shane Black, Sharlto Copley, Tom Sizemore, Walt Disney, William Blake, William Buckley, Willy Brandt, Yasiin Bey Tyra Banks, Zara Larsson.

SAGITTARIUS
QUALITIES
CHEERFULNESS, OPENHANDEDNESS,
SOLICITUDE, VALOR, HONOR, REASON
QUIRKS
OUTSPOKENNESS, RECKLESSNESS,
BAD MANNERS, VACILLATION,
CARELESSNESS, CONTRADICTION
Motto: *"I see"*
Elements: *Fire, Jupiter, Mutable*

--

TIGER
QUALITIES
FERVOR, BRAVERY, MAGNETISM,
GOOD LUCK, BENEVOLENCE, AUTHORITY
QUIRKS
IMPETUOSITY, HOTHEADEDNESS,
DISOBEDIENCE, SWAGGER, INTEMPERANCE,
ITINERANCY
Motto: *"I Watch"*
Elements: *Positive Wood, Yang*

The Sagittarius born Tiger is a person who stubbornly, but charmingly, wishes to remain a child. These people love all the trappings of adventure and gadgets, space races and long journeys to faraway lands. Of course, children cannot realize such dramatic dreams. They only imagine what it's like to ride in a space ship or dive thousands of feet into the ocean's depths. Well, Sagittarius/Tigers are exactly the same. They fantasize about great adventures. But they never go further than their own backyards. Oh, yes, they will take long walks into the mountains, discover ruins and memorize each stone. But these very dear, funny people never leave home for long.

Not that Sagittarius/Tigers don't move around a lot. They most certainly do. They're the drive-overnight-to-Jerry's-and-hurry- back-twelve-hours-of-winding-roads-to-be-on-time-to-open-the-store-at-eight-in-the-morning type. Or they can take trips for business purposes and not ever feel homesick. Sagittarius/Tigers are not sticky barnacles. But they favor the path of least resistance. They'd rather stay with those of whom they are sure than go hunting up new friends or trying to seduce an unfamiliar partner. Even though adventure remains the biggest part of the Sagittarius/Tiger's life, it almost always remains inside his mind.

Socially the Sagittarius/Tiger is by turns extroverted and withdrawn. This unevenness comes, I believe, from the fact that frequently this person is forced out of his environment by his impetuous Tiger side, yet when he gets to the party, he's instantly bored and wishes he were home inside his head again. Tiger keeps trying to erupt this person onto the social scene but Sagittarius is more interested in keeping him occupied with books and causes. It happens that the Sagittarius/Tiger grows so uncomfortable with the pressures of interaction in society—especially with unfamiliar people—that, out of embarrassment, he misbehaves. The Sagittarius/Tiger can be that woman in the center of the room with the big mouth, telling off-color jokes and secretly wishing she were anywhere but there.

This person is a keen observer. He or she may attend gatherings or join in group activities solely for the purpose of watching. Sagittarius/Tiger is aware of everything, sensitive to a forearm hair to tone and atmosphere. He or she will be fascinated by novelty and eccentricity. If the Sagittarius/Tiger becomes interested in something, he or she will usually track it down and find out all there is to know about it. In this way the Sagittarius/Tiger builds an inner library of characters about whom he knows everything. It's a singular hobby, but one native to the Sagittarius/Tiger. I call it "people-collecting."

Of course this person is dealt a reckless and outspoken personality by birth. He is a victim of both Sagittarian and Tiger recklessness and swagger hotheadedness and vacillation. This makes him sometimes seem interfering when he's only trying to be helpful. But these character traits also give punch to whatever the Sagittarius/Tiger does in his life. As with other Tiger subjects, the inner goal must begin with temperance. Slow down, Sagittarius/Tiger, and think before you leap, turn your tongue around seven times before speaking and don't be so sure that public opinion is all wet. Every time you venture out into the world, try to remember to pick up a quart or two of wisdom.

Love

The romantic sector is a difficult one for the Sagittarius/Tiger. First of all, he or she will not trust easily. Tigers are always watching for flaws and picking up subtle little negative signs from others. Tigers are magnetic. Sagittarians are open-handed and solicitous. This person will seem amenable to starting a relationship. But don't get her wrong. What you can see is only the very tippy-top of a very complex iceberg. The Sagittarius/Tiger's easy generosity can quickly turn sour. She may grow cynical if disappointed. This person wants to be handled with utmost care. "Don't take me for granted!" should be inscribed on all her T-shirts. Sagittarius/Tiger is a false grandee. But then, this bumptious, kindly sort never wears her heart on her sleeve.

Should you be attracted to one of these people, step carefully. Manipulate deftly, and proceed with caution. The Sagittarian Tiger needs reassurance and loving care, but he or she will never come right out and ask for it. If I were you, I would offer this light- of-your-life type a good logical excuse for coming around to your place: Ask her if she can teach you to cook, or get him to come over and show you how to parallel park.

Compatibilities

You can depend on the love of Aries, Leo, Libra and Aquarius/ Horses. They serve your causes well, and give good sound advice. Leo, Libra and Aquarius/Dogs warm your cockles as well. You can relate to their devotion. No cigar with Virgos, Geminis or Pisces born in Ox, Cat or Snake years. Virgo and Pisces/Monkeys rub you the wrong way. And Geminis born in Sheep years strike you as irretrievably frivolous.

Home and Family

The Sagittarius/Tiger's home doesn't matter much to him. He would surely like it comfortable and easy to live in. But as this person is often a bachelor until middle years and doesn't really want to grow up, he or she may not bother with interior decoration. There will always be cold drinks in the fridge and a good stereo system playing fine music. But the most a Sagittarian Tiger needs is a nest for dreaming of desert islands where the nests are made of straw and the sun never sets.

This person is not overly family-oriented. Everybody can have children, however, so if he or she becomes a parent I'd reckon they would be the kind to be pals with their kids, taking them to baseball games and teaching them how to water ski. The Sagittarius/Tiger is a bit of a worrywart about others and will always take time to listen to children's woes, comfort them when they're sad and truly empathize when they are feeling misunderstood. The Sagittarian Tiger parent won't be a disciplinarian. He thinks everybody—especially he—should be free.

The Sagittarius/Tiger child will be warm and loving company for parents. He will enjoy homely pleasures like playing Monopoly with Mom and Dad, or the joys of preparing for Christmas together. The best thing about this child is his willingness to watch out for danger and to look after himself and other kids. This child will be inventive and hardworking. He or she will love electronic games.

Profession

This native is both hard-driving and tireless when at work. Sagittarius/Tigers are ambitious people who don't much care for what others think of the means they employ to achieve their ends. For this last reason, these folks are especially able to take over on unproven projects that observers may not approve of. Sagittarian Tigers often undertake ventures of vast scope. Breadth of field appeals to their dauntless explorer side. They like to envision grandeur and pomp but don't much care for chains of command or hierarchic hypocrisies,

The Sagittarius/Tiger is not usually concerned about who's boss. He or she is most interested in getting on with work on a scale unconnected to routine. Their hope is always to escape the humdrum and somehow transcend workaday jobs.

Although they can be efficient employees, Sagittarius/Tigers may feel they know better than their boss. These natives are best off on their own, doing their own things, running businesses or writing poems. They are good at jobs requiring frequent travel. No matter what career this fiery subject chooses, you can be sure that his life itself, morning till night, is a trip. Work is his or her best form of expression.

Jobs that might suit this person are: physicist, city planner, postman, roadie, preacher, actor/actress, athlete, journalist, fund-raiser, traveling salesperson, NASA engineer.

Famous Sagittarius/Tigers:
Alec Newman, Andrew McCarthy, Beethoven, Ben Browder, Cristina Onassis, Darleen Carr, Ed Harris, Emily Dickinson, Emma

Bell, Felicity Huffman, Giovanni Ribisi, Hailee Steinfeld, Heather Donahue, James Hinchcliffe, Janine Turner, Johnny Simmons, Joseph Gatt, Katie Cassidy, Leonard Maltin, Liane Foly, Liv Ullmann, Margaret Whitton, Marissa Ribisi, Martin Van Buren, Ralph Fiennes, Sammy Davis, Sarah Paulson, Stephen Merchant, Tracy Austin, Trevor Morgan, Wassily Kandinsky, Wendie Malick.

SAGITTARIUS
QUALITIES
CHEERFULNESS, OPENHANDEDNESS,
SOLICITUDE, VALOR, HONOR, REASON
QUIRKS
OUTSPOKENNESS, RECKLESSNESS,
BAD MANNERS, VACILLATION,
CARELESSNESS, CONTRADICTION
Motto: *"I see"*
Elements: *Fire, Jupiter, Mutable*

--

CAT/RABBIT
QUALITIES
TACT, FINESSE, VIRTUE,
PRUDENCE, LONGEVITY, AMBITION,
QUIRKS
SECRETIVENESS, SQUEAMISHNESS,
PEDANTRY, DILETTANTISM,
HYPOCHONDRIA, COMPLEXITY
Motto: *"I Retreat"*
Elements: *Negative, Wood, Yin*

The prudent Cat side of this couple tugs at the Sagittarian's carefree arrow till he snaps it loose. It falls to the ground before leaving the bow. In other words, in this person the recklessness of Sagittarius is defused by the Cat's virtue and sense of measure. This Sagittarian is not so brash as his brothers and sisters. A Sagittarian born in a Cat year will be sensitive to his real surroundings, aware of the need for diplomacy and, because of the Cat's serious ambition, sagaciously yoked to his or her career.

There is a spirited melancholy in this person's makeup. The Sagittarian born Cat seems to have been improved or pepped up through sorrow, tempered by loss or hurt. He is buoyant yet resigned to certain bitter truths that others prefer to ignore. The Sagittarius/Cat does not surrender to this mournful air, but rather exploits it well, using a sad smile to appeal to millions. This Sagittarian, honed to a fine edge by his careful Cat side, is able to synthesize his energies sufficiently to create a powerful self-image. Armed with this overwhelming sense of self, the Sagittarian Cat can confront almost any form of opposition. Not that he goes looking for trouble, but he is not afraid of adversity. Defiance is his natural habitat. He is bold and dares to achieve dominance and to overcome competition.

The Sagittarius/Cat is also clever enough to know how to hold on to his hard-earned position. He feeds his public just what they need to continue to be addicted to his wares. The Sagittarius/Cat dispenses great gobs of understated love to his fans and, as a result, he keeps them on his side. People believe in the Sagittarius/Cat because he understands the delicate blend of solicitude and command necessary to seduce throngs.

Taking oneself seriously can be a giant pain in the neck for intimates and onlookers. But in the case of such directed people as Sagittarius/Cats, arrogance and an air of self-satisfaction seem natural. Or at least this character knows how to make them seem natural. It's true that the Sagittarian born Cat puts himself on a pedestal and renders his person untouchable. But that's all part of the mystique that works so well. The Sagittarius/Cat is highly individualistic. His or her methods are always unusual. They may be unscrupulous, and if they don't succeed (and many don't) in enticing their audience, in captivating crowds and convincing millions, Sagittarius/Cats are wise enough to know when they are beaten.

Generally, the Sagittarius/Cat is an amiable fellow. Good cheer emanates from his aura. The Cat's sense of elegance and presentation quells almost all the Sagittarian's natural bumptiousness, and leaves us just that smidgen of vulgarity we like to call "the common touch." Cats born in Sagittarius conform to social norms and care deeply about what others think of them. They are not easy to figure out and have no intention of becoming so. This is a brave Cat and a toned-down Sagittarian. It's a very strong marriage held together by a bond of self-interest.

Love

This person tends to engage in multiple subsequent relationships. There is a great deal of sexual energy here. Much of the energy is, of course, covert and pent up. One doesn't think of any Cat subject as a sex maniac. But the Sagittarius/Cat is a bit of a tom. He skulks about marking territories and claiming some that don't even belong to him. By the same token, she may not hesitate to "cat around" with other people's mates. The Sagittarius/Cat is not really unfaithful. But the need to be admired is so enormous here that sexual fidelity is impossible. Personal fidelity is, however, very serious for this character. He may love 'em and leave 'em, but he never forgets those he has cared for, and is careful to keep old friendships alive.

So you are in love with a Sagittarius/Cat? My suggestion is that you look up to him or her. Stroke and cuddle this mettlesome Cat, but don't try to keep her by the fireside. You must remember that your admiration is pleasant to her, but it's never going to be enough. This person needs to be loved by a cast of thousands. If you can keep from being jealous of your Sagittarian Cat's large following and put up with her constant primping and preening in front of prospective admirers, I guess you can take the heat. But I don't think long-term affairs or marriages with this crowd-pleaser are meant to be shared by any but self-sacrificing types.

Compatibilities

Aries, Leo and Aquarius/Dogs know instinctively how to touch your deepest emotions and make wonderful lovers for your personality type. Leo, Libra and Aquarius/Pigs are also on sympathetic terms with you, as are Aries and Aquarius/Sheep. The Aries/Snake woos you without half trying. But Gemini, Virgo and Pisces/Roosters and their Tiger counterparts conspire to put you on edge. Tell them to pick on somebody their own size.

Home and Family

The Sagittarian Cat's home will be in many places at once. This nature is itinerant, and for the enormous objectives of the Sagittarius/Cat to be fulfilled, he or she must be able to travel—first class all the way. No question about that. Because he is, after all, a Cat, this person may well have one place he considers home. It will most likely be situated in the deep, remote countryside. There, he or she will have installed many comforts, a few domestics or even a second family—and of course, I almost forgot, the bodyguards.

The Sagittarius/Cat parent is very self-involved. These people often marry and have kids but they will probably leave the rearing of children to a homebody mate. This person won't be available to small fry. But as the children grow and become really able to communicate, the Sagittarius/Cat parent is likely to take a friendly interest. This parent is of the do-what-I-say-and-not-what-I-do school of education. Strict and even, boarding-school oriented.

The Sagittarius/Cat child is certainly talented for theater or music, athletics or even public speaking and debate. The ability to captivate audiences is what shows through first with this smiling babe. He or she must be encouraged to pursue these talents and given every opportunity to use them in a disciplined fashion. Try, while your Sagittarius/Cat child is still malleable and young, to increase his or her willingness to communicate on a one-to-one level. You may find this child introverted except when called upon to perform. He or she will aspire to greatness and have much appeal.

Profession

The talents of the Sagittarius/Cat, be they artistic or commercial, mechanical or technical, are all-encompassing. In other words, this person will have a major gift and be able to exploit that main talent. He or she must be very careful not to disperse energies in personal dramas or dilute talents by trying to do a variety of unrelated things. They can and will go far if they keep their sights fixed on success in one well defined area—theirs.

The Sagittarian Cat is a loner. He or she can open a business, or run a factory and manage almost any amount of work. Too, these people have a special appeal for groups. They can take charge in an office situation. But they must be allowed free rein, and as that is not always possible, I suggest this person try to be self-employed. Sagittarians born in Cat years want their own way too much to knuckle under to systems and strict hours. They are self-directed.

Some suitable careers for Sagittarius/Cats might be: politician, jockey, tour guide, diplomat, actor/actress, dancer, singer, restaurant owner, supermarket manager, religious leader, musician.

Famous Sagittarius/Cat/Rabbits:

Aaron Carter, Arjuna Ranatunga, Augusto Pinochet, Ben Tudhope, Benjamin Bratt, Brad Pitt, Brendan Coyle, David Yates, Edith Piaf, Elena Satine, Emmanuelle Chriqui, Fisher Stevens, Frank Sinatra, Hallee Hirsh, Helen Slater, James Mangold, Jennifer Beals, Jonathan Scarfe, Joshua Sasse, KaDee Strickland, Karen Gillan, Kathryn Bigelow, Mayim Bialik, Michael Angarano, Michael Socha, Milla Jovovich, Morgan Brittany, Paula Patton, Sia, Sonja Morgan, Sunny Mabrey, Til Schweiger, Tina Turner, Treat Williams, Ulrich Thomsen, Wendell Pierce.

SAGITTARIUS
QUALITIES
CHEERFULNESS, OPENHANDEDNESS,
SOLICITUDE, VALOR, HONOR, REASON
QUIRKS
OUTSPOKENNESS, RECKLESSNESS,
BAD MANNERS, VACILLATION,
CARELESSNESS, CONTRADICTION
Motto: *"I see"*
Elements: *Fire, Jupiter, Mutable*

--

DRAGON
QUALITIES
STRENGTH, SUCCESS, GOOD HEALTH,
ENTHUSIASM, PLUCK, SENTIMENTALITY
QUIRKS
RIGIDITY, MISTRUST, DISSATISFACTION,
INFATUATION, BRAGGADOCIO, VOLUBILITY
Motto: *"I Preside"*
Elements: *Positive Wood, Yang*

An admirable but not always gentle character, the Sagittarius/ Dragon is a warrior on the grand scale. These people are attractive and ambitious. They believe in success and forge ahead with bravura toward that aim. Never bullish or hotheaded, this character's style is gentlemanly and dignified. Sagittarius/ Dragons are not afraid of danger. They take great risks and even court peril. They dance around the flame of adventure and derring-do but they rarely get seriously burned. Dragons born in Sagittarius outwit their enemies, hoist them on their own petards and invite them to lunch the next day. Victory, after all, calls for a celebration.

There is no arrogance in this method. The Sagittarius/Dragon sees no reason to snub people or lord his superiority over them. On the contrary, this character will be the jolly sort of idealist who beckons one and all to follow his dreams, brandish his flags and fly his colors. Sagittarius/Dragons are not selfish or stingy. They want the best for everybody involved—yet they definitely feel that everybody should be involved in the Sagittarian Dragon's project.

This person is a visionary and can initiate enterprises single-handedly. He or she can carry off deals and draw conclusions and make decisions without raising an eyebrow. But they don't like complication. They deplore deceit. Woe unto him who cheats a Sagittarian Dragon. The Dragon won't harm the offender. Not on your life. She will simply never trust him again, which, coming from this honorable character, is a low blow.

You see, the Sagittarius/Dragon is an optimist. He or she wants to believe in the basic goodness of mankind. These people are not naive, nor are they innocents who need protection. Rather, Sagittarius/Dragons are natural leaders who need good lieutenants, whips, exchequers, advisers, cabinet ministers, wives, husbands and careful, deliberate and faithful helpers who protect this hasty idealist from himself.

Sagittarius is outspoken and open-handed. Dragons are also very generous and giving. They both love parties and want to make life more festive. The Sagittarian and the Dragon both want to increase the scope of their operations, to encompass larger and larger groups and spheres of influence where they can impose their theories and try their methods. If left completely to their own devices, these benevolent despots might glad-hand themselves out of the race. So they must seek wise counsel and follow the advice of more conservative souls.

The combination of Sagittarius and Dragon must struggle against a little voice inside them which urges them onward no matter what. This person wants more than anything to prove that he or she can. Usually, there is no doubt in anybody's mind but that of the Sagittarian Dragon himself. Nonetheless, this person can be overly optimistic and enterprising because he wants to show the world how right he is. And very often he is right. But once in a while the Sagittarian Dragon has to pick himself up and straighten out his disjointed nose because of hasty decision-making or acting on false hunches.

The Dragon born in Sagittarius can be snappish and sometimes caustic, but is most often merciful and kind toward others. His is not a cozy fire but rather a crackling, vigorous conflagration that burns as a beacon for people he likes and wants to help. There is something of the Dragon Prince here, something noble and mythical that bespeaks munificence and power. A mightier combination one can hardly hope to find.

Love

The Dragon born in the sign of Sagittarius will marry when the time is right. Of course these people, with their hearty enthusiasms and eager aspirations, are appealing. Yet, the Sagittarius/Dragon himself is not interested solely in attraction. He will go looking for a true helpmate when he sets out in adult life. No Dragon—especially a Sagittarian Dragon—ever thinks small. This one imagines a giant future with scads of children and horses and businesses and expanded families. This Dragon is not about to marry Mickey Mouse. This Dragon wants quality. And don't you know, he or she usually gets just that.

If one of these swashbucklers has caught your eye, I daresay you are in for quite a ride. The Sagittarius/Dragon mate will keep you on your toes, busy, busy, busy. If you are in the least phlegmatic, stay away from this vivacious dynamo. But if you want to work side by side with someone whose ideals appeal to you and whose cause you are not afraid to champion, then go after your Sagittarius/Dragon love. But don't ever disappoint this character or fail to keep your part of the bargain. Sagittarius/Dragon is sentimental and devoted to those closest to his or her heart.

Compatibilities

You are a very popular partner indeed. Aries, Leo, Libra and Aquarius are your compatible western astrological signs. From within their ranks you can best be loved by Aries/Ox, Tiger, Monkey and Pig; Leo/Rat, Monkey or Rooster; Libra/Tiger and Monkey, or Aquarius/Rat and Monkey. These are your allies. Now for your detractors: all of them Dogs of the Gemini, Virgo and Pisces persuasions. Now that wasn't so hard, was it?

Home and Family

Luxury doesn't come first for the Sagittarius/Dragon. But status does. The Sagittarius born under the sign of Dragon will not be likely to hang his coat of arms over a door in just any old part of town. This subject wants to live in the "best" neighborhood, send his or her kids to the "right" schools, and will be sure to shop in all the "finest" emporia. Pared-down opulence and originality will characterize the abode of Sagittarius/Dragon. "Let's turn the attic into an office and tear up the bathroom tile and put in an aquarium." Sagittarius/Dragon likes to do things with imagination and style.

The Sagittarius/Dragon is a born parent. This person leads well and takes responsibility seriously. Moreover, parenting and protecting, nurturing and looking after others gives the Dragon born Sagittarius real personal gratification. He or she will be firm and insist kids stay close to the family circle while growing up. No child will be made to feel insecure so long as he has a Sagittarius/Dragon for a Mom or Dad. These folks are notorious for taking care of their own. They pile everybody in the car and leave on vacation as a gang, pack picnic lunches, and hike up the mountainside along with the best of them.

As a child this person will probably be bubbly and enthusiastic. She will invariably get involved in group projects of which she is the chief. These kids are usually popular with school friends and playmates. Teachers appreciate their willingness to lead, but may sometimes feel a shade threatened by the Sagittarius/Dragon's sense of superiority. There is nothing this child feels he or she cannot accomplish, so sometimes they are sorely disappointed in themselves. You can talk to them directly and not fear breaking their spirit; these little people are tough and capable. They should be taught patience.

Profession

What a Dragon born in Sagittarius sets out to do, he means to see accomplished. This person manifestly wants what he wants when he wants it. Now, obviously this self-belief has its drawbacks. Nobody is invincible, least of all the most sentimental Dragon of them all, Sagittarius. But that deeply emotional foible is precisely what makes him or her so charming. Many of the Sagittarian Dragon's battles are inadvertently won by virtue of this happy personality quirk. What looks like a rock is actually a marshmallow. But as it talks and acts like a rock, nobody can tell the difference. Tricky, no?

The Sagittarius/Dragon will probably not want to play any game where he or she is not the leader. This is a beloved boss, a person who commands great respect from employees and associates. Another cleverness of this combined sign is that he or she knows when to stand back and let events take over. This character can be hasty but is sometimes surprisingly wise as well.

Careers that suit this person are: nursery school director, bookstore owner, TV producer, insurance magnate, banker, entrepreneur, builder, politician, senator, lawyer, theologian, business consultant, writer, editor, publisher.

Famous Sagittarius/Dragons:
Alfred Enoch, Amy Acker, Anna Faris, Anna Popplewell, Ashley Grace., Betty Grable, Bruce Lee, Chadwick Boseman, Chuck Man-

gione, Conleth Hill, Dominic Monaghan, Don Cheadle, Emily Browning Zoë Kravitz, Francisco Franco, Frank Zappa, Garret Dillahunt, Jenny Agutter, Louisa May Alcott, Mandy Patinkin, Marisa Tomei, Mark Duplass, Michael Dorn, Nathan Adrian, Noam Chomsky, Richard Brake, Richard Pryor, Robert Laffont, Ross Bagley, Ryan Kwanten, Samantha Lewes, Susan Dey, Tamsin Egerton, Teri Hatcher, Vanessa Hudgens, Zachary Taylor.

SAGITTARIUS
QUALITIES
CHEERFULNESS, OPENHANDEDNESS,
SOLICITUDE, VALOR, HONOR, REASON
QUIRKS
OUTSPOKENNESS, RECKLESSNESS,
BAD MANNERS, VACILLATION,
CARELESSNESS, CONTRADICTION
Motto: *"I see"*
Elements: *Fire, Jupiter, Mutable*

--

SNAKE
QUALITIES
INTUITION, ATTRACTIVENESS, DISCRETION,
SAGACITY, CLAIRVOYANCE, COMPASSION
QUIRKS
DISSIMULATION, EXTRAVAGANCE,
LAZINESS, CUPIDITY, PRESUMPTION,
EXCLUSIVENESS
Motto: *"I sense"*
Elements: *Negative, Fire, Yin*

Solicitude personified, the Sagittarius/Snake cares for those he loves and admires, and looks after everything from home to car interior with a sense of concern that makes Florence Nightingale look like a slouch. This is a creature of dignity and bearing whose manners and taste for refinement are second only to an unparalleled devotion to virtue. The Sagittarian Snake is a human luxury item, without the expensive price tag.

This character is never noisy or boisterous. Yet much gets said. The Sagittarius/Snake waves no banners, makes no waves. Yet he is zealously involved in championing causes. This person keeps his counsel and recoils before conflict. Yet he communicates expertly, untangles complex arguments, and just about never loses an inning.

Thing is, people born in this combination of signs are singularly motivated to rise above their station or birthright. The average successful Sagittarius/Snake is someone who has started small and known how to slither up and through the ranks without hue or cry because he or she wanted a better life. This person is an idealist. He or she is pure of heart and straightforward, yet discreet.

To the Snake born in Sagittarius, the act of exerting oneself is visible proof of moral rectitude. Unlike so many of their serpentine counterparts, Sagittarius/Snakes are not lazy, and sincerely do not mind getting up to fetch you that drink or going out in the snow to run four miles a day. In their quiet way, these people are powerhouses of energy. As they are stealthy and never seem in a hurry, you would never guess at their efficiency. But what they can accomplish in one day without a sound or a hair out of place is astounding.

Too, Sagittarius/Snakes are organizational wizards. Give them a broken-down office structure or an unruly bunch of children for a few days and they will put everything to rights. Their manner is never splashy or harsh. But the firm set of their mouths tells you that these pristine characters don't fool around. When it comes to getting the basement cleaned, watch their style.

Sagittarius/Snakes are not ones to take risks. They are neither cowardly nor fearful. They like sports and practice everything from skiing to skydiving without a second's hesitation. But they don't go around jousting with danger or looking for adventure in speleology or big game hunting. Similarly, in their daily life, Sagittarius/ Snakes don't go tempting the devil. They are wont to enjoy the comforts of a good thing, and readily know when they have caught one by the tail.

The Snake born in Sagittarius doesn't meddle. He will not gossip or mix in affairs that don't directly involve him. These people are curious enough, but will not go out of their way to uncover someone's motives. They are not uninterested in the business of others, but they are by nature judicious. The Sagittarius/Snake feels that each of us has carved out a niche in life and that he likes his just fine. He hopes you are also comfy in yours, but he will probably not pry far enough to find out.

Love

Sagittarians often marry late. Sagittarius/Snakes sometimes don't marry at all. They do tend, however, to enjoy a few high-quality long-term relationships of a profound and intimate type. Often, Sagittarius/Snakes engage lovers and/or mates in long, serious discussions. They have a confidential air about them that awakens the snoop in some. "What can he be thinking?" one may wonder. "Such a strong silent type," others may remark. When they are in love, Sagittarian Snakes exhibit amazing dedication. They are usually faithful because to be promiscuous would strike them as vulgar and superficial.

If you love one of these classy types I advise you to clean up your act fast. If you want to keep the Sagittarius/Snake in the style to which he has accustomed himself, you will have to learn how to live quietly and elegantly, never to raise your voice and even learn how to jog and stay on a diet. Wisdom above all is the Sagittarius/Snake's motto. Carelessness offends his sensibilities. So be cool and don't show your hand. The Sagittarius/Snake loves mystery.

Compatibilities

Affiliations with Oxen of the Leo, Libra and Aquarius schools will be positive and engender prosperity. You'll also establish complicity with Aries and Aquarius/Roosters. Such relationships flourish best in urban environments. Virgos, Geminis and Pisceans are not your favorite people, particularly Gemini/Monkey, Virgo/ Tiger and Pig, and Pisces/Tiger, Monkey and Pig natives.

Home and Family

This person's home will be first, last and always attractive. The basis of his or her lifestyle is peacefulness and a constant quest for refinement. The Sagittarius/Snake will prefer antiques to modern furnishings. He or she will go in for the real thing in jewelry, paintings, and even in roofing and siding. The Sagittarius/Snake is an authenticity freak. He pursues the truth right down to the last mohair on his overcoat. She only wears cashmere sweaters if she can help it. With Sagittarius/Snake, it's no glitz all the way.

This person will make a fabulously creative and interested parent. The comforts of home will be offered little Cameron and Olivia by the dozen. Each child will be carefully followed by everybody, from allergists to pierced-ear specialists. Perhaps the Sagittarius/ Snake can be accused of "overgreenhousing" his or her kids. The bathtub doesn't really have to be scrubbed with a velvet sponge after each use, does it? Seriously, children are extemporaneous at best; let them take risks even if they break a bone or two. It helps them learn about life outside the greenhouse.

A baby Sagittarius/Snake will show early signs of meticulousness, and suffer enormously from discord and household disruptions. This child needs a quiet intellectual environment and plenty of countrified experience to ease him into the future. He or she will be outgoing and loving toward other kids. Also, parent-pleasing is a by-product of this kid's whole persona. The little Sagittarius/Snake wants his folks to be proud of him or her. They will bend over backwards to make a sad Mom or Dad smile.

Profession

All jobs that require caring for others are suitable for this solid citizen type. He or she will naturally prefer careers that allow for dealing with people, organizing or solving sticky human problems. Paperwork doesn't annoy the Sagittarius/Snake outrageously, and he or she works well in all areas demanding attention to detail.

The Sagittarius/Snake makes an excellent, sane, and quiet-spoken boss. He or she will endeavor to be just in all delegation of labor, and will probably not play favorites. This person is a model employee. As long as their hair doesn't get too messed up or their personal routine disrupted, Sagittarius/Snakes move along smoothly and rarely balk. This person makes an excellent entrepreneur, as he or she will be a self-starter—and finisher!

Jobs that best suit the Sagittarius/Snake are: maître d'hotel, hostess, physician, nurse, philosopher, psychiatrist, decorator, surgeon, dentist, gardener, florist, dog trainer, astrologer, researcher, chef, shepherd.

Famous Sagittarius/Snakes:

Adelaide Clemens, Antoine de Caunes, Ashley Benson, Beatrice Rosen, Beau Bridges, Ben Stiller, Bess Armstrong, Bill Pullman, Colin Hanks, David Harewood, Dionne Warwick, Dougray Scott, Eddie Rabbit, Emily Wheaton, Francis Cabrel, Geoff Stults, Howard Hughes, Jeffrey Wright, Jessica Steen, Jill Flint, John Davidson, John Malkovich, Katheryn Winnick, Kim Basinger, Leslie Stahl, Matthias Schoenaerts, Nate Torrence, Nicholas Hoult, Nichole Bloom, Ossie Davis, Pierre Brasseur, Pope John XXIII, Ryan Murphy, Shirley Henderson, Taylor Swift, Ted Raimi, Vijay Amritraj.

SAGITTARIUS
QUALITIES
CHEERFULNESS, OPENHANDEDNESS,
SOLICITUDE, VALOR, HONOR, REASON
QUIRKS
OUTSPOKENNESS, RECKLESSNESS,
BAD MANNERS, VACILLATION,
CARELESSNESS, CONTRADICTION
Motto: *"I see"*
Elements: *Fire, Jupiter, Mutable*

--

HORSE
QUALITIES
PERSUASIVENESS, UNSCRUPULOUSNESS,
POPULARITY, STYLE, DEXTERITY,
ACCOMPLISHMENT
QUIRKS
SELFISHNESS, AUTONOMY, REBELLION,
HASTE, ANXIETY, PRAGMATISM
Motto: *"I demand"*
Elements: *Positive Fire, Yang*

A great striding Horse figure, the Sagittarius/Horse is three-quarters Horse and only one part man. As they say in westerns, "That's a lot of horse!" Interestingly, this person is more head than beast. The Sagittarian born Horse operates first out of homespun values, next in search of self-control, and thirdly he concentrates on finding and achieving a goal.

Sagittarius/Horses are never tired. Black circles under their eyes, facial features dragging on the sidewalk and skin the color of pigeon feathers mean nothing to this veritable generator of a person.

"You must be exhausted," one says after they have stayed up three days and nights working on a schedule that would have long since silenced Brazil. The Sagittarius/Horse glances at you as though you'd asked her name. "Me? Tired? Never!" And it's true. These people work until they drop.

The Sagittarius/Horse has good manners. These develop quite naturally through the years because Sagittarian Horses are concerned with social graces and involve themselves readily in matters of social class. I won't say the Sagittarian born Horse is a snob, but almost. In any case, he or she is a person who longs to be set apart from the horde. Sagittarius/Horse takes pleasure in being different.

Born under this dual sign of caring and pragmatism, the Sagittarius/Horse subject represents the perfect blend of these two qualities. He or she will take up causes and go for broke on committees the way Sagittarians do, but they will only sacrifice their time to such "isms" and beliefs that they expect to have feasible outcomes. These people are too practical to dream the utterly impossible dream.

The Horse born in Sagittarius wants to be the star of his or her own life. They are not particularly attracted by worldly celebrity, but rather forge ahead for the purpose of gaining self-respect through their success. The Sagittarius/Horse has high ideals for himself, for his work and for the work of those close to him. Pleasure is important only insofar as it gives release from tension and anxiety, and in that way increases productivity in work. This Horse will be the pivotal element in his home or workplace; those who circulate around him or her will do so by virtue of the Sagittarius/Horse's generosity of both spirit and pocketbook.

If poverty could bring the Sagittarius/Horse happiness and freedom from worry, I don't think he would mind being without money. But this is a person who requires a solid framework where he feels in control. Frameworks don't come cheap these days. Somebody has to pay the rent and insurance, utilities and cleaning people. For this reason penury threatens the well-being of Sagittarius/Horse. His security comes from without. So it must be bought.

The Sagittarius/Horse may seem marginal to some. He or she sometimes has outrageous notions. Thing is, their type of nonconformity is only strange and outlandish insofar as it reflects off something more traditional. Hence the Sagittarius/Horse may seem weird and unusual sometimes, but his style of weirdness is dependent on the contrast to society's humdrum. Sagittarius/Horses are not so bohemian as to become hermits or poets who move to remote places and avoid all worldly contact. They are so tempted to put in their two cents that they cannot remain forever out of the mainstream.

Early recklessness can prompt unwise judgments. But the Sagittarius/Horse grows wiser with age. He soon learns how to keep his word, to provide and care for family and close collaborators, to stand quietly back waiting for the right opportunity. Galloping is for kids. Life, according to the mature Sagittarius/Horse, should be lived at a pleasant canter, never too fast and never too slow, but always going in the same direction—forward.

Love

Early on, the Sagittarius/Horse will make at least one or two false moves in romance. This character is born ardent. His wild oats are plentiful. But when age creeps up, the Sagittarius/Horse learns to control his or her beastly side and seeks a partner who can fit into the framework of which I spoke earlier. Sagittarius/Horse does not want a namby-pamby, obedient partner who never questions her opinions. But he may want someone to look after the details of home and family while Sagittarius is busy providing for everybody's porridge. Above all, this person wants no interference, and prefers to make it clear from day one that love is serious business for him or her. Hanky-panky will be excluded in favor of application of fanny to seat of chair or nose to grindstone.

If you care for a Sagittarius/Horse, don't get hung up on him or her. Be your own person. Represent a mental challenge. Play a little hard to get. But don't ever think you will turn this autonomous person around to your way of living. It is you who will have to learn to get up at five A.M. and let the cat in, make the coffee, and pack Sagittarius/Horse's suitcase for a trip to Dallas. And where is the Sagittarius/Horse all this time? On the phone to Bonn or Rome or London, jabbering on about deals and plans and more deals. Sagittarius/Horse's mission comes first. Whatever yours is will automatically be less important.

Compatibilities

With your drive for personal success, you'll be needing a patient, serious partner to share your life. Take a mate from Aries, Libra, Leo or Aquarius, who was hatched in a Tiger year. Or better still, if you can trap one, get an Aries, Leo or Libra/Sheep. They are ever so much more patient with your comings and goings. A Libra or Aquarius/Dog will stand by you through thick and thin, too. Contrarily, I advise you against Virgo, Gemini or Pisces/Rats.

Home and Family

The homes of Sagittarians born in Horse years are either somebody else's rented taste, and decor or, at best, decorated by their mate. The only part of his home that really interests the Sagitta-rius/Horse is the work area. It can be a den or a basement tool room or atelier or studio or office or utility room, but it must be all his own. Here, the stamp of equine practicality will shine. High tech is an understatement: track lighting, and Formica desks with large-surfaced tops, and computer terminals galore! The rest? Those cou-ches you wanted from *Roche et Bobois...* all right, sure, buy them. Sagittarius/Horse is generous but he or she is not up to paying at-tention to fripfrap. Clothes will follow the same pattern: comfort-able and classical with the odd departure from beige and navy blue into gray flannel. Yellow? Only for costume balls.

The Sagittarius/Horse parent provides. Kids will be seen and even heard, but Mom or Dad Sagittarius/Horse may not have scads of time to play tiddlywinks with them. These are busy, energetic par-ents whose athletic talents are reserved for their own sports inter-ests and who, anyway, have a bit of difficulty stooping to crawling on the floor with toddlers. Noblesse prevents.

As a child this person will be talented for all sports activities. Teachers may accuse the Sagittarian Horse of adding fantasy to her work. This is the kid who repeatedly draws pictures of her dog in the margin of her math papers. It doesn't occur to the teacher that maybe she's bored out of her mind. Instead this kid is often scolded for daydreaming.

At home this child will be obedient and loving. He or she wants to be included in all activities and may even seek to take over the management of group efforts. Frankly, the Sagittarius/Horse woul-dn't mind being an only child. These people love control.

Profession

This person's talents lie in areas requiring insight and a keen sense of observation and caring. All careers involving people and their tri-als and tribulations will suit the Sagittarius/Horse. They are gifted for organization and management. They have natural presence and poise and know how to meet the public. Bossing comes naturally to this leader type. But the Sagittarius/Horse is not classically bossy. He or she will be directive and mutely authoritarian. A smile always ac-companies an order or request. The Sagittarius/ Horse makes a terri-fic employee, too. They are serious and responsible people who care about getting ahead. What more could any employer want? As for working alone, the Sagittarius/Horse can be a creative self-starter, but he prefers working in groups to functioning alone.

Some suitable careers for Sagittarius/Horses are: physical educa-tion teacher, cattle rancher, real estate developer, writer, diplomat, golf pro, football coach, actor, actress, journalist, market analyst, politician, orchestra leader, psychiatrist.

Famous Sagittarius/Horses:

Aimee Garcia, Alexander Solzhenitsyn, Andy Williams, Billy Burke, Bob Guccione, Buck Henry, C. Thomas Howell, Diego Boneta, Don Yesso, G. Gordon Liddy, Ian Somerhalder, James Thurber, Jean-Louis Trintignant, Jean-Luc Godard, Jimi Hendrix, Joanna 'JoJo' Levesque, Joel Coen, Katherine Heigl, Katherine LaNasa, Katie Holmes, Kiefer Sutherland, Kimmy Robertson, Kristin Bauer van Straten, Lauren German, Leonid Brezhnev, Maximilian Schell, Pierre Desgraupes, Rachel Brosnahan, Ray Liotta, Rita Ora, Sarah Hyland, Sinéad O'Connor, Tony Todd, Tyler Mane, Vincent Cassel.

SAGITTARIUS
QUALITIES
CHEERFULNESS, OPENHANDEDNESS,
SOLICITUDE, VALOR, HONOR, REASON
QUIRKS
OUTSPOKENNESS, RECKLESSNESS,
BAD MANNERS, VACILLATION,
CARELESSNESS, CONTRADICTION
Motto: *"I see"*
Elements: *Fire, Jupiter, Mutable*

--

SHEEP
QUALITIES
INVENTION, LACK OF FORESIGHT,
PERSEVERANCE, WHIMSY, GOOD MANNERS,
IMPRACTICALITY
QUIRKS
PARASITISM, SENSITIVITY,
TARDINESS, PESSIMISM, TASTE, WORRY
Motto: *"I depend"*
Elements: *Negative, Fire, Yin*

Sagittarius/Sheep enjoys a giant creativity. Invention and enterprise are second nature to this dynamic, clear-thinking soul. Yet, there is one rub. Sheep only function well when they feel secure. Lack of means or the threat of financial ruin, family schisms and personal jeopardies of all sorts will flummox this Sheep and throw him off his feed. The major struggle for this valiant and courageous character will revolve around getting and keeping protection for himself and family and friends.

The Sheep personality, with its built-in grace and charm, brings mannerliness and a taste for style to the sometimes overly rustic Sagittarius. In the case of this double sign, the Sagittarian gets to keep all of his solicitous instincts and shows great willingness to help others. But this Sheeply Sagittarius is not recklessly or inter-feringly helpful. This Sheep has finely tuned antennae that tell him when he is needed. Then, in a wink, he hops in the driver's seat and dashes to rescue the fair maiden in distress. Sagittarian Sheep have solutions for all your problems. They may suggest weirdo answers to dilemmas you would never dream up in a lifetime of cogitating. Or they may simply take your problem home with them and unravel it at their ease until three in the morning.

Time and schedules, hours for work and hours for play, and so on don't mean anything to Sagittarius/Sheep. They are relatively prompt as they care for and are polite to others. But chunks of organized time don't really exist in the minds of these altruistic creators. Sag-ittarius/Sheep like to catnap between four and six A.M., get up and drive through from California to Florida, and then go to sleep for three straight days. If she needs to sleep, she will. But in the mean-time, more important, is the project, the enterprise, the venture at hand. When that's done they can rest. Not before.

And with these perseverant innovators, whose enthusiasm for de-tail and works of great intricacy is dauntless and whose creativity is boundless, there is always another endeavor in the wind. Don't look now, but that Sagittarius/Sheep who just finished building her own ten-room house from scratch out of non-returnable soda bottles is about to embark on a study trip to Tibet. Of course, she won't leave until she has directed a new musical comedy show for the church benefit and installed her own central heating system. The Sagitta-rius/Sheep is indefatigably constructive.

The Sagittarius/Sheep is also a good judge of usefulness. He or she will be able to tell right off if a new lighting system or a pair of sawhorses will serve a defined purpose. These people have a good memory for detail, and yet sometimes slack off when it comes to attending to them. Final touches are not the province of the Sheep born in Sagittarius. He or she will be happy to think up the plot and work out the architecture and even draw you a plan for your next book, but when it comes to correcting spelling errors, they want someone else to take over. Their business is imagination.

Sometimes, because these people are so specifically conception-oriented, they come up with impractical schemes. There is not just one unfinished project in this subject's closet, there are thirty-one. Some plans just don't pan out. Sagittarius/Sheep never cry over spilt effort. They'd sooner think up some new earth-shaking device and go about gathering parts to put that together.

Love

Oddly circumspect in love relations, the Sagittarius/Sheep doesn't fit into the child bride or groom category. As we already know, the Sheep must have security. Without it, he flails and flounders and flubs. So until this person has amassed sufficient means and sorted out enough of life's daily problems to suit his or her need for self-safety, he will not be likely to take on the responsibility of someone else. This person has an independent streak where love is concerned, too, and doesn't want to be held down or limited in any way. Freedom is almost as important to the Sagittarius Sheep as love.

If you love a Sagittarius/Sheep person, you will certainly esteem him first. These inventive, interesting folks can always boast admirers by the dozen. They are mostly faithful in love affairs, as they are usually too busy with their projects to go bird-dogging. Besides, they have enough to worry about with one person to help and care for and drive and be interrupted by. You will best serve this character by learning how to take care of details he or she eschews. If you cook and clean as well, you can very quickly render yourself indispensable. The Sagittarian Sheep sometimes forgets to eat, and dirty dishes are his or her constant companion. Tiptoe a lot. Genius at work.

Compatibilities

Liaison is readily established between you and members of the Aries, Libra and Aquarius/Cat set. Leo, Libra and Aquarius/Pigs make excellent mates for you. They encourage your creative side. For some extra action, try an Aries/Horse. They inspire your admiration. A Gemini, Virgo or Pisces/Dog person will nag you and drive you to drink. Stay out of the way of Gemini/Tigers, and Virgo and Pisces/Oxen too.

Home and Family

If possible, this person will invariably choose to live in the countryside. Cities, with their noise and clatter, get in the way of the Sagittarius/Sheep's calm center. This character is attracted by solitude and silence. Starry nights tranquilize him. Thunder and lightning excite his poetic spirit. Sagittarius/Sheep need the proximity of the elements to help them restoke furnaces of energy depleted by the inhuman efforts for which they are so famous. So the Sagittarius/Sheep's house may not be fancy, but it will surely be solid and comfortable, and as isolated as possible.

This person makes a terrific parent. He or she really cares for children and is interested in what makes them tick. The Sagittarius/ Sheep likes the way kids' minds work, and admires childlike spontaneity and verve. The Sagittarius/Sheep, despite his advanced creative mind, will not be a permissive parent. Instead, this person's kids will be called upon to be courteous and curious. Sagittarius/ Sheep is progressive, however. He or she works alongside kids to teach them crafts or help them with school projects. The Sagittarius/ Sheep child is removed from the group vector by virtue of his exceptional views. This little person may feel "out of it" a lot of the time, and suffer from loneliness in a crowd. Parents are well advised to encourage this child in creative pursuits, providing lessons and tutors where possible. There is often real genius in this child's mind. But insecurity is the enemy of that spark. All family disruptions and parental discord upset this sensitive kid's nerves. He or she takes everything to heart and wants to help to make it better. Protect this child if you can.

Profession

Ordinarily Sheep subjects suffer from lack of foresight. They are the people who buy one quart of milk for a set of hungry sextuplets. But here Sagittarius, with his drive to change the future, is heeded by the Sheep, so Sagittarius/Sheep are rather careful souls. They are family-oriented and security-minded and thus less dependent or parasitic than many other Sheep natives. They have a keen eye for social commentary. They are cooperative in the extreme, and certainly not afraid of hard labor—on their own terms, of course. They often know how to turn a little bit of wealth into a lot of money.

The Sagittarius/Sheep boss is well loved by employees. He or she may be criticized for not being harsh enough. But the Sagittarius born Sheep rules by sweetness. His orders are sugarcoated and the results are sometimes not half bad. If he is employed in a lucrative job he will be greatly appreciated by superiors. Sagittarius/Sheep are a great addition to any office situation. They are good at jobs requiring individual effort and offering personal gain. The Sagittarius/Sheep cares what others think and always tries to please.

Careers that may fit into the Sagittarius/Sheep's life are: psychiatrist, insurance agent, artist (all sorts), house painter, choreographer, wine grower, doctor, lawyer, missionary, farmer, designer, musician, teacher, clergyman, seamstress, picture framer.

Famous Sagittarius/Sheep:
Adam Brody, Alberto Moravia, Alexandra Stamler, Anna Freud, Anna Nicole Smith, Bill Wilson, Billie Jean King, Billy Idol, Busby Berkeley, Charlie Puth, Deborra-Lee Furness, Dennis Chris-

topher, Emily Swallow, Georges Seurat, Jamie Foxx, Jane Austen, Jane Kaczmarek, Jennifer Carpenter, Jillian Rose Reed, Jim Morrison, Joel Kinnaman, Jonathan Sadowski, Judd Apatow, Kelly Brook, Kevin Conroy, Marcus Butler, Mark Twain, Michael Owen, Miranda Otto, Mo'Nique, Nestor Carbonell, Nick Thune, Priscilla Barnes, Randy Newman, Rita Moreno, Robert Wahlberg, Salli Richardson-Whitfield, Samantha Burton, Sun Yang, Tamara Duarte, Wallis Currie-Wood, Xander Berkeley.

SAGITTARIUS
QUALITIES
CHEERFULNESS, OPENHANDEDNESS,
SOLICITUDE, VALOR, HONOR, REASON
QUIRKS
OUTSPOKENNESS, RECKLESSNESS,
BAD MANNERS, VACILLATION,
CARELESSNESS, CONTRADICTION
Motto: *"I see"*
Elements: *Fire, Jupiter, Mutable*

--

MONKEY
QUALITIES
IMPROVISATION, CUNNING, STABILITY,
SELF-INVOLVEMENT, WIT, OPPORTUNISM
QUIRKS
DECEIT, RUSE, LOQUACITY,
LEADERS, SILLINESS, ZEAL
Motto: *"I plan"*
Elements: *Positive, metal, Yang*

S agittarians are always freethinkers. They blaze trails and shoot for the future. They are glib and humanitarian. They are direct and cheerful. Much of the above description also fits the Monkey character. So, in some ways, the Sagittarian Monkey is in harmony with both sides of his nature. His outgoing side doesn't have to do daily battle with some introverted tendency to hide under rocks when company comes. Sagittarius/Monkey is comfortable in his skin.

But a basic rift exists between the Sagittarian and his Monkey counterpart. Sagittarians are altruistic and other-oriented. Sagittarians are truthful and like to play daredevil. The Monkey is not a bit like that. The Monkey is cunning itself, careful never to be too direct, and capable of epic feats of circuitousness. He rarely tempts the devil unless he knows he can beat him, and his orientation is toward himself rather than toward others.

So what happens? Well, it's quite simple. Monkey turns Sagittarius into a natural leader. This person has the necessary ardor and force to move a mountain, and he also possesses the guile and opportunism needed to establish his own government on the same site. Sagittarius/Monkeys take over. They like to run things and make decisions and order people around and make laws and initiate changes and make alterations. And before you can say "Sagittarius/ Monkey" this tricky little number is having a street named after himself—and while he's at it, maybe he'll name one after his girlfriend, too.

Huge efforts don't bother the Sagittarius/Monkey either. These capable people are organized and go right to the heart of any given problem. They are earnest and believe fervently in their creeds and ideals. They are attractive. And they are very convincing. Sagittarius/Monkeys naturally love to speak in public and debate prickly subjects with aplomb and common sense. They like money and know how to spend it wisely and generously.

Silliness, for the Monkey born in Sagittarius, will be reserved for private parties. The public image of this power-seeking dynamo will be grave. Sagittarius/Monkey wants to be taken seriously. With friends or intimates this character may be a perfect clown, dancing on tables and enlivening gatherings with witty comments and crazy antics. But image-wise, this bright person is nobody's fool.

Sagittarius/Monkeys think big. They never putter around with small potatoes. These folks are interested in gain and authority. They are excellent administrators and just about never enter into direct conflict. These people are essentially conservative, and even if they have a streak of the liberal in them, they will be careful to cloak it in middle-of-the-road clothing. Monkeys born in Sagittarius like hefty challenges. They are expert at public relations. They are their own best ambassadors and seem to know instinctively how to gently sway public opinion in their own favor.

Love

Sagittarius/Monkeys are a bit uncomfortable in intimacy. They don't give easily of their emotions, and tend to shrink from the bonds that coupledom imposes. The Sagittarius/Monkey will be hesitant about marrying or hitching up with someone for life. This character sees beyond each relationship, and wonders whether or not in a few years' time she will become bored with the loved one. There is a refusal in this character to take on emotional responsibility for anything other than his missions. He will be fun to hang around with but I'm not sure I'd want him to marry my sister.

If you are attracted to the challenging Sagittarius/Monkey, use wiles to fight wiles. Don't be too declarative or easy for this person to bag. Otherwise, he will lose interest overnight. You will best charm this difficult subject by challenging her mind, testing her mettle and taking little trips by yourself from time to time just to keep her on her toes. For heaven's sake, don't say you are only going to the neighboring village. Pretend you've been called away on affairs of state.

Compatibilities

Aries, Libra and Aquarius/Rats spur you to greater heights. You'll not be sorry for taking up with Leo, Libra or Aquarius/ Dragons either. There's no future for you with Virgo, Gemini or Pisces/Pigs. Gemini and Pisces/Oxen demand far too much stability for your taste. And Virgos of both the Cat and Tiger persuasions prevent you from advancing on your own terms. Pisces/Snakes are lovely. But you can't have one. It just won't work.

Home and Family

This person's interior will be practical and sensible. He will probably own a number of *objets d'art* picked up in his many travels. But there is not much showiness in the Sagittarius/Monkey's taste. He or she does not want to impress through furnishings. A comfortable and well-organized, functional home is this person's aim. The Sagittarius/Monkey's wardrobe will be publicly bourgeois old-line and privately casual.

The Sagittarius/Monkey is not apt to marry young and have a slew of stairstep babies trotting around underfoot by age twenty-five. No. This person has personal advancement in mind before everything else. Then, once he or she is established in a solid career, it will be time enough for making babies. And one or two will suffice, thank you. Sagittarian Monkeys will be careful parents who provide handsomely for their children's futures. They are concerned with public appearances and will make their children behave.

If you have a Sagittarius/Monkey child, you have probably already noticed how serious he or she threatens to become. Although at home these little kids can be very rough-and-tumble, they can usually contain themselves in school. This child will have talent for organization and leadership. They can benefit from early training in public speaking or theater work. They are sensitive but private about their emotions. It's rather difficult to know what they are thinking. Never pry. Question gently.

Profession

The Sagittarius/Monkey rarely takes the path of least resistance. He or she will be, adept at managing and has great organizational acumen. These people are problem solvers. They see concrete solutions to puzzles that stymie whole commissions of specialists. "Why don't we turn it into a stadium then?" they will suggest at the town planning board meeting. "We can make it profitable by building a parking lot underneath."

The Sagittarius/Monkey always has an answer. And if he doesn't know what he's yammering about—it certainly sounds as if he does. Of course this person is a leader and will want to boss. The Sagittarian Monkey is not sarcastic or mean to his subordinates. But he does sometimes have a blustery way of acting superior that gets under the skin of employees. Largely, he can be trusted to take over in all areas requiring common-sense administration. This person doesn't stay an underling for long, but he or she knows how to be flexible for promotional purposes and cooperative for gain. These folks work very well alone.

Careers that suit the Sagittarius/Monkey are: politician, writer, ambassador, office manager, account executive, lobbyist, negotiator, personnel director, economist.

Famous Sagittarius/Monkeys:

Adam Hicks, Anna Chlumsky, Beatriz Corrales, Brendan Fraser, Bridgit Mendler, Casper Van Dien, Chris Carmack, Christina Aguilera, Claire Chazal, Claude Levi-Strauss, Dave Brubeck, David Lambert, Dina Meyer, Don Lake, Ellen Burstyn, Enrio Macias, Isabel Cueto, Jacques Chirac, Jake Gyllenhaal, Janina Gavankar, Jenna Dewan Tatum, Jessica Paré, Jill Hennessy, John Milton, Katarina Jezic, Larry Bird, Lisa Marie, Lucy Liu, Mark Rolston, Marla Sokoloff, Melissa Roxburgh, Michael Vartan, Miley Cyrus, Rachel Griffiths, Rena Sofer, Ric Felix, Ricardo Montalban, Sean Grandillo, Simon Helberg, Steven Bauer, William Fichtner

SAGITTARIUS
QUALITIES
CHEERFULNESS, OPENHANDEDNESS,
SOLICITUDE, VALOR, HONOR, REASON
QUIRKS
OUTSPOKENNESS, RECKLESSNESS,
BAD MANNERS, VACILLATION,
CARELESSNESS, CONTRADICTION
Motto: *"I see"*
Elements: *Fire, Jupiter, Mutable*

--

ROOSTER
QUALITIES
RESILIENCE, ENTHUSIASM, CANDOR,
CONSERVATISM, CHIC, HUMOR
QUIRKS
COCKINESS, BOASTFULNESS, BLIND FAITH,
PEDANTRY, BOSSINESS, DISSIPATION
Motto: *"I overcome"*
Elements: *Negative, Metal, Yin*

B uoyancy characterizes the Sagittarian Rooster. He's atwitter with chitchat and agog with stories of adventure. This subject, born under two of the most high-strung signs, will be nervous, frank, candid, and a bit carried away with himself. The word is enthusiasm but it's more than that. Sagittarius/Roosters are full of dash and élan. They cut an impressive figure wherever they go—and they go everywhere!

Despite the Sagittarius/Rooster's determination to cover half the globe by age thirteen, this person is deep-down sensible and lives far more carefully than the impression implies. He or she will have noble aims. They entertain a kind of Robin Hood objective to rob from the rich and give to the poor. Not that Sagittarius/Roosters are thieves. There is no evidence to that effect. But they can be secret pirates, leering at those ships that pass in the night loaded with jewels and furs yet denying themselves chicanery. The Sagittarian Rooster is a lover of truth. He deplores phoniness.

Sagittarius/Roosters are beset by their noble aims at a very young age. They would like to "do good" in the old-fashioned missionary sense. They may travel to Africa or India to help poor people, or they may stay closer to home and hire on as listeners in a suicide center. But whatever they undertake is often disappointing to their starkly honest natures. No charity can be perfect. There's always a hitch. Somebody has a hand in the till or funds are being misused or poor people in some distant land refuse help for religious reasons. Philanthropy is mined with disappointment.

For this reason, the Sagittarius/Rooster is often seen as disenchanted, locked in an ideal that won't let him or her loose, but that doesn't work either. For some less resilient souls this sort of disillusion could lead to dejection and even self-pity. But not for the Sagittarius/Rooster. In a matter of days you will find this character back on his feet, packing a suitcase for yet another foray into the wilds of humanitarianism. It's the old story: You can't keep a good man down.

Withal, the Sagittarius/Rooster has fairly good sense. He only seems reckless and acts boasting and cocky. Underneath, this person has his eye on the needle at all times and is monitoring his own progress critically. These people realize that freedom and adventure are too attractive to them, and know that one day they must settle down or become patently ridiculous. When that day comes, Sagittarius/Roosters land themselves cushy jobs with serious titles on the doors, or simply sit down and start writing books about their many exploits.

Sagittarius/Roosters have good manners, yet sometimes they can be snappy and brusque. A harsh remark in the midst of a seemingly ordinary calm conversation is not unusual coming from these people. They are brutally frank. They thrive on adversity and challenge. They are not afraid to stoop to conquer, and they care greatly for friends and family. In fact, I would say that no matter where this person journeys in a lifetime, he or she will remain forever tied to duty and responsibility at home, a free spirit locked in the body of a dutiful do-gooder. Maybe that's why Sagittarius/Roosters are always departing and leaving the barnyard door ajar, so they can return to their favorite prison when the chips are down.

Love

Sagittarius/Roosters are not always lucky in love. They are by turns too demanding or too docile. In love affairs there is always a delicate gray area of deceit. Some things are better not discussed when it comes to passions and jealousies. Well, the Sagittarius/Rooster can't hack the deceit part. He or she wants all the cards on the table and no double-dealing. Moreover, as this person is so indomitable and fiercely dynamic, he or she often takes up with someone who needs help, someone whose aims are not fixed, and who seems so adorably lost. This is what I call the Sagittarius "Popeye" complex. Good Samaritan time. Of course, pity is not love. But sometimes Sagittarius/Roosters can't tell the difference.

If you love a Sagittarius/Rooster, try to jolly her out of a rigid sense of duty by tickling or amusing her in some fashion. Take him to the theater and buy him pop-up toys. Get these people out of their duty rut, And most of all, don't take advantage of this person's kindly, caring nature. A hurt Sagittarius/Rooster is not a pretty sight.

Compatibilities

Aries Leo, Libra and Aquarius/Snakes find you irresistible, and the feeling is mutual. Leo, Libra and Aquarius/Oxen provide you with both pleasure and safety from harm. And the real joys of romance arrive in the form of Leo and/or Libra/Dragons. They are so-o-o-o-o impressive. Virgo and Gemini/Rooster subjects are no fun for you to keep around. Pisces/Dogs drive you mad with their incessant worrying, and Virgo and Pisces/Cats are far too bossy and unadventurous for you to put up with them for long.

Home and Family

The Sagittarius/Rooster's home will be spare yet elegant. Comfort is not the primary goal. Appearance and attractiveness come first. Having a "good address" helps, too. Not that Sagittarius/Rooster is a snob—far from it. But this person is essentially conservative, prefers security to danger, and cannot tolerate messiness or disorder. So the Sagittarius/Rooster often sets up shop in a reputable area. He or she is gone much of the time so "home" is a dubious term at best to describe Sagittarius/Rooster digs.

This person would love to be a parent. But where to find the time? They have their Indians in Bolivia, their Puerto Ricans in Harlem and their immigrants in Texas to attend to first. After that, they have to hurry home to spend Christmas with the folks and buy all those toys for the nieces and nephews. And if Sagittarius/ Rooster does settle down, how will he or she ever get free again to go trotting off to Brazil? The subject of children is a tricky one for the

Sagittarian born Rooster. It's yes and no and yes and no until one day it seems impossible. Sagittarius/Rooster is too peripatetic to be a parent.

The Sagittarius/Rooster child will play at adventurous games. You may try to interest him or her in piano lessons or needlepoint, but it probably won't take. And if it does, it's because this kid is wholeheartedly dutiful and doesn't want to hurt parents' feelings. This child is a maverick. He may not get along well in the confined ambience of a schoolroom. She's always dreaming of becoming a famous ballerina who gives all her money to the poor. They will stick out education if parents make it clear there is no other route. Otherwise, the Sagittarius/Rooster is likely to go far away from home in an attempt to find himself in the eyes of strangers.

Profession

All careers involving movement and travel suit this person. Sagittarian Roosters are talkative and frequently never shut up in three languages. They have a natural ability to sort out details, are visionary about future trends and tuned in to fashions. The Sagittarius born Rooster seeks to have a cosmic view of his environment and indeed of the whole universe. He's got good sense and doesn't hesitate before making decisions. Sagittarius/Roosters get on with things. Born bossy, the Sagittarius/Rooster nonetheless is not sure if he wants that top job all that much. If he agrees to be the chief in Chicago, then what will happen to the Indians in the Andes? The answer is a job where Sagittarius/Rooster travels a lot and gets to see a lot of progress in a short time. As an employee, this person is happy as long as he sees a light at the end of the tunnel—a promotion to tour guide, for example.

Jobs that may please the Sagittarius/Rooster are: photographer for National Geographic, UNESCO or peace corps volunteer, publisher of travel books, writer, performer, journalist, geologist, cartographer, doctor, missionary, roadie, pirate, prospector, logger, travel agent.

Famous Sagittarius/Roosters:

Deanna Durbin, Adan Canto, Alicia von Rittberg, AnnaSophia Robb, Ashley Madekwe, Brendan Fletcher, Britney Spears, Caroline Kennedy, Colin Mochrie, Courtney Henggeler, Denise Crosby, Flip Wilson, François de Closets, Hermione Corfield, Jay Z, Kiersey Clemons, Kristy Swanson, Krysten Ritter, Laurie Holden, Max Martini, Michael Clarke Duncan, Michelle Dockery, Natascha McElhone, Prince Nicolas of Belgium, Ray Romano, Ricky Whittle, Stefania Pirozzi, Steve Buscemi, Tim Conway, Vishwanathan Anand.

SAGITTARIUS
QUALITIES
CHEERFULNESS, OPENHANDEDNESS,
SOLICITUDE, VALOR, HONOR, REASON
QUIRKS
OUTSPOKENNESS, RECKLESSNESS,
BAD MANNERS, VACILLATION,
CARELESSNESS, CONTRADICTION
Motto: *"I see"*
Elements: *Fire, Jupiter, Mutable*

--

DOG
QUALITIES
CONSTANCY, UNSOCIABILITY,
RESPECTABILITY, SELF-RIGHTEOUSNESS,
INTELLIGENCE, TACTLESSNESS
QUIRKS
UNEASINESS, CRITICISM, DUTY,
CYNICISM, HEROISM, MORALITY
Motto: *"I worry"*
Elements: *Positive, Metal, Yang*

The dry hero that is Sagittarius/Dog embodies all of the Sagittarian's idealist traits, the adventurousness, the future vision, the bravura and the fire. But this person also takes on those creditable qualities native to all born under the sign of the Dog: honor and sincerity, loyalty and respectability. Both signs are endowed with a loose tongue. Sagittarians like to be frank and to expound. Dogs, although circumspect and mistrustful, tend to lash out with words, toppling adversaries like tenpins. This is a worthy person whose nose for what's happening on the world scene and how to fix it is enviably accurate.

Sagittarius/Dog is a brash and opinionated sign. This person has an idea about everything and as his integrity is unquestionable, people tend to take what he or she says as gospel. Too, the Sagittarius/Dog is the opposite of cowardly. He or she dares much that others consider sheer madness. They speak out openly on all their ideas and they meet challenge with challenge. Ask a Sagittarius/Dog a question and he may toss you one right back. This character is a no-nonsense forger of ideals in his or her public life. They move in the best circles and make it their business to be seen in the "right" dinner parties and colloquiums. The Sagittarius/Dog is always taken seriously.

The nature here is generous. The soul is sensitivity itself. The Sagittarius/Dog champions honor and sticks close to duty. He never shirks what he feels is the virtuous sector of life. However, as this person attaches so much importance to respectability, when he or she does let loose in private situations, the sky is the limit. This person indulges in pleasure as avidly as he or she plies a trade. Sagittarius/Dogs work at having a good time. And as they are thorough people, they leave no stone unturned in the debauchery department.

Sagittarius/Dog is a sign of leadership and fresh viewpoints. There is much creative thought in these people, and they will be able to apply that inventiveness to a career, since they are earth-connected and strict with themselves. These people know how to blend the Sagittarian's desire for expression and daring with the Dog's innate caution. They often become celebrated thinkers, writers, or linguists. They know how to align ideas and put them into words with flair and logic.

The Sagittarius/Dog is actually quite optimistic. The Dog's natural pessimism is jollied by Sagittarius's cheerfulness. Sagittarius also brings the Dog a certain cavalier attitude toward neatness and housekeeping. But never mind, the Dog returns the favor by making this Sagittarian more critical and less impetuous than normal. The marriage of Sagittarius to Dog gives us a powerful figure who sits comfortably on his or her throne.

If wronged, the Sagittarius/Dog will bite. This person does not take kindly to improbity. His methods are brash and his weapons king-sized. Never cross a Sagittarius/Dog unless you want to feel the sting of his slap for the rest of your born days. This person is basically peaceable, but approach him gently and don't try any funny business or he'll have your right leg. And if that doesn't make you understand, he'll take the left one too.

Love

In private situations these forceful people are remarkably sweet-natured. They sincerely want to be liked and despite a one-on-one shyness, they know how to involve themselves in a passionate way and can be faithful to that passion for a long time. They usually choose to keep their private affairs out of the public eye. They are masters of discretion in romantic matters. Sagittarius/Dogs never air their dirty linen for the world to see. They find "open soap operatics" vulgar and dull.

Should you be smitten by this feisty character, you will not be able to keep him or her at home for long. The Sagittarius/Dog is always on the move. He or she takes on huge projects in public life and has stamina to burn for digging and turning over the earth to get to treasured goals. Your job will be to comfort and solace this nervous, sometimes disquieted soul. Your best bet is to have plenty to do on your own and not to wait up for your Sagittarius/Dog lover to get home. They cannot recall when they rolled in before three A.M.

Compatibilities

You are a Tiger fan. Together you and the Tigers from Leo, Libra and Aquarius will go far. You also make beautiful music with Horse natives born in those same western astrological signs. Leo/Cats make you happy, too. They offer you optimism. You don't get much out of love affairs with Dragons, especially Gemini, Leo, Virgo and Pisces/Dragons. Gemini, Virgo and Pisces/Sheep don't add anything to your life except anxiety, which you don't need. You just plain don't get on with Gemini/Monkeys.

Home and Family

The Sagittarius/Dog's family, its traditions and manners, its feast days and funerals, its ideals and coat of arms, will matter enormously to this person. However, in his own life, home is of practically no importance. He will want a nicely decorated flat or house near his office or place of work. But he doesn't want to fool around with putting up wallpaper or tiling the kitchen himself. This person is interested in his outside life and his work. If he can afford to, he will have maids and butlers to take care of housekeeping details.

Provided she can employ the best people to raise her children, this person will be a serious yet demanding parent. As respectability means a great deal to the Sagittarius/Dog, he will want kids to practice good manners and have gracious ways. As there is a bit too much crispness in the Sagittarius/Dog's emotional makeup, she must make a decided effort to be cuddly and warm with little ones. Also, if they are too conservative and strict with kids, these people can unwittingly form rebels who will return home at age twenty waving the banners of anarchy.

The Sagittarius/Dog child is a brittle little thing whose earnestness and desire to please and excel is touching. I would say this kid needs to be softened by nature and exposed to a little funk while still young in order to instill knowledge of how the other half lives. This child may be picky and nervous. Parents should encourage his or her writing talents and urge this child to achieve in areas where he can shine. No matter what you do, what interests the Sagittarius/ Dog child is precisely what he or she will end up doing. They're like that—very directed, and independent as all get-out.

Profession

This character works very well in jobs that challenge his or her intellect. Sagittarius/Dogs have no time for pandering to obstreperous bosses or listening to office gossip. They go right to the desk and work till they drop. Then they leave their desks. They are abrupt and short-tempered in business dealings. Effectiveness is the single objective of this sharp-witted creature with the taste for freedom. He doesn't want to be tied to a job longer than he has to. She doesn't want to be restricted to her business except when necessary.

These people can make efficient bosses. They are, however, sarcastic and biting. Their manner is tough and no-nonsense, but their spirit is kindly. Understanding employees like them very much indeed. But weak people don't take well to the harsh environment engendered by this boss.

The Sagittarius/Dog will probably be serious in his work if employed, but he will surely be disobedient about trivial rules and flout them. Actually, the Sagittarius/Dog's dream is to work alone in some self-perpetuating pursuit or other like writing or running a hotel—or both.

Some suitable careers for Sagittarius/Dogs are: journalist, politician, novelist, linguist, translator, researcher, dramatist, activist, artist, lawyer, diplomat, speechwriter, professor.

Famous Sagittarius/Dogs:
Benny Andersson, Brooke Langton, Charlene Tilton, Charlie Cox, Dame Judi Dench, Darlanne Fluegel, David Kersh, Elisha Cuthbert, Gemma Chan, Gianni Versace, Griff Jenkins, Hannah Endicott-Douglas, Jake T. Austin, Jean Genet, Jennifer Connelly, Julie Condra, Lynn-Holly Johnson, Mädchen Amick, Nat Wolff, Oded Fehr, Regina Hall, Sarah Silverman, Sheree J. Wilson, Sophie Daumier, Steven Spielberg, Tom Payne, Winston Churchill, Wyatt Smith.

SAGITTARIUS
QUALITIES
CHEERFULNESS, OPENHANDEDNESS,
SOLICITUDE, VALOR, HONOR, REASON
QUIRKS
OUTSPOKENNESS, RECKLESSNESS,
BAD MANNERS, VACILLATION,
CARELESSNESS, CONTRADICTION
Motto: *"I see"*
Elements: *Fire, Jupiter, Mutable*

--

PIG
QUALITIES
SCRUPULOUSNESS, GALLANTRY, SINCERITY,
VOLUPTUOUSNESS, CULTURE, HONESTY
QUIRKS
CREDULITY, WRATH, HESITATION,
MATERIALISM, GOURMANDISM, PIGHEADEDNESS
Motto: *"I civilize"*
Elements: *Negative Water, Yin*

S till waters run deep. The Sagittarian Pig, above reproach in moral conduct and beyond social disapprobation, makes it his or her business to maintain a spotless reputation. Don't think the Sagittarius/Pig is a Pollyanna and only capable of Boy Scoutism. Not at all. But this person attends to his or her public name by staying clear of trouble and acting the role of moralist.

Sagittarius/Pigs are born observers. They see everything that goes on around them and then some. They pick up on details and record speech patterns and tics. They recognize flaws and foibles in a wink and they find it all very amusing. When they are ready, armed with their closetful of human frailties, they synthesize their accumulated findings and send them back to us in the form of art. Sagittarius/Pig is a popular artist. Never too abstract or labyrinthine in his style, the Sagittarius/Pig's aim is to poke fun at society and, in turn, at himself.

These people have enormous public appeal. Nobody ever really feels threatened by a Sagittarius/Pig. The character is so constituted as to be unafraid of giving and caring openly about others. The Sagittarius/Pig is virtuous by nature and has an attractiveness that transcends physicality. In fact, I daresay, most Sagittarius/Pigs are not classically good-looking. But they have such honest, forthright charm that they can send entire populations swooning over their simple style.

They are sincerely interested in others. And what do people like better than talking about themselves? Sagittarius/Pig is an excellent listener who nods in all the right places and gives terrific, sound advice to people in trouble. Too, the Sagittarian Pig is indulgent with human failings. He or she truly can see why you argued with your baby sister on her wedding day. They are even touched by your weakness. How can anyone resist? Sagittarius/Pig is father and mother confessor in one and you don't have to recite any prayers as penance. I call Sagittarius/Pigs big-hearted.

But they can also be pigheaded. The Sagittarian born in a Pig year can get so caught up in his virtuousness that sometimes he forgets to be flexible. This causes plenty of trouble around the ranch. Of course the Sagittarius/Pig's sense of humor saves him from total rigidity. But his resistance to the ideas of others, or their suggestions, can be exasperating, to say the least.

Sagittarian Pigs are sometimes quixotic—and although their intentions are honorable, their attitudes can be brash or invasive. There is a tiny tendency here to engage in pratfall humor. I recommend intravenous subtlety. And attention. If the Sagittarius/Pig claims not to need applause, it's because he or she is ashamed to admit how much he thrives on it. Don't forget, Pigs are very cultivated people. The Pig born in Sagittarius must sometimes wonder who this rash and fiery beast he got into bed with at birth really is. Dauntless and even power-hungry, the Sagittarius/Pig runs a tight ship. But below decks there may be a party in full swing, the magnitude and exoticism of which would make Fellini faint from shock.

Love

Sagittarius/Pigs marry for love and often stay that way. These people are truly generous of spirit and giving of themselves. They are also utterly discreet and sincere. Of course the Sagittarius/Pig is interested in challenge from a lover or mistress, especially on an intellectual level. He will never be fully satisfied sharing a life with someone whose opinions he doesn't respect. Some great couples are half Sagittarius/Pig.

If you have fallen for one of these professional good guys, I know you must have a fine sense of humor. The Sagittarius/Pig is funny. He or she finds comedy everywhere. They are also gut-level appealing with their constant observations and their sense of humanity. Your position as the mate or companion of this finely tuned recording device will be to maintain your own autonomy and your reputation so that your Sagittarius/Pig can be proud of you. This person is not only interested in whether or not your tie is straight. The Sagittarius/Pig wants you to say clever things and know how to present your point of view. For Sagittarius/Pig, the image you present reflects directly on his sterling idea of self. To love you, the Sagittarius/Pig must believe in you too.

Compatibilities

You love the countryside. You cleave unto nature and sensuality, and extol the value of the hearth. Cats suit your need for household tranquility. Choose your own Cat from Aries, Leo, Libra or Aquarius. Leo and Aquarius/Sheep are fine associates for you, too. Escape the clutches of Gemini, Virgo and Pisces/Snakes before they squeeze you to death. Gemini/Roosters are too scatty for your solid side, and Virgo/Monkeys too possessive.

Home and Family

The Sagittarian born in Pig years is such a busy person that his home will have to be first and foremost a functional place to work in. This is not the sort of person who comes home and takes off his shoes and flops onto a couch. He or she invariably goes straight from work to work. The desk may be plunk in the middle of the living room. This person loves precious things, but can dispense with opulence in favor of productivity.

Parenting interests the Sagittarian Pig because he's curious about human nature and fascinated by all its aspects. He will be generous with the time he spends with kids. She will read to them and listen sympathetically to their tales of school rivalries and difficult teachers. The Sagittarius/Pig is one of the most cuddly of the Sagittarian smoothies. Kids whose parents are born in this sign have a lot to live up to.

The Sagittarius/Pig child will show early signs of curiosity about the world. He will not be introverted or sulky. You can expect this child to work well in school and have fun with all things theatrical and creative. Too, his or her cynical comments will make you roar with laughter. These kids will survive almost all squabbles and family discord. They are uniquely self-propelled.

Profession

Reserve and will are the bywords of the Sagittarian Pig. He or she ought not to have very much trouble with career choices. They will be artistic for sure and able to turn their creative notions into viable vehicles for use in anything from business to entertainment or services. This person can be a winning performer or deft puppeteer. Whatever he or she does will be accompanied by good taste and a hearty dose of cheerfulness.

The Sagittarius/Pig is a fair and generous boss. He only demands perfection from people who work with and for him. But Pigs are honest and so are Sagittarians. Nobody can hate such a gallant soul.

The Sagittarian Pig employee is serious and reputable. You can trust him or her with the payroll. Of course, these people work splendidly alone. They undertake complex and difficult projects and over and over again make them successful.

Some careers suitable for the Sagittarius/Pig are: dramatist, film or theater director, actor, opera singer, composer, TV personality, lobbyist, clergyman, ecologist, cinematographer, photographer, inventor.

Famous Sagittarius/Pigs:

Alain Bashung, Amy Locane, Camilla Luddington, Chet Huntley, Chris Hardwick, Christina Applegate, Claire Forlani, Claude Casadessus, Daniela Ruah, Dilma Rousseff, Dominique Dunne, Emily Mortimer, Emun Elliott, Francis Huster, Freeman Dyson, Gigliola Cinquetti, Hector Berlioz, James Viscount Severn, Jana Kramer, Jane Birkin, Jean Pierre Foucault, Joe Dinicol, Johnny Whitaker, Jonah Hill, Judd Nelson, Jules Dassin, Kali Rocha, Karine Vanasse, Lee L. Cobb, Léon Schwartzenberg, Maria Callas, Maxwell Caulfield, McKayla Maroney, Michael McCary, Noël Coward, Nostradamus, Patrick John Flueger, Petra Kelly, Spike Jonz, Steven Yeun, Tatiana Casiraghi, Utkarsh Ambudkar., Willy Brandt, Woody Alien, Xavier Samuel.

CAPRICORN
QUALITIES
RESOLVE, WISDOM, AMBITION,
GENEROSITY, SUPERIORITY,
DEPENDABILITY
QUIRKS
STIFFNESS, CLUMSINESS, PRETENSION,
LONELINESS, EPICUREANISM, SELF-DOUBT
Motto: *"I use"*
Elements: *Earth, Saturn, Cardinal*

--

RAT
QUALITIES
NERVOUSNESS, INFLUENCE,
ACQUISITIVENESS, THIRST FOR POWER,
INTELLECTUAL SKILL, CHARISMA
QUIRKS
APPEAL, VERBOSITY, THRIFT,
SOCIABILITY, GUILE, MEDDLING
Motto: *"I rule"*
Elements: *Positive Water, Yang*

Both Capricorn and Rat want to achieve success. Rat wants power. Capricorn wants sway over others. Together the covetous Rat and the solitary mountain Sheep that is Capricorn will go far (many times to the detriment of anything from reputation to family or even health). The Capricorn born in Rat, like the Tiger only more so, is in constant, grievous danger.

The old song goes, "Everybody loves a lover." And it's partly true. Love is a contagious disease. Nobody, however, loves a power - monger. Power is not a jolly communicable feeling. Power signifies that someone else had to be squashed on the way up. Power implies greed and avidity. Rats born in Capricorn live to achieve power. They want to dominate their peers and want to be the best at whatever they are doing. They are insanely competitive.

There are no bad signs, remember? But Capricorn/Rat does have the potential for badness. He's slippery and dignified at the same time. He gives the appearance of being solely on the up and up. He even attracts by means of a phony "limpid mountain stream" approach. His speeches are clear-cut and easy to follow. These people send out dependability rays. I'm sure they even believe that their self-seeking projects are for the good of all, for the best, for the sake of humanity.

This is a difficult sign to live in, even harder to live with. The success of this complex and grand human being depends entirely on how impregnable he or she was to childhood lessons in morality. If he has evolved beyond the "gimme" stage it's usually because of firm and loving tutelage in youth.

Most Capricorn/Rats have, of course, developed well beyond the primitive grabby stages and hold positions of remarkable importance in their own realms. They are thorough and efficient. They are congenial and industrious. They are careful and conservative, yet generous and quietly loving. The talents of Rat/Capricorns lie in areas where tremendous application is necessary for mastery of the art. They balk at nothing, are afraid of no one, and often, despite perilous brushes with the pavement, know how to keep coming back smelling like expensive perfume.

Wells of new ideas, projects, and wily great plans hatch in the busy head of this character. Capricorn/Rats are never afraid of having an invention filched or a notion pilfered by someone less scrupulous than themselves (yes, such people exist). They have such a well-developed sense of personal eminence that they give away their genius schemes like kisses at a church bazaar. "Step right up and rip off one of my incredible creative notions," says the Capricorn/Rat, "There's more where that one came from." Moreover, as Rat/Capricorns themselves have sticky fingers, they understand.

Having the idea is one thing. Carrying it through is quite another. But not to worry. One of the major strengths of Capricorns born in Rat years is their ability to take their ideas through to a solid conclusion. The Capricorn is a concrete person. Dreams are not enough for the Capricorn/Rat. He or she is gifted for applying abstract concepts to real life situations. The contrary is not true. Capricorn/Rats handle emotional or subjective events poorly. They are uptight about feelings and grapple all the time with rigidity and stiffness. It is precisely this static or unbending approach that will ultimately betray Rat/Capricorn. He needs flexible, conscientious counselors around him to keep him out of the hoosegow.

Love

A sincere need for long-standing love matches characterizes this person's romantic portrait. As emotion is not of primary importance to this person, the Capricorn/Rat is only tepidly attracted to moon-light and roses (unless he's buying or selling one or the other of these commodities). What he wants in a mate is help, real bedrock devotion and true grit. The Capricorn/Rat knows full well that she cannot depend uniquely on her own energies to accomplish the mil-lions of necessary details involved with home and family. They are lucid creatures, these Capricorn/Rats. They don't attempt anything sentimental unless they are very sure they can handle it.

Should you care for one of these giant-of-industry types, I suggest you be somebody quite wonderful yourself. No Capricorn/Rat worth his salt will take up with a nudnik. The sign implies strength. You'll best meet the needs and standards of this demanding person by be-ing strong yourself. Capricorn/Rat loves first and foremost because he admires or looks up to his lover. If you don't feel particularly equal to the Capricorn/Rat in your life, if he or she makes you feel small and insignificant, move on. Capricorn/Rat is capable of re-ducing the faint of heart to a smudge.

Compatibilities

The Ox and you together know how to seek and achieve power and security. Find your Ox among the following signs: Taurus, Leo, Virgo, Scorpio or Pisces. Monkeys of the same signs make you happy, ex-cept, perhaps, the Virgo/Monkey, whose meticulous ardor irritates you. Taurus, Virgo and Pisces/Dragons make you smile a lot. You can take a chance on one of these. Horse or Rat combos are never ideal, as a power struggle inevitably ensues. So hands off Horses, particularly Aries, Cancer or Libra/Horses. It's doubtful you will be drawn to Aries or Libra/Cats. But if you are, don't say I didn't warn you.

Home and Family

Capricorn/Rats never deprive themselves of comforts. These folks like to decorate their lives to suit their high opinions of themselves. The home environment will drip with conveniences. Also, Capri-corn/Rats are strongly attached to tradition, so the furnishings are likely to be antique but not rustic or countrified. The Capricorn/Rat wants a certain sophistication to inform his decor. You can find hordes of Capricorn/Rats at chic furniture auctions and estate sales.

As the average Capricorn/Rat is not physically demonstrative, you may imagine he or she does not love children. This is, of course, nonsense. Capricorn/Rats adore their kids and want to protect and nurture them carefully. This person will hunger for companionship with his or her offspring. Long talks and activities done as a unit will attract this family-oriented Capricorn. He or she will be strict. No question about that. But there is a deep devotion here that the loving child will instinctively feel.

The Capricorn/Rat child requires early moral training in order to temper his overwhelming need to overwhelm. Let's just say this kid is determined to reach the top and knows few bounds in this resolve. Discipline of the corporal sort will do no good. This child will react strongly to any attempt at physical restraint. Capricorn/ Rats have a decided talent for reasoning and logic. So it's easy to know how to proceed. "I love you but sometimes I don't love the things you do," is a good start. Explain the difference between good and evil. Don't be afraid to give this kid a sound ethical or religious upbringing. Emphasize the Golden Rule.

Profession

The victorious Capricorn/Rat is the happiest one. This person needs to arrive at goals, one after the other, gamboling lickety-split up the cliff toward the isolation of domination. Once in awhile this person should take a quick glance behind him. He or she is at all times and in all circumstances pursued by at least one dedicated enemy. Getting places in life means toppling a few colleagues and stepping on your share of toes. Capricorn/Rats are surrounded by brooding people who have never forgotten that day back in 1948, "when she got the manager's office and I got the lowly switchboard job." Ah me. Vengeance. Yes. People are gunning for Capricorn/ Rats all over the lot. These subjects must be perspicacious. I'd advise them to be a little less ambitious, but I know it's out of the question.

Capricorn/Rats are bosses. They will only take employee jobs that guarantee promotion within minutes after hiring. As authority figures they are able to run a tight ship. But their subordinates don't ever really learn to adore them.

These people are so naturally dominant that I give the following careers as possibles: university administrator, executive officer, writer, performer, politician, musician, entrepreneur, attorney, banker, newscaster.

Famous Capricorn/Rats:
Adriana Ugarte, Alison Sudol, André Michelin, Andy Kaufman, Caroline Munro, Chad McQueen, Cynthia Addai-Robinson, Da-

mien Chazelle, Dan Harmon, Danny Lloyd, Donna Summer, Gabrielle Carteris, Gerard Depardieu, Graham McTavish, John De-Lorean, Josie Davis, Jude Law, Julia Louis-Dreyfus, Kelli Maroney, Konrad Adenauer, Lawrence Kasdan, Lenora Crichlow., Leonor Varela, Lewis Hamilton, Linda Lovelace, Lucy Davis, Michel Debré, Pablo Casals, Paul McCrane, Queen Mathilde of Belgium, Rakesh Sharma, Richard Nixon, Rod Serling, Steven Williams, Temuera Morrison, Thomas Wilson Brown, Vanessa Paradis, William Ragsdale.

CAPRICORN
QUALITIES
RESOLVE, WISDOM, AMBITION,
GENEROSITY, SUPERIORITY,
DEPENDABILITY
QUIRKS
STIFFNESS, CLUMSINESS, PRETENSION,
LONELINESS, EPICUREANISM, SELF-DOUBT
Motto: *"I use"*
Elements: *Earth, Saturn, Cardinal*

--

OX
QUALITIES
STUBBORNNESS, STRENGTH OF PURPOSE,
ELOQUENCE, STANDOFFISHNESS, INNOVATION,
VINDICTIVENESS
QUIRKS
INTEGRITY, BIGOTRY, PLODDING,
DILIGENCE, BIAS, STABILITY
Motto: *"I preserve"*
Elements: *Negative Water, Yin*

The Capricorn born Ox is a down-home conservative thinker. He's persistent and poky, stubborn and resolute. The Capricorn/Ox entertains solely his own highly individualistic opinions on everything, takes little time to consider the "other guy," and can even be accused of a certain spiritual brutality. Capricorn/Oxen are not violent types. But they can be crude—even cruel—in their methods.

Talk about strength of purpose! The Capricorn/Ox is a monster of determination and diligence. He never gives up on a project till he's pushed it to its absolute limit. He'll take all the hairs off the dog, if necessary, to find the one flea that's biting him. He's a mountain upon which I do not advise you to depend for casual skiing or sledding. This mountain will be choosy about whom it allows to hike up and down its craggy face. And as for seeking its shelter from the elements, you'd better come well recommended or else be family. Otherwise this persnickety, snobbish Capricorn may summon the north wind to whisk you to Siberia.

You see, this very vital yet bleak monolith is a veritable alp of a person. You never get to know all of his valleys or study the chasms he'll have hidden away in his bag of tricks. Some days you'll think he's the jolliest, sunniest, most pleasant person you have ever met. The next—gloom and doom. And neurosis. "I can't and I won't and I didn't and I wouldn't . . .." Oh Zeus! As solid and concrete and tangible as the Capricorn/Ox seems to be, he is really quite fragile. There is a poet living in every cavern of his mind and a sensitive artist perched in his soul. Yet, on the inscrutable surface you may at times wonder whether this person's heart is still beating.

The average Capricorn/Ox is bright. I'd even venture that most Capricorn/Oxen who have the opportunity to further their education do so. There are scads of intellectuals among these penetratingly ambitious souls. The Capricorn/Ox is nimble with words, will be drawn to the classics and is knowledgeable about things traditional. Here is a person who can turn a run-down railway depot in darkest Slovenia into an internationally photographed showplace for Architectural Digest's most demanding readers. Everything will be restored with scale-model perfection to its original ethnicity. Capricorn/Oxen are perfectionists for themselves as well as for the rest of us humble creatures.

Food is the realm that impassions the gourmand Capricorn born Ox. We are not, however, dealing with your run-of-the-mill glutton. The Capricorn/Ox couches his ungainly eating habits in the most elegant aura. Every bite of what goes onto the Capricorn/Ox's table must meet exigent standards of excellence. This person does not want to eat junk food. He or she longs, rather, to be immersed knee-deep in *foie gras*. The Capricorn/Ox's taste buds are as stubbornly standoffish as the rest of his substantial makeup.

It's difficult to sway this person from any preconceived notions he might cherish. The Capricorn/Ox is the undisputed ruler of the kingdom of *idées fixes*. What he or she learned at Granny's knee is etched in the stone mind of your Capricorn/Ox, never to stray further than the brain cell cluster where it lives happily ever after. "You take the Fifth Avenue bus uptown. Then you hop a crosstown at Fifty-ninth," he insists. "But there is no Fifth Avenue uptown. Fifth Avenue is one way downtown," you may protest.

My advice? Take the Sixth Avenue bus uptown and don't mention it again. Capricorn/Oxen are much more pleasant when they think they're right.

Love

Steadfast and remarkably sex-oriented, the Capricorn/Ox enjoys a lusty and action packed love life. Marriage is a must. The Capricorn/Ox's sense of family is much too strong to abandon the idea of an enduring kith and kin relationship. Outside of marriage, the Capricorn/Ox may have other fish to fry. Don't worry, though. The earnest and solid-citizen Capricorn/Ox won't leave home for one of these little minnows. In fact, if Capricorn/Ox notices a minnow trying to become a shark, he scampers off home where he feels he belongs. Divorce could shatter this delicate hunk of density. Divorce, for the Capricorn/Ox, means failure. Capricorns of all persuasions hate failure and take it personally. So if you're looking for a steady lover who'll bring home the bacon for life, get yourself a sober, forthright Capricorn/Ox. Pardon them their occasional peccadilloes and give them lots of reasons to respect you. Capricorn/Ox also responds well to heavy doses of his own medicine. Don't be afraid to live a little.

Compatibilities

Taurus, Leo, Virgo, Scorpio and Pisces are most harmonious for you in their Snake incarnations. The Scorpio/Snake may strike you as a bit much. Otherwise you might like to chance it with a Rooster from any of the above-mentioned astrological groups. Taurus, Leo, Virgo or Pisces/Rats would do nicely as well. And then there's always either Leo/Pig or Scorpio/Dragon to amuse you. Aries/Dragons are too hasty for you, and Cancer/Dragons too moody. Cancer or Libra/Sheep is not good for you. Libra/Ox, Tiger and Monkey are out, too, as is the stalwart (and competitive) Cancer/Pig.

Home and Family

The word is swanky. Inside and out, the Capricorn/Ox's place will reek of swank. He always boasts a good address and he's invariably proud to announce just how old the building where he lives is. At no extra cost he will furnish the name of the historically famous architect who designed it. If he has a country house (what am I saying? Of course he has a farm!), it will be authenticity itself. A restored stone mill that still works, grinding the wheat he grows, to make it into flour, which he uses to bake that spectacularly tasty bread you're eating. Or maybe it's an old church with handcrafted Gothic stained-glass windows brought direct from Chartres by antique sailing vessels. These characters like the real thing, and will accept no substitutes.

The Capricorn born in Ox years is a proud parent. He or she will parade baby Julia and little Alexander in the specially imported pram from London in the finest park right up there with the best of them. As far as Capricorn/Ox is concerned, his or her child can do no wrong. Fact is, in the interest of saving his skin, this person's child is likely not to commit a heck of a lot of naughty crimes in his life so long as Dad or Mom is there watching. Capricorn/Ox is a driving taskmaster who gives in both time and effort as much as he asks for in return.

Our Capricorn/Ox child will first of all be serious. Then, as he gets a bit older and goes to school, he will become more serious. The little scholar. The valedictorian. The goody-goody. Then, as adolescence approaches and the vision of love halos her horizon, the Capricorn/Ox child will begin to adapt herself to some new demands. Her sexual charm and satirical humor are the fruits of early adulthood when she learns how to be appealing. This kid doesn't need much more than a roof over his head and plenty of good things to eat. His path is already traced from birth. He'll grow up to be a Capricorn/Ox. Inflexible but funny.

Profession

Fame is not in the cards for this goal-oriented grind. It happens that a Capricorn/Ox reaches celebrity, but it is not one of his or her real objectives, and since Capricorn/Ox lives for his objectives, well, celebrity doesn't often occur. This person will, however, reach a respectable position in his or her job life. People will certainly look up to him and wish to be like him. In this way, by sterling example, the Capricorn/Ox obtains sufficient recognition to satisfy whatever small need he or she has for attention from peers. The main worry of every Capricorn/Ox is a fear of not living up to his or her own very high standards of excellence in the career of his/her choice. The Capricorn/Ox wants to feel he has used every ounce of talent and brains he was born with before he dies. He rides himself hard and long in order to achieve this very worthy end.

The Capricorn/Ox works best alone. He's such an individual that working with groups sometimes rubs him the wrong way. It can be hard on the group, too. Capricorn/Oxen always know best and stick relentlessly to their ideals and choices and habits. They will make intransigent bosses and huffy employees, unless, of course, they are given carte blanche to advance at their speed (slow) and use their methods (deliberate).

As for careers, I think the ones most applicable here are: teacher, farmer, theologian, food critic, fashion journalist, picture framer, architect, art director, consultant.

Famous Capricorn/Oxen:
Alison Arngrim, Anthony Hopkins, Ashton Locklear, Beth Behrs, Chuck Berry, Colin Morgan, David Johansen, Debbie Allen, Deepika Padukone, Denis O'Hare, Elisabeth Teissier, Erin Gray, Hrithik Roshan, Irina Shayk, Jason Behr, Jemaine Clement, Jessy Schram., Jim Carrey, John Lynch, Kate Moss, Kevin Durand, Mark Steger, Marlene Dietrich, Mary Tyler Moore, Melanie C, Omari Hardwick, Pierre Beregovoy, Sappho, Sissy Spacek, Suzy Amis, Thomas Watson Jr, Victoria Principal, Wade Williams.

CAPRICORN
QUALITIES
RESOLVE, WISDOM, AMBITION,
GENEROSITY, SUPERIORITY,
DEPENDABILITY
QUIRKS
STIFFNESS, CLUMSINESS, PRETENSION,
LONELINESS, EPICUREANISM, SELF-DOUBT
Motto: *"I use"*
Elements: *Earth, Saturn, Cardinal*

--

TIGER
QUALITIES
FERVOR, BRAVERY, MAGNETISM,
GOOD LUCK, BENEVOLENCE, AUTHORITY
QUIRKS
IMPETUOSITY, HOTHEADEDNESS,
DISOBEDIENCE, SWAGGER, INTEMPERANCE,
ITINERANCY
Motto: *"I Watch"*
Elements: *Positive Wood, Yang*

This whirlwind of staccato remarks and brusque gestures is a living tower of amiable good will. Now you see him, now you don't. And what you see is exactly what you get—congenial speed. The Capricorn born Tiger is easily bored. The concrete density of Capricorn's ambitious nature meets here with the hasty and sympathetic Tiger's bohemian nonsense. How this person even has so much as a second to stop and pet a puppy or kiss a baby is beyond me. The Capricorn/Tiger is jet-propelled. He has the metabolism of four hummingbirds and the true gift of sincere bonhomie.

Like all Capricorns, our Tiger subject is a bit awkward. When smoothness or suppleness might be in order to stem the flow of some clumsy social goof, count on the Capricorn/Tiger to end up chewing on his big toe. This character never sees the social amenities as anything more than what he basically thinks of them—hogwash! He's always in too much of a rush to stoop and kiss Madame Whatsername's be-ringed hand or hang about outside waiting for the butler to let him in. The Capricorn/Tiger is the person you are most likely to find standing dripping wet in the middle of your living room carpet, having just barged through your front door. "Hi!" he says cheerily. "How's the weather treatin' you?"

As Capricorn/Tigers are disdainfully oblivious to the tide of society and carry on at their own hasty pace, they tend to live a parallel existence to the one we know. Their work may take them through insufferably protracted periods of inhuman effort. But they come up smiling. They like a challenge. They prefer results to applause. The Capricorn/Tiger is out for real, tangible proof of his own powers. What other people think is of practically no importance to him at all.

Capricorns born in Tiger years frequently have sinewy, strong bodies that carry them through their race with life in top physical shape. As fast as they run and as manic as they appear, these people are surprisingly comfortable in their own vibrant skins. They are delightful company and attractive to the opposite sex. Is there nothing wrong with this engaging roadrunner? Of course there is. This is astrology. Nobody gets off scot-free. Capricorn/Tigers' energies are easily dispersed. They go in so many directions at once that they often get confused as to what the pertinent direction was in the first place. They also have expensive tastes and are wasteful with their wealth. They tend to lose track of material things.

But in the overall scheme, these people are amazingly all right. They are reasonable, and sufficiently successful to provide a good home for their family. They are naturally empathetic and truly like their fellow man. They have more confidence than the average Capricorn, who doubts himself and his own motives. For a Tiger, this character is rather sedate. He or she will be reliable and dependable (when not distracted) and will always do what he or she is asked in order to assist a fellow human being in need.

Love

Behind the casual air of dishevelment that is native to Capricorn/Tigers lies a profound sensitivity to all living things. There is a noble savage quality to this character. He will probably love animals and tend to take in strays. Yet, as a life partner, she will carefully select a person who can represent her deepest notions of how folks should live. These people want to create a healthy environment for raising a family. The Capricorn/Tiger needs a nucleus from which he can dash off to act on this or that new idea or plan. He needs to be loved oodles, and, in return, he dispenses buckets of generosity and lots of opportunity for fun.

If you have one of these creatures for your very own, hang onto him! Don't be a fool. Just because she's gone off to Chile to hunt skunks for an interplanetary deodorizing project, don't despair. Your Capricorn/ Tiger will bounce back into the middle of your trundle bed with all her lights on in a matter of days. Your job as the mate of one of these delectable nutcases is to keep yourself busy while he's gone, and most of all to learn to enjoy yourself without leaning on old Capricorn/Tiger. This person hates to be tied down, but loves to be married. It's a shade paradoxical, but it's very real to him or her. Don't be a grouch. It will get you nowhere fast.

Compatibilities

You are a natural-born Dog lover. Choose your pet from among Taurus, Leo, Virgo, Scorpio and Pisces breeds. If that doesn't do the trick, then pick up with a Leo, Virgo, Scorpio or Pisces/Horse. A Scorpio/Dragon may cause your eventual romantic demise, but the journey is half the fun. Aries, Cancer or Libra/Sheep are not on your sweetheart list. Nor are Aries or Cancer/Cats, Aries or Libra/Monkeys, Aries/Pig or Cancer/Oxen or Snakes.

Home and Family

The Capricorn/Tiger will want to own things and hold property of all kinds, but he won't be the sort to fiddle with looking after it. This native wants no part of do-it-yourself jobs. Call in an expert. Get a specialist. But don't ask your carefree Capricorn/Tiger to fix anything more than your broken heart. This person's house will be unpretentious and comfy. Take off your shoes and put your feet up. This hostess wants her guests to relax. She'll take care of the racing about, thank you.

In a family situation the Capricorn/Tiger will, of course, provide. His or her children represent stability and even reality to this jumpy sweetheart. Capricorn/Tigers will be snappy to their kids if made impatient, and can do a fine job of yelling at them at the climax of a crisis. But mostly Capricorn/Tigers don't pay all that much attention, and let their kids run a bit wild. They can't help it. They equate freedom with love in their own lives. Why should it be any different for their offspring?

The Capricorn/Tiger child will have all the earmarks of hyperactivity. He or she may be giddy and rambunctious and clown a lot. The best thing to do with this type of kid is to let him be giddy. But of course this isn't always possible. We don't all live in the vast countryside where we can dump Jason's kinetic excesses into the garden till he pipes down. My advice is to occupy this child with as many different projects as he or she can accomplish. There will be much innate intelligence available, so if it is properly applied (guide with a tender but firm hand), Jason should become a fine specimen of hyperkinetic adult with a head on his shoulders.

Profession

This person is cut out for working at the kind of job that allows freedom of movement. He can adapt his mind-set to someone else's rules, provided he sees the wisdom of the rule. Tigers are not very obedient. Capricorn helps here. But still, a Tiger is a Tiger; liberty of action and lots of challenge will keep this person content. His talents are innumerable and, oddly enough, he likes competition. Whatever the obstacle, count on the Capricorn/Tiger to try to locate a fast and efficient solution. Capricorns born Tiger feel that the most important thing is happening right now. They'll worry about next time, next time.

Of course, if you can pin them down long enough to install them behind a big mahogany desk, these people will make just and compassionate bosses. These bosses are the type who keeps the same secretary for a hundred and fifty years.

Capricorn/Tigers also adapt well to employee positions. These folks don't have any social axes to grind, and as long as they are satisfactorily productive, underling jobs will do fine. Capricorn/ Tigers are devoted and constant workers.

Careers that might apply here are: doctor, physical education teacher, veterinarian, cattle rancher, cowboy, forest ranger, book reviewer, translator, script writer, actor, actress.

Famous Capricorn/Tigers:

Bradley Cooper, Caity Lotz, Charo, Cristina Umaña, Crystal Gayle, Danica McKellar, Dave Foley, Dax Shepard, Evan Peters, Faye Marsay, Freddie Stroma, Gunnhild Øyehaug, Jason Connery, Jason Marsden, John McTiernan, Jon Polito, Jon Voight, Jordan Ladd, Kathleen Bradley, Kirstie Alley, Kit Harington, Kristin Cavallari, Lester Speight, Lucien Bodard, Lyndsy Fonseca, Mekhi Phifer, Naya Rivera, Patricia Neal, Ralph Fiennes, Richard Antony, Richard Widmark, Rush Limbaugh, Shelley Hennig, Steven Soderbergh, Thure Lindhardt, Yvette Mimieux, Ellie Goulding, Zane Holtz.

CAPRICORN
QUALITIES
RESOLVE, WISDOM, AMBITION,
GENEROSITY, SUPERIORITY,
DEPENDABILITY
QUIRKS
STIFFNESS, CLUMSINESS, PRETENSION,
LONELINESS, EPICUREANISM, SELF-DOUBT
Motto: *"I use"*
Elements: *Earth, Saturn, Cardinal*

--

CAT/RABBIT
QUALITIES
TACT, FINESSE, VIRTUE,
PRUDENCE, LONGEVITY, AMBITION,
QUIRKS
SECRETIVENESS, SQUEAMISHNESS,
PEDANTRY, DILETTANTISM,
HYPOCHONDRIA, COMPLEXITY
Motto: *"I Retreat"*
Elements: *Negative, Wood, Yin*

In this alloy the cautious Cat blends with the prudent Capricorn and creates a person whose ambition is second only to his gift for success. Endowed from the outset with traits that drive him or her toward slow but sure prosperity, the Capricorn/Cat never makes an important decision rapidly, never leaps wildly into any plan or project, never dashes into relationships without running a marketing study on them first. This person possesses natural wisdom. He's dynamic, vigorous and up-to-the-minute modern. But he's also heedful of possible dangers, and can read a threat from miles away.

The personality of Capricorn born in Cat years is pleasant. For a normally retiring Cat subject, this person is outgoing, extroverted. Nothing cheers up the Capricorn/Cat like the prospect of an evening spent at his place with friends, sitting around drinking and eating and having a jolly time. He will put on the record of your choice and show you his latest photos. But he will never monopolize the conversation or attempt to wrench center stage away from anyone else. It's true about Cats born in Capricorn: They need comfort first. Before this person can feel that he or she belongs to the world, he must have a material bastion of some sort to protect him from the outside. He doesn't like to face dull reality head on. Moreover, he is too busy working on tactics and strategies, adding and subtracting and figuring out his percentages, to take dull realities in hand. He needs protection from the day-to-day, boring "get the car fixed, buy the groceries and tell me your sob stories" life. For this purpose, Capricorn/Cat usually surrounds himself with people who will perform the dismal chores in order that he can get on with more important factors relative to his ascent to the summit of his profession.

Although the Capricorn/Cat may well succeed so resoundingly as to rise to the position of monarch, he or she will never be called the king of tact. Our hero blurts out just exactly what nobody needs to hear at all the wrong moments. "Hey! Where did you get that jagged scar?" or "Did you notice how much weight you have gained?" Such remarks could alienate the best of friends. But that doesn't happen with our slightly bumptious Capricorn/Cat. People enjoy this creature despite his occasional uncomfortable comments and his general clumsiness. The Capricorn/Cat has the endearing ability to laugh at himself, to poke fun at his own mistakes and to remain stable and sure of himself through it all.

The Capricorn/Cat is altruistic and sentimental. But he will not be the type to give away his shirt to a charity. There is a nice balance in this character's approach to friendship.

Panic is a major emotion native to the Capricorn/Cat. He is not basically changeable or flighty. So when confronted with the probability of a sudden shift or instant novelty, the adrenalin races him around in too many directions at once. Some say the Capricorn/Cat panics over nothing. The Capricorn/Cat likes to sleep late in the morning, tends to be messy about the house, and is hopelessly non-manual. This Capricorn is perhaps the most physically graceful of any.

Love

A Capricorn born in a Cat year will be cuddly and loving. But never in public! This person maintains a dignified surface and will not slobber over love affairs. Essentially, Capricorn/Cats are practical people. They will be attracted to mates who do things. They admire the tangible and seek results in all areas of their lives. A Capricorn/Cat will hardly ever take up with someone for the sake of mere beauty or good looks. They are interested in involvement with the person's self. They are also fascinated by the exotic, and may well take up with someone utterly different, whose artistic or gypsy like approach amuses and astonishes the Capricorn/Cat.

If you love a Capricorn/Cat, prove yourself useful and creative in your own field. Show them what a "mensch" you are. Don't shrink or be shy. The Capricorn/Cat recognizes skittishness as a fault he himself has had to overcome. He is not interested in what he already knows too well. Be your own person and think up ways to surprise the Capricorn/Cat. He likes surprises. He hates to be bored.

Compatibilities

Taurus, Leo, Virgo, Scorpio and Pisces/Dogs settle comfortably into your refined lifestyle. Taurus, Leo and Virgo/Pigs answer your need for wealth and culture. Leo, Virgo and Pisces/Sheep are capable of providing you with a creative and gentle partner. To avoid conflict (and you do avoid it!) eschew the Gemini, Cancer and Libra/Rooster. The Cancer and Libra/Rat don't suit you at all. Nor does the Libra in its Tiger or Dragon form.

Home and Family

Home for the Capricorn/Cat should be both comfortable and personal. There is, in this ambitious, upwardly mobile person, a streak of snobbery. How can I say this? Capricorn/Cats want to impress you. They will go out of their way to decorate their homes in a plush, almost lavishly comfortable manner. First of all, they want you to feel at ease. But they also want you to notice that their sofa is made of finest Cordoba leather and that those candlesticks are real brass. Impressive surroundings give the Capricorn/Cat confidence. He likes things to seem proper. I won't say he's bourgeois, but almost.

The Capricorn/Cat parent wants a child who can live up to his own self-image. No whining or sniveling allowed. This person will provide handsomely and give baby Alexander the best education available. But woe unto the lazy child who doesn't perform in school, bring home good grades, and measure up to Mom or Dad Capricorn/Cat's standards of virtue. The Capricorn/Cat wastes no time in making his or her position clear. "If you live here, you must do me proud. Otherwise—there's the door."

The Capricorn/Cat child is wiser than his years. He or she recognizes early on the necessity for paying attention to business. He or she will not take kindly to the interfering brand of parent. Capricorn/Cats are secretive about their feelings and don't appreciate meddling. This child will give a kind parent very little trouble. He wants to please and to fit in. He needs lots of comforts and will probably favor stuffed animals to live pets. The Capricorn/Cat child is humble, yet sure of himself. You will not have to prod him to do what he likes doing. As for practicing the piano . . .

Profession

Professions requiring a high degree of seriousness and an overdose of raw ambition will suit this character. Social acceptance is of paramount importance to the Capricorn/Cat. He doesn't want to be connected with shady or even untoward or unsuitable deals. Whatever goes on underneath the table will be considered taboo for discussion. The Capricorn/Cat wants no part of lawsuits or even fiscal audits. Mind you, should he have to entertain a tax inspector or two, all will prove to be in tiptop shape. Capricorn/Cat may be messy about the house but you can be sure that his papers are in order.

The subject born in Capricorn/Cat will make a sincere effort not to ruffle employees' feathers by shouting or ranting orders at them. This person operates best in a cooperative atmosphere and prefers that his workers smile. As he applies himself to routine well and makes great sacrifices to his goals, he has no time for subordinates who don't give their all in both labor and devotion.

This person won't buck the system if he is employed by someone else. Sure, he or she will try by all acceptable means to find a way to regain a certain job independence. But if they have to work for others, they know how to take orders and at least appear to toe the mark. Capricorn/Cats are born starved for success—personal and integral success. Nothing short of unmitigated professional fulfillment will satisfy this craving.

Winner jobs will best suit our Capricorns born in Cat years. Entrepreneur, writer, leader, politician, negotiator for international relations, hotshot lawyer, franchise owner, executive officer of a bank, general, sports commissioner, president of a university.

Famous Capricorn/Cat/Rabbits:

Andrew Lawrence, Dedee Pfeiffer, Ernesto Zedillo, Frank Sivero, Fritz Mondale, Gary Grant, Gaspar Noé, George Balanchine, Georges Balanchine, Haley Bennett, Heather O'Rourke, Henry Miller, Iain De Caestecker, Jeff Bezos, Jess Harnell, Jonathan Keltz, Joseph Stalin, Judith Krantz, Kacey Clarke, Kala Sosefina, Kevin Reynolds, Mark Addy, Marsha Thomason, Maurice Béjart, Michael Peña, Michelle Fairley, Michelle Obama, Mileniume Kaukava, Nicolas Cage, Paz Vega, Penelope Ann Miller, Robert Hossein, Robert Sheehan, Sammo Kam-Bo Hung, Sophia Umansky, Stephanie Faracy, Steve Bisley, Thomas Dekker, Tiger Woods, Yolanda Hadid.

CAPRICORN
QUALITIES
RESOLVE, WISDOM, AMBITION,
GENEROSITY, SUPERIORITY,
DEPENDABILITY
QUIRKS
STIFFNESS, CLUMSINESS, PRETENSION,
LONELINESS, EPICUREANISM, SELF-DOUBT
Motto: *"I use"*
Elements: *Earth, Saturn, Cardinal*

--

DRAGON
QUALITIES
STRENGTH, SUCCESS, GOOD HEALTH,
ENTHUSIASM, PLUCK, SENTIMENTALITY
QUIRKS
RIGIDITY, MISTRUST, DISSATISFACTION,
INFATUATION, BRAGGADOCIO, VOLUBILITY
Motto: *"I Preside"*
Elements: *Positive Wood, Yang*

Nobody condemns mediocrity the way the Capricorn/Dragon can. For people born in this combination of signs, prosperity as a result of personal toil amounts to the strongest hedge against the ordinary. The Capricorn/Dragon is special. He or she feels that peculiarity from a young age, realizes its terrible fragility and wants more than anything to be able to hang on to uniqueness forever. Capricorn/Dragon is aware of the pitfalls of upward mobility. He or she knows full well how much of a struggle is required to reach a peaceable victory and call a truce with adversity. But this knowledge does not daunt this angular Dragon subject. Threats and red flags cannot deter the true zealot.

Capricorn austerity is not very obvious here. When first you meet this sunny person with the hearty handshake and open ready smile, you'd almost believe you had been greeted by a glib Gemini or a munificent Leo. But no. Capricornian Dragons are naturally bright and cheerful—unless they are contradicted. Then suddenly you will note a clear aura of cool tension rising from this subject's epidermis. That's rigidity and stiffness.

The Capricorn/Dragon is talented for projects that ask for vehemence and gusto. He likes to be thoughtful of others and gets a real charge out of the expressions of gratitude they shower on him in return. He's a crowd-pleaser, but not for gain. His motives are personal. He wants attention and knows how to go after it in a positive fashion. Dragons love festivals and holidays, parties and crowds. The Capricorn/Dragon is no exception. The only difference is that Capricorn likes to give the parties himself, take care of guests with that special appeal native to his sign, and make certain that everyone is comfortable and having a good time. The Capricorn/Dragon is the caterer of the double zodiac. He's always up for a get-together and he'll do the shopping and cooking and even the cleaning afterwards, so long as you promise to go home happy.

The main drawback of this character's personality is his or her inability to say out loud what he or she feels inside. Don't misunderstand. The Capricorn/Dragon is a competent and eloquent communicator for all that relates to the outside. But when it comes to intimacy, the Capricorn born in Dragon years stalls out. He or she cannot trippingly spill the words "I love you" or "You have beautiful hair" or "Don't ever leave me" or "My darling Adam, you're the best ever." Capricorn/Dragons are privately reserved. They are forever being accused of coldness in matters of the heart.

This very genuine person makes a good lifelong friend. He or she will keep all commitments to loved ones and even stick out a neck once or twice if necessary. If a Capricorn/Dragon likes you, he will go through fire to see you thrive. He's not only loyal but he carries out his beliefs. If you have a problem collecting a radio you loaned someone a year ago, tell the Capricorn/Dragon of your woe. He'll tie himself to the person's house in the name of what's right. He'll take the matter to court. Capricorn/Dragons make terrific chums. But God help you if you do them wrong: The Capricorn/Dragon loses interest in traitors as swiftly as he demonstrates his devotion to those he cares for.

Love

The purity streak is very strong in Capricorn/Dragons. They are painfully honest about their preferences, and although diplomatic in every other, area of life, in love they sometimes make terrible romantic faux pas. I think the Capricorn/Dragon would love to settle down and marry and have a family—period! Yet, this person is too appealing for his/her own good. And pleasing is their pleasure. So when someone is too pleased for words and wishes to push the pleasure a bit further, Capricorn/Dragon is sorely tempted. Thing is, Capricorn/Dragons are quite conservative. If they do get involved in extramural sex, they like to think the devil made them do it. Their seething jealousy in love situations is positively frightening. They rant!

If you love a Capricorn/Dragon, don't hesitate to be firm with them. Make them understand that you love them for something more basic than their good looks or sex appeal. And put your foot down about all those parties, too. With this good-hearted soul you will have to wear the heaviest shoes. Capricorn/Dragons are too busy being nice to realize they haven't remembered to tell you how much they adore you. They must be reminded. But they don't hate being prompted. They are the type who might consider backseat driving a favor. "Oh, really? A stop sign? Where?" They really are too cute.

Compatibilities

Dragons are immensely popular. So are Capricorns. There are masses of people for you to try getting along with. Start with Rats. A Leo, a Virgo, a Scorpio or a Pisces will do. Or put a Taurus or Leo/Tiger in your tank. Taurus, Leo, Scorpio and Pisces/Roosters excite the adventurer in you. Same goes for Snakes born in those four signs. As for Monkeys, you prefer Virgo, Scorpio or Pisces to all other types. Who you don't get on with is limited to Gemini, Cancer and Libra/Dogs and Gemini and Cancer/Oxen. Otherwise the world is your playground. Enjoy.

Home and Family

Most Capricorn/Dragons wish they lived in well-appointed surroundings. And most Capricorn/Dragons live in bohemian pads. Their chairs don't match, their cat uses the table top as a bed, their baby has been eating the telephone book again, and darn! Where is the mate to this green sock? Capricorn/Dragons are messy about the house. They like pretty things but can do without. If you want an example, I'd say the average Capricorn/Dragon would rather invest in a magnum of expensive champagne than buy a snazzy couch or an antique chair. They are not really very materialistic people. They like nice things for practical purposes. But they care not about impressing or being like someone else.

These people make happy parents. The Capricorn/Dragon, with his slightly stiff upper-lip air and restrained laugh, is thoroughly amused by kids. They represent innocence and creativity and a carefree life. Capricorn/Dragon's dream is to have care lifted from his shoulders, to really fly like Peter Pan away from responsibility and worry. Of course, he does precisely the opposite and plunges head first every time into the role of Reliable Roger. So kids, to the Capricorn/Dragon, mean potential freedom. He wishes his little Melody or Mary Lee would grow up to be a great artist so that she would never have to buckle under to dull routines and smile at half-wit superiors. Heaven help the kid whose own lifelong dream is to be an accountant for Xerox.

As a child, no matter his place in the family, this kid will unconsciously take on the role of eldest. He or she slips readily into positions of command, and if siblings and parents see no objection to Capricorn/Dragon taking over the running of the household, he or she will make short work of setting an example for the others. He is not one to lord his power over others. But this child will be a natural leader. And winning? You'll fall directly in love with this tot. Capricorn/Dragons are irresistibly attractive.

Profession

Capricorn/Dragons recognize their own little foibles and are intensely interested in who they are and how they got to be like that. You will often find them in careers where the mirroring of human nature is the vector. They understand themselves and seek to understand the needs of others. They are generous but nonetheless careful with their money. They have natural talent for directing operations and managing people. When crossed, they can be pitilessly vengeful. The Capricorn/Dragon makes an interesting, lovable boss. He or she encourages subordinates to work rather than ordering them around. And as the Capricorn/Dragon often prides himself on his good manners, he or she will be courteous as well. As an employee this person is always biding time, waiting till he or she gets the big promotion. The Capricorn/Dragon is decidedly not interested in lowly jobs.

Suitable careers for this valuable person are: journalist, painter, astrologer, psychiatrist or psychologist, counselor, fundraiser, editor, clergyman, lobbyist, negotiator, public relations person, professor, caterer.

Famous Capricorn/Dragons:
Abigail Klein, Alex D. Linz, Andrew Johnson, Beau Mirchoff, Bernard Blier, Bobby Goldsboro, Brendan Hines, CCH Pounder, Conor Dwyer, Daniel Filipacchi, Danny McBride, Devin Ratray, Eddie Vedder, Emily Meade, Evelyne Thomas, Faye Dunaway, George Newbern, Hayley Williams, Ian Gomez, J.R.R. Tolkien, James Nesbitt, Jena Sims, Joan Baez, Joan of Arc, Joe Manganiello, Joely Richardson, Julia Ormond, Kohei Uchimura, Mark Valley, Michael Cudlitz, Michelle Forbes, Nicolas Cage, Nina Dobrev, Orlando Bloom, Pamela Sue Martin, Rebecca Dalton, Rhoda Griffis, Rob Zombie, Sophie Ward, Steve Lund, Susannah York, Tori Anderson, Vinnie Jones, Woodrow Wilson, Yvonne Zima.

CAPRICORN
QUALITIES
RESOLVE, WISDOM, AMBITION,
GENEROSITY, SUPERIORITY,
DEPENDABILITY
QUIRKS
STIFFNESS, CLUMSINESS, PRETENSION,
LONELINESS, EPICUREANISM, SELF-DOUBT
Motto: *"I use"*
Elements: *Earth, Saturn, Cardinal*

--

SNAKE
QUALITIES
INTUITION, ATTRACTIVENESS, DISCRETION,
SAGACITY, CLAIRVOYANCE, COMPASSION
QUIRKS
DISSIMULATION, EXTRAVAGANCE,
LAZINESS, CUPIDITY, PRESUMPTION,
EXCLUSIVENESS
Motto: *"I sense"*
Elements: *Negative, Fire ,Yin*

An arrogance and aplomb that would frighten Godzilla characterize this match. Capricorn practices what he preaches, puts his ideas to use and is not afraid of his own ambition. Snakes sense things, sniff out solutions and spend a large portion of their lives slinking in and out of crises on the way to the bank, the jeweler's, the airport, their lawyer's office or jail. Snakes often have more flair than brains. But with Capricorn as a mate, who needs brains?

The Capricorn born a Snake is in a class by himself. Not only does he feel superior to everyone in sight, but he also looks better than anyone else. These are stately people with built-in stature and class to burn. Their wardrobes alone cost half the national budget of Monaco—not to mention their cars and homes, their boats and their hairstyles.

Capricorn/Snakes are wildly loving of those less fortunate than themselves (everybody) and take in strays, adopt poor kids, hire on slothful employees, and the like. Some say they surround themselves with slobs so they will feel all the more superior. I don't quite agree with that theory. Capricorn/Snakes are deeply caring. They are often born luckier than other people. Things come to them easily. So my theory is that Capricorn/Snakes like to share their wealth and don't much care what anyone else's opinions are.

This person's very presence is powerful. Capricorn/Snakes are show-stoppers. They catch the eye of a whole room at once, and by their very carriage manage to keep it riveted on them until they are through basking in the attention. Oh yes. Attention is the Capricorn/Snake's drug. He wants to be looked at, hugged, talked and listened to, scolded and spanked, and fed and bathed first. Nobody and nothing will be allowed to come between this haughty character and the audience he's looking to get attention from. Real star quality.

The underside of the Capricorn/Snake's grand generosity is his appalling wastefulness. These people buy three tuxedos for every one they might need to go to that charity ball next week. They'll get two different kinds of car for your birthday, just in case you didn't like the first one. Also, in their eagerness to please and preside, to own the moment in which they live, Capricorn/Snakes are not above any sort of ruse. If smiles don't work then tears it will be, or fits of rage, hysteria or psychosomatic illness. They want to be noticed. At any cost. If they hate you, you certainly won't be able to be indifferent to their distaste, either. They will find ways to remind you. Capricorn is a purposeful little critter. And Snakes are so darn clever. A brush with one of these monsters will never leave you indifferent.

There is, in every Capricorn/Snake, the gift of the supernatural. These people could probably live a very full life just following hunches and answering premonition's call. It's spooky but true. There is a foresight here unequaled by any other sign. Intuition is even too mild a word. The Capricorn/Snake senses trends, dangers, political movements, events of all natures.

As tough as nails and as sweet as pie, the Capricorn/Snake operates almost exclusively out of a thirst for power, for celebrity, for true greatness in the eyes of his contemporaries. No posthumous kudos for this person! "Give me those dozens of roses right now," commands the startling Capricorn/Snake. "I shall distribute them to people less fortunate than myself. " And so she does. Off goes the Capricorn/Snake with her diva personality to draw crowds elsewhere, to throw kisses to her entranced audience, and to sow peace and love among men (as long as they live by her rules). This character is so charmingly bossy you hardly notice you have been given the job as the head of the cleanup committee.

Love

A romantic if there ever was one, the Capricorn/Snake is forever imagining himself "in love" with somebody. Every relationship that comes along feels as if it must be the perfect one. Each stray just needs a little fixing up here and there and before you can say "Mao Tse-tung" he or she will be the perfect lover or mistress, obedient and sane and healthy and brilliant by virtue of his ability to stand on his own feet. (Ordinarily, the people Capricorn/Snakes pick up are quasi-bedridden.) In other words, Capricorn/Snakes are promiscuous by default. They are always losing their lovers to dissipation and sloth. But not to worry. There are more where they came from. People go mad for this creature. He or she is never at a loss for tenderness. They are affection consumers. Capricorn/Snakes eat love.

If you love a Capricorn/Snake, you will be in awe of him or her. If you care to keep your Capricorn/Snake, don't stay that way. This person ends up fixing his affections on the most demanding of his admirers. Capricorn/Snakes need to be confronted daily by a strong and severe judge who helps them get a bead on their mirror image, who knows how to reach their epicenter of softness and true enlightenment. All the scruffy strays in the universe won't do. Capricorn/Snake needs a tough, no-nonsense partner who knows how to keep him or her in line and who, most importantly, doesn't let him or her get away with duplicity. Fibbers to a man, Snakes must be constantly monitored for signs of dissimulation.

Compatibilities

Taurus, Leo, Virgo, Scorpio and Pisces/Oxen and their Rooster brothers and sisters are all possibles. You may swoon for a Leo/Dragon or Monkey. They have enormous charm and vitality. Besides, they like you too. You're not likely to get the same flash from Cancer or Libra/Pigs. Aries and Gemini/Tigers and Monkeys are on another wavelength as well. Don't bother with Aries/ Roosters. They go too fast and, to you, seem to get nowhere.

Home and Family

The Capricorn/Snake home will not be merely elegant. It will be a bastion, a model, a paragon of studied posh. And why do I even use the word "home" in the singular? Capricorn/Snake people never have just one house. At the very minimum this person will have a town and a country home. From then on, as they acquire the funds, they have one in the Caribbean, a little place in Goa and a condo in Saint Moritz. And the boat? That's in the Bahamas. To this natural classicist, no number of Corinthian columns on the front veranda will be too many, no carpet too thick, no antique too dear. The best of everything for this character is never good enough. And messy? My God. Miasmatic in the dressing room. Never mind. The maid comes every day. Twice. Sometimes three times.

These people make wonderful parents. Having kids is a bit like taking in stray puppies. Capricorn/Snakes hover and comfort, and stay up all night and wrap their puking infants in the nearest sable stole at hand. Little Lauren or Jimmy should never want for anything. That is the Capricorn/Snake ideal—and if the nanny is nice, the kid is in good shape. Count on the Capricorn/Snake to be gone a lot of the time. When he's there, he'll spend intense quality time with the kids. But we are talking about a world-class busy person. The kid should be spared too much of the Capricorn/Snake parent's vast shadow, anyway. It's not healthy trying to live up to such a monolith.

The Capricorn/Snake child is first of all loving—graspingly so. Secondly he is loving—sweetly so. And thirdly he is loving—endearingly so. Most of all he likes to be the most adored child in the family. He needs all of his parents' attention, and if he doesn't get it, he finds ways. He is a dutiful child and very bright, of course. But if he isn't first at everything he gets stomachaches, has nightmares, and bites his nails. This never lasts long, as the Capricorn/Snake child always triumphs sooner or later over whatever his or her family was. But while he's small this kid must be nurtured as though he were a future prize orchid that takes twenty years to come to flower and in the meantime must be worn on your wrist—even as you sleep.

Profession

Most Capricorns born in Snake are destined for some form of prominence. They may be a political leader one day or they may just shine head and shoulders above their peers for some professional or humane reason. Whatever it is that gets them there, they get there. They sincerely believe that they are the best and the greatest at their craft or field, and because of this fervent belief, they of-

NEW ASTROLOGY FOR THE 21ST CENTURY

ten convince both themselves and others of that fact. Capricorn/ Snakes aspire to greatness—and they often get it.

The Capricorn/Snake knows how to take orders if he or she knows it's only temporary. These people are good workers (if they can get out of bed) and find brilliant solutions to problems for bosses who know how to use them properly. Capricorn/Snakes do not, however, want to remain employees forever. They like their bread buttered far too thickly to put up with floor-scrubbing for long. When they do get to be boss, they will play boss. There is never any question who runs the show and there is never any doubt the show is best run by Capricorn/Snake. The Capricorn/Snake should not attempt to slither out from under his destiny. It will only come back to haunt him.

Suitable careers for Capricorn/Snakes are: entrepreneur, president, millionaire, heiress, movie star, top model, advertising director, religious leader, oil magnate, choreographer, film director.

Famous Capricorn/Snakes:
Adrian Waller, Antoine Fuqua, Aristotle Onassis, Camryn Grimes, Cheryl Howard, Eddie Cahill, Edgar Allan Poe, Edwin (Buzz) Aldrin, Glen Yarborough, Grant Gustin, Howard Hughes, Howard Stern, James Remar, Jamie Clayton, Jane Badler, Jane Levy, January Jones, Jodi Long, Joshua Malina, Kailash Satyarthi, Katey Sagal, Katherine Moennig, Liam Aiken, Liam Hemsworth, Lucy Punch, Mackenzie Rosman, Mao Tse-tung, Maria Pitillo, Martin Luther King, Michael Raymond-James, Michelle Mylett, Mohammed Ali, Nicolette Scorsese, Olivier Martinez, Patrick Dempsey, Régine, Richard Clayderman, Rod Taylor, Salman Khan, Sarah Miles, Stefan Edberg, Stephen Hawking, Tovah Feldshuh, Trudie Styler, Vanessa Ferlito, Vernee Watson.

CAPRICORN
QUALITIES
RESOLVE, WISDOM, AMBITION,
GENEROSITY, SUPERIORITY,
DEPENDABILITY
QUIRKS
STIFFNESS, CLUMSINESS, PRETENSION,
LONELINESS, EPICUREANISM, SELF-DOUBT
Motto: *"I use"*
Elements: *Earth, Saturn, Cardinal*

--

HORSE
QUALITIES
PERSUASIVENESS, UNSCRUPULOUSNESS,
POPULARITY, STYLE, DEXTERITY,
ACCOMPLISHMENT
QUIRKS
SELFISHNESS, AUTONOMY, REBELLION,
HASTE, ANXIETY, PRAGMATISM
Motto: "I demand"
Elements: Positive Fire, Yang,

"Count on me!" says the reliable Capricorn/Horse. And believe me, you can. Here is a marriage made in heaven. Capricorn lends solidity and staying power to the somewhat dandified and often insecure Horse character. In his turn, Horse gives this Capricorn manual dexterity and a finely developed sense of his or her own popularity.

Here we have a subject whose personal development is often subjugated to the needs of others. Capricorns born in Horse years are good people. They take care of the less fortunate in minutest clothes-brushing detail. They know how to love. They set a fine example to more selfish sorts and, because of their semi rigidity and somewhat forbidding air, are frequently misunderstood. Capricorn/ Horses seem snappish and even a bit rough on their entourages. They are essentially peace-loving people, of course. But their manner is dry and their demeanor brittle.

Capricorn/Horses are conscientious and painstaking to a fault. If at first they don't succeed, they have infinite resources for trying again. These people are believers in humanity. They are rigorous for themselves and only indulgent with others if others show promise. Do-nothings and layabouts abstain. The Capricorn/Horse has no time for indolents. He wants to surround himself with unusual and creative people. This character is perpetual motion incarnate. He or she never sits still unless the project being worked on demands a sitting position. They are doers of deeds and setters of cornerstones. They get things going every day, over and over, and they somehow manage to inject fantasy, excitement and creativity into any kind of routine.

The ingenuousness of Capricorn/Horses is both touching and admirable. Despite all that can happen in a lifetime—illness, setbacks, poverty, loss, and so on, these folks manage to view life as an inevitable continuum, a clock that needs to be wound daily no matter the weather in order to give proper service. Capricorn/Horses treat life gently, as though it belonged to them only for a short while. They seem to sense that one day they too will have to pass away. This combination of innocence and resignation can bring with it an excessive awareness or fear of aging. The Capricorn/Horse is a secret wrinkle-watcher.

Curiously, this person rarely achieves anything grand or of cosmic import until late in life. As there is great deliberation in this character's makeup and an attention to detail rare indeed, his works often require years to germinate and be tested and finally to blossom forth. Early success is not instantly given to retiring, self-effacing souls. But, in the case of the talented and even unwittingly brilliant Capricorn/Horse, fulfillment always arrives sometime. How could such cleverness and creativity go eternally overlooked?

Finally, most appealing about the personality of the Capricorn/Horse is that he is not out to prove anything to anyone. He's living his old life at his pace in his way and something invisible tells him it's just fine like that. He's neither demonstrative nor really extroverted. Rather, the Capricorn/Horse exhibits a certain pleasant reserve, which, although close to shyness, does not qualify as shrinking timidity. Capricorn/Horses are not as self-aware as the average Horse person. But they are equally hardworking, practical and noble.

Love

This generous, peaceful nature revels in love. Moreover, people love Capricorn/Horses easily. They respect them too; admire their spunk and talent. In fact, I don't know any Capricorn/Horse people who aren't overrun by suitors or fawned upon by ladies. Thing is, Capricorn/Horse is basically faithful. He or she has no eye for promiscuity or lighthearted one-night stands. Who would watch the laboratory while Monsieur Pasteur is out back flirting with the goose girl? No, sir. Capricorn/Horse keeps his own eye on his own test tubes and trusts nobody else with the serious side of his life. His romantic goal? To find someone funny to love, who will offer distraction and loyalty forever.

If you love a Capricorn/Horse, I can understand you. If he or she can't love you back, I know you must be crushed. But you do, of course, see that this citadel of integrity and enticing diffidence cannot possibly maintain the image of which you are so enamored if he or she leaves an active affair to take up with you. Unless you corral this colt from the cradle or catch him or her on the rebound or coming into the stretch, you will have to get up pretty early in the morning to win a Capricorn/Horse's love. If, by some fluke, you find one of these desirable mates roaming around free, tell him or her a joke. Capricorn/Horses are serious folks. Anything that jollies them up gets an instant A+.

Compatibilities

Sheep coexist peacefully with Horses born in Capricorn. The best choice of Sheep persons for you will be found among Taurus, Leo and Pisces natives. Virgo, Scorpio and Pisces/Tigers lend pizzazz to your workday, and you cannot go wrong with Dogs born in those same signs. On the other hand, if I were you I would avoid close contact with Aries, Cancer or Libra/Horses (all Horses can be left out of your intimate secrets with impunity). Cancer and Libra/Monkeys leave you cold.

Home and Family

Capricorn/Horses like traditional surroundings. They enjoy function and give it precedence over form in decoration. Like all Horse subjects, they are attracted by bright colors and yet, because they are Capricorn, these people use fuchsias and cadmium yellows in a less cavalier fashion than most flashier Horses. An ornate shawl is thrown over an overstuffed couch; a hand-made patchwork quilt in crazy colors adorns their bed. But all in all, the decor at Capricorn/ Horse's house is natural and practical. Wood, stone, plants and more wood.

Capable of enormous self-sacrifice for family needs, the Capricorn/Horse makes a terrific parent. He or she is sufficiently sentimental to remember to hug and compliment little ones for achievement. And the Capricorn/Horse is also strict and teaches by example. His or her time, again the Capricorn/Horse's strongest resource, belongs to the nurturing process. This parent doesn't take any back talk from kids but has, nonetheless, a relaxed and familiar rapport with them. The Capricorn/Horse takes great pride in his children's achievements. But if a child fails, he knows he can always run first to a Capricorn/Horse Mom or Dad for comfort.

The Capricorn/Horse child gives parents much pleasure. This is the one kid in the family who stays close to home even after he or she is grown. The Horse born in Capricorn doesn't mind rules and understands parental regulation. His aim as a child will be to please his family, to make them proud and to make sure he receives an extra pat on the head for his efforts. You can give the Capricorn/ Horse lots of education. He is bright and willing to learn. Also, as he will tend to be silent, he should be encouraged to participate in home productions of plays and readings. He has the talent for great performance but he's too conservative to show off.

Profession

Service professions suit the Capricorn/Horse. He or she will be drawn to jobs that require experimentation and demand steadiness and routine. The Capricorn/Horse is creative. But he or she is essentially a plough horse. The spotlight? Get it out of his eyes, please. Capricorn/Horse wants only to know that what he works at is worthwhile. He doesn't fancy frivolous careers in glamour professions. He's after results. He's socially conscious and very humane.

Jobs this subject might excel at are: minister of health, scientist, chef, veterinarian, craftsperson, fabric designer, furniture builder, architect, lawyer, nurse, dog trainer, wine grower.

Famous Capricorn/Horses:

Aaliyah, Andy Rooney, Annie Lennox, Anwar Sadat, Ben Hardy, Bill Goldberg, Cash Warren, Charles Nelson Reilly, Denzel Washington, Derek Riddell, Diedrich Bader, Dominika Figurska, E. L. Doctorow, Emily Watson, Ennis Esmer, Estella Warren, Eva La-Rue, Gayle King, Hans van Arum, Harriet Sansom Harris, Irrfan Khan, Isaac Newton, J.K. Simmons, James Earl Jones, James Marshall, Jay Chou, Jill Wagner, Johannes Sellin, Kevin Costner, Kiefer Sutherland, Louis Pasteur, Mendes France, Odetta, Paul Rodriguez, Puccini, Robert Duvall, Rowan Atkinson, Samantha Sloyan, Sandra Taylor, Sarah Polley, Sarah-Sofie Boussnina, Sir Alvin Ailey, Stacy Martin, Tia Carrere, Tippy Hedren, Tyrese Gibson.

CAPRICORN
QUALITIES
RESOLVE, WISDOM, AMBITION,
GENEROSITY, SUPERIORITY,
DEPENDABILITY
QUIRKS
STIFFNESS, CLUMSINESS, PRETENSION,
LONELINESS, EPICUREANISM, SELF-DOUBT
Motto: *"I use"*
Elements: *Earth, Saturn, Cardinal*

--

SHEEP
QUALITIES
INVENTION, LACK OF FORESIGHT,
PERSEVERANCE, WHIMSY, GOOD MANNERS,
IMPRACTICALITY
QUIRKS
PARASITISM, SENSITIVITY,
TARDINESS, PESSIMISM, TASTE, WORRY
Motto: *"I depend"*
Elements: *Negative, Fire, Yin*

The normally lackadaisical Sheep personality gets a run for his money when his birthright links him forever to the rigid, dependable, and ambitious Capricorn mountain-climbing Sheep. The Chinese Sheep and the occidental one are poles apart. The oriental Sheep drips with sensitivity and thinks only of whimsy and invention. The other is an uphill skier whose ambition is to be ambitious. "Get there or die!" says the dogged Capricorn. "Ouch! My feet hurt," whines the sensitive Sheep. Inner discord is no stranger to people born under the dual sign of Capricorn/Sheep. The push-me-pull-you effect that two directly opposite vectors produce in this character causes him or her a lot of personal anguish. Capricorns born in Sheep years know they must be serious. They work to get into a position of power. They struggle through studies and often come up the hard way, through the ranks. Both signs are persevering.

Lucky for the Sheep to be born Capricorn. This addition of a little earth to the capricious Sheep's personality doesn't spoil his high quality and even puts a fair amount of starch in his otherwise flimsy sails. Capricorn/Sheep remain (for Capricorns) the crazies of the Capricorn race. But they manage to keep their feet on the ground about ninety percent more than other Sheep. Of course, they pay for this security. Capricorn/Sheep don't have time to be as creative as they'd like. They are preoccupied with success. They are driven by a need for recognition. They are even a tiny bit pretentious and want to be rich enough to show off once in awhile. Naturally all the industriousness they must employ in the drive to become somebody in their chosen profession takes time away from invention. As a result, the Capricorn/Sheep is given to daydreaming and imagining a better world wherein he or she would be able to fly or to paint or to play at Carnegie Hall or to win the Davis Cup.

In the long run, this person grows elastic. He or she will learn as time goes along to abstract the day-to-day and to live solely in anticipation of short periods of blissful irresponsibility. This Sheep is too reliable for his own good. Since his dependability cuts down on his creativity, his Capricorn wisdom and sense of what is right gives this Sheep a pain in the neck. But no matter how vigorously he denies it, his first duty is to his work. Capricorn sees to that from the word go.

What's most delectable about this person is that although he is an almost religiously strict Capricorn (all the more severe because he is a convert), he knows better than all other Capricorns how to let loose. In his off-duty moments, you would guess him to be a wild-eyed Taurus/Dragon or at least a murky Scorpio. He loves to dance and sing and generally carry on. Capricorn/Sheep have huge reserves of charisma. They are both elegant and sensitive. They love company. They covet power and they are remarkably verbal. They are spendthrift and rarely prompt.

Love

Capricorn/Sheep is a romantic idealist. He or she believes in fairy tales. Although these subjects will not be terribly verbose about lovemaking, they are eager and enthusiastic sex partners. The Sheep born in Capricorn is given to great displays of affection through gifts or even pranks or loving surprises. No matter how serious they may seem, they are just itching to get out of their Capricorn suit and into their Sheeply rags so they can rush off into the woods like Pan and woo little unsuspecting creatures into their lair. These people are mightily attractive. And promiscuous? Well, a little—no, a lot. But they know how to be discreet.

If you love a Capricorn/Sheep, remember he or she is a Sheep. Remember that if you marry or live with one of these people you will most likely be (subtly, of course) wearing the pants. The Capricorn/Sheep comes on very strong and seems to be authoritarian. But what he really wants is to be left alone to play with his toys and gambol through the woods. If you can improve his lot by undertaking the details of householding or bringing home the bacon, this person will not love you less for doing so.

Compatibilities

It looks to me as though you favor Pigs, and I can almost guarantee that your special favorite will be born in Taurus, Leo, Virgo, Scorpio or Pisces. You will flip for Cats born in Leo, Virgo, Scorpio or Pisces, and you will not kick the Horses of the Leo, Scorpio or Pisces variety out of bed for eating crackers. Less likely to keep you awake nights are natives of Aries, Cancer or Libra born Tiger. Aries and Libra/Dogs unnerve you with their gab about causes and charity. And Aries and Libra/Oxen strike you as stodgy and stubborn and no fun at all. Libra/Horses won't work. Too self preoccupied.

Home and Family

When the Capricorn/Sheep is at home, he wants it beautiful and well kept. Mostly, he's out. This person is quirky. He is capable of suddenly deciding to renew all the furniture in the whole house. Out with the old and in with the new. Capricorn is, after all, the sign of the New Year. And Sheep? Well, they are all whacked out of their skulls when it comes to material wealth. So burn the old couches and sofas or put them out on the sidewalk. "And the new furniture, madam? Where shall I put it?" "Why, on my American Express, of course," says the Sheeply Capricorn. *Luxe* and debt. The bylaws of the Capricorn/Sheep home life.

The Capricorn/Sheep parent is loving but not always giving. He or she can be impatient and even sarcastic with kids. The Capricorn/Sheep parent is always champing at the bit herself because she isn't free to be free the way kids are. Her children's comparative liberty rankles the Capricorn/Sheep parent. Let's say he or she is a devoted but difficult parent who needs understanding from kids, who are not, as we know, always compassionate with a troubled or busy parent. Capricorn/Sheep parents especially adore their kids when the kids are old enough to look after themselves.

The Capricorn/Sheep child will have the potential to be the light of his parents' life. Talented and creative, intelligent and whimsical, this kid's winsomeness makes you want to chew him up alive. But try and get him to settle down to work on his math. This kid is a handful. Rewarding, and very, very conscientious about parents later in life. But when they are small, Capricorn/Sheep kids know how to keep adults hopping. They should be disciplined early on and never allowed to think anything in life worth having comes cheap. This kid needs a sound religious education, too.

Profession

I hesitate to say that this person is a born leader. Yet, despite all the whimsy and the flimsy, this character is a veritable monument of magnetism. Properly applied, the blend of wise Capricorn and sensitive Sheep is unbeatable. There's something about the very disparity of characters involved that creates a synergy capable of uncanny attraction. The inventiveness of Sheep can best be put to material use by the steady Capricorn. If the combination works, that is if Sheep is controlled most of the time by Capricorn, the charge is electric, to say the least.

In a position of power this person will be just plain bossy. He or she directs operations almost by second nature. "Get me this and bring me that." However, as the Capricorn/Sheep is more humanitarian than he is bossy, his employees will adore him. He never forgets their birthdays and gives quick promotions for the sake of morale building. This person can be an employee. But not for long.

Some jobs that might appeal to the Capricorn/Sheep are: performer, physician, surgeon, politician, producer, dean of a university.

Famous Capricorn/Sheep:
Andre Holland, Ben Kingsley, Cardinal John O'Connor, Carlos Saura, Chad Lowe, Chloe Bridges, Clarence Gilyard Jr., Cuba Gooding Jr., David Caruso, De Forest Kelley, Diego Luna, Eden Sher, Elaine Cassidy, Frida Farrell, George Burns, Grand L. Bush, Imelda Staunton, Janet Hubert, Jason Segel, Jeff Chase, Jenson Button, Joe Frazier, Joey Lauren Adams, John Denver, Justin Welby Archbishop of Canterbury, Lilly Wachowski, LL Cool J, Logan Lerman, Louis Tomlinson, Luke Macfarlane, Maurice Utrillo, Mel Gibson, Millard Fillmore, Noomi Rapace, Paul Young, Phyllis Logan, Professor Jean Barnard, Rachel Nichols, Ravish

Malhotra, Robert Lamoureux, Salvatore Adamo, Sam Riley, Sarah Shahi, Shawn Johnson, Sofia Black-D'Elia, The Reverend Moon, Yves Berger, Zooey Deschanel.

CAPRICORN
QUALITIES
RESOLVE, WISDOM, AMBITION,
GENEROSITY, SUPERIORITY,
DEPENDABILITY
QUIRKS
STIFFNESS, CLUMSINESS, PRETENSION,
LONELINESS, EPICUREANISM, SELF-DOUBT
Motto: *"I use"*
Elements: *Earth, Saturn, Cardinal*

--

MONKEY
QUALITIES
IMPROVISATION, CUNNING, STABILITY,
SELF-INVOLVEMENT, WIT, OPPORTUNISM
QUIRKS
DECEIT, RUSE, LOQUACITY,
LEADERS, SILLINESS, ZEAL
Motto: *"I plan"*
Elements: *Positive, metal, Yang*

A certain indefinable air of resigned melancholy pervades the portrait of Capricorn born in Monkey. Although I cannot say why, the combination of Capricorn-the austere and Monkey-the-problem-solver creates in its natives a queer brand of personal anguish. These people are not obviously nervous. Indeed, their smart demeanor and distinguished bearing bespeak an attitude of self-assurance. Capricorn/Monkeys send out dignity vibes. They are what my mother used to call debonair. Nevertheless, underneath the smooth, mannerly veneer lives a tortured soul.

Perhaps the Monkey's self-assuredness and basic temperance clash with Capricornian stiffness. Maybe, instead of Capricorn benefiting gaily from Monkey's silly side and incorporating a bit of that simian loquacity, the Capricorn element is intimidated by its Monkey side. Sometimes I think that Capricorn/Monkeys must feel like one of those good-looking, beribboned, shiny cardboard boxes from fancy shops, inside of which sits a naughty, tricky and giggling live baboon. The package, in other words, doesn't at all reflect its contents.

Capricorn/Monkeys like to appear serious. In fact, unless you know them intimately and become privy to their secret life, you will probably only know the grave side of this person's nature. Superficially they are the most presentable people in captivity. Inside the home, they can be absolute rotters. I do not wish to suggest dual natures. But the Monkey born in Capricorn suffers from a form of public shyness rare among men. If you meet him or her in a bar where the atmosphere is jolly and tongues are loosened by exotic elixirs, you will probably not notice this clammed-up side. You will see a jolly, story-telling performer with a sly twinkle in his eye and a memory for narrative that astounds as well as amuses. He will be bright and dapper, sharp-witted, slightly bitchy and really very witty.

The Capricorn/Monkey's timing is perfect. Yet you take this character home and put her or him into a living room situation and the picture goes all fuzzy. Somehow Capricorn/Monkeys imagine they must create the order and handle the planning and running of whatever it is that constitutes private life. They take this responsibility terribly seriously. "Where are the groceries? Why isn't dinner ready? Why didn't Maria clean the library? What happened to your socks? Have you lost your mind? You can't spend your whole week's allowance on comic books!" It's obvious that their jaunty Monkey side doesn't cotton to this burdensome Capricorn severity. Nonetheless, there it is. Capricorn/Monkey is a hell of a cop.

Essentially, the Capricorn/Monkey is theatrical. He has an agile and exacting mind. He has a superlative talent for expression. He enjoys sinewy, lanky good looks with a bone structure that would make Greta Garbo weep with envy.

Capricorn/Monkeys see human situations in a special light all their own. They understand and are compassionate with all variety of personal joy and suffering. They know how to translate these emotions for others' appreciation. Capricorn/Monkeys are interpreters. They are not simple, nor are they easy, laid back or bohemian. Façade is important to them. Social graces and custom will continue to die hard so long as they keep making Capricorn/ Monkeys.

Love

Quality takes precedence over quantity in the rather abstemious romantic life of Capricorn/Monkeys. This subject would always prefer to be deeply in love forever than passionately in love for a split second. Moreover, the Capricorn/Monkey's standards of excellence are high. He won't be happy with somebody who looks as if the cat dragged him in when he gets out of bed. Capricorn/ Monkey will make no bones about sporting velvet dressing gowns and matching slippers. He or she will enjoy the trappings of a life with someone else, share intimacies of a secret and (for the Capricorn/ Monkey) terrifying nature only with the loved one, and dream of the old adage: "Live hidden, live happy."

Should you be caught in the charm vortex of this spruce and dashing personage, I suggest you toy with the idea of being at least as meticulous as a Virgo. You will need all the resourcefulness you can gather for this romantic experiment. But remember, if the Capricorn/Monkey loves you, there is no love more fervently pure than his. As the object of a Monkey born in Capricorn's affections, you will be the light (and the dark) of your admirer's life—forever. It's a very big job. The emotional rewards are many. Ditto the sleepless nights.

Compatibilities

You'll go looking for happiness among the Rats. Choose carefully out of the batch by preferring a Leo, Virgo, Scorpio or Pisces. A Taurus, Virgo or Pisces/Dragon will captivate you as well, and you can freely involve yourself with anyone born in either Taurus/Sheep or Scorpio/Tiger. Aries/Tigers don't set well with you, though. Nor do Cancer/Horses or Libra/Snakes and Pigs. You want to be the noble member of your couple. Don't precipitate marriage.

Home and Family

Plenty of room to breathe and relax—not to mention perform— at home is what the Monkey born in Capricorn dreams of. This subject feels everyone ought to have his or her own space to be alone in. Houses will be large and furnished in excellent taste. This Capricorn is rather more manual than most, as Monkey lends him dexterity and grace. Even in his strict, almost uniform-type manner of dress, this person cleaves to traditional colors and easy to manage shapes. Beiges and navy blues will predominate. Grays, too, will be worn discreetly and cool dark greens favored by the Capricorn/Monkey. It's almost as though the Capricorn/Monkey has such a multicolored circus going on inside his head that he wants peaceful surroundings in which to find repose.

This person will be a conscientious parent but is not likely to hatch multiple broods. The Capricorn/Monkey has limited patience with the frivolities of childhood. Babies will probably not bother the Capricorn/Monkey, as he or she will find them endearing and innocent. But as a child grows and needs guidance, the Capricorn/Monkey parent will prove short-tempered at times. This native has all he can do to hold himself together. All transgressions on the part of offspring will represent a personal failure to keep order in the universe. The advantage to having such a parent is, of course, the example set by his or her general good behavior in the world. Capricorn/Monkeys are far from being mother hens. They love their kids—that's enough.

This child, on the other hand, will be quite adorable. A born performer and lover of everything to do with spectacle, this kid will probably want to watch TV nine hours a day and go to the movies the rest of the time, that is when he's not at theater camp or directing operations in the school production. The behind-the-scenes quality of this person's nature makes for an interesting, somewhat secretive and solitary child whose monkeyshines will always surprise those close to him or her. Too, this is a cerebral child whose studies will play a leading role in his activities. A gratifying little person to have around, this kid learns fast and enjoys the company of adults.

Profession

Jobs and career-oriented pursuits are the flames that ignite this character's whole existence. Capricorn/Monkeys are the opposite of lazy. They are creative and know how to tell stories and captivate audiences. Their expression is very emotional and their sufferings moving. They are dry and almost brittle at times. But for all his or her superficial aridity, the Capricorn/Monkey is able to transpose the wall-to-wall mosaic show inside his mind into viable vehicles for others to view and enjoy. He or she is a gifted interpreter of human life.

As a boss, the Capricorn/Monkey will be steady and able to laugh with his subordinates. People like this person's compassionate authority in job situations. The Capricorn/Monkey deals well with rank. He doesn't mind being a member of a group at work on a special project. As long as his creativity and artistry are not threatened, he can take orders with especial good humor.

Jobs that are likely to please the Capricorn/Monkey are: film or theatrical director, actor or actress, performer (singer, dancer, comedian, and the like), writer, gossip columnist, TV producer, TV commercials director, historian, psychologist, astrologer, cinematographer, photographer.

Famous Capricorn/Monkeys:

Aaron Schwartz, Anil Kapoor, Antje Traue, Dalida, Dave Bautista, Dave Grohl, Eliza Dushku, Françoise Hardy, Franz Drameh, Genevieve Padalecki, Heather Dubrow, Helena Christensen, Jade Thirlwall, Jason Bateman, Joanna Pacula, John Lasseter, Jonas Armstrong, Katie Couric, Kyle Richards, Marilyn Manson, Mario Van Peebles, Max Gallo, Max Whitlock, Mel Gibson, Michael Schumacher, Morgan York, Morris Chestnut, Naveen Andrews, Norman Reedus, Paulina Vega, Ricardo Darín, Rod Stewart, Sean Keenan, Shea Whigham, Simone de Beauvoir, Trieste Kelly Dunn, Verne Troyer, Yousuf Karsh, Zayn Malik.

CAPRICORN
QUALITIES
RESOLVE, WISDOM, AMBITION,
GENEROSITY, SUPERIORITY,
DEPENDABILITY
QUIRKS
STIFFNESS, CLUMSINESS, PRETENSION,
LONELINESS, EPICUREANISM, SELF-DOUBT
Motto: *"I use"*
Elements: *Earth, Saturn, Cardinal*

--

ROOSTER
QUALITIES
RESILIENCE, ENTHUSIASM, CANDOR,
CONSERVATISM, CHIC, HUMOR
QUIRKS
COCKINESS, BOASTFULNESS, BLIND FAITH,
PEDANTRY, BOSSINESS, DISSIPATION
Motto: *"I overcome"*
Elements: *Negative, Metal, Yin*

D ignified and impeccable, the Capricorn born Rooster cuts a dashing figure. He will be well turned out, strong of opinion and honest to a fault. Capricorn's reserve matches the conservative side of the Rooster nature harmoniously. There is little conflict and lots of restraint. The Capricorn/Rooster possesses integrity and autonomy. He functions well alone if he has to. But he prefers to be surrounded. Count on the Capricorn/Rooster to do the "done" thing. This person's charm is increased by his excellent manners, his careful use of words, and his ability to find the best in each situation. Capricorn/Roosters worry about how others see them and make heroic efforts to please those who judge their behavior. These people care greatly for appearances but are never guilty of pretension.

The Capricorn/Rooster is a born traveler. His alert mind and keen curiosity are forever sending him off somewhere to try new experiences. He's jaunty and openly interested in meeting new people, hearing about different customs and learning about other cultures. As he or she is supremely presentable, the Capricorn/Rooster will be a frequent guest. People invite her to dine in the best restaurants and urge her to join them in Mediterranean spas and Caribbean watering places for a bit of fun-sharing. Her enthusiasm for novelty guarantees her host or hostess a willing and cheerful participant in all activities—especially meals!

The Capricorn/Rooster character is somewhat inflexible. It is nigh unto impossible to convince this apparent master of the concrete that he or she may have embarked on a suicide path. Capricorns born in Rooster years not only think they know best, they flatly refuse to take advice. Their lives will move ahead at a jagged pace, which suits their rather clumsy emotional structure. It's no use trying to hurry them along or cheer them when they are down. "Time," says the philosophical Capricorn/Rooster, "heals all wounds."

Roosters born in Capricorn often complain of boredom. Routine is their enemy. So are formalities and red tape. Nothing infuriates a Capricorn/Rooster more than labyrinthine bureaucracy. He or she will simply not tolerate the filling out of intricate forms, the standings-in-line, the numerous hurry-up-and-waits that go along with securing anything official, from a marriage license to a theater ticket. In short, these busy folks love to go places but they don't always adore the means one must employ to get there.

Of the Capricorn/Rooster's many attractions, perhaps the most outstanding is versatility. This character is accomplished at a wide variety of different pursuits. It is not unusual to meet Roosters born in Capricorn whose avid interest in medieval religious art overlaps their passion for raising the perfect Cabernet grape, their talent for baking bread, and their flair for occasional freelance brain surgery as well. These are skillful, accomplished people.

Love

The art of loving, however, is one that doesn't come easily to the Capricorn/Rooster. There is a separateness about these souls that incites them to maintain a certain distance from emotion. They are not wild about public display of affection, and although they feel deeply, they are hesitant about showing it.

Should you be in love with a Capricorn/Rooster, I suggest you learn first to deal with the bevy of close friends this gregarious person will have on permanent tap. There is no reason for jealousy in their regard. Your Capricorn/Rooster really loves you best. But through the smoke-screen of his or her delight in being surrounded, you may have some trouble discerning that special tenderness. Keep busy and don't demand too much attention. Better still, learn how to prune grape vines.

Compatibilities

I see you with a Snake mate. You would be well advised to seek one of these among members of the Leo, Scorpio, Sagittarius or Pisces set. You'll also match perfectly with Taurus, Scorpio or Pisces/Oxen. A Taurus/Horse can also turn you on. Cancer and Libra/Cats annoy the hell out of you. Aries and Cancer/Pigs make you wonder: why bother being sexy at all?

Home and Family

Your average Capricorn/Rooster is not very manual or artsy-craftsy. She will definitely not be the type to run up the curtains and make her own guest towels. He will probably steer clear of hammer, screwdriver and wrench. The Capricorn/Rooster likes comfort but cannot create it alone. He or she will be materialistic enough to want solid and traditional furnishings, but the interior decorating instinct is not one of this person's main talents.

The Capricorn/Rooster is often a shade too otherwise-occupied to settle down and have a family. If he does have kids, he will not be too patient with childish pranks and will want his children to act as closely as possible like his adult friends. Capricorn/Rooster is an exacting fellow and doesn't let his sentiments get ahead of his intellect.

This child will probably astound you with his many talents and his bright enthusiasms. Capricorn/Rooster kids are bright and sometimes cranky to boot. They need much patient affection and training, as they will go alone into the world to seek their fortunes.

Profession

The Capricorn/Rooster, like all Roosters, has his professional highs and lows. The variety of jobs he or she can do ensures that this person will be oft tempted to change careers in midstream. Naturally, if you know how to pilot a space ship and write symphonies, it follows that you might become confused as to your direction from time to time. Capricorn/Rooster is able to apply himself to difficult studies and achieve status and prestige in a chosen field. He or she will have difficulty asserting preferences and will balk at demanding favors or promotions. Capricorn/Rooster is self-destructively modest. He or she is not proficient at sports or jobs where physical prowess is required.

If authority is conferred on this person, he or she will carry out the role of boss scrupulously and in all fairness. She may be guilty of impatience with silly mistakes and especially with laziness on the part of subordinates. The Capricorn/Rooster drives himself very hard and cannot abide indolence in others. His innate desire to shine makes this person an asset to any employer. The Capricorn born in a Rooster year will give eons of good service—if he is not bullied. Bullying makes him quit on the spot. He hates people to take unfair advantage of power.

There are myriad career possibilities for this many-faceted subject. He or she might choose from optometrist, physicist, opera singer, ornithologist, auditor, tree surgeon, novelist, composer, talk show host, journalist, editor, set designer, geneticist. I could go on.

Famous Capricorn/Roosters:
Ariadna Gutierrez, Catherine Duchess of Cambridge, Charlotte Best, Charlotte Riley, Chris Laurita, Christian Galenda, Dolly Parton, Eddie Redmayne, Emilie de Ravin, Gabriel Jarret, Gaby Hoffmann, Jean Chrétien (French Canada), Jennifer Ehle, Jodie Sweetin, Josh Stamberg, Julian Sands, Keith Coogan, Lara Fabien, Lauren Cohan, Linda Kozlowski, Matt Ross, Meghan Trainor, Molière, Olivia Cooke, Patrick Fischler, Rudyard Kipling, Ruth Wilson, Sam Strike, Shonda Rhimes, Sienna Miller, Steve Allen.

CAPRICORN
QUALITIES
RESOLVE, WISDOM, AMBITION,
GENEROSITY, SUPERIORITY,
DEPENDABILITY
QUIRKS
STIFFNESS, CLUMSINESS, PRETENSION,
LONELINESS, EPICUREANISM, SELF-DOUBT
Motto: *"I use"*
Elements: *Earth, Saturn, Cardinal*

--

DOG
QUALITIES
CONSTANCY, UNSOCIABILITY,
RESPECTABILITY, SELF-RIGHTEOUSNESS,
INTELLIGENCE, TACTLESSNESS
QUIRKS
UNEASINESS, CRITICISM, DUTY,
CYNICISM, HEROISM, MORALITY
Motto: *"I worry"*
Elements: *Positive, Metal, Yang*

This is a flinty cobblestone of a person. A mixture of the cozy concrete and the cynical concrete, whose main aim in life is independence and peace-keeping. The Capricorn/Dog is relatively fearful of the abstract, the vague, the metaphysical, and spends a great portion of his life ensuring that what belongs to him stays where it belongs. To clarify, these people are cautious, conservative and conscious of society's demands. They are far from snobs. Instead, they watch and worry while the rest of us debauch and destroy ourselves. The Capricorn/Dog loves order and wishes to preserve it.

Now, this strong-minded and revolutionary character is not above a good fight. If he or she believes firmly enough in an ideal, or must come to the fore to protect a family member or friend, his engagement in the fray knows no limits. The Capricorn/Dog seeks justice in a stony and scratchy manner. He is rarely guilty of extraneous diplomacy and cannot be accused of having excessive reserve, either. For a Capricorn, this person is quite outrageous. He's given to barking—even baying—at the moon. He's spindly and agile. He'll frequently be found performing some unusual act of courage or daring uncharacteristic of both Capricorns and Dogs.

So the force created by the mating of Dog with Capricorn gives us a conservative yet silver-tongued and magnetic human being. This person will disguise herself readily behind masks and throw up smokescreens so that we cannot tell who she really is. Capricorn/Dogs are unique and mysterious. They are self-seeking but manage to hide this under a semblance of congeniality and even wit. Theirs is a biting humor. Sarcasm abounds. This Dog tears phoniness and facsimile to shreds. He wants the real thing out of life and—oddly for a shrinking Dog character—knows how to go after it.

Normally these people have a gourmet streak. They enjoy fine cuisine and don't hesitate to indulge in it. Sometimes they make excellent cooks as well. They have a talent for respecting detailed directions in recipes and are born with regard for the way things ought to be. In later life, the Capricorn/Dog may develop a weight problem.

This native is capable of doing without. He is attracted by money and even by the luxuries it may buy. But comfort is secondary in the life of Capricorn/Dogs. They can exist as comfortably in a messy house trailer as in a palace. Something about their shiny veneer allows for a strain of carelessness in regard to luxury. They may drive an expensive car or ride around in an old pickup truck. It's pretty much all the same to them.

These folks do, however, have a fancy side. Glitter and sparkle attract them. They are curious about the spangled life of show biz and fascinated by panache. Usually they do not go so far as to speckle their eyelids with sequins, but it's been done.

Love

The love lives of these metallic paper cutout people are very stormy and complex. Often the Capricorn/Dog will remain celibate for most of a lifetime. Not that he or she doesn't enjoy sex, it's just that it's so ... well, sex is so messy! The Capricorn/Dog sports an almost compulsive cleanliness. He is not really attracted to complexity in emotion. The stormy part comes from the fact that he occasionally tries to fit in romantically, gets married, or settles down to live with a companion. It just about never works. Capricorn/Dogs live for their independence. If they are tied up, they bark incessantly till somebody comes and frees them. Then they hide.

If you are in love with a Capricorn/Dog, you will surely find him or her interesting and never be bored. The Capricorn/Dog boasts a rich culture and cares enormously about refinement of the spirit. Your sex life might be a bit odd, as this character is a mite kinky. But surely you will never go without something to ponder. I advise you to feed this Rock of Ages person well, and don't let him or her wear his mask at the table.

Compatibilities

Horses from Taurus, Leo, Virgo and Pisces will give you a good ride. You will also find pleasure with Taurus, Virgo, Scorpio and Pisces/Cats. You get on famously with Leo, Virgo, Scorpio and Pisces/Tigers too. Cancer/Roosters, both moody and peripatetic, will frustrate your sense of what is right. You won't like their Aries counterparts much, either. Aries, Cancer and Libra/Sheep annoy you with their shilly-shallying. Cancer and Libra/Dragons are not for you. Nor is the emotive Cancer/Monkey.

Home and Family

The family takes first place in this person's heart. He or she may not be adept at creating a nest, but where the Capricorn/Dog lives is part and parcel of his personality. There will certainly be walls full of books. This subject reveres knowledge and loves to learn as much as to teach. The kitchen will be in good working order and he or she will want to own the right pots and pans for cooking matchless sauces and soups. As for living space, it probably won't be very luxurious. This creature is more cerebral than sensuous. His idea of comfort derives from whatever he can plunk down and sprawl on for the purpose of reading.

The Capricorn/Dog parent cares for his children as a German shepherd dog cares for sheep. He moves them efficiently from place to place and keeps them rigorously safe from harm. He's not the clownish or jolly type of parent who takes Kitty and little Matthew on the loop-the-loop. Rather, the Capricorn/Dog will spend a whole day building a sandcastle complete with moats and damsels in distress just to awaken his child's love of history.

A little Capricorn/Dog will not be quite so austere as his grownup counterpart, but almost. You may sometimes wonder what makes this kid tick. He's acerbic if scolded. He's quiet and ever so nervous. Never you mind, he's cooking up a future for himself wherein he will be independent of society, wear a disguise when he goes out in public, and ride around in a broken-down Ford for life.

Profession

The career of this weirdo (and Capricorn/Dogs are weird!) will usually take an intellectual turn. By the time he or she reaches college age, the Capricorn/Dog person has come to terms with the lack of desire for nose-to-nose contact and day-to-day routine in an office hierarchy. Hence the Capricorn/Dog may see himself in an academic career, writing and teaching in relative peace and quiet. Or he may find that even the university atmosphere weighs on his freedom-from-constraint center. In this case, the Capricorn/Dog may simply strike out on his own, become an artist or a Bohemian, a beach bum intellectual or a famous athlete.

I don't know what kind of boss this person would be, but I suspect sarcastic and caustic. In any case, it isn't likely to happen because the Capricorn/Dog hates authority in all forms. His political ideas border on anarchy. He can take orders so long as he doesn't have to be pleasant to coworkers or answer the telephone gaily and cheerily.

Jobs that may possibly work for this subject are: playwright, monk, nun, missionary, adventurer, hermit, carpenter, mason, teacher, professional student, coupon clipper, sailor.

Famous Capricorn/Dogs:

Al Capone, Albert Schweitzer, Alison Brie, Amaury Nolasco, André Bergeron, Ava Gardner, Beau Garrett, Bebe Neuwirth, Ben Franklin, Brett Dalton, Butterfly McQueen, Carlos Morales Quintana, Chandra West, Clancy Brown, Danielle Cormack, David Bowie, David Yost, Diane von Furstenberg, Dizzy Dean, Elaine Hendrix, Ellen Sandweiss, Elvis Presley, Gary Barlow, Georgia Hirst, Heather Thomson, Jacques Anquetil, Jann Wenner, Jeremy Renner, Joan Severance, Jonathan Davis, Julian Morris, Kate Bosworth, Kerry Condon, Kevin Rahm, Kevin Weisman, Kid Rock, Kristin Kreuk, Lauren Adams, Maggie Smith, Moliere, Nicola Peltz, Regina King, Robert Schwartzman, Sade, Samantha Boscarino, Sarah Alexander, Shawn Wayans, Taye Diggs, Ted Cruz.

CAPRICORN
QUALITIES
RESOLVE, WISDOM, AMBITION,
GENEROSITY, SUPERIORITY,
DEPENDABILITY
QUIRKS
STIFFNESS, CLUMSINESS, PRETENSION,
LONELINESS, EPICUREANISM, SELF-DOUBT
Motto: *"I use"*
Elements: *Earth, Saturn, Cardinal*

--

PIG
QUALITIES
SCRUPULOUSNESS, GALLANTRY, SINCERITY,
VOLUPTUOUSNESS, CULTURE, HONESTY
QUIRKS
CREDULITY, WRATH, HESITATION,
MATERIALISM, GOURMANDISM, PIGHEADEDNESS
Motto: *"I civilize"*
Elements: *Negative Water, Yin*

This mix creates a being of infinite talent and aspirations to match. The sky is the limit. Capricorn/Pigs never see themselves as less than monstrously famous and hugely wealthy. These are grandeur specialists, whose personal goals of cosmic proportions don't stand in the way of their equally epic egos. There is, in the Capricorn/Pig makeup, a certain refreshing purity of desire. No Capricorn/Pig ever underestimates him- or herself. Some claim that such a clearheaded attitude toward blatant self-seeking ambition is healthy. I guess maybe it is—for the Capricorn/Pig, anyway.

As we already know, Pigs tend to credulity and lawfulness. They almost always do things the "right" way. They work long and hard. They study. They do their homework. They take care of their families and properties. They are responsible citizens. They usually even vote. Capricorns, too, are solid citizens. They also like to abide by rules and regulations. They work hard and they study well. Capricorns also vote.

So, the Capricorn born Pig is pure of heart and as determined as a bulldozer in a demolition derby. Capricorn/Pigs take the prize for great know-how and an unparalleled willingness to share their abilities with the world. They are compassionate and hardly ever say no to a cry for help. They are generous, yet careful not to waste. They are extraordinarily cultivated and forever seek to increase their knowledge, as they are wildly curious.

As the Capricorn/Pig is self-sacrificing and rarely strays from the path of righteousness, it is perplexing to her that others can be less scrupulous than she and still stay out of prison. No scofflaw, this character. In fact, Capricorn/Pigs are shocked by shady dealings and untruths. They hardly know what to make of improbity and are even a little bit fascinated by it. You watch and see if a Capricorn/ Pig doesn't one day whisper confidentially to you that he knows of a place you can get a "real deal on a color TV ," implying that this TV may be stolen. Ask him if he has one of those hot TVs at his place. "Oh no!" he'll burst out, fearing you might think him capable of such knavery. Capricorn/Pigs never descend to perfidy.

Hardheaded and traditional, the Capricorn/Pig is a bit of a prude. He or she will be sensitive and drawn to artistic endeavor. Manners are important to the Capricorn/Pig, and exemplary behavior in public goes right along with them. This subject boasts a gigantic ego. Nothing daunts him. He is confident and clearheaded. He wants to go far and he does. Modesty does not roil the limpid waters of this person's soul.

Love

The Capricorn/Pig invests him- or herself totally in romantic affairs. Yes, he or she is pure of spirit and by nature a giving person. But such dedication and fervent commitment to the emotional side of life can burden the object of this person's vast affections. The Capricorn/Pig is a faithful and passionate lover. But he or she is also a smothering one. These people want to own those they love and are terrified of losing them. Jealousy and rage, scenes and scandals, are not beneath their dignity.

This possessiveness makes it very much of a responsibility to be loved by or to love such a character. They are tempting and wonderful to hang out with. But Capricorn/Pigs want to protect their loves from all outside influence. They may be jealous of your friends and of your extracurricular activities. They may have tantrums and embarrass you in public. The only defense against this tidal wave of love is to let it wash over you and wait till you bob to the surface. If you ever try to break up with one of these people—good luck!

Compatibilities

You will not go wrong by picking a mate from the Cat family who was born in either Taurus, Leo, Virgo, Scorpio or Pisces. You admire the Taurus/Tiger and he admires you right back. You'll get on in a home-loving way with a Leo, Virgo, Scorpio or Pisces/Sheep. Don't dally with the inexorable Cancer or Libra/Snake. They are after your gold. Aries and Cancer/Horses will not work for you either. Too much tension.

Home and Family

The surroundings of Capricorn/Pigs will be less opulent than those of other, more comfort-conscious Pig subjects. The Capricorn likes a pleasant home but can live without three satin cushions under his derrière at all times. So the interior of a Capricorn/Pig house will be cozy but have a tinge of austerity to its style. Hard-edged paintings (of great value, of course) and sculptures, geometric fabric designs and plenty of grays and primary reds and blues. Green is a color the Capricorn/Pig likes, too. There will be thriving houseplants everywhere.

The Capricorn/Pig is a little on the busy side to end up having a large family to raise. More likely, this person will prefer not to marry at all. In deference to his mission or career, the Capricorn/Pig may forego the pleasures of parenthood. If, however, he or she does have a child, it will of course be raised with great care and enormous, passionate, suffocating love. If you are a Capricorn/Pig parent and you have a tendency to be a little rigorous and overly protective of your bairns, buy a dog and give the kids a break.

Capricorn/Pig children will be driven by their desire to arrive at excellence in a field they will probably choose very young. They are certainly talented for learning and for all things cultural. You can take this child to museums and galleries and theatrical productions and operas until your feet wear off. Capricorn/Pig children are baby culture vultures. They are clingingly sweet as well. Watch their candy intake.

Profession

The subject we are discussing here is an interpretive genius. His or her talents rarely lie in creative areas. The strength of Capricorns born in Pig years is their ability to emote for public consumption. They accumulate enormous stores of artistic know-how through reading and learning and watching others. Then they show their vision to the world. They don't have much inventive or abstract gift. But they are brilliant at reflecting the world's own image to itself.

I expect this person would make a very demanding yet respectable boss. It wouldn't do to betray him in business. Capricorn/Pigs become hysterical over betrayal. They beat their breasts and keen. As an employee this person will be dutiful because all Capricorn/Pigs are that way. But he won't want to be an underling and he won't hesitate to try to wrench the boss's job away—not forcibly, fairly and squarely. But wrench he will, nonetheless. Scrupulously.

Some jobs that might suit this subject's talents are: actor, musician, dancer, singer, doctor, linguist, clergyman (bishop), gallery owner.

Famous Capricorn/Pigs:

Alain Affelou, Albert Schweitzer, Amanda Peet, Andrea Thompson, Anthony Andrews, Ashley Zukerman, Brooke Williams, Calvin Harris, Corey Haim, Daniel Sunjata, David Marciano, Drea de Matteo, Gabby Douglas, Hilaria Baldwin, Humphrey Bogart, Jared Leto, Jean-Pierre Aumont, Jennifer Hale, Justin Trudeau, Kalki Koechlin, Kate McKinnon, Kevin Anderson, Kim Jong-un, Kristen Hager, Marc Blucas, Maria Callas, Mark Rylance, Max Riemelt, Michael P. Anderson, Michael Stipe, Nicole Eggert, Oliver Platt, Patricia Clarkson, Pulkit Samrat, Richard T. Jones, Ricky Martin, Roland Petit, Sophie Dee, Toto Wolff, Val Kilmer, Weronika Rosati, Will Rogers.

AQUARIUS
QUALITIES
VISION, ORIGINALITY, CHARITY,
TOLERANCE, INDEPENDENCE,
INDIVIDUALITY
QUIRKS
ECCENTRICITY, SEPARATENESS,
NEUROSIS, DISOBEDIENCE,
THOUGHTLESSNESS, CRUELTY
Motto: *"I know"*
Elements: *Air, Saturn/Uranus, Fixed*

--

RAT
QUALITIES
NERVOUSNESS, INFLUENCE,
ACQUISITIVENESS, THIRST FOR POWER,
INTELLECTUAL SKILL, CHARISMA
QUIRKS
APPEAL, VERBOSITY, THRIFT,
SOCIABILITY, GUILE, MEDDLING
Motto: *"I rule"*
Elements: *Positive Water, Yang,*

"Onward and upward" should be the motto of this completely idealistic and experimental character. Aquarius the individualist married to the aggressive and charming Rat character affords us a being of immense personal magnetism and derring-do. On the one hand, the Aquarian born Rat seeks to accumulate material possessions. On the other, this person cares less about tangibles than I do about Eskimo fertility rites. He's a bohemian with a bourgeois streak. A hippie sophisticate. He wants to be free and unencumbered. But he cannot stand to be alone. He wants to ride a black stallion on the beach in the wind, but he's not mad about horses. A contradictory nature full of excellent intentions, the Aquarius/Rat somersaults through life, stopping only to exhibit the fruits of his immense talent here and there as he tumbles along. .

Aquarians want to be different. They have vision and are tolerant. Rats have lots of personal appeal and long to wield power. Of course, in this duo, the Rat is neutralized by the altruistic Aquarian, who tells him to get his mitts off the power switch until such time as man will love man and no wars will be fought. The effect is startling. Real force emanates from within this person. Watch him try to take over the reins in a given situation. He can strike a deal, even a slightly shady deal. Then, suddenly out of nowhere, he may back down. Under the influence of Aquarius, the Rat's cupidity deflates. Good-bye, trickery. Hello, freedom and love.

As the Aquarius/Rat thinks he wants to see around corners toward a better world, he will frequently become involved in spiritual searches for truth and equilibrium. The Aquarian is first a thinker. The Rat, too, is cerebral. Both signs are borderline neurotic. So, rather than looking for stability on travelled paths, they are attracted by the cosmic, the extra-sensory and supernatural methods of mind control. Aquarian Rats are forever taking courses in ESP, EST, Hatha, Mudra and Zen. They want to depart from the humdrum, avoid having to live a bourgeois routine existence. They long to find peace through spiritual enlightenment.

No matter the degree of clear thinking attained by this character, he or she is nonetheless always a Rat. Rats sooner or later cleave to the middle-class life. Rats are acquisitive and driven by a thirst for power. Aquarius may force the Rat to a clear mountain stream but he cannot make him drink. This essential disagreement causes further loss of security for our native. He makes rash moves and grows moody and distant. Emotions are not his favorite province, so how can he say he's sorry? How can he adapt to the workaday world with its stringent and inhuman demands? Why is life so stiflingly boring?

Well, as this offbeat subject will be the first to tell you, "The answer is blowing in the wind." Other people never live up to the Aquarius/Rat's high standards. He is often disappointed by the failure of group efforts and hurt by the selfishness of intimates. Yet he watches even himself fall short of the mark. Then he is really desolate and confused. Where did he go wrong? Although "application of derrière to seat of chair" is one of my stock bits of advice, I dare advance it here more particularly. Aquarian Rats must learn to slow down, to feel their way instead of trying to "think" their way, to sit still long enough for the lead to set between those ears. They must-n't dabble in mind-altering substances or freaky movements unless there is a concrete and earthbound reason to do so. Sailing off into space without a seatbelt is a very dangerous business.

Love

As the Aquarius/Rat mixes fancy with charisma and neurosis with nervousness, you can imagine the troubled waters of emotion at work here. This person will be both attractive and vulnerable. The attractiveness shows. The vulnerability hides. His or her emotional needs will be best met by coupling with solid citizen types who are willing to tether their Aquarius/Rat firmly to earth. Of course, square peg drudges hardly excite this rabid metaphysician. It's a di-lemma.

If you love an Aquarius/Rat, don't fence him or her in. But do tie your loved one down. I know this sounds contradictory, but think of Aquarius/Rats as morning glories. For morning glories to thrive, their feet must be firmly planted in the shade and their heads con-stantly exposed to the brightest sunlight. That's how you have to treat your Aquarius/Rat. Let him or her feel as free as a hot air bal-loon, but keep the lines drawn taut and don't take any nonsense. Your Aquarius/Rat will love you all the more for caring.

Compatibilities

Oxen like to be with you. They are inspired by your rapacity and swift dispatch. Choose an Ox from Gemini, Libra, or Sagittarius if you want to be sure of compatibility. The same western astrological signs lend you their Dragons on a silver platter. This time it's you doing the admiring. Aries, Libra and Sagittarius bestow Monkeys on your lifestyle. They too bring you joy—and good advice. Don't be led down the aisle by Taurus, Leo or Scorpio/Horses, and get out of the way of Leo/Cats and Scorpio/Roosters.

Home and Family

Although erratic when flying loose in the world, the Aquarius/Rat somehow does not display this eccentricity at home. Here, in the privacy of his abode, the Aquarius/Rat decorates tastefully, simply and with a spareness that hints at his or her penchant for Oriental thought. Too much material wealth makes the Aquarius/Rat nerv-ous. If he is flashy or showy, it will be in his dress. At home, things will be kept simple and elegant.

This person is a remarkably good parent. You see, kids have a tethering influence on Aquarius/Rats. For that security the Aquarius/Rat parent is grateful, and in his turn stretches the parental role as far as it will go. He or she gets very involved with kids' activities and feelings. The Aquarius/Rat discusses everything in greatest detail with his children, and imparts a world view of broad scope to his kids long before they are old enough to leave the nest.

The Aquarius/Rat child is, most of all, interesting. He may be slightly daredevil and will surely be drawn to the unusual. Again, the role of intimates (in this case parents) is to focus the terrestrial aspect of this subject. Never allow his or her attraction to the otherworldly to overcome the attachment felt for family. The talented and intelligent Aquarian Rat child must be hitched to a solid post but never hobbled.

Profession

Of course, as for all Aquarians who struggle with the emotional side of life, work is health. If this sometimes cranky and irrepressible Rat subject is able to fix his or her attention on one professional passion, authentically ingenious projects can be realized. The Rat/Aquarian has such a unique perception and is so close to madness and extraterrestrial thought at all times that if these qualities are applied to earthly pursuits, the result is unbeatable. But watch that freaky side. This person can go bonkers in a wink if allowed too much leeway.

The Aquarius/Rat is more of a creative than a bossy type. He or she will be glad to try to run an office or shop. But the result will never be spectacular—competent, but not fabulous. The same goes for employment. This person's strength is in his or her individuality and personal approach to problems of at least cinemascopic proportion. Punching time clocks just won't do.

Some possible professions for the Aquarian Rat are: politician, artist, journalist, genius, designer, musician, film maker, hair stylist, actor, writer – and other creative pursuits too numerous to mention.

Famous Aquarius/Rats:
Adlai Stevenson, Alan Alda, Andrew Duke of York, Arielle Kebbel, Billie Joe Armstrong, Carey Lowell, Cecily Strong, Clark Gable, Countess Mountbatten of Burma, Cristiano Ronaldo, Crystal Reed, David Strathairn, Deborah Ann Woll, Doutzen Kroes, Frankie Wright, Galileo, George Stephanopolous, Greg Louganis, Greta Scacchi, Henry Rollins, Isabel Lucas, James Spader, Jamie Brewer, Jean-Jacques Servan Schreiber, Jenette Goldstein, John Belushi, Josh Trank, Jubilee Jenna Mandl, Jules Verne, Keanu Staude, Keith Gordon, Lauren Lane, Louis Renault, Meg Tilly, Megan Gallagher,

Michael Trevino, Nastassja Kinski, Portia de Rossi, Richard Tyson, Rosa Parks, Sarah Clarke, Stephanie Leonidas, Tim Meadows, Tina Majorino, Vanessa Redgrave, Wayne Gretsky, Wolfgang Amadeus Mozart.

AQUARIUS
QUALITIES
VISION, ORIGINALITY, CHARITY,
TOLERANCE, INDEPENDENCE,
INDIVIDUALITY
QUIRKS
ECCENTRICITY, SEPARATENESS,
NEUROSIS, DISOBEDIENCE,
THOUGHTLESSNESS, CRUELTY
Motto: *"I know"*
Elements: *Air, Saturn/Uranus, Fixed*

--

OX
QUALITIES
STUBBORNNESS, STRENGTH OF PURPOSE,
ELOQUENCE, STANDOFFISHNESS, INNOVATION,
VINDICTIVENESS
QUIRKS
INTEGRITY, BIGOTRY, PLODDING,
DILIGENCE, BIAS, STABILITY
Motto: *"I preserve"*
Elements: *Negative Water, Yin*

A strong-minded and loving bully, the Aquarian born in Ox years is destined to a lifetime of slog and struggle uphill against his own unwillingness to conform. Oxen, as you know, always think that the road to happiness is through retirement from the hub of popular activity. Oxen want to be left alone in the country somewhere. Aquarius is more affable, outgoing, flexible, less tundra-like than the Ox. Their marriage can be a rocky one.

Basically, the Ox does not agree with his flighty Aquarian side. And the Aquarian? Well, he sort of doesn't give a damn. Aquarius is the out-of-this-world fantasy person whose spirit is almost as monumentally elastic as the Ox's is rigid. The cool-headed Aquarian who never gets lost in trivial emotion is here suddenly confronted by his own tendency toward bigotry and stick-in-the-mudism. The result? Grumpy moods. Suppressed anger. Bitterness. Feigned apathy about almost everything and everybody. The image, then, is one of a fiercely productive person who appears not to give two hoots. His "like it or lump it" attitude lives very close to the feisty surface. This person cannot hide his latent belligerence.

What saves our character from stewing for too long in his own acrid juice is a razor sharp sense of humor. The Aquarius/Ox is a great storyteller, a stunning performer, and a laugh-a-minute companion. He benefits from an excellent memory for detail, and can grip your attention for hours with just one anecdote about his gay cousin from Australia who rides a unicycle. Ordinarily boring stories become jewel-studded tales from the Arabian Nights. When the eloquence of the Ox meets with Aquarius's originality of thought, the result is Scheherazade.

Too, the Aquarian profits from being brought to earth by his Ox side. Oxen of no matter what persuasion know how to apply the work ethic. Aquarians long to be free and roam about dreaming up the undreamed-of. This person will never stop working until he or she drops. Work, for the Aquarius/Ox, no matter how thankless or routine, represents salvation. Work keeps one from flying too close to the sun.

The Aquarius/Ox doesn't bother with social approval. He cares not for judgments coming from people he considers beneath him anyway. This character blazes his own trails in life by slow and sure methods, keeping the zippy Aquarian mind operating at full tilt and never letting up on the elbow grease for a second. Of course, people become inflamed at this creature's brutish determination. But as they are almost never as dutiful and laborious as he, they must concede Aquarius/Ox the victor, hands down all around.

Despite the Aquarius/Ox's uncanny talent for work, he or she will surprise you by exhibiting a silly side. The Aquarius/Ox loves to have fun. He or she will cook and decorate and stay up trimming trees till four A.M. for the sake of communal joy. The self-sacrificing person he or she is, although it doesn't carry over much into the world at large, will animate many a soirée and fill many little hearts with delight. The Aquarius/Ox's imagination for surprises and goodies is enormous, and it is generous, too.

Love

The Aquarius/Ox has a difficult private life. First of all, being Aquarian, he needs mental stimulation and finds himself quickly bored. Then the home-loving Ox side rears his head and says, "I want to settle down. I'm tired of being so insecure. Too bad about your need for intellectual clear-headedness. I want a home." So they get a home, and maybe a child or two. But before you know it, all they can think of is that old mental stimulation again. The ups and downs of Aquarian Ox love life are epic. And the Aquarius/Ox doesn't seem to mind. He is often able to live without much sex and to drown whatever sorrows or regrets he might have in work.

If you are attracted to one of these extraordinary people, you will first have to realize that no matter how much you count, you will never take first place over either Aquarius/Ox's children or his work. This person is addicted to the love of his family and is a workaholic as well. Sex and affection, tenderness and romance, are secondary to this person's well- being. He or she will have affairs and be a competent lover. But they are not sentimental. They hate syrupy sweet billings and cooings and don't have time for Valentines.

Compatibilities

You're a fool for Snakes. Their very style drives you mad with desire. Stick to Aries, Gemini, Libra or Sagittarius/Snakes. They are the most likely to stick to you. Gemini, Libra and Sagittarius/ Roosters also attract you. You are drawn to their frank, open ways. Taurus, Leo and Scorpio/Dragons exact too much from your patience. Taurus and Leo/Tigers don't turn you on. Leo and Scorpio/ Sheep are not good either. And whatever you do, don't take up with a Scorpio/Monkey or a Taurus/Horse.

Home and Family

The Aquarius/Ox's home is very comfortably furnished. As they are traditionalists and love art, they will own quality objects and care much for the welfare of such items. They are not showy people, so the furnishings will be sober yet welcoming. There may be some gold pieces sewn into the green velvet armchair, so mind the lumps under your seat. Aquarius/Oxen are shrewd with money, and know how to keep what they earn. Between sweat of brow and merchant's hand spans an eternity. Their money motto: "You've got it. Keep it."

Aquarian Oxen make fabulous parents. They know how to allow for fancy and imagination in their kids, and yet they always have the best-mannered and the nicest children around. First of all,

NEW ASTROLOGY FOR THE 21ST CENTURY

Aquarius/Oxen crave the company of kids, and little kids love them right back. They know how to teach children as well as to delight them. They spoil them, but they also make them obey. It's miraculous the way Aquarius/Oxen can handle children. Not having kids would be a terrible shame for this loving, caring, sweet, parental type.

The Aquarius/Ox child will seem dreamy and idealistic. He or she will of course be loquacious, but only when telling a story. Otherwise he may not be terribly communicative. This tyke should be offered lots of security. He doesn't take well to brusque changes in personnel at home. He will love spectacle and enjoy being taken to shows and plays. Don't try to force him or her into groups. These people don't function well in hierarchies.

Profession

Aquarius/Oxen are very manual people. They can fix anything, build anything, and are inventive to boot. As this subject is also expedient and practical, there are few labors that he or she cannot undertake and achieve at. The Aquarius/Ox is thorough and conscientious. He or she will be attracted by high salaries and able to adhere to routines. These folks are socially conscious, too. They often end up working for the betterment of mankind in international organizations and foundations.

The Aquarius/Ox boss will not be contradicted. You work for him. He calls the shots. You get your pay and keep your comments to yourself. If she likes you, you've got a friend (and a banker) for life. But if she doesn't, pack it in. You'll never penetrate her iron curtain of disdain. As an employee this person will perform duties with exceptional ability and perseverance. He or she will be slow. And he or she will basically not give a damn what you think. But the work will get done—and it will be done better than if you did it yourself. If you have hired such a person, give him his head about his work. You cannot tell him how to do anything. He always knows best.

Some jobs for this behemoth of diligence are: farmer, boat-builder, cabinetmaker, nursery school teacher, physical therapist, TV repairman, professor, counselor, activist.

Famous Aquarius/Oxen:

Alex Borstein, Anna Hutchison, Anne Jillian, Brent Spiner, Brooke Adams, Charles Lindbergh, Chloë Grace Moretz, Colin Egglesfield, Creflo Dollar, Dane DeHaan, Daniel Auteuil, Frank Collison, Gemma Arterton, Jack Lemmon, Jim Sheridan, Judith Light, King Abdullah of Jordan, Mark Spitz, Maxime LeForestier, Michael Ironside, Michael T. Weiss, Mischa Barton, Morgan Fairchild, Morgan Fairchild, Natalie Cole, Nicholas Turturro, Paul Newman, Peter Gabriel, Pierre Mondy, Richard Dean Anderson, Richard Roxburgh, Sarah Wynter, Tara Strong.

AQUARIUS
QUALITIES
VISION, ORIGINALITY, CHARITY,
TOLERANCE, INDEPENDENCE,
INDIVIDUALITY
QUIRKS
ECCENTRICITY, SEPARATENESS,
NEUROSIS, DISOBEDIENCE,
THOUGHTLESSNESS, CRUELTY
Motto: *"I know"*
Elements: *Air, Saturn/Uranus, Fixed*

--

TIGER
QUALITIES
FERVOR, BRAVERY, MAGNETISM,
GOOD LUCK, BENEVOLENCE, AUTHORITY
QUIRKS
IMPETUOSITY, HOTHEADEDNESS,
DISOBEDIENCE, SWAGGER, INTEMPERANCE,
ITINERANCY
Motto: *"I Watch"*
Elements: *Positive Wood, Yang*

A more speculative Tiger than we already know is personified by this clear-thinking, zigzag personality. Aquarius lends Tiger vision. Tiger congeals some of the free-floating mental jelly that characterizes Aquarians. This combination sign provides the world with many innovators. Aquarius/Tigers go crazy for modern methods. They are purveyors of all sorts of new ways of accomplishing old tasks. They are into everything from the dernier cri computer setup for pet training to obscure relaxation techniques developed by astronauts in zero gravity.

Aquarius/Tigers like to stay young. For this reason they don't often get married early and settle down to raise a family. Not that the Aquarius/Tiger is especially promiscuous, but his sexual adventures do smack of the miscellaneous. He is erratic, and even addicted to change for its own sake. Count on the Aquarian Tiger to switch domiciles whenever he feels the urge. Take him or her with you on holiday to the Alps and the next day you may wake up and find him/her gone. Aquarius/Tigers hate to be confined—even for fun! Spontaneity is the Aquarius/Tiger's favorite play-thing.

This person lives to be impetuous. He or she spends far too much energy dashing hither and thither in too many directions at once. Many times the Aquarius/Tiger is disappointed by the results. He's exhausted. Yet where is the booty? Who took the achievement? This person must learn to slow down and consider the alternatives to racing ahead of time. He ought to think more and dash less. Otherwise, he will spend much of his life in a state of confused jitters.

As Aquarius/Tigers are not terribly balanced people, they are sometimes influenced by oddball cult-mongers. They may take up with a crazy religious group or involve themselves in shady activities for the thrill of it. What is urgently important for natives of this sign is that they cultivate wiser souls than themselves, who will guide them and know how to put their genius to best use. Of course, the Aquarian Tiger sometimes rebels against wisdom or measure. He or she itches to try something entirely different, to leap from the beaten path onto the moving sidewalk of excitement. Staying straight and acting sane is the cross this person must learn to bear with dignity. Otherwise, he or she cannot produce for the world as it truly exists. Freakiness doesn't pay.

In all of this brouhaha, the Aquarian born Tiger manages to maintain very high ideals. He or she believes, nay, knows what is right and best for the people he or she loves and cares about. This Tiger longs to help his family and to comfort his friends. But often, the practical wherewithal just isn't there. Aquarius/Tigers are not what you would call selfish, exactly. They often entertain complex schemes and carry them out most effectively. But those same schemes tend to take all the Aquarius/Tiger's time and since something has to give, both family and friends are given short shrift. There is a certain genius in Aquarius/Tigers. This genius must be pampered and ministered to. The Aquarian Tiger is his own best publicity agent. If you aren't sure whether or not the next Aquarius/Tiger person you meet is marvelous, ask him. He will be the first to assure you that he is.

Love

Long-lasting passion is difficult to maintain – even for this zany character. You may stand by and watch him or her go up in flames over a lover for a matter of months or even years. So long as there are elements of honeymoon left in the relationship, Aquarius/Tigers take delight in romance. But don't ask them to tie the knot. Don't even mention marriage. Steer clear of jewelry store windows and take back streets to avoid churches, temples and justices of the peace. It is rare, but if he or she does marry, the average shelf life of wedlock for this heady person is about three weeks.

If you love one of these dashing creatures, you must not expect anything eternal from your relationship. Aquarius/Tigers are mavericks. Their pattern is to step in puddle after puddle just to test the water. Your heart will be fast broken should you put your hopes where your head should be. Be a good audience and never ask them to settle down. They cannot tolerate being caged in.

Compatibilities

Dogs and you see eye to eye. There's complicity between you, and real sympathy on a human level. Try picking a Dog person from out the signs of Aries, Gemini, Libra or Sagittarius. Horses, too, understand you. They won't stand by you as faithfully as Dogs but they may give you better advice. Try Horses from Gemini, Libra and Sagittarius. Shun Taurus and Leo/Cats, Virgo and Scorpio/Oxen, Taurus and Scorpio/Sheep—and run when you meet a Taurus/Snake. Your intuitions collide with disastrous results.

Home and Family

The Aquarius/Tiger will have a home. The fact that these people tend to like motion for its own sake doesn't mean they don't want a place of their own. The decor here will be simple and comfortable enough, but there will probably not be any studied refinement about the place. A medieval Spanish chest may be open to display the latest laser beam music player. Or a fancy modern kitchen may cook everything by robot while Aquarius/Tiger sits reading Hegel in his favorite gadget armchair with the built-in bar. As for clothes, I'd guess sober and classical, with very occasional flights of fancy.

The Aquarius/Tiger parent is not terrifically patient with the tumult of children. This person, if he ever had any, might treat his children as equals. He or she will expect the kids to live up to his standards rather than the opposite. No goo-goo and gaga baby talk for these people. They respect their children as adults. Unfortunately, not all kids want to be treated like grownups when they are only three years old.

The Aquarius/Tiger child is impressive. He or she will behave in a very clear-cut manner. There is no need for subterfuge when you know flat out what you want. This kid is interested in everything new. Electronics and science, modern literature and new ways of riding a bike will capture his attention. No matter how you raise this child, you should try to show him the value of wisdom, and the wisdom of taking advice from people more experienced than himself. He or she will always buck the system. But sometimes the results are very interesting.

Profession
Inventive in the extreme, and gifted with a certain genius for seeing through walls, the Aquarius/Tiger can be well employed in jobs requiring a different view of old methods. No matter what this person attempts, he or she will bring to it a sense of innovation and exaggerated free-thinking. Once their madcap ideas are toned down for actual use and application, they can be smashing. Give this character an office or laboratory of her own and let her experiment till the cows come home. Money? Never heard of it.

This boss will be scatty, unpredictable... and annoyingly changeable. He likes acclaim and will react well to flattery. As an employee this person will prove brilliant as an idea person. But nine to five? I'm not so sure. Perhaps the happiest Aquarius/Tigers are those who work on their own, applying their genius and modern notions to creating artistry.

Some occupations for Aquarius/Tigers are: philosopher, writer, inventor, hairdresser, fashion designer, politician, masseur, acupuncturist, psychiatrist, computer nerd.

Famous Aquarius/Tigers:
André Citroën, Ariel Winter, Balthazar Getty, Boris Pasternak, Charles S. Dutton, Christian Bale, Cybill Shepherd, David Patrick Kelly, Diane Franklin, Eddie Izzard, Elizabeth Banks, Evan Peters, Gail O'Grady, Garth Brooks, Georges Simenon, Germaine Greer, Ivy Levan, James Denton, James Murray, Jemima Khan, Jennifer Jason Leigh, Jerry O'Connell, John Hughes, Judy Blume, Kevin Dilworth, Lou Diamond Phillips, Mahershala Ali, Mia Kirshner, Nadine Labaki, Natalie Imbruglia, Ophelia Lovibond, Oz Perkins, Patrick Bergin, Phil Collins, Robbie Williams, Sakina Jaffrey, Sara Gilbert, Scott Elrod, Seth Green, Sheryl Crow, Tiffani Amber Thiessen, William Burroughs, William McKinley, Yabov Smirnoff.

AQUARIUS
QUALITIES
VISION, ORIGINALITY, CHARITY,
TOLERANCE, INDEPENDENCE,
INDIVIDUALITY
QUIRKS
ECCENTRICITY, SEPARATENESS,
NEUROSIS, DISOBEDIENCE,
THOUGHTLESSNESS, CRUELTY
Motto: *"I know"*
Elements: *Air, Saturn/Uranus, Fixed*

--

CAT/RABBIT
QUALITIES
TACT, FINESSE, VIRTUE,
PRUDENCE, LONGEVITY, AMBITION,
QUIRKS
SECRETIVENESS, SQUEAMISHNESS,
PEDANTRY, DILETTANTISM,
HYPOCHONDRIA, COMPLEXITY
Motto: *"I Retreat"*
Elements: *Negative, Wood, Yin*

Here is your true to life, one hundred percent virgin intellectual. The Aquarian Cat accumulates knowledge for the fun of it. He is curious about everything, and makes indiscriminate studies of practically everyone he comes in contact with. It doesn't matter whether the subject is edifying or not, Aquarius/Cat wants to know all about it in goriest detail. He's fascinated by knowledge, facts, information, learning, erudition—and experience. He or she spends a lifetime leaping from book to book, from museum to museum, and from discipline to other discipline. It's what Cats born in

Aquarius like to do—know more.

They are not particularly competitive in their quest for savvy. The Aquarius/Cat really needs to know more just for the sheer pleasure of acquiring facts. However, he or she may have a smarty-pants side that with a little practice they would do well to eliminate altogether. It is lovely to know scads of interesting things, to recall passages from great poetry, even to be able to recite whole scenes from Shakespeare. But knowledge (especially someone else's) can be very boring. Aquarius/Cats tend to pedantry. When they flaunt their information ad nauseam, Aquarius/Cats are patently annoying.

Better to apply this knowledge to practical exploits. The concrete use of understanding ought to be the goal. But here is where the Cat born Aquarius begins to falter. This person cannot decide what he or she wants most out of life. They are perpetually seeking outlets of acceptable magnitude and scope in order to apply their huge bank of smarts. The Aquarius/Cat suffers from a condition I like to call "too much choice." He can do almost anything he wants, so he rarely knows what he wants.

This character operates a lot on hunches. He or she will possess a very specialized and refined vision of others. Aquarius/Cat can locate a specific flaw or a need in a person's character through pure insight. Perhaps this gift comes from the Aquarius/Cat's odd way of studying everyone he meets. But it seems spookier than that. Aquarius/Cat is the one who says, "Hey, you didn't tell me that Jane was divorcing Frank." Your mouth drops open. That was classified information. "How did you know?" you ask the Aquarian Cat, who waits, licking his chops. "Just guessing," he'll tell you with that Cheshire smile.

One striking thing about Aquarius/Cats is their apparently carefree nature. These people appear to be totally without hang-ups or complexes. They travel a lot, and they find human contact a breeze. Aquarius/Cats are always picking up new friends and enthusing over how perfectly delightful and terrifically interesting So-and-so is. They are awash in friends. Actually, however, they are quite conservative underneath and worry about their effect on others. The Aquarius/Cat is less of a free spirit than even he believes.

For a Cat subject, the Aquarian is adventurous. He does things normal Cats wouldn't hear of. He takes up kooky hobbies like being a magician or learning to dance the flamenco. He doesn't fancy danger, mind you. But the Aquarius/Cat is easily seduced by the arcane. If it's unusual, he or she will try it at least once.

The most striking quality in this person is his or her desire to undertake projects or great designs. The Aquarius/Cat never imagines him- or herself in some lowly, underling, hack job making a living and waiting to retire. No. Aquarius/Cats only imagine themselves as grand experimenters with challenges. The Aquarius/Cat is born to rise above the average herd. He doesn't even bother to detest mediocrity. He doesn't recognize it. He sees only lofty, cosmic images and leaves the petty, scruffy side of life to those of less elevated aspirations.

Love

The Aquarius/Cat will want to live as half of a couple in marriage and have children. As she will be the emissary-to-the-world type, she will surely seek a calm and sensitive partner who comprehends her need for attention and comfort. These people eschew harshness in partners, as they don't like conflict and avoid it at all costs. The Aquarius/Cat is looking for an intellectual equal who knows how to be entertained—a nice, open-minded person who will laugh at the Aquarius/Cat's jokes.

Should you have chosen to love an Aquarius/Cat, I wish you well. This person will never bore you. Sometimes you may want to turn off the plethora of information spilling forth from their mouths. But mostly this person is steady and oh, so respectable. Aquarian Cats are fairly even-tempered, too, and only ever-so-slightly neurotic.

Compatibilities

You'll be happiest with Aries, Gemini, Libra or Sagittarius/Pig partners. Aries, Gemini, Libra and Sagittarius proffer their Sheep subjects for your pleasure too. You can also count heavily on Librans born in Dog years. Taurus, Leo and Scorpio/Rats are not tuned to your channel. Taurus and Leo/Roosters never notice you, nor you them. And Scorpio/Horses are on their own trip, which does not include you.

Home and Family

Home for this character will be a useful place in which to read comfortably and house his or her family intelligently. Most everything about the Aquarius/Cat's exterior appearance is classical. The decor should be sane and refined, but not ornate or showy. Aquarius/Cat is a hearth sign. This person will be drawn to coziness and a propitious ambience for gabbing. The Aquarian born Cat is a tiny bit of a snob. Look for sheets made from the finest cottons, hand-embroidered pillow slips and elegant thirsty, big bath towels.

The Aquarius/Cat parent is slightly eccentric, in that he or she will want to start children learning a mite too early. As their goal is always to know more, they feel kids, too, should benefit from floods of knowledge. For this purpose they spend lots of time with their little ones, poring over alphabet books and guiding pudgy little patties through writing exercises. As for tenderness, the Aquarius/Cat is a tad distant with kids. Head in the clouds time.

This child Cat born in Aquarius gives no trouble to his or her folks as long as he or she is occupied twenty-four hours a day. This kid is bright. You have to feed his vacuum-cleaner mind with knowledge. The choice is vast. He may want to learn hieroglyphics or voodoo. You just stand by ready to pay for all the lessons, please. Watch this child's diet, too. He or she may tend to snack while reading all those tomes.

Profession

You cannot expect this grand person to be willing to work in a garage and like it. I can practically guarantee that the Aquarius/Cat's job choice will involve the use of brains first and brawn second. Not that the Aquarius/Cat is precious or even that skittish about physical labor. But repeating the same gesture over and over dulls the vivified sensors of this person's active mind. He wants challenge. And what's more, Aquarian Cats want money—lots of it. They are close with their wealth and do not spend lavishly on others. Whatever job they have, they will often think of exchanging it for something even more enormous and complex.

The Aquarius/Cat is a natural authority but does not take his position seriously. He or she will not be the domineering type. After all, if you are so darned terrific in your own head, what is there left to prove? I am not suggesting that Cats born in Aquarius are haughty. But they emanate a certain superiority of affect. They won't be bossy, but rather so there as to be unavoidably dominant. These people make fine employees for empires that need to hire kings and queens, governments looking for chancellors, universities head hunting a new president - even for secret service agencies looking for top level spies.

Some jobs that might go well with the Aquarius/Cat nature are: head of state, prime minister, historian, psychoanalyst, politician, novelist, double agent, performer (stars only need apply), preacher, oil magnate, shipping magnate, professor, Trust Fund manager.

Famous Aquarius/Cat/Rabbits:
Alexandra Krosney, Bridget Fonda, Curtis Dale Roberts, Dave Fennoy, David Jason, David Naughton, Edouard Manet, Emma Bunton, Enrico Colantoni, Faran Tahir, Fran Tarkenton, H.R.Giger, Jack Nicklaus, Jacques Villeret, James Cromwell, Jane Seymour,

Jessica De Gouw, John Hurt, John Michael Higgins, Juliette Gréco, Laura Linney, Linus Roache, Mariska Hargitay, Melissa Manchester, Michael B. Jordan, Michael Jordan, Paul Johansson, Philip Glenister, Ronda Rousey, Rose Leslie, Seal, Stendhal, Tom Brokaw, Valene Kane, William Katt, Zosia Mamet.

AQUARIUS
QUALITIES
VISION, ORIGINALITY, CHARITY,
TOLERANCE, INDEPENDENCE,
INDIVIDUALITY
QUIRKS
ECCENTRICITY, SEPARATENESS,
NEUROSIS, DISOBEDIENCE,
THOUGHTLESSNESS, CRUELTY
Motto: *"I know"*
Elements: *Air, Saturn/Uranus, Fixed*

--

DRAGON
QUALITIES
STRENGTH, SUCCESS, GOOD HEALTH,
ENTHUSIASM, PLUCK, SENTIMENTALITY
QUIRKS
RIGIDITY, MISTRUST, DISSATISFACTION,
INFATUATION, BRAGGADOCIO, VOLUBILITY
Motto: *"I Preside"*
Elements: *Positive Wood, Yang*

"I know" and "I preside" were walking across the bridge. One of them fell in. Who was left? That's correct! No matter which way you look at this character, he's right up there in the top twenty. You see, Aquarius/Dragon always takes over. Nothing can stop him, as he both knows and presides better than everybody else. There is a driving, steady quality to this personality. No matter what he or she does it will be accomplished with flourish and style. Aquarius/Dragons are know-it-alls, yet circumspect about showing it. They are family-oriented and respect social conventions.

This person's nature is both hard-nosed and unswayable. Once he has declared something, it's impossible to change his mind. Aquarius/Dragons give off severity rays. They are powerhouses who will stoop to anything in order to conquer their prey.

Aquarius/Dragons want things done their way. They hate competition. They are capable of enormous hoaxes to get control over others. When the Aquarius/Dragon is looking for followers, anything goes: poetry, humor, logic, charisma, noise, favors, money and so on. Of course, what I call hoax may really be charm and diplomacy, but whatever you call it, this character uses liters of it daily. He really lays it on. He is polite and well spoken. He is proper and mannerly. Frankly, I think he's a bit much. But you cannot take away the fact that the Aquarius/Dragon is enormously successful.

This subject is an organizer. He is sharp-minded and goes straight to the point. Other, more fiery, self-involved Dragons sometimes miss the mark because of their uppity egos. The Dragon born Aquarius doesn't have that problem. Aquarius lends clarity to the dynamic Dragon. This person is a cool customer. People are attracted to his air of protectiveness and his earnest desire to please.

Despite his gift for achieving easy glory, the Aquarius/Dragon remains a worrier, Inside an outer shell of self-confidence, this subject gnaws at himself about eventualities. He is a shade pessimistic about the future. He does not like to lose control. Therefore, whatever is out of his hands, as yet unformed and uncertain, troubles this mistrustful character. He may become frantic and even neurotic over events that seem to be shifting away from his sphere of influence.

In worldly matters this niggling dread can be useful. It keeps the Aquarian Dragon on his toes. But in the personal realm, where romance or sentiment is concerned, this feeling of impending loss panics the soul of our hero and threatens to develop into real hysteria. When emotions are at stake, Aquarius/Dragon loses his cool in seconds. He is vastly sentimental and not always secure about his place in the heart of the loved one. His apparent calm then serves as a cover for this bottomless pit feeling of possible loneliness that stalks the Aquarius/Dragon's private hell. He cannot be alone.

The Aquarius/Dragon is never intentionally mean or petty. His pleasure is in serving as control center. He wants to be mother, boss, chief, owner, handler, manager and everything else. His aim is to protect and to serve. He or she wants to watch things grow, to improve or to allow to flower elements over which he or she has this famous control. As the Dragon born in Aquarius is not particularly creative himself, his objective in love or friendship or even in work situations is to implement improvement. Aquarius/Dragons don't mind running the show from the wings.

Love

In romantic situations, the Aquarius/Dragon is ruthless for power. He wants to get and keep a lover forever. Of course, his desire for emotional dominion has nothing to do with evil or wickedness. The Aquarius/Dragon wants to help a loved one to realize his or her own dreams. . The happier the loved one is, the happier the Aquarius/Dragon will be. There is however a potential for blind jealousy. Should you be in the clutches of an Aquarius/Dragon, I suggest you never mention the name of another possible lover or mistress in his fragile, incendiary presence. These folks suffer immense anxiety about losing you. Don't play with their delicate heartstrings. You will be afforded much mental leeway in your couple, but if you stray, your giant green Dragon will first fly into a rage, then melt into a puddle of sobbing green goop.

Compatibilities

Aries and Gemini/Tigers are fun for you. So are Libra and Sagittarius/Rats. Gemini, Libra and Sagittarius/Monkeys provide fascinating company and keep you on your toes. You might also be attracted to an Aries/Rooster. The reciprocity quotient is low, but the game's a treat. Taurus, Leo and Scorpio/Dogs don't approve of you. And Taurus born Monkey finds you too much of a challenge.

Home and Family

The home of the Aquarius/Dragon tends to favor the practical over the aesthetic. Although this person is sensitive to beauty and reacts positively to artistic creation, the interior of his or her home will not necessarily indicate a search for loveliness. This is a practical person. The ovens will work well and the sinks will be ample.

As these persons are family-responsible in the extreme, they will probably not only assist parents and siblings but will also want to have children of their own. They are reliable parents, and even have a bit of Pygmalion streak. In lieu of being creative themselves, they wish to shape and mold human beings as though they were dolls. They will care for their offspring, worry, fret, cook, sew, earn, comfort, protect, teach—you name it. They do it in spades!

Little Aquarius/Dragon kids also fret a lot. They are concerned about their own futures and worry that parents may not be well or happy. They take on lots of personal guilt for what happens at home, and must be reasoned with about assuming too much responsibility. They are good workers in school and very attached to their family unit's strength. Sometimes as young adults they leave home for a while to test their iconoclastic secrets. But rebellion in the case of clear-thinking Aquarius/Dragons doesn't go very far. Parents who have an Aquarian Dragon child should think twice about divorce. Schism is hard on this clinging nature's nerves.

Profession

Talented for organizing anything from office structures to personnel duties, the Aquarius born Dragon can function in most any job requiring leadership and equanimity. This person is clever and moderate with money, and knows how to increase his earnings through investment. He is usually a serious student and will begin achieving in the real world at a young age.

The Aquarius/Dragon is a natural boss. People like and respect his opinions. He is very diplomatic, remember? He is peripatetic by nature, too, and can work comfortably at different rungs of the hierarchal ladder. The Aquarius/Dragon is destined for a long-term job as well as personal commitment. He will not be tempted to change careers on a whim.

Employment is no problem for this highly employable character. He'll do anything on his way up—sweep, push a pencil, run elevators—but he won't have to do any menial job for long, as his superior executive talents are recognized soon enough. Promotion every two or three years is common for these people.

The Aquarius/Dragon may enjoy the following jobs: householder, stockbroker, banker, vice-president in charge of investments, company director, personnel manager, hospital administrator, librarian, writer.

Famous Aquarius/Dragons:
Aaron Neville, Alan Cumming, Anton Lesser, Ayn Rand, Boris Pickett, Brandon Lee, Carol Ann Susi, Charlie Day, Christopher Eccleston, Ciarán Hinds, Diane Lane, Erin Cleaver, Françoise Dorin, Garry Chalk, Gong Li, Isla Fisher, Jeanne Moreau, Jenny Shipley, Jeremy Sumpter, Jim Jarmusch, JM Coetzee, Joanna Kerns, Josh Stewart, Justin Hartley, Keeley Hawes, Kelly Carlson, Kerry Washington, Khleo Thomas, Kim Ji-min, Kylie Bunbury, Maiara Walsh, Maitland Ward, Marcel Dassault, Mary Steenburgen, Matt Dillon, Michel Galabru, Michel Serrault, Neil Diamond, Nick Nolte, Pierre Tchernia, Placido Domingo, Princess Stephanie of Monaco, Roger Mudd, Roger Vadim, S. J. Perelman, Sam Jaeger, Sarah Sutherland, Shakira, Sherilyn Fenn, Smokey Robinson, Steven Zaillian, Ted Koppel, Tony Jaa, Zach Galligan.

AQUARIUS
QUALITIES
VISION, ORIGINALITY, CHARITY,
TOLERANCE, INDEPENDENCE,
INDIVIDUALITY
QUIRKS
ECCENTRICITY, SEPARATENESS,
NEUROSIS, DISOBEDIENCE,
THOUGHTLESSNESS, CRUELTY
Motto: *"I know"*
Elements: *Air, Saturn/Uranus, Fixed*

--

SNAKE
QUALITIES
INTUITION, ATTRACTIVENESS, DISCRETION,
SAGACITY, CLAIRVOYANCE, COMPASSION
QUIRKS
DISSIMULATION, EXTRAVAGANCE,
LAZINESS, CUPIDITY, PRESUMPTION,
EXCLUSIVENESS
Motto: *"I sense"*
Elements: *Negative, Fire, Yin*

Sunshine incarnate, the Snake born in Aquarius has the double luck to be able to think clearly and to intuit things with rare finesse. This "up" person is firmly planted in reality, yet manages to keep smiling. He is a natural optimist and stubborn about maintaining that image. The Aquarius/Snake never bothers to want what he knows he cannot have. Nonetheless, he is avid for what he desires and can get. By this I mean that the Serpent born in Aquarius is chillingly lucid. He or she will attempt to seduce and conquer others for the sheer excitement of the dance. But before attempting to seduce or entice, enchant or charm, this person will know well ahead precisely what his chances are. Snakes born in Aquarius do not play losing games.

This sureness of self is, of course, part of the charm of the Snake/ Aquarius. He is never without a slew of hot spots in his life, wherein occur the most exorbitant variety of events. He tries everything new; he leaps about from lair to lair like Santa Claus, bringing joy and good will to every life he touches. He is not really materially gener- ous, nor is this person attracted to ownership of tangibles. The Aquarius/Snake doesn't care about the concrete. In fact, he'd rather not own anything at all to take care of or dust. The plush and sensu- ous inner life of this utterly charismatic creature goes on without in- terference from the outside. His adventures and dreams, his travels and his plans, all take place inside the head. Aquarius/Snake is the day dreamer of the double zodiac. If someone yells at this character because she is late and lazy and forgets dates and is careless about facts, Aquarius/Snake takes a mental trip. She just drifts off. While the scolder stands there railing away, Aquarius/Snake basks in the imaginary sunshine of a desert island—all alone without a soul for company or interference. To Aquarius/Snakes what is real is what they declare to be real. The rest is fantasy.

These clever people can work very hard at complicated and diffi- cult jobs. They can also perform breakthrough experiments, and cre- ate beautiful art. The Aquarius/Snake's imagination is fertile, and his sense for saying or doing the proper thing at the proper time (not for social advancement or out of respect for manners) is infallible.

The Aquarius/Snake is the kindest of Snakes. He or she will be charitable, and feel pity for the sorrows and pain of others. She is not so empathetic as she is sympathetic and willing to help in a practical way. Having a Snake born in Aquarius for a friend is en- viable. They are caring and loving, generous with their time, and truly good-hearted. They not only take in strays but they keep them warm and fed for however long is necessary. Also, the lucid Aquar- ius/Snake knows how to let go gracefully. When he has fixed the wounded bird's wing and he can fly alone, Aquarius/Snake takes him outside and lets him go. No rewards wanted. No thanks either, other than the pleasure Aquarius/Snake gets from performing a charitable act. This Snake is not looking for glory, applause, or rec- ognition for heroism.

The Aquarian Snake is eccentric and slightly outrageous. He or she will definitely lean to irresponsibility and have a running battle with laziness. Too, all Snakes fabulate. This one may only fib to make someone feel better. But lies come easily to this slippery sort. Lies, and a temptation to truancy. Not that any great criminals were ever born under this sign combination. But the temptation to be marginal is very strong.

Love

The Aquarius/Snake knows how to control his emotions with cold, logical reason. He is first a thinker, then a sensor and finally he allows himself to feel. Feeling is not of primary urgency and will not take precedence over reason. Moreover, with such a mosaical life structure, this person cannot help getting involved with more than one person at a time. He or she will be promiscuous but jealous of mates.

Should you love an Aquarius/Snake, let me give you some advice. Don't ever tie him or her down. Don't ask for account of time spent away from you. Give out no information at all on your own private affairs. Keep things mysterious and shrouded in secrecy. The Aquarius/Snake is a sucker for enigma. Keep him guessing and he'll slide along after you forever. Don't try to corral him. It's fatal. He'll move off like an eel, never to be heard from again.

Compatibilities

Gemini, Libra and Sagittarius/Oxen make the safest partners for you. Wisdom and cool headedness being some of your highest priorities, you settle well with Oxen. Aries, Libra and Sagittarius/Roosters make you a bit more nervous and insecure, but they are fun and you do share a good giggle from time to time. Aries/Cat can be stimulating to your cultural side. You won't last long with Taurus, Leo or Scorpio/Pigs. They're onto your game and you to theirs. Boredom. Taurus/Tigers and Leo/Monkeys amuse you, but you prefer stargazing to earthly pursuits and so will ultimately clash.

Home and Family

The Aquarius/Snake doesn't care much for interiors. He wants them to function and be attractive, but he doesn't really want to have to check up on them and worry about whether they are despoiled or robbed. His is a cerebral, not a material, nature. What this character does care about is how comfortable the people he loves and cares for and protects are. He will go out of his way to house loved ones properly, building them a bathtub in their bedroom if they think it's fun, tearing out walls to make room for another family member. The Aquarius/Snake dresses sexily and has garish tastes.

Family is everything to this humane and self-sacrificing person. She will look after aging parents and call on old people in homes. He will take his kids to the ice rink, the roller rink, the circus, and every other possible point of interest imaginable and wait patiently for them to finish playing. These people are exaggeratedly infatuated with their offspring but they still manage to make them behave. They dream about how wonderful it would be if their whole family were happy and healthy. Aquarian Snakes would do almost anything to see their dream come true.

The Aquarian Snake child is close to perfect. He or she will care intensely for family unity. He will be sunny and optimistic and cute. His talents for philosophy and metaphysics should be educated and encouraged. This person needs sound instruction and a secure home life-- otherwise he or she may really end up on that fictional desert island. They are over-imaginative and need lots of reassurance and love. Without it, they could be attracted to a life of petty crime or dissolution. The Aquarius/Snake's backbone must be tenderly imposed from without by means of a code of behavior demanded by family and home life.

Profession

Usually, Aquarian Snakes have brilliant imaginative and philosophical minds. They are adventurous and reasonable. They like to feel free within a structure. As they are curious about everything, and are both manual and artistic, there are few creative doors they cannot open.

Aquarius/Snakes would have to be persuaded to be the boss of any enterprise, big or small. These people prefer the wings to the stage. They like to manipulate others and to toy with their emotions and thoughts, but they are not authoritarian for the sake of wielding control. They will work well in groups if necessary, but they will show only the tiniest part of themselves to each group involved. Their greatest joy is in helping others. They work best on their own, at their own speed, while their imagination transports them to tropical parts unknown.

Some careers they might want to try are: social worker, undercover policeman, lawyer, diplomat, preacher, political activist, travel agent.

Famous Aquarius/Snakes:
Abraham Lincoln, Charles Darwin, Chaim Potok, Carole King, Bertrand Poirot Delpech, Dick Cheney, James Joyce, Oprah Win-

frey, Placido Domingo, Richard Gephardt, Sergio Mendes, William H. Harrison, Danielle Haim, Elizabeth Olsen, Charlene Princess of Monaco, Dean Muir, Oprah Winfrey, Sergio Perez, Becky Ann Baker, Maura Tierney, Kathleen Kinmont, Michael Bay, Julie Warner, Christine Elise, Chris Rock, Ike Barinholtz, Chord Overstreet, Ken Page, Christie Brinkley, Bill Mumy, Rainn Wilson, Kristen Schaal, Omar Sy, Kelly Stables, Rich Sommer, Stephen Farrelly, Yousef Erakat.

AQUARIUS
QUALITIES
VISION, ORIGINALITY, CHARITY,
TOLERANCE, INDEPENDENCE,
INDIVIDUALITY
QUIRKS
ECCENTRICITY, SEPARATENESS,
NEUROSIS, DISOBEDIENCE,
THOUGHTLESSNESS, CRUELTY
Motto: *"I know"*
Elements: *Air, Saturn/Uranus, Fixed*

--

HORSE
QUALITIES
PERSUASIVENESS, UNSCRUPULOUSNESS,
POPULARITY, STYLE, DEXTERITY,
ACCOMPLISHMENT
QUIRKS
SELFISHNESS, AUTONOMY, REBELLION,
HASTE, ANXIETY, PRAGMATISM
Motto: *"I demand"*
Elements: *Positive Fire, Yang*

To this alert and energetic Aquarian, variety and movement represent freedom. The Horse lends rebellion to the clear-minded Aquarian, and pushes him to stride ahead. Horses are hasty and gifted for easy accomplishment. The Aquarian wants an original life. When the two are matched by birth, an eccentric, fleeting sort of being evolves. The Aquarius/Horse never lights for long.

There is much manual skill in this person. No job or task requiring digital dexterity is beyond his capabilities. He is also distinctively talented for using words well, and may even be multilingual. As one of his first priorities is to travel about and indulge in varied experiences, he picks up quickly on uncommon phenomena and dives headlong into exotica.

This person craves the artistic in life, longs for the world to be a more beautiful and caring place and spends much time and thought trying to improve it. Aquarius/Horses are concerned, active citizens who know how to go to work for what they believe in.

And this character believes in eccentric schemes. She may want to have a babbling brook in her living room. He may long to own a huge castle in Bulgaria with forty rooms where people get together to stage sing-alongs. These Aquarius/Horses are dreamers and plotters of vast plans that can take a lifetime to realize. Not to worry. The Aquarius/Horse will carry out his plan in his own sweet time-preferably with his own hands. Vast scope doesn't faze this valiant subject. He knows he can work it out in detail all alone. All he asks for is a little cooperation. And, of course, money.

Often the Aquarius/Horse's source of income is really somebody else's. Not that this native is dependent—far from it. But the Aquarius born in Horse cannot imagine why anyone should refuse him the funds he needs to start the relief organization for errant minstrels. It's a perfectly valid cause. Besides, the Aquarius/Horse is among the most persuasive of signs. He listens—but mostly to himself. What he wants he must have. Otherwise? Well, there is no otherwise.

This character is essentially freelance. Salaries and nine-to-five jobs seem silly to him. He's only after the jackpot or the big deal to come through. If he can't have a lot of money he'd just as soon starve—or mooch. The Aquarius/Horse is a liberal thinker who truly cares about the downtrodden and the poor. But often he misses seeing the forest and forgets about the trees altogether. In any case, with Aquarius/Horse it's all or nothing. They are either right there with all the facts in hand delivering a seductive speech on their latest passion, or else they've drifted off somewhere to take a look at the sunsets in Malaysia.

The Horse born in Aquarius is slightly loony, too. Eccentricities abound in this person's nature. And as Aquarius/Horses are truly visionary people, they may suffer from a surfeit of insight, which, if improperly applied, can develop into madness. Mostly though, the Aquarius/Horse makes excellent use of his peculiarities. The edge of craziness always present in Aquarians serves to enlighten the overly pragmatic Horse nature. Horse, in his turn, helps the distant

Aquarian to gain a sense of belonging, and brings him safely back to earth from his frequent flights. This person promises to add magic to the lives of those who surround him or her. An Aquarius/Horse usually has a finely honed sense of self-derision, and can amuse either on purpose or simply because he is irretrievably astonishing. What you see of the Aquarius/Horse is only about one-tenth of what is actually present in this dense and zany personality.

Love

Here the Aquarius/Horse firmly believes he or she can do no wrong. When they love someone, they feel that whatever the loved one receives from them ought to be sufficient. This character decidedly does not want to be bothered with complicated love affairs. From the beginning, it ought to be clear that Aquarius/Horse runs the show, calls the shots and even sets the pace. Either his partner accepts being flexible enough not to panic each time this person floats off on some new adventure (whether romantic or not), or he'll get a different partner. Sentimentality is not one of this person's foibles.

The difficulty with loving an Aquarius born in a Horse year is immaterial. The only important thing about being mad for this nut is that he or she is so wonderfully kooky and fascinatingly interesting. If you have the hots for an Aquarius/Horse, look on the bright side. You cannot change them. Never hound or nag them. Nothing you can do or say will make a dent, anyway. Just try to keep your own head above water, and most of all—enjoy them.

Compatibilities

Gemini and Sagittarius/Dogs are loyal and have their wits about them. You need such steady intelligent partners. A Libra/Sheep will need your protection and for that reason may appeal to you. Sagittarius/Tigers are good rebound romance prospects for you. They're so very flexible and independent. Taurus, Leo and Scorpio/Rats are not on your list of romantic associates. Nor should you bother to take up with a Leo/Monkey.

Home and Family

Talk about funky! This person's house will be a museum of found objects and weirdo styles. The Aquarius/Horse is a collector. As he or she travels outrageously much, they are always bringing back some trinket or geegaw bartered from a Sikh in a souk or filched from a sheik's dining tent. It's a riot of color. Imagine Horse and Aquarius together and see what comes out in the wardrobe. Flash and sash with rank panache. Get those red leather riding boots and the paisley scarf wrapped fetchingly around the jodhpur tops. Wow!

The Aquarius/Horse may be crazy, but he's not all that bananas about having barrels of kids. Children in numbers threaten his freedom of movement. This person must move. If ever he or she does settle down to have children, it will tend to be late in life. Then, watch out! This person can get so involved in the details of parenthood as to be a perfect bore. Parenting is a challenge, but viewed with the passion and potential for ecstasy of the excitable Aquarius/Horse—whew! Kids, if you want to have a great childhood, get yourself born to this wonderful cuckoo Mom or Pop. Forget bedtimes and chores forever. As a parent the Aquarius/Horse is permissive, modern, avant-garde, and utterly subjugated by childish charms.

This artsy child will amuse parents with pranks and original tricks. His creative attributes will be many. He prefers to be spoiled and pampered rather than to have to adhere to a lot of silly rules. He's persuasive, and finds remarkably plausible excuses for his kinks. Training and manners will add polish to this character's exterior. Otherwise, there is not much you can do except lavish attentions on this sweet creature.

Profession

So much talent should not go unrewarded. This person will not be particularly ambitious for gain in his life. The Aquarian Horse is not an investor or even a saver. He is not really much interested in money, but knows he must have lots to carry out his drastically expensive projects. Normally he doesn't have a "job" but works in some marginal, lucrative capacity that permits him to travel to exotic lands.

The Aquarius/Horse boss will be fair and just but severely self-involved. You can fully expect this character to get to the office late and leave early, and still expect you to be there on the minute and work overtime to boot. He's a little crazy, remember? But oh, so interesting. And talented. This person can be gainfully employed provided the boss lets him or her go on trips every three or four days. The talents of Aquarius/Horse are intense and ephemeral. Use sparingly.

Jobs that might appeal to the Aquarian Horse are: movie star, photographer, interpreter, speechwriter, traveling salesperson, fundraiser, art teacher, mercenary.

Famous Aquarius/Horses:

Amy Jackson, Ashton Kutcher, Boris Yeltsin, Brett Dier, Bryan Callen, Chris Parnell, Claire Bloom, Claude Rich, Craig Roberts, Danai Gurira, Dean Jones, Don Coscarelli, Eiza González, Emma Roberts, Ernie Banks, Franklin D. Roosevelt, Gahan Wilson, Gene Hackman, Jackie Robinson, James Dean, John Travolta, John

Wesley Shipp, Julie Dreyfus, Justine Bateman, Lochlyn Munro, Luke Pasqualino, Mamie Van Doren, Marthe Keller, Neal McDonough, Nia Sanchez, Rachel DiPillo, Rene Russo, Rip Torn, Robert Wagner, Rory Kinnear, Rosamund Pike, Sara Rue, Stacey Dash, Tamlyn Tomita, The Weeknd (Abél Makkonen Tesfaye), Thomas Edison, William Levitt, Zach Grenier.

AQUARIUS
QUALITIES
VISION, ORIGINALITY, CHARITY,
TOLERANCE, INDEPENDENCE,
INDIVIDUALITY
QUIRKS
ECCENTRICITY, SEPARATENESS,
NEUROSIS, DISOBEDIENCE,
THOUGHTLESSNESS, CRUELTY
Motto: *"I know"*
Elements: *Air, Saturn/Uranus, Fixed*

--

SHEEP
QUALITIES
INVENTION, LACK OF FORESIGHT,
PERSEVERANCE, WHIMSY, GOOD MANNERS,
IMPRACTICALITY
QUIRKS
PARASITISM, SENSITIVITY,
TARDINESS, PESSIMISM, TASTE, WORRY
Motto: *"I depend"*
Elements: *Negative, Fire, Yin*

A quarius weds the Sheep. Clarity and sensitivity, knowledge and whimsy. This solid marriage of complementary signs is rich with possibilities. Aquarius brings a dowry of independence to the inconsistent Sheep, whose byword is dependency. Sheep carries emotional depth with him to the wedding. This Aquarius can feel more profoundly than most. And his Sheep identity benefits from an electrical charge of true Aquarian autonomy. This person will be gifted for futuristic planning, oblivious to social criticism, and capable of maddening individuality.

The Aquarian born Sheep lives for and in the moment. What is going on now is what is going on—period! Such spontaneity is, of course, a double-edged sword. On the one hand, creativity is heightened. Nothing like regret or apprehension stands in the way of invention and breakthrough. Yet this person may be so unconstrained as to leap into sizzling soups he'd have avoided by applying a moment or two of forethought. The Aquarius/Sheep must learn caution and perspective. If not, his exaggerated taste for the heat of the moment may lead him astray.

A penchant for profligacy may also hinder this person's progress. The Aquarian Sheep is openhearted and open-minded. He will be tempted to allow almost anyone into his life just for the pleasure of knowing them. In theory, the glad hand is lovely. But we all know that the world is full of parasites and sycophants. The Aquarius/ Sheep sometimes falls victim to the more ruthless of this lot and is hard put, because of his kindly and sensitive nature, to dig in his hooves and rid himself of sycophantic creeps.

The wise Aquarius/Sheep will recognize his shortcomings and seek direction from family or structure from an outside influence. This person requires a framework in which to evolve his theories and practice his innate genius. He must have peace of mind, and no interference or distraction. Isolation, of course, frightens this essentially gregarious soul—so he or she may bolt once or twice before settling down to business.

People sometimes accuse this charmer of quirkiness. Some think Aquarian Sheep are not really serious people because they seem lighter than air. It is true that Sheep born in Aquarius love to have fun and clown around. But of course this is only their public or social image. These people are secret grinds. They can live on bread and water and work round the clock on some unlikely experimental creation for days without coming up for air. They are other. They are true artists and visionaries. They don't dream of approval or applause, but rather take pleasure only in what they are about.

Besides being innovative and eccentric, the Aquarian Sheep is self- indulgent. He may come out of a work tunnel after a month or so and lunge lickety-split into some passionate dumb love affair that lasts two and a half seconds, or decide to eat himself sick. Aquarians born Sheep are excessive, but have no lust for excess. Their joy in glut comes from heedlessness and sheer caprice.

Love

Well, this is a tough one. Poor old Aquarius/Sheep never seems to get enough love. They are fickle people out of a need to give and take pleasure now without malice aforethought. This laxity in romance unfortunately gives the Aquarius/Sheep a bad reputation. He or she is basically not even aware of the need for something as restrictive as sexual fidelity. Why? Whatever for? thinks the Aquarian Sheep freethinker. For this person, love is for sharing the moment.

If you love one of these sweet-natured darlings, I can certainly understand your dilemma. The best (and only) thing to do is stand by and wait for your Aquarius/Sheep to come rolling home. If you are the wise type of person he or she really needs, the Aquarius/Sheep will be grateful for your steadfastness and constancy. Your job is to nurture this great talent. Competition is out of the question—and yes, you can live your own life and not fear this person's disapproval. Freedom, for the Aquarius/Sheep, is a two-way street.

Compatibilities

Your favorites among the animal signs are usually found in the Cat category. Look for your personal Cat among Geminis, Librans and Sagittarians. Those same signs provide you with your next best choice, which is a sensual and wealthy Pig person. Aries/Horses will do nicely as well. Give short shrift to Taurus or Leo/Oxen, and don't gamble on a Leo or Scorpio/Dog's good nature. Scorpio/ Monkeys and you are on the permanent outs.

Home and Family

The Aquarian Sheep is at home wherever he feels welcome and comfortable. Whether the home belongs to him or to his mate or family is all the same to him. This character can settle in wherever his whimsy leads him. Decor is as important to this beauty-loving sign as it is to the next guy. But if the Aquarius/Sheep has to actually go out and choose the fabric, then measure and sew up the drapes, and worry about whether or not they hang straight—forget it. "Throw a scarf over that window and lie down here on this mattress, honey," says the devil-may-care Aquarius/ Sheep. "And while you're up, hand me that can of peanuts.. I haven't eaten in three days."

A delicious parent for the progressive child, the Aquarius/Sheep will dabble in all childhood pleasures with energy and spunk. As this character is spontaneous and doesn't care much for social approval, he fits right in with kiddish ways. The discipline level will probably be at about minus zero in this household. But there will be fun aplenty.

The Aquarius/Sheep kid should be very talented for things artistic. You can derive great satisfaction from his or her efforts at musical or artistic endeavor. Their sense of time is nonexistent. You'll have to buy them several alarm watches if you want them home from school on time.

Profession

This person is in no hurry to achieve anything. He defies convention, and couldn't care less for routine. He's slightly greedy, but that doesn't help him to be ambitious. Mostly the Aquarius/Sheep cares about what's going on right now inside his sensitivity zone. Art and art-related careers are the safest ones for him or her. But whatever this person chooses to do, he will only do it as well as the exterior structure demands. They are not leaders. And they are not terrific followers either. Ask for starch in the collars.

I don't really see this person bossing anyone seriously. He may well assume the role of leader or authority figure in a venture. But he won't mean it. As with everything they do, if it pleases them and satisfies their need for pleasure, these people will gladly take over. They are capable but capricious. If I had an Aquarius/Sheep employee, I should surely need to be at least a Leo/Dragon. The Aquarius/Sheep responds well to strength.

Some possible careers for the Aquarian Sheep are: artist, fashion designer, decorator, industrial designer, potter, art critic, illustrator, animator, window dresser, toy designer, inventor, musician, actor, actress.

Famous Aquarius/Sheep:
Benicio Del Toro, Bonnie Wright, Cerina Vincent, Charles Dickens, Charles Shaughnessy, Charlotte Ross, Christina Ricci, Christopher Masterson, Christopher McDonald, Ed Sheeran, Edward Burns, Ethan Phillips, Federico Fellini, Geena Davis, James Michener, Jeff Daniels, Jennifer Candy, Jesse Spencer, Laura Dern, Lauren Hall, Louis Féraud, Malese Jow, Margarita Levieva, Matthew Lawrence, Mena Suvari, Miguel Ferrer, Miki Furukawa, Mimi Rogers, Mo Yan, Nathan Lane, Nicolas Sarkozy, Rachelle Lefevre, Raquel Cassidy, Robby Benson, Robert Hersant, Rutina Wesley, Sarah Lancaster, Serge Lama, Stéphane Grappeli, Vince Gilligan, Wilmer Valderrama, Ziyi Zhang.

AQUARIUS
QUALITIES
VISION, ORIGINALITY, CHARITY,
TOLERANCE, INDEPENDENCE,
INDIVIDUALITY
QUIRKS
ECCENTRICITY, SEPARATENESS,
NEUROSIS, DISOBEDIENCE,
THOUGHTLESSNESS, CRUELTY
Motto: *"I know"*
Elements: *Air, Saturn/Uranus, Fixed*

--

MONKEY
QUALITIES
IMPROVISATION, CUNNING, STABILITY,
SELF-INVOLVEMENT, WIT, OPPORTUNISM
QUIRKS
DECEIT, RUSE, LOQUACITY,
LEADERS, SILLINESS, ZEAL
Motto: *"I plan"*
Elements: *Positive, metal, Yang*

A person of exceptional breadth and depth arises from the un-ion of Aquarius and Monkey. The natural detachment of Aquarius assists the Monkey in forging his destiny without cumbersome sentiment or extraneous emotion. Monkey gives the visionary Aquarian a sound sense of fact and helps him to deal with the present. The combination is harmonious and promising.

He or she will be aggressively verbal. Words are the vehicle of this clear-thinking soul. Also, an air of revolution, or at least a sensitivity to social change or breakthrough, colors every Aquarius/

Monkey creation. He or she may choose to exercise power over others, but if so, the goal is never power for itself. Rather, the Aquarius/Monkey seeks to lead or advise, judge and guide his fellows toward a more perfect world where truth gets more airtime than falsehood.

The basic methods of the Aquarius/Monkey have to do with zeroing in on human behavior, be it fictional or real, and synthesizing events into a digestible form. The ideal is verisimilitude. The plan is to so cleverly reflect real life by means of a unique personal vision that finally teaches human beings about themselves. History, literature, the law, journalism and cinema are all possible vehicles for this person's huge talent.

The Aquarian's natural clarity and the Monkey's brilliance join hands in this sign. They are strong, hard-working people who long to achieve the unlikely, and often do. Too, they are versatile. An Aquarius/Monkey poet doesn't necessarily only write poetry. He or she may also design skyscrapers or own an elephant farm in Africa. The Aquarius/Monkey is most of all a doer. He cares more for his work and the advancement of the human race than he does for material wealth or celebrity. As long as the Aquarius/Monkey is professionally active, he is content.

This character is, moreover, zealous. In some signs dedication can take on fanatical proportions. But not here. The Aquarius/ Monkey is a cool customer. If he is zealous, it is because he wants to get more done than is humanly possible in a normal eight-hour workday. So the Monkey born in Aquarius frequently works a twelve-hour day. "He's killing himself," clucks his mother-in-law. "She'll die young at this rate," worries the anxious boyfriend. "But," thinks the wiry Aquarius/Monkey, "so what? At least I will have contributed my view, set down my picture of the world." Accomplishment, for the Aquarian Monkey, is what life is all about.

This native seems to have been born "out on a limb". He or she takes chances. These people are not in the least afraid to dream up or plan great deeds. They are essentially self-confident and have great personal integrity. Aquarius/Monkeys are wise and gifted. What's more, they are noble people, whose dignity impresses friend and enemy alike. They are clever tacticians and always prefer to make a deal rather than to confront an adversary head-on in a lawsuit or duel.

Love

This person tries unconsciously not to embroil him- or herself in emotional complexity. Normally, the Aquarius/Monkey avoids mires of all sorts. He is lucid, remember. And achievement-oriented. Of course he needs love, and will seek a partner to share his burdens as well as his joys. But this person doesn't usually look to personal passion as a panacea. He doesn't need to feel exalted by a great love affair in order to survive and feel comfortable about himself. The Aquarius/Monkey is unfaithful. For the fun of it.

What he or she will most need from a lover is comfort and stewardship. The busy, ingenious Aquarius/Monkey loves beauty but is more interested in quality than in the physical aspect of a partner. His or her choice of a lover or mistress, wife or husband, will invariably depend on the intrinsic value of the potential mate as a person, not as an object.

The Aquarius/Monkey needs help. He or she is too busy to do it all alone. If you love one, be of assistance, be discreet, and learn how to get around on tiptoe while your genius is at work.

Compatibilities

Suitable for your emotional needs are Gemini, Libra and Sagittarius/Rats. Aries, Libra, Scorpio and Sagittarius/Dragons motivate you, too, and will answer your serious questions seriously. You'll not be excited by Taurus, Leo or even Scorpio/Pigs. Your goals are opposed. Taurus and Leo/Tigers irk you with their self-importance, and Scorpio/Snakes may turn you on but they have no staying power for your kind of mind.

Home and Family

The home of an Aquarius/Monkey will be rational, useful and without pretension. This person's surroundings usually bespeak his sensible character and are solid yet not traditional. He will probably lean toward the modern and practical in decor. His wardrobe will be suitably elegant but never showy. This person usually doesn't need to impress. And if he does? It's probably an indication that his career is slipping.

The Aquarius/Monkey parent is sincere and serious about raising kids. She will have high aspirations for her children and will attempt to teach the little ones how to use their talents wisely. This is a patient person who will put on little Lucas's skis and help Britanny off with her parka and leggings when he fetches her from school. The Aquarius/Monkey is a rather undemonstrative parent, however, and not hug-'em-up loving. He or she will communicate best with children through words.

This child is a treat. His many talents and multiple curiosities will surface early in life. School should be a breeze (unless, of course, teachers won't allow the Aquarius/Monkey to show how exceptional he is). He may be slightly disobedient, as he is far from cowardly or even malleable. His mature ideas will astound adults. He will not take unfair advantage of a loving Mom or Dad. Aquarius/Monkey's a good scout.

Profession

This character is essentially cerebral. I don't peg him or her for a merchant or even a civil servant. There's too much revolutionary thought going on for conformity to sit comfortably. An independent, the Aquarius/Monkey sets about his or her own projects rationally, seeking funds from outside sources and using them wisely in order to be sure to be welcome to borrow the next time.

The Aquarius/Monkey makes an excellent boss. He is lovable, and employees and assistants will respect this interesting person's views and creations. As an employee, the Aquarius/Monkey will be scrupulously concerned with giving value for wages. He may prove rebellious in the long run and wish to branch out on his or her own. With such a gift for encompassing grand projects of a very personal nature, this wish for independence is no surprise.

Some professions that might appeal to the Aquarius/Monkey are: writer (novelist, script writer, poet, composer, journalist, playwright), film director, theater director, actor or actress, public speaker, judge or lawyer. All word-related professions are suitable.

Famous Aquarius/Monkeys:

Akio Morita, Alice Walker, Alicia Keys, Angela Davis, Anton Chekhov, Axelle Red, Betty Friedan, Bob Marley, Brandy Ledford, Brian Krause, Carl Bernstein, Charlotte Rampling, Colette, Colin O'Donoghue, Darren Aronofsky, Donna Reed, Eddie Barclay, Elijah Wood, Emily Rose, François Truffaut, Freddie Highmore, Gary Coleman, Gay Talese, Harley Jane Kozak, Jason Ritter, Jenifer Lewis, Jennifer Aniston, Johnny Lang, Josh Brolin, Justin Timberlake, Karen Fukuhara, Kathryn Morris, Kelly Hu, King Felipe of Spain, Learned Hand, Lisa Marie Presley, Logan Miller, Mario Lanza, Mary McCormack, Michael Sheen, Milos Foreman, Molly Ringwald, Morgane Polanski, Neymar, Olivia d'Abo, Patton Oswalt, Paulina Gaitan, Richard Karn, Taylor Lautner.

AQUARIUS
QUALITIES
VISION, ORIGINALITY, CHARITY,
TOLERANCE, INDEPENDENCE,
INDIVIDUALITY
QUIRKS
ECCENTRICITY, SEPARATENESS,
NEUROSIS, DISOBEDIENCE,
THOUGHTLESSNESS, CRUELTY
Motto: *"I know"*
Elements: *Air, Saturn/Uranus, Fixed*

--

ROOSTER
QUALITIES
RESILIENCE, ENTHUSIASM, CANDOR,
CONSERVATISM, CHIC, HUMOR
QUIRKS
COCKINESS, BOASTFULNESS, BLIND FAITH,
PEDANTRY, BOSSINESS, DISSIPATION
Motto: *"I overcome"*
Elements: *Negative, Metal, Yin*

First of all, the Aquarius born in a Rooster year often succeeds. And second of all, he frequently fails. The Rooster's swings of good and bad luck go on through the whole of his life, no matter what astrological sign he was born under. However (and here's the big however), Aquarius, the offbeat and aloof sign of brotherly love and general good will, possesses just the quality Roosters have been waiting for to keep them from scratching around in the dust for an errant grain of corn for years until their luck returns. Aquarians are lucid visionaries whose very detachment, although at times maddening, saves the Rooster.

This person never gets too emotionally attached to good fortune. Something tells him or her that the only thing permanent about life is change. The Aquarius/Rooster knows better than to invest his soul in any one of his myriad projects and plans, be they emotional, artistic or purely mercantile. The Aquarian born Rooster understands the ephemeral nature of happiness. Oh, he or she will crow a bit when times are good and complain bitterly when the chips are down. But something always belies their resignation. Something tells you that he or she never believed in that eternal bliss baloney in the first place.

Not that the Aquarius/Rooster is blasé. Far from it. This person is generally of cheerful demeanor, and personifies enthusiasm and involvement. But look a little deeper. The scars are cleverly hidden under natty dressing habits and a smart wardrobe of accessories. The Aquarius/Rooster's disenchantment may be camouflaged by a cushion of glorious pink roses, but it's still there.

The Rooster's love of appearances is at war here with the Aquarian's sense of what is right. Trouble is, the Rooster is stubborn and won't give up his craving for exterior signs of success. Remember that Roosters revel in the external and are not particularly driven by the search for emotional truth or understanding. Roosters just want to get on with it. Poor old lucid, Boy Scout, clairvoyant Aquarius hasn't a chance in the skin of a conservative and show-offy Rooster. When Aquarius pushes the brotherhood button, narrow-minded Rooster comes blustering up to warn, "Are you crazy? Don't let those oddballs in here. Before you know it the place will be crawling with religious fanatics and hippies!" Slam! So much for Aquarian altruism.

What happens finally is that Aquarius calls a truce with the feisty, bossy Rooster side of his nature and tries to be satisfied with enlightening each successive effort at success with a certain humanistic quality. Both of these characters are candid and frank. The Aquarius/ Rooster has the gift of gab and will know how to put it to good use.

This subject falls victim only to himself in life. He knows his faults, as he is lucid and aware. But he can become neurotic if he won't face facts. And facing facts is not an Aquarius/Rooster talent. These people like to sugar the pill, brighten the tarnished image and even go so far as to pretend that what exists for everybody else patently and openly doesn't pertain to them. Am I saying that the Aquarius/Rooster is a bit of a trickster? Does he lie to himself for

his own peace of mind? Yes. Precisely. The Aquarius/Rooster dis-
simulates truth to protect himself. He may twist the law ever so
slightly, or only manipulate a rule once in awhile. But the demon
temptation is always there. Aquarius/Roosters are cavalier about
truth, and bend it to fit their needs.

The Aquarius/Rooster is somewhat old-fashioned and tradition-
loving. He is pulled at all the time by social mores and custom. He
is tormented by a mixture of guilt and fibs. He's tricky and ruseful
but he doesn't want anybody to notice—least of all himself.

Love

The Rooster born in Aquarius appears so fantabulous that one
may imagine him engaged to marry some marvelous, exciting creature, the envy of his less adventurous friends. But don't be fooled.
The Aquarius/Rooster will never allow himself to be dragged into
affairs unless those same affairs bring him some emotional, financial, professional or even spiritual gain. The Aquarius/Rooster
would like to be taken care of at home so he or she can go out and
boss the world and make scads of money. This subject will be attractive for sure, and take excellent care of his physique.

If you are flat-out crazy about one of these dashing persons and
show it too much, they may lose interest. The Rooster/Aquarius
needs a challenge. He and she may not admit it, but they are bored
by obedient slave types. Be outwardly gentle and inwardly steely
and tough. And if you want to get and keep this fascinating customer's sentiments, set limits. Be demanding. Insist on first place.
Stomp your feet and don't let up till you get what you want. He or
she will only admire you the more for your mettle.

Compatibilities

Snakes make excellent sidekicks for Aquarians born Rooster.
You'll be most likely to find yours among Aries, Gemini, Libra or
Sagittarius. Oxen, too, please you and give you a sense of belong-
ing. Try Oxen born in Gemini, Libra or Sagittarius. Unsatisfactory
mates for you are lurking in the Taurus, Leo and Scorpio/Cat camps.
Avoid them. You'll get nothing but flak from a Taurus/Pig.

Home and Family

The place where Aquarius/Rooster lives is very important to his
or her self-image. It will no doubt be situated in an upwardly mobile, safe neighborhood. This person likes to show off and will
decorate accordingly. But he or she is also conventional. His home
will appear staid. No avant-garde futilities will clutter the horizon.
The Rooster/Aquarius's abode is his castle. You don't just drop in
on the organized abundance that reigns herein.

The Rooster/Aquarius parent is passionately fond of his or her kids, but doesn't much fancy wiping fannies or playing nursery school taxi driver. This is not the baby talk type of Mom or Dad. He or she will instead be interested in the growth and development of the offspring and act as curious onlookers, excited by the prospect that little Lisa or Shawn or baby Matthew might become a movie star or a radio disc jockey. He'll help kids out but he doesn't want to have to wash their diapers.

The Rooster/Aquarius child disobeys and often makes trouble for parents. This child needs more than his share of private, intimate attention. If he or she is denied it, trouble ensues. This kid will be bright and charming, but hard to manage. No amount of discipline or punishment will solve the basic problem of need for extra affection and parental time. If you plan to have a lot of children, don't have a Rooster/Aquarius. This little one functions best as either an only child or half of a matched set.

Profession

Words come easy to the Aquarius/Rooster. And successes are guaranteed. He or she will be persuasive and convincing, generous and amiable. The Rooster/Aquarius is ever so slightly lazy about paperwork, tax returns, and the like. He'll need a prod to get down to business, as he is also given to excessive self-indulgence followed by agonizing regret. All careers are open to this clever and wily person. Before they die, you can be sure they'll have found a way to succeed. These folks really love to be rich.

As a boss, the Aquarius/Rooster will be likable, if a bit hard-driving. This character doesn't mind telling people what to do, and has a remarkable gift for making them think they're having fun doing him or her favors. Aquarius/Roosters are also a bit cocky and tend to flaunt their power if not checked. As an employee, this person may not be very compliant. He questions methods and wants to use his own. But the personality is a plus here. People like this smartly dressed, patronizing character. Give him an inch and he'll take a mile. But never mind. He's so nice. And he does very competent work.

Some careers for Aquarius/Roosters are: entrepreneur, advertising campaign manager, attorney, politician, writer, composer.

Famous Aquarius/Roosters:

André Cayatte, Booboo Stewart, Brenda Fricker, Cameron Bright, Costa-Gavras, Edith Cresson, Ellen DeGeneres, Eva Gabor, Gabrielle Anwar, Gertrude Stein, Harry Styles, Heather Graham,

Hugh Downs, Ice-T, Jennifer Stone, Joseph Gordon-Levitt, Kathy Najimy, Lana Turner, LeVar Burton, Lisa Loring, Lorenzo Lamas, Matthew Lillard, Michael Wincott, Minnie Driver, Paris Hilton, Prince Hans-Adam II of Liechtenstein, Ray Winstone, Shane Harper, Skeet Ulrich, Susan Sontag, Susanna Thompson, Taylor Dearden, Tom Hiddleston, Tracy Middendorf, Vanna White, Victoria Justice, Warwick Davis, Will Poulter, Yoko Ono.

AQUARIUS
QUALITIES
VISION, ORIGINALITY, CHARITY,
TOLERANCE, INDEPENDENCE,
INDIVIDUALITY
QUIRKS
ECCENTRICITY, SEPARATENESS,
NEUROSIS, DISOBEDIENCE,
THOUGHTLESSNESS, CRUELTY
Motto: *"I know"*
Elements: *Air, Saturn/Uranus, Fixed*

--

DOG
QUALITIES
CONSTANCY, UNSOCIABILITY,
RESPECTABILITY, SELF-RIGHTEOUSNESS,
INTELLIGENCE, TACTLESSNESS
QUIRKS
UNEASINESS, CRITICISM, DUTY,
CYNICISM, HEROISM, MORALITY
Motto: *"I worry"*
Elements: *Positive, Metal, Yang*

The Aquarius is a Dog of the Saint Bernard persuasion. He caretakes. She lends a hand, holds a weary head and comforts those less lucky than herself. In the process of all this philanthropic service and apparently selfless loving, the Aquarius/Dog takes great pains to look after himself as well. He can be bossy and power-hungry and, what's more, the Aquarius/Dog makes no bones about masking his ambitions in charity's raiment. He may be making a million dollars a year, but since he's doing it for a cause or teaching somebody something, or bringing them pleasure, why shouldn't he live in abject luxury?

It's an odd mix indeed, this clear Aquarius with testy Dog. The tongue is always sharper than the heart is kind, the drive for personal achievement stronger than the Golden Rule. With Aquarian as a mate, the Dog's respectable nature is compromised by Aquarian desire for his or her individuality to reign supreme. The Dog born in Aquarius may well be kind and caring, and willing to stick out his neck for a friend. But his eye is nonetheless on the doughnut and not on the hole. This person's missionary identity does not spring full-blown from a humane spirit. The Aquarius/Dog gets thrills out of sorting through other people's dirty linen. He and she seek the company of people who need help. They go hunting for messy emotional situations in which their mettle and will are tested over and over. They love to give advice and express their opinions. Aquarius/Dogs are noisy and brash. They go after what they want and are not afraid to take the advantage. Almost without meaning it, they can be rash and cruel.

The Dog has a penchant for cynicism. He is critical and feisty. He's almost self-righteously moralistic. But he's a worrier. Angst is the Dog's middle name. Now along comes Aquarius. He wants to help the Dog out, give him a break, show him how to be cool and how not to nosedive into anxiety. "Detach yourself, old boy, from all this materialistic anguish. Free your mind through philosophy and dig your sensitivity, go with the flow of your complexity, understand and accept yourself." The Dog brightens. Maybe he really is as terrific as his Aquarius side would have him believe. Maybe he doesn't have to worry so much and can just "go for it" in the cool department. So he tries. He gets out there into the stratosphere and starts grooving on lucidity and clairvoyance. Then bam! His ulcer starts acting up. Did he really attack that woman who ran over his toe with her supermarket cart? Oh my God. What will people think? What have I done? Nothing new. You were simply your normal rude, harsh and abrasive self, Doggie. Not to worry. But you always do.

The Aquarius/Dog combats neurosis with productivity. This person is a mine of brutally hard labor. He or she is energetic, although somewhat sporadic, and constantly in motion. He is essentially unstable and thrives on undoing the complicated knots into which he gets tied. He's tactless and overly frank. He is a social climber and cares for the approbation of his contemporaries. Although he often whines because life is so oppressively unfair, he's the first to take profit from the situation. His humor will be wry and satirical.

Love

As snarls entertain this character, and entanglement serves as a magnet to his Good Samaritan side, the Aquarian Dog usually attaches him- or herself to romantic situations heavy with impending complications. He may take up with a married person and convince that person of how badly she's been treated, urge her into divorce and then announce that he himself is married. Or else she might marry someone to try to save him or her from alcoholism, fail, and end up bitter and complaining. These people look out for their own interests but do so in complex ways. They are faithful by nature, but if they happen to be married to three people at once, well, you can't expect miracles.

If you love one of these perplexing people, I dare suggest that you yourself must be fairly loony. I agree that Aquarius/Dogs are mighty attractive. But they seek out deranged people. If you're very apple-pie normal, forget this person. But if you can manage to become an overnight drug addict, or pretend to suffer from the interference of voices on your balcony or emanating from a back tooth, you're about to be irresistible to the Aquarius/Dog. In any case, unless you enjoy domestic spats, you will be required to pledge unswerving allegiance to your Aquarius/Dog's quirky ideals.

Compatibilities

You'll hit the spot with Aries, Gemini and Sagittarius/Tigers. Don't be shy. They really do like you. Horses from the Gemini, Libra and Sagittarius families are attracted to you as well. Aries/Rats need your sound-minded assistance. You'll enjoy Cat company from both Librans and Sagittarians. Don't leap into the arms of a Taurus, Leo or Scorpio/Dragon. You'll not be comfortable there. Leo/Sheep and their Rooster counterparts are no dice either.

Home and Family

The average Aquarius/Dog has at least two separate homes. These people love variety, and choose dramatic and socially "in" places to live. They will have rather lavish tastes and believe strongly in the value of thirsty big bath towels by the Jacuzzi and flowers on the grand piano. Carpets three inches thick don't make them sick either. It's funny, but practically none of the abstemiousness of other Dog characters rubs off on this one. The Aquarius/ Dog likes to have his pipe and slippers brought by the butler. He spends a lot of money on his lifestyle.

The Aquarius/Dog parent is distant and yet sentimental about his kids. Of course he or she is always busy or traveling or racing to the scene of an accident, so there isn't always too much time to spend on a day-to- day basis with children. But the idea of family picnics and reunions and splashy Fourth of July celebrations makes the Aquarius/Dog's heart pound and his tail wag with delight. All of the ex-wives can come and bring their husbands and their subsequent kids, too. After all, one is either caring or one is not. The Aquarius/Dog really cares.

The Aquarius/Dog child will be strangely disconnected from the crowd. He seems to carry the weight of the world on his shoulders. These children are usually slight of build and hugely sensitive. They cry easily, and need lots of urging not to be shy. They read a lot, and worry, too. Security is ultra-important to this nervous kid. No sudden jolts or surprises, please. Just nice petting and sweetness. Otherwise you'll have a neurotic little rebel on your hands.

Profession

The Aquarius/Dog, like most Aquarians, prefers to work alone. He will not be afraid to take the reins in a business situation. This character is gifted for interpretation and will excel at all social work. He's resolutely modern-thinking and sincerely wishes the world were not such a rotten place. He will achieve best if left alone to impose his own sort of discipline.

If accorded authority, this person unflinchingly takes over. He or she promises to be snappish and bark out an order a minute. His or her office is a one-man show. No comments or advice needed, thank you. Meddlers abstain. The Aquarius/Dog can be employed by others, but he must feel needed and receive a measure of autonomy. Otherwise, he may sulk and pout and eventually quit.

Some suitable careers for this character are: fisherman, cattle rancher, social worker, doctor, writer, editor, publisher, recording engineer, psychiatrist or psychologist, teacher, clergyman.

Famous Aquarius/Dogs:

Adam Lambert, Alan Bates, Alexander Dreymon, Alice Eve, Alicia Keys, Allie Grant, Anthony LaPaglia, Bellamy Young, Berthold Brecht, Bridget Regan, Camila Alves, China Kantner, Christophe Dechavanne, Craig Horner, Daiane dos Santos, Danielle Campbell, Denis Bushuev, Dominic Purcell, Dylan Everett, Frédéric Rossif, Gérard Lenorman, Helen Gurley Brown, John Anderson, Justin Gatlin, Kelly Lynch, Laure Marsac, Lauren Ash, Liam McIntyre, Linda Blair, Makenzie Vega, Marie-Paule Belle, Matty Cardarople, Natalie Dormer, Niki Koss, Norman Mailer, Paco Rabanne, Paul Cezanne, Paulina Gerzon, Sara Malakul Lane, Shawna Waldron, Simon Pegg, Svetlana Khodchenkova, William Schockely, Zsa Zsa Gabor.

AQUARIUS
QUALITIES
VISION, ORIGINALITY, CHARITY,
TOLERANCE, INDEPENDENCE,
INDIVIDUALITY
QUIRKS
ECCENTRICITY, SEPARATENESS,
NEUROSIS, DISOBEDIENCE,
THOUGHTLESSNESS, CRUELTY
Motto: *"I know"*
Elements: *Air, Saturn/Uranus, Fixed*

--

PIG
QUALITIES
SCRUPULOUSNESS, GALLANTRY, SINCERITY,
VOLUPTUOUSNESS, CULTURE, HONESTY
QUIRKS
CREDULITY, WRATH, HESITATION,
MATERIALISM, GOURMANDISM, PIGHEADEDNESS
Motto: *"I civilize"*
Elements: *Negative Water, Yin*

There evolves from the blend of Aquarius with Pig a brash quality that borders on lumpishness. Perhaps the Pig's naturally pastoral, countrified side imitates Aquarius's openness. Or maybe the Aquarian subject picks excess sincerity from the Pig and becomes too direct. But whatever the mechanics, this subject comes up both bold and forward.

More than any other, this Aquarius will be capable of giant outbursts of rage and indignation. Usually, as the Aquarian nature is tolerant and detached, he prefers that confrontation roll over him and pass to the other side before reacting to it. But here, with the sometimes belligerent Pig added, the Aquarian can be downright bellicose. He has all the extra force and push of the Pig character to define his ambitions for him. The Aquarius/Pig is a determined sort who wants to get places in life and, typically Aquarius too, ignores limits. So here is a dynamic, clear-thinking powerhouse, both gallant and wrathful at the same time, whose capacity for vision is blurred only by his own exaggerated sense of self-importance.

Despite this egotistical disposition, the Aquarius born Pig has many friends. He's a bit of a goof and people like to laugh at his reckless silliness, feeling that they are part of his or her in-jokes and giggles. The Aquarius/Pig draws an audience in, and has both charm and strength to impart. As the Pig born in Aquarius is both domineering and likable, he can expect to go far in his life. This subject can definitely be a winner. But God forbid he should not vanquish and triumph—Aquarius/Pigs are sore losers.

There is something of the prima donna in the Aquarius/Pig's giant sense of self. Even his carriage and bearing are obvious attempts at majesty. "Watch out for me!" says the Aquarius/Pig, shoulders rolling menacingly. "I'm comin' through." Not like a Mack truck or even like a bulldozer—more like a very puffed up Piggie Wig strutting along on hind legs toward the palace wearing purple satin running shorts and sporting a jaunty, tilted gold crown. Grandeur with a common touch.

Now, the hitch with our friend the Aquarius/Pig as a leader or ruler is that although he loves the glory and the applause, rolls around in sycophancy and wallows in success, he cannot stop preaching to the masses. Soon enough the masses get tired of listening to his sermons, and weary of his squeals of glee, and of kissing the hem of his running shorts and they want a new king. "Not by the hair of my chinny-chin-chin," blusters the by now complacent monarch. "I'll huff and I'll puff and I'll blow your house in." And he frequently will.

But enough of fairy tales. This person is saved from Pigly excesses by his cool Aquarian side. He's bossy, but amiable and cheery (when he's not angry). He needs direction and knows how to take advice from those wiser than himself. Aquarius/Pigs are somewhat fickle by nature, and must be kept on the path of righteousness by outside influences.

Most of all, Aquarius/Pigs are aggressively charismatic. They know how to attract crowds and please them. They are reckless, but only for gain. They are always more prosperous than they appear. They are fascinating and capable of initiating trends of universal scope.

Love

The Aquarius/Pig has the gift of knowing how to seem to care. He or she will be a stroker, an overt demonstrator of affection. Expect pats on the head and nuzzles in the neck region from this subject. But don't expect lifelong fidelity or fifty years of self-sacrifice. Uh-uh. The Aquarius/Pig whispers sweet nothings in your ear about how sensuous he is. Then you get him in bed and he proceeds to tell you about his latest coup on the playing field or in his office hierarchy. Aquarius/Pigs talk a big story.

If you love an Aquarius/Pig, prepare to be a true helpmate, booster and man-of-all-work. This person is not interested in being subjugated to passion. He or she will require lots of tender loving care and listening to. Aquarius/Pigs are not especially attentive to what others say. Try setting fire to their purple running shorts.

Compatibilities

You're the type to choose Cats and Sheep as partners. They are natural and cautious, sexy and non-interfering. Try the Cats and Sheep born in Leo, Gemini, Libra and Sagittarius first. If you don't find your life mate therein, then give an Leo/Tiger a call. You have plenty to say to each other. Contrary to everything you represent (yet mighty attractive I admit) are Snakes born in Taurus, Leo or Scorpio. Taurus born Horse does nothing for your self-image either.

Home and Family

The digs of our Aquarius born Pig will want to be opulent and vast—like a palace—to match the ambitions of this grandiose character. There ought to be a room similar to a throne room (we'll call it his office) and many telephones for "important" meetings. Primarily, this person will want comfort and culture to surround him, will have a fine touch for decorating lavish abodes, and yet will retain a pleasant countryside aura about the place. The Aquarius/Pig is not crazy about metropolises. But noblesse oblige.

The Aquarius/Pig's rapport with children is rather more authoritarian than is advisable. Don't forget this person is much of the time preoccupied by his or her own advancement. A lot of the care that goes into raising kids will be left up to the Aquarius/Pig's mate. Then, if things go awry, Aquarius/Pig will be called in to consult. There's not enough warmth here for both the crowd and the kids. Aquarius/Pig usually chooses the crowd.

This child has aspirations you never dreamed of. He or she will know how to undertake tasks and persevere in avenues of great difficulty that require enormous concentration and grit. He or she will undoubtedly be athletic. This kid will be popular, too, and a ringleader of the best kind—she'll keep everybody in line. This child may prove cuddly and snuggle up to parents, but he or she is always thinking about the future.

Profession

Silly question. The Aquarius/Pig is a chosen person for career advancement and growth. He or she wants to have money and will turn life upside down to get both wealth and power. This character always shines brightest when challenged by some job decision or potential promotion. The Aquarius/Pig's visionary abilities are least fogged over in this area. She knows what she wants and figures out in no time how to get it.

The Aquarius/Pig is always a boss. Even if he or she is serving as employee or hired hand, underling or extra, the term of subordination is limited. Of course if they think subjugation and obedience will net them advancement, Aquarius/Pigs will dig right into those piles of dirty dishes and get them cleaner faster than anybody else. This person is not afraid to appear humble for a while in order to get places. The basic Aquarian Pig dream is stardom and top dollar. Watch his dust.

Some careers that will suit the Aquarius/Pig are: pope, king, champion, movie star, diva, president, prime minister, all executive slots, and high-handed career posts.

Famous Aquarius/Pigs:

Barbara Hershey, Christopher Guest, Damian Lewis, Denise Richards, Essence Atkins, Ewen Bremner, Farrah Fawcett, Gabriel Macht, Gillian Vigman, Henry Czerny, Ian Hyland, John McEnroe, Jon Button, Jordan Todosey, Josh Randall, Jules Verne, Justin Baldoni, Lisa Zweerman, Lucas Mayer, Luke Arnold, Luke Gregory Crosby, Luke Grimes, Michael C. Hall, Michael Jonasz, Michael Kelland Hutchence, Michel Sardou, Mikhail Baryshnikov, Minnie Driver, Nastassia Kinski, Patricia Velasquez, René Barjavel, Renee O'Connor, Robyn Lively, Ronald Reagan, Sasha Pieterse, Sigrid Thornton, Sonny Bono, Tom Wilkinson, Tomasz Szmidt, William Leymergie.

PISGES
QUALITIES
UNDERSTANDING, PERCEPTION, CREATIVITY,
COMPATIBILITY, AWARENESS, SPIRITUALITY
QUIRKS
DIFFIDENCE, LACK OF WILL, FEARFULNESS,
SMUGNESS, RAGE, INDECISION
Motto: *"I believe"*
Elements: *Water, Jupiter/Neptune, Mutable*

--

RAT
QUALITIES
NERVOUSNESS, INFLUENCE,
ACQUISITIVENESS, THIRST FOR POWER,
INTELLECTUAL SKILL, CHARISMA
QUIRKS
APPEAL, VERBOSITY, THRIFT,
SOCIABILITY, GUILE, MEDDLING
Motto: *"I rule"*
Elements: *Positive Water, Yang*

This incisive character, a wizard by combination of receptivity and offense, serves best as half of a team. If there is one person who can play the game in hand with a partner and win almost every time, due to the very energy created by the partnership, it's the Pisces/Rat. Neither Pisces nor Rat characters are natural hermits. The Pisces, extra sensitive and watery, when allied to the power-hungry Rat gains a certain perspective on the finite that assures him an exceptional ability to make wise choices.

For the basically indecisive Pisces, the addition of Rat will to his character helps him to set goals and adhere to limits. Pisces/Rats are dependent. They don't operate alone. For the most part they form the other half of a couple where they assume a role as "better half" or "good cop" or "spokesman" or "whip." Pisces/Rat doesn't want the whole pie. Nor does he want the responsibility that goes with administering or engineering enterprises on his own. Pisces/Rat is a born sidekick. He or she will be caring and nurturing of the chosen partner. Pisces/Rat will be faithful to his other half's ideals, and never openly deride him or her. Pisces/Rat may appear to follow the leader half of his duo but in fact he may very well be the secret ringleader himself. In private, the Pisces/Rat confides his doubts and warnings to his closest associate, serves as counselor and sage. But in public, Pisces/Rat takes a back-row seat and surrenders the stage to his leader.

Pisces/Rats are sharp-tongued. They never defend, but always jump quickly to offend before they are attacked. These people affect snobbishness and seem status-conscious. But behind an air of self-importance and near haughtiness, the Pisces/Rat is a softie. If you looked in his or her most hidden cupboards, you would be likely to find stacks of old teddy bears and sweet little dog-eared books of maudlin poetry. The Pisces epidermal sensitivity is not annihilated by the Rat's aggressivity, but it can easily be camouflaged in subjects born under these two signs.

Pisces/Rats tend to be jealous of the fortunes of those more basically daring and brash than themselves. They attempt to justify their envy of those they dislike by denigrating their talents or questioning their morality. Pisces/Rats are a shade self-righteous and won't hesitate to take an attitude of holier than thou in order to quell the enthusiasm of someone they feel is a potential threat. They need not, of course, waste time on such drivel, as they themselves are supremely talented and often, if given the opportunity, excel at arts and letters, musical careers or business.

The major talent of this attractive and trenchant person is his or her ability to adapt to the demands of any human situation that presents itself. Pisces/Rats skitter about from circumstance to circumstance without flinching or showing their hands. They are skillful and devoted, thrifty and aware. The Pisces/Rat's perception makes him or her an invaluable asset to stodgier and pushy yet less sensitive people. Pisces/Rat wants power for the group, success for the community, advancement for the team.

Love

Sometimes, if they are particularly lucky, a Pisces/Rat falls in love with his chosen partner or team mate, marries her, and lives happily ever after as the towering sidekick. But many times it doesn't happen this way, and Pisces/Rat must choose his or her leader from platonic sources. Love, then, becomes but a cozy place to go home to from the real relationship, which is where Pisces/Rat assists and advises. As these people suffer from hypersensitivity and nervousness, they prefer lovers or mistresses of calm and collected natures.

Should you fall for one of these hugely perceptive hired guns, I suspect you will find them both amenable and indispensable to your own advancement. Ply them with common sense. Seduce them by taking them into your confidence and exposing your vulnerable side. Pisces/Rat falls flat for a strong person with a sentimental streak. Don't be afraid to lay it on thick. Pisces/Rats love drama.

Compatibilities

You'll get on with Oxen and Dragons like a house afire. But you must try to pick your Ox or Dragon partner from out of available Taurus, Cancer, Scorpio and Capricorn subjects. You can also expect great moments from Scorpio/Monkeys and their Capricorn counterparts. On the other hand, you may expect nothing (if not less) from Gemini, Virgo or Sagittarius/Horses.

Home and Family

The household of Pisces/Rat will revolve around the couple who lives there. The Pisces/Rat will defer to his partner's tastes and be satisfied to decorate his own room or office in a cluttered, artsy style, pleasing to himself. If the team in question exists only outside the household, the Pisces/Rat may be counted on to live alone in a cosy, rather offbeat decor. The vector here is always the best interest of the Pisces/Rats' relationship. If the group needs a new carpet, we will get us a new carpet, and so on.

Now, as a parent this person will certainly be competent. Pisces/Rats are very responsible and reliable people. They have a quick sense of humor and will enjoy playing with kids and making them giggle. But this person also has much to interest him or her other than the child, and will often be forced to relegate the child's day-to day care to someone more drudgery-oriented. After all, if Sancho Panza stops to burp the baby, who will look after Don Quixote?

The Pisces/Rat child will no doubt astonish by his mature perceptions and his incisive and appropriate wit. He may be long in coming to what he wants to do later on in life. He wants to stay a child as long as possible, as he depends more easily than he "independs." Of course, all Pisces children are artistic and want lessons in their area of talent. Be patient with this sensitive kid. Don't push him out of the nest too soon.

Profession

Pisces born in Rat years don't trust others easily. They are critical, and not without guile. They tend to be smug and enjoy the bandwagon feeling of belonging to a unit that excludes others. They are extremely security-conscious, and although they give utter devotion and service to any group effort, Pisces/Rats want their fair share of all booty acquired by the group. They are community-minded yet personally motivated.

The Pisces/Rat will never be the apparent boss. This is a background person who will perhaps only once or twice in a lifetime allow his ego out of its cage for public viewing. Mostly he or she will run the show from the wings, avid for power but not for notoriety. These people want to express themselves, but not for glory. Their use of authority is rarely abusive, but it can be abrasive. They make fabulous, devoted employees. As artists they function well in group efforts.

Some suitable careers for this subject are: producer, artist, actor, editor, journalist, writer, nurse, physical therapist, police detective, consultant, buyer, importer/exporter, travel agent.

Famous Pisces/Rats:

Adam Clayton, Alain Jérôme, Anthony Robbins, Arye Gross, Billy Crystal, Brandon T. Jackson, Claude Sautet, Courtney B. Vance, Dina Manzo, Douglas Hodge, Finn Carter, George Washington, Gloria Vanderbilt, Ivan Lendl, Jaimie Alexander, James Taylor, Jason Beghe, Jean Louisa Kelly, Jean-Edern Hallier, Joseph Gilgun, Kerr Smith, Lawrence Durrell, Luis Bunuel, Madeleine Renaud, Matt Nable, Michael Chang, Noel Fisher, Noureen DeWulf, Olivia Wilde, Patricia Nixon, Richard Coyle, Robert Altman, Robert Glenister, Rory Cochrane, Shaquille O'Neal, Sophie Turner, Susan Yeagley, Taylor Marie Hill, Ursula Andress, Vicki Lewis, Wilson Bethel.

PISCES
QUALITIES
UNDERSTANDING, PERCEPTION, CREATIVITY,
COMPATIBILITY, AWARENESS, SPIRITUALITY
QUIRKS
DIFFIDENCE, LACK OF WILL, FEARFULNESS,
SMUGNESS, RAGE, INDECISION
Motto: *"I believe"*
Elements: *Water, Jupiter/Neptune, Mutable*

--

OX
QUALITIES
STUBBORNNESS, STRENGTH OF PURPOSE,
ELOQUENCE, STANDOFFISHNESS, INNOVATION,
VINDICTIVENESS
QUIRKS
INTEGRITY, BIGOTRY, PLODDING,
DILIGENCE, BIAS, STABILITY
Motto: *"I preserve"*
Elements: *Negative Water, Yin*

The Pisces born in an Ox year is quite a character. Just when you think this person is nothing more than froth and furbelow, thwack! He or she floors you with a remark that would knock the wind out of Chicago. The gap between the basic slugger nature of Oxen and Pisces ephemeral personality misleads one. Never forget that you can't judge a book by its cover. The Pisces/Ox seems for all the world the *artiste*, the stereotypical Pisces dreamer. But wait! Pisces/Ox is perhaps even more of a schemer than a poet.

This person's enmity is a force to be avoided at all costs. The Pisces/Ox has the capacity for sarcasm but prefers another, more insidious weapon. This subject is a card-carrying member of the "erosion school of winning." Pisces/Ox doesn't stoop to fisticuffs or intimidation. He is too sensitive for such vulgar means. Instead, when Pisces/Oxen seek to overcome a hurdle or fell a bastion, they wait. They scheme and plot and deviate and cogitate. But they don't make a move. They busy themselves with knitting or crossword puzzles, letting time slip by.

You see, the Pisces sensitivity and the Ox's strength of purpose can make an unbeatable match. If properly handled, the combination of signs guarantees success. I say success instead of happiness because the Pisces/Ox is still a fluid, aquatic creature no matter how many hooves he has on the ground. This person may never be perfectly, blissfully content. Yet, thanks to his supersensitive natural antennae about people, the Pisces/Ox can reach a point where he never makes an error in judging others. This person senses what's weakest about his adversaries. So he plans strategies. Then, without hue or cry, he sits back and giggles while he watches his enemy paint himself into a corner.

Pisces/Oxen have strong opinions on many subjects. People are drawn to them by virtue of their sense of compassion and understanding. This person almost never lives alone, but rather is surrounded by family and a few privileged friends to whom he or she is devoted, and vice versa. Pisces/Oxen are loved and looked up to and respected. They don't take any guff from losers, nor do they tolerate insubordination. They are exclusive and jealous about those close to them. But, as they give their all for the sake of perpetuation of family and tradition, they plainly do not comprehend treachery or betrayal. Mutual respect is paramount to this solid citizen.

The Pisces born in an Ox year likes to be listened to. He tells terrific tales. Moreover, without their ability to develop plots and expound juicy details, Pisces/Oxen would be rather shy. The Pisces/Ox's eloquence is the key to his or her social success. Financial success comes rather naturally to this steady and innovative person. The ingredients for riches are all here: determination, ambition, know-how and, most of all, love of comfort and security.

Love

This person often has a busy sex life. Pisces injects the Ox's normally so-so libido with extra emotional get up and go. Since much of the activity of this person is covert anyway, secret affairs and labyrinthine, sentimental plots will play a large role in his love life. Marriage is of course important to the Pisces/Ox. He cannot survive without a family. But curiously, his family's opinions of his extracurricular activities don't always jibe with what he wants. This can create conflicts and engender much dissatisfaction in the Pisces/Ox heart.

If you love a Pisces/Ox, be grand. The Pisces born in Ox years craves scope and looks for a complementary broad-minded soul with whom to share his or her life. As this person often feels her own values are stodgy or old-fashioned, she is attracted to eccentricity and even kinkiness in lover. If you're a little odd and marginal, you risk being tailed by a steady-gaited Pisces/Ox.

Compatibilities

Rats are your favorites. Try staying within the families of Taurus, Cancer, Scorpio or Capricorn/Rats if you want concord to reign in your life. Beyond Rats you can seek your pleasures among Snakes and Roosters of the same four families I mentioned above. A Scorpio/Dragon will also excite you. On the down side I'd advise against Gemini and Virgo/Dragons. Don't take up with Sagittarius/ Sheep or Monkeys. You need calm and they cannot offer that commodity.

Home and Family

The Pisces/Ox's home is his chateau. For the sake of his home and the symbol it represents of cohesion and reputation vis-à-vis the world, this person will kill. You must not be surprised to find deep classical sofas and carpets, marbles and period furniture in this grandeur-addict's home. Scale is of major importance to him also. He favors symmetry and soft colors. The artwork will be mostly representational; the Pisces/Ox is not comfortable with the abstract. He's sensitive to material beauty of a concrete nature.

This parent is demanding and intransigent. He or she loves the children so fiercely as to feel the need to keep them forever. The Pisces/Ox family image is central to his equilibrium. He can see himself forever involved with his kids. She doesn't ever envision their total independence from her, nor does she see the need for children to move away from parents when they are married. A family is a family, and the Pisces/Ox is a dutiful and generous monarch.

This child's sensitivity will be apparent from an early age. All that is pretty and feminine will appeal. Gentleness is assured. Disciplines that require long-lasting, detailed application are open to this receptive talent. He will probably be gifted for languages, and can be encouraged in all things literary and artistic. Don't divorce on this kid's account. He'd prefer a fighting family to no family at all.

Profession

The stable, steady and courageous Pisces/Ox can go very far and become really, really rich if he or she so chooses. They are, first of all, creative and innovative. Secondly, they possess giant strength and dedication. They want luxury and they know how to win through patience and forbearance. Should they put all of these talents to work, they have to succeed. They can, however, because of their loyalty to family and tradition, be steered by unscrupulous or thoughtless parents into careers that don't suit their need to be first.

Pisces/Ox's integrity is so apparent that as a boss, he is first of all respected. He or she will want everything well done—the corners all neat and those copies crystal clear. Not an easy superior to work for, but certainly not wishy-washy. This person makes a reliable, if a bit slow, employee, too. Pisces born in Ox years don't have to own the company. They may be content to earn as much money as the owners but to stay out of the public eye. There is little desire for fame in this person. If it happens, fine. If not, anonymous wealth will be all right.

Some careers that might please this creature are: lawyer, artist (all kinds), cinematographer, company director, writer, administrator, stockbroker, banker, office manager, *éminence grise*.

Famous Pisces/Oxen:
Annie Dufresne, Anson Mount, Bingbing Li, Boris Kodjoe, Camila Cabello, Camryn Manheim, Christopher Atkins, Edward Gorey, Elias Koteas, Emile Hirsch, Emily Cox, Erik Estrada, Eva Amurri Martino, Fabio, Gates McFadden, George Frideric Handel, Isabelle Fuhrman, Ivana Trump, Jack Davenport, John Erlichman, Katie Ledecky, Kellan Lutz, King Harald of Norway, Kirby Puckett, Larry Drake, Laurel Clark, Len Wiseman, Linus Pauling, Nathalie Kelley, Ólafur Darri Ólafsson, Patrick Duffy, Pierre-Auguste Renoir, Rae Dawn Chong, René Clément, Rob Cohen, Scott Michael Foster, Shiloh Fernandez, Simone Biles, Steven Weber, Titus Welliver, Victor Garber, Vincente Minnelli, Yael Stone, Zach Roerig, Zeppo Marx.

PISCES
QUALITIES
UNDERSTANDING, PERCEPTION, CREATIVITY,
COMPATIBILITY, AWARENESS, SPIRITUALITY
QUIRKS
DIFFIDENCE, LACK OF WILL, FEARFULNESS,
SMUGNESS, RAGE, INDECISION
Motto: *"I believe"*
Elements: *Water, Jupiter/Neptune, Mutable*

--

TIGER
QUALITIES
FERVOR, BRAVERY, MAGNETISM,
GOOD LUCK, BENEVOLENCE, AUTHORITY
QUIRKS
IMPETUOSITY, HOTHEADEDNESS,
DISOBEDIENCE, SWAGGER, INTEMPERANCE,
ITINERANCY
Motto: *"I Watch"*
Elements: *Positive Wood, Yang*

This plucky Pisces character spends a large chunk of his energy and time trying to achieve closer rapport with himself. Pisces born in Tiger years often feel confined by their spunky feline side and sometimes wish to shake the Tiger off their backs. Pisces likes to swim in limitless time and move through infinite space. Constraints are of no interest to the Fish. He longs to be free to float unbound. His goal is spiritual enlightenment.

Pure Pisceans have no ear for the roar of the crowd. The Tiger, on the other hand, hankers for drama and dreams of the drastic. Tigers drink adrenalin for breakfast. They are magnetic and vain. They are hasty and rash and world-connected. They don't really fancy constraints any more than Pisces or anybody else. But Tigers are motivated to gain ground. Tigers are frontiersmen with muskets on their shoulders. They are true pioneers in the Conestoga wagon tradition and are so danger-loving that they almost prefer being pursued by Indians to coming to a nice quiet place to settle in. So this Pisces will only come to inner peace when he can finally put his terrible Tiger away for a rainy day. Then, in relatively calm and serene circumstances, the Pisces born Tiger may continue his quest for self-awareness.

The Pisces/Tiger is very giving. This person gets joy out of sharing his bounty. He will take pleasure in preparing food for people he likes. He will often lend a hand to a needy neighbor or pal. She will be sincerely interested in the welfare of others, and will go out of her way to remember to ask how they are. Because of this readiness to open his or her heart and take others in, the Pisces/Tiger is vulnerable. A misplaced word or phrase, a barb or harsh criticism can crush the Pisces/Tiger's sensitive soul and leave him reeling. Not only does the Pisces/Tiger take umbrage at sarcasm, but he reacts to it by means of an odd sort of aggressiveness that takes an interlocutor by surprise.

In other words, Pisces/Tigers look much more placid than they are. Behind that cheery "Good morning" might lie an accusing remark just itching to be fired at somebody who dares to challenge. Pisces/Tigers rarely attack. But they are ever watchful and ready to catapult an aggressor into next weekend. This person can shrug off a bad love affair, resign himself to a failed carrot cake or sit back and laugh at his own mistakes, but don't count on the Pisces born in a Tiger year to indulge anybody who pushes too hard.

Proud and sometimes comical, this person has something of the appeal of the weeping clown. His sensitivity seems to sit right up there on the front of his sleeve. He often sports a crooked and touching smile that says "fragile." Essentially the Piscean Tiger feels shy. But he doesn't like being thought of as timid. His emotions are profound and complex. He's open to suggestion, but he doesn't want to appear to be influenced. He's anxious to please, but he will only play the fool for gain. In fact, this graceful subject with the gift of social sparkle is slightly lunatic, deliciously unpredictable and wildly attractive.

Love

There is much tenderness in this aqueous Tiger. But the flip side of his or her pastel-sweet sensuousness may be coated in bitter chocolate.

The Pisces born Tiger bounces back elegantly from romantic disappointment. But they also develop scars from each subsequent sentimental wound and may eventually become skittish about falling in love. If you love one of these amusing giants, keep him or her guessing. You will not be nearly so attractive to the Pisces/Tiger if you supplicate or beseech him to love you. Play a little hard to get. And learn how to laugh at his or her jokes. Don't be aggressive, and exert diplomacy rather than strength when you want to sway your Pisces/Tiger's views.

Compatibilities

Horse people are practical. If you hitch up with a Horse, you will benefit from this pragmatism. Choose especially a Taurus, Cancer, Scorpio or Capricorn/Horse subject. Harmonious, too, with your kind of person is a Cancer, Scorpio or Capricorn/Dog. Dogs lend you their sense of measure and help you to find temperance. A healthy Scorpio/Dragon will also do nicely. Gemini, Virgo and Sagittarius/Snakes and Sheep all work against your best interests. Virgo and Sagittarius/Oxen do likewise. Virgo/Monkeys want your sensitive soul and you are not eager to give it away.

Home and Family

This subject is at home almost everywhere. As they are not drawn to material thrills, and look for comfort in their friends and the companionship of groups, Pisces/Tigers' home environments may only be relative to whatever project they are engaged in at the time. Of course these active people need space to prowl around in. They are not comfortable when hemmed in. They are somewhat bohemian, and although they may own lovely objects and furniture, they can probably take them or leave them alone.

The Pisces/Tiger parent would love his or her child to be an artist, a free spirit and, most of all, happy. These parents are permissive with kids. Yet, they exercise a powerful emotional hold over children and are not likely to stand for either sass or rebellion. Tigers, even in Fish clothing, are rigorous when it comes to making rules and applying them. Undoubtedly the Pisces/Tiger Mom or Dad will provide little Emma and baby Oscar with scads of opportunities to expand their minds and use their talents.

This child is hypersensitive. You should handle him or her with double velvet gloves. You may have a great artist or musician, dancer or actor on your hands. Try not to impose your will openly, but rather offer this youngster the chance to develop whatever gifts may lead to potential careers at a very early age. This kid needs to feel secure and revels in lots of generous parenting.

Profession

The Pisces/Tiger's ultrasensitive nature doesn't prevent him or her from being quite a fighter in the professional world. Tiger endows this watery subject with drive beyond the call of duty, and Pisces gains energy here, too. With Pisces in tow, the Tiger will be less headstrong and lurching. A congenial person, the Pisces/Tiger is well able to deal with both public and private career demands without losing sight of goals.

The Pisces/Tiger is too shy to be bossy. The role of authority figure doesn't really appeal to him or her anyway. Pisces/Tiger will enjoy the fruits of his labors best when he works on his own and uses his artistic talents for profit. Otherwise, this person can, of course, work for someone else and fit in without difficulty. He or she is adaptable and wise enough to know the value of conforming to discipline. Early training is always essential to Pisces' destiny..

Some possible careers for Pisces/Tigers are: artist (actor, painter, writer, and so on), artisan (weaver, jeweler, potter, and the like), musician (instrumentalist or composer), dancer or choreographer, filmmaker, piano tuner, art teacher, costume designer, homeopath, acupuncturist, astrologer

Famous Pisces/Tigers:

Adam Baldwin, Alexandra Daddario, Barbara Alyn Woods, Brad Dourif, Brittany Snow, Elizabeth Barrett Browning, Ethan Wayne, Eva Mendes, Evan and Jaron Lowenstein, Grace Park, Grant Show, Jai Courtney, Jameela Jamil, James Phelps, Jamie Bell, Jasmine Guy, Jenna Fischer, Jerry Lewis, John Steinbeck, Jon Bon Jovi, Julia Campbell, Julie Sinmon, Julie Walters, Julius Erwing, Kalpana Chawla, Larry Bagby, Laure Adler, Marisa Zanuck, Mark-Paul Gisselaar, Miko Hughes, Miou-Miou, Neil Jordan, Nijinsky, Olesya Rulin, Oliver Phelps, Pete Rozelle, Ruby Rose, Rudolf Nureyev, Stéphane Mallarmé, Stephen Sommers, Teresa Palmer, Tobias Menzies, William H. Macy, William Hurt.

PISCES
QUALITIES
UNDERSTANDING, PERCEPTION, CREATIVITY,
COMPATIBILITY, AWARENESS, SPIRITUALITY
QUIRKS
DIFFIDENCE, LACK OF WILL, FEARFULNESS,
SMUGNESS, RAGE, INDECISION
Motto: *"I believe"*
Elements: *Water, Jupiter/Neptune, Mutable*

--

CAT/RABBIT
QUALITIES
TACT, FINESSE, VIRTUE,
PRUDENCE, LONGEVITY, AMBITION,
QUIRKS
SECRETIVENESS, SQUEAMISHNESS,
PEDANTRY, DILETTANTISM,
HYPOCHONDRIA, COMPLEXITY
Motto: *"I Retreat"*
Elements: *Negative, Wood, Yin*

D oes the Cat eat up the Fish? No. This lovely couple has a happy beginning and equally felicitous ending. Pisces' sensitivity blends swimmingly well with the Cat's love of hearth and home, caution and modesty. The Piscean born in a Cat year will probably enjoy a long and productive career as a guardian of refinement and elegance. He or she is almost assured of having artistic talents and, moreover, can count on knowing how to put those same talents to practical and profitable use.

Natural noblesse belongs to this Cat subject. There is little that the expanded Pisces spirit cannot receive, and with the sensible Cat to keep the fluid Fish in dry-dock for at least part of his life, much can be accomplished. Both of these signs are noted for their abilities to avoid conflict, to flee confrontation and to eschew revenge or pettiness. No unnatural encumbrances impair this person's progress. The Pisces/Cat gets precisely where he or she wants to go without ever entering the traffic pattern.

This person remains circumspect most of his life. Pisces/Cats are silent until they know their audience. When they feel secure, they speak up. They are not very sociable, and shrink from fashion and trends. Simplicity is their aim, complexity their enemy. The Pisces/Cat is a seeker of order and reason whose definite personal views are his or her security blanket. What strikes one as indecisiveness on the part of Pisces/Cat people stems from an unwillingness to participate in anything that doesn't jibe with their definite way of thinking.

Pisces/Cats are often, either directly or indirectly, responsible for the aggrandizement of someone they feel is more worthy than they. Glory, to the Pisces/Cat, can be a handicap, an embarrassment. Nonetheless, many natives of this sign gain fame. They are incisive observers of every aspect of human life, and frequently know how to interpret what they see in a unique manner. They can be witty and don't hesitate to use their humor to get a point across. Never brash or forward, the Pisces/Cat tiptoes along. "little cat feet" applies nicely here.

The Pisces born in Cat may not be particularly creative and can be guilty of idea-snitching. But the degree of admiration he can proffer and the seriousness he employs make startling innovations seem unnecessary. This Cat's ambition is discovery or disclosure. He will want to clarify those things he sees as murky. He understands secrecy, and knows how to use discretion to his own advantage. In the worldly sense, the Pisces/Cat is a bit of a loner. He is a home-dependent soul who clings to all that is familiar and safe. He or she functions well in community living situations. This person can be accused of snobbishness, as he tends to be smug and self-satisfied. He abhors sudden shifts or lifestyle changes and treats them as though they were earthquakes.

Love

The Pisces/Cat is not a warmhearted, outgoing, glad-handed, or (God forbid!) promiscuous person. Usually, these people keep their own counsel about what they are looking for in a mate and can hang out alone for years before they have satisfied their desire for Prince or Princess Charming. The white charger image dies hard with tradition-loving people like Pisces/Cat. He or she is, moreover, a born romantic and nobody is ever perfect enough to fulfill the ideal.

Your lover or mistress is a Pisces/Cat? Lucky you. You should have your doors and windows boarded up so the soft tough guy you have chosen doesn't escape through the cracks. You will be required to furnish boatloads of reassurance and tenderness. You will be called upon to serve as spokesman for this sometimes timid person. But behind the scenes he or she will very likely be the soul mate of your life. Don't let your Pisces/Cat languish without your cozy company. He will never cause a scene or scandal, but if you stray, when you get home he may be out—for keeps.

Compatibilities

Taurus, Cancer and Scorpio/Pigs will bring you the peace of mind you so earnestly seek. Or try a Cancer or Scorpio/Sheep for a creative holiday from routine. Scorpio or Capricorn/Dogs can invest your life with plenty of new ideals. A Cancer/Cat is enough like you to produce a marriage of near twinship. Too, Cancer/Cats bring you their tempting goals and love of home.

Home and Family

The family urge is very strong in the Pisces/Cat. He or she will want to have and nurture children. In order to carry out this dream she will, of course, need a home. Count on the Pisces/Cat to insist on a well-appointed, comfortable and safe house in a "good" neighborhood. These people are upwardly mobile and depend greatly for their image on where and how they live. This person wants peaceful surroundings and will probably prefer the country to the city.

The Pisces/Cat parent is primarily interested in his or her child's personal welfare. Pisces/Cats will overprotect their kids, but will be quietly firm and rather rigid in their demands. They don't like things that protrude from respectability. Pisces/Cat parents will insist on manners. They are tender and loving with kids. He may not take them on roller coasters, but he'll be happy to read them a bedtime story.

If you have a Pisces/Cat child, you will notice very early on that he doesn't like noise or commotion. He or she will not be the kind of baby you throw into the air for squealing purposes. This child needs a gentle environment and comfort in order to grow up healthy and strong. He must be taught never to blame his own shortcomings on others. Pisces/Cat kids also need encouragement so they won't grow up timid. Tell this child how attractive he or she is. Pisces/Cats love to be admired.

Profession

A certain reticence may keep this clever and agreeable person from rising in the ranks. The Pisces/Cat is extremely nervous and worries a lot about status and appearance in society. Work doesn't frighten this person a bit. But sticky involvement or possible conflict does. Because of this retiring quality, the Pisces/Cat may have to choose a well-paid but routine job over a dashing career full of ups and downs.

The Pisces/Cat boss is serious and rather severe. As this person suffers from acute vulnerability to stress and strains, he or she may camouflage sensitivity under a facade of coldness. Although this distant attitude may be false, it is nonetheless the only contact the Pisces/Cat can allow. Independent work suits the Pisces/Cat. He goes along at his own sweet pace without prodding. As an employee this person is quiet and reserved, diligent enough but not always willing to initiate tasks.

Jobs that might please the Pisces/Cat are: mathematician, computer specialist, art curator, designer, translator, writer, wine grower, landscape architect.

Famous Pisces/Cat/Rabbits:

Albert Einstein, Alex Kingston, Anaïs Nin, Ashley Greene, Audrey Marie Anderson, Bertrand Blier, Brooklyn Beckham, Bryan Batt, Chase Masterson, Chelsea Handler, Daniel Roebuck, David Sarnoff, David Thewlis, Debra Jo Rupp, Drew Barrymore, E.L. James, Ellen Greene, Ellen Page, Erma Bombeck, Eva Longoria, Eve Ruggieri, George Plimpton, Greg Nicotero, Harry Belafonte, Helen Shaver, Hubert Givenchy, Jacques Chaban-Delmas, Jerome Flynn, Joel Osteen, Jolene Blalock, Kathy Ireland, Kevin Smith, Kurt Russell, Laurent Ruquier, Maurice Benard, Milana Vayntrub, Miles Teller, Natalie Zea, Patricia Richardson, Peter Fonda, Raymond Queneau, Régis Crespin, Russell Wong, Sienna Guillory, Sutton Foster, T.J. Thyne, Tommy Tune, Tuppence Middleton, Vanessa Williams, William Baldwin, Yves Boisset, Zero Mostel.

PISCES
QUALITIES
UNDERSTANDING, PERCEPTION, CREATIVITY,
COMPATIBILITY, AWARENESS, SPIRITUALITY
QUIRKS
DIFFIDENCE, LACK OF WILL, FEARFULNESS,
SMUGNESS, RAGE, INDECISION
Motto: *"I believe"*
Elements: *Water, Jupiter/Neptune, Mutable*

--

DRAGON
QUALITIES
STRENGTH, SUCCESS, GOOD HEALTH,
ENTHUSIASM, PLUCK, SENTIMENTALITY
QUIRKS
RIGIDITY, MISTRUST, DISSATISFACTION,
INFATUATION, BRAGGADOCIO, VOLUBILITY
Motto: *"I Preside"*
Elements: *Positive Wood, Yang*

The Fish born in Dragon cares greatly for his or her own advancement. This person needs to feel progress. Standing still renders him nervous and edgy. So, when there is no progress, if he is not moving ahead, he travels. One thing is sure, the Pisces/Dragon is a mover. He may be running or walking, swimming or taking a train, but the Fish born a Dragon ambulates.

From the Pisces side of his nature, this subject gains perspective. For a Dragon, who knows better than anyone how to brag himself into first place, the tepid waters of Pisces are a boon. Pisces cools the Dragon's exaggerated gusto and dampens his fire. In certain cases, Pisces slows the Dragon too much and the green scaly monster becomes an appealing but rudderless wastrel, a shadow of his effusive Dragonesque self. This last state can be dangerous to the Pisces/Dragon's well-being as dampened Dragon spirits may increase the Pisces' "don't give a damn" attitude. What should be emphasized for the benefit of the Pisces/Dragon is self-discipline and perseverance. Both of these signs are past masters at slinking out of practice sessions. This person will surely try to have him or herself excused from drills and rehearsals. The Dragon born in Pisces thinks he knows enough already and were others to ask his advice, a lot more could be accomplished in a shorter time. So why hang around being bored?

Aha! Here's the rub. Pisces/Dragons always think they know best. They barge ahead in almost every situation they encounter, doing exactly as they please. They may think they are barging in the name of some ideal. But they give no thought to whether the rest of us agree with said ideal. In other sign combinations Dragons, who push and shove and take over, can be told off. "Go back to your cave, Dragon, and wait till we call you." But it's very difficult to tell off a Pisces/Dragon. He is narcissistic and defensive in the extreme. He is unsure of himself and may compensate by designing and constructing emotional storms, the tears from which might extinguish the sun itself.

This person spins a web of charm so attractive and convincing that even he believes init. He or she will come on so strong with an idea or plan that you cannot possibly doubt its feasibility. Pisces/Dragon doesn't know about halfway measures. He or she will be going to do it all. Then, one day, you see him in the street and say, "Hey Dragon/Pisces, old boy, how's that company you were putting together?" or, "What about your skyscraper out in the backyard?" The Pisces/Dragon pulls himself up tall and looks disdainfully downward. "Which one was that, pal?" he wonders.

Now what is so exciting about this character is his or her charm and good health. The Pisces/Dragon may be bumptious and a bit too plucky at times, but the real Pisces self, that Lucy-in-the-Sky-with-Diamonds faraway look in the long-lashed eye, the laughs and the jokes and the giggles and pokes—ah, there is what makes a Pisces/Dragon a joy to be around. He's always got a quip for you. She's always on the verge of dashing off to do her jogging and then to the health club and afterward to the vegetarian restaurant in a flourish. Pisces/Dragons (when they don't lay it on too thick) are adorable companions.

But they are not world-beaters. They can live quite happily in the background once they get it through their heads that skyscrapers in backyards are impractical and overblown. They can rely on advisers and live from dispensing smiles to people who love their *dolce far niente* approach.

Pisceans born in Dragon years will be touchy and argumentative until they finally stop trying to prove themselves. Then they will become efficient in a chosen profession, stay in a pleasant rut, and cruise around all day dreaming about what to make for dinner.

Love

The Pisces/Dragon is not constant in love matters. Very often these people are born smashingly attractive. They don't have an easy time growing up with their beauty, since their ego needs a bit of taming in the first place. So the beauty feeds the ego and vice versa. But, and this is a breakthrough but, Dragons, especially Pisces/Dragons, are enormously sentimental. They may indulge in adventure upon sexual adventure and engage in the most rococo of emotional turmoil. Breakups and reconciliations galore pepper their diaries. But they always return to the scenes of their emotional crimes. Once a Pisces/Dragon has loved, he or she always loves— forever. Sentiment is this person's most powerful quality. Because of it, he forgives and excuses and goes on loving—and never forgets the good times.

If you are smitten by the wiles of a Pisces/Dragon person, I think I can give you some good advice. First off, don't ever nag them. Cajoling is the method best utilized in the case of Piscean Dragons. They love to be coaxed. Be as much of an "up" person as you can, laughing at their jokes and telling them how hilarious they are, but don't ever fall completely under their spell. As they get carried away with their own marvelousness, you (of all people) must keep your feet firmly planted in reality.

Compatibilities

Oh, you Dragons and your popularity charts! Taurus, Cancer, Scorpio and Capricorn give you Monkey admiration. Tiger love comes from Taurus, Cancer, Libra and Scorpio. Then of course there are the Taurus and Scorpio/Snakes, who go mad for you. Not to forget both Scorpio and Capricorn/Rats who adore you, too. You won't get much applause from Gemini or Virgo/Cats, who fear your rashness. Virgo and Sagittarius/Dogs don't appreciate you much either. Alas! Virgo/Pig and Sagittarius/Ox think you are for the birds.

Home and Family

The Pisces/Dragon is not a homemaker. He or she will be happy to live in modest but decent surroundings. The territory that interests this person is elsewhere, outside the home, in the world. Pisces/Dragon is inordinately idealistic and can spend his whole lire dreaming of having his own place in the sun. But for the moment, he's off to Greece with a friend who's got a house on an island. Poor old Pisces/Dragon, he sometimes waits to go after what he dreams until it's patently too late. But never mind; he didn't really care in the first place.

As a parent this person will be fun loving. The Pisces/Dragon will enjoy kids, and their shenanigans will delight him. As he takes great pleasure from being the leader of a group and doesn't often get to the top in adult life, parenting is really a dandy outlet for this character. He must be careful not to overindulge kids in wild schemes. But otherwise, he can be a loving and very affectionate parent.

This Pisces/Dragon child will not be easy to raise. He or she is by turns enthusiastic and lackadaisical. This child will seem, vocally at least, to know what she wants. She will be vehement and have a strong will. But getting their own way is just about the worst thing that can happen to these darling Pisces/Dragons. Instead, they must be patiently and carefully guided. Don't leave them on their own to decide for themselves; they cannot always steer a straight course. If you neglect them they will never forgive you.

Profession

Does the Pisces/Dragon really want a profession? That is the question. I know this sounds insane in a world so drowning in the zeal of ambition and success, but unless I miss my mark, I feel that Pisceans born in Dragon years would rather sit back and watch the parade go by. They like activity. They are not lazy people. But there is something other-worldly about this character. Something non-involved. I reckon his best shot is independent work, but then he'll need a watcher and a guide.

It's useless to talk of this person as boss. He can get to be a boss by inheritance or fluke, but although he can be bossy, I cannot imagine him seriously coveting the head honcho's job. Too much flak. Of course the Pisces/Dragon can be employed. But he'll want a job that gives him room to breathe and not too much direction all at once.

Careers that might please the Pisces/Dragon are: philosopher, professor, photographer, producer, cinematographer, writer, linguist, roadie, traveling salesperson, circus performer.

Famous Pisces/Dragons:
Al Jarreau, Alexander Koch, Ali Larter, Ariel Sharon, B. F. Skinner, Bernardo Bertolucci, Chuck Norris, Corey Stoll, Daniel Gillies,

Daniel J. Travanti, Danny Masterson, Douglas Adams, Edward Albee, Freddie Prinze Jr., French Stewart, Gore Verbinski, Greg Berney, Gretchen Christopher, Harvey Weinstein, Howard Hesseman, Irving Wallace, James Fleet, James Robert Bruce Ogilvy, Jennifer Capriati, Johanna McGinley, John Pyper-Ferguson, Jonathan Fumeaux, Josh Bowman, Juliette Binoche, Kelly Macdonald, Laraine Newman, Laura Harring, Lee Evans, Mario Andretti, Mark Dacascos, Mimi Kuzyk, Paul Schneider, Peter Berg, Phil Lesh, Rachel Blanchard, Rashida Jones, Raul Julia, Rihanna, Rob Lowe, Ronn Moss, Sasha Grey, Willie Garson.

PISCES
QUALITIES
UNDERSTANDING, PERCEPTION, CREATIVITY,
COMPATIBILITY, AWARENESS, SPIRITUALITY
QUIRKS
DIFFIDENCE, LACK OF WILL, FEARFULNESS,
SMUGNESS, RAGE, INDECISION
Motto: *"I believe"*
Elements: *Water, Jupiter/Neptune, Mutable*

--

SNAKE
QUALITIES
INTUITION, ATTRACTIVENESS, DISCRETION,
SAGACITY, CLAIRVOYANCE, COMPASSION
QUIRKS
DISSIMULATION, EXTRAVAGANCE,
LAZINESS, CUPIDITY, PRESUMPTION,
EXCLUSIVENESS
Motto: *"I sense"*
Elements: *Negative, Fire, Yin*

This deep thinker is bubbly and graceful but only on the strict surface. Underneath roil philosophies and perceptions too otherworldly to share with any but the most enlightened. Pisces/ Snake feels everything profoundly and intuits each situation with such force and lucidity that he almost winces at the power of human contact. Sensitivity takes on a whole new meaning in the case of the Pisces/Snake. Intuition is redoubled, second sight emphasized and presentiment so powerful as to be considered a gift. Pisces/Snake is a kind of witch in sheep's clothing.

Trouble is, the world is no fit place for such sentient souls. There are no jobs for witches currently. Oh, I suppose these people might choose astrology or crystal ball gazing if they had their druthers. But Pisces/Snake people are decidedly not "druthers" types. They don't want to make waves. They don't want to impress anyone with their importance, and they have no axes to grind in the big bad world. The Pisces/Snake can be content to live away from it all, protected by a family unit to which they are both soul and solace. Pisces/Snakes, whether they like it or not, take care of their own.

Now none of this solace that I speak of is given away without a fight. The Pisces/Snake is a deep thinker and quite a loner within the crowd. He or she claims to take part in group life because it's there and it's necessary. The whole while he or she complains, "I do this and I do that. I am the only one around here who . . . Why doesn't somebody else notice this or that? How can anybody be so careless? Why should I be nice to that fool or this ingrate?" Pisces/ Snake doesn't yell or scream and throw things. Oh no. He rails. He kvetches. He groans and grumbles, and occasionally thrusts out his viper tongue to lash at some unfortunate soul. Yet, two minutes later, when backs are turned, Pisces/Snake will gather the object of his wrath in his arms and apologize. Pisces/Snake is a sweetie-pie, a natural-born creative thinker, and as attractive as two Super Glue surfaces.

Pisces/Snake doesn't particularly like the real world. These people don't want responsibilities, and most of all they don't want to have to succeed on their own. Paperwork (unless it's poetry or pages of metaphysics) galls them. Laziness stalks their every step. They are wise and perceptive. But it just isn't in them to carry through with their wisdom. They can accept being cutting, but they cannot be cruel. They may be fascinated with improbity, but they are incapable of committing crimes. Some may call them wishy washy. I call them just plain nice.

The Pisces/Snake is very easily hurt. Sensitivity is so close to the surface that it shows in her eyes. If a harsh remark or nasty comment is made about them, these people take it quickly to heart. Then, they may nurture private hatreds. People are quickly jealous of the sunny public image affected by Pisces/Snakes. Too, as the Pisces/Snake is always the best-looking and most popular person in the room by sole virtue of their artless personal magnetism, pretentious people envy them. How can such a simple-looking person have such appeal? Magic. Despite all this charisma, the Pisces/ Snake lacks confidence. He is never quite sure of himself and always steps lightly around newcomers. He's interested in everything pertaining to nature, animals and the supernatural. Pisces/ Snakes are achingly compassionate and understanding of others. They are frequently moody, but very easily jollied out of their grumps.

Love

For the Pisces/Snake, true love has no bounds. If this person marries or chooses someone as a mate, it is forever. The bond will not be broken. Pisces/Snakes like to stay at home and enjoy filling their houses with friends and neighbors. But they are not very social in the "Come on, honey, let's go out to dinner" sense. Pisces/Snakes need long periods of calm to restoke their furnaces, because when they are "on" they spend a lot of their energy. It's possible that their mate will be unfaithful, since Pisces/Snakes do not fancy crowds or adhere to trends. They will not go out dancing or wear trendy clothes if they don't feel like it—and they scarcely ever feel like it.

If you want to gain the affection of one of these fascinating magicians, learn how to listen. You can gain great emotional ground with a Pisces/Snake by lending him your ear for an hour or two. Pisces/Snakes are terribly sensual, but their sensuality is both reserved and modest. They will only be swept off their feet once in a lifetime. Then, after they have learned their lesson the hard way, Pisces/Snakes become extremely careful about people to whom they confide their hearts. If they decide to love you, you have a friend for life.

Compatibilities

Taurus, Cancer and Capricorn/Roosters are your secret admirers. You will be able to find happiness with them. Cancer and Capricorn/Oxen and Dragons covet your beauty and enjoy your incisive wit, too. Gemini, Virgo and Sagittarius/Tigers are not on your side at all. Nor should you consider cohabitation with Pigs of the same three signs. Virgo/Monkeys will squeeze you harder than you can squeeze them back—don't tempt them.

Home and Family

The Pisces/Snake is home-connected. No matter how far he or she goes in life, the basic family bond will never be stretched or broken. This is a dutiful and loving person whose home counts for nothing if it doesn't house the people he loves. If you find a Pisces/Snake in his or her own home, you will notice comfortable yet spare surroundings. Pisces/Snake is a cautious spender. Luxury for parents or spouse or children may be important. As for Pisces/Snake? He or she can live in one room with a bed and a large closet. Pisces/Snakes don't often look gussied up, but they secretly like to own lots of becoming clothing.

The Pisces/Snake parent doesn't love the pain connected with parenting. This person is a walking open wound of sensitivity. A child's cry, to this person, sounds like a Boeing 707 passing through his eardrums. The clank of a baby's spoon against a highchair top might put the fragile Pisces/Snake into a coma. If he or she has children, it would be a good idea to have plenty of help, too.

The Pisces/Snake child is the mother's pet type of kid. They are so liquid and malleable, so wise for their years, and so endearingly snuggle-able, that any Mom's heart will go out to this cutie. He or she will suffer from rude remarks at school, and they buckle if forced to undergo rough treatment from teachers. The best medicine for the Pisces/Snake's hyper-nervous and sensitive nature is education. The acquisition of knowledge helps the Pisces/Snake to channel his philosophies and attach his profundities to reality. Without a sound basis in learning, this person will always be at loose ends. Emotional games are not sufficiently challenging to keep him occupied.

Profession

This careful and compassionate person can do many jobs in life. But first, he or she must get over the major hurdle of not wanting to leave home. With a good educational background the Pisces/Snake may be willing to go out and make his fortune alone. But without it, this person will have to be pried loose from his Mom's apron strings at age thirty. Pisces/Snake deals well with the public, and is strong and resistant to physical labor as well.

As a boss this person is effective but unloved. As he is too kind and giving to employees, they tend to take advantage of the Pisces/Snake's good nature and then criticize him for not being strong enough. Nobody loves a benefactor. As an employee, so long as Pisces/Snake feels secure and well liked, and can go home when he's finished work, his career will run smoothly. The Pisces/Snake is an excellent independent worker.

Careers for the Pisces/Snake might be: scholar, researcher, historian, philosopher, writer, builder, social worker, veterinarian, journalist, astrologer, theologian.

Famous Pisces/Snakes:

Aamir Khan, Alison Becker, Andres Segovia, Angelababy, Anthony Burgess, Anton Yelchin, Barbara Feldon, Barbara Niven, Bree Turner, Brian Tee, Buffy Sainte-Marie, Chris Eigeman, Chris Martin, Christine Ebersole, Corbin Bleu, Daniel Woodrell, Heather McComb, Isabelle Huppert, Isabelle Huppert, Jack Falahee, James Van Der Beek, James Wan, Jennie Jacques, José Maria Aznar

(Spain), Kay Lenz, Kristin Davis, Lily Collins, Nathalie Emmanuel, Noah Emmerich, Paul W.S. Anderson, Raymond Aron, Robert Lowell, Ron Eldard, Ron Jeremy, Scout Taylor-Compton, Steve Bacic, William Petersen, Willie Stargell, Wilson Pickett, Xavier Dolan.

PISCES
QUALITIES
UNDERSTANDING, PERCEPTION, CREATIVITY,
COMPATIBILITY, AWARENESS, SPIRITUALITY
QUIRKS
DIFFIDENCE, LACK OF WILL, FEARFULNESS,
SMUGNESS, RAGE, INDECISION
Motto: *"I believe"*
Elements: *Water, Jupiter/Neptune, Mutable*

--

HORSE
QUALITIES
PERSUASIVENESS, UNSCRUPULOUSNESS,
POPULARITY, STYLE, DEXTERITY,
ACCOMPLISHMENT
QUIRKS
SELFISHNESS, AUTONOMY, REBELLION,
HASTE, ANXIETY, PRAGMATISM
Motto: *"I demand"*
Elements: *Positive Fire, Yang*

The apparent peacefulness of this combination of Fish and Horse is but a fine shell surrounding a highly fragile and spiritual nature. Pisces/Horse people are both clairvoyant and humanistic. They give of themselves without expecting more than a pat on the head in return. In this double sign, the Horse's ordinarily selfish push for autonomy is quieted. Pisces keeps the Horse's dander down, teaches him to be self-effacing, and shows him the wonders of clairvoyance.

The average Pisces/Horse is far too nice. Many of the pleasant aspects of Pisces (creativity, compatibility and understanding), are heightened by the Horse's peppy style. Pisces/Horses sometimes sacrifice too much of their own time, forgetting to take enough for themselves. They tend to be reserved, and to prefer popularity over self-determination. If Pisces/Horse can be protected by a strong and worthy person who wants to see them achieve their goals, Pisces/Horse can really go places in the world. Their indubitable specialness and rare gifts need only find a safe path that leads them out of the darkness. Then, these people can earn high honors in the world.

This talented Pisces person is born with the equine traits of dexterity and brilliance. He can even learn from his Horse side to be ruthless and pragmatic. But sometimes the Pisces shrugs off these potential tools of success, preferring anonymity to fame. The road to notoriety or even private success in his or her chosen field seems to the thin-skinned Pisces too long and uncomfortable. Pisces/Horse has a singular handicap in being able to see beyond now. The moment he's living in fades in light of the glaring future. Pisces/Horse can foretell the rough spots and preview the snags. So he often gives up before he begins.

Life and all of its wild peregrinations seems almost futile to the sometimes fatalistic Pisces/Horse. Other people with their inextricably tangled lives make him want to giggle and poke fun. As he observes the degree to which some humans take themselves seriously, this ephemeral seahorse is tickled. He wonders to himself, "Can't they see how silly they look? Aren't they aware of ridicule? Why are these people so upset? It's only life, after all."

It's natural for Horse people to be a bit rebellious. When you add Pisces, who meanders, and Horse, who may at any moment bolt, you might come up with a kind of pleasure-seeking bohemian who's looking for nothing more than a place to sleep under the stars for the night. Should this devil-may-care attitude dominate the Pisces/Horse's personality, he or she can become a victim, resigned and uncomplaining. There is not a whole lot of combativeness in Pisces/Horse. They may flare up for a little while when they're young, affecting revolution and playing hotshot? But by age twenty these characters are mostly either engaged in practicing their skills for eventual profit or they are off "finding themselves" in Kathmandu. The Pisces/Horse must find a passion early and follow it for a lifetime.

Love

The Pisces/Horse serves love well. He or she has the capacity for bottomless devotion. The Pisces/Horse knows how to minister to others, and sincerely cares whether or not you take that aspirin for your headache. He or she is a bit on the shy side and will probably not be a demonstrative lover. If this person has chosen you, you can count on being admired as well as adored.

If you are the lover of this worshipful type, you must never take advantage of his or her kindness. The Pisces/Horse will idolize you. He or she can be counted on for loyalty and fair play. Your job is to draw this timid soul out of his or her cocoon with imaginative and generous foreplay. The Pisces/Horse needs seduction: moonlight, flowers, candles on the table, a spot of champagne... lay it on thick and your Pisces/Horse will follow you anywhere.

Compatibilities

You're off and running with Cancer, Libra. Scorpio and Capricorn/Tigers. Those are healthy and loving matches. Taurus, Scorpio and Capricorn/Dogs love you to pieces as well. And you'll get on swimmingly with Taurus or Capricorn/Sheep. You are not apt to enjoy the favors of Rats—especially Gemini, Sagittarius or Virgo/Rats, Monkeys born in either Sagittarius or Gemini will not give you a fair shake. Stay clear of them.

Home and Family

The Pisces/Horse's favorite home will probably be somebody else's. This character is not particularly acquisitive, nor does he or she care about impressing others. He doesn't want to be cold or wet and would prefer to eat rather than not. But faring well to this airborne person doesn't necessarily include reclining on furniture signed by a fancy designer or gazing at wallpaper hand-printed in Italy. The Pisces/Horse's natural habitat is amid the ethers, up there inside his or her head. Even cleaning out gutters brings him far too close to the earth.

As a parent this person will surely be involved. The very spontaneity of kids attracts this heady person and he seeks to understand his kids. I don't however, figure him or her for a homebody nesting type who runs a tight ship. Oh no. A household run by the Pisces/ Horse will be a gypsy's dream. Neatness and orderliness seem to this creative soul but trivial restrictions. Pisces/Horse seeks an environment without bonds in which to raise a family. No fences, please.

The Pisces/Horse child will surely obey and conform so long as he or she is comfortable and well fed. Not that this kid will decide to stay at home forever—far from it. But until adolescence you can look forward to a peaceful and yielding child who is more than interested in the supernatural. Because of a tendency toward real clairvoyance, this child could be subject to disturbing dreams or waking moments of illumination. Teach him or her to treat this presentiment as a talent, to accept its aid. Don't be afraid. Sometimes Pisces/Horses really can foretell the future or are in touch with forces beyond our ken.

Profession

The Pisces/Horse is not very effective in the business or professional world. He or she shies from entrapment in deals, and laughs at the image of four telephone receivers under one chin. Life, for this other-worldly soul, has little to do with questing after wealth or gain. However, as the Pisces/Horse is always artistic and visionary, careers in the arts often allow them to succeed despite their penchant for non-involvement. Should they arrive at a lofty position, they handle fame with dignity.

The Pisces/Horse boss? Well, at most this person may hire somebody to type his manuscripts or transcribe his compositions onto lined music paper. He will probably not be very demanding. But as an employee, as long as he's challenged, the Pisces/Horse can move through routines without bucking the system If he becomes dissatisfied with a job it is usually because he has lost admiration for the boss, or else his creativity has not been put to good use. Pisces/ Horse needs encouragement and even some faint applause in the background in order to work well alone.

Applicable careers for this subject are: psychic, florist, gardener, bookstore owner, astrologer, psychologist, psychiatrist, witch, musician, writer, movie director, artist, poet .

Famous Pisces/Horses:

Alexis Denisof, Andrea Bowen, Anthony Head, Antonio Vivaldi, Ben Miller, Billy Zane, Brooke Burns, Catherine Bach, Catherine O'Hara, Cindy Crawford, Clara Lago, Donal Logue, Elise Neal, Emory Cohen, Frédéric Chopin, Gary Anthony Williams, Gavin MacLeod, Jay Hernandez, Jennifer Grant, Jensen Ackles, Joanne Woodward, John Irving, Lauren Ambrose, Lesley-Anne Down, Lindsey Morgan, Lord Snowdon, Lorin Maazel, Luc Plamandon, Madison Riley, Michel Magne, Mickey Spillane, Nick Zano, Patty Hearst, Plastic Bernard, Prince Ernst August of Hanover, Princess Sophie of Prussia, Rachel Dratch, Reiley McClendon, Ron Howard, Sherrie Rose, Sophie Hunter, Téa Leoni, Virginia Williams, Zack Snyder.

PISCES
QUALITIES
UNDERSTANDING, PERCEPTION, CREATIVITY,
COMPATIBILITY, AWARENESS, SPIRITUALITY
QUIRKS
DIFFIDENCE, LACK OF WILL, FEARFULNESS,
SMUGNESS, RAGE, INDECISION
Motto: *"I believe"*
Elements: *Water, Jupiter/Neptune, Mutable*

--

SHEEP
QUALITIES
INVENTION, LACK OF FORESIGHT,
PERSEVERANCE, WHIMSY, GOOD MANNERS,
IMPRACTICALITY
QUIRKS
PARASITISM, SENSITIVITY,
TARDINESS, PESSIMISM, TASTE, WORRY
Motto: *"I depend"*
Elements: *Negative, Fire, Yin*

This person, a combination of the two most sensitive, feeling signs of both zodiacs, is what the French call "un grand sensible." This character's sensitivity comes first. The rest—the genius, the ability to apply talents, the romance and the soul—come later. I always used to imagine that a person born under this ensemble of signs might prove so hypersentient as to be perfectly useless in the real world. But now I realize, after collecting a bunch of these people and watching them live, that my image of the writhing poet in pain from the very sound of his own inspiration is totally false. Pisces born in Sheep are some of the most powerful Pisces.

The reason for this? Well, you see, Pisces most often finds himself born into an astrological scheme containing some aggression-directed sign. Pisces/Tiger, for example: supposing he finds himself linked not only to Tiger but with a Leo or a Virgo Ascendant? Pisces' receptivity and emotion may be squashed before it has a chance. Whereas, with the Sheep as a partner, the dependent, whimsical, sensual, tasteful and non-pushy Sheep, Pisces can finally swim unhindered in the direction of his choice. No stricter influence tries to place unwanted limits on him. If Pisces feels like singing off key, the Sheep will gladly harmonize.

So Pisces/Sheep is a positive marriage of two very feeling and creative signs. What can they do with all this invention and emotion? How can they manage to tame all the fluidity into some manageable form? It's easy. They don't. Pisces doesn't like molds. Nor does Sheep. As a team they do away with them. They ramble around and meander and climb and descend and go back and forth and in and out capriciously—but never uselessly. Pisces/Sheep are living antennae. They pick up on everything they see and hear. They recall details of color and texture. They remember places, and record sizes and shapes. Pisces/Coats, my friend, are artistes of the highest order. They ingurgitate, cogitate and dispense emotion.

How does this apply to daily life? It doesn't. Forget daily life. Pisces/Sheep is a wanderer. He or she is not really interested in routine or repetition of experience. Their primary goal is getting through till the next experience washes over them. Their meals can be snacks or gourmet repasts. Their hair may fail to get combed or else is coiffed to the nines. Their clothes are either gorgeous or grungy. But either way, it's all the same to the Pisces born Sheep. He or she has time to burn. They disdain criticism and meddling. They go about their lives precisely as they see fit. And if you don't like it, you can make your own music.

Don't get me wrong. Pisces/Coats are anything but disobedient. For there to be disobedience there has to have been obedience. Not for the Pisces/Sheep. He never adhered to dumb customs, but went along with the crowd. He's not rebellious because he never paid attention to rules in the first place. Pisces/Sheep is a born outsider. And what about the Sheep? Who will he lean on? What will he cling to? Why, the Fish, of course. In Pisces' waters, the Sheep is no longer considered a parasite but a welcome guest. Here is symbiosis in its purest form.

Love

Hmmmm. Yes. Love and the Pisces/Sheep . . . let's just say that if

Pisces/Sheep falls in love, it is extremely difficult for him to fall out again. Many times, because of a certain separateness that comes naturally because of the psychic distance between Pisces/Sheep and his peers, this person will be able to avoid long-term entanglements. Yet, if only for the perpetuation of the race, he or she will, at some point, become totally engrossed in another. He or she will probably settle on some tougher person who guides and regulates the Pisces/Sheep's life/career/bath-taking/meals, and so on. The Pisces/Sheep is a passionate soul whose thunderous lovemaking gets novels written about it. But this person will not even try to be faithful. "What's faithful?" he or she will pop down off a cloud to wonder. Oh, never mind.

Should you be the chosen person or wish to be attached to this heap of human creativity, I suggest you be the type who takes over. Even the most rigid of tyrants has trouble domesticating Pisces/Sheep. They don't understand schedules. They have no routines but their own to adhere to. Time means nothing to a Pisces/Sheep, or at least, nothing we ever heard of. So if you are attracted to this wonderful loony, don't hold him down. Pamper him. But sit on him too. Who knows? You might be seatted on Michelangelo.

Compatibilities

A real Cat lover are you! Take a chance on a breed that suits you, like Taurus, Cancer, Scorpio or Capricorn/Cats. They offer good, secure returns for your charms. The same breeds offer you their Horse subjects for love and romance. A Taurus, a Scorpio or a Capricorn/Pig would be able to make you happy, too. And the fun you can have with a sexy Scorpio/Sheep is not even printable. May I suggest you avoid Aries, Gemini and Virgo/Oxen? It's in your best interest, believe me. Virgo/Dogs won't be able to deal with you at all.

Home and Family

If the Pisces/Sheep ever gets this far, if he or she actually settles down to a life of family and housekeeping, he or she will thrive in luxury and beautiful surroundings. Also, this person is often handy with tools and can invent effective lighting effects and plan interesting rooms. The artistry for which they are famous allows Pisces/Sheep to apply their talents anywhere. The furnishings will probably not be too practical. The Pisces/Sheep will benefit from organizational assistance from a more material-minded mate or companion. He or she will love having scads of terrific, dramatic clothes.

This person will endure his children and certainly love them madly. He or she will, however, be easily exasperated with their frequent childish interruptions and lack of common sense. The Pisces/Sheep is like everybody else in this way, he sees his own faults first in others. But for this extremely artistic soul, interference and noise is truly too much to bear.

Pisces/Sheep should be protected from their offspring. And vice versa! If you are thinking about having a Pisces/Sheep child, get your life ready to welcome a vastly undisciplined—not necessarily turbulent or violent—person. This kid will be amazing, and so drawn to things creative and natural as to fascinate you. He will require acres of comfortable grazing and swimming areas. I'd move to the country and buy a big house with a room just for this artistic wonder child. Then let him or her loose on a box of paints or a library full of poetry. You won't be sorry.

Profession

The best jobs for this person are those allowing travel and requiring creativity. This person needs to move about freely. He or she also wants to avoid routine, and would prefer not to have to be on the cleanup committee. Finding a career for this art-oriented soul is not a snap job. Most often, if he or she is directed early on, or even apprenticed while young to a greater artist, the problem of job choice will solve itself. This person wants to apply his talents, is truly a driven artist, and if he doesn't give in to a nasty streak of pessimism, all will go well.

The Pisces/Sheep boss is a seer of situations. As he or she floats about on a cloud, their overview of what's really happening is lofty and accurate. Pisces/Sheep are capable of filling authoritarian positions. They handle people deftly. This person does not, however, make a solid and drudge-oriented office or factory employee. The Pisces/Sheep is best employed at a job that allows some contact with people but mostly space to move about in, both figuratively and literally.

Some applicable careers are: artist (all kinds), musician (all kinds), artisan (all kinds), costume designer, makeup artist, theatrical set designer, hairdresser, seamstress, writer (all kinds).

Famous Pisces/Sheep:
Adam Levine, Bianca Lawson, Bruce Willis, Chris Klein, Connie Britton, Currie Graham, Danneel Ackles, David Herman, Erika Ervin, Gary Sinise, George Eads, George Harrison, Glenne Headly, Hal Linden, Hanna Mangan Lawrence, James Madison, Jennifer Love Hewitt, John Barrowman, John McPhee, Kelsey Grammer, Lauren Graham, Lili Taylor, Marc Warren, Marcel Pagnol, Mark Boone Junior, Max Lloyd-Jones, Michelangelo, Mikhail Gor-

bachev, Muti, Nina Hagen, O'Shea Jackson Jr., Oscar Isaac, Patrick Renna, Paul Lieberstein, Riki Lindhome, Rupert Murdoch, Sam Taylor-Johnson, Sarah Bolger, Sir Timothy Laurence, Steve Jobs, Tom Wolfe, W. H. Auden.

PISCES
QUALITIES
UNDERSTANDING, PERCEPTION, CREATIVITY,
COMPATIBILITY, AWARENESS, SPIRITUALITY
QUIRKS
DIFFIDENCE, LACK OF WILL, FEARFULNESS,
SMUGNESS, RAGE, INDECISION
Motto: *"I believe"*
Elements: *Water, Jupiter/Neptune, Mutable*

--

MONKEY
QUALITIES
IMPROVISATION, CUNNING, STABILITY,
SELF-INVOLVEMENT, WIT, OPPORTUNISM
QUIRKS
DECEIT, RUSE, LOQUACITY,
LEADERS, SILLINESS, ZEAL
Motto: *"I plan"*
Elements: *Positive, metal, Yang*

The merry Monkey finds a new, more elegant external image under the influence of unrestrained Pisces. The Monkey is normally level-headed. His job in the Chinese Zodiac is to solve problems, big and small. Monkeys are born with common sense. Monkeys are natural leaders but not power seekers. They have cunning and stability. A rare combination. Pisces lends spiritual grace and beauty to the nimble and spirited Monkey. The result is a handsome person whose reputation for charm precedes him or her everywhere.

This character loves loveliness, and knows where to find it. What the Piscean Monkey wants, he or she usually gets. They have natural style and class. People give Pisces/Monkeys elegant wardrobes and pretty jewelry, castles to live in and honors to be proud of. There is something about the matching of creative perception with ruse and opportunism that makes for a very cosmopolitan character. The Pisces/Monkey is sophisticated without being a snob. He or she will be well attired without bothering to be on the list of the ten best dressed. The Pisces/Monkey comes closest to one of those swashbucklers or princesses in gothic novels—they have spunky flair.

Now this elegance might be merely veneer. The Pisces/Monkey is a bit of a parvenu, and one of the all time great pretenders. But nonetheless, image is reality. And these people have got that noblesse image down to a science.

The Pisces/Monkey charms and calculates his or her way through life. He shifts and squiggles and wriggles and slaloms his thoughts and investments, his loves and his hates, to suit the needs of the moment. She knows how to get the best of most people she tussles with. This Pisces is a born wheeler-dealer whose class act dupes throngs and skyrockets him or her to the desired slot in what seems like minutes. You see, Monkeys are already cleverer than most of us. Monkeys usually have a good grip on their lives. But when Pisces joins forces with them, they become just that dab more fugitive and a tiny bit dreamy. The Pisces wistfulness, that dollop of eyelash-batting modesty, is what clinches the deal every time.

The Pisces/Monkey is peripatetic. He has a tendency to excess and may have health problems with anything from alcoholism to overeating. Pisces/Monkeys are not, however, self-destructive. They know when they must blow the whistle on their indulgences. The Pisces/Monkey always recovers lost stability.

Piscean Monkeys are very sentimental. They know how to grab onto the feelings of another and hold them fast. In friendship as in love, the Pisces/Monkey sticks like day-old porridge.

Pisces' usual liquid regard, with Monkey incisiveness added, becomes a kind of tender glare. The general attitude of this Monkey Fish says, "I love humanity, but if it tries to hurt me I shall be forced to gobble it up." Piscean Monkeys are never guilty of intentional heavy-handedness. They are jealously aware of their own seductive powers. But oftentimes they are lazy about seeking dominion over others, preferring the vicissitudes of intricate personal relationships to the flat adulation of the public eye.

Love

The love stories of Pisces/Monkeys are as epic as those in the Gothics I spoke of before. These people involve themselves in passionate affairs of dramatic proportion and Biblical scale. Pisces/

Monkeys are more than attractive. They are alluring and mysterious. People fall fanny over teakettle in love with them. Pisces/ Monkey's a bit vain so he or she is pleased to be the object of someone's affection. But because this person is Pisces and sometimes appears passive, lovers may try to take advantage of the Piscean Monkey's good nature. Then, sparks fly. Misuse of Monkey Fish emotions is a no-no.

If you are enamored of one of these rakish aristocrats, I suggest you get yourself lots of money. Pisces/Monkeys like money. They know how to get it and keep it. You share yours. They get to keep theirs. One for you and two for me. You will not have a dull life with this mover and shaker. They respond well to tenderness but freak if they are made fools of. Step lightly.

Compatibilities

Taurus, Cancer, Scorpio and Capricorn give you the loving Dragon. Your Rat lovers should be found among Taureans, Cancers and Capricorns. You might even get on with a Taurus/Monkey. Don't ask me why, but my charts tell me you should avoid Virgo and Sagittarius/Tigers; Gemini and Sagittarius/Snakes, and Virgo/ Horses and Pigs.

Home and Family

Luxury is the order of the day in Piscean Monkey home decor. These folks like things ruffled and satiny. They favor lace on velvet - the latter preferably made of pure silk. They are attracted to traditional furniture and large rooms with marble fireplaces. It's the chateau complex. Piscean Monkeys are hedonists, and will enjoy living in luxury hotels almost as much as in their posh homes.

The Pisces/Monkey parent improves with age. As a young person, this parent may indeed be distracted from the serious side of parenting by his or her own good looks and success in the sexual sense. As they grow older, though, Pisces/Monkeys take increasingly responsible care of their kids. They are curious about their children's opinions and are receptive to criticism. The Pisces/ Monkey parent will provide. Good schools and the lot. But he may be too busy to play checkers all afternoon with a sick kid.

The Pisces/Monkey child is a sparkling little imp of a teddy bear. You will want to either hug or tickle this bright little tyke. He or she will be something of a daredevil, and may clown around in school. The Pisces/Monkey is a social kid. Watch for signs of impending fame and fortune. And don't get yourself talked into things. This child at age three can already persuade you his bedtime ought to be moved to midnight.

Profession

There are few jobs closed to the Pisces/Monkey. He is versatile in the extreme, and able to carry out orders with agility and zeal. He is physically able, although subject to frequent accidents due to his mobile lifestyle. And his mental abilities are sharp and attuned to what's happening in the world. He's strong-minded, too, and talented in both creativity and interpretation.

The Piscean Monkey boss will be loved by his employees and underlings. This person exerts charm before exerting authority. He or she will never stoop to humiliating the help. They are very humanistic, and although Pisces/Monkey probably can lay down the law, he or she will prefer to command through reason and good sense. The Piscean Monkey employee is serious and willing to pitch in. He or she may not take to anonymous jobs where people work in cubicles. The Pisces/Monkey must be seen to be appreciated.

Some careers for the Piscean Monkey are: politician, insurance sales, admiral, actor, actress, ski instructor, artist, TV personality.

Famous Pisces/Monkeys:

Aaron Eckhart, Balthus, Bel Powley, Bryan Cranston, Charlelie Couture, Chelsea Clinton, Dana Delany, Daniel Craig, Ed Quinn, Emily Osment, George MacKay, Hank Ketcham, Ingrid Bolsø Berdal, James Dooham, James Frain, Jean Lecanuet, Jeri Ryan, Jessie T. Usher, John Boyega, John Updike, Justin Roiland, Katherine Waterston, Kaya Scodelario, King Jigme Khesar Namgyel Wangchuck of Bhutan, Laura Prepon, Lesley Manville, Liz Taylor, Liza Snyder, Maisie Richardson-Sellers, Matthew Gray Gubler, Megan Follows, Michel Legrand, Michele Morgan, Moira Kelly, Patsy Kensit, Piet Mondriaan, Ranulph Fiennes, Rebel Wilson, Renzo Olivo, Rex Harrison, Rohan Bopanna, Samara Weaving, Sean Bridgers, Sophia Myles, Ted Kennedy, Tim Daly, Tommy McCarthy, Tony Randall.

PISCES
QUALITIES
UNDERSTANDING, PERCEPTION, CREATIVITY,
COMPATIBILITY, AWARENESS, SPIRITUALITY
QUIRKS
DIFFIDENCE, LACK OF WILL, FEARFULNESS,
SMUGNESS, RAGE, INDECISION
Motto: *"I believe"*
Elements: *Water, Jupiter/Neptune, Mutable*

--

ROOSTER
QUALITIES
RESILIENCE, ENTHUSIASM, CANDOR,
CONSERVATISM, CHIC, HUMOR
QUIRKS
COCKINESS, BOASTFULNESS, BLIND FAITH,
PEDANTRY, BOSSINESS, DISSIPATION
Motto: *"I overcome"*
Elements: *Negative, Metal, Yin*

The greatest quality of the combination of Fish and Rooster is adaptability. This thorough and self-directed person feels instantly at home wherever he or she happens to be sitting. They like change, and move quickly to adjust and acclimatize. Roosters are adventurous. Pisces like to wander. Moving through space attracts this enthusiastic character. Discord causes Pisces/Rooster to flee. Unrequited love makes him weep.

Pisces born in Rooster years secretly doubt their ability to please others. They are never sure of their charms, and worry unduly about appearances. On the surface they will not like to show this apprehension. So, superficially, the Pisces/Rooster is cocky and absolute.

He invariably shows his best side, and is not afraid to tell you how perfect he is. Soooo... the greatest fault of the Pisces/Rooster could be arrogance. The most grievous error he ever commits is born of pretense. You don't have to plumb very deep to discover that this person's modest inner self does not, however, approve of haughtiness.

Rooster is a down-to-earth, no-nonsense adventurer. Pisces is quite the opposite. So what evolves here is a type who alternately behaves outrageously by blurting, "I am the mistress of Mr. Slade," when she should be keeping her counsel. Then she realizes she has made a booboo and retreats into the background, wishing the storm were over and that Mr. Slade had never come into her life.. The Pisces/Rooster is uneven and a tad neurotic. On the one hand he longs for peace and pastoral walks. On the other he's out chopping wood till three in the morning so he can get ahead.

Pisces/Rooster is a closet zany. He claims he doesn't like to have fun. But he's aching to escape his own act, to explode his bubble. Ups and downs are characteristic of Roosters. Pisces suffer from highs and lows of mood. If the Roosterish up isn't in conjunction with the Piscean high, watch out for signs of inner conflict, nail-biting and thumb-sucking not excluded.

The Pisces/Rooster is clever. His best shot is to try to capitalize his serious side by exposing his zany, funny self. By this I mean that Pisces/Roosters can feel at ease in the world if they decide to show the world who they really are. They can be both daring and resourceful. But they are also creative and spiritual. It's very simple. They should write a breakthrough book, or direct a fun-filled film, or join a motorcycle club, or do skydiving for money. "But I'm not like that!" says the Pisces/Rooster. "I'm a hard worker who likes to be alone to hike the mountainsides with my dogs."

Perhaps. But I think if you stopped feeling sorry for yourself and emphasizing the differences between you and the rest of the world you might come out of that self-imposed closet and have a good time. You are talented and efficient. Everybody tells you that. You are attractive and adaptable. So why are you so stingy with yourself? Why don't you relax and have some fun? Don't count on others to make your fun for you.

Love

Outwardly, Pisces/Rooster suffers from being underloved. He or she says nobody ever really cares, that true love never works, and that it's all a sham anyway. Shrug shrug. Underneath (again!), this person is a romantic, an idealist, a true believer in the enduring forever-after kind of passion. But in the best of relationships clashes will arise. Pisces/Rooster is easily discouraged. He or she has trouble sticking to relationships. Remember, the only fault a Pisces/Rooster thinks he has is that he's perfect. So how can he or she accept having been rude or short-tempered or unfaithful? The Pisces/Rooster is always advertising his or her imperfections and feeling unworthy as a result. What this person needs is constant challenge.

If you love a Pisces/Rooster and want to keep her near you for a while, don't let her get away with complaining. Don't let him feel sorry for himself, nor demand faultless behavior from either you or himself. These people tend to be bossy and moody by turns. Call their bluff. Don't sit by and weep. It brings out the worst in Pisces/ Roosters. Sniveling is too much like something they might be capable of. They hate that.

Compatibilities

You'll be blissful around Taurus, Cancer, Scorpio and Capricorn/ Oxen. Cancer, Scorpio and Capricorn/Snakes excite you, too. Also, Taurus and Capricorn/Dragons will admire your direct approach. Gemini, Virgo and Sagittarius/Cats are your incompatible signs, and Gemini/Rooster gets on your nerves. Gemini/Pigs are your nemesis.

Home and Family

The Pisces/Rooster is usually fairly neat. His or her rooms will be effectively furnished in warm, bright colors. They will want to own much that impresses. They favor shiny objects. As Pisces, these folks love everything natural and safe. They will probably prefer a large, rambling country house to an exiguous city apartment. And they love to dress—good taste in conservative clothes. The Pisces/ Rooster is never sure he or she wants to have kids. These people have enough trouble convincing themselves to get along with themselves without adding the burden of another whole person to their sensitive personal load. This person is not made for nurturing. Should he or she have children, the raising of those kids may be left to a mate.

A Pisces/Rooster child is highly sensitive and very capable. No matter how he grows up, he will be sure to find fault with parents' demands. Yet, this highly artistic kid is obedient and idealistic about his folks. At adolescence, when Pisces/Roosters suddenly notice that their parents are only human, they suffer severe disappointment. The best way to raise this child is with lots of reassuring hugs and encouragement. Self-doubt is the enemy, confidence the goal. Never humiliate this proud child.

Profession

The multitalented and adventurous Pisces/Rooster demands much of himself from a career point of view. Jobs requiring the deciphering of complex plans will challenge the Pisces/Rooster. This person is effective and efficient. She likes to do things the "right way." Pisces/Roosters are not adept at business dealings. They are executors. They carry out other people's creations. Creativity for its own sake doesn't interest this person. His or her artistic talents will want applying to some concrete project.

The Pisces/Rooster boss will be demanding. He or she is a perfectionist and quite cocky and proud. These people can, however, understand others' problems and yield to others' methods with ease. As they are not made for scrappy fighting, these subjects will get along well in ready-made slots in offices and factories. Otherwise, they are very capable of working alone, and need no prodding. The Pisces/Rooster is ambitious for knowledge more than for gain.

Some jobs that might suit the Pisces/Rooster are: optometrist, fisherman, writer, electrician, engineer, photographer, computer programmer, piano tuner, recording engineer, pharmacist, skin diver, historian.

Famous Pisces/Roosters:
Abe Vigoda, Alexander McQueen, Amy Pietz, Aunjanue Ellis, Bryce Dallas Howard, Chaz Bono, Christophe Lambert, Dave Sheridan, David Anders, Ellen Muth, Elodie Yung, Grover Cleveland, Javier Bardem, Jenna Boyd, Jodie Comer, John Turturro, Josh Gad, Julia Winter, Kevin Curran, Kim Raver, Lee Radziwill, M.C. Solaar, Majandra Delfino, Marlon Jackson, Michael Caine, Mouna Ayoub, Mykelti Williamson, Osama bin Laden, Paget Brewster, Paul Blackthorne, Philip Roth, Philippe de Broca, Quincy Jones, Robert Sean Leonard, Roger Gicquel, Ryan Cartwright, Spike Lee, Taylor Dooley, Terrence Howard, Theresa Russell, Thomas Jane, Timothy Spall.

PISCES
QUALITIES
UNDERSTANDING, PERCEPTION, CREATIVITY,
COMPATIBILITY, AWARENESS, SPIRITUALITY
QUIRKS
DIFFIDENCE, LACK OF WILL, FEARFULNESS,
SMUGNESS, RAGE, INDECISION
Motto: *"I believe"*
Elements: *Water, Jupiter/Neptune, Mutable*

--

DOG
QUALITIES
CONSTANCY, UNSOCIABILITY,
RESPECTABILITY, SELF-RIGHTEOUSNESS,
INTELLIGENCE, TACTLESSNESS
QUIRKS
UNEASINESS, CRITICISM, DUTY,
CYNICISM, HEROISM, MORALITY
Motto: *"I worry"*
Elements: *Positive, Metal, Yang*

The Pisces born in a Dog year, like all Pisceans only more so, has a tender side that must be nurtured and treated with sincere affection.. Their sensitivity takes the form of nervous touchiness. They don't like to be questioned or contradicted. They are strong-minded but can be weak-willed.

Take the Pisces side of this person's nature, for example. Pisces is all receptiveness and permeability. Pisces lives to perceive and become more aware. Pisces often has no fixed aspiration. He is spiritual and understanding. He is also vulnerable and sometimes bitter. Frequently, Pisces lacks the ability to make decisions. Dogs are noted for their constancy. Dogs are devoted and loyal and trustworthy.

Dogs are dutiful and respectable. They are even heroic. But they, not unlike Pisceans, can also be insecure, cynical and self-righteous. When the two signs get together, the character evolves as testy and sarcastic, critical and worried. The Pisces/Dog is always on the defensive. He doesn't make friends easily. New people flummox him. He or she may attempt to ignore social intercourse altogether in favor of peace at any price.

In this sign, talents are many. The person born Pisces/Dog will have myriad attitudes and oodles of potential. Providing there exists a sound basis in family training and background, this person can go very far in a chosen field. But for a Pisces/Dog person, security comes first. These folks don't like the unknown. He or she will drive very hard to achieve superiority in a chosen area of interest. But his or her real goal is always safety and asylum, freedom from anxiety.

Pisces born in Dog years can be very amusing. They zero in on foibles or details of human behavior and have a knack for satire and mimicry. Their wit is wry and snappy, like dry kindling. It can sliver the thickest of skins.

The sense of responsibility with which the Pisces/Dog is born can be a millstone around his or her neck. Duty is everything to this tender-hearted and reliable character. Sometimes, in the execution of their obligations, these people push themselves too hard. Their fragile nerves cannot resist the pressures and stress sets in. Pisces/Dogs must watch out for signs of depression and despair due to overwork, exhaustion and worry. This character is a flimsy giant. From the sturdy-looking outside you would never guess at his delicacy of feeling or imagine for a minute that she cries herself to sleep at night over unexpressed sorrow. But as these people are basically humble and don't flaunt their emotions, they are sometimes misunderstood.

Pisces/Dogs never growl or snarl if they can smile instead. They only bark at danger. But then, they see danger where it is not. The Pisces born a Dog is an artless fellow who has nothing to prove and plenty to worry about.

Love

The Pisces/Dog is usually married. There is security in wedlock and the Pisces born Dog needs lots of that. These people (For Dogs) are quite faithful in love, and have very high standards for their choice of mate. The Pisces/Dog needs much reassurance and has to be encouraged to dare new things. He needs comfort and tenderness in giant doses, as sensitivity and piano-wire taut nerves may cause him or her to suffer from lack of self-confidence.

For this gingerly person there is no substitute for a loving pep talk. If you fancy one of these high-strung people, you will need to employ patience and to have your own life under control. The quality of sentiment in Pisces/Dog, be it exhilaration or despair, is crisp and brittle. Should you disappoint this sentient person of sterling character, you may ultimately destroy him or her. Pisces/Dogs are not real fighters. They like calm and need a Rock of Gibraltar type for a mate or lover. If you are in the least unscrupulous, keep your hands off this innocent puppy. He or she deserves better.

Compatibilities

Taurus, Libra and Capricorn/Tiger people like your style. You have that little air of tenderness and vulnerability that appeals to Scorpio and Capricorn/Cats. Scorpio/Horses want to take care of you. And vice versa. Gemini, Virgo and Sagittarius/Dragons, Sheep and Roosters are out of the running across the board.

Home and Family

The Pisces/Dog can live almost anywhere. This person does not depend on his or her surroundings for well-being. Of course they like things to be orderly and pleasant. But we don't always find them nattering about their choice of couch pattern or the color of the lampshades. The Pisces/Dog is discreet and takes good care of others' belongings. But he can manage without too much luxury, and will be loath to spoil him or herself by creating a fancy environment.

The Pisces/Dog parent is a monolith of caring. This person is naturally uneasy. Don't be surprised if you find him or her running to the crib every five minutes to see if little Isabelle is still breathing. The Pisces/Dog parent will want his or her child to excel at schoolwork and sports and outside activities. If you are a Pisces/ Dog and have children, take the pressure off once in awhile, huh? They're only kids, you know.

This sign makes nervous little children. Most important is to make this child feel safe and secure. Coziness really counts for a Pisces/ Dog kid. Don't force them into ridiculous positions or ask them to perform in public unless they really want to. They are not so much shy as they are allergic to indiscretion.

Profession

The Pisces/Dog is a person of great ability. The native talent here combines with a sharp mind and plenty of cynical wit. A wisp of an idea or plan can be turned into a complex project overnight by this clever soul. The Dog's sense of duty and Pisces' sensitivity form a person of abundant resource, who is tireless in his quest for the right link to complete a chain. The Pisces/Dog is an able worker who doesn't give up easily. His fatal flaw is hypersensitivity. If scorned or insulted, the Pisces/Dog may crumble. He is a gentle pooch. Handle with care.

The Pisces/Dog boss will be fair and just and even comical in his methods. He doesn't want to make any enemies among employees, and always finds something encouraging to say to them. He may use biting sarcasm in some cases. Ignore it. He or she doesn't have a mean bone. The Pisces/Dog is a respectful worker. He may get carried away on some seemingly zany idea but don't worry, he'll always come back to earth. The Pisces/Dog is a serious person with earnest ideals. This person doesn't work well alone. He or she will need cheering along from time to time and prefers to cooperate rather than work in solitude.

Some careers for Pisces/Dogs are: writer, actor, actress, cartoonist, professor, dancer, singer, art director, secretary, graphic artist, nursery school teacher.

Famous Pisces/Dogs:
Aislinn Paul, Alan Rickman, Albert of Monaco, Andrea Parker, Ansel Elgort, Cameron Palatas, Christina Grimmie, Dakota Fanning, David Niven, Dichen Lachman, Edoardo Ballerini, Greg Germann, Hayley Orrantia, Holly Hunter, Jack Kerouac, Jacques Séguéla, Jean-Michel Folon, Jeanne Mas, Jed Rees, Jessica Biel, Julie Bowen, Justin Bieber, Kat Von D, Kate Maberly, Kim Coates, Kofi Siriboe, Linda Fiorentino, Lindsey McKeon, Lisa Robin Kelly, Liza Minnelli, Meredith Salenger, Michael Rapaport, Miranda Richardson, Niecy Nash, Patricia Heaton, Prince Albert of Monaco, Queen Latifah, Rachel Weisz, Samm Levine, Samuel Barber, Sandy Duncan, Sharon Stone, Thora Birch, Tim Kaine, Victor Hugo, Yanic Truesdale, Youri Gagarine.

PISCES
QUALITIES
UNDERSTANDING, PERCEPTION, CREATIVITY,
COMPATIBILITY, AWARENESS, SPIRITUALITY
QUIRKS
DIFFIDENCE, LACK OF WILL, FEARFULNESS,
SMUGNESS, RAGE, INDECISION
Motto: *"I believe"*
Elements: *Water, Jupiter/Neptune, Mutable*

--

PIG
QUALITIES
SCRUPULOUSNESS, GALLANTRY, SINCERITY,
VOLUPTUOUSNESS, CULTURE, HONESTY
QUIRKS
CREDULITY, WRATH, HESITATION,
MATERIALISM, GOURMANDISM, PIGHEADEDNESS
Motto: *"I civilize"*
Elements: *Negative Water, Yin*

The degree of permeability in the Pisces/Pig subject is so elevated as to cause him or her a real burden. This person feels more deeply than we do. Pisces/Pigs are gentle souls with unlimited ambition. They are sensualists who love *luxe* and care immensely for tradition and custom. I'd say without hesitation that the Pisces/Pig's biggest stumbling block is the modern world. He is old-fashioned and firmly rooted in time-honored ways. Shortcuts irritate the Pisces/Pig. Nicknames grate on his nerves. Gadgets bore him.

Because of this "handicap", the Pisces/Pig, who is nonetheless eager for gain and advancement, must work harder than others. He imposes this yoke of extra labor on his own neck. His ideas are as stationary as his feelings, which are both dense and delicate. If he thinks he's right, he will not budge a bristle. And even if he's wrong, he still doesn't budge. He placates or he excuses or finds some gracious way out, pride intact.

Of course, what can happen to a pigheaded person with heightened sensibilities is that others may tease and misuse him. This only exacerbates the situation and makes our Pisces/Pig furious. But his is not an expressive rage. It's a long, low seethe. No tantrums or scenes. Just steam emanating from the ears.

The Pisces born Pig is a good-hearted character, so his sulks don't last long. He or she harbors true and profound affection for friends and loved ones and is scrupulous about respecting loyalties. He is a peacekeeper and a diplomat. The Pisces/Pig knows how to "handle" testy, difficult people. He is wise and he is ever so blasé. It's almost as if the Pisces/Pig knew better than other people and indulged the rest of us in our childish whims. "Finally," thinks the Pisces/Pig, "what does it all matter?"

What interests this Pig most is culture and convention. History will fascinate him or her. Stories told by grandparents and tales and legends of all sorts captivate this laudable type. He or she often stays close to home as an adult and marries someone of similar background. The Pisces/Pig doesn't make waves, nor is he wont to splash wantonly in the surf where he risks being toppled by one. This character is not timid. Oh no. Nor is he or she squeamish. But he is a bit thin-skinned and prefers to take the paved road home, avoid pitfalls, skirt craters and duck slings and arrows.

This subject benefits from the final position in both zodiacs. Both Pisces and Pig wrap up their ancient systems. As a result, Pisces/Pig has both the perspective of a very old sage and the misfortune to have had to amass all the flotsam of a twelve-year, twelve-month cycle. In other words, there is plenty going on inside these rich and comfort-loving people. But some of what's happening is not so savory. The life of a Pisces/Pig has to be devoted to sorting through the rubble and figuring out what's best for his or her use.

The world is almost too much for this person. His heart is frequently heavy with awareness. He or she is sentimental and yet resigned. His parents are a disappointment and Pisces/Pig adores them. Her lovers are less than perfect but she cares for them passionately. Kids grow up and leave home and that's another letdown. What's left? Money. Luxury. Paintings. Sculpture. The chateau. The Rolls. The library. The thousands of musical phrases Pisces/Pig has retained. "Perhaps," says the old aesthete, "I shall become a Sunday painter."

Love

People accuse this person of being a clinging vine. It is true that the Pisces/Pig adores security and feels that much of his or her attachment to the earth comes through the one he or she loves. Without full-time affection and tenderness, this person has a sensation of being shipwrecked and alone. As he or she is both hyper sensual and voluptuous, this person will sacrifice a lot to hang onto an object of passion. Let's just say that in love matters this person is a receiver- not a taker. A receiver.

Should you be the better half of one of these obdurate ladies or gentlemen, you may say something unkind, yet they will receive your remarks with a smile. Pisces/Pigs pick up on other peoples' needs and sense their deepest feelings. They like to do for others and are apt to give presents and fuss over whether or not you're comfortable. Should you be tempted to take advantage of this person's kindness, think twice. Pisces/Pigs don't stand for nonsense. They will drive you mad with their disenchantment. Oh, and you'd better like making love. Pisces/Pigs wallow in it.

Compatibilities

Cats and Sheep belong to your league. They like the way you view life and are anxious to please you. You'll admire them, too. Choose from Cats and Sheep born in Taurus, Cancer, Scorpio and Capricorn. For a bit more exciting—but less stable by far—relationship, try a Cancer/Tiger. Moody but fascinating. As for your incompatible signs, you are advised to forget about love with Virgo or Sagittarius born Snakes. (Leave Snakes alone altogether if you can stand it.) Don't chase after a Gemini/Horse or a Sagittarius/Monkey, either. You'll be wasting precious time you could spend with a nice Cat or Sheep.

Home and Family

The domesticated Pisces/Pig is an inveterate nester. They wriggle their curly little tails all over town fetching home antiques and carpets and dimmer switches till everything is just right. The Pisces/Pig is handy and dexterous. The ambience *chez lui* will bespeak a cultivated and genteel lifestyle. No Pisces/Pig lives in a barn unless said barn has been painstakingly restored by gnomes from the Black Forest who scrape paint off old beams with baby toothbrushes. This person is continually concerned about improving his surroundings. And they are always perfect.

This parent nurtures and fusses and fumes over children and their welfare and happiness. If I had to find myself a "wife and mother" in the traditional sense of the word, I'd put an ad in the paper asking specifically for a Pisces/Pig—gender indifferent. This character is built to serve and enjoys caretaking. Kids get their meals on time and the holes in their socks darned. For family purposes, a Pisces/Pig for me.

The Pisces/Pig child may at first strike you as rather too susceptible to criticism. He or she will probably not be rebellious, but naughtiness or overindulgence is a definite possibility here. The Pisces/Pig likes a good joke. His or her pranks will be of the "Surprise!" variety. This is a kid who will stick by you in your old age. Whatever hypersensitivity he or she exhibits while small will pay off as loyalty in later years. Bundle this little one up and cuddle him or her a lot. Without parental affection this Pisces/Pig is at sea.

Profession

This well-adjusted solid citizen fits into almost any profession. The urgency here is that he or she find a career slot early and stick to it. As the Pisces/Pig will enjoy many talents, he or she may be tempted to vacillate from one to the other. This won't do. A Pisces/Pig needs security. If properly guided from an early age, he or she can find and keep a good position in life. Pisces/Pigs make excellent executives and are scrupulous in their dealings with others. They are good negotiators, seeing every side of all problems and able to understand various points of view. Of course, they are superbly artistic. They are both Pisces and Pig!

This person will be a loving, concerned and sociable boss. He can also make an excellent sidekick or personal assistant. The Pisces/Pig is not necessarily after the job of head honcho. He'd almost rather play second fiddle so he can have a bit more fun. This person is a fine, reliable and even inventive employee, especially if highly paid.

A list of suitable careers for the Pisces/Pig might go on forever, but to name a few: restorer of paintings or antiques, museum curator, personal assistant, gallery owner, painter, sculptor, fashion designer, hairdresser, beauty counselor, stylist, architect, builder.

Famous Pisces/Pigs:
Andrew Jackson, Andre Courreges, Cyd Charisse, Emmanuel Lewis, Jean Harlow, L. Ron Hubbard, Lea Salonga, Luc Besson, Maurice Ravel, Emily Blunt, Brett Davern, Cierra Ramirez, Christoph Genz, MC Mary Kom, Kyle MacLachlan, Aidan Quinn, Talia Balsam, Donna Murphy, Beth Broderick, Tom Arnold, Glenn Close, Nina Hartley, Jon Hamm, Cara Buono, Peter Sarsgaard, Charlie Brooker, Sean Astin, Alan Tudyk, Kate Mara, Mélanie

Laurent, Rafe Spall, Lupita Nyong'o, Mercedes Mason, Michael Cassidy, Aziz Ansari, Haley Lu Richardson, Julia Goldani Telles, Quinn Shephard.

The Chinese Horoscope Historical Reference Chart

1600-1699

Year	Sign	Element	Year begins	Year ends
1600	Rat	Metal	2/14/1600	2/2/1601
1601	Ox	Metal	2/3/1601	1/22/1602
1602	Tiger	Water	1/23/1602	2/10/1603
1603	Cat	Water	2/11/1602	1/30/1604
1604	Dragon	Wood	1/31/1604	2/17/1605
1605	Snake	Wood	2/18/1605	2/6/1606
1606	Horse	Fire	2/7/1606	1/27/1607
1607	Goat	Fire	1/28/1607	2/15/1608
1608	Monkey	Earth	2/16/1608	2/3/1609
1609	Rooster	Earth	2/4/1609	1/24/1610
1610	Dog	Metal	1/25/1610	2/12/1611
1611	Pig	Metal	2/13/1611	2/1/1612
1612	Rat	Water	2/2/1612	2/18/1613
1613	Ox	Water	2/19/1613	2/8/1614
1614	Tiger	Wood	2/9/1614	1/28/1615
1615	Cat	Wood	1/29/1615	2/16/1616
1616	Dragon	Fire	2/17/1616	2/5/1617
1617	Snake	Fire	2/6/1617	1/25/1618
1618	Horse	Earth	1/26/1618	2/13/1619
1619	Goat	Earth	2/14/1619	2/3/1620
1620	Monkey	Metal	2/4/1620	1/21/1621
1621	Rooster	Metal	1/22/1621	2/9/1622
1622	Dog	Water	2/10/1622	1/30/1623
1623	Pig	Water	1/31/1623	2/18/1624
1624	Rat	Wood	2/19/1624	2/6/1625
1625	Ox	Wood	2/7/1625	1/27/1626
1626	Tiger	Fire	1/28/1626	2/15/1627
1627	Cat	Fire	2/16/1627	2/4/1628
1628	Dragon	Earth	2/5/1628	1/23/1629
1629	Snake	Earth	1/24/1629	2/11/1630
1630	Horse	Metal	2/12/1630	1/31/1631
1631	Goat	Metal	2/1/1631	2/19/1632
1632	Monkey	Water	2/20/1632	2/7/1633
1633	Rooster	Water	2/8/1633	1/28/1634
1634	Dog	Wood	1/29/1634	2/16/1635
1635	Pig	Wood	2/17/1635	2/6/1636
1636	Rat	Fire	2/7/1636	1/25/1637
1637	Ox	Fire	1/26/1637	2/13/1638
1638	Tiger	Earth	2/14/1638	2/2/1639
1639	Cat	Earth	2/3/1639	1/22/1640
1640	Dragon	Metal	1/23/1640	2/9/1641
1641	Snake	Metal	2/10/1641	1/29/1642
1642	Horse	Water	1/30/1642	2/18/1643

1643	Goat	Water	2/19/1643	2/7/1644
1644	Monkey	Wood	2/8/1644	1/27/1645
1645	Rooster	Wood	1/28/1645	2/15/1646
1646	Dog	Fire	2/16/1646	2/4/1647
1647	Pig	Fire	2/5/1647	1/24/1648
1648	Rat	Earth	1/25/1648	2/10/1649
1649	Ox	Earth	2/11/1649	1/31/1650
1650	Tiger	Metal	2/1/1650	1/20/1651
1651	Cat	Metal	1/21/1651	2/8/1652
1652	Dragon	Water	2/9/1652	1/28/1653
1653	Snake	Water	1/29/1653	2/16/1654
1654	Horse	Wood	2/17/1654	2/5/1655
1655	Goat	Wood	2/6/1655	1/25/1656
1656	Monkey	Fire	1/26/1656	2/12/1657
1657	Rooster	Fire	2/13/1657	2/1/1658
1658	Dog	Earth	2/2/1658	1/22/1659
1659	Pig	Earth	1/23/1659	2/10/1660
1660	Rat	Metal	2/11/1660	1/29/1661
1661	Ox	Metal	1/30/1661	2/17/1662
1662	Tiger	Water	2/18/1662	2/7/1663
1663	Cat	Water	2/8/1663	1/27/1664
1664	Dragon	Wood	1/28/1664	2/14/1665
1665	Snake	Wood	2/15/1665	2/3/1666
1666	Horse	Fire	2/4/1666	1/23/1667
1667	Goat	Fire	1/24/1667	2/11/1668
1668	Monkey	Earth	2/12/1668	1/31/1669
1669	Rooster	Earth	2/1/1669	1/20/1670
1670	Dog	Metal	1/21/1670	2/8/1671
1671	Pig	Metal	2/9/1671	1/29/1672
1672	Rat	Water	1/30/1672	2/16/1673
1673	Ox	Water	2/17/1673	2/5/1674
1674	Tiger	Wood	2/6/1674	1/25/1675
1675	Cat	Wood	1/26/1675	2/13/1676
1676	Dragon	Fire	2/14/1676	2/1/1677
1677	Snake	Fire	2/2/1677	1/22/1678
1678	Horse	Earth	1/23/1678	2/10/1679
1679	Goat	Earth	2/11/1679	1/30/1680
1680	Monkey	Metal	1/31/1680	2/17/1681
1681	Rooster	Metal	2/18/1681	2/6/1682
1682	Dog	Water	2/7/1682	1/26/1683
1683	Pig	Water	1/27/1683	2/14/1684
1684	Rat	Wood	2/15/1684	2/2/1685
1685	Ox	Wood	2/3/1685	1/23/1686
1686	Tiger	Fire	1/24/1686	2/11/1687
1687	Cat	Fire	2/12/1687	2/1/1688
1688	Dragon	Earth	2/2/1688	1/20/1689

1689	Snake	Earth	1/21/1689	2/8/1690
1690	Horse	Metal	2/9/1690	1/28/1691
1691	Goat	Metal	1/29/1691	2/16/1692
1692	Monkey	Water	2/17/1692	2/4/1693
1693	Rooster	Water	2/5/1693	1/24/1694
1694	Dog	Wood	1/25/1694	2/12/1695
1695	Pig	Wood	2/13/1695	2/2/1696
1696	Rat	Fire	2/3/1696	1/22/1697
1697	Ox	Fire	1/23/1697	2/10/1698
1698	Tiger	Earth	2/11/1698	1/30/1699
1699	Cat	Earth	1/31/1699	2/18/1700

1700-1799

Year	Sign	Element	Year begins	Year ends
1700	Dragon	Metal	2/19/1700	2/7/1701
1701	Snake	Metal	2/8/1701	1/27/1702
1702	Horse	Water	1/28/1702	2/15/1703
1703	Goat	Water	2/16/1703	2/4/1704
1704	Monkey	Wood	2/5/1704	1/24/1705
1705	Rooster	Wood	1/25/1705	2/12/1706
1706	Dog	Fire	2/13/1706	2/2/1707
1707	Pig	Fire	2/3/1707	1/22/1708
1708	Rat	Earth	1/23/1708	2/9/1709
1709	Ox	Earth	2/10/1709	1/29/1710
1710	Tiger	Metal	1/30/1710	2/16/1711
1711	Cat	Metal	2/17/1711	2/6/1712
1712	Dragon	Water	2/7/1712	1/25/1713
1713	Snake	Water	1/26/1713	2/13/1714
1714	Horse	Wood	2/14/1714	2/3/1715
1715	Goat	Wood	2/4/1715	1/23/1716
1716	Monkey	Fire	1/24/1716	2/10/1717
1717	Rooster	Fire	2/11/1717	1/30/1718
1718	Dog	Earth	2/12/1718	2/18/1719
1719	Pig	Earth	2/19/1719	2/7/1720
1720	Rat	Metal	2/8/1720	1/27/1721
1721	Ox	Metal	1/28/1721	2/15/1722
1722	Tiger	Water	2/16/1722	2/4/1723
1723	Cat	Water	2/5/1723	1/25/1724
1724	Dragon	Wood	1/26/1724	2/12/1725
1725	Snake	Wood	2/13/1725	2/1/1726
1726	Horse	Fire	2/2/1726	1/21/1727
1727	Goat	Fire	1/22/1727	2/9/1728
1728	Monkey	Earth	2/10/1728	1/28/1729
1729	Rooster	Earth	1/29/1729	2/16/1730
1730	Dog	Metal	2/17/1730	2/6/1731
1731	Pig	Metal	2/7/1731	1/26/1732
1732	Rat	Water	1/27/1732	2/13/1733
1733	Ox	Water	2/14/1733	2/3/1734
1734	Tiger	Wood	2/4/1734	1/23/1735
1735	Cat	Wood	1/24/1735	2/11/1736
1736	Dragon	Fire	2/12/1736	1/30/1737
1737	Snake	Fire	1/31/1737	2/18/1738
1738	Horse	Earth	2/19/1738	2/7/1739
1739	Goat	Earth	2/8/1739	1/29/1740
1740	Monkey	Metal	1/30/1740	2/15/1741
1741	Rooster	Metal	2/16/1741	2/4/1742
1742	Dog	Water	2/5/1742	1/25/1743

1743	Pig	Water	1/26/1743	2/13/1744
1744	Rat	Wood	2/14/1744	2/1/1745
1745	Ox	Wood	2/2/1745	1/21/1746
1746	Tiger	Fire	1/22/1746	2/8/1747
1747	Cat	Fire	2/9/1747	1/29/1748
1748	Dragon	Earth	1/30/1748	2/16/1749
1749	Snake	Earth	2/17/1749	2/6/1750
1750	Horse	Metal	2/7/1750	1/26/1751
1751	Goat	Metal	1/27/1751	2/14/1752
1752	Monkey	Water	2/15/1752	2/2/1753
1753	Rooster	Water	2/3/1753	1/22/1754
1754	Dog	Wood	1/23/1754	2/10/1755
1755	Pig	Wood	2/11/1755	1/30/1756
1756	Rat	Fire	1/31/1756	2/17/1757
1757	Ox	Fire	2/18/1757	2/7/1758
1758	Tiger	Earth	2/8/1758	1/28/1759
1759	Cat	Earth	1/29/1759	2/16/1760
1760	Dragon	Metal	2/17/1760	2/4/1761
1761	Snake	Metal	2/5/1761	1/24/1762
1762	Horse	Water	1/25/1762	2/12/1763
1763	Goat	Water	2/13/1763	2/1/1764
1764	Monkey	Wood	2/2/1764	1/20/1765
1765	Rooster	Wood	1/21/1765	2/8/1766
1766	Dog	Fire	2/9/1766	1/29/1767
1767	Pig	Fire	1/30/1767	2/17/1768
1768	Rat	Earth	2/18/1768	2/6/1769
1769	Ox	Earth	2/7/1769	1/26/1770
1770	Tiger	Metal	1/27/1770	2/14/1771
1771	Cat	Metal	2/15/1771	2/3/1772
1772	Dragon	Water	2/4/1772	1/22/1773
1773	Snake	Water	1/23/1773	2/10/1774
1774	Horse	Wood	2/11/1774	1/30/1775
1775	Goat	Wood	1/31/1775	2/18/1776
1776	Monkey	Fire	2/19/1776	2/7/1777
1777	Rooster	Fire	2/8/1777	1/27/1778
1778	Dog	Earth	1/28/1778	2/15/1779
1779	Pig	Earth	2/16/1779	2/4/1780
1780	Rat	Metal	2/5/1780	1/23/1781
1781	Ox	Metal	1/24/1781	2/11/1782
1782	Tiger	Water	2/12/1782	2/1/1783
1783	Cat	Water	2/2/1783	1/21/1784
1784	Dragon	Wood	1/22/1784	2/8/1785
1785	Snake	Wood	2/9/1785	1/29/1786
1786	Horse	Fire	1/30/1786	2/17/1787
1787	Goat	Fire	2/18/1787	2/6/1788
1788	Monkey	Earth	2/7/1788	1/25/1789

1789	Rooster	Earth	1/26/1789	2/13/1790
1790	Dog	Metal	2/14/1790	2/2/1791
1791	Pig	Metal	2/3/1791	1/23/1792
1792	Rat	Water	1/24/1792	2/10/1793
1793	Ox	Water	2/11/1793	1/30/1794
1794	Tiger	Wood	1/31/1794	1/20/1795
1795	Cat	Wood	1/21/1795	2/8/1796
1796	Dragon	Fire	2/9/1796	1/27/1797
1797	Snake	Fire	1/28/1797	2/15/1798
1798	Horse	Earth	2/16/1798	2/4/1799
1799	Goat	Earth	2/5/1799	1/24/1800

1800-1899

Year	Sign	Element	Year begins	Year ends
1800	Monkey	Metal	1/25/1800	2/12/1801
1801	Rooster	Metal	2/13/1801	2/2/1802
1802	Dog	Water	2/3/1802	1/22/1803
1803	Pig	Water	1/23/1803	2/10/1804
1804	Rat	Wood	2/11/1804	1/30/1805
1805	Ox	Wood	1/31/1805	2/17/1806
1806	Tiger	Fire	2/18/1806	2/6/1807
1807	Cat	Fire	2/7/1807	1/27/1808
1808	Dragon	Earth	1/28/1808	2/13/1809
1809	Snake	Earth	2/14/1809	2/3/1810
1810	Horse	Metal	2/4/1810	1/24/1811
1811	Goat	Metal	1/25/1811	2/12/1812
1812	Monkey	Water	2/13/1812	1/31/1813
1813	Rooster	Water	2/1/1813	1/20/1814
1814	Dog	Wood	1/21/1814	2/8/1815
1815	Pig	Wood	2/9/1815	1/28/1816
1816	Rat	Fire	1/29/1816	2/15/1817
1817	Ox	Fire	2/16/1817	2/4/1818
1818	Tiger	Earth	2/5/1818	1/25/1819
1819	Cat	Earth	1/26/1819	2/13/1820
1820	Dragon	Metal	2/14/1820	2/2/1821
1821	Snake	Metal	2/3/1821	1/22/1822
1822	Horse	Water	1/23/1822	2/10/1823
1823	Goat	Water	2/11/1823	1/30/1824
1824	Monkey	Wood	1/31/1824	2/17/1825
1825	Rooster	Wood	2/18/1825	2/6/1826
1826	Dog	Fire	2/7/1826	1/26/1827
1827	Pig	Fire	1/27/1827	2/14/1828
1828	Rat	Earth	2/15/1828	2/3/1829
1829	Ox	Earth	2/4/1829	1/24/1830
1830	Tiger	Metal	1/25/1830	2/12/1831
1831	Cat	Metal	2/13/1831	2/1/1832
1832	Dragon	Water	2/2/1832	2/19/1833
1833	Snake	Water	2/20/1833	2/8/1834
1834	Horse	Wood	2/9/1834	1/28/1835
1835	Goat	Wood	1/29/1835	2/16/1836
1836	Monkey	Fire	2/17/1836	2/4/1837
1837	Rooster	Fire	2/5/1837	1/25/1838
1838	Dog	Earth	1/26/1838	2/13/1839
1839	Pig	Earth	2/14/1839	2/2/1840
1840	Rat	Metal	2/3/1840	1/22/1841
1841	Ox	Metal	1/23/1841	2/9/1842
1842	Tiger	Water	2/10/1842	1/29/1843

1843	Cat	Water	1/30/1843	2/17/1844
1844	Dragon	Wood	2/18/1844	2/6/1845
1845	Snake	Wood	2/7/1845	1/26/1846
1846	Horse	Fire	1/27/1846	2/14/1847
1847	Goat	Fire	2/15/1847	2/4/1848
1848	Monkey	Earth	2/5/1848	1/23/1849
1849	Rooster	Earth	1/24/1849	2/11/1850
1850	Dog	Metal	2/12/1850	1/31/1851
1851	Pig	Metal	2/1/1851	2/19/1852
1852	Rat	Water	2/20/1852	2/7/1853
1853	Ox	Water	2/8/1853	1/28/1854
1854	Tiger	Wood	1/29/1854	1/16/1855
1855	Cat	Wood	1/17/1855	2/5/1856
1856	Dragon	Fire	2/6/1856	1/25/1857
1857	Snake	Fire	1/26/1857	2/13/1858
1858	Horse	Earth	2/14/1858	2/2/1859
1859	Goat	Earth	2/3/1859	1/22/1860
1860	Monkey	Metal	1/23/1860	2/9/1861
1861	Rooster	Metal	2/10/1861	1/29/1862
1862	Dog	Water	1/30/1862	2/17/1863
1863	Pig	Water	2/18/1863	2/7/1864
1864	Rat	Wood	2/8/1864	1/26/1865
1865	Ox	Wood	1/27/1865	2/14/1866
1866	Tiger	Fire	2/15/1866	2/4/1867
1867	Cat	Fire	2/5/1867	1/24/1868
1868	Dragon	Earth	1/25/1868	2/10/1869
1869	Snake	Earth	2/11/1869	1/30/1870
1870	Horse	Metal	1/31/1870	2/18/1871
1871	Goat	Metal	2/19/1871	2/8/1872
1872	Monkey	Water	2/9/1872	1/28/1873
1873	Rooster	Water	1/29/1873	2/16/1874
1874	Dog	Wood	2/17/1874	2/5/1875
1875	Pig	Wood	2/6/1875	1/25/1876
1876	Rat	Fire	1/26/1876	2/12/1877
1877	Ox	Fire	2/13/1877	2/1/1878
1878	Tiger	Earth	2/2/1878	1/21/1879
1879	Cat	Earth	1/22/1879	2/9/1880
1880	Dragon	Metal	2/10/1880	1/29/1881
1881	Snake	Metal	1/30/1881	2/17/1882
1882	Horse	Water	2/18/1882	2/7/1883
1883	Goat	Water	2/8/1883	1/27/1884
1884	Monkey	Wood	1/28/1884	2/14/1885
1885	Rooster	Wood	2/15/1885	2/3/1886
1886	Dog	Fire	2/4/1886	1/23/1887
1887	Pig	Fire	1/24/1887	2/11/1888
1888	Rat	Earth	2/12/1888	1/30/1889